SERVICE MARKETING

SERVICE MARKETING

ROLAND T. RUST
Madison S. Wiggington Professor of Management,
Director, Center for Service Marketing,
Vanderbilt University

ANTHONY J. ZAHORIK
Burke Institute

TIMOTHY L. KEININGHAM
CEO, Copernican Systems, Inc.

HarperCollinsCollegePublishers

Executive Editor: Anne Elizabeth Smith
Senior Editor: Michael Roche
Developmental Editor: Becky Kohn
Project Editor: Ellen MacElree
Cover Designer: John Callahan
Text Designer: A Good Thing, Inc.
Cover Photograph: Tony Stone Images
Art Studio: Vantage Art, Inc.
Photo Researcher: Michelle E. Ryan
Electronic Production Manager: Su Levine
Desktop Administrator: Laura Leever
Manufacturing Manager: Willie Lane
Electronic Page Makeup: Interactive Composition Corporation
Printer and Binder: R. R. Donnelley & Sons Company
Cover Printer: New England Book Components

SERVICE MARKETING

Library of Congress Cataloging-in-Publication Data

Rust, Roland T.
   Service marketing / Roland T. Rust, Anthony J. Zahorik, Timothy L. Keiningham.
      p.   cm.
   Includes bibliographical references and index.
   ISBN 0-673-99145-8
   1. Service industries—Marketing. 2. Customer service.
I. Zahorik, Anthony J.   II. Keiningham, Timothy L. III. Title.
HD9980.5.R87 1996
658.8—dc20   95-38909
                                                    CIP

96 97 98 99   9 8 7 6 5 4 3 2 1

TO CHIHARU, DONNA, AND MICHIKO

Contents

PART III
LISTENING TO THE CUSTOMER 153

PART IV
MEASURING CUSTOMER SATISFACTION 225

Chapter 9
THE PSYCHOLOGY OF CUSTOMER SATISFACTION 227

Chapter 10
DESIGNING CUSTOMER SATISFACTION SURVEYS 240

Chapter 13
THE COST OF QUALITY 321

Chapter 14
RETURN ON QUALITY 331

PART VI
IMPROVING SERVICE 349

Chapter 15
MOMENTS OF TRUTH 351

PART VII
THE FUTURE OF SERVICE MARKETING 483

Chapter 19
IMPLICATIONS OF TECHNOLOGY 485

P r e f a c e

Why write a new book on service marketing? The quick answer is that service is increasingly important because the information age is making service a much larger and more important part of every advanced economy. So much has happened in service marketing in the last 10 years that a new book incorporating modern developments was sorely needed. In the United States, for example, current estimates place 75 percent of the economy in the service sector, with service also making up about 75 percent of the product sector. In other words, there is very little happening in the U.S. economy that is *not* service. Similar percentages are seen in most other developed economies.

SERVICE MARKETING IN A HISTORICAL CONTEXT

Before the late 1970s, it was thought that traditional marketing techniques worked just as well for service as they did for toothpaste or laundry detergent. That was the era of the "4 Ps"—the marketing mix elements of price, product, promotion, and place. The assumption was that service was just an augmentation of the physical product, or that service could be considered a product itself if no physical product was involved. The implied task was "marketing a service."

In the late 1970s and early 1980s, scholars such as Lynn Shostack began to question the applicability of standard product marketing techniques to services. These thinkers noted that services were different in many ways from physical products; for example, services are intangible, and production and consumption of services are often simultaneous. Therefore, marketing a service involves different techniques than marketing a product. Services marketing texts that originated in the period up to the mid-1980s reflected this point of view.

In the mid-1980s, as the quality movement became influential throughout the world, scholars such as Len Berry and Christian Gronroos began to realize that service delivery was the critical factor in successful service. The emphasis in thinking shifted, as a result, to service quality. The 1990s are bringing an increasing recognition among service scholars that service and service quality are important throughout the economy, not just in the service sector. One of our major reasons for writing this book is to bring the thinking of the last 10 years into a service marketing textbook, fully incorporating the advances brought by the quality revolution, and recognizing explicitly that service marketing is important in any organization, and not just in the service sector.

THE NEW VIEW OF SERVICE MARKETING

The recognition that service is vital to the product sector as well as to the service sector led us to title our book *Service Marketing* rather than the more usual "Services Marketing." We wanted to make it clear that we were interested in service *wherever* it occurs—not just in the service sector. This point was brought home to us recently when Fleetguard, a subsidiary of Cummins Engine, joined Vanderbilt's Center for Service Marketing. Fleetguard makes filters for diesel engines, and thus is a full-fledged member of the smokestack economy. Nevertheless, Fleetguard realizes that its success depends on the quality of its service. In fact, of the 12 current Partners of the Center for Services Marketing, only nine (75 percent) may be said to be in the service sector, about the same as the percentage of the economy *overall* that is in the service sector.

EVERY ORGANIZATION IS A SERVICE

The title *Service Marketing* also accentuates the fact that our book is not just about "marketing services." We are also interested in such things as service delivery and improving service over time. Our view is that *every* organization is a service, which may or may not (and usually doesn't!) include a physical product. At Vanderbilt we advise students to take the service marketing course concurrent with, or in some cases even prior to, the traditional introductory course, principles of marketing or marketing management, thus implying that this course is just as fundamental to marketing as the two basic introductory courses.

A MULTIFUNCTIONAL PERSPECTIVE

Another important aspect of our book is its multifunctional perspective. Business executives continually complain that students too often learn subjects in isolation, while in the business world everything connects to everything else. We have worked hard to make this book cross functional boundaries, and overlap in natural ways with related areas. It is impossible to talk seriously about service without considering the relationship to strategy, human resources and organizational behavior, accounting, finance, and operations. Our book reflects the multifunctional nature of service by daring to stray from the marketing "silo" when it is useful to do so. For example, Chapter 4, "Focusing and Positioning," is to a large extent a strategy chapter; Chapter 17, "Employee Empowerment," discusses topics that are often considered human resources; Chapter 13, "The Cost of Quality," shares many elements with cost accounting; Chapter 14, "Return on Quality," has financial content; Chapter 15, "Moments of Truth," involves a number of operations issues; and Part 7, "The Future of Service Marketing," includes a great deal about how management information systems are evolving. We consider service as a whole, and do not shy away from relevant topics just because they involve knowledge and skills that are "not marketing."

CUSTOMER SATISFACTION AND SERVICE QUALITY

The last 10 years have brought tremendous attention to the issues of customer satisfaction and service quality. The quality movement and the Malcolm Baldrige National Quality Award in particular have succeeded in making the majority of companies and nonprofit organizations more aware of how important it is to satisfy the customer, and how important it is to measure and monitor customer satisfaction and/or service quality. Our book brings customer satisfaction and service quality to the forefront as central concepts that are vital to any organization's success. For example, Part 4, "Measuring Customer Satisfaction," and Part 5, "Determining Financial Impact," emphasize customer satisfaction and service quality and link them to financial return. We give these topics more emphasis than they have ever received before in any services marketing text, consistent with the importance they now command in the business world.

ORGANIZATION OF THE TEXT

The text is divided into 7 parts, which include 19 chapters, as follows:

Part 1: Service Marketing: The Traditional and Emerging Views connects the traditional view of *services* marketing with the emerging view of *service* marketing. Chapters 1 and 2 explain the differences between goods and services and the nature of demand for services. Chapter 3 provides an overview of the central issues in service marketing management as even companies in the goods sector find effective service increasingly important. Chapter 3 also presents the central assumptions and guiding principles of the emerging view of service marketing, and provides a blueprint for the remainder of the book.

Part 2: Focusing the Organization includes two chapters that show how the definition of the business determines its goals and objectives, and how its identification of its customer groups determines the tactics it will use. Our consideration of such groups as suppliers, governmental regulators, and employees as customers is consistent with the concept the Europeans refer to as *relationship management*. (In the United States, this term is often used more narrowly, to describe only the relationship between the producer and the direct customer.) The idea of identifying and satisfying specific customer groups is central to the thrust of the book.

Part 3: Listening to the Customer includes some of the various ways that information can be obtained from customers and used to serve them. Chapter 6, "Methods of Listening to the Customer," emphasizes preliminary and exploratory methods of listening. Chapter 7, "Complaint Management," and Chapter 8, "Service Guarantees," emphasize methods an organization can use to turn around a dissatisfied customer and learn from the experience.

Part 4: Measuring Customer Satisfaction is an example of material that differentiates this book from earlier texts. Given the profound impact of the quality revolution and the explosion of customer satisfaction measurement programs, no book on service marketing can fail to make customer satisfaction measurement an integral part of the course material. Chapter 9 describes the psychology of customer satisfaction, and Chapters 10 and 11 discuss how to design and analyze customer satisfaction surveys. Among corporate recruiters, we have found that these skills are among the most valued in new hires.

Part 5: Determing Financial Impact arises from the 1990s brand of the quality movement, the movement toward "Return on Quality" and financial impact. Part 5 gives students a financial accountability mindset, and some tools they can use to address the issue.

Part 6: Improving Service shows how management can implement service improvements. Chapters 15–18 include such topics as designing processes that satisfy customers, using internal marketing to improve service, developing customer relationships, empowering employees, and devising a business plan that emphasizes customer satisfaction and service. This part is a collection of modern topics that would not have appeared as prominently in a text from the 1980s.

Part 7: The Future of Service Marketing recognizes that changes in the technological environment are having a profound impact on how service is supplied and performed. With the advent of the "information superhighway," the Internet, the World Wide Web, video dial tone, and interactive television, all converging on an interactive, digital, information infrastructure, there will be huge changes in how marketing is done and a further shift toward the importance of service. Chapter 19 gives some ideas of the ways service marketing will be affected.

IMPORTANT FEATURES

The text includes many features that enhance students' ability to learn.

1. *Chapter outlines* provide an overview of what topics will be covered.

2. *Tables and figures* provide graphical explanation of important and/or difficult concepts.

3. *Photographs* are extensively used to demonstrate concepts and to make the text more lively.

4. *Discussion questions* at the end of each chapter are designed to make students think deeply about what has been studied, and to provoke active participation in the course content.

5. *Cases* at the end of each part provide realistic scenarios that test the ability of students to integrate the course material into situations of realistic complexity and ambiguity.

To increase the value of the learning experience for students and to maximize flexibility for course design to instructors, a companion volume *Readings for Service Marketing* is also available. This selection of 30 readings can be used by instructors who wish to expose their students to current research and the thoughts of leading researchers in the field of service marketing. To get further information about packaging the readings with this volume, please contact your HarperCollins representative.

Course Materials

We have worked hard to satisfy the professor by providing an instructor's manual that includes an extensive set of course materials:

1. *Lecture transparency masters* make preparing the course lectures simple.

2. *Suggested class projects* can provide practical experience for the students.

3. *Suggested exam questions* make it easy to build exams.

4. *Suggested homework questions* provide useful practice in the course material.

5. *Suggested class schedules* for courses of different duration make it easy to adapt the class to either a semester or a quarter system.

6. Case notes provide guidance about how best to use the cases in class.

The Supplementary Manual: "Computer Exercises for Service Marketing"

For classes wishing to investigate customer satisfaction measurement and return on quality in more depth, we provide a supplementary manual to the instructor. This manual, bound into the instructor's manual, includes text, software, and cases. It includes a description of a computer decision support for return on quality, with a demo version of the system that students can actually run, and a case that the students can use with the system. There is also customer satisfaction measurement data on computer disk for students to analyze, along with two cases that provide managerial contexts to make the data meaningful. The DOS-compatible disk can be duplicated for student use, as can the perforated sheets that make up the manual. At Vanderbilt, we find that the students benefit greatly from these computer exercises, both in terms of their grasp of the course content and in the expansion of their computer skills.

ACKNOWLEDGMENTS

We could not have written the book without the outstanding help and encouragement of many people. Thanks especially to HarperCollins Executive Editor Anne Smith, who was most encouraging throughout the project, helped us in countless ways, and was an endless source of wisdom, and to Senior Editor Mike Roche, who helped orchestrate production and marketing. Thanks also to our editor, Becky Kohn, who made our writing look better than it really is, and contributed many helpful suggestions about how to improve the book. Thanks also to the staff at HarperCollins, including Ellen MacElree, Lisa Pinto, Matthew Rohrer, and Mary McGeary. Thanks to Steve Clemens for all of his work on the ROQ decision support system. Thanks to Chase Manhattan Bank, Chemical Bank, the Promus Companies, Union Planters Bank, USAA, and several clients of Copernican Systems, Inc., for acting as "beta tests" for the ROQ system.

A number of reviewers in the United States, Canada, and Europe also provided extremely valuable input, which helped us polish drafts of this manuscript, in order to communicate our ideas more clearly. These reviewers, who often worked under tight guidelines with rough manuscript, include the following: Laurette Dubé, Université de Montréal; Raymond Fisk, University of Central Florida; Paula A. Francese, University of New Hampshire; Stephen J. Grove, Clemson University; Evert N. Gummesson, Stockholm University-Sweden; Dawn Iacobucci, Northwestern University; Jan Mattsson, Gothenburg University, Sweden; Banwari Mittal, Northern Kentucky University; John C. Mowen, Oklahoma State University; Adrian F. Payne, Cranfield University-School of Management- United Kingdom; Thomas L. Powers, University of Alabama-Birmingham; Teresa Swartz, California Polytechnic State University-San Luis Obispo; Steven A. Taylor, Illinois State University; and Theo Verhallen, Tilberg University-the Netherlands.

Thanks to Dr. Germain Boer, who was helpful to us in producing our chapter on the cost of quality. Thanks also to Marshall Weems of Financial Selling Systems and Donald Jackson of the Jackson Consulting Group for contributing to our knowledge of quality improvement implementation. Thanks to all of our students at Vanderbilt (and the University of Texas) for providing the "market test" of the course material over nine years of teaching. Thanks to the Partner Companies of Vanderbilt's Center for Services Marketing for their real-world testing of many of the ideas in this book. Special thanks to Ray Kordupleski of AT&T for working closely with us, coauthoring with us, and giving us the benefit of his considerable wisdom and experience. We also would like to thank our families and loved ones for putting up with us while we spent time on the book that we could have spent with them. In particular we thank Michiko Keiningham for the hard and thankless work she contributed to many of the figures in the book.

Roland T. Rust
Anthony J. Zahorik
Timothy L. Keiningham

PART I

SERVICE MARKETING: THE TRADITIONAL AND EMERGING VIEWS

Chapter 1

SERVICES VS. GOODS

1.1 INTRODUCTION

This book is about the marketing of service. As such, it differs from traditional marketing texts in several ways. First of all, traditional marketing texts present material about marketing that was developed during an era when the so-called industrialized nations thought of themselves as providers of goods. The emphasis on the four P's (product, price, place, and promotion), particularly on product and place, or distribution, shows the roots of marketing thinking in the design and selling of goods. This approach is not wrong, in that a significant share of our economy is devoted to the marketing of goods. However, the production and marketing of intangible services, as opposed to physical goods, puts different demands on marketers and on the entire service firm, from the executives to the service delivery people. As such, it requires special coverage beyond that in standard texts.

There is a second way in which this book differs from standard texts. The basic emphasis of the four P's is on designing, delivering and marketing products that will win new customers, an enterprise we will refer to as "offensive marketing." While winning new customers is vital to the long-term success of any organization, many firms have come to realize that survival and profits also are critically dependent upon keeping the customers they already have, or "defensive marketing." And since the key to retaining customers is often found in after-sale service, this book will devote much more attention than traditional texts do to the monitoring of customer satisfaction and the development of long-term relationships with customers.

So is this a specialized textbook? We would argue that it is not. We see it, rather, as an essential complement to standard marketing texts. A detailed study of the special requirements of service marketing is essential for any marketer for two reasons: First, as we are about to point out, most students of business are likely to be working for firms that identify themselves as part of the service sector. Second, we will argue that even those students who intend to work for firms that manufacture goods will find that, more and more, the competitive edge and long-term profitability of those firms depend on the attendant services that the firms provide to their customers.

The most marked change in the structure of developed economies in the twentieth century, particularly in the latter half, has been the transformation from an emphasis on the manufacture of physical goods to the production of intangible

FIGURE 1.1

INCREASING PERCENT OF EMPLOYMENT IN THE SERVICE SECTOR IN TEN INDUSTRIALIZED COUNTRIES

	U.S.	Canada	Aus-tralia	Japan	France	Germany	Italy	Nether-lands	Sweden	U.K.
1970	63.94%	62.57%	56.98%	47.41%	48.04%	42.84%	40.13%	55.45%	53.86%	53.59%
1975	66.44	65.82	61.22	51.95	51.88	48.80	44.00	60.83	57.72	58.62
1980	67.11	67.18	64.58	54.78	56.27	51.88	47.69	65.09	62.89	61.15
1985	70.00	70.56	68.27	56.97	61.43	55.42	55.34	68.30	66.06	68.89
1990	72.04	72.25	70.36	59.23	64.98	57.59	58.64	69.50	67.92	69.66

Source: Todd M. Godbout (1993), "Employment change and sectoral distribution in 10 countries, 1970–90," *Monthly Labor Review* (October), p. 8.

services, as shown in Figure 1.1. In the United States, a leader in the transformation to a service economy, the percentage of workers employed in the service sector has risen from a mere 30% in 1900 to an estimated 80% by 1995.[1] Even this number underestimates the true number of service employees in the economy, because as many as three-fourths of the workers in manufacturing firms are actually engaged in support services such as maintenance, research, accounting, marketing, personnel management, and information processing, rather than in the direct production of goods. More than ever, firms have come to realize that the increased value and competitiveness of the goods they sell are likely to come from the attendant services offered with them rather than the products' physical properties. The quality of goods produced is no longer a source of differential advantage in most industries: More and more it's a basic requirement to enter the market. Unique and powerful strategies are more likely to come from hard-to-duplicate, value-enhancing services than from the goods themselves.[2] For example, services now account for 74% of the U.S. gross national product, and resulted in a balance-of-trade surplus for the United States of $55.7 billion in 1993, helping to offset a trade deficit of $132.4 billion in the goods sector.[3] A similar shift is occurring in all developed or developing nations.

There are several reasons for the growing emphasis on services in developed economies. The reason cited most often by politicians and labor leaders is the transfer of manufacturing operations from developed nations with high labor rates to third-world economies with lower wage rates. This once impractical strategy has been made financially attractive by the growth of automation, cheap transportation, and global communications. On the other hand, service jobs are much harder to export, so the makeup of the domestic economy that remains becomes correspondingly more service-oriented.

But shrinkage of the manufacturing sector is not the only reason for an increasing percentage of the GNP being provided by services. The service sector has experienced dramatic absolute growth, as shown in Figure 1.2. For example, new technologies, such as information processing and telecommunications, have created enormous new industries and a massive restructuring of the economy. Many aspects of these technologies are so specialized that even when manufacturers incorporate them into their own production processes, it is better to purchase them from outside

FIGURE 1.2

GROWTH OF EMPLOYMENT IN THE SERVICE SECTOR OF TEN INDUSTRIALIZED COUNTRIES (IN THOUSANDS)

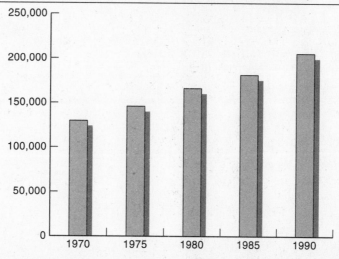

Source: Todd M. Godbout (1993), "Employment change and sectoral distribution in 10 countries, 1970–90," *Monthly Labor Review* (October), p. 8.

vendors than to adopt them in-house.[4] The growth of the data processing industry is one example of a service industry that would have grown regardless of the fate of the heavy industry sector. So too is the growth of leasing, as many organizations and individuals have discovered the accounting advantages of leasing rather than purchasing. In fact, the growth of specialization in support services has made it cost-effective for firms to outsource everything from strategic planning to building maintenance. A host of new service industries has sprung up to meet the demand, thereby allowing firms to concentrate on what they do best. Pepsico's Taco Bell restaurant chain now hires outside vendors to do its initial food preparation, so that its employees can concentrate most of their efforts on serving customers rather than on chopping vegetables.[5]

Simultaneously, other factors have spurred growth in the service economy and in the use of marketing by service firms. One of these factors, particularly in the United States, has been the deregulation by government of service industries that were at one time severely constrained by law from developing new products or opening new markets. Banking is one of the most dramatic examples. At one time the government basically told banks what limited sets of services they could offer and what interest rates they could pay or receive. Efficiencies of scale were limited because banks were constrained to operate within the borders of their own state. In the past decade banks have been allowed to expand their operations into a whole new realm of services, across state lines. The result has been a fiercely competitive arena in which marketing, once an unknown and unneeded activity, is now of central importance. Similar transformations have taken place in the airline, insurance, and telecommunications industries. The demand by these

Formerly highly regulated service industries have become sophisticated marketers due to intense competition.

industries for marketing expertise tailored to their specific situations has grown enormously.

Another stimulus to service industry growth has been the growing acceptance of marketing by various professional groups, such as lawyers and doctors, that at one time considered marketing—generally mistakenly used to mean advertising and promotion—to be unseemly. However, the saturation of certain markets and other economic factors have forced many of these professions to become much more competitive to survive. As a result, most of these industries have begun to embrace marketing, in its full range of activities, as both acceptable and essential for survival. The result has been a corresponding growth in these services.

Finally, many manufacturing firms have realized that many of the support service skills they developed in-house have value on the outside. Many have sold computing and data processing capabilities, sales force training programs, facility management skills, and other internally grown skills to other firms.

Another major contributor to the growth of the service sector has been the increasing demand for healthcare, driven primarily driven by the aging of the population. In fact, the U.S. Bureau of Labor predicts that six of the top ten fastest growing occupations until the year 2005 will be in medical services, generally increasing by amounts ranging from 70 to 90 percent over their 1990 levels.[6]

Even though the U.S. economy was dominated by services as early as the 1940s, until quite recently the development of the discipline of marketing was focused on the sale of goods. A few lonely voices were heard addressing the unique problems of service marketers before 1980, but it has only been in the past 15 years that ser-

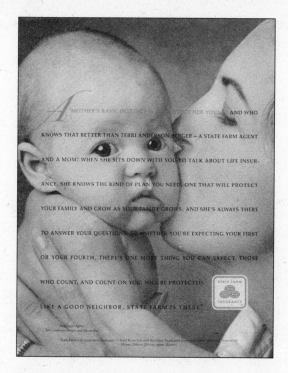

Some services attempt to reduce customer risk by "tangibilizing" their highly intangible services.

vices have received special attention from marketing scholars and practitioners.[7] New marketing paradigms have been developed to reflect what many service marketing professionals have identified as the unique aspects of selling services that were not addressed by traditional goods-based marketing concepts. In this chapter we discuss some of the commonly cited distinctions between goods and services and their implications for marketers.

1.2 UNIQUE CHARACTERISTICS OF SERVICES

Exactly what is a service, and why should services receive special treatment from marketers? A popular definition describes service as "any act or performance that one party can offer to another that is essentially intangible and does not result in the ownership of anything. Its production may or may not be tied to a physical product."[8] Although we will see that the distinction between goods and services is somewhat artificial, since the success of goods manufacturers is vitally dependent on the services they provide, there are four commonly cited characteristics of services that make them different to market from goods: *intangibility, inseparability, variability, and perishability.*

Intangibility

Pure services such as baby-sitting cannot be seen or touched. They are ephemeral performances that can be experienced only as they are delivered. As the above definition of a service suggests, intangibility may represent the most critical difference between services and goods, and its implications for marketing are great.

Intangible services are difficult to sell because they can't be produced and displayed ahead of time. They are therefore harder to communicate to prospective customers. A hobbled weekend athlete can't see the results of elective knee surgery beforehand. The person may be able to talk to other patients who have experienced the same procedure, but their operations don't necessarily reflect the outcome of *this* particular surgery. There are no tires to kick, no samples to taste, no test drives available. The prospective surgery patient must commit to the process before seeing what he or she is getting, and therefore has higher perceived risk. Marketers of services can reduce this risk by stressing tangible cues that will convey reassurance and quality to prospective customers. These tangible cues range from the firm's physical facilities to the appearance and demeanor of its staff to the letterhead on its stationery to its logo.

Life insurance companies are particularly savvy about this problem. Their service is, after all, the most intangible of services: by definition, the buyer will *never* know the ultimate result of what he or she has bought! To compensate for this intangibility the major companies have all developed strong visual symbols for their firms. What comes to mind when you run down the names of the major insurance firms? Prudential (the rock of Gibraltar), Allstate (protective hands), Travelers (a red umbrella), Nationwide (a blanket), Wausau (a train station). One exception in the auto and property insurance business, which illustrates another approach to handling intangibility, is State Farm Mutual. Its symbol is usually three red ovals— not particularly memorable or meaningful. However, its advertising portrays actual agents and the work they do for customers in time of need, creating a strong image of a caring company made up of real people.

Indeed, another common method for reducing the uncertainty that intangibility generates in the minds of customers is to stress the professionalism of the firm's staff, with its implications for successful service outcomes. In general, developing a strong corporate image is a great help in overcoming customer resistance. For high-risk services, personal selling may be more necessary than with goods that can be examined and sampled. Word of mouth can also be especially important, and service firms are advised to undertake activities that will stimulate positive word of mouth, such as developing postpurchase follow-up programs.

Intangibility creates other management problems as well. It makes services impossible to protect through patents. It also makes it very difficult to determine actual production costs, and services are therefore often thought to be harder to price than goods.

Inseparability

This characteristic is interpreted differently by different service marketing writers, but all interpretations point out that special operations problems exist for the firm's managers. One interpretation of this term is the inseparability of customers from the service delivery process. In particular, many services require the participation of the customer in the production process. A child getting a haircut must sit still; otherwise, the family photo may have to be delayed for a month. The person who comes to a tax preparer at the last minute with boxes of disorganized records may cause the preparer to overlook some possible deductions. An overdemanding restaurant patron may fluster or aggravate the waitstaff so badly that service quality is reduced for customers at several tables.

These examples illustrate the fact that, unlike goods, which are often produced in a location far removed from the customer and totally under the control of the manufacturing firm, service production often requires the presence and active participation of the customer—and of other customers. Depending upon the skill, attitude, cooperation, and so on that customers bring to the service encounter, the results can be good or bad, but in any event are hard to standardize.

A second interpretation of inseparability refers to the fact that in some service industries the service delivered is inextricably tied to particular individual service providers. Customers may have grounds for complaint if their service is not provided by, for example, the surgeon or lawyer or professor they thought they were paying for. This strong link between individual provider and service product creates severe capacity problems for a service firm, since one individual can be stretched only so far. Capacity can be stretched farther by training assistants who can free the star performer for all but the most essential tasks, or it can be expanded indefinitely by standardizing the service and training other experts to provide it.

Training personnel to provide the same standard of service is essential if a service is to grow successfully. The multilocation service firm is acutely aware of this need for training. Uniform quality of services cannot be guaranteed by carefully controlled, centralized mass production as it can with goods. Instead, because services are produced individually at each location by different individuals, often with little or no direct supervision, careful selection of job candidates and continuous training of employees in production techniques, quality standards, and corporate policies become particularly critical to ensure uniform quality. As a result, successful service firms spend a great deal of time, effort, and money on human resources activities.

Variability

The fact that service quality is difficult to control compounds the marketer's task. Intangibility alone would not be such a problem if customers could be sure that the services they were to receive would be just like the successful experiences their neighbors were so pleased with. But in fact, customers know that services can vary greatly. Different front-line personnel have different abilities. Even the same service provider has good days and bad days, or may be less focused at different times of day. Services are performances, often involving the cooperation and skill of several individuals, and are therefore unlikely to be the same every time. This potential variability of service quality greatly raises the risk faced by the consumer.

The service provider must find ways to reduce the perceived risk due to variability. One method is to design services to be as uniform as possible—by training personnel to follow closely defined procedures, or by automating as many aspects of the service as possible. This isn't always a good strategy, however. The appeal of some service personnel—particularly, those involved in such expensive personal services as beauty parlor treatments or home decorating—lies in their spontaneity and flexibility to address individual customer needs. The danger with too much standardization is that these attributes may be designed right out of the services, therefore reducing much of their appeal. A second way to deal with perceived risk from variability is to provide satisfaction guarantees or other assurances that the customer will not be stuck with a bad result. In Chapter 8 we will discuss the growing use of unconditional guarantees for services. Finally, even for highly customized services, advertising alone may be able to reassure prospective customers that the organization is capable of and committed to doing an excellent job.

Perishability

The fourth characteristic distinguishing services from goods is their time dependence. Services cannot be inventoried, since they are performed in real time. And time periods during which service delivery capacity sits idle represent revenue-earning potential that is lost forever. Periods of peak demand can't be prepared for in advance by producing and storing services, nor can they be made up for after the fact. A service opportunity occurs at a point in time, and when it's gone, it's gone forever. This can present enormous difficulty in facilities planning. A survey of service firms found that the greatest operational challenges facing them were posed by the perishability of their products.[9]

Matching service capacity to demand patterns can involve managing one or both elements. Perishability often puts a greater burden on service marketers to manage demand than it does on goods marketers, who can build up inventories to meet peak demand or can reduce prices later to move unsold inventory. The cited survey found that firms' principal method for controlling demand was to increase personal selling during potentially slow periods. Surprisingly, few firms claimed to use the standard economic solution of price changes to increase or decrease demand, although some service industries, such as resort hotels with seasonal demand, do this routinely. Few respondents said they developed alternative, counterseasonal service products to use slack capacity, although that has long been a common practice by goods marketers. Many service providers also control demand by requiring appointments.

The alternative to controlling demand is to make service capacity flexible. Some service firms keep on call frontline personnel who can arrive on short notice to meet surges in demand, or crosstrain support personnel to assist with customer service during busy periods. Chapter 2 will address the nature of demand for services in more detail.

1.3 MARKETING MANAGEMENT FOR SERVICES: EXPANDING THE MARKETING MIX

Service marketing managers have found that the traditional four P's of marketing are inadequate to describe the key aspects of the service marketer's job. The traditional marketing mix is said to consist of the following elements of the total offering to consumers: the *product* (the basic service or good, including packaging, attendant services, etc.); its *price;* the *place* where the product is made available (or distribution channels—not generally a real issue for most services, except perhaps for repair and maintenance[10]); and *promotion* (marketing communication: advertising, public relations, and personal selling). Some marketers suggest that the unique requirements of

FIGURE 1.3

THE EXPANDED MARKETING MIX FOR SERVICES

selling services require the manager attend to three additional P's.[11] These are *people, physical evidence,* and *process,* as shown in Figure 1.3.

People

Many services require personal interactions between customers and the firm's employees, and these interactions strongly influence the customer's perception of service quality. For example, a person's stay at a hotel can be greatly affected by the friendliness, knowledgeability, and helpfulness of the hotel staff—in most cases the lowest-paid people in the organization. One's impression of the hotel and willingness to return are determined to a large extent by the brief encounters with the front-desk staff, bellhops, housekeeping staff, restaurant waitstaff, and so on, many of which take place outside the direct control of hotel management. In fact, the average hotel patron has very little contact with hotel supervisors and managers. Therefore, management faces a tremendous challenge in selecting and training all of these people to do their jobs well, and, perhaps even more important, in motivating them to care about doing their jobs and to make an extra effort to serve their customers. After all, these employees must believe in what they are doing and enjoy their work before they can, in turn, provide good service to customers.

For this reason, human resources management policies and practices are considered to be of particular strategic importance for in delivering high-quality services. Establishing a customer-oriented culture throughout the firm and empowering employees to provide quality service cannot be established merely by putting up inspiring posters. Management leadership, job redesign, and systems to reward and recognize outstanding achievement are among the issues that a successful service manager must address. The term "internal marketing" has been coined to characterize the sets of activities a firm must undertake to woo and win over the hearts and minds of its employees to achieve service excellence. We will discuss these issues further in Chapter 20.

The "people" component of the service marketing mix also includes the management of the firm's customer mix. Because services are often experienced at the provider's facilities, one's satisfaction with a service can also be influenced by other customers who are being served there. Ill-mannered restaurant customers at the next table, crying children in a nearby seat on an airplane, and commercial bank customers whose lengthy transactions take up the tellers' time are all examples of unpleasant service conditions caused by a firm's other patrons. On the other hand, the right mix of customers can greatly increase the enjoyment of experience—for example, at entertainment services, such as nightclubs or sporting events. Determining the desirable customer mix for a service, segmenting the market into compatible groups, and managing customer arrivals to avoid conflict and enhance the service experience are essential components of service management and will be discussed further in Chapter 2.

Physical Evidence

This element of the expanded marketing mix addresses the "tangible" components of the service experience and firm's image referred to earlier. Physical surroundings and other visible cues can have a profound effect on the impressions customers form about the quality of the service they receive.[12] The "servicescape"—that is, the ambience, the background music, the comfort of the seating, and the physical layout of a service facility—can greatly affect a customer's satisfaction with a service experience. The appearance of the staff, including clothes and grooming, may be used as important clues. Promotional materials and written correspondence provide tangible evidence of the firm's professionalism. To the extent that these elements provide reassurance, they can be incorporated into the firm's marketing communications to help reduce customer anxiety about committing to the purchase. Service firms should design these items with extreme care, since they will play a major role in influencing a customer's impression of the firm. In particular, all physical evidence must be designed to be consistent with the "personality" that the firm wishes to project in the marketplace.

Process of Service Production

Because customers are often involved in the production of services, the flow and progress of the production process is more important for services than it is for goods. A customer who buys a television set is not particularly concerned about the manufacturing process that made it. But the customer at a fine restaurant is not interested merely in the end result—the cessation of hunger. The entire experience of arriving at the restaurant—of being seated, enjoying the ambiance, ordering, receiving, and eating the meal—is important. The pace of the process and the skill of the providers are both apparent to the customer and fundamental to his or her satisfaction with the purchase.

The importance of the process is true even for less "sensual" experiences. A customer who applies for a loan at a bank evaluates the purchase not only by the amount of the loan received and the interest rate paid. The speed and sensitivity of the approval process, the interaction with bank officers, the accuracy of bank statements, and the ease of getting redress if mistakes are found all affect the person's attitudes about doing further business with the bank and his or her willingness to recommend it to others.

Therefore, when designing service production processes, particular attention must be paid to customer perceptions of that process. For this reason, marketing and operations are closely related in service management. In Chapter 16 we will describe some techniques for laying out service processes so that the customer's point of view is adequately considered.

1.4 THE IMPORTANCE OF SERVICE QUALITY AND CUSTOMER SATISFACTION MEASUREMENT

The application of quality management methods illustrates another obvious difference between goods and services. Top service companies spend much more time measuring customer satisfaction with service quality than do goods marketers, in general. Most quality control methods were originally developed to monitor the extent to which manufactured goods meet the specifications that have been set for them. Goods can be weighed, measured, put under stress, and so on, before they are sold. Services, on the other hand, are produced as they are consumed, and this changes the focus of standard quality control methods. Although some objective measures of service quality can be taken as they are performed, such as time spent waiting, number of errors in filling an order, and the like, it becomes quickly apparent that such measures do not adequately capture the real test of a service's quality—whether the customer was satisfied. Goods marketers have come to accept the fact that they too must ultimately define quality in terms of customers' subjective opinions, but service marketers came to this conclusion very early when they tried to apply standard quality methods.

Managing service quality is, in fact, a major part of service marketing. Providing services that consistently meet or exceed customers' expectations is key to overcoming most of the major problems unique to services. For example, service reliability has been found to be the most important dimension of quality to consumers, so improving quality generally means improving the reliability of service outcomes.[13] And, because reliability directly addresses customer concerns about service variability and intangibility, a reputation for high quality directly reduces the purchase risk for new customers, whereas a poor reputation makes selling the service much more difficult. High-quality services are also more likely to stimulate positive word of mouth by current customers, reinforcing the firm's own advertisements by giving them more credibility and further improving the firm's reputation. Moreover, success at producing high-quality service helps to build enthusiasm and higher morale among staff members, a factor that we have already seen is essential to delivering still better service.

Because of the central role that quality plays in service marketing, much of this book will be focused on the improvement and measurement of the many dimensions of service quality.

1.5 ALL MARKETERS MUST BE SERVICE MARKETERS

In spite of the sharp distinctions that have been drawn between services and goods, very few examples of pure services or pure goods exist. Restaurants are typically classified as service businesses, and yet they certainly sell tangible goods. (At the

Lexus planned the physical layout, selling approach, and service procedures of its dealer-ships with as much care as the engineering design of its luxury automobiles.

extreme, the drive-through window of a fast food restaurant is almost entirely devot-ed to the transfer of goods.) On the other hand, the auto industry is often cited as an exemplar of the "hard-core" manufacturing sector, and yet General Motors would have difficulty selling any cars without offering customers a wide range of support-ing services, such as warranties, financing programs, and repair facilities. Toyota's Lexus line has established strong customer loyalty as much for its extraordinary cus-tomer service system as for the quality of its automobiles. Lexus was intended to compete with other cars of extremely high quality, so its management saw no obvi-ous competitive edge in product excellence, although it was considered essential just to enter the market. Instead Toyota seized an opportunity for differentiation by treat-ing its customers much better—from the way its sales people approach prospective customers to the way owners are treated during maintenance visits.[14]

Actually, the distinction between the goods sector and the service sector in the economy is artificial. Most "products" have both service and goods components. Consider the difference between a dealer who sells cars and a leasing agency that leases cars. Under the traditional classification, the former is considered a goods business because it transfers ownership of physical goods. The latter is considered a service business because it merely provides transportation, rather than ownership. But aside from the piece of paper that states that the leasing company will get its car back in a few years, the activities and benefits provided by the two firms are identi-cal. In both cases customers drive away with new cars and are required to send back monthly payments. The goods-service distinction is all but meaningless to the mar-keting activities of the two firms.

Clearly, even a "goods business" such as the automotive industry has many service components to worry about, long before a customer needs the "service department," whose purpose is to repair and maintain the cars after they are sold. It is interesting to note that many auto companies make more money from financing, extended warranties and maintenance services than they do from the sale of the cars. In fact, these services can generate profits large enough to offset losses in the sales division of the company. For example, General Motors Acceptance Corporation (GMAC), the loan-financing arm of GM, has recently been healthier and more successful than the manufacturing division.

The objective of any firm is to fill its customers' needs profitably, and those needs are rarely satisfied by physical goods alone. Marketing's role is to find out what the needs are, whether they are being met, and how to meet them better. More than ever, meeting customer needs and staying competitive requires providing intangible services. Therefore, services marketing does not just refer to the advertising and selling of services. It is the managerial process of ensuring that the organization's offerings are serving customer needs—whether it sells telephone service or dump trucks. In this sense, every organization is in the service business.

1.6 THE COMPONENTS OF A SERVICE

The products that firms market do differ in the extent to which they involve the transfer of ownership of physical goods. However, intangible components inevitably play a pivotal role in winning and maintaining a satisfied customer. To stress this point, we will refer to all the market offerings of firms as their services, and point out that these services (Figure 1.4) can be broken down into four main components:

FIGURE 1.4

THE FOUR COMPONENTS OF A SERVICE

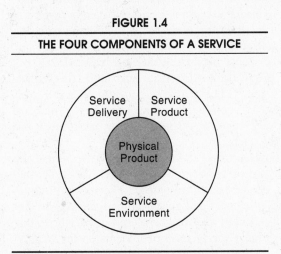

Source: Adapted from Roland T. Rust and Richard L. Oliver (1993), "Service quality: Insights and managerial implications from the frontier," in *Service Quality: New Directions in Theory and Practice.* Copyright © 1993 by Roland T. Rust and Richard L. Oliver. Reprinted by permission of Sage Publications.

physical product, service product, service environment, and service delivery.[15] All of them must be managed to meet customer needs.

The *physical product* is whatever the organization transfers to the customer that can be touched. It is tangible and physically real. Examples include houses, automobiles, computers, books, hotel soap and shampoo, and food. As with the rest of the service offering, product design must be customer-oriented. There is a well-developed method for ensuring that product design matches customer needs, called *Quality Function Deployment (QFD)*, or more popularly in the United States, the *House of Quality*.[16] The procedure was developed in Japan in the 1970s as a way to help marketing managers and engineers to talk to each other and to work toward a common goal of meeting customer needs. By linking engineering design features to specific customer needs QFD assures that design improvements improve the product's value to customers. At the same time, it helps the firm to avoid costly engineering improvements that are "better engineering" but do not meet customer needs. Spending time and effort on unnecessary engineering is known as "overengineering," and it is seen most often in technology-driven companies. QFD will be discussed further in Chapter 16.

The *service product* is the core performance purchased by the customer, the flow of events designed to provide a desired outcome. It refers to that part of the experience apart from the transfer of physical goods and typically includes interactions with the firm's personnel. For example, General Motor's Saturn division offers what is intended to be a nonintimidating purchase process. At each Saturn dealership customers are allowed to look at the cars in the showroom without being approached by sales representatives. Only when shoppers ask to speak to someone will a sales rep speak to them. To further reduce anxiety, actual sales prices, set to be competitively low, are posted on the cars, so that customers don't have to worry about negotiating the price, as at most other auto dealerships. The cars come with strong service guarantees, and dealer personnel are trained and empowered to make exceptional efforts to keep customers happy and solve their problems. All of these aspects of the firm's interaction with customers must be planned, and they help determine the nature of the overall service experience. We will discuss the design of the service product further in Chapter 16.

The *service environment* is the physical backdrop that surrounds the service, sometimes referred to as a "servicescape."[17] For example, going to see a movie is more enjoyable if the theater is clean, has comfortable seats, and has a spacious, well-lit parking lot. Even though the customer doesn't take any of that home, it has an important impact on the service experience.

Besides being pleasant or unpleasant in its own right, the service environment can influence how customers respond to "critical incidents"—that is, service events that may result in the customer becoming dissatisfied or delighted.[18] The service environment can also signal the intended market segment and position the organization.[19] For example, a restaurant near a university campus might signal that it is catering to college students by putting college memorabilia and pictures of students on the walls. A car dealer might use its service environment to position itself as upscale by decorating its showroom in a tasteful and elegant manner. There are three distinct elements that can be manipulated in the service environment: the ambient conditions, the spatial layout, and the signs and symbols.[20] The ambient conditions include things such as the lighting and background music. What may be appropriate for some businesses may be inappropriate for others, depending upon the market positioning. For example, bright lighting is appropriate for fast food restaurants, but would be inappropriate for an expensive, romantic restaurant. The spatial layout can also influence customer satisfaction. For example, Disney World found that long waiting lines seem shorter if the lines go around frequent turns, and there is some entertainment along the way. Signs and symbols are also important. For example, a car dealer selling American cars may fly a big United States flag to remind potential customers "to buy American."

The *service delivery* refers to what actually happens when customers buy the service. The service product defines how the service works in theory, but the service delivery is how the service works in actual practice. We often hear the adage, "Plan your work, and work your plan." The service product is the result of "planning your work," and the service delivery is the result of "working your plan." For example, the service design may be that a fast-food customer is greeted cheerfully within ten seconds, but the actual service delivery may be hindered by the counter employee joking in the back of the store for five minutes with other employees. What is designed does not always occur.

Most services are decentralized. That is, although the quality of the physical product can be relatively easily maintained at the factory through the careful use of statistical quality control techniques and the service product can be carefully designed and tested before multiple installations are built, the actual service delivery is much more geographically dispersed and much harder to monitor. Think for example of a huge retailer such as Wal-Mart. Wal-Mart has stores all across the United States. Decisions about store layouts, product mix, return policies, and other basic components of the physical and service product offerings are made at corporate headquarters to obtain the best results. However, when there is high service delivery at a particular store, it is due in large part to the actions of management and front-line employees at the local level. Guaranteeing sustained high-quality service delivery is an ongoing management activity, including the training and motivating of personnel and continuous monitoring of customer satisfaction.

Figure 1.5 shows examples of the four components of a service for several large industries. For example, a university provides primarily intangible benefits, including

FIGURE 1.5

COMPONENTS OF SERVICE: INDUSTRY EXAMPLES

Industry	Physical Product	Service Product	Service Environment	Service Delivery
Auto	The car	Title transfer Warranty Loans	Showroom Grounds Car lot	Test drive and sales pitch Repair time Negotiation
Hotels	Shampoo, etc. Food	Messages Shuttle Wake-up calls	The room Pool Lobby	Front desk performance Room cleaning Promptness of room service
University	Diploma	Majors Residence Placement	Classrooms Dormitories Sports fields	Teaching performance Janitorial Job interview schedules
Retail store	Goods	Assistance Credit Inventory	Sales floor	Knowledgeability Friendliness Speed

an education in a particular discipline, living quarters, and job placement. The physical good provided on graduation day, a diploma, has largely symbolic value only. The quality of the education can be very much enhanced or detracted from by the service environment, consisting of the physical facilities. The actual service delivered, as opposed to what the course catalog described, depends upon the quality of teaching, maintenance of the facilities, and the actual performance of the other attendant services.

The relative importance of these components to meeting customers' needs varies over industries. In fact, marketers have long recognized that services can be organized on an "intangibility continuum."[21] On one end of this scale are those that are "tangible-dominant," where the physical product is the primary concern of the customer. Purchasing table salt is an example. At the other end of the continuum are the "intangible-dominant" services, involving little or no transfer of title to physical goods, such as receiving a medical diagnosis. In fact, few services are purely intangible-dominant or tangible-dominant, but depend on some combination of both.

Even manufacturers of simple, highly tangible consumer products have found that service is essential to their survival, particularly those directed to organizations in their distribution channel. Organizations like Procter & Gamble distinguish between their *consumers* (the end users of their products) and their *customers* (the wholesalers and retailers who purchase directly from P&G). The company's relationship with its consumers is based on the sale of highly tangible, simple products such as detergents, prepared foods, and paper products (although in each case the firm provides an 800 telephone number that consumers can call for information on product use). However, P&G's critical relationships with its channel members, from its partnership with Wal-Mart to its dealings with small wholesalers, are based entirely on services.

What does this mean for marketers? It means that, to the extent that the characteristics of services mentioned above pose marketing management problems that have not been recognized in the past by goods-focused marketers, these are problems that all marketers must learn to face.

1.7 CUSTOMER EVALUATION OF SERVICES

Intangibility and service complexity also combine to determine how customers evaluate the services they buy, and can provide some insights into how best to market different types of offerings.[22] The quality of highly tangible services is generally easier to evaluate than is that of services that are primarily intangible. The attributes that customers use to evaluate tangible goods are mostly those known as *search qualities,* properties that can be evaluated by the purchaser before the sale is made. More intangible services possess a greater number of *experience qualities,* properties that can be evaluated only after the purchase. This increases the buyer's risk, and requires that the marketer provide some of the reassurances mentioned earlier. At the extreme are certain attributes that a buyer may not be able to evaluate even after purchase. These are usually possessed only by technically complex, intangible services. For example, many medical procedures fall into this category, since even after receiving treatment patients must still rely on their doctors to know whether the service was a success. Such attributes are called *credence qualities,* because

FIGURE 1.6

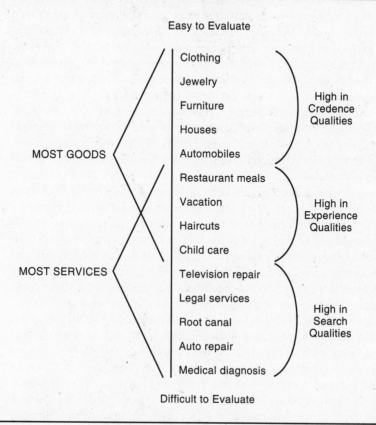

Easy to Evaluate

Clothing

Jewelry

Furniture

Houses

MOST GOODS   Automobiles

High in
Credence
Qualities

Restaurant meals

Vacation

Haircuts

High in
Experience
Qualities

Child care

MOST SERVICES   Television repair

Legal services

Root canal

High in
Search
Qualities

Auto repair

Medical diagnosis

Difficult to Evaluate

Source: Adapted from Valarie A. Zeithaml (1981), "How consumer evaluation processes differ between goods and services," in *Marketing of Services,* James H. Donnelly and William R. George, eds., Chicago: American Marketing Association, pp. 186–190.

customers must believe the presence of these qualities on faith based on the word of others. Figure 1.6 shows how these concepts are related to the complexity of product evaluation and its position on the intangibility continuum.

The moral for marketers is that the more a service possesses experience and credence qualities, the more one must take steps to reduce potential buyers' perceived risk by providing information, by paying careful attention to the image projected by the service's tangible cues, and by maintaining a reputation for quality.

1.8 DEFENSIVE MARKETING

The rising emphasis on customer service reflects, in part, a shift in understanding of the role of marketing in general, from a primarily offensive (new customer) orientation to a more defensive (customer retention) perspective. In the past decade firms have come to realize the importance not only of winning new customers but also of keeping them as long-term partners. The great population and economic growth of the post–World War II era, when marketing concepts were first refined, have given way to much slower growth. However, customer demands for improved quality and rapid technological development have led to shortened product life-cycles and intense global competition. Companies can no longer afford to assume that new customers can be found to replace those who have become dissatisfied and left. In fact, a survey done by the U.S. government revealed that it costs the average firm five times more to win a new customer than it does to do whatever is necessary to keep a current customer happy.[23] As a result, customer retention and the development of long-term relationships, referred to here as defensive market-ing, have become the focus of many companies. For manufacturing and pure ser-vices firms alike, defensive marketing generally means a focus on customer service rather than on physical products.

Successful customer retention programs extend the set of skills required of mar-keting managers, beyond merely requiring them to be more conscious of customer service. In particular, a retention orientation requires firms to be responsive to cus-tomer concerns by keeping open dialogues with them. This approach involves effec-tive programs for receiving and responding to complaints, active solicitation and analysis of customer satisfaction data, and the development of long-term strategic relationships with customers by evolving to meet their changing needs. Each of these activities will be dealt with in more detail in later chapters of the book.

With this expanded list of activities done on the customer's behalf, the ques-tion of costs naturally arises. When is responding to customers' requests good busi-ness, and when is it "giving away the store"? The fundamental credo of defensive marketing is that when dealing with a customer a firm must consider the "lifetime value" of a satisfied customer, rather than the profit to be gained from any indi-vidual transaction. The grocery store's response to a customer's complaint about a 69-cent head of lettuce, if properly handled, may represent thousands of dollars in future profits over the course of her relationship with the store. This perspective shows that short-term, tight-fisted solutions can be more damaging to profits than generous approaches to keeping customers happy. It explains why the Ritz-Carlton hotel chain has granted each of its employees on-the-spot authority to solve cus-tomer problems costing up to several thousand dollars. We will discuss further the calculation of the lifetime value of customers in a later chapter.

But how much is the right amount to spend to keep customers happy? It is cer-tainly possible to lavish too much on customers or to spend money on improving the wrong things. Part VI of the text is an optional section in which we will discuss some methods for determining the appropriate areas and amounts to be spent on quality improvements to improve customer retention, while keeping an eye on their effects on profit.

1.9 THE ORGANIZATION OF THIS BOOK

This book is intended to prepare students to market services in the broadest sense of the term—that is, to win and retain customers by developing a strong customer service orientation both before and after sales are made. It is our belief that this orientation is essential preparation for managers to succeed in the new world of marketing in the twenty-first century.

In Part I of the book we present the traditional view of service marketing, describing the unique aspects of services that require managers to alter the standard practices associated with the marketing of goods. In Part II we enlarge upon our position that *all* marketers must be experts at service marketing, and that the dichotomy between goods and services is an artificial one. Part III describes the marketing activities necessary to give the organization more of a customer service orientation—namely, the staking out of a market positioning and the identification of appropriate customer segments. Once the organization has identified its markets, it must be prepared to listen to its customers. Part IV describes the various programs required to solicit customer input about product quality. A key component in any customer retention program is the monitoring of customer satisfaction through regularly administered surveys. Theoretical background for, and practical implementation of, such surveys are covered in detail in Part V. The findings obtained from such surveys can suggest a wide number of possible quality improvement efforts that might be employed to improve customer satisfaction and retention, but which ones are cost-effective? A variety of procedures for estimating the effect on profits of service quality improvement efforts are described in Part VI. The chapters in Part VII discuss a range of topics related to the implementation of quality improvement efforts, including the design of service encounters, the empowerment of employees to respond to customer needs, and issues involved in establishing long-term relationships with customers. Finally, Part VIII covers the future of service marketing, particularly the extraordinary changes in marketing that will be brought about by the ability of technology to help firms monitor and have dialogs with individual customers on a mass scale.

1.10 SUMMARY

The service sector now dominates the economies of developed and developing nations. The traditional view of service marketing has stressed that services are different from goods in ways that require different management activities. In particular, services are intangible, inseparable, variable, and perishable. To successfully address the marketing complexities posed by these characteristics, the service marketing mix must go beyond the usual four P's to include three additional mix elements: people, physical evidence, and the service process. In addition, the management of service quality through the monitoring of customer satisfaction is perhaps more critical to the success of service marketing than to the marketing of goods.

In fact, we have argued that the distinction between service- and goods-producing sectors of the economy is an artificial one in that *every* firm sells service to its customers. That service consists of four components: the physical product, the service product, the service environment, and service delivery. Services differ on the relative role and importance of the physical product component. But the maintenance of loyal customers requires that even the most goods-oriented firm must understand and adopt service marketing skills.

REVIEW QUESTIONS

1. Some legal and medical firms now advertise their services on television. What do these firms do specifically to address the issue of the intangibility of their services? What could they do better? How are they addressing variability, and how could they improve that aspect of their marketing?

2. Service marketing often involves "tangibilizing the intangible."[24] Some marketers argue that goods marketing attempts to do the opposite: to intangibilize the tangible. Can you provide some examples to illustrate this difference.

3. Marketers often find that the cost of establishing a brand name for a product is well worth the promotional costs involved. Customers often prefer branded products and are willing to pay extra for them because of what the brands represent. For what kinds of services is it possible or desirable to establish brand names? Why do you suppose H&R Block was able to successfully brand tax preparation services while an attempt several years ago to brand dental clinics was a dismal failure?

4. What elements make up the four service components for the following business: a hair salon, a manufacturer of drill presses, a construction company, a producer of canned vegetables?

5. Can tangible products have credence qualities?

6. What is meant by the distinction between offensive and defensive marketing?

ENDNOTES

1. James Brian Quinn (1992), *Intelligent Enterprise,* New York: The Free Press, p. 4, and Stephen M. Shugan (1993), "Explanations for the Growth of Services," in *Service Quality: New Directions in Theory and Practice,* Roland T. Rust and Richard L. Oliver, eds., Newbury Park, CA: Sage Publications.

2. James Brian Quinn, Thomas L. Doorley, Penny C. Pacquette (1990), "Beyond Products: Service-Based Strategy," *Harvard Business Review,* 68 (March–April), 58–68. Also, read the introduction of William R. Davidow and Bro Uttal (1989), *Total Customer Service,* New York: Harper & Row.

3. Ronald Henkoff (1994), "Service is Everybody's Business," *Fortune,* (June 27), 48–60.

4. For an excellent discussion, see J.B. Quinn (1992), *Intelligent Enterprise,* New York: Free Press.

5. Henkoff (1994), *op. cit.*

6. Arsen J. Darnay (ed.) (1992), *Service Industries USA: Industry Analyses, Statistics and Leading Organizations,* Detroit: Gale Research Inc, p. xix.

7. Raymond P. Fisk, Stephen W. Brown, Mary Jo Bitner (1993), "Tracking the Evolution of the Services Marketing Literature," *Journal of Retailing,* 69 (Spring), 61–103.

8. Philip Kotler (1994), *Marketing Management: Analysis, Planning, Implementation, and Control,* 8th ed., Englewood Cliffs, NJ: Prentice-Hall, p. 464.

9. Valarie A. Zeithaml, A. Parasuraman, and Leonard L. Berry (1985), "Problems and Strategies in Services Marketing," *Journal of Marketing,* 49 (Spring), 33–46.

10. Christopher H. Lovelock and John A. Quelch (1983), "Consumer Promotions in Service Marketing," *Journal of Marketing* 49 (Spring), 33–46.

11. Bernard H. Booms and Mary Jo Bitner (1981), "Marketing Strategies and Organizational Structures for Service Firms," in *Marketing of Services,* James H.

Donnelly and William R. George, eds., Chicago: American Marketing Association, 47–51.

12. Mary Jo Bitner (1990), "Evaluating Service Encounters: The Effect of Physical Surroundings and Employee Responses," *Journal of Marketing,* 54 (April), 69–82; Mary Jo Bitner (1992). "Servicescapes: The Impact of Physical Surroundings on Customers and Employees," *Journal of Marketing,* 56 (April), 57–71.

13. Valarie A. Zeithaml, A. Parasuraman, and Leonard L. Berry (1990), *Delivering Quality Service: Balancing Customer Perceptions and Expectations,* New York: Free Press and Leonard L. Berry and A. Parasuraman (1991), *Marketing Services: Competing Through Quality,* New York: Free Press.

14. Henkoff (1994), *op.cit.*

15. Roland T. Rust and Richard L. Oliver (1993), "Service Quality: Insights and Managerial Implications from the Frontier," in *Service Quality: New Directions in Theory and Practice,* Roland T. Rust and Richard L. Oliver, eds., Newbury Park, CA: Sage Publications.

16. See John R. Hauser and Don P. Clausing (1988), "The House of Quality," *Harvard Business Review,* 66 (May–June), 63–73, John R. Hauser (1993), "How Puritan-Bennett Used the House of Quality," *Sloan Management Review,* 35 (Spring), 61–70, and Abbie Griffin and John R. Hauser (1992), Patterns of Communication Among Marketing, Engineering and Manufacturing—A Comparison Between Two New Product Teams," *Management Science,* 38 (March), 360–373.

17. Mary Jo Bitner (1992), "Servicescapes: The Impact of Physical Surroundings on Customers and Employees," *Journal of Marketing,* 56 (April), 57–71.

18. Mary Jo Bitner (1990), "Evaluating Service Encounters: The Effects of Physical Surroundings on Customers and Employees," *Journal of Marketing,* 54 (April), 69–82.

19. Mary Jo Bitner (1992), *op. cit.*

20. Mary Jo Bitner (1992), *op. cit.*

21. Lynn Shostack (1977), "Breaking Free from Product Marketing," *Journal of Marketing,* 41 (April), 73–80.

22. Valarie A. Zeithaml (1981), "How Consumer Evaluation Processes Differ Between Goods and Services," in *Marketing of Services,* James H. Donnelly and William R. George, eds., Chicago: American Marketing Association, pp. 186–190.

23. TARP (1986), *Consumer Complaint Handling in America: An Update Study,* Washington, DC: White House Office of Consumer Affairs.

24. Theodore Levitt (1981), "Marketing Intangible Products and Product Intangibles," *Harvard Business Review* (May–June), 94–102.

Chapter 2

THE NATURE OF DEMAND
FOR SERVICES

2.1 INTRODUCTION

Demand for products generally has a certain amount of unpredictability. Even when management can forecast demand well, precise estimates are generally not possible. Changing economic conditions, unexpected competitive behavior, the weather, and the inevitable unpredictability of human behavior all contribute to a certain level of randomness in demand patterns. Forecast inaccuracies incur two kinds of costs. The first occurs when management plans for more demand than actually materializes. In this case, costs arise from paying for idle capacity (paying full rent for a half-full restaurant) or from having an excess inventory of goods (including inventory holding costs, spoilage and theft losses, and the possible cost of markdowns to sell them). In the second case, when management underestimates demand, possible costs include lost and dissatisfied customers, or high costs required to supply products on an emergency basis. In both cases, producers of both goods and services suffer. However, producers of goods often have a hedge against demand forecast errors that service providers do not have: the ability to carry inventory.

The perishability of services, described in Chapter 1, makes it very difficult for service managers to provide appropriate production capacity when demand fluctuates. For highly intangible services there is no way to build inventories to prepare for predicted increases in demand, much less hold buffer stocks to cover unpredicted surges. Nor is there any way to save unsold inventory—time and capacity—for use later. Even for many services with tangible components, such as fine restaurants, the shelf life of those components may be very short. Therefore, the service firm's window of opportunity to meet customer demand is very small. A mismatch between service capacity and demand therefore results in lost sales.[1]

The capacity/demand mismatch is important for other reasons as well. When demand becomes too great for current service capacity, service quality levels often fall because delays increase and errors occur. Similarly, service quality can degrade when facilities are underutilized, if personnel become bored or if part of the ambience is supplied by the presence of other patrons.

Clearly then, service managers are under greater pressure to predict demand accurately than are managers of primarily tangible goods. In addition, to understand and forecast demand, service managers must also find ways to make capacity flexible, and to monitor capacity usage carefully to keep the organizational profitable.

In this chapter we describe these responsibilities in detail. We begin by describing the components of demand for services and what marketing managers can do to understand and predict them. We then describe ways to use marketing tools to match the timing of demand to the firm's capacity to provide service in an effective way. However, demand can be influenced, but not controlled. To get the most from its assets and to provide consistently high quality the firm must also develop the means to change capacity to meet demand fluctuations. In the final sections of the chapter we discuss techniques for achieving this flexibility and for committing capacity to the most profitable uses.

2.2 WHAT DRIVES DEMAND FOR SERVICES

Variation in demand can be caused by many factors, some of which are predictable and some of which are not. Predicting fluctuations in demand can be greatly improved by decomposing demand into predictable and unpredictable components and by understanding the forces driving each. Figure 2.1 shows how demand may be the net result of three different factors. Figure 2.1a shows an underlying growth trend in demand, perhaps attributable to an increase in population or an upswing in the economy. Figure 2.1b shows how total annual sales are unevenly distributed throughout the year, with the peak selling season occurring during the summer, a slow season during the winter, and two "shoulder" seasons in the spring and autumn. Finally, on top of these predictable patterns there is a certain level of unsystematic and unpredictable "random" variation, depicted in Figure 2.1c. The net effect of these patterns is the actual demand over time depicted in Figure 2.1d.

Many businesses are subject to periodic cycles such as that in Figure 2.1b— for example, increased traffic at a dry cleaner during daily rush hours, decreased patronage of a business-oriented hotel on weekends, or heavier traffic at a tourist destination during the summer. In many cases, a service may be subject to several cycles at once. Consider a roadside diner whose business follows an annual tourist season cycle, a weekday-weekend cycle, and a daily cycle that varies over mealtimes. The various combinations of peaks and valleys of these cycles require different marketing activities to use the facility productively while providing good service. For example, a program to market the restaurant during midafternoons on weekdays in the off-season will be very different from one used on Friday evenings during the height of the tourist season. Preparation for these different periods will require that the manager understand and be able to predict the demand for each.

Random variation in demand is a fact of life for virtually every service. Even when *average* levels of patronage can be predicted rather well, customer arrivals or phone calls don't arrive at a constant rate, but may tend to arrive in "lumps" separated by periods of lighter activity. This situation can be due to simple random variation in traffic levels or may be due to identifiable but hard-to-predict causes,

FIGURE 2.1

DECOMPOSING DEMAND INTO PREDICTABLE CYCLES AND RANDOM VARIATION

(a) Basic growth in demand because of population increase

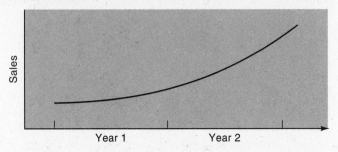

(b) Annual seasonal demand cycle

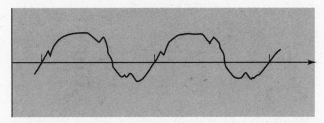

(c) Random fluctuation in demand

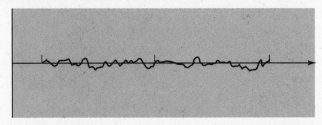

(d) Net effect: Total demand

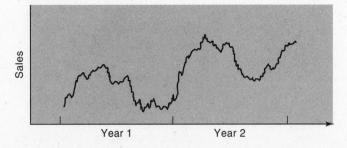

*Restaurants and many other service businesses must
be prepared for unpredictable surges in demand.*

such as bad weather, traffic jams, natural disasters, flu outbreaks, and so on. Although these variations cannot be predicted or controlled, management should nevertheless understand the underlying factors that typically cause them and be prepared to deal with the results so that profitability and appropriate levels of service quality will be maintained.

Some further understanding of sales variation may be attained by decomposing sales by customer segment. To perform segmentation analysis, information must be kept about each transaction that can allow it to be properly classified: customer information, services purchased, purpose for the purchase, whether the visit was by appointment, and the like. Although this information may be costly and difficult to gather for some businesses, others routinely collect it already.

Such detailed data on transactions may provide several key insights. First, it may be possible to pinpoint the underlying causes of demand fluctuation if certain clumps of demand are primarily from a few segments whose causes can be better understood and predicted, even if they can't be controlled. For example, much of the variation in an accounting firm's demand over a year may be due to the various fiscal year-ends of its major clients, and these needs can be planned for well in advance. The firm's demand will also include an unpredictable amount of business

FIGURE 2.2

HYPOTHETICAL DEMAND PROFILE OF AN ACCOUNTING FIRM

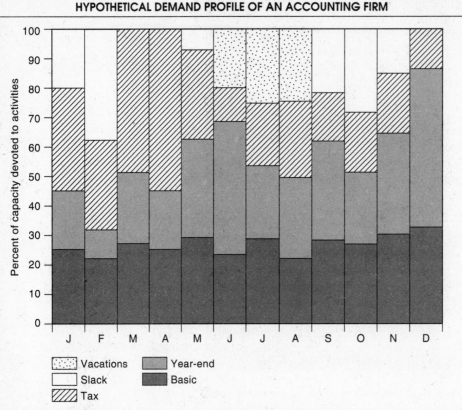

Vacations   Year-end
Slack   Basic
Tax

at tax time, as well as unscheduled demands by its regular clients for help with business crises. The precise volume of demand from these quarters will be harder to anticipate, so the firm must still carry some excess or flexible capacity. A planning diagram such as that in Figure 2.2 can be used to analyze capacity needs over a planning horizon. The firm has anticipated the percent of its capacity that will be devoted to contracted basic services and year-end closing activities, and has estimated the demand for tax-filing assistance (some of which could also be determined in advance by contracts with corporate clients). After including reduced capacity as the result of vacations during the summer months, the remaining capacity is available for new clients and for unanticipated demands by current clients.

Second, such analysis may also reveal that certain sales at peak demand are from segments that are not profitable, are inconsistent with the service image, or are in other ways undesirable. It may be possible to discourage these customers from using the services, at least at peak periods, thereby reducing the strain on capacity and the resulting degradation of service quality. For example, in the wake of a disastrous ice storm that recently caused massive power outages throughout the Southeast, emergency police and fire telephones were swamped with calls from citizens whose electric power was out but who otherwise had no life-threatening emergencies. Announcements were quickly made in all media to discourage these calls and to inform people of the appropriate numbers to call. In preparation for any similar emergencies in the future such information should be broadly communicated in advance, for example, by being prominently displayed in phone books or explained in public service announcements.

Finally, identifying the reason for individual transactions may show that sales to certain segments could be easily diverted to off-peak periods, while others cannot. For example, an outdoor adventure outfitter may find that some of the people who purchase its services during the peak summer months are adults who are not constrained by school schedules and could be persuaded to shift their visits to spring and autumn programs. On the other hand, if the data show that most of the demand is from college students on summer vacation, then it would be clear that there will be no chance of diverting these sales to the "shoulder" seasons.

2.3 WHAT MARKETING CAN DO TO SHAPE DEMAND

Choosing Levels of Demand for a Given Capacity

Although random fluctuations in demand cannot be entirely eliminated, there are steps that service marketers can take to smooth or otherwise manipulate the level of demand over time. Some methods are intended to move demand from peak periods; others are intended to increase demand at slow periods.

The first stage in demand management is to decide on the level of demand desired. It is not necessarily true that a service organization wants to be running at full capacity at all times. The amount of capacity available to accommodate demand is a strategic question, intimately linked to the corporation's positioning, or publicly presented image. For example, some services intentionally set capacity below demand.[2] This practice is common in status-oriented services, such as exclusive country clubs and high-profile nightclubs, which are able to charge high prices from those select few who are chosen to be customers.

Even in these high-status services, the organization's actual capacity to serve customers is usually designed to exceed the number of customers admitted, since service quality often tends to deteriorate when operations are run at or near full capacity. Of course, for some services running at full capacity is acceptable and even preferable. Sporting events and some popular music concerts are considered more enjoyable by all concerned if there is a "packed house." However, many other services suffer from operational problems when systems are pushed too hard. A rule of thumb across many service industries is that quality degrades if more than 75 percent of theoretical capacity is used.[3] Consistently high quality can be provided at that level, but if usage increases beyond it, inefficiencies, errors, bottlenecks, and long waits are likely to result, and the quality of service suffers. In determining the optimal level of demand for a given capacity, the firm must weigh its desire for short-term revenue (and the urge to "pack 'em in") against its need to protect its reputation for high-quality service and its long-term viability.

At the other extreme is demand which is far below capacity. Not only does low demand cost the firm money, in that revenues may not be sufficient to support fixed costs, but it also can have a detrimental effect on customer satisfaction. To the extent that the presence of other customers contributes to the ambience of the service experience, low demand negatively affects perceived service quality. Going to a poorly attended ball game or concert can certainly detract from the excitement that customers expect to experience. Moreover, service quality may also suffer if service personnel become bored, and lose their enthusiasm for doing a good job. This can lead to a vicious cycle, as poor performance will only lead to still lower demand, further demoralizing the staff. Service reputation may also suffer if the firm acts rashly in its attempt to "fill seats" by attracting a mix of customers who are not compatible with the regular clientele or to whom the service staff cannot relate well.

The manager's job in this case is to find ways to stimulate greater demand while protecting the service's positioning in the minds of its regular customers. Some of this new demand may be current customers shifted from high demand periods, or it may come from new customers generated by marketing efforts. Alternatively, the firm may use these periods of slack capacity for facilities maintenance and repair, restocking of tangible good inventories, and other tasks that are essential to operations but are difficult to perform during periods of high traffic.

Using the Marketing Mix to Manage Demand Levels

Once an optimal level of demand has been determined for the given level of capacity at various times, the elements of the marketing mix can be manipulated to alter demand to meet those target figures.

Price   The standard economic solution to over- or underutilized services is to alter the price to change demand. Resort hotels routinely raise prices during "the season" and charge lower rates during the off-season to attempt to level the use of facilities. Movie theaters charge lower prices for matinees to encourage people to attend during usually slow daytime hours. Health clubs often offer reduced rates to senior citizens, provided they use the facilities only at off-peak hours such as mid-mornings or midafternoons. Some barbershops charge more for children's haircuts on weekends than on weekdays to free up the facilities for adults who have trouble getting away from work during the week.

These examples illustrate several factors about the use of pricing as a demand leveler. Economic theory tells us that to maximize profits one must understand demand curves, the relationship between prices and the number of customers willing to pay those prices. It's obvious that for most nonstatus products, as price goes up, demand goes down, as in Figure 2.3. What the marketer must know to maximize profits is (1) how many people will pay a particular price, and (2) if the price is changed, will the loss (gain) of some customers be more than offset by the increased (decreased) revenue from each of the customers who buy at the new price. This information is essential, but getting it is extremely difficult. Some sense of what the market will bear can be obtained by studying competitive prices and similar markets, but experimentation and research may also be required to develop a complete understanding of demand.

Determining demand curves for services is complicated by several factors. First of all, since services are time-dependent and cannot be stored for later use, demand curves can vary over time. The resort hotel demand curves in Figure 2.3 show that the market is much less price-sensitive during prime vacation months than it is in

FIGURE 2.3

A DEMAND CURVE FOR A RESORT HOTEL

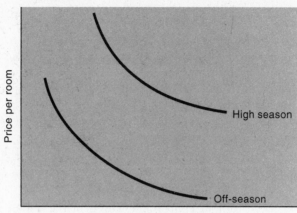

the off-season, so different demand curves must be determined. (Perishable goods also have time-dependent demand curves, of course. How much would a Chicagoan pay for a fresh vine-ripened tomato in January?)

Second, at any point in time different customer segments can have different demand curves. Business travelers (and others who book on short notice or who do not stay at their destinations over Saturday night) can be induced to pay more for airline tickets than vacation travelers. Movie theaters and hair salons charge lower rates for children because they (or their parents) may be less willing to use the services as heavily at full price. (The lower prices in these instances certainly don't reflect lower variable costs or less wear-and-tear on the facilities.)

The firm's objective is usually to obtain maximum profits from the various segments while maintaining the integrity of the firm's quality level. The existence of multiple demand curves complicates this process.

When multiple segments are served at the same time, the challenge for the marketer is to keep those customers willing to pay top dollar from choosing lower-priced alternatives instead. This result is usually achieved by separating service levels into classes and by providing value enhancements to the higher-priced classes. For example, airlines provide earlier boarding, wider seats, free drinks, and better food for first-class passengers to justify considerably higher ticket prices. Still, not all segments of the market perceive the additional value, and many passengers prefer to pay less and fly coach. (Witness the oft-heard comment of the utilitarian coach flier, that "both ends of the plane arrive at the same time.") Service marketers must be certain that the amenities provided justify the additional price to its customers, so that the higher-paying segments will not settle for the less expensive class of services.

Firms may be able to enforce price discrimination among segments by restricting access to various prices, such as the "Saturday night stay" requirement used by airlines to segment price-sensitive and price-insensitive customers. Many restaurants and other services offer special discounts for students and senior citizens, who are less able to pay full price, but some sort of identification is usually required. This device can also be used to smooth demand if these discounts are restricted to off-peak times.

Finally, some services that have long-term, "membership" relationships with customers use "initiation fees" to maintain demand by discouraging customers from switching away. Many health clubs, for example, charge sizable one-time fees upon joining in addition to monthly membership charges. Although these fees are actually "sunk costs" to customers, they do tend to discourage customers from switching or quitting because of the money they have "invested." If all competitors also charge initiation fees, switching is further suppressed.

Products   Price is not the only way to manage demand. In fact, in some cases it has no effect at all. For example, the Greenbriar resort in White Sulphur Springs, West Virginia, is a luxury destination hotel with extensive grounds, most of which are devoted to world-class golf courses. However, in the winter months and in inclement weather these facilities are obviously not an attraction to (most) golfers, no matter how much prices are discounted. The hotel's only recourse was to offer additional services that certain segments of its clientele will find attractive. It has responded to the challenge with a host of indoor and outdoor sporting activities, cultural events, cooking seminars, and other attractions and amenities that will support demand even when golf is out of season.

Altering the product mix is a common approach used by many services to even demand, whether to meet the changing tastes and needs of its clientele over time, or to reach different segments at different times. For example, some Colorado ski resorts that appeal to wealthy skiers in the winter months become havens for backpackers and white-water rafters in the summer months. Some 7 Eleven stores in Japan change the entire stock on their shelves three times a day to appeal to the different needs of morning, midday, and evening customers.

Again, the challenge is to be certain that the image of the service is not confused by these different services and the possibly incompatible segments to which they are targeted. To take an extreme example, a movie theater that shows children's movies on Saturday morning and family pictures during the week would undoubtedly jeopardize its standing with these customers if it decided to show hard-core pornography on late Saturday nights. Choosing countercyclical products must be done with extreme care for the image and strategic focus of the firm. Smoothing demand does not mean taking on any business one can get or getting involved with segments and technologies where the firm is at a competitive disadvantage. These decisions must be made within the context of the firm's overall image strategy.

Marketing Communications   In some cases, advertising or personal selling can be used to persuade customers to shift demand to low periods. Con Edison, New York City's electric utility, must provide capacity to meet tremendous daytime demand by commercial and public users, while much of this capacity lies idle at night. To avoid having to build even more capacity to serve nonessential domestic daytime use Con Ed has occasionally run advertising messages asking consumers

Many ski resorts have develop summertime activities to keep their facilities generating revenues all year round.

to run their appliances at night whenever possible. The implied payoff for consumers is lower utility rates. In other cases, it may be sufficient to remind customers that they can avoid long lines or receive more personal service if they come at off-peak hours.

In addition to shifting demand, more intense communication may be able to generate more new business to fill slow periods. Although firms often allocate advertising, promotion, and selling budgets to mirror the current patterns of demand,[4] marketing should consider the possibility of increasing the intensity of communication in slow periods. In particular, service firms should explore ways to induce trials using sales promotions techniques that reduce risk, including limited free trials (when possible) and discount coupons, or programs that attract attention and generate excitement, such as contests and premiums.

Distribution   Management can also consider increasing demand by adjusting the places and times at which services are offered. The development of satellite offices, mobile units, and home delivery are all ways to access to a service more convenient for the customer. Many hospitals have created satellite clinics to deal with minor emergencies and routine consultations. The Red Cross uses mobile blood donation centers that can drive to offices and factories to allow donors to fit donations into their schedules. This simultaneously encourages higher levels of donation and helps to shift some of the evening and weekend demand for services. Similarly, more convenient hours of operation may also increase the number of customers who can purchase a service. Wal-Mart, a leader in customer service, now keeps many of its stores open 24 hours per day to accommodate its customers who have day and/or evening jobs. Lotus Corporation's telephone support for its 1–2–3 spreadsheet software is also available 24 hours a day, seven days a week.

Other Methods of Managing Demand

Even when demand is well matched to capacity *on average,* random fluctuations in arrival rates can result and can cause waiting lines or periods of idle capacity. The unevenness of customer arrivals can be handled in a variety of ways: by insisting that customers have reservations, by asking customers to wait for a service opening, by asking them to come back later, by sending them to another company unit, or even arranging for them to go to a competitor.

Reservations   One way to smooth demand and to reduce customer discomfort associated with waiting is through the use of reservations. The system can often direct customer arrivals into time periods that would otherwise be slow. However, the downside of a reservation-based system is that customers occasionally fail to show up for appointments. This typically results in lost revenues, since there is too little time to contact and reschedule other customers to fill the gaps in the schedule. For this reason services that are able to do so demand prepayments that are not refundable unless adequate cancellation time is given. Hotels usually offer a mixture of reservation agreements. Because those that take reservations also have many unscheduled arrivals as well, they do not generally penalize customers who fail to arrive, since reserved rooms are not held past 6 P.M. and can often be resold if unclaimed. Only so-called guaranteed reservations, which are held all night, require nonrefundable deposits because they provide the hotel with no chance of filling the lost capacity if the customers fail to show up.

A common strategy to deal with no-shows when customers suffer no penalties for not appearing is to overbook—that is, to promise more reservations than there is capacity available. If the firm has a good understanding of the percent of customers who tend not to show up and uses this information to limit the amount of overbooking, then this policy can work most of the time. However, given the nature of random variation, the number of arrivals will occasionally exceed available capacity. In those cases the firm must be ready to assuage angry customers with some form of recompense. Airlines, whether justified or not, are notorious among customers for overbooking, but are usually prepared to pay excess passengers with valuable free tickets to take later flights.

Waiting Lines   Intangible services cannot be inventoried in advance, but once a customer arrives he or she may be willing to wait for service to begin: In effect one can inventory customer arrivals instead. Making a customer wait for service is the equivalent of a backorder to a manufacturer. However, the length of time a customer is willing to wait for service is generally much shorter than the time one is willing to wait for an ordered product to arrive. If a service firm can determine the maximum length of time that customers consider to be acceptable and can predict the probability distribution of arrivals, it is then possible to use an area of applied mathematics called queuing theory to design the service delivery system's capacity to keep queue lengths to generally satisfactory lengths.

Waiting lines are the service marketer's alternative to holding inventory.

It is also possible to affect the perceived length of time that customers must wait by providing diversions. For example, many restaurants offer lounges where patrons can pleasantly pass the time (and provide additional profits for the firm) until they are ready to be served. At Disney World's Epcot Center in Florida, waiting areas for some of the attractions provide high-quality entertainment such as short films to help visitors pass the time until the actual shows begin. Many companies play recorded music or advertising messages for telephone callers who have been put on hold. And of course, doctors stock their waiting rooms with magazines and children's toys to help waiting patients pass the time.

Although many queues operate on a first-come, first-served basis, other priority arrangements (known as "queue disciplines") are possible. Certain services, such as emergency rooms, provide service on the basis of critical need (using a "triage" system) rather than order of arrival. Retail stores with express lanes are segmenting customers into separate queues based on estimated length of service time. Some services also divide customers by segment, such as banks that have separate teller lines for retail and commercial customers, a good but imperfect predictor of the actual time needed to complete transactions.

In each of these queue disciplines, the marketer must balance the overall level of service provided against the aggravation of those who must be forced to wait the longest. If a customer feels that he or she has been forced to wait an unreasonable amount of time, there is usually an option of leaving the system and going to a competitor. By segmenting customers into different queues, overall customer satisfaction can be maximized: With a few exceptions, grocery customers with full shopping carts expect to wait longer, whereas customers buying "six items or less" may be generally less tolerant and in more of a hurry.

Letting the Market Figure It Out

It is not absolutely necessary that the service organization take upon itself the task of smoothing demand. To some extent it can be left to the customers to learn when the facilities are crowded and when they aren't. This allows customers to self-select the level of waiting and crowding they can tolerate. Those who are sensitive to these matters will have an incentive to come at less busy times, whereas those who don't mind will continue to arrive at peak periods. This approach assumes that demand will remain high and that customers will continue to find the effort involved worthwhile. Clearly some government offices use this approach, because their customers have no alternatives when demand is high and the managers do not have to worry about covering their fixed costs when demand is low. But commercial services that are truly concerned about customer satisfaction and profits must take active steps to match demand to available capacity.

2.4 MANAGING SERVICE CAPACITY

In the previous section we spoke of attempting to manage the demand for a service. But, since demand cannot be perfectly controlled, efficient management of resources requires that the firm also consider changing capacity by increasing it to meet high demand and contracting it in slack periods. Service capacity has several components that can be altered to match changes in demand.[5]

People   For many services, the most easily changeable component is people, the service providers. In some instances it is easier to hire and fire people than it is to purchase and divest buildings and machinery. This approach can be costly, however, if employees require extensive training to provide the service or if hiring and layoff costs are high. In such cases firms may prefer to supplement their permanent workforces with cadres of part-time employees who work fewer hours, but who are employed often enough to keep their skills sharp. For example, the retailer Nordstrom's is able to adjust to increases in customer traffic by keeping lists of part-time salesclerks who can help out on short notice. However, the fact that part-time workers often have high turnover rates can run up expenses if training costs are high.

Another solution that avoids training and hiring costs is to simply increase the work hours of the regular staff during periods of high demand. This policy provides high flexibility in matching short-term demand fluctuations, but it cannot be sustained for long periods of time. The cost of overtime pay and the effects on service quality of tired employees can overwhelm the benefits. Moreover, when demand falls below desired levels, labor capacity can't be correspondingly reduced by shortening the hours of full-time employees. However, labor hour capacity can be reduced by scheduling vacations and alternative maintenance duties during such periods.

The capacity of the workforce can also be made more flexible through extensive crosstraining, which enables employees to perform several different jobs. This approach allows management to reassign those working at less essential tasks to assist temporarily at points of high demand. For example, many retail stores have people working in backroom operations who can assist in serving customers when traffic becomes too great for the regular sales staff.

It is also possible to increase the productivity, and hence work capacity, of a staff without adding more people through training in improved job skills and by motivating personnel through inspiring leadership.

Facilities Physical facilities are often more difficult to adjust. Adding a building tends to increase capacity by large amounts, and moving to new quarters of appropriate size is an impractical solution if done too frequently. However, a service firm with multiple outlets may be able to accommodate excess demand at one facility by sending it to other units. Firms may also have the option of renting temporary facilities.

Facilities can also contribute to the improvement of productive capacity by providing a comfortable, efficient environment in which to work.

Equipment and Tools Productivity enhancement tools can increase the capacity of a fixed work force by freeing the staff from time-wasting, repetitive tasks. These tools can be as simple as an envelope for storing receipts given to H&R Block customers at the beginning of each year, which greatly reduces tax preparation time.[6] Or they can be as elaborate as the extensive systems of automatic teller machines that banks have built to allow their counter people to devote more time to customers needing more complex services. Manufacturers of sophisticated computer and electronics products build self-diagnostic components into their products to avoid sending costly engineers into the field to do routine analyses. Computers that automate ordering and billing activities and keep track of customer purchase histories have transformed operations performed by the clerical staff in many kinds of firms. However, some equipment can be extremely expensive and only available in increments that add large units of capacity and thus make the firm less flexible. In such cases, firms may be able to rent the equipment or share ownership with other firms.

Time Time is the most perishable component of service capacity. Time capacity can be increased by simply operating for longer hours, although this is not an option if those times do not match customer needs. Increasing hours of operations also produces some of the complications with personnel mentioned above. Time capacity can also be increased by shortening the time required to serve customers— that is, by shortening the length of time customers spend in the service (for example, by shortening the rides at an amusement park). It can also be done by reducing the amount of time customers spend with the most time-constrained assets (increasing the capacity of the hospital's best surgeon by assigning all but the most essential tasks to other staff).

Time can also be saved by using periods of slack demand for other uses, particularly for maintenance and repair. These functions must be performed at sometime or other; however, if they can be scheduled away from peak demand periods, the overall productivity of the service's facilities will be improved.

One way to level the demand on time is to try to convince customers to wait for service during less hectic periods. This option may be undesirable or even impossible for certain customers, however, and can result in loss of sales to competitors.

Matching Capacity to Demand

Management must analyze these components of capacity, particularly at periods of maximum demand to determine which ones are causing service bottlenecks (Figure 2.4). A technique called blueprinting, to be discussed later, can be used to identify critical stages. Those points that are constraining capacity should then be altered to provide the level of service desired.

Strategies for Capacity Flexibility   The amount of flexibility a firm should build into its capacity is a strategic decision, which is determined by the type of service offered, costs, labor availability and other factors. At one extreme is a level-capacity strategy, in which the firm designs its systems to provide a constant level of capacity and absorbs the costs when demand is far above or far below that level. At the other extreme is the strategy to "chase demand" with capacity that can be rapidly expanded or contracted to meet current needs. A given firm's optimal level of flexibility to match capacity to demand will fall somewhere between those two extremes.

A firm should tend toward a level-capacity strategy, particularly in its personnel policies, when employees are required to have high skill levels and to work with minimal supervision and must exercise personal discretion in dealing with customers. Such jobs typically have high recruitment and training costs, so low turnover is essential. These firms may also require long lead times to change facility or equipment capacity, and these changes can only be made in large, discrete increments. This strategy is also more acceptable if operations are automated to the extent that the marginal cost of dealing with additional customers is low.

FIGURE 2.4

USING THE MARKETING MIX TO MATCH DEMAND AND CAPACITY		
	When Demand Is Too High	**When Demand Is Too Low**
Price	Raise prices, in general, or to certain segments Use price promotions to shift demand to off-peak times	Lower prices, in general, or to certain segments Offer price promotions
Promotion	Encourage off-peak usage	Encourage trial
Product/Process	Schedule reservations Alter process to allow more customer involvement Standardize or simplify to increase productivity and production capacity Use waiting lines	Add new services to use slack capacity and attract new users
Distribution	Extend hours Add additional sites, if possible	Make hours more convenient Offer more convenient locations
People	Train more people to perform parts of process Keep part-timers available Segment customers by time-sensitivity and encourage less sensitive to come at off-peak times	Keep inappropriate segments from mixing together

A chase strategy is more appropriate for firms with labor-intensive operations requiring low-skilled employees who require little training and where part-time employees can be quickly brought in. High labor turnover is actually an advantage in this case, because capacity can be quickly reduced without incurring layoff costs.

Customer Involvement   Another source of additional capacity is the customer himself or herself. By converting certain operations to self-service, the firm's own personnel can be diverted to other functions. Buffets and salad bars at restaurants are a common example. Discount investment brokers, who leave researching of investment alternatives to the customer, have been remarkably successful, now accounting for more than 30% of the broker business.[7] The Shouldice Hospital in Toronto, a facility that deals exclusively with hernia operations, requires its patients to perform a wide number of tasks that are typically done by staff in other hospitals—from self-diagnosis in the application process to pre-op preparations to counseling of other patients. Although this involvement works well for Shouldice's patients, and in fact adds an important sense of reassurance and control to the patient's experience, asking paying customers to perform some of the service tasks can often lead to dissatisfaction. In general, requiring customers to provide their own service must be reflected in lower prices or they tend to feel they are being cheated. Self-service firms also lose a certain measure of control over service quality when customers are asked to perform key steps, so managers must be careful to transfer only easily accomplished tasks to their patrons.

Other Methods to Alter Capacity   In addition to adjusting the various components of capacity listed above, services have developed other ways to increase capacity. One is to use subcontractors to bolster service capacity. This can give the firm access to highly-trained employees for short periods of time. Similarly, the firm may be able to rent facilities and equipment on short notice.

2.5 GETTING THE MOST OUT OF CAPACITY

Consider a typical problem faced by hotel managers. An airline headquartered in the area would like to book a large number of rooms for a week next spring to house flight attendant trainees during their orientation program. The airline is demanding a rate considerably below standard rates, but the income would be guaranteed. On the other hand, there is a chance—but no guarantee—that a medical convention scheduled at another hotel for the same time will spill over to other sites at the last minute, and doctors attending the convention will be willing to pay top dollar for rooms in the hotel. What should the manager do to improve the odds of making the highest profits: lock in the guaranteed but low rate on the rooms, or hold out in hopes of realizing much higher profits from the medical convention? The manager's success will be determined not by the percent of rooms filled, but by the profit that can be generated for the firm.

Similar dilemmas are faced on a regular basis by managers of many services, including restaurants, airlines, trucking and printing firms, broadcasting networks, and so on. The markets for each of these services contain customers with widely varying abilities (or willingness) to pay. Price sensitivity generally decreases the closer to the time for service delivery the decision is made. These service firms have capacity that can neither be increased nor decreased easily, so booking the mix of customers that maximizes profits takes careful advanced planning of the use of their limited facilities. Moreover, since the costs of serving customers from different segments do not usually vary as widely as the prices paid, the firm does better the higher the amount it can charge, all other things being equal. The challenge is to know when to lock in certain business early and when to refuse such business in hopes of big spenders showing up later. Of course, sometimes the hoped-for high-priced business will not appear, and the service capacity will go to waste. Management must understand that taking risks doesn't pay off every time. The object is to understand the odds well enough that the *average* yield over time is maximized.

The key to making good decisions about advance reservations is having good information. To generate the highest possible profits from their service assets managers need accurate forecasts of demand as well as sound information on price sensitivity and the costs incurred in serving various market segments. In particular, marketing research and experience in the market are necessary to develop a sense of the probability of arrivals of customers from different price segments and at different times. This information can then be used to set limits on the number of units which will be presold at various prices by particular points in time. For example, a resort hotel planning its summer sales might determine from past data that it has a strong possibility of selling 25% of its rooms on short notice to customers who will pay high rates for rooms. This information can in turn be given to the sales force and reservations clerks to guide their selling efforts, and with the policy that its staff refuse to book reservations for that percent of its rooms at prices below the anticipated high rates.

Because different segments have individual demand patterns, these optimal sales allocation profiles generally vary over time, which adds an additional dimension to the information that service marketers must collect. The ideal mix of classes of business may differ by week, by day of the week, even by the hour of the day. Management must therefore develop a selling plan with different sales targets for each segment of customers at different times.

Even with this information, the allocation decision cannot be an objective profit-maximizing exercise. Subjective factors must also play a part in allocating capacity to various segments. For example, the effect on long-term customer relationships of refusing business must be considered. As we will discuss later in the book, one must consider the lifetime value of a customer, not merely the profit to be obtained from a particular transaction. Another issue to consider is the interaction among customers, and the effect on the firm's strategic positioning that can result from allocating too much capacity to segments that do not interact well with others or with the staff. For example, in the case of the hotel mentioned earlier, a high percentage of corporate trainees among the guests might adversely affect the hotel's image as an upscale facility, even though it may be most profitable in the short run to do so.

2.6 SUMMARY

Unlike goods, which usually have relatively long "shelf lives," services must be produced at the moment they are consumed. Therefore service marketers must match their productive capacity to increases and decreases in demand. Too little capacity to meet demand may mean lost sales and lower-quality service for those who are served. Too much idle capacity can cost the firm if fixed costs are not being covered by revenues and can also reduce service quality. Service firms must therefore understand what drives demand fluctuations. There are actions they can take that may be able to alter demand fluctuations so as to improve the firms' abilities to meet it. On the other side, firms can design their services to have more flexible productive capacity.

To understand what causes changes in demand, fluctuations should be decomposed into separate parts, particularly the systematic and random components. Demand should also be disaggregated by market segment to determine which purchases can possibly be shifted in time and which cannot. Once demand patterns are understood, marketers can use a variety of standard marketing tools to influence them. Price discounting at off-peak hours is the most obvious way to smooth demand; however, it is not the only tool available, and in some cases it will not be effective at all. Product changes, communication appeals, and changes in distribution strategy can also be used to manage demand. Requiring customers to make reservations or designing waiting-line systems are also used to match demand to capacity. In all cases, management must strike a balance between managing demand and negatively affecting the strategic positioning of the firm.

Since demand cannot be perfectly controlled, firms must also find ways to adjust service capacity. Capacity consists of several components, each of which may be adjusted to change total service throughput. These components include the people in the organization, the firm's facilities, its equipment and tools, and time available to serve customers. Choosing the level of capacity flexibility a firm wishes to possess is a strategic decision that depends on market conditions and on components of the service delivery process. Some firms may choose to provide a constant level of capacity, but most develop varying abilities to "chase demand."

Service capacity is a scarce resource, and customers vary in their willingness to pay premium prices. Therefore, service firms with profit-maximizing objectives must develop strategies to allocate their capacity optimally to serve different segments. This is particularly true for firms that sell services in advance. The key to making good decisions is having accurate information about the likelihood of purchase and likely contribution margins for each of the different segments. However, short-term profit maximization goals should also be tempered by long-term considerations, which are often much harder to quantify.

REVIEW QUESTIONS

1. What measures does the U.S. Postal Service take to smooth demand for its services at Christmas time? How might each of the four P's be used to reduce peak demand for these services?
2. Federal Express, the overnight package delivery firm, has a huge fleet of aircraft that sits idle during daylight hours. At one time the firm considered

using its fleet for daytime passenger service to make use of this enormous idle capacity. Upon further review they scrapped the idea. Why do you suppose they did so?

3. A café in a city business district is a popular lunch place for merchants and business executives during the day. At night the café features a blues band and caters to a fairly rough crowd, occasionally requiring police to break up fights. This arrangement has been successful for many years. How is that possible?

4. What are the components of capacity for supermarkets, haircutting salons, professional football stadiums, universities, radio stations? How do these organizations adjust their capacity to meet predicted and unpredicted fluctuations in demand?

5. Hotels sometimes measure their success in terms of their occupancy rates—that is, the percent of rooms rented. Why is this measure incomplete?

6. Airline A posts fares between Chicago and New York of $350 but, because of a variety of promotional programs, sell its seats for average fare of $275. It is flying at load factors of 75%. Airline B also posts a price of $350 and offers comparable service, but does far less discounting. It receives an average ticket price of $327, but has load factors of only 65%. Which airline is more efficient at generating revenues from its assets.

ENDNOTES

1. Much of this chapter is based upon material in W. Earl Sasser, Jr. (1976), "Match Supply and Demand in Service Industries," *Harvard Business Review* (November–December), 133–140; Robert G. Murdick, Barry Render, and Roberta S. Russell (1990), *Service Operations Management,* Boston: Allyn and Bacon; and Christopher H. Lovelock (1991), *Services Marketing,* Englewood Cliffs, NJ: Prentice-Hall.
2. Murdick, Render, and Russell, *op. cit.,* p. 214.
3. James L. Heskett (1986), *Managing in the Service Economy,* Boston: Harvard University Press, p. 38.
4. Ray Schudson (1985), *Advertising: The Uneasy Persuasion,* New York: McGraw-Hill.
5. Murdick, Render, and Russell, *op. cit.*
6. Heskett (1986), *op. cit.,* p. 60.
7. Heskett (1986), *op. cit.,* p. 105.

Chapter 3

A FRAMEWORK FOR SERVICE MARKETING MANAGEMENT

3.1 INTRODUCTION

Chapters 1 and 2 described the traditional view of service marketing, including such topics as the difference between services and products, how to price and promote a service, and the nature of customer demand in services. A new view of service marketing is currently emerging, which complements (but does not replace) the traditional view. This emerging view incorporates many of the principles of customer service, customer orientation, and quality management, which became widely applied in the late 1980s and early 1990s. The emerging view is well-suited to a world in which even product companies must compete on the basis of service and in which the environment is changing rapidly. The emphasis of the emerging paradigm is that of continually improving services to increase customer satisfaction and thus revenues, market share, and profits.

The emerging view of service marketing is not to be confused with the quality movement of the 1980s or the reengineering movement of the 1990s, even though it borrows many quality improvement and reengineering techniques. Both the quality movement of the 1980s and the reengineering movement had primarily an *inward* focus, trying to streamline business processes to drive down costs. That much is fine, but there is only so far that costs can be reduced. As one major corporation told us, "We discovered that we couldn't shrink our way to profitability." Ultimately the shareholders want profitability *growth,* and that is possible only through expanding sales. Usually companies that want to expand sales think in terms of advertising more or cutting price. But advertising is increasingly ineffective (see the Rust and Oliver article, "The Death of Advertising," in the readings), and price cutting directly decreases margins, which, all other things being equal, also tends to reduce profits. Thus we need an alternative approach to expanding revenues and profits, and that is what this book is about.

We first discuss some central assumptions that drive the emerging paradigm. These assumptions lead to some guiding principles that help determine the topics service marketing should address, and describe a managerial philosophy for modern service marketing. Finally we describe a blueprint for action, which shows the steps management can take to implement the new approach to service marketing management.

3.2 CENTRAL ASSUMPTIONS

The central assumptions of the emerging view are statements that most leading corporations would accept as truths. Even so, the consequences of fully acting upon these assumptions are profound. What makes these assumptions especially powerful in suggesting the direction of change in service marketing is that each of them is becoming increasingly true over time. In other words, the managerial principles resulting from these assumptions will become increasingly appropriate, given the current trends in the business environment. The three central assumptions are outlined in Figure 3.1.

The first assumption is that *every organization is a service*. By this we do not mean that every organization avoids physical products. Rather, what we mean is that although not every company produces a physical product, every company produces a service. For example, suppose Nissan decided that it was a product company and could ignore service. To cut costs, it would quickly sell off its dealerships and repair shops. It would also stop shipping its cars around the world, because that too is a service. Ultimately, Nissan would be a collection of manufacturing plants, in places such as Japan and Smyrna, Tennessee, waiting for customers to come to the plant to buy a car.

The reason this strategy appears so absurd is that we all expect even manufacturing firms to supply a wide array of services to customers. In fact, it is easy to see that what the customer really demands is the service of transportation, and Nissan is wise to supply that service as completely as possible. (See Shugan's article in the readings in Part I for another view of how the auto industry is really a service.)

FIGURE 3.1

CENTRAL ASSUMPTIONS OF THE EMERGING VIEW

1. Every organization is a service.

2. The primary purpose of the organization is to satisfy customers.

3. Customer requirements are constantly changing.

This assumption is becoming increasingly true as two major trends accelerate. First, as discussed earlier, the service sector itself is becoming much more important. Second, the service content of products is becoming greater as computerization and new communications networks make possible a much higher information content in every product, and as flexible manufacturing methods make it possible to customize products to a much greater degree. Thus we call what we are doing "service marketing" instead of "services marketing" so as to emphasize that service is important for both services and goods.

Note that if every organization is really a service, then management's emphasis naturally moves to satisfying the customer. This is the second assumption of the emerging view: *that the primary purpose of any organization is to satisfy its customers*. It is easy to see how this assumption is becoming a competitive necessity. Imagine, for example, two companies (Company A and Company B), which have equal resources that they can spend on either satisfying customers or doing other things. Suppose Company A spends more on satisfying customers than does Company B. A's customers become more satisfied, and tend to stay with Company A at a higher rate, resulting in steadily increasing market share for Company A, and eventually driving Company B out of the market. "Survival of the fittest" thus ensures that satisfying customers will become the leading priority of organizations if there is a competitive market. Because we know that markets are increasingly becoming global, as information transfer becomes more efficient and as intangible goods become a larger percentage of the economy, we know that markets are becoming increasingly competitive, and therefore satisfying customers will become more and more important in the coming years.

The third assumption is that *customer requirements are constantly changing*. Management must continually adapt to a changing marketplace because the only constant is change. Thus a premium is placed on continuously monitoring and adapting to the changing marketplace. For this reason these issues are given increased emphasis in the emerging view of service marketing. It is important to recognize that the assumption of constantly changing customer needs is increasingly true over time. The causes are the acceleration of technological change, especially with respect to communications, and profound social changes caused by an increasing rate of world population growth. The net result is that few cultures of the world are really stable, and the people who make up those cultures have dramatically different needs and wants than their own grandparents had. Consider, for example, how much U.S. society has changed since the 1930s. If a modern consumer were suddenly restricted to the consumption options of the 1930s, that consumer would likely feel very unhappy and deprived.

As another example, consider South Africa. Until the 1990s that country was governed by the principle of apartheid, which kept blacks separate from whites in many respects. The dismantling of apartheid brought black people into the mainstream of South African society, bringing dramatic changes to the needs, wants, and expectations of consumers in that country.

Likewise, New Zealand has experienced dramatic change, albeit from an explicitly economic rather than social upheaval. Until the 1980s New Zealand was one of the most socialistic countries in the world. In the 1980s that country moved strongly toward a free-market economy, resulting in a dramatic increase in economic competition. The expectations of consumers rose greatly as the increased competition increased the consumption alternatives available. At the same time, the range of incomes dramatically increased, as it became possible to be very poor or very rich, for the first time. This wider range of incomes in turn produced a wider range of consumer needs.

3.3 GUIDING PRINCIPLES

The central assumptions suggest the appropriateness of a new approach to service marketing management, which can be characterized by five guiding principles, as shown in Figure 3.2. Methods of implementing these principles then become a blueprint for action.

The first principle is to *improve service continually.* No matter how good a job the organization is doing of supplying service, it must continually improve. This is essential because of the assumption that customer requirements are constantly changing. As a result, what is good today may be bad tomorrow. Service must change to accommodate changing customer needs. Note that the emphasis is somewhat changed from the manufacturing quality control concept of continual improvement. Here our emphasis is on customers and their changing needs, rather than the efficiency of internal processes.

The second principle is to *concentrate on the areas most important to customer retention.* This principle consciously rejects the idea of improving everything all at once. Resources are instead focused on the areas that will have the greatest impact.

FIGURE 3.2

GUIDING PRINCIPLES FOR THE EMERGING VIEW

1. Improve service continually.

2. Concentrate on the areas most important to customer retention.

3. Use customer satisfaction to expand revenues.

4. Make sure service improvement efforts are financially accountable.

5. Delight—don't just satisfy—the customer.

The emphasis is also on customer retention rather than customer attraction. This is not to denigrate the importance of such marketing mix issues as advertising, pricing, and promotion, but rather to recognize that the primary purpose of the organization is to satisfy customers, and that the bottom-line measure of customer satisfaction is usually customer retention.

The third principle is to *use customer satisfaction to expand revenues*. Revenue expansion results from customer satisfaction through the mechanisms of customer retention and word of mouth. The key here is that service improvement efforts are not just for cost cutting. We emphasize instead the marketing side of service improvement, which is revenue expansion through customer satisfaction. Higher revenues in turn produce increased market share and larger profits, thereby resulting in growth for shareholder investments.

The fourth principle is to *make sure that service improvement efforts are financially accountable*. Not all service improvement efforts pay. Any expenditure for the improvement of service may be viewed as an investment. Because the primary purpose of the organization is to satisfy its customers, and one of its important customer groups is its shareholders, investments made by the firm must satisfy return targets set by the shareholders, as represented by the board of directors. Thus expenditures must all be made with consideration of the rate of return, and service improvement efforts are no exception.

The final principle is to *delight—not just satisfy—the customer*. Mere satisfaction is generally thought of as resulting from problem avoidance. But all good organizations seek to avoid problems, which means that in many mature markets the surviving competitors will all be relatively problem-free. This means that any competitive advantage from customer satisfaction will often have to be based on a higher order of customer satisfaction, which is commonly called "customer delight," and arises from surprising and exceptional service.

It should be clear that these five principles have considerable synergy. For example, customer delight helps expand revenues by producing high levels of customer retention. Concentrating on the areas which impact customer retention makes it easier to generate a sufficient financial return. A philosophy of continual improvement and attention to changing customer needs leads to customer satisfaction and delight, revenue expansion, and financial accountability.

Taken together, these principles describe a managerial philosophy which is at once hard-nosed (financial accountability), optimistic (revenue expansion), and altruistic (customer delight). The next section shows how these principles can be implemented by service marketing management.

3.4 A BLUEPRINT FOR SERVICE MARKETING MANAGEMENT

The emerging view of service marketing is increasingly customer-oriented, with relatively more attention paid to retaining existing customers than to attracting new ones. The reason for this is economic: It is well known that most businesses find it several times cheaper to retain an existing customer than it is to attract a new one. The blueprint for service marketing management that arises from this realization is

FIGURE 3.3

A BLUEPRINT FOR SERVICE MARKETING MANAGEMENT

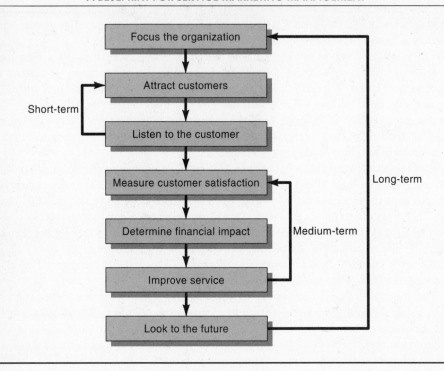

therefore much more concerned with keeping customers happy. The key tasks of service marketing management under the emerging paradigm are shown in Figure 3.3. These tasks are listed in roughly the logical order in which they would be accomplished by a start-up organization, although an ongoing organization would essentially do all of these things continuously.

The remainder of the book is organized around the essential tasks of service marketing management, as summarized in the blueprint. The first task is to focus the organization. This involves figuring out the purpose of the organization, how the organization should be positioned against competition, and which customer groups will be targeted. These issues are addressed in Part II. The second task is to attract customers.

The third task is to listen to the customer. This phase is inherently informal, and is not the same as conducting customer surveys. The idea here is to let the customers determine the areas that the organization should care about the most. Part III discusses methods of listening to the customer, including such nonstandard listening techniques as complaint management systems and service guarantees. This leads to the fourth task, which is to measure customer satisfaction. Satisfaction is measured on those areas which customers have identified as being important. Methods for making these measurements are discussed in Part IV.

At this point, based on the results of the customer satisfaction surveys, management may propose actions to improve service, satisfaction, and customer retention. But it is important to implement only those improvements that have a sufficient return on investment. Methods of determining financial impact, the fifth task, are discussed in Part V; they include traditional cost of quality computations, as well as more recent methods, such as the evaluation of "return on quality" (ROQ).

Improvements that stand the test of financial accountability must then be implemented in the workplace. This sixth task is that of improving service, to which many issues are relevant. Included are flowcharting the service processes from the customer's perspective, using methods such as relationship management and employee empowerment to establish close, flexible links to the customer, and incorporating service and ROQ-related concepts in the business planning process. These issues are discussed in Part VI.

Finally, any organization that desires to be successful in the long run must always look to the future, which is task seven. This involves to a great degree determining the implications of changing technology. Part VII discusses these issues.

The tasks, as set out above, define a logical flow by which service marketing management should proceed. But we need to be aware that there are also some very important feedback loops. For example, in the short term, listening to the customer can help the organization attract customers more successfully. Advertising might concentrate on themes that have been identified by customer interviews, or pricing might be informed by the results of brand choice studies. There is a potential pitfall here, however. Too many companies simply tell customers what they want to hear, without actively improving service. Empty promises such as these may work in the short term, but they are long-term poison. The organization must be sure to keep its long-term actions consistent with its short-term communications.

In the medium term, it is important that the service improvements be monitored for effectiveness. Thus one of the major uses of customer satisfaction measurement is determining whether service quality efforts have been successful or not. This feedback is essential for determining whether or not to make further changes. In the long term, considerations of the future, and especially the trends in technology, are essential in focusing the organization, as well as adopting a market positioning that will not quickly become obsolete. Thus we see that service marketing management involves short-term, medium-term, and long-term concerns, and that the main tasks of service marketing management work together as a recursive system.

3.5 CONCLUSIONS

The emerging view of service marketing management is different in many ways from the traditional view. The differences result primarily from permanent changes in the business world. They especially reflect the pervasive influence of the information revolution, which has greatly increased the importance of service, and the extent to which products are dominated by their service components. Essentially the shift has been from a product world to a service world. Once we thought of service as a small and relatively inconsequential part of the "augmented product," but now we think of a physical product as a small (and usually missing altogether!) part of the service.

The differences may appear to be semantic, but they are not. The profound shift in perspective leads to an important change in emphasis in service marketing management, with greatly increased attention to satisfying the customer.

REVIEW QUESTIONS

1. Figure 3.1 lists the central assumptions of the emerging view of service marketing. What would the central assumptions of the traditional view be? Why are they now no longer as relevant as they once were?
2. Similarly, Figure 3.2 lists the guiding principles of the emerging view. What would the guiding principles of the traditional view be? Why have they become obsolete?
3. The blueprint for service marketing management includes several tasks that are given greater emphasis than they received in the traditional paradigm. Which are they? Why are they becoming more important? What traditional tasks have been given less emphasis? Why?

CASE

CLUB MED (A)

In January 1987, Jacques Giraud, president and chief executive officer of Club Med, Inc., was reflecting upon his first year at the company's helm. He was pleased with the company's financial performance in 1986, and he was excited about its prospects for future growth. His optimism was tempered, however, by the knowledge that competition was growing. Until now, Club Med had faced only a handful of competitors throughout the world and almost no direct competition in what was referred to as the "American Zone." In recent years, however, several organizations had attempted to duplicate the Club Med experience, among them SuperClubs, Jack Tar Villages, Sandals, and Eden II resorts, all based in the Caribbean. In Germany, Robinson's had captured an estimated 75% to 80% of the German market for all-inclusive vacation packages. Giraud swiveled his chair and turned to gaze out over Central Park. He mused:

> We have done well so far in the North American Market—our success seems virtually assured. But are we really as competition-proof as some people think? Or are we going to wake up one day to a big surprise—like the U.S. auto companies did? Has the lack of competition until now inflated our egos, fattened our bellies, and blinded us to internal weaknesses? We have been successful for so long, and have taken so many things for granted, that I wonder what our strengths really are. And where our problems lie. As Molière said, "It is not only what we do, but also what we do not do, for which we are accountable."

COMPANY BACKGROUND AND HISTORY

Often referred to as "the Club," Club Méditerranée was the ninth-largest hotel company in the world in 1986. It had been founded by a group of friends in 1950 as a nonprofit sports association. The group was led by Gerard Blitz, a Belgian diamond cutter and water-polo champion, who, like the others in the group, was on a tight budget and had an affinity for sports and vacations in scenic seaside locations. Members of the association

This case was prepared by Assistant Professor Christopher W. L. Hart, with the research assistance of Dan Arczynski, Dan Maher, and Lucy N. Lytle, as the basis for class discussion rather than to illustrate either effective or ineffective handling of an administrative situation.

slept in sleeping bags and took turns cooking meals and washing dishes. As the association grew, running it as an informal, loosely organized group became increasingly difficult.

In 1954, Blitz invited his close friend, Gilbert Trigano—an active association member whose family business had been supplying the group with U.S. Army-surplus tents—to join the association on a full-time basis. Trigano, who saw commercial potential in the concept, became managing director and set out to transform the association into a business. In 1985, Club Méditerranée S.A., a publicly owned company traded on the Paris Stock Exchange, had 108 resort villages throughout the world and hosted 820,000 vacationers annually. Exhibit 1 shows the locations of the company's villages.

Throughout this growth, the "family spirit" endured among the Club's managers, and was a significant part of the company's culture. All of the top managers at Paris headquarters had formerly worked in the villages, many in the position of general manager ("village chief" in the Club's parlance).

In 1972, Club Med, Inc. was formed as a U.S. subsidiary of Club Méditerranée. Gilbert Trigano's son Serge, 39, who had worked his way up in the firm, became president and chief executive officer of Club Med, Inc., in 1982. The subsidiary sold the company's vacation packages and operated its resorts in North America, the Caribbean, South America, Asia, and the South Pacific. Exhibits 2, 3, and 4 show selected operating data for Club Med, Inc.

In 1984, about 25% of the subsidiary's shares were sold in a public offering on the New York Stock Exchange. They sold at a hefty price-earnings multiple of 16, which many people thought was too high. The stock became a favorite of several influential Wall Street analysts, however, who realized that Club Med had several operational features that differed significantly from traditional hotel chains. First, the company earned $3 million per year just in interest

from customers' prepaid vacation deposits. Second, capacity was measured as the number of beds in a village, not the number of rooms. (Singles were assigned roommates.) Third, a respected analyst, who specialized in the gaming and lodging industries, projected strong sales growth for the U.S. subsidiary, based on a historical analysis of the Club's market penetration in other countries. (See Exhibit 5.)

In 1985, Jacques Giraud, who had been *directeur général* of Club Méditerranée, moved from Paris to New York to take over as president and chief executive officer of Club Med, Inc. from Serge Trigano, who moved back to Paris to head the parent firm.

INDUSTRY STRUCTURE

Club Med was in a strong position with respect to buyers, suppliers, and labor. (See Exhibit 6.) Buyers, for example, could buy the "true formula" only from the Club. According to company management, it would cost a consumer 50% to 100% more to attempt to replicate the Club Med experience through other vacation options. The price of a week's vacation during the winter season at Club Med's Caribbean villages, including round-trip airfare from New York, ran from $1,000 to $1,400 per person.

Second, the company enjoyed a strong bargaining position with its suppliers. Commercial airlines jumped at the opportunity to sell seats to Club Med at volume discounts, which Club Med sold as part of vacation packages at a substantial profit. Because the Club's villages created jobs and tourism revenue, economically depressed countries in exotic locations competed fiercely to become the sites of new Club Med villages. The benefit packages they offered often included low-cost financing, foreign-worker agreements, tax breaks, and, in some cases, direct equity investment.

Club Med also possessed considerable leverage with labor. A surprisingly large number of young and talented people were eager to work as Club Med "GOs."[1] In 1984, the company received 35,000 GO applications for 2,000 positions worldwide. Turnover was high, however—nearly 46% among newly recruited American GOs in their first season, and 27.6% overall. Additionally, the company enjoyed a strong bargaining position in negotiating the wages of local village workers.

Exhibit 7 gives comparative performance data for Club Med and the two industries in which it operates: lodging and air transport.

DISTRIBUTION NETWORK

Club Med bundled the ground portion of its vacation package (i.e., lodging, meals, sports activities, ground transportation) with air transportation and sold the complete packages either through travel agents or directly to consumers. Direct sales were made through its reservations center in Scottsdale, Arizona, or through "vacation stores" it had established in several large North American cities.

Club Med management recognized that the number of travel agencies had increased enormously during the 1970s and early 1980s, jumping from approximately 6,700 in the United States in 1970 to over 24,000 by 1983. This growth was largely due to airline deregulation. The end result was that an average of 80 travel agencies opened or went out of business each day, travel increased, and travel-agent commissions went up as competing airlines tried to capture a larger share of the travel-agency market. It appeared that the travel-agency business would become increasingly concentrated; a protracted market shakeout was expected, and would lead to the demise of many small, undercapitalized operations. Conversely, large firms with scale economies (i.e.,

American Express, Thomas Cook) were expected to capture an increasing share of the travel market.

Club Med vacation packages were widely distributed, with 12,000 agencies booking 115,000 customers in 1982. However, approximately 50% of the Club's nondirect sales were booked by only 2,000 agencies. Unfortunately, turnover among these top-sellers was high—half of the top 2,000 agencies in 1982 were not among the top agencies in the previous year.

In 1983, Club Med's strategy for dealing with the fast-changing distribution network was to increase the loyalty to Club Med of top-selling travel agencies by:

- educating their travel agents about the Club Med vacation package;
- designating top-selling chains as "Club Med experts" and have Club Med's sales representatives direct most of their attention to these chains;
- tying in Club Med's promotional efforts exclusively with the "expert" agencies;
- rotating a "flying team" of GOs who hold informational seminars throughout North American cities;
- creating travel-agent schools and placing the graduates with "expert" agencies.

COMPETITION

By 1986, Club Med was no longer the only successful chain of all-inclusive, club-style resorts. Other companies in the western hemisphere had entered the all-inclusive resort market. Moreover, new competitors were appearing on the scene at an alarming rate.

---

[1] The term "GO" (pronounced "gee-oh") stands for "gentils organisateurs" in French, "congenial hosts" in English. Each Club Med village employs a team of about 80 GOs who handle all jobs other than housekeeping and maintenance. GOs organize the activities in a Club Med village and mingle freely with guests (called "GMs": "gentils membres" in French, "congenial members" in English).

The advertisement of one competitor is featured in Exhibit 8.

Nonetheless, over the years many companies that had tried to compete with Club Med had failed. This led to much speculation throughout the lodging industry: Why was the record of would-be competitors so dismal? No known analysis of this topic had yet been published.

As opposed to pay-as-you-go traditional hotels, all-inclusive (AI) resorts offered lodging, all meals, recreational activities, and airport transfers for one preset price. Airfare was usually offered as an option, at charter rates. Except for a few optional activities (i.e., deep-sea fishing, day excursions), guests usually did not need to make any purchases while staying at the resort. Most AI resorts offered a wide range of recreational activities, with specially selected staff members acting as activity directors, organizing games and teaching sports like windsurfing and scuba diving.

The Jamaica-based Jack Tar Village company operated AI resorts in Grand Bahama, Montego Bay, Runaway Bay, Puerto Playa, and Saint Kitts. Its village in Grand Bahama featured 12 tennis courts, 27 holes of golf, a shopping arcade, and "the largest swimming pool in the western hemisphere." The hotel facilities in Saint Kitts included a movie theater, a beauty salon, and a casino featuring blackjack, roulette, and slot machines. A new 250-room hotel, featuring a duty-free shopping zone and an aquarium, was scheduled to be built in Frigate Bay in the fall of 1986.

Jack Tar's glossy color advertisements, implicitly criticizing Club Med's spartan rooms and its methods of operation, promised that their all-inclusive price "covers virtually everything, including unlimited wine, beer and cocktails . . . You'll get a nicer room with full size beds, air-conditioning, and other first-class hotel amenities rarely found at other 'all-inclusive' resorts . . . You won't have to carry cash to the beach, sign vouchers, or keep up with drink tokens or

beads." (At Club Med, GMs purchased plastic "bar beads" which were exchanged at the bar for drinks.)

This advertisement prompted one executive at Club Med to remark:

> So what if Jack Tar Villages includes the price of cigarettes and drinks at the bar in their package? [At Club Med these items were not included in the all-inclusive price.] A customer who would choose them over Club Med for that reason is what we would consider an undesirable customer. Our clientele generally doesn't include people whose aim is to drink a lot of free booze. We serve free wine at dinner because that is the European way.

Another competitor was the SuperClubs organization, which operated four AI resorts in Jamaica: Couples I; Hedonism II; Jamaica, Jamaica; and Boscobel Beach. Couples I, located in Ocho Rios, was the first couples-only resort in the Caribbean when it opened in 1978. After a slow start (occupancy dipped as low as 10% the first year), the resort gained acceptance among travel agents and, by June 1982, management reported its 50th consecutive week of 100% occupancy, at least 18% of which was repeat business. Couples I boasted the highest year-round occupancy of any hotel in Jamaica—95%.

Hedonism II, a 20-acre, 280-room resort located in Negril Bay on the west coast of Jamaica, appealed to a slightly different market. It opened in 1974, and, according to its management, enjoyed 90% occupancy during the winter season, dropping to 60% in the off-peak seasons. With its beach equally divided between nude bathing and normal beachwear, and a windowed bar looking into a pool where nude swimming was allowed late at night, Hedonism II had a reputation as Jamaica's most uninhibited and sex-oriented resort. The available activities included tennis, basketball, exercise rooms, jet skiing, and parasailing (the latter two available off-site for an extra charge).

Two major operational distinctions between Club Med and SuperClubs were drinks and staff. First, whereas Club Med required guests to purchase drinks at the bar (with "bar beads"), SuperClubs included all drinks in its AI price. Second, the staff at Club Med villages was composed primarily of its GO team, the members of which rotated to different villages every 6 months, forming entirely new teams. The SuperClubs operations had a much smaller number of GOs—called "activity directors." Ordinarily they were individuals recruited from the local area; they did not rotate among SuperClubs' properties on a scheduled basis.

Another major distinction between Club Med and SuperClubs was packaging and distribution. As mentioned previously, Club Med bundled the ground portion of the vacation package with air transportation and sold the complete packages either through travel agents or directly to consumers. SuperClubs, on the other hand, bundled complete ground packages and sold them through large tour wholesalers—operations that combined the ground packages with airline seats purchased in bulk—and then sold the complete vacation packages through travel-agency chains. SuperClubs paid a 20% commission for this service.

When a Club Med executive was asked about the Club's strategy for dealing with such competitors as Jack Tar and SuperClubs, he explained that Club Med was "currently discussing how to deal with this issue." He added:

> This much is certain: Traditionally, Club Med's strength has been that our customers recommend us to their friends. Word-of-mouth business is very important to us. Where we risk losing business is with people who have never visited a Club Med, and who don't have any friends who've come here. That's the kind of people our competition might attract.

Granted, the Club Med concept no longer is unique. Our competitors have copied the key ingredient—an all-inclusive price and an enthusiastic, pampering staff. *The difference is that they generally operate within a traditional hotel context.*

THE CLUB MED SERVICE CONCEPT, OPERATING STRATEGY, AND SERVICE DELIVERY SYSTEM

Club Med's rapid growth and dominance in the resort-vacation business was the product of its unique vacation concept. The Club Med concept has been described as the process of transforming a group of uptight, urban professionals—who start out as total strangers—into a fun-loving, relaxed group of friends and acquaintances, "converts" who assist the GOs in welcoming the next group of uptight, urban professionals into the village.

Club Med GMs (guests) truly were "members" in the sense that they paid a $25 initiation fee and annual dues of $40. Members received newsletters and high-quality catalogs featuring the Club's villages, and were given the opportunity to purchase such ancillary services as travel insurance.

Club Med villages were designed and operated to create an atmosphere in which the GMs had nothing to worry about except relaxing and enjoying themselves. One female GM, reclining in a poolside chaise longue, observed, "I figured I was a workaholic because I could never forget about my job when I went on vacation. I always felt kind of uneasy. But I've only been here for two days and I've completely *forgotten* about work!" She sat up and called out to a group of men and women playing water volleyball: "Hey honey, do you remember what company I work for?" Multiple responses from the pool indicated that the question was irrelevant and not to be repeated. The case writer admitted to himself that he was having trouble remembering why he came to Club Med. "I guess I won't need my calculator," he mused.

Each Club Med village was organized along similar lines. The chief of the village had overall responsibility for village operations. Reporting to the village chief were seven chiefs of service, each of whom was in charge of a different functional area. The 80 or so GOs in a village reported to their respective chiefs of service.

The GOs received a salary of about $400 a month, and were given room and board which was estimated to cost Club Med an additional $250 per month. GO-related expenses were considered to be a fixed cost, since the company's policy was to keep the number of GOs in any village fixed, regardless of occupancy percentage.

Club Med village sites were selected for their natural beauty, good weather, and recreational potential. Each facility typically had 150 to 300 rooms laid out around a central core of facilities that included a large pool, an outdoor bar, a theater, a main dining room, shops, and offices. The architectural design was intended to facilitate interaction among GMs and GOs. Villages were built on properties of 40 acres or so to provide plenty of space for such sporting activities as windsurfing, sailing, waterskiing, snorkeling, archery, soccer, basketball, volleyball, tennis, and, in some villages, scuba diving. Additionally, each village had landscaped areas with walkways to give GMs plenty of room to roam without having to forgo the village's safety and ambiance.

The rooms in Club Med villages were spartan, but clean. They lacked such traditional conveniences as clocks, TVs, radios, telephones, postcards, and writing paper, the intent being to separate GMs as much as possible from the demands of civilization. One GM, an investment banker, cracked, "Three days ago, I was having telephone withdrawal symptoms. . . . I *craved* a phone! Today, I wish the damn things had never been invented. It must have been great in the old days when

you made a decision, mailed a letter, and headed for the links." To promote a sense of trust in the village, there were no room keys (although rooms could be locked from inside). Unfortunately, theft was not unknown, especially in certain villages.

Everything in a village was organized to promote social intercourse. Meals were buffet style, and the buffet tables were elaborately laid out to convey a sense of variety and abundance. GMs and GOs were randomly seated together in groups of six or eight, again to promote interaction, and they could fill up on a wide variety of cheeses, fruits, breads, salads, vegetables, entrees, and desserts. Conversations among those seated at a table were spontaneous, especially after a few glasses of beer or wine (which were available in unlimited quantities at lunch and dinner). One GM commented, "I felt uncomfortable at first, being seated with people I didn't know. It's not a problem, though. A lot of the people I've met have turned out to be really nice. And, if you don't like certain people, it's easy to get away from them at the end of the meal." To give GMs the option of enjoying a quiet meal away from the crowd, most villages had at least one separate specialty restaurant where reservations were required.

Each village was equipped with a state-of-the-art sound system. An expert sound engineer kept music playing throughout the day and evening in the core area around the pool and bar. The music, which was selected by the sound engineer with the approval of the village chief, varied from village to village. Classical music was not the norm (although each village had an area where taped classical music was played while the sun set).

Club Med promoted social interaction not only in the public areas but also in the rooms, assigning roommates to unaccompanied singles (always of the same sex). This concept was foreign to many GMs, but most did not find it to be a serious problem. Few would have *preferred* roommates, but it was generally recognized that "doubling up" held down the price of a Club Med vacation. An impromptu focus group assembled at the bar generated the consensus opinion that Club Med vacations were indeed inexpensive in comparison to the price of vacations at traditional Caribbean resorts (i.e., pay-as-you-go).

The Club's vacation concept was designed to eliminate the need for GMs to make any financial decisions during their stays. Except for bar drinks and items purchased in village shops (e.g., suntan lotion, clothing), the entire vacation was paid for in advance. GMs charged extras to their rooms and settled their accounts at the end of the week, when they picked up their passports and airline tickets at the village "bank" (where all valuables were to be stored, to minimize the possibility of theft). Drinks were purchased with colored-plastic pop beads that could be strung together or worn around the neck (except that the beads often did not hold together). A scotch and soda cost ten 40-cent orange beads; a Coke went for four orange beads. According to Club Med management, the beads were a popular symbol of the Club and an effective way to keep GMs' thoughts off monetary concerns.

GMs could choose from many individual and group recreational activities scheduled during the day. The Club was famous for sports, but it also offered such activities as arts and crafts, cards, and, in some villages, computer workshops. At designated times, lessons taught by professionally qualified GOs were available for all major sports. Group activities included volleyball, softball, aerobics, bicycling, basketball, and picnics. Many GMs enthusiastically participated in as many of these activities as possible; others preferred to engage in individual pursuits (e.g., reading a book by the pool). In general, GMs settled into vacation routines that met their individual preferences after two or three days of investigating their options.

While the flexible daily schedule was always changing, nighttime activities usually followed a single pattern. Every evening started with the GMs congregating around the bar for a happy hour of pre-dinner drinks and semi-organized group games (e.g., Trivial Pursuit). Drinks were liberally awarded as prizes. Dinner started at 7:30 or 8:00, depending on the village. After dinner, GMs and GOs reconvened around the bar for a half hour or so of after-dinner drinks and dancing in a large patio area bordered by the bar, pool, and theater. Next came a Club tradition: the GO show. Each night, the GO team (all amateurs) put on a stage show, typically involving dancing, lip synch, and slapstick comedy. The shows were of varying length and quality, and GMs' reactions were mixed.

One new GM, Edward Robinson from New York, was delighted with the shows. "To see those kids putting out that kind of energy and enthusiasm, especially after doing a full day's work, makes *me* feel like a kid again. I think these GOs are fantastic."

At the end of each show, another Club ritual began: the "crazy-signs dance." All the GOs took to the stage and led the GMs in a set of animated hand motions performed to French songs. Most GMs joined in enthusiastically, although many found the hand motions difficult to master. One GM, Mike O'Brien from New Jersey, commented sourly: "I've been to three Club Meds and still can't get the crazy signs down. I feel stupid screwing up in front of the other guests. Most of them screw up too, though."

In general, however, the crazy-signs dance generated an up-tempo mood. Those who wished to continue dancing would next trek over to the disco, which opened shortly after the "show" ended. The disco was usually isolated at one end of the village to reduce the noise level for those GMs who preferred to go to bed.

The disco GO, a sound engineer, played taped music of current hit songs, occasionally broken up with an "oldies review." There was also a bar, plenty of seats, and easy access to the beach. The disco was open until the last GM left, which could be around dawn. Then the daily routine started again, with a tempting breakfast buffet set up in the dining room.

This set of activities was predictable—unlike the environmental and political conditions Club Med had to contend with in its far-flung destinations. Some of the local airports' facilities were barely adequate to handle a full load of vacationers. Some villages had physical problems, making them harder to manage than other villages with better design and facilities. Additionally, if Club Med struck a deal with a host government in a joint venture, with the local government agreeing to maintain the facility, and for some reason such upkeep became impossible to provide (i.e., a severe economic downturn, as in Mexico), the Club occasionally had difficulty keeping its facilities in top condition.

Mother Nature didn't always cooperate with the Club, either. One GM, Eddie Lewis from Boston, arriving at the village in Cancun, was miserable as a result of a long flight and transfer delays. His frustration was compounded when he saw that it was raining and learned it was expected to rain his whole vacation week. Yet, by the end of that time, he said, "I just had a great vacation—one of the best ever. It didn't even matter that I couldn't go windsurfing. I had a wonderful time anyway. Those Club Med people—and especially Sylvio de Bortoli, the village chief—sure know what they're doing.

"In fact," he continued, "I heard a story this week about the tradition the Club has when its time to turn over the village to a new chief. One particularly creative village chief, Michel Simon, decided it would be fun to play a practical joke on his replacement, who was coming in that evening from Tahiti. Michel gathered the entire village, all the GOs and GMs—we're talking several hundred people here—and took them across the bay in Playa Blanca, Mexico—to an empty hotel!

"He had everyone pretend this was the *real* Club Med village. When the unsuspecting new chief arrived, he was treated to a sumptuous dinner, a wonderful show, and, of course, a few glasses of wine. Everyone played along until the new chief went to bed, whereupon the group returned, en masse, to the real Club on the other side of the bay. Boy, was that guy surprised when he woke up in a *deserted* hotel!"

CUSTOMER PROFILE

A market survey exploring the profile of a typical Club Med GM was completed in September 1986. The results were based on responses to an eight-page self-administered questionnaire mailed to 50,000 GMs who had visited a Club Med village in the past year (i.e., in the summer of 1985 or in the winter of 1985–86). The questionnaire covered a range of topics, including demographics, lifestyle, experience with Club Med, and Club Med imagery. The response rate was in excess of 40%.

Club Med had worked hard to change the swinging-singles, sex-oriented image it had acquired in the 1970s. Ongoing market research showed the success of their efforts. Demographic data on Club Med's clientele revealed the average age to be 37, with a median income of $39,000 and an average income of $54,000. More than 70% were aged 25 to 44. Half were married, and 40% had children. More than 75% were college graduates and 28% held advanced degrees. For selected results of a 1986 GM survey, see Exhibit 9.

CUSTOMER SATISFACTION

Club Med's most important marketing tool was satisfied GMs. An industry rule-of-thumb was that people returning from vacation would tell an average of ten others about their experiences, either pro or con. The importance of word-of-mouth to Club Med was evidenced by the 65% of first-time GMs who decided to go primarily on the basis of recommendations from friends and acquaintances. These first-time GMs accounted for 60% of all GMs. During the past several years, approximately 25% of all new GMs had become repeat customers. Repeat GMs took an average of four additional Club Med vacations. The Club estimated its contribution margin at 60%.

To monitor GM satisfaction, each GM received a mail questionnaire immediately after returning home. (Exhibit 10 shows the questionnaire.) Roughly 50% of the questionnaires were returned to Club Med headquarters, where the data were entered into a computer and summarized on a weekly basis, by village. (The average response rate for guest surveys in the lodging industry, by contrast, was 2% to 4%.) These statistical summaries were taken very seriously. Examples of guest-satisfaction ratings are shown in Exhibit 11. Exhibit 12 shows a compilation of qualitative comments written on the questionnaires used to generate these ratings.

BACK IN NEW YORK

"It's that Club Med 'magic,' " Jacques Giraud laughed, when told of the GM in Cancun who had a great vacation despite flight problems and horrible weather. "In fact, there was a lot of magic in Cancun *that* season when Sylvio was the village chief. The physical circumstances were unusually difficult, yet he managed to boost the GM satisfaction ratings fifteen points higher than they were the year before. But I would like to know exactly *what* the Club Med magic is. I recently held an informal brainstorming session with my managers, including all the village chiefs in the American zone. They came up with some interesting observations about our strengths and weaknesses." (For a summary of these points, see Exhibits 13 and 14.) Winking, he suggested to the case writer, "Maybe we should have your students visit a Club Med village for a week, to give them a better sense of what the Club is about. Yes ... a field study!" Giraud turned back to the panoramic view of Central Park. "Then *they* could clarify and resolve the issues that I face."

EXHIBIT 1

LOCATIONS OF CLUB MÉDITERRANÉE VILLAGES, WORLDWIDE

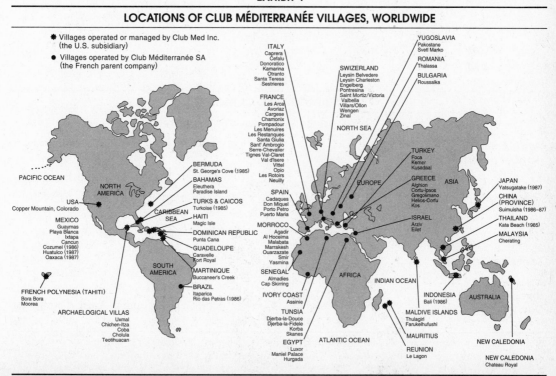

EXHIBIT 2A

CLUB MED, INC. OPERATING DATA (*U.S. DOLLARS*)

	1981	1982	1983	1984	1985	1986
Sales						
Revenue (millions)	$180	$207	$212	$235	$280	$337
Net Income (millions)	7.9	7.1	9.7	12.0	15.6	18.0
Guests (000)	169	196	208	238	282	332
Net Income/Sales	4.4%	3.4%	4.6%	5.1%	5.6%	5.3%
Sales/Guest	$1,065	$1,056	$1,019	$987	$993	$1,015
Net Income/Guest	47	36	47	50	55	54

Selected Financial Performance Results of U.S. Lodging Firms

	Return on Sales*			Return on Equity		
	1984	1985	1986	1984	1985	1986
Marriott	—	—	—	22.1%	22.1	20.6
Ramada	1.5%	3.0	1.5	3.6	6.7	3.6
Hilton	16.6	14.1	13.2	18.6	16.1	14.4
LaQuinta	—	—	—	7.9	4.9	3.5
Four Seasons	—	—	—	—	—	22.2

Note: 1984 sales in the U.S. resort-lodging industry were approximately US$10 billion.

EXHIBIT 2B

OCCUPANCY AND CAPACITY

	1984	1985	1986
North America			
Number of Beds:			
All Areas	9,602	11,052	12,384
North America	470	470	470
Mexico/Caribbean	7,332	8,632	9,364
Total	7,802	9,102	9,834
Occupancy:	64.2%	62.2%	60.9%
North America	72.7%	63.5%	65.4%
Mexico/Caribbean	63.4	64.2	64.4
Asia			
Number of Beds	1,800	1,950	2,550
Occupancy	65.5%	52.9%	47.3%
Total	63.6%	64.2%	64.4%

Note: Club Med reports occupancy in terms of beds available for guests. This method is significantly different from that generally used in the hotel industry, which expresses occupancy in terms of rooms available for guests.

EXHIBIT 3

CONSOLIDATED INCOME STATEMENT FOR CLUB MED, INC., *YEAR ENDED OCTOBER 31, 1986 ($000)*

REVENUES	$336,950
Cost of revenues[a]	221,613
Gross profit	$115,337
Sales, general & administrative expenses	83,989
Depreciation and amortization	11,544
OPERATING INCOME	$ 19,804
Interest income (expense)	418
Foreign currency exchange gains (losses), net	(1,135)
Income before taxes and extraordinary items	$ 19,087
Provision for taxes[b]	(1,714)
Income before extraordinary items	$ 17,373
Extraordinary items	682
NET INCOME	$ 18,055
	= 11.6% ROI

Source: 1986 Annual Report, p. 23.

[a]Cost of revenues includes wages.

[b]Club Med operates in a number of countries and consequently is taxed according to rules of various jurisdictions, some of which do not impose an income tax. The company's effective tax rate in 1986 was 5.4%.

EXHIBIT 4

CONSOLIDATED BALANCE SHEET FOR CLUB MED, INC., *YEAR ENDED OCTOBER 31, 1986 ($000)*

Assets		
Current Assets:		
Cash and Marketable Securities	$ 53,621	17.1%
Accounts Receivable	15,358	4.9
Inventories	8,292	2.6
Other	13,808	4.4
Total Current Assets	$ 91,079	29.0%
Property and Equipment:		
Villages	$214,193	68.3%
Other	7,596	2.4
Construction in Progress	27,638	8.8
	$249,427	79.5%
Less Depreciation and Amortization	(47,274)	−15.1
Net Property and Equipment	$202,153	64.4%
Other Assets	20,591	6.6
TOTAL ASSETS	$313,823	100.0%

(Continued)

EXHIBIT 4 (Continued)

Liabilities and Shareholders' Equity

Current Liabilities:

Accounts Payable	$ 12,061	3.8%
Amounts Received for Future Vacations	22,470	7.2
Current Maturities of Long-Term Debt	1,695	0.5
Accrued Expenses	14,842	4.7
Other	9,086	2.9
	$ 60,154	19.2%
Long-term Debt[a]	$ 91,151	29.0%
Minority Interest and Other	3,506	1.1
Shareholders' Equity	159,012	50.7
TOTAL LIABILITIES	$313,823	100.0%

Source: 1986 Annual Report, p. 24.

[a]$39.6 million is at or below the London Inter-Bank Offering Rate (LIBOR, the rate at which banks lend money to each other), and $26 million is at LIBOR plus 1/2% to 5/8%.

EXHIBIT 5

POTENTIAL SIZE OF MARKETS IN VARIOUS COUNTRIES

	Approximate Current Number of GMs	Estimated Potential	Estimated % Growth Potential	Approximate Growth as a % of Total Growth Potential
Europe/Middle East				
France	356,000	356,000[a]	0%	0.0%
Israel	19,000	19,000	0	0.0
Belgium	38,000	39,600	4	0.1
Switzerland	20,800	25,200	21	0.3
Italy	106,000	114,200	8	0.6
Austria	7,500	19,000	153	0.8
West Germany	35,000	215,250	515	12.6
Great Britain	7,500	123,400	1,545	8.1
Scandinavia	11,400[a]	68,400	500	3.9
Netherlands	7,200[a]	43,200	500	2.5
Spain	9,600[a]	57,600	500	3.4
Ireland	900[a]	5,400	500	0.3
Total Europe/Middle East	620,600	1,087,150	75%	32.7%
North America				
U.S.A./Canada	179,800	780,050	334%	42.1%

(Continued)

EXHIBIT 5 (Continued)

	Approximate Current Number of GMs	Estimated Potential	Estimated % Growth Potential	Approximate Growth as a % of Total Growth Potential
Asia/South Africa				
Japan	12,000	229,250	1,810%	20.1%
Australia	18,000	38,750	115	1.5
New Zealand	4,000	6,600	65	0.2
Hong Kong	1,600	5,400	237	0.3
Taiwan	3,700[a]	9,400	154	0.4
Malaysia	4,600[a]	4,600	0	0.0
Singapore	4,100	4,100	0	0.0
South Africa	5,000	12,300	146	0.5
Total Asia/South Africa	53,000	380,400	618%	23.0%
All Other	46,600	78,300	68	2.2
Club Med, Inc. Region	279,400	1,238,750	343	67.3
Entire World	900,000	2,325,900	158	100.0

Source: Drexel, Burnham, Lambert, Inc.

[a]Based on propensities to vacation at Club Med (x.x people/1,000). Propensity of French citizens to vacation at Club Med divided in half to generate demand estimates for other nations.

EXHIBIT 6

STRUCTURAL ANALYSIS MODEL: CLUB MED.

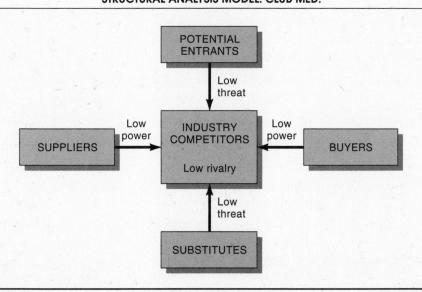

Source: Dan Arczynski, "Club Méditerranée: A Competitive Analysis." Competitive Analysis Course, Harvard Business School, May 5, 1986.

EXHIBIT 7

COMPARATIVE COST DATA: CLUB MED AND INDUSTRY AVERAGES

	Club Med	Industry Average
Lodging Industry		
Sales[a]	100%	100%
Cost of goods sold	(48)	(40)
Labor	(27)	(36)
Sales, general and administrative	(9)	(5)
Advertising	(5)	(3)
Interest	(3)	(7)
Depreciation	(4)	(6)
Profit before taxes	4%	3%
Air Transport Industry		
Sales[b]	100%	100%
Cost of goods sold	(89)	(98)
Profit before taxes	11%	2%

[a]Club Med's revenue from land packages and village operations was $227.6 million in 1986 (68% of total revenue).

[b]Club Med's revenue from air transportation was $92.6 million in 1986 (27% of total revenue).

Club Med's other revenue came primarily from membership, management, and cancellation fees.

EXHIBIT 8

How Perillo sold 10,000 tours in 100 days and how he will do it again

by Mario Perillo

I'm not much for bragging but I can't resist taking credit for so monumental an accomplishment.

I created probably the fastest selling tour program ever launched. Maybe the best selling in history.

Club Perillo at the Paradise Island Resort & Casino in the Bahamas

Started 100 days ago, 10,000 people paid from $599 to $1199 to be in Paradise. And reservations are still pouring in by the hundreds each day. Why?

1. They love my new concept. You pay one low price and leave your wallet at home.

2. Everything's included: Pan Am airfare from New York, deluxe balconied rooms, 3 sumptuous meals each day, free wines, cocktail parties, multi-million dollar shows, theme parties, sightseeing, catamaran cruises, transfers, gaming chips, baggage handling, room tax, hotel tax —even the tips.

3. The resort. It has everything. If you travel the world you'd be hard put to find a more complete and exotic haven...Our stays are 4, 5, and 6 days.

4. Two professionals. I sent my son Steve and lifetime friend Joe Fusco to Paradise Island to treat each guest as my best friend. And they're doing it.

5. Reputation. Perillo reputation. 43 years of straight dealing...Take a look at my free brochure and I guarantee you will want to make a reservation...May I now introduce another exciting Club Perillo.

4 pros who have made me famous by making sure my promises are kept. Lucio Massari (Italy Chief) Steve Perillo, Joe Fusco and Mike Castrignano, Club Perillo head hosts.

Club Perillo cruises the Caribbean on the deluxe Italian liner— S.S. Costa Riviera

I fully intend to book 10,000 lucky people on the Costa Riviera in the next 100 days. Maybe more. How can I be so sure?

1. Because the Club Perillo concept works. You pay one price and leave your wallet at home.

2. The Ship. 30,000 tons of elegance. Italy afloat. A warm, magnificent work of art. The ultimate in food and service. Proud of her Italian registry...7 days as a millionaire sailing from Ft. Lauderdale every Saturday, to St. Thomas, St. Croix and Nassau.

3. The cabins. You get the very best on the ship. The top deck. All outside with private bath, fully airconditioned, stereo and private telephone. The best.

4. Your hosts. Besides a staff of 500, you will have your own private host, adviser, concierge and friend on board in the person of Mike Castrignano, Joe Fusco or Steve Perillo.

5. What's included? Everything. Airfare from New York, the best cabins, the shore excursions, port taxes, unlimited wines with dinner, cocktail parties, transfers—EVEN THE TIPS.

6. The prices. You pay $1299 or $1399 per person (double occupancy) including airfare from New York depending on the season. If you get to Ft. Lauderdale on your own (without using our New York airfare) deduct $200 a person...But you must act immediately.

Italy. Our first love and major destination

Italy sells itself. Like front row seats at a Pavarotti concert...500,000 people have gone with us. We are the leaders to Italy in the world.

Italy is a treasury of art and natural beauty. An architectural masterpiece. The home of the Pope. The fashion capital of the world.

Our fantastic tours range from 8 to 15 days to all the "must see" places from the Alps to Sicily. Fully escorted by the finest professionals in Europe—headed by a Master of Tourism—Lucio Massari...We have even created a select Club Perillo on the Isle of Capri. A jewel.

One low price includes everything: Round trip NY/Rome on Pan Am, free dinner wines in flight, free stereo and movies, first class and deluxe hotels, meals, Gala Dinners in a palace dancing to our own orchestra, sightseeing, deluxe motorcoaches, transfers, baggage handling, taxes, hotel service charges, worry free and completely escorted...Depart year-round. Low season prices from $1099 to $1199 for 10 days.

Please request our free brochures with full details on all I have written about. Telephone us today or see your travel agent.

CLUB PERILLO

In New York
(212) 584-8300
(914) 735-2000
Outside N.Y. State toll-free
1-800-431-1515

Or please complete and mail the coupon below.

SOURCE: *The New York Times*, February 1, 1987.

EXHIBIT 9

SELECTED MARKET RESEARCH RESULTS

Sex of Respondent

	Total	Summer	Winter
Base-Total Sample	(19,527)	(8,408)	(11,119)
• Male	47%	48%	46%
• Female	53	52	54

Age of Respondent

	Total	Summer	Winter
Base-Total Sample	(19,527)	(8,408)	(11,119)
• 18 to 24	8%	8%	8%
• 25 to 29	22	23	21
• 30 to 34	22	22	22
• 35 to 39	18	19	18
• 40 to 44	13	12	14
• 45 to 49	7	6	8
• 50 to 54	5	4	5
• 55 +	5	5	5

Marital Status

	Total	Summer	Winter
Base-Total Sample	(19,527)	(8,408)	(11,119)
• Married	48%	48%	48%
• Single	36	37	36
• Divorced	11	11	10
• Other	5	4	6
• Have children	40%	38%	42%

Geographic/Sales Region, U.S. Market

	Total	Summer	Winter
Base-Total Sample	(19,527)	(8,408)	(11,119)
• Northeast	34%	28%	38%
• Pacific	23	28	19
• New York	20	19	21
• Midwest	10	9	12
• Southeast	5	7	4
• Southwest	4	6	3
• Mountain	4	4	3

EXHIBIT 9 (Continued)

Likelihood of Vacationing at Club Med in Future

	Total	Summer	Winter
Base-Total Sample	(19,527)	(8,408)	(11,119)
• Extremely/Very	74%	77%	72%
—Extremely	48	53	44
—Very	26	24	28
• Somewhat	18	16	19
• Not Too/Not at All	8	7	9
—Not Too	6	6	7
—Not at All	2	1	2

EXHIBIT 10

GM QUESTIONNAIRE

Club Med Village: _____

Dates of your stay: From: _____ to: _____
Month/Day/Year   Month/Day/Year

Name: _____ Member # _____

Address: _____

City: _____ State: _____ Zip: _____

Rating grid (columns: Overall Impression, Organization, Team of G.O.s, Food, Bar, Sports, Daytime Ambiance, Evening Entertainment, Music and Dance, Mini Club, Excursions, Accommodations, Club Flights and Transfers, Cleanliness):

	OVERALL IMPRESSION	ORGANIZATION	TEAM OF G.O.s	FOOD	BAR	SPORTS	DAYTIME AMBIANCE	EVENING ENTERTAINMENT	MUSIC AND DANCE	MINI CLUB	EXCURSIONS	ACCOMMODATIONS	CLUB FLIGHTS AND TRANSFERS	CLEANLINESS
EXCELLENT	6	6	6	6	6	6	6	6	6	6	6	6	6	6
VERY GOOD	5	5	5	5	5	5	5	5	5	5	5	5	5	5
GOOD	4	4	4	4	4	4	4	4	4	4	4	4	4	4
FAIR	3	3	3	3	3	3	3	3	3	3	3	3	3	3
POOR	2	2	2	2	2	2	2	2	2	2	2	2	2	2
VERY POOR	1	1	1	1	1	1	1	1	1	1	1	1	1	1

Your Comments: _____
_____
_____
_____

1. Did Club Med meet your expectations?
   ☐ Far below expectations   ☐ Surpassed expectations
   ☐ Fell short of expectations   ☐ Far surpassed expectations
   ☐ Met expectations

2. If this was not your first Club Med, how many other times have you been to a Club Med village? _____

3. How did you make your Club Med reservations?
   ☐ Through a travel agent   ☐ Through Club Med Reservations

4. Quality of your reservations handling (pre-travel information):
   ☐ Very Poor   ☐ Poor   ☐ Fair   ☐ Good   ☐ Excellent

5. Which one factor was the most important in your choosing Club Med for your vacation?
   ☐ Previous stay with us   ☐ Advertisement   ☐ Editorial Article
   ☐ Travel Agent Recommendation
   ☐ Friend/Relative Recommendation

6. Kindly indicate your age bracket:
   ☐ Under 25   ☐ 25-34   ☐ 35-44   ☐ 45-54   ☐ 55 or over

7. Kindly indicate your marital status: ☐ Married   ☐ Single

8. Would you vacation with Club Med again?   ☐ Yes   ☐ No

9. If you answered yes to question 8, where would you like to go on your next Club Med vacation?
   ☐ U.S.A.   ☐ Mexico   ☐ French West Indies   ☐ Caribbean
   ☐ Europe   ☐ Other: _____

EXHIBIT 11

GUEST SATISFACTION RATINGS: IXTAPA, CANCUN, AND PARADISE ISLAND VILLAGES[a]

	Ixtapa, Mexico (n = 654)	Cancun, Mexico (n = 856)	Paradise Island, Bahamas (n = 512)
Overall Impression	95.7%	92.3%	81.4%
Organization	92.8	90.7	80.1
Team of GOs	94.1	93.3	79.0
Food	80.8	65.8	82.6
Bar	74.4	70.6	72.5
Sports	97.2	95.6	93.8
Daytime Ambiance	96.3	93.2	91.1
Evening Entertainment	89.4	83.3	70.9
Music and Dance	85.1	80.9	77.5
Rooms	87.4	61.5	78.0
Flights and Transfers	75.5	56.7	61.7
Cleanliness	94.5	77.3	78.5

Notes:

1. Data disguised; from one season.

2. During this season in Cancun: weather was terrible; tennis courts in bad need of repair; major renovation of facility under way.

[a]Percentages of respondents who checked "excellent," "very good," and "good" on questionnaire in Exhibit 10.

EXHIBIT 12

SUMMARY OF QUALITATIVE COMMENTS FROM QUESTIONNAIRES: IXTAPA, CANCUN, AND PARADISE ISLAND VILLAGES

	Ixtapa, Mexico (n = 654)	Cancun, Mexico (n = 856)	Paradise Island, Bahamas (n = 512)
Overall Vacation Rating			
Excellent/Good	125	174	77
Disappointing/Poor	10	15	20
GO Team			
Friendly/Good	182	215	83
Rude/Unhelpful	24	32	65
Village Chief "Great"	8	105	3
Miscellaneous			
Air Charter Poor	10	151	27
Transfers Poor	4	30	5
Need Room Keys	6	5	43
Reported Theft	7	11	23
Rooms Uncomfortable	32	154	52
Food Average/Poor	42	118	30
Bar Drinks Overpriced/Weak	42	49	20
Bar Beads a Hassle	12	12	7

Note: Many questionnaires were returned without comments, and many were returned with multiple responses. In other words, of the 856 questionnaires returned by GMs who visited Cancun, many had no qualitative comments on them, while others had multiple comments.

EXHIBIT 13

SUMMARY OF MAIN POINTS LISTED BY CLUB MED MANAGERS

Strengths

- GOs
- Company spirit; a "family"
- Understanding customer needs
- Innovator
- All-inclusive concept
- "Float" (i.e., customer pays before taking the vacation)
- Marketing and distribution strategy
- Size (economies of scale)
- Wide choice of destinations
- Excellent locations
- Low capital-intensity (due to funding from host governments, etc.)
- Ability to manage in diverse international settings
- Service concept appeals to broad market
- Experience
- Open communication throughout company
- Leadership

Weaknesses

- Subject to political problems in countries where villages located (e.g., Haiti)
- Subject to foreign-exchange fluctuations
- GO turnover
- Cultural differences between management and employees (e.g., European managers and American GOs)
- Remoteness of villages (communication difficult)
- Singles-oriented image
- Broad market appeal could allow competition to specialize
- Spartan accommodations

EXHIBIT 14

COMMENTS FROM CLUB MED MANAGERS CONCERNING COMPANY STRENGTHS AND WEAKNESSES

Strengths

- "Club Med understands the needs of its customers, which translates into satisfied customers. And satisfied customers are particularly important for a company, like ours, that depends on repeat business."

- "Our services are constantly evolving. For example, as various sports gain popularity, we start offering them at Club Med."

- "The Club is an innovator."

- "Our policy of nomadism (i.e., rotating the GOs every six months) leads to flexibility, variety, and it insures that the villages have an international flavor."

- "There is a high level of commitment among Club Med employees. It is like family—and *is* the family for many employees."

- "We have an adaptable management style. We can operate the Club in many diverse international settings."

- "Our service concept appeals to a very broad market. Club Med is for everybody, not just for a specific kind of customer."

Weaknesses

- "The company has been criticized for having a strong French-orientation."

- "Having such a broad market appeal might leave other companies room to specialize. They could go after niches in the market."

- "If I were working for a competitor of Club Med, I might recommend that my company be *completely* all-inclusive. No charge for cigarettes or drinks at the bar."

- "Club Med's accommodations are very spartan. And we don't offer double beds for couples, or single rooms for singles."

- "If Club Med doesn't continue to change and adapt to the demands of the market we would hurt ourselves more than any of our competitors ever could."

PART II

FOCUSING THE ORGANIZATION

Chapter 4

FOCUSING AND POSITIONING

4.1 THE PURPOSE OF THE ORGANIZATION

Clearly defining the purpose of an organization enables the organization to focus its efforts and accomplish more than it otherwise could. Failure to clearly define the organization's purpose, or defining the organization's purpose poorly, can result in lost opportunities. For example, the railroad companies in the United States defined their purpose as supplying train transportation. Had they viewed their purpose as supplying transportation, not necessarily on trains, they might have been in position to become the dominant airline companies as well, insuring additional years of revenue expansion and profitability.

The purpose of the business is often referred to as a "service strategy" in the service sector, or a "business strategy" in the product sector. Because our viewpoint is that all businesses are really services, we will refer to the "service strategy" for both sectors. The service strategy is described by a vision statement, mission statement, goals, and plans of the firm. Figure 4.1 shows how the core strategies of the organization (the vision and the mission) form the basis for the goals and plans of the organization. Figure 4.2 gives examples of how the organization works from the general (vision and mission) to the specific (strategic goals and short-term plans).

Depending upon how the organization is positioned, it either may share a market or it may create one. In a competitive marketplace it is usually advantageous to create a market, through the mechanisms of niching (choosing a very narrow and specific market) or radical innovation (creating a completely new market).

4.2 THE SERVICE STRATEGY

Any organization is more effective if everyone is working to accomplish the same goals. We often hear about getting everyone "rowing in the same direction." But how can everyone have the same goals? Goals must be articulated precisely and communicated early. This result can be achieved through the service strategy, which tells employees and customers exactly what the organization is, what the organization

FIGURE 4.1

ELEMENTS OF THE SERVICE STRATEGY

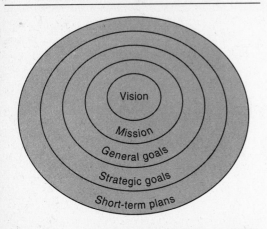

Source: *Juran's Quality Control Handbook*, Fourth Edition by J.M. Juran and Frank Gryna. Copyright © 1988 by J.M. Juran and Frank Gryna. Reprinted by permission of McGraw-Hill, Inc.

FIGURE 4.2

VISION, MISSION, GOALS, AND PLANS (WITH SOME EXAMPLES)

Vision	To be the leading supplier of baseball bats in the world
Mission	To provide high quality baseball bats, at a reasonable price, to schools, clubs, and recreational players
General Goal Example	To be the leading supplier of bats to Little League baseball teams
Strategic Goal Example	Devise a high-quality aluminum bat for Little League play
Short-Term Plan Example	Determine what Little League players want in an aluminum bat
Vision	To be a "landmark restaurant" in Nashville, Tennessee
Mission	To provide excellent food and the most efficient and professional service in town, at a moderate to high price
General Goal Example	To achieve higher ratings on service satisfaction (rated by "mystery shoppers") than those of the major competitors
Strategic Goal Example	Ensure that the waiters and waitresses are thoroughly trained
Short-Term Plan Example	Have each new waiter or waitress serve an apprenticeship under the supervision of an experienced "mentor"

does, and what the organization believes in. The service strategy must also identify the customers who will be served, and the value they will receive.

A good service strategy produces several important benefits. First, it *communicates to potential customers* exactly what the organization is and what it will provide. This is referred to as "positioning" the firm in the market. Second, it *communicates to employees* exactly what the company stands for, and is trying to do. Third, it *produces operating efficiencies* by eliminating activities that are not focused on the organization's main tasks. A good service strategy has several characteristics. It is clear, specific, and unambiguous. It is equally relevant to both customers and employees. It is articulated concisely. It is based on knowledge of customer needs, obtained through some form of market research. We will now consider the elements of the service strategy: the vision statement, mission statement, general goals, medium-term strategic goals, and short-term plans.

The Vision Statement

The vision statement describes the lofty aspirations of the organization. It represents an ideal that the organization may never actually be able to accomplish but serves as an image of desired perfection. For example, Martin Luther King, Jr.'s "I have a dream" speech was a vision statement for race relations in the United States. He did not actually expect the racial harmony he was describing to be accomplished any time soon. But he thought if he could get people to visualize it, then constructive action was more likely.

Vision in a business is in many ways analogous to the individual technique of visualization, a technique often used by athletes wishing to attain peak performance. For example, world-record high jumper Dwight Stones would stand on the runway and visualize himself running down the runway, leaping in the air, and successfully clearing the bar, several times before each jump. As he visualized, Stones's head would bob up and down with each step and then his eyes and head would go way up as he visualized the jump itself. Studies of world-class athletes have shown that visualization is very commonly used to improve performance. The vision statement is the organization's way of visualizing success and may help it to attain heights that otherwise would not be possible. In fact, some managers *deliberately produce a divergence between the projected image and what actually currently exists,* in the hopes that reality will then be subsequently transformed to be consistent with the vision.[1] For example, a company's vision might be to be the friendliest bank in the industry. This vision, communicated effectively to all employees, can be a self-fulfilling prophecy. Let us consider some examples of vision statements. Bill Gates, the CEO of software giant Microsoft, is a business leader with strong foresight and high aspirations. Microsoft has always had a clear vision. After the company became dominant in the computer software industry, Gates announced a new vision for Microsoft; the company would seek to become dominant in home and office interactive communication. As Gates put it, he wanted Microsoft to become in office equipment and home communication what it currently was in computers. This vision tells consumers what to expect and focuses the work of Microsoft employees. This lofty goal provides the basis for the mission, strategy, and tactics of the organization.

As another example, consider another visionary thinker, Walt Disney. He wanted to build a city in which the latest of everything was present. It would essentially be a "world of tomorrow." Disney died before his vision could be implemented, but it helped shape the construction of EPCOT Center, the popular tourist attraction in which technological marvels and the latest in knowledge are displayed.

Great vision statements are often futuristic. If a vision is not futuristic, it is likely to have been accomplished in some form already. What is the difference between a weak or poor vision statement and a good one? Consider, for example, the vision of "supplying our customers with the highest quality products, with the best service, at the lowest price." Nothing in this "vision" expresses desired direction. The company wants to be better rather than worse on everything of importance. This approach is not likely to inspire either employees or customers. Instead, an effective vision statement guides the behavior of the firm by articulating an ideal to which each employee can aspire. It is ambitious and futuristic. It inspires the imagination.

The Mission Statement

The mission statement makes the vision more realistic and concrete. Although the vision statement may describe a glittering corporate utopia, the mission statement is ambitious but practical. To be effective, the mission statement needs to say what the organization is, what it intends to do, and who it intends to serve. Almost all companies recognize this much. But too often companies fail to recognize that the mission statement must also involve *trade-offs*. No company is all things to all people. To be effective, the statement must also state what the organization *is not*, what the organization *does not* intend to do, and whom the organization *does not* intend to serve.

Let us consider a hypothetical mission statement from a hotel chain: "Our mission is to provide the highest-quality accommodations, outstanding service quality, and the best value." (The word "value" in a mission statement generally means reasonable price.) Essentially the mission statement above is promising highest quality at lowest prices. But if that were possible, they would get 100% market share. Who would stay anywhere else? The mission statement is not specific enough because it does not express any trade-offs or hard decisions. It does not help guide employee behavior. For example, suppose a manager needs to make a decision about bathroom fixtures. A nicer shower will cost more, but will be higher quality. What should the manager do? The mission statement is of no help whatsoever.

Let us now imagine how a mission statement for a hotel chain might be better. Consider: "Our mission is to provide medium-priced accommodations for business travelers, with high-quality furnishings, responsive service, but few amenities." That sounds mean and gritty. But it is a very effective statement, because it gives guidance about how to make decisions. The bathroom fixture decision would be relatively clear. The mission statement demands high-quality furnishings. The trade-off is that there will probably not be a restaurant or swimming pool. It is clear who the primary customer is (the business traveler) and who the primary customer is not (the vacation traveler).

Often the mission statement will also include corporate values. Ben & Jerry's ice cream shops post their mission statement prominently in every store. (This demonstrates conclusively that although management may be "old hippies," they are also knowledgeable business people.) Their mission statement talks a lot about the values of the company, in addition to their business goals. For that company, values such as environmental awareness and treating employees well are central to their corporate identity, and thus to their service strategy. Shared values can be a very powerful bond, drawing employees together, and also attracting customers who hold similar values.

The Holiday Inn brand name, once used to identify a chain of motels with full service, reasonable price, and good quality, was used on both an upscale business chain (Crowne Plaza), and an economy chain (Express). It was not apparent that Holiday Inn retained its formerly clear focus. For this reason Holiday Inn eliminated the Holiday Inn brand from Crowne Plaza, hoping that this change would help position its brands more clearly.

What happens if a company doesn't have a clear mission? A classic example is Sears. Sears became prominent as a mail order company. Then, when shopping centers proliferated, after World War II, Sears made the move into mass retail. But the company lacked a clear mission, and seemed to target both everybody and nobody. Low-priced goods and high-priced goods were offered haphazardly and the store's image became confused. Gradually, companies with better-defined missions picked up market share from Sears. High-end specialty retailers could provide better service and higher quality. Discount stores, such as Wal-Mart and Kmart, which lacked upscale pretentions, had lower overhead and therefore could beat Sears on price. Sears was not positioned to appeal to any particular customer group, and became a spectacular failure.

In summary, the mission statement is a powerful tool, but too few companies take full advantage. To be successful the mission statement must state what the organization is, and *what it is not*. This contrast is what creates the ability to make managerial trade-offs, and thus derive benefit from the mission statement.

General Goals

Within the mission, goals must be set to accomplish the mission. Referring to Figure 4.2, we see two examples of how general goals are derived from the mission of the organization. In the first example, the mission is to provide bats to clubs, recreational players, and other nonprofessionals. One goal growing out of this is to be the leading bat supplier to Little League teams. The goal is specific, and it is measurable. It is not the only possible goal that would be compatible with the company's mission, but it will help the company achieve its mission.

The second example is the restaurant that seeks to provide the most efficient and professional service in town. A general goal related to this mission is to achieve higher ratings on the service satisfaction of the major competitors. Again, this goal is concrete and measurable.

Medium-Term Strategic Goals

These goals make the general goals more specific. They provide the method by which the general goals are to be accomplished. In the baseball bat example, the strategy for becoming the leading supplier of Little League bats is to devise a high-quality aluminum bat. That is not the only strategy that could have been selected. Other possible strategies might include advertising heavily, providing free coaching videos, hiring former major league stars to travel the country touting the bats, providing the cheapest bat on the market, or any one of a number of possible strategies. Nevertheless, because aluminum bats are what Little Leagues use, devising a high-quality aluminum bat is a reasonable strategy for increasing Little League sales.

In the restaurant example, the general goal of achieving high ratings on service satisfaction results in a strategic goal of a greater emphasis on training the staff. Again it is not the only possible strategic goal that could have grown out of the mission. The restaurant could have offered the highest salaries in town, or linked compensation directly to the satisfaction ratings, of any one of a number of possibilities. The important thing is that concrete, specific action is taken to try to achieve the general goal.

Short-Term Plans

In this implementation phase the strategic goals are accomplished by specific action. In the case of the baseball bat company, research is done to determine what Little League players want a bat to be like so as to achieve the strategic goal of developing a high-quality bat. In the restaurant example, an apprenticeship program is started to help new waiters and waitresses become better trained.

4.3 MARKET SHARING AND MARKET CREATION

The service strategy dictates one of two alternative approaches to market positioning: either *market sharing* or *market creation*. Market sharing means jumping into an existing market, and dividing it with the existing competitors. Market creation means building a unique market that the organization can dominate.

American Airlines provides a good example of market sharing. The U.S. full-service business air travel market is shared by several competitors that are virtually indistinguishable from American. The result is that customers perceive a commodity market, in which choice is based on price, and thus competition drives prices down, making the industry a very difficult one in which to make a profit. Most of the companies in that market segment are, in fact, losing money. On the other hand, consider Southwest Airlines. They essentially created their own market by providing a unique service (efficient, no-frills air service, at a low price). Because they were the innovator, and are still the dominant player in that segment, they are able to be very profitable, largely because of a lack of significant competition.

Economic theory explains why a company may wish to create a market rather than share a market. A firm that has a monopoly can charge higher prices than a firm competing for business. Being the only firm in an industry is an ideal position from the point of view of the firm, because it has the entire market and high profits. Of course, we must realize that the company is monopolizing only its market niche and not the entire industry, which means that anti-trust problems may usually be avoided as well! The following sub-sections show some of the ways that market creation can be accomplished.

Market Creation Through Niching

Niching means carving a small, specialized piece (niche) out of the existing market. Niche competitors can always take share away from competitors who don't have a clear mission. For example, aggressive niche competitors such as Wal-Mart have lured customers away from Sears, an entrenched, but sluggish, competitor. Figure 4.3 gives examples of successful niche competitors.

Whole Foods Market is a good example of a business that created a niche. Whole Foods began as a typical small natural-foods store. The owners envisioned the possibility of a gourmet, natural-foods supermarket. As it turned out, the concept worked. Why was Whole Foods successful? Although most people prefer standard food at low prices, there is a segment of the population that attaches greater value to quality and healthfulness. Whole Foods moved aggressively to attract this segment, hiring nutritionists, seeking suppliers of organic produce, and stocking premium brands, even though all of these things increased costs. Their competitors were

FIGURE 4.3

EXAMPLES OF SUCCESSFUL NICHE COMPETITORS

Company	Industry	Niche	Vulnerable Competitors
Wal-Mart	Mass retail	Low price OK quality	Sears, J.C. Penney
Wyndham Hill	Records	New age	Columbia, Warner Brothers
Rolls-Royce	Automobiles	Luxury	Cadillac, Lincoln
CNN	TV	News	ABC, CBS, NBC
Switzerland	Banking	Privacy	U.S. banking system
Southwest	Airlines	Low price	American, Delta, United
Whole Foods	Grocery	Natural foods supermarket	Kroger, A&P
AT&T	Telephone	Service quality	MCI, Sprint
Microsoft	Computers	Operating systems	IBM, Apple
Sun City, Arizona	Condominiums	Senior citizens	Other Sun Belt condos

unable to respond effectively without losing track of their own service strategy, which was to supply acceptable quality at a low price. Whole Foods grew to three large supermarkets in Austin, Texas, and then expanded to California, New Orleans, and the Midwest. Whole Foods was listed as one of the top 100 small businesses by *Business Week* magazine. The business is extremely successful, because they chose a clear niche, targeted their efforts to support that niche's strategy, and monopolized their portion of the market. By the way, as would be predicted by economic theory, their prices are higher than those of the competition.

Companies that are unable to change and unable to specialize are especially vulnerable to niche competitors. A classic example is IBM. Until the PC revolution, IBM was the dominant company in the computer industry. Then the market shifted to personal computers. First, Microsoft niched as an operating system and software supplier. Meanwhile, Intel was niching as a mother board supplier, providing the integrated circuits that form the brains of the PC. Small (but growing) players like Apple, Compaq, and Dell niched by assembling the computers themselves, at a low price. At that point, IBM was left with no market to dominate. Niche players had taken all of it! IBM is now suffering record losses and laying off massive numbers of employees for the first time in its history. The trade press is referring to IBM as a "dinosaur."

Niching is a very good idea, but there are some pitfalls. For one thing, the niche must be large enough to support a company. A restaurant that served only beans might have trouble in the market. Even a large city is unlikely to have enough customers who would chose a meal of only beans. Also the niche must be meaningful to the customers. Suppose, for example, an art gallery showed only paintings of artists whose middle name began with "R." That would be a unique positioning, but it would be unsuccessful because the way in which the gallery is unique does not relate in any way to customer needs.

Finding Niches Using Mapping Techniques

One of the best ways to find a niche in an existing market is to employ a mapping technique. There are several approaches that may be used. In each, the general idea is to build a picture (map) of the market, showing where market opportunities lie. Some show the competing firms, some show the customers, and some show both. Statistical details of these methods are beyond the scope of this book, but we will look at the pictorial outputs of the techniques to show each method's potential usefulness.

One of the most popular techniques is *multidimensional scaling* (MDS). Figure 4.4 shows an application of MDS to the positioning of cable television channels. The dots indicate cable channels, and the circles indicate clusters of viewer "ideal point." (Technical details are beyond the scope of this book, but a map may be obtained easily using one of many MDS software packages.) In other words, the closer the channel is to a viewer's ideal point, the more likely the viewer is to choose that channel. Note that there is a large region in the space that appears to be unoccupied by any existing cable channel. This region represents a market opportunity. A new channel positioned in this area would have good prospects, because a large customer group is not currently being well served. An investigation of these

FIGURE 4.4

MDS PERCEPTUAL MAP OF 14 CABLE TV CHANNELS WITH CONSUMER IDEAL POINTS (CIRCLED)

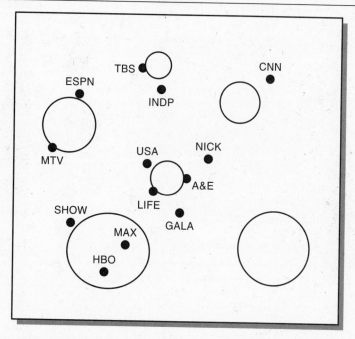

Source: Roland T. Rust and Naveen Donthu (1988), "A programming and positioning strategy for cable television networks," *Journal of Advertising* (No. 4), pp. 5–13. Reprinted by permission.

consumers indicated that a news show or detective show would be successful in this market. In fact, the major broadcast networks moved to fill this void by creating docudrama shows that mixed dramatic reenactments with factual accounts.

Another popular method is *conjoint analysis.* (A technical description of conjoint analysis is beyond the scope of this book, but any of several commercial software programs may be used.) A conjoint part-worth space is shown in Figure 4.5. The part-worth is the relative value placed on that variable. In the map shown (simplified to show only a handful of respondents) we see what appear to be three distinct segments: one of which values both extracurriculars and academics (3, 7, and 8), one of which values only extracurriculars (4 and 6), and one of which values only academics (1, 2, and 5). A college wishing to niche should apparently choose one of these possibilities. For example, a college that provided great extracurriculars and mediocre academics would appear to have possibilities, based on this map.

The simplest mapping approach is the *compositional mapping approach* (see Figure 4.6). In this approach, respondents rate various aspects, which are then used as the dimensions of a map, to reveal customer segments. In this example, respondents

FIGURE 4.5

A CONJOINT PART-WORTH SPACE FOR COLLEGE ATTRIBUTES WITH A SAMPLE OF PROSPECTIVE STUDENTS (NUMBERED)

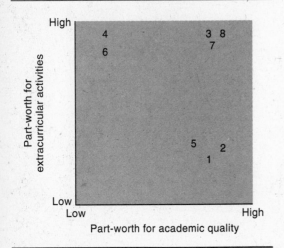

FIGURE 4.6

COMPOSITIONAL MAP OR APARTMENT ATTRIBUTE IMPORTANCES WITH A SAMPLE OF PERSPECTIVE RENTERS

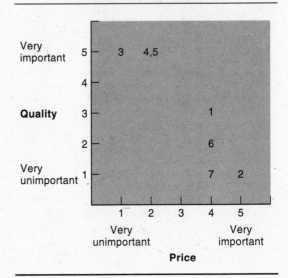

rated the importance of quality and price in apartments, each on a 5-point rating scale. It would appear that there are two distinct segments (again based on a simplified map, showing only a handful of respondents). One segment cares a great deal about price, but not about quality. The other cares a great deal about quality, but not much about price. *Correspondence analysis* is a method that has become popular in industry in the past few years. This method is used to show customer segments and their characteristics in the same map. The method assumes that responses are categorical (can be grouped). Figure 4.7 shows an example of a map produced by this method.

Another technique recently introduced to the business literature is *density mapping*. This method shows the relative concentration of customers in a geographic space (or perceptual space). Figure 4.8 shows the density map of existing hospitals in a large city. The dots represent existing hospital locations, and the contours represent the density of the population. From the density map it is clear that a large population peak (the dark area where the contour lines are close together) is not served by a nearby hospital. It would make sense to explore the possibility of building a hospital in this area.

Mapping techniques, though very useful in identifying market niches, have some limitations. Truly unique ideas will be "off the map." For example, suppose you were mapping broadcast network preferences in 1940. Radio preferences would be reflected. TV would be "off the map." Once TV was introduced, the perceptual map of broadcast networks would change completely.

FIGURE 4.7

CORRESPONDENCE ANALYSIS SPACE

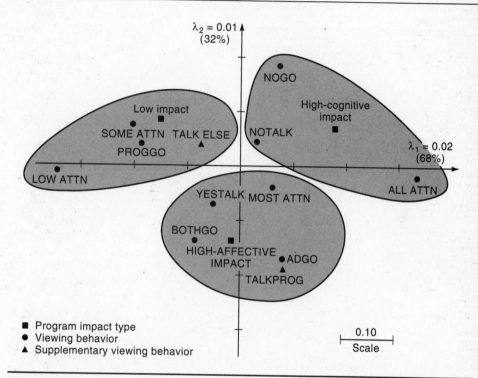

Source: Donna L. Hoffman and Rajeev Batra (1991), "Viewer response to programs: Dimensionality and concurrent behavior," *Journal of Advertising Research*, August-September, pp. 46–56.

Market Creation Through Radical Innovation

Upjohn Corporation used radical innovation to create a market. Based on corporate research and development, Upjohn discovered that a previously well-known drug, for which Upjohn held the patent, could be used to grow hair and partially cure baldness. The company then used advertising to inform the target market (balding men) that a radically new market (hair-growing medicine) was being created. The profit potential in such a (monopolistic) situation is enormous. Radical innovation is a way of creating a market. Simply invent something that doesn't exist, that people will like and pay for. Of course it is not always easy to be innovative, and even harder to make the innovation profitable.

One of the best approaches to devising a radical innovation is to follow technological changes. Technology is the skeletal system of business. Muscle and flesh can only go where the skeleton goes, but where a new skeleton goes there is generally a new opportunity for muscle and flesh to follow. In other words, the implications of new technology are fertile fields for market creation. Of course, such

FIGURE 4.8

CONTOUR MAP OF CUSTOMER DENSITY FOR LOCATING A NEW HOSPITAL (CURRENT HOSPITALS NUMBERED)

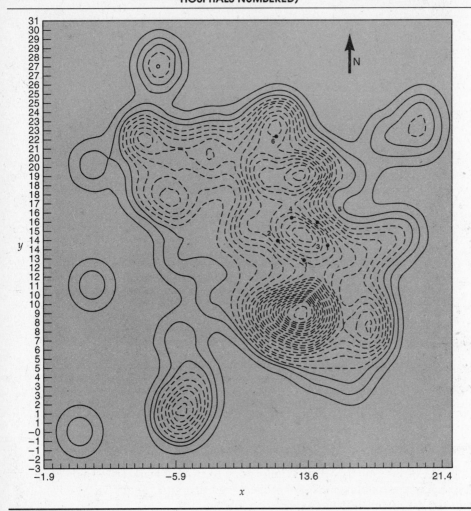

Source: Naveen Donthu, and Roland T. Rust (1989), "Estimating geographic customer densities using kernel density estimation," *Marketing Science* (Spring), pp. 191–203. Reprinted by permission of Marketing Science. All rights reserved.

innovations are prone not to be market-driven, strictly speaking, but rather capability-driven. They are sometimes derided as a result.[2] Nevertheless, as Deming says, "new types of service are generated, not by asking the consumer, but by knowledge, imagination, innovation, risk, trial and error."[3]

An example of technology-driven innovation is the billboard in space.[4] It became technologically feasible to build a billboard in space, readable from earth, and several Japanese companies hurried to take advantage of the opportunity, in spite of spirited opposition. This project gives new meaning to the term "advertising

The airplane is one example of a technology-driven innovation.

space." Another, perhaps more benign, example of technology-driven innovation is interactive telecommunications services. Advances in signal reduction technology made the "bandwidth" (amount of information) of regular telephone cable effectively much larger, permitting these new services. Companies then rushed in with extensive interactive service networks, such as movies on demand and interactive shopping.

Radical innovation has its perils. Inventing new services can be difficult and risky, especially when the business is not sure beforehand that consumers want or need the service.[5] Creating demand for a new service is costly in terms of advertising and marketing research. Nevertheless, as the pace of technology change increases, technologically driven radical innovations seem likely to become more prevalent and more profitable.

A Paradigm for Innovation

A company wishing to innovate may benefit from adhering to several principles which may increase the probability of success. These are:

1. Follow technology.
2. Niche.
3. Experiment, but keep the trials cheap and small.

4. Try many ideas simultaneously.

5. Learn from failure.

REVIEW QUESTIONS

1. Apply the chapter material to your professional identity. Write a mission statement that communicates your intended uniqueness and professional identity. Is your uniqueness sufficiently unique? If so, write down some general goals, medium-term strategic goals, and short-term plans that support your professional mission.

2. Think of a company in your region that is not doing well. What is it doing wrong in terms of market positioning? Write a mission statement for this firm that you think might set the firm in the right direction. What would be some immediate implications of this mission statement?

3. Think of another major company in your area. What are the most important technological trends that are likely to change that industry? What sorts of market innovations can you imagine arising?

4. Think of the last big company you heard on the news that was not doing well. How could that company niche more completely? Would it help?

5. Think of the last new service you became aware of. How was it derived? Did it result from a niching strategy or a radical innovation?

ENDNOTES

1. Richard Normann (1983), *Service Management,* New York: Wiley, 72–80.
2. Eberhard E. Scheuing and Eugene M. Johnson (1987), "New Product Management in Service Industries: An Early Assessment," in *Add Value to Your Service,* Carol Surprenant ed., Chicago: American Marketing Association, 91–96.
3. W. Edwards Deming (1986), *Out of the Crisis,* Cambridge, MA: MIT Center for Advanced Engineering Study, p. 192.
4. Steven W. Colford (1993), "Blasted Space Ad!" *Advertising Age* (June 7), p. 46.
5. Karl Albrecht and Ron Zemke (1985), *Service America! Doing Business in the New Economy,* Homewood, IL: Dow-Jones-Irwin, 63–76.

Chapter 5

IDENTIFYING CUSTOMER GROUPS

5.1 OVERVIEW

We can think of a customer as any individual or group with which a service provider has an exchange. That is, the service provider gives something and receives something; presumably, both parties to the exchange are better off. Because the service provider is better off from the exchange, the relationship has value and should be protected. In other words, the other party in the exchange should be treated well, as a customer. Thus we see that a person eating in a restaurant needs to consider the waiter a customer, to increase the odds of getting good service; similarly, a student should treat the professor as a customer, to increase the odds of getting good grades, help with placement, and the like. Traditionally we have thought of a customer as someone who gives money in exchange for a product or service. But money is not the only thing of value that can be obtained in an exchange.

Figure 5.1 shows some of the customers a service provider may have. This list is by no means complete, but it highlights the fact that service providers must consider many diverse customer groups. We will be concerned with these principal customer groups:

1. Direct customers

2. Indirect customers

3. Decision makers

4. Supplier customers

5. Opinion leaders

6. Regulators

7. Competitors

8. Internal customers

FIGURE 5.1

CUSTOMERS OF A TYPICAL SERVICE PROVIDER

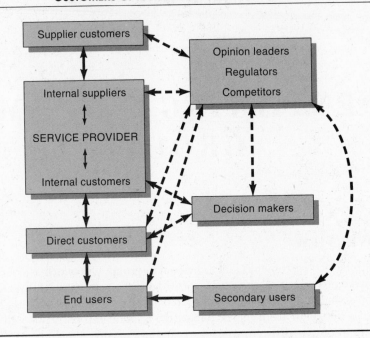

This list includes some groups not traditionally thought of as customers, such as suppliers and competitors. We will see that the typical service provider's exchanges with these groups affects the health of the organization.

The *direct customer* is what we typically think of as a customer. It is the individual or group that directly pays for our service (e.g., a car buyer). The *indirect customer* is someone who buys or uses our service through someone other than the service provider (e.g., the baby who eats the food her mother bought). *Decision makers* are those who do not themselves buy the service, but determine the buying decision of a paying customer (e.g., the doctor who writes a prescription). *Supplier customers* are those who the service provider pays for services (e.g., the steel company who sells steel to the car company). *Opinion leaders* are those who affect others" purchase decisions, often through the media (e.g., *Consumer Reports* magazine). *Regulators* determine the governmental or legalistic ground rules of the service (e.g., the Food and Drug Administration for food products). Service providers fight with *competitors* for market share (e.g., MCI vs. AT&T). *Internal customers* are those units within the organization with which the service provider has an exchange (e.g., top management). All of these customer groups are important, and neglecting any one of them can have disastrous consequences. We will examine each of them in turn. We will also discuss how to avoid the "customer blind spot" of neglecting one of these customer groups.

5.2 DIRECT CUSTOMERS

Did you buy a cup of coffee this morning before going to class? Perhaps you stopped by the bookstore to pick up a new text. Maybe after class you withdrew some money from an ATM machine, got your hair cut, and went to lunch with some friends. In each of these transactions, you were a *direct customer*.

Direct customers are the most obvious customers of a service provider, because they are where the money comes from. Even so, an organization often underestimates the importance of a direct customer. Consider, for example, a new-car buyer. The customer is obviously important, because the sale of a car worth thousands of dollars is a significant transaction. But is this the sole value of the customer? If the customer is satisfied, then that same customer is more likely to return and purchase *another* car in a few years. The customer may come back again and again. This multiplies the customer's value, and makes clear the importance of increasing repurchase by improving customer satisfaction.

This multiplied value, though more realistic, still underestimates the true value of the customer. The customer can influence others through word of mouth. Positive word of mouth can generate additional sales from relatives, friends, and colleagues, whereas negative word of mouth can erase sales that would have happened. The word-of-mouth factor makes the direct customer even important beyond direct sales to that customer. A direct customer does not cease to be a customer after a particular transaction is concluded.

Programs for strengthening relationships with direct customers are often very effective. One example of relationship strengthening that has proliferated in recent years is frequent-flyer programs available from most airlines. These programs encourage repurchase and customer loyalty by giving free tickets for various mileage targets, as well as service prerequisites such as upgrades and preference on boarding. It is now not uncommon for many passengers to book inconvenient flights rather than use a different airline, to help the frequent-flyer miles accumulate faster.

Unfortunately, many businesses don't understand or appreciate the value of a customer. One of the authors recently had an experience that dramatized this. The author had a coupon for dry cleaning at a nearby dry cleaner. When he presented the coupon, he was told that it had expired, although there was nothing about any expiration date on the coupon. Being somewhat sensitive to the abuse of consumers by business, he insisted that the company honor the coupon, pointing out that not honoring the coupon would mean the company was engaging in deceptive advertising. The company refused. He then went outside and spent the next hour making sure the company received the negative word of mouth it deserved, as potential customers approached the area. He also filed complaints with the Better Business Bureau, the state consumer protection agency, the local chamber of commerce, and the coupon company. Actually the dry cleaner did good work. The customer would have remained a customer for years, had he not been mistreated. There is no telling how much damage resulted from negative word of mouth.

5.3 INDIRECT CUSTOMERS

Indirect customers may also include end users (those who actually use the product), and secondary users (those who are the second, third, or subsequent users of

FIGURE 5.2

EXAMPLES OF INDIRECT CUSTOMERS

Company	Indirect Customer	Possible Relationship Maintenance
Ford	Car buyer	Ford Owners magazine
Coca-Cola	Grocer	Slotting allowance
Procter & Gamble	End consumer	(800) hot line
Sports Illustrated	Doctor's office patient	Subscription cards in magazine
University	Spouses of students	Spouse support groups

the product.) Figure 5.2 lists some examples of indirect customers. Consider a manufacturer of laundry detergent. The company most likely sells its product to large retailers (e.g., grocery chains) or distributors. While the large retailers and distributors are the direct customers, the manufacturer's indirect customers include those who buy from the retailers and distributors. Such indirect customers include retail customers and small, independent grocery stores. Even though the indirect customers do not buy their laundry detergent directly from the manufacturer, their satisfaction will have a huge impact on the manufacturer's sales and profitability.

Why would some companies pay little attention to end users? They may focus only on the fact that the direct customers are retailers or wholesalers. For example, one shoe company pays considerable attention to retailer needs. The end users, those who buy the shoes to wear, are almost completely ignored. The result is predictable: the shoes do not sell well because they do not meet the wearer's needs. The retailer then becomes unhappy with the shoe company, and sales suffer.

A manufacturer often ignores the end consumer because obtaining market research may be politically tricky. Northern Telecom, for example, sells much of its telecommunications equipment through the "baby Bells." Those companies do not want Northern Telecom to use their customer lists to sample customers, because Northern is also a direct competitor. Northern sells some equipment direct to the end customer, and they do not want Northern to steal their customers. In fact, most manufacturers scare retailers by the implicit threat to sell direct, often through direct mail and database marketing. Thus retailers are often reluctant to help get the manufacturers close to the customer. Nevertheless, manufacturers must obtain a good sense of the needs, wants, and desires of the end customers.

Another kind of end user is the *secondary user*. If you have ever read magazines in a doctor's office, you have been a secondary user. The magazines actually count on these secondary readers to boost their readership figures, by the number of readers per copy. Thus it is important to a magazine to attract secondary readers. In fact, there is considerable variation among magazines in readers per copy.

A good example of cultivating secondary users is the use of computer software site licenses. These licenses permit multiple users of computer software at one site to enjoy a greatly reduced price. Secondary customers are more likely to pay the site license than purchase multiple copies, and this practice cuts down on illegal copying.

In this way, site licensing increases revenues, and also increases individual usage, thus contributing to increased future sales.

Secondary users are as important to consider as end users. For example, the federal government's Department of Energy, faced with a steadily increasing volume of radioactive waste, needed to find some way to reuse the material. It therefore supported the irradiation of food. Unfortunately, irradiating food destroys important nutrients and leads to much poorer control of the disposal of the radioactive materials because they are distributed to widely dispersed irradiation facilities. As a result, many consumer groups are up in arms over this practice, defending the secondary users. Moreover, the government reinforces its image of not caring about its citizens. It is important to identify secondary customers explicitly, and to devise programs that reinforce the relationship with them. Examples of some possible programs are given in Figure 5.2 in the column headed "Possible Relationship Maintenance."

5.4 DECISION MAKERS

Decision makers may not actually pay, but because they determine the choice, they are just as important as the customers who do. Figure 5.3 lists examples of situations in which decision makers are important. One of the most typical cases is that of hospital choice. On many occasions, the actual choice of hospital is made by the patient's doctor. Therefore the doctor is an extremely important customer to any hospital.

A hospital can maintain relationships with its physicians in many ways. For example, it may supply expensive equipment that makes the doctor more effective. It may pay the doctor to practice at the hospital. It may provide comfortable lounges and special parking facilities for doctors. All of these programs are designed to bring in business by cultivating the hospital-physician relationship.

5.5 SUPPLIER CUSTOMERS

We might not naturally consider a supplier to be a customer. After all, the company gives money to the supplier in exchange for a service or product. Nevertheless,

FIGURE 5.3

EXAMPLES OF DECISION MAKERS

Company	Indirect Customer	Possible Relationship Maintenance
Hospital	Physician	Special medical equipment
Ballpoint pens	Purchasing manager	Gifts, meals
Textbook publisher	State Board of Education	Identify problem topics
University	Parents	Parents' weekend
Hotel	Travel agent	Free stays for referrals

the key concept is that of a mutually beneficial exchange. The supplier provides the supplies, service, or whatever necessary to make the organization function properly. The organization, on the other hand, reciprocates by making payments.

Having a positive relationship with one's suppliers is beneficial in several ways. An organization will do a greater percentage of its business with suppliers that they have good relations with and these favored suppliers will become more dependent on their customer, the organization. The supplier and buyer become more like partners, and the terms of such a partnership are usually predictable: The supplier may charge a higher price, but in return the organization may demand more, in terms of product and service quality, from the supplier. The supplier is also expected to become part of the organization's planning team, and anticipate future changes in needs. This characterization describes the Japanese system of *keiretsu,* which has been so successful. Such partnering relationships are less common among U.S. businesses, but are gaining popularity.

The U.S. alternative shows what negative consequences stem from poor supplier relations. Around 1990, General Motors decided that the appropriate way to deal with suppliers was to get tough. Rather than seeing the suppliers as customers, GM saw them as adversaries. They insisted on huge price cuts and higher quality. GM's large market share made this power play feasible, at least in the short run. Of course, the suppliers were alienated. Some chose to make more attractive relationships with the other car companies, turning their back on GM. Also those competitors, having better partnerships with their suppliers, found it easier to improve supplier quality and cut costs. As a result, with the exception of the Saturn division, GM found itself falling behind its major competitors in both quality and cost control.

The lesson is clear. Suppliers are customers; companies that fail to recognize the importance of this relationship will lose ground. The key word is cooperation, not conflict, and the goal is a harmonious, long-term relationship, in which the company can obtain increasing levels of performance from its suppliers, not because the suppliers are coerced but rather because they understand their own customer's needs very well.

5.6 OPINION LEADERS

Some customers don't buy the product, don't use the product, and don't make the decision to choose the product. Yet they can make or break the product. Consider a Broadway play, for example. When the play opens, it is reviewed by critics in the major papers. If the play receives poor reviews, would-be playgoers who read the reviews are less likely to attend. The play may have poor attendance, and close quickly. On the other hand, if it receives rave reviews, many people will want to see it. Attendance will be good, and the play generally will have a long run.

As we can see from this, the media and certain individuals can have a large impact on the behavior of others. They become important customers, even if as individuals their economic decisions may be negligible. Companies clearly must devise programs that produce good relations with opinion leaders. Figure 5.4 gives a few examples of opinion leaders, and how a company might build a positive relationship with them.

FIGURE 5.4

EXAMPLES OF OPINION LEADERS

Company	Indirect Customer	Possible Relationship Maintenance
GM	*Consumer Reports*	Emphasize *CR* Criteria
Brooks	*Runners World*	Advertising in *RW*
Restaurant	Critic	Recognize and dote upon
Apple	College professors	Free equipment
President of the United States	News reporters	Regular access

Sometimes just being outstanding is not good enough, without the extra boost that an opinion leader can supply. Jimi Hendrix, probably the greatest rock guitarist of all time, was an unknown for many years. He had an obscure band in the army, another obscure band in Tennessee, and traveled as a sideman for several years with such artists as the Isley Brothers and Little Richard. They were happy to have a great guitar player in their band, but did not provide Hendrix with the benefit of their position as opinion leaders. Little Richard, for example, used to insist that the stage lights be turned off where Hendrix was so the audience could not see Hendrix playing impossibly difficult passages behind his back or with his teeth. Finally Hendrix moved to New York and cultivated the friendship of some influential opinion leaders who convinced a record company to put together a band around Hendrix. The result was spectacular financial success. Without the influence of the New York opinion leaders, Hendrix probably would have been the greatest unknown guitarist in the world.

Another example is Brooks shoes. Brooks was a minor player in the running-shoe market in the 1970s. Then one year *Runners World* magazine made a Brooks model its top-rated running shoe. Brooks's sales took off, and the company became one of the world's leading manufacturers of running shoes. Some critics complained that there was an apparent conflict of interest, because the shoes that advertised heavily in *Runners World* seemed to be the shoes that did best in the shoe rankings. No such link was ever established. Nevertheless, there was no disputing the power of the opinion leader, *Runners World,* in influencing sales, and the smart companies hedged their bets by making sure they had a healthy advertising budget in the magazine.

President Bill Clinton provides an example of what can happen if one alienates opinion leaders. Clinton decided to have very few news conferences and generally to deny access to White House reporters. He apparently did not realize that the White House press corps was a very important group of opinion leaders. As a result, Clinton got hammered by the press; everything he did was criticized unmercifully. This poor press contributed to the public's perception that Clinton was incompetent and weak, doing great damage to his effectiveness as a leader. If Clinton had instead provided regular access, giving the press the stories they needed to report fully from the White House, they would undoubtedly have covered his presidency in a much more sympathetic manner.

5.7 REGULATORS

Regulators define the governmental or legalistic ground rules by which an organization operates. Thus the regulators are very important customers, and must be treated with care. Figure 5.5 gives examples of regulators, and organizations that they affect. It also gives examples of some ways in which the relationship with the regulators can be improved.

One of the most successful examples of a relationship with a regulatory body is the National Rifle Association's relationship with Congress. The NRA, supported financially by the gun industry, opposes (for obvious financial reasons) any form of gun control. The American people have been overwhelmingly in favor of more gun control for many years. Yet the people's elective representatives, the Congress, do very little. Why? The NRA spends large amounts of money lobbying Congress, and giving money to congressional candidates. This time and money is not wasted. Gun control is killed time after time, and the NRA's interests are upheld.

An example of an unsuccessful relationship with regulators is given by Florida Power & Light, a power utility. In the 1980's Florida Power & Light embarked on what appeared to be one of the most successful quality programs in the world. They achieved impressive efficiencies and process improvements. They were ultimately awarded Japan's Deming Prize, the top quality award in Japan. Florida Power & Light was the only American firm to ever have been so honored. Unfortunately, Florida Power & Light had forgotten about one of its most important customers, the state public utility commission. The commission thought the large amounts of money FP&L was spending on quality improvement, and the Japanese consultants that had been hired, were wasteful. FP&L had never conclusively demonstrated the positive financial impact of their quality effort, and financial impact (especially price reduction) was the primary concern of the regulatory body. To avoid its fate, FP&L needed to monitor the needs and wants of its regulators on a continuing basis. The result was that the CEO was fired, and the award-winning quality program was scrapped. An organization ignores its regulators at its own peril.

FIGURE 5.5

EXAMPLES OF REGULATORS

Company	Indirect Customer	Possible Relationship Maintenance
Energy utility	State Utility Commission	Frequent contact to avoid conflict
Chrysler	EPA	Political pressure
College athletics	NCAA	Self-policing and full disclosure
Insurance	Congress	Lobby for safety laws
Serbia	United Nations	Compromise in conflict resolution

5.8 COMPETITORS

How can one possibly call a competitor a customer? After all, every competitor would probably like to see its competition failed and bankrupt. Again one gets some insight by examining the mechanism of exchange. Does a company get anything positive from an exchange with competitors?

Cooperation among competitors is actually encouraged in some cultures. In Japan, for example, there are many examples of industry initiatives that involve sharing technological information. That is part of what has led to the characterization of the Japanese industrial system as "Japan, Inc." Such initiatives are also beginning to find favor in the United States, as the government realizes that markets now stretch well beyond national boundaries, and that larger coalitions are sometimes necessary for companies to be globally competitive. For example, MCC, a computer consortium involving several U.S. companies, was welcomed by the government, in spite of the fact that considerable technology sharing would occur. Even Apple and IBM, cutthroat rivals, have formed a working relationship in which they share technology with one another. The obvious implication is that it now pays to treat the competition as a customer, so that when collaborative opportunities arise, the well will not have been poisoned.

5.9 INTERNAL CUSTOMERS

One of the most important customer groups is not outside the organization at all. The organization itself runs more smoothly if everyone in the organization treats the other employees as customers. Figure 5.6 gives a few examples of internal customers, and how a positive working relationship with them can be maintained.

To illustrate the importance of internal customers, consider Bill Arnold, the former CEO of Centennial Medical Center, a large healthcare complex in Nashville, Tennessee. Arnold was one of Nashville's leading proponents of Total Quality Management (TQM), and he wrote a book about his experiences with it at Centennial.[1] Arnold did a number of flamboyant things to improve his relationships with his internal customers, whom he called "associates." For example, he took the door to his office off its hinges and hung it from the ceiling, dramatically symbolizing

FIGURE 5.6

EXAMPLES OF INTERNAL CUSTOMERS

Service Supplier	Indirect Customer	Possible Relationship Maintenance
Marketing research	Marketing management	Regular informal meetings
Payroll	Employees	Identify customer needs
CEO	Management	Adopt service attitude
Salesperson	Sales manager	File call reports promptly
VP	Middle management	Return phone calls

his accessibility. To further reinforce the image, he put a coffeepot and bowls of M&M's in his office. Most employees were captivated by the new approach.

On the other hand, some of the internal customers had a problem. The doctors did not seem to understand his "crazy" methods, and especially did not understand why other employees were taking the CEO's time. A few started talking among themselves, and began sniping at Arnold when they got the chance. An even more important internal customer, the top management of HCA, of which Centennial Medical Center was part, was distressed by Arnold's failure to produce results at the bottom line. Arnold's brand of quality improvement emphasized human relationships, not financial performance, and that approach did not match top management's needs. Ultimately Arnold was forced out, and his novel management techniques were scrapped.

5.10 AVOIDING THE CUSTOMER BLIND SPOT

The examples of failure we have seen have a common theme. In every case the organization is doing good things, but develops a fatal blind spot. The blind spot generally involves a customer group that has been ignored or whose needs have not been met. If sufficiently important and sufficiently neglected, one customer group is enough to destroy the organization's effectiveness. Systematic attention to customer groups is required to avoid the customer blind spot. Figure 5.7 details a systematic approach for maintaining customer relationships with the key customer groups. The

FIGURE 5.7

MAINTAINING CUSTOMER RELATIONSHIPS

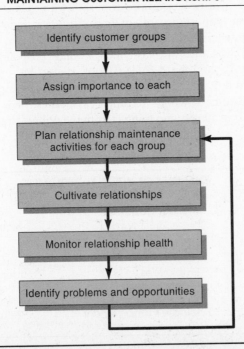

first step is to identify the relevant customer groups. This chapter could be used as a checklist to accomplish the identification. Second, importance must be assigned to each. There are sometimes customer groups that are of no real importance or require only a minimal amount of attention. In the Bill Arnold situation, for example, a systematic investigation would have revealed top management as a vitally important internal customer and would have resulted in considerably more attention to the bottom line, their chief concern.

The third step is to plan relationship maintenance activities that target each group. These maintenance activities are then implemented and monitored for effectiveness. Inevitably, not every activity is successful. Problems and opportunities must be identified, and these in turn are used to replan the customer relationship maintenance activities. It is truly amazing how many organizations (and individuals) fail to maintain successful relationships with key customer groups. In many cases it is caused by a failure to manage the relationship systematically.

REVIEW QUESTIONS

1. Think of the biggest employer in your city. Who are that organization's direct customers, indirect customers, decision makers, supplier customers, opinion leaders, regulators, and competitors? Which customer groups are most important? Least important? Where is that company's biggest customer blind spot? What could be done about it?
2. Think of yourself, a student. Who are *your* customers? Does that make you think about some of those groups differently? How should you change your behavior as a result?
3. Think of the company in your city that is in the most financial difficulty. What is its customer blind spot?

ENDNOTE

1. William W. Arnold and Jeanne M. Plas (1993), *The Human Touch: Today's Most Unusual Program for Productivity and Profit,* New York: Wiley.

SHOULDICE HOSPITAL LIMITED

Two shadowy figures, enrobed and in slippers, walked slowly down the semidarkened hall of the Shouldice Hospital. They didn't notice Alan O'Dell, the hospital administrator, and his guest, who had just emerged from the basement boiler room on a tour of the facility. Once they were out of earshot, O'Dell remarked good naturedly, "By the way they act, you'd think our patients own this place. And while they're here, in a way they do."

Following a visit to the five operating rooms, also located on the first of three levels, O'Dell and his visitor once again encountered the same pair of patients still engrossed in discussing their hernia operations, which had been performed the previous morning.

HISTORY

Born on a farm in Bruce County, Ontario, Dr. Earle Shouldice, who was to found the hospital bearing his name, first displayed his interest in medical research at the age of 12. He performed a postmortem on a calf that, he discovered, had died from an intestinal obstruction. After a year of following the wishes of his parents that he study for the ministry, Shouldice persuaded them to let him enroll in medicine at the University of Toronto.

An attractive brochure that was recently printed, although neither dated nor distributed to prospective patients, described Earle Shouldice as follows:

While carrying on a private medical and surgical practice in the years between the two World Wars and holding a post as lecturer in anatomy at the University of Toronto, Dr. Shouldice continued to pursue his interest in research. He did pioneer work towards the cure of pernicious anemia, intestinal obstruction, hydrocephalic casesand other areas of advancing medical knowledge.

Professor James L. Heskett prepared this case as a basis for class discussion rather than to illustrate either effective or ineffective handling of an administrative situation. Some of the data in this case are disguised. To order copies, call (617) 495–6117 or write the Publishing Division, Harvard Business School, Boston, MA 02163. No part of this publication may be reproduced, stored in a retrieval system, or transmitted in any form or by any means—electronic, mechanical, photocopying, recording, or otherwise—without the permission of the Harvard Business School.

His interest in early ambulation stemmed, in part, from an operation he performed in 1932 to remove the appendix from a seven-year-old girl and the girl's subsequent refusal to stay quietly in bed. In spite of her activity, no harm was done, and the experience recalled to the doctor the postoperative actions of animals upon which he had performed surgery. They had all moved about freely with no ill effects. Four years later he was reminded of the child when he allowed washroom privileges immediately following the operations to four men recovering from hernia repair. All had trouble-free recovery.

By the outset of the Second World War in 1940, Shouldice had given extensive thought to several factors that contributed to early ambulation following surgery. Among them were the use of a local anesthetic, the nature of the surgical procedure itself, the design of a facility to encourage movement without unnecessarily causing discomfort, and the postoperative regimen designed and communicated by the medical team. With all of these things in mind, he had begun to develop a surgical technique for repairing hernias[1] that was superior to others. He offered his services in correcting hernias for army inductees who otherwise would not qualify for service. Because hospital beds often were not available, sometimes the surgery took place in the emergency department of the Toronto General Hospital, and the patients were transported later in the day to a medical fraternity where they were cared for by medical students for two or three days.

By the war's end, word of the Shouldice technique had spread sufficiently that 200 civilians had contacted the doctor and were awaiting surgery upon his discharge from the army. Because of the scarcity of hospital beds, particularly for an operation that was considered elective and of relatively low priority, he started his own hospital. Dr. Shouldice's medical license permitted him to operate anywhere, even on a kitchen table, and consequently he received authorization from the provincial government to open his first hospital in a six-room nursing home in downtown Toronto in July 1945. As more and more patients requested operations, Dr. Shouldice extended his facilities by buying a rambling 130-acre estate with a 17,000-square-foot main house in the suburb of Thornhill, 15 miles north of downtown Toronto. Initially, a 36-bed capacity was created in Thornhill, but after some years of planning, a large wing was added to the house to provide a total capacity of 89 beds.

At the time of his death in 1965, Dr. Shouldice's long-time associate, Dr. Nicholas Obney, was named surgeon-in-chief and chairman of the board of Shouldice Hospital Limited, the corporation formed to operate both the hospital and clinical facilities. Under Dr. Obney's leadership, the volume of activity continued to increase, reaching a total of 6,850 operations in the 1982 calendar year.

---

[1]Most hernias, known as external abdominal hernias, were protrusions of some part of the abdominal contents through a hole or slit in the muscular layers of the abdominal wall which was supposed to contain them. Well over 90% of these hernias occurred in the groin area. Of these, by far the most common were inguinal hernias, many of which were caused by a slight weakness in the muscle layers brought about by the passage of the testicle in male babies through the groin area shortly before birth. Aging also caused inguinal hernias to develop. The other, much less common, external hernias were called "femoral," in which a protrusion appeared in the top inch or so of the thigh. Because of the cause of the affliction, 85% of all hernias occurred in males.

THE SHOULDICE METHOD

Only external types of abdominal hernias were repaired at Shouldice Hospital. Internal types, such as hiatus (or diaphragmatic) hernias, were not treated. As a result, most first-time repairs (called primaries) involved straight-forward operating procedures that required about 45 minutes. Primaries represented approximately 82% of all operations performed at Shouldice in 1982. The remaining 18% involved patients suffering recurrences of hernias previously repaired elsewhere.[2]

In the Shouldice method, the muscles of the abdominal wall were arranged in three distinct layers, and the opening was repaired—each layer in turn—by overlapping its margins in much the same manner as the edges of a coat might be overlapped when buttoned. The end result was to reinforce the muscular wall of the abdomen with six rows of sutures (stitches) under the skin cover, which was then closed with clamps that were removed within 48 hours after the operation. (Other methods might not separate muscle layers, often involved fewer rows of sutures, and sometimes involved the insertion of screens or meshes under the skin.)

The typical first-time repair could be completed with the use of preoperative sedation (sleeping pill) and analgesic (pain killer) plus a local anesthetic, an injection of Novocain in the region of the incision. This allowed immediate patient ambulation and facilitated rapid recovery. Many of the recurrences and the very difficult hernia repairs, being more complex, could require up to 90 minutes and more. In some circumstances, a general anesthetic was administered.

THE PATIENTS' EXPERIENCE

It was thought that most potential Shouldice patients learned about the hospital and its methods from past patients who had already experienced them. Although over 1,000 doctors had referred patients, doctors were less likely to recommend Shouldice because of the generally regarded simplicity of the surgery, often considered a "bread and butter" operation. Typically, many patients had their problem diagnosed by a personal physician and then took the initiative to contact Shouldice. Many more made this diagnosis themselves and contacted the hospital directly.

The process experienced by Shouldice patients depended on whether or not they lived close enough to the hospital to visit the facility to obtain a diagnosis. Approximately 42% of all Shouldice patients came from the United States. Another 2% originated from provinces other than Ontario and from European countries. These out-of-town patients often were diagnosed by mail, using the Medical Information questionnaire shown in Exhibit 1.

Of every eight questionnaires sent, seven were returned to the hospital in completed form. Based on information in the questionnaire, a Shouldice surgeon would determine the type of hernia the respondent had and whether there were signs that some risk might be associated with surgery (for example, an overweight or heart condition, or a patient who had suffered a heart attack or a stroke in the past six months to a year, or whether a general or local anesthetic was required). At this point, a patient was given an operating date, the medical information was logged into a computerized data base, and the patient was

---

[2]Based on a careful tracking of its patients over more than 30 years, it was estimated that the gross recurrence rate for all operations performed at Shouldice was 0.8%. Recurrence rates reported in the literature for these types of hernia varied greatly. However, one text published around that time stated, "In the United States the gross rate of recurrence for groin hernias approaches 10%."

sent a confirmation card; if necessary, a sheet outlining a weight loss program prior to surgery and a brochure describing the hospital and the Shouldice method were also sent. A small proportion was refused treatment, either because they were too fat, represented an undue medical risk, or because it was determined that they did not have a hernia.

If confirmation cards were not returned by the patient three days or more prior to the scheduled operation, that patient was contacted by phone. Upon confirmation, the patient's folder was sent to the reception desk to await his or her arrival.[3]

Arriving at the clinic between 1:00 P.M. and 3:00 P.M. the day before the operation, a patient might join up with 30 to 34 other patients and their friends and families in the waiting room. After a typical wait of about 20 minutes—depending on the availability of surgeons—a patient was examined in one of six examination rooms staffed by surgeons who had completed their operating schedules for the day. This examination required no more than 15 to 20 minutes, unless the patient needed reassurance. (Patients typically exhibited a moderate level of anxiety until their operation was completed.) At this point it occasionally was discovered that a patient had not corrected his or her weight problem; others might be found not to have a hernia after all. In either case, the patient was sent home.

Following his or her examination, a patient might experience a wait of 5 to 15 minutes to see one of two admitting personnel in the accounting office. Here, health insurance coverage was checked, and various details were discussed in a procedure that usually lasted no more than 10 minutes. Patients sometimes exhibited their nervousness by asking many questions at this point, requiring more time of the receptionist.

Patients next were sent to one of two nurses' stations where, in 5 to 10 minutes and with little wait, their hemoglobin (blood) and urine were checked. At this point, about an hour after arriving at the hospital, a patient was directed to the room number shown on his or her wrist band. Throughout the process, patients were asked to keep their luggage (usually light and containing only a few items suggested by the hospital) with them.

All patient rooms at the hospital were semiprivate, containing two beds. Patients with similar jobs, backgrounds, or interests were assigned to the same room to the extent possible. Upon reaching their rooms, patients busied themselves unpacking, getting acquainted with roommates, changing into pajamas, "prepping" themselves (shaving themselves in the area of the operation), and providing a urine sample.

At 5:00 P.M. a nurse's orientation provided the group of incoming patients with information about what to expect, the drugs to be administered, the need for exercise after the operation, the facility, and the daily routine. According to Alan O'Dell, "Half are so nervous they don't remember much from the orientation." Dinner was served from 5:30 to 6:00 P.M. in a 100-seat dining room on a first-come, first-served basis. Following further

---

[3]Patients living within 50 miles from the hospital (about 40% of all patients) were encouraged to come to the clinic on a walk-in basis for an examination, usually requiring no more than 15 or 20 minutes for the physical and completion of an information questionnaire. If the doctor performing the examination diagnosed the problem as an external hernia, the individual could obtain immediately a future booking for the operation. On occasion, when a previously booked patient canceled at the last minute, a walk-in patient, or one selected from a special waiting list, could be scheduled for the next day. At the time of booking, the potential patient was given a specific date for the operation, a letter estimating the total cost of the operation (as required by the Ontario provincial government for all Ontario residents), and information supplied to out-of-province patients.

recreation, tea and cookies were served at 9:00 P.M. in the lounge area. Nurses emphasized the importance of attendance at that time because it provided an opportunity for preoperative patients to talk with those whose operations had been completed earlier that same day. Nearly all new patients were "tucked into bed" between 9:30 and 10:00 P.M. in preparation for an early awakening prior to their operations.

Patients to be operated on early in the day were awakened at 5:30 A.M. to be given preop sedation and to be dressed in an O.R. (operating room) gown. An attempt was made to schedule operations for roommates at approximately the same time. Patients were taken to the preoperating room where the circulating nurse administered Demerol, an analgesic, 45 minutes before surgery. A few minutes prior to the first operation at 7:30 A.M., the surgeon assigned to each patient administered Novocain, a local anesthetic. During the operation, it was the responsibility of the circulating nurse to monitor the patient's comfort, to note times at which the Novocain was administered and the operation begun, and to arrange for the administration of Demerol to the patient scheduled next on the operating table, depending on the progress of the surgery under way. This was in contrast to the typical hospital procedure in which patients were sedated in their rooms prior to being taken to the operating rooms.

Upon the completion of the operation, during which a few patients were "chatty" and fully aware of what was going on, patients were invited to get off the operating table and walk to the post-operating room with the help of their surgeons. According to Ursula Verstraete, director of nursing:

Ninety-nine percent accept the surgeon's invitation. While we put them in wheelchairs to return them to their rooms, the walk from the operating table is for psychological as well as physiological [blood pressure, respiratory] reasons. Patients prove to themselves that they can do it, and they start their all-important exercise immediately.

Throughout the day after their operation, patients were encouraged to exercise by nurses and housekeepers alike. By 9:00 P.M. on the day of their operations, all patients were ready and able to walk down to the dining room for tea and cookies, even if it meant climbing stairs, to help indoctrinate the new "class" admitted that day.

Patients in their second or third day of recovery were awakened before 6:00 A.M. so they could loosen up for breakfast, which was served between 7:45 and 8:15 A.M. in the dining room. Good posture and exercise were thought to aid digestion and deter the buildup of gas that could prove painful. After breakfast on the first day after surgery, all of the skin clips (resembling staples) holding the skin together over the incision were loosened and some removed. The remainder were removed the next day. On the fourth morning, patients were ready for discharge.

During their stay, patients were encouraged to take advantage of the opportunity to explore the premises and make new friends. Some members of the staff felt that the patients and their attitudes were the most important element of the Shouldice program. According to Dr. Byrnes Shouldice, the 53-year-old son of the founder and vice president of the corporation—a surgeon on the staff and a 50% owner of the hospital:

Patients sometimes ask to stay an extra day. Why? Well, think about it. They are basically well to begin with. But they arrive with a problem and a certain amount of nervousness, tension, and anxiety about their surgery. Their first morning here they're operated on and experience a sense of relief from something that's been bothering them for a long time. They are immediately able to get around, and they've got a three-day holiday ahead of them with a perfectly good reason to be away from work with no sense of guilt. They share experiences with other patients, make friends easily, and have the run of the hospital. In summer, the most common after-effect from the surgery is sunburn. They kid with the staff and make this a positive experience for all of us.

The average patient stay for comparable operations at other hospitals was thought to be five to seven or eight days, but it had been declining because of a shortage of beds and the tendency to give elective surgery a low priority for beds. Shouldice patients with jobs involving light exercise could return to work within a week after their operations, but those involved in more strenuous work, whose benefits were insured, received four weeks of benefits and recuperation. All self-employed persons returned to work much earlier. In general, typical times for recuperation from similar operations at other hospitals were two weeks for those in jobs requiring light exercise and eight weeks for those in more strenuous jobs, due largely to long-established treatment regimens.

THE NURSES' EXPERIENCE

The nursing staff comprised 22 full-time and 18 part-time members. They were divided into four groups (as shown in Exhibit 2), with supervisors for the hospital, operating room, laboratory, and central supply reporting to Ursula Verstraete, the director of nursing.

While the operating rooms were fully staffed from about 7 A.M. through the last operation ending in the mid- to late afternoon, the hospital was staffed with three shifts beginning at 7 A.M., 3 P.M., and 11 P.M. Even so, minimal patient needs for physical assistance allowed Shouldice to operate with a much lower nurse-to-patient ratio than the typical hospital. Shouldice nurses spent an unusually large proportion of their time in counseling activities. As one supervisor commented, "We don't use bedpans." In a typical year, Verstraete estimated that she might experience a turnover of four nurses.

THE DOCTORS' EXPERIENCE

The hospital employed 12 full-time surgeons, 7 part-time assistant surgeons, and one anesthetist. Each operating team required a surgeon, an assistant surgeon, a scrub nurse, and a circulating nurse. The operating load varied from 30 to 36 operations per day. As a result, each surgeon typically performed three or four operations each day.

A typical surgeon's day started with a *scrubbing* shortly before the first scheduled operation at 7:30 A.M. If the first operation was routine, it usually was completed by 8:15 A.M. At its conclusion, the surgical team helped the patient walk from the room and summoned the next patient. While the patient was being prepared and awaiting the full effects of the Demerol to set in, the surgeon completed the previous patient's file by dictating five or so minutes of comments concerning the operation. Postoperative instructions were routine unless specific instructions were issued by the surgeon. After scrubbing, the surgeon could be ready to operate again at 8:30 A.M.

Surgeons were advised to take a coffee break after their second or third operation. Even so, a surgeon could complete three routine operations and a fourth involving a recurrence (a 60- to 90-minute procedure) and still be finished in time for a 12:30 P.M. lunch in the staff dining room.

Upon finishing lunch, as many as six of the surgeons not scheduled to operate in the afternoon moved upstairs to examine incoming patients between 1:00 and 3:00 P.M. A surgeon's day ended by 4:00 P.M. In addition, a surgeon could expect to be on call one week-day night in ten and one weekend in ten. Alan O'Dell commented that the position appealed to doctors who "want to watch their children grow up. A doctor on call is rarely called to the hospital and has regular hours."

According to Dr. Obney, chief surgeon:

When I interview prospective surgeons, I look for experience and a good education. I try to gain some insight into their domestic situation and personal interests and habits. Naturally, as in any field, we try to avoid anyone with a drinking or drug problem. Oftentimes these people can hide their illness very well and it can take a while before it is detected. Here, sometimes, recommendations can be of great help. I also try to find out why a surgeon wants to switch positions. And I try to determine if he's willing to perform the repair exactly as he's told. This is no place for prima donnas.

Dr. Shouldice added:

Our surgeons enjoy operating, but sometimes are less interested in the more mundane office routines that all vocations have. Traditionally a hernia is often the first operation that a junior resident in surgery performs. Hernia repair is regarded as a relatively simple operation compared to other major operations. This is quite wrong, as is borne out by the resulting high recurrence rate. It is a tricky anatomical area and occasionally very complicated, especially to the novice or those doing very few hernia repairs each year. But at Shouldice Hospital a surgeon learns the Shouldice technique over a period of several months. He learns when he can go fast and when he must go slow. He develops a pace and a touch. If he encounters something unusual, he is encouraged to consult immediately with other surgeons. We teach each other and try to encourage a group effort. And he learns not to take risks to achieve absolute perfection. Excellence is the enemy of good.

Dr. Obney assigned surgeons to an operating room on a daily basis by noon of the preceding day. This allowed surgeons to examine the specific patients that they were to operate on. Surgeons and assistants were rotated every few days. Scrub nurses and circulating nurses were assigned to a new operating room every two weeks and four weeks, respectively. Unless patients requested specific doctors, cases were assigned to give doctors a nonroutine operation (often involving a recurrence) several times a week. More complex procedures were assigned to more senior and experienced members of the staff, including Dr. Obney himself. Where possible, former Shouldice patients suffering recurrences were assigned to the doctor who performed the first operation "to allow the doctor to learn from his mistake."

As Dr. Obney commented:

If something goes wrong, we want to make sure that we have an experienced surgeon in charge, and we don't like surgeons who work too fast. Experience is most important. The typical general surgeon may perform 25 to 50 hernia operations per year. Ours perform 600 or more.

The 12 full-time surgeons were paid a straight salary. A typical starting salary at that time for someone with 5 to 10 years of experience was $50,000. In addition, bonuses to doctors were voted by the board of directors twice a year, depending on profit and performance. The total bonus pool paid to the surgeons in a recent year was approximately $500,000. Assisting surgeons were part-time, and they received 51% of the $60 fee that was charged to patients who received their services.

The anesthetist was hired for $300 per day from a nearby partnership. Only one was required to be on duty on any given day and could supervise all five operating rooms in addition to administering an occasional general anesthetic to a patient with a complex case or to a child.

Training in the Shouldice technique was important because the procedure could not be varied. It was accomplished through direct supervision by one or more of the senior surgeons. The rotation of teams and frequent consultations allowed for an ongoing opportunity to appraise performance and take corrective action.

According to Dr. Obney:

We haven't had to let anyone go because they couldn't learn, or continue to adhere to, the method. However, a doctor must decide after several years whether he wants to do this for the rest of his life because, just as in other specialties—for example, radiology— he loses touch with other medical disciplines. If he stays for five years, he doesn't leave. Even among younger doctors, few elect to leave.

THE FACILITY

A tour of the facility with Alan O'Dell yielded some interesting information. The Shouldice Hospital comprised two basic facilities in one building—the hospital and the clinic.

On the first-level opening to grade at the back of the building, the hospital contained the kitchen and dining rooms as well as the office of the supervisor of housekeeping. The second level, also opening to grade but at the front of the building, contained a large, open lounge area, the admissions offices, patient rooms, and a spacious glass-covered Florida room. The third level had additional patient rooms, a large lounge, and a recreational area.

Throughout the tour, patients could be seen visiting in each others' rooms, walking up and down hallways, lounging in the sunroom, and making use of light recreational facilities ranging from a pool table to an exercycle.

Alan O'Dell pointed out some of the features of the hospital:

The rooms contain no telephones or television sets. If a patient needs to make a call or wants to watch television, he or she has to take a walk. The steps are designed specially with a small rise to allow patients recently operated on to negotiate the stairs without undue discomfort. Every square foot of the hospital is carpeted to reduce the hospital feeling and the possibility of a fall. Carpeting also gives the place a smell other than that of disinfectant.

This facility was designed by Dr. Byrnes Shouldice. He thought about it for years and made many changes in the plan before the first concrete was poured. A number of unique policies were also instituted. Because Dr. Shouldice started out to be a minister, ministers are treated gratis. And you see that mother and child in the next room? Parents accompanying children here for an operation stay free. You may wonder why we can do it, but we learned that we save more in nursing costs than we spend for the patient's room and board. Children may present difficulties in a hospital environment, but when accompanied by a parent, the parent is happier and so is the child.

While patients and staff were served food prepared in the same kitchen, the staff was required to pick up its food from a cafeteria line placed in the very center of the kitchen.

This provided an opportunity for everyone to chat with the kitchen staff several times a day as they picked up a meal or stopped for coffee. Patients were served in the adjoining patient dining room.

According to O'Dell:

We use all fresh ingredients and prepare the food from scratch in the kitchen. Our kitchen staff of three prepares about 100 breakfasts, 200 lunches, and 100 dinners each day at an average raw food cost of $1.10 per meal.

Iona Rees, director of housekeeping, pointed out:

We do all of our own laundry in the building with two full-time employees. And I have only three on my housekeeping staff for the entire facility. One of the reasons for so few housekeepers is that we don't need to change linens during a patient's four-day stay. They are basically well, so there is no soiling of bed linens. Also, the medical staff doesn't want the patients in bed all day. They want the nurses to encourage the patients to be up socializing, comparing notes [for confidence], encouraging each other, and walking around, getting exercise.

Of course, we're in the rooms straightening up throughout the day. This gives the housekeepers a chance to josh with the patients and to encourage them to exercise.

The bottom level of the clinic housed five operating rooms, a laboratory, the patient-recovery room, and a central supply area where surgical instruments were cleaned and sterilized. This was the only area of the entire facility that was not carpeted, to prevent static electricity from forming in areas where potentially explosive anesthetics might be used. In total, the estimated cost to furnish an operating room was no more than $30,000. This was considerably less than for other hospitals requiring a bank of equipment with which to administer anesthetics for each room. At Shouldice, two mobile units were used by the anesthetist when needed. In addition, the complex had one "crash cart" per floor for use if a patient should suffer a heart attack or stroke during his or her hospital stay.

The first floor of the clinic contained admissions and accounting offices, a large waiting room with a capacity for as many as 50 people, and 6 examination rooms. On the second floor of the clinic, situated in much of what was the original house, was found the administrative offices. A third floor contained 14 additional hostel rooms where patients could be held overnight awaiting the assignment of a room and their operations. At such times when the hospital was particularly crowded, doctors were asked to identify those postoperative patients who could be released a day early. Often these were local residents or children.

ADMINISTRATION

Alan O'Dell, while he walked, described his job:

I'm responsible for a little of everything around here. We try to meet people's needs and make this as good a place to work as possible. My door is always open. And members of our staff will come in to seek advice about everything from medical to marital problems. There is a strong concern for employees here. Nobody is fired. [This was later reinforced by Dr. Shouldice, who described a situation involving two employees who confessed to theft in the hospital. They agreed to seek psychiatric help and were allowed to remain on the job.] As a result, turnover is low.

We don't have a union, but we try to maintain a pay scale higher than the union scale for comparable jobs in the area. For example, our nurses receive from $15,000 to $25,000 per year, depending on the number of years' experience. We have a profit-sharing plan that is separate from the doctors'. Last year the employees divided up $65,000.

If work needs to be done, people pitch in to help each other. A unique aspect of our administration is that I insist that each secretary is trained to do another's work and in an emergency is able to switch to another function immediately and enable the more vital workload to proceed uninterrupted. With the exception of the accounting staff, every secretary, regardless of her or his position in the hospital, is trained to handle the hospital switchboard and work at the reception desk. If necessary, I'll go downstairs and type billings if they're behind. We don't have an organization chart. A chart tends to make people think they're boxed into jobs.[4]

In addition to other activities, I try to stay here one night a week having dinner and listening to the patients to find out how things are really going around here.

Administrative Structure

The hospital was operated on a nonprofit basis and the clinic on a for-profit basis. Dr. Shouldice and Mrs. W. Urquhart, his sister, each owned 50% of each.

O'Dell, as administrator of the hospital, was responsible for all of its five departments: surgery, nursing, administration, maintenance, and housekeeping. Medical matters were the domain of Dr. Obney, the chief surgeon. Both Alan O'Dell and Dr. Obney reported directly to an executive committee composed of Drs. Shouldice and Obney, Alan O'Dell, Ursula Verstraete (director of nursing), and Mrs. Urquhart. The executive committee met as needed, usually twice a month, and in turn reported to an inside board (as shown in Exhibit 2). In addition to executive committee members (except Ursula Verstraete), the board included the spouses of Dr. Shouldice and Mrs. Urquhart, two former long-time employees, and Jack MacKay. The board met three times per year, or when necessary.

Operating Costs

It was estimated by the casewriter that the 1983 budgets for the hospital and clinic were close to $2.8 million and $2 million, respectively.[5]

THE MARKET

Hernia operations were among the most common performed on males. In 1979, for example, it was estimated that 600,000 such operations were performed in the United States alone. Only in the early 1980s had the hospital begun to organize information about either its client base of 140,000 "alumni" or the market in general.

According to Dr. Shouldice:

When our backlog of scheduled operations gets too large, we begin to wonder how many people decide instead to have their local doctor perform the operation. Every time we have expanded our capacity, the

---

[4]The chart in Exhibit 2 was prepared by the casewriter, based on conversations with hospital personnel.
[5]The latter figure included the bonus pool for doctors.

backlog has declined briefly, only to climb once again. Right now, at 1,200, it is larger than it has ever been at this time of year [January].

The hospital relied entirely on word-of-mouth advertising, the importance of which was suggested by the results of a poll carried out by students of DePaul University as part of a project (Exhibit 3 shows a portion of these results). Although little systematic data about patients had been collected, Alan O'Dell remarked that "if we had to rely on wealthy patients only, our practice would be much smaller."

Patients were attracted to the hospital, in part, by its reasonable rates. For example, charges for a typical operation were four days of hospital stay at $111 per day, a $450 surgical fee for a primary inguinal (the most common hernia) operation, and a $60 fee for the assistant surgeon.[6] If a general anesthetic was required, an additional fee of $75 was assessed. These were the charges that compared with total costs of $2,000 to $4,000 for operations performed elsewhere.

Round-trip fares for travel to Toronto from various major cities on the North American continent ranged from roughly $200 to $600.

In addition to providing free services to the clergy and to parents of hospitalized children, the hospital also provided annual checkups to its alumni, free of charge. Many of them occurred at the time of the annual reunion. The most recent reunion, featuring dinner and a floor show, was held at a first-class hotel in downtown Toronto and was attended by 1,400 former patients, many of them from outside Canada.

The reunion was scheduled to coincide with the mid-January decline in activity at the hospital, when an average of only 145 operations per week were performed. This was comparable to a similar lull in late summer and contrasted with the peak of activity in September, when as many as 165 operations per week might be performed.

It was thought that patients from outside Canada were discouraged from coming to Toronto in midwinter by often misleading weather reports. Vacations interfered with plans in late summer. For many of the same reasons, the hospital closed for two weeks late in December each year. This allowed time for major maintenance work to be performed. Throughout the year, no operations were scheduled for Saturdays or Sundays, although patients whose operations were scheduled late in the week remained in the hospital over the weekend.

PROBLEMS AND PLANS

When asked about major questions confronting the management of the hospital, Dr. Shouldice cited a desire to seek ways of increasing the hospital's capacity while at the same time maintaining control over the quality of the service delivered, the future role of government in the operations of the hospital, the use of the Shouldice name by potential competitors, and the selection of the next chief surgeon.

As Dr. Shouldice put it:

I'm a doctor first and an entrepreneur second. For example, we could refuse permission to other doctors who want to visit the hospital. They may copy our technique and misapply it or misinform their patients about the use of it. This results in failure, and we are concerned that the technique will be blamed for the recurrences. But we're doctors, and it is our obligation to help other surgeons learn. On the other hand, it's quite clear that others are trying to emulate us.

---

[6]At the time this case was written, a Canadian dollar was worth about 80% of an American dollar.

Look at this ad. [The advertisement is shown in Exhibit 4.]

This makes me believe that we should add to our capacity, either here or elsewhere. Here, for example, we could go to Saturday operations and increase our capacity by 20% or, with an investment of perhaps $2 million and permission from the provincial government, we could add another floor of rooms to the hospital, expand our number of beds by 50%, and schedule the operating rooms more heavily.

On the other hand, with government regulation being what it is, do we want to invest more money in Toronto? Or should we establish another hospital with similar design outside Canada? I have under consideration a couple of sites in the United States where private hospital operations are more common. Then, too, there is the possibility that we could diversify at other locations into other specialties offering similar opportunities such as eye surgery, varicose veins, or hemorrhoids.

For now, I have my hands full thinking about the selection of someone to succeed Dr. Obney when he retires. He's 65, you know. And for good reason, he's resisted changing certain successful procedures that I think we could improve on. We had quite a time changing the schedule for the administration of Demerol to patients to increase their comfort level during the operation. Dr. Obney has opposed a Saturday operating program on the premise that he won't be here and won't be able to maintain proper control.

Alan O'Dell added his own concerns:

How should we be marketing our services? Right now, we don't. We're even afraid to send out this new brochure we've put together for fear it will generate too much demand. We know that both patients and doctors believe in what we do. Our records show that just under 1% of our patients are medical doctors, a significantly high percentage. How should we capitalize on that? And should we try to control the misuse of the hospital's name by physicians who say they use our techniques but don't achieve good results? We know it's going on, because we get letters from patients of other doctors claiming that our method didn't work.

On the other hand, I'm concerned about this talk of Saturday operations. We are already getting good utilization of this facility. And if we expand further, it will be very difficult to maintain the same kind of working relationships and attitudes. Already there are rumors floating around among the staff about it. And the staff is not pleased.

We still have some improvements to make in our systems. With more extensive computerization, for example, we could improve our admitting procedures.

The matter of Saturday operations had been a topic of conversation among the doctors as well. Four of the older doctors were opposed to it. While most of the younger doctors were indifferent or supportive, at least two who had been at the hospital for some time were particularly concerned about the possibility that the issue would drive a wedge between the two groups. As one put it, "I'd hate to see the practice split over the issue."

EXHIBIT 1

MEDICAL INFORMATION QUESTIONNAIRE.

SHOULDICE HOSPITAL

7750 Bayview Avenue

Box 370, Thornhill, Ontario L3T 4A3 Canada
Phone (416) 889-1125

(Thornhill - One Mile North Metro Toronto)

MEDICAL INFORMATION

Patients who live at a distance often prefer their examination, admission and operation to be arranged all on a single visit — to save making two lengthy journeys. The whole purpose of this questionnaire is to make such arrangements possible, although, of course, it cannot replace the examination in any way. Its completion and return will not put you under any obligation.

Please be sure to fill in both sides.

This information will be treated as confidential.

FAMILY NAME (Last Name) | FIRST NAME | MIDDLE NAME

STREET & NUMBER (or Rural Route or P.O. Box) | Town/City | Province/State

County | Township | Zip or Postal Code | Birthdate: Month Day Year | Married or Single | Religion

Telephone
Home ....
Work ....
If none, give neighbour's number ....

NEXT OF KIN: Name | Address | Telephone #

Date form completed

INSURANCE INFORMATION: Please give name of Insurance Company and Numbers.

HOSPITAL INSURANCE: (Please bring hospital certificates) | OTHER HOSPITAL INSURANCE

O.H.I.P. | BLUE CROSS | Company Name
Number | Number | Policy Number

SURGICAL INSURANCE: (Please bring insurance certificates) | OTHER SURGICAL INSURANCE

O.H.I.P. | BLUE SHIELD | Company Name
Number | Number | Policy Number

WORKMEN'S COMPENSATION BOARD | Approved | Social Insurance (Security) Number
Claim No. | Yes No

Occupation | Name of Business | Are you the Owner? If Retired — Former Occupation
Yes No

How did you hear about Shouldice Hospital? (If referred by a doctor, give name & address)

Are you a former patient of Shouldice Hospital? | Yes | No | Do you smoke? | Yes | No

Have you ever written to Shouldice Hospital in the past? | Yes | No

What is your preferred admission date? (Please give as much advance notice as possible)

No admissions Friday, Saturday or Sunday.

FOR OFFICE USE ONLY

Date Received | Type of Hernia | Weight Loss | lbs.

Consent to Operate ☐ | Special Instructions | Approved
Heart Report ☐ | | Operation Date
Referring Doctor Notified

(Continued)

EXHIBIT 1 (CONTINUED)

MEDICAL INFORMATION QUESTIONNAIRE.

PLEASE BE ACCURATE!: Misleading figures, when checked on a admission day, could mean postponement of your operation till your weight is suitable.

HEIGHT ...... ft ...... ins. WEIGHT ...... lbs. Nude   Recent gain? ...... lbs.
or just pyjamas   Recent loss? ...... lbs

Waist (muscles relaxed) ...... ins.   Chest (not expanded) ...... ins.

GENERAL HEALTH

Age ...... years is your health now GOOD ☐ . FAIR ☐ . or POOR ☐

Please mention briefly any severe past illness — such as a "heart attack" or a "stroke", for example, from which you have now recovered (and its approximate date) ......

We need to know about other present conditions, even though your admission is NOT likely to be refused because of them.

Please tick ☑ any condition for which you are having regular treatment:

Blood Pressure ☐
Excess body fluids ☐
Chest pain ("angina") ☐
Irregular Heartbeat ☐
Diabetes ☐
Asthma & Bronchitis ☐
Ulcers ☐
Anticoagulants
(to delay blood-clotting
or to "thin the blood") ☐
Other ...... ☐

Name of any prescribed pills, tablets or capsules you take regularly: —

Did you remember to MARK AN "X" on your body chart to show us where each of your hernias is located? ☐

THIS CHART IS FOR EXPLANATION ONLY

Ordinary hernias are mostly either at the navel ("belly-button") - or just above it

or down in the groin area on either side

An "incisional hernia" is one that bulges through the scar of any other surgical operation that has failed to hold - wherever it may be.

Left Groin

Right Groin

THIS IS YOUR CHART — PLEASE MARK IT!

(MARK THE POSITION OF EACH HERNIA YOU WANT REPAIRED WITH AN "X")

Left Groin

Right Groin

APPROXIMATE SIZE . . . .
Walnut (or less)
Hen's Egg or Lemon
Grapefruit (or more)

ESSENTIAL EXTRA INFORMATION

Use only the sections that apply to your hernias and put a ✓ in each box that seems appropriate.

NAVEL AREA (AND JUST ABOVE NAVEL) ONLY
Is this navel (bellybutton) hernia your FIRST one?   Yes ☐   No ☐

If it's NOT your first, how many repair attempts so far? ☐

GROIN HERNIAS ONLY

	RIGHT GROIN		LEFT GROIN	
	Yes	No	Yes	No
Is this your FIRST GROIN HERNIA ON THIS SIDE?	☐	☐	☐	☐

How many hernia operations in this groin already? Right ☐   Left ☐

DATE OF LAST OPERATION

INCISIONAL HERNIAS ONLY (the ones bulging through previous operation scars)
Was the original operation for your Appendix? ☐ . or Gallbladder? ☐ .
or Stomach? ☐ . or Prostate? ☐ . or Hysterectomy? ☐ . or Other? ...... ☐

How many attempts to repair the hernia have been made so far? ☐

EXHIBIT 2

ORGANIZATION CHART

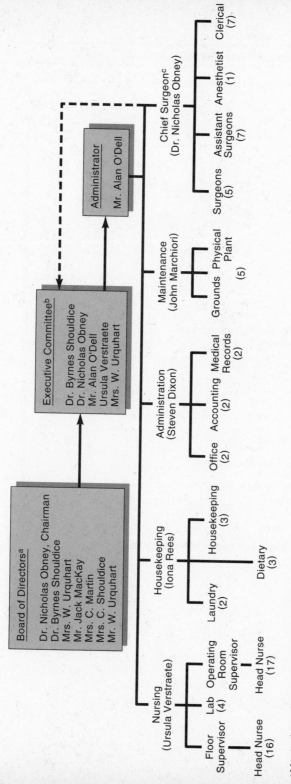

Board of Directors[a]

Dr. Nicholas Obney, Chairman
Dr. Byrnes Shouldice
Mrs. W. Urquhart
Mr. Jack MacKay
Mrs. C. Martin
Mrs. C. Shouldice
Mr. W. Urquhart

Executive Committee[b]

Dr. Byrnes Shouldice
Dr. Nicholas Obney
Mr. Alan O'Dell
Ursula Verstraete
Mrs. W. Urquhart

Administrator
Mr. Alan O'Dell

Chief Surgeon[c]
(Dr. Nicholas Obney)

Surgeons (5)   Assistant Surgeons (7)   Anesthetist (1)   Clerical (7)

Maintenance
(John Marchiori)

Grounds   Physical Plant (5)

Administration
(Steven Dixon)

Office (2)   Accounting (2)   Medical Records (2)

Housekeeping
(Iona Rees)

Laundry (2)   Housekeeping (3)

Dietary (3)

Nursing
(Ursula Verstraete)

Floor Supervisor   Lab (4)   Operating Room Supervisor

Head Nurse (16)   Head Nurse (17)

[a]Meets three times a year or as needed.
[b]Meets as needed (usually twice a month).
[c]Informally reports to Executive Committee.

113

EXHIBIT 3

SHOULDICE HOSPITAL ANNUAL PATIENT REUNION, JANUARY 15, 1983.

Direction: For each question, please place a check mark as it applies to you.

1. <u>Sex</u>   Male _41_ 95.34%
               Female _2_ 4.65%

2. <u>Age</u>   20 or less _·_
               21-40   _4_   9.30%
               41-60   _17_ 39.54%
               61 or more _22_ 51.16%

3. <u>Nationality</u>

   Directions: Please place a
   check mark in nation you
   represent and please write in
   your province, state or
   country where it applies.

   Canada _38_ Province _88.37%_
   America _5_   State   _11.63%_
   Europe ___   Country ___
   Other   ___

4. <u>Education level</u>

   Elementary   _5_   11.63%
   High School   _18_   41.86%
   College   _1330_ 30.23%
   Graduate work   _7_   16.28%

5. <u>Occupation</u> _____

6. Have you been overnight in a hospital other than   Yes _31_
   Shouldice before your operation?   No _12_

7. What brought Shouldice Hospital to your attention?

   Friend _23_ Doctor _9_   Relative _7_ Article ___ Other _4_____
          53.49%   20.93%   16.28%   (Please explain) 9.30%

8. Did you have a single _25_ or double _18_ hernia operation?
                          58.14%   41.86%   _2-5 reunions — 11 47.83%_

9. Is this your first Annual Reunion? Yes _20_   No _23_ / _6-10 reunions — 5 21.73%_
                                          46.51%   53.49% _11-20 reunions — 4 17.39%_
                                                             21-36 reunions — 3 13.05%

   If no, how many reunions have you attended? _____

10. Do you feel that Shouldice Hospital cared for you as a person?

    Most definitely _37_ Definitely _6_ Very little ___ Not at all ___
                    86.05%   13.95%

EXHIBIT 3 (CONTINUED)

SHOULDICE HOSPITAL ANNUAL PATIENT REUNION, JANUARY 15, 1983.

11. What impressed you the most about your stay at Shouldice? Please check one answer for each of the following.

A. Fees charged for operation and hospital stay

Very Important _10_   Important _3_   Somewhat Important _6_   Not Important _24_

B. Operation procedure

Very Important _33_   Important _9_   Somewhat Important _1_   Not Important ____
76.74%   20.93%   2.33%

C. Physician's Care

Very Important _31_   Important _12_   Somewhat Important _–_   Not Important _–_
72.10%   27.90%

D. Nursing Care

Very Important _28_   Important _14_   Somewhat Important _1_   Not Important ____
65.12%   32.56%   2.32%

E. Food Service

Very Important _23_   Important _11_   Somewhat Important _7_   Not Important _2_
53.48%   25.59%   16.28%   4.65%

F. Shortness of Hospital Stay

Very Important _17_   Important _15_   Somewhat Important _8_   Not Important _3_
39.53%   34.88%   18.60%   6.98%

G. Exercise; Recreational Activities

Very Important _17_   Important _14_   Somewhat Important _12_   Not Important _–_
39.53%   32.56%   11.63%

H. Friendships with Patients

Very Important _25_   Important _10_   Somewhat Important _5_   Not Important _3_
58.15%   23.25%   11.63%   6.98%

I. "Shouldice Hospital hardly seemed like a hospital at all."

Very Important _25_   Important _13_   Somewhat Important _5_   Not Important ____
58.14%   30.23%   11.63%

12. In a few words, give the MAIN REASON why you returned for this annual reunion.

_____

_____

_____

EXHIBIT 4

ADVERTISEMENT BY A SHOULDICE COMPETITOR

NORDSTROM

Bruce Nordstrom, age 45, cochairman of Nordstrom, and the eldest of the Nordstroms, typified the modest, unassuming attitude of the company's management. "There is nothing special or difficult about what we do," he said. "I mean, none of us has been to Harvard, Stanford, etc. We are all graduates of the University of Washington here." He almost painted a picture of being "just plain country boys."

However, there was nothing modest about Nordstrom's success. It had grown from sales of $67 million in 1970 to sales of $250 million in 1977 (January 31, 1978); 1978 sales were just under $300 million. Earnings too had increased from $2.8 million in 1970 to $13.7 million in 1978. From 1970 to date (April 1979) the company had built three Nordstrom stores and four Place Two stores in Washington State and three Nordstrom stores and one Place Two in Oregon. It had also expanded and remodeled existing stores. And in addition to its growth in its traditional trading areas, Nordstrom had acquired a department store company in Alaska in 1975 and had opened its first store in California in 1978. In May 1979 the company planned to open its first store in Utah. Nordstrom also operated leased shoe departments, but it was gradually phasing out this business. By the end of 1978, Nordstrom maintained only eight leased shoe departments, all in Hawaii. About 90% of its business came from its 16 Nordstrom stores, 6% from its 10 Place Two Units, and the balance from its leased departments. Exhibit 1 provides a five-year summary of financial results and other data.

All through their expansions, the Nordstroms had maintained their philosophy of offering a wide selection, exceptionally attractive shopping surroundings, good service, and competitive prices. At the same time, the organization offered its employees a decentralized management environment where initiative tended to be directly and strongly rewarded. If only one word could be used to describe the atmosphere within

Associate Fellow Manu Parpia prepared this case under the supervision of Professor Walter J. Salmon, as the basis for class discussion rather than to illustrate either effective or ineffective handling of an administrative situation. To order copies, call (617) 495–6117 or write the Publishing Division, Harvard Business School, Boston, MA 02163. No part of this publication may be reproduced, stored in a retrieval system, used in a spreadsheet, or transmitted in any form or by any means—electronic, mechanical, photocopying, recording, or otherwise—without the permission of Harvard Business School.

Nordstrom, it would have been "vitality." An extract from management's written statement of philosophy is shown in Exhibit 2.

The Nordstroms were confident that their philosophy and methods of operation could be transferred to their new locations. They recalled that a noted West Coast retailer had told them to "wait until you are a hundred million dollar company," implying they could not maintain their philosophy in a larger organization. Yet the Nordstroms noted with pride that they were at $300 million and still going strong.

Could they continue to use this philosophy successfully? What should they be alert for? What changes should they expect, and what effect would they have on Nordstrom's performance? To answer these questions, it was important to identify why Nordstrom was successful.

NORDSTROM'S BACKGROUND

In the late 1880s, a 16-year-old boy left Sweden for the United States, arriving in the Midwest with five dollars in his pocket and a determination to succeed. His name was John W. Nordstrom. The young immigrant worked in the mines, in the logging camps, and at manual labor in Michigan, Colorado, California, and Washington before heading north to the Alaskan gold rush in 1896. He returned to Seattle two years later with a $13,000 stake, ready to settle down.

Carl F. Wallin, a Seattle shoemaker he had met in Alaska, offered Nordstrom a partnership in a shoe store, and in 1901 the store opened in downtown Seattle. The first day it made one sale and took in only $12.50, but the two men worked hard and lived thriftily, and gradually the business grew. In 1929 Wallin sold his interest to Nordstrom, and in 1930 John W. sold the company to his sons, Elmer, Everett, and Lloyd. Although the three had worked for Nordstrom earlier, they were not working for him in 1930. As Jim Nordstrom tells it, "Grandpa rang up Everett,

who was working here in Seattle, and asked him if he and his brother would like to take over the business. Once they took over the store, Grandpa handed over the keys and just walked away."

The three brothers had built the single shoe store into a 27-unit operation with sales of $12 million by 1963. At this stage the next generation, Bruce and John Nordstrom, as well as their brother-in-law Jack McMillan, were working for the company, and Jim Nordstrom was about to join on a full-time basis. Each of the young Nordstroms had worked from stock boys on up in the shoe stores. They knew the fashion shoe business intimately. However, it was clear that to employ the young Nordstroms gainfully, the company would have either to expand the shoe business to other geographic regions or diversify into another business within the state. An expansion of the shoe business would mean, for at least some of the young Nordstroms, a permanent move to another region—the idea of establishing stores elsewhere without the presence of a Nordstrom was, at that time, unthinkable. But all the family enjoyed the outdoor life in Washington. They were very comfortable in Seattle and really didn't want to move. So Nordstrom had to diversify out of shoes.

In 1963 Nordstrom purchased Best's Apparel in downtown Seattle and in Lloyd Center in Portland, Oregon. Best's had an established reputation in fashion apparel and was considered one of Seattle's leading fashion stores. The Nordstroms reasoned that because they were familiar with shoes, a highly fashion-related business, fashion apparel would be relatively easy for them to retail successfully. It did not, however, turn out to be as easy as they had expected, and, in Bruce Nordstrom's words, "We took some tremendous markdowns." However, the family learned quickly, and profits soon recovered. In the late sixties, Nordstrom began to introduce men's clothing into some of its stores, and it found good customer acceptance. By 1971 there were seven Nordstrom-Best stores, with sales of nearly $80 million.

Nordstrom management again changed hands in 1970. Since 1963 the present generation of Nordstroms had been prominent in the management. Their fathers wanted to retire, and they faced three alternatives: sell to their sons as their father had done, sell out to an established company, or let their sons take over. They also wanted their estates to have an easily established market value. The first alternative was not feasible; it would have required more funds than the young Nordstroms had. The senior Nordstroms were inclined to sell out, but the younger Nordstroms prevailed on them to—as Bruce put it—"entrust their fortune to us." Once this decision was taken, the older Nordstroms quickly withdrew from day-to-day responsibilities—in fact, Elmer and Everett retired and Lloyd became chairman of the board. The company also went public, thus fulfilling the senior Nordstroms' desire for a market value to their estate. Thus, once again the transition between generations was accomplished smoothly, leaving the younger generation in full control.

The Nordstroms attributed their success in apparel to having applied the principles of the shoe business. Nordstrom shoe stores had offered an exceptionally wide selection of merchandise, attractive surroundings, a high level of service, and competitive prices. A broad selection of merchandise was a must for a successful, family shoe store. Operators had to ensure (within reason) that any customer who walked in could choose from a variety of appropriately styled shoes that would fit. As shoes were often branded merchandise, operators also had to ensure in catering to the mass market that they met competitors' prices. Finally, selling shoes is a service-intensive business. Store salespeople had to be willing to identify a customer's needs and tastes, locate appropriate shoes, and finally try them on the customer's feet.

The Nordstroms believed that they had effectively transferred these principles to apparel retailing. Nordstrom stores stocked a wide variety of depth of merchandise. Their inventory per square foot averaged almost twice that of comparable classifications in department stores. Nordstrom also had an established policy of meeting competitors on price. If a customer told a Nordstrom salesperson that he or she had seen the same item of apparel at a competitor's for $25 and the store was selling it for $26, the salesperson was authorized to sell the customer the merchandise for $25. After a suitable (but quick) check on the validity of the customer's claim, the entire stock would be marked down. Finally, Nordstrom management took pride in the fact that a customer would always find helpful and knowledgeable salespeople in their stores. Salespeople were encouraged to develop client lists and telephone their "regular" clients if new merchandise that would suit them had been delivered to the store. If merchandise to suit a customer's needs was not available, salespeople were encouraged to follow up with the buyers.

Even the Nordstrom policy of decentralized decision making was an offshoot of its shoe store origin. As a family shoe store operator, Nordstrom had believed that it had to allow the store manager flexibility in ordering, and particularly reordering, because Store A might have clientele with different tastes and different size needs than Store B. Initially the Nordstroms exercised control by having a "Nordstrom in every store," but soon this was not possible, so they had to delegate responsibilities to the store managers. As one Nordstrom put it, "Our objective is to transmit the entrepreneurial feeling to the store level—that's why we keep it decentralized." Another "transfer" from the shoe business was Nordstrom's policy of paying the majority of its salespeople commissions—common practice in shoe retailing.

The success of these transfers was apparent, and Nordstrom-Best continued to grow.

In 1971 it substantially remodeled the headquarters store in downtown Seattle. Though it continued to expand, the company faced constraints, particularly in 1974. Concern about the environment resulted in a slowdown in building of new shopping centers and expansion of old ones. Money, too, became scarce. The Nordstroms found few opportunities to grow. They did note that many customers from smaller towns in the Northwest often asked why Nordstrom did not "come to their town." These towns could not support a full-fledged store, so Nordstrom examined what it could transfer, in its entirety, from its larger stores.

> The examination culminated in the establishment of Place Two Stores. These were 15,000–20,000 sq. ft. stores to be located in towns with populations of 25,000–50,000. The stores stocked young men's and women's clothing. Ultimately they were placed under a separate general manager and given their own buying organization. The Nordstroms found this concept successful in locations with exceptionally high concentrations of young people, including college communities and locations in large standard metropolitan statistical areas where Nordstrom could not find a site for a full-scale store. Nonetheless, in the changed environment of the late 1970s, management felt that they should concentrate on the larger stores and that Place Two expansion should basically be limited to what the Place Two organization could itself finance.

In 1979 Nordstrom was recognized as Seattle's leading women's apparel store and a strong second choice in men's clothing. The store offered a wide variety of apparel, accessories, and, of course, shoes. It was Seattle's leading store for fashion shoes for both men and women. In fact, Nordstrom inevitably dominated the fashion shoe market once it was established in a location. The store did not offer major appliances, furniture, health and beauty aids, and the like, nor did it intend to.[1] In addition to its own charge cards, Nordstrom accepted Master Charge and VISA. Some idea of Nordstrom's market strengths can be gained from the results of a survey conducted by a marketing organization (Exhibit 3). The survey covered six counties around Seattle-Tacoma and consisted of 1,000 interviews over the telephone, lasting approximately 20 minutes each.

Nordstrom advertising strategy emphasized image advertising. Although the company used newspaper advertising to help achieve its goal, it did not aim to dominate newspaper advertising in its merchandise categories. Nordstrom also used direct mail advertising, sending catalogs and brochures to its active accounts about five to six times a year. And the company always inserted a few pamphlets advertising merchandise in its monthly customer statements. Nordstrom spent 2.1% of sales on advertising in 1978 and 2.2% in 1977—these figures excluded suppliers' promotional allowances.

Nordstrom had gone public in 1971; its stock was traded in the over-the-counter market. In 1976 and in 1978, the company had tapped the equity market, issuing 900,000 shares of common stock on each occasion.[2] As of January 31, 1979, the company believed it

---

[1]The Alaska division, which had been acquired in 1975, had sold a range of major appliances, but the Nordstroms had gradually phased out the appliances. The Alaska division stores still offered televisions and microwave ovens but did not sell refrigerators, cooking ranges, and so on. The company intended to move out of this category altogether.

[2]Adjusted for stock splits.

was in a strong financial condition with a long-term debt to capital ratio of 29%.[3] The company also believed that it could sustain a growth rate of two to three stores a year with internally generated funds. As its store base increased, the company believed it could accelerate its growth rate if it desired. As of April 1979, the Nordstrom family owned 57% of the common stock.

THE ORGANIZATION

The Nordstroms did not have an organization chart. As one of them put it, "It would be too confusing." However, all the managers knew that the top management consisted of "the five": the three Nordstroms—referred to widely in the company as "Mr. Bruce," "Mr. John," and "Mr. Jim"; John A. (Jack) McMillan, related to the Nordstroms by marriage; and Robert E. Bender, a close family friend. Each was responsible for a merchandise group. (Exhibit 4 gives their individual backgrounds and responsibilities.)

The company was divided into four regions: Washington, Oregon, Alaska, and California. There were three regional managers; the Washington division reported to "the five." Except in Washington State, all the store managers reported to the regional manager. There Ray Johnson, the downtown store manager, was considered more equal than the others (mostly because he was Nordstrom's personnel manager, too). However, if a store manager had any questions, he or she would ring up one of "the five," or, as Mr. Jim put it, "talk to any one of us who picks up the phone."

The regional managers were given a great deal of autonomy, including, in general, buying autonomy. There was, however, no hard and fast rule on the degree of buying autonomy delegated to the regions and, within each region, how much the buying was centralized.

Under each store manager were department managers and a personnel manager. Although department managers did report to the store managers, they also had to work with and work within guidelines given by their merchandise managers or buyers.

Nordstrom's buying organization was unusual if not unique in the industry. Four of "the five" had working for them general merchandise managers for each of the merchandise categories for which they were responsible. The organization within each category varied according to its needs. However, the guiding principle was to ensure the greatest extent of decentralization to allow initiative at the lower levels. The organization under John Nordstrom typified the variations that existed within the buying pyramid.

Mr. John was responsible for the men's clothing and the men's shoe divisions. In men's clothing, buying was completely centralized. One buyer bought for the whole company and was responsible for the inventory levels at each store. The company had tried to decentralize the buying function by delegating authority to regional buyers, but it had found that this did not work. The company kept experimenting, though, by giving buying authority to the regions. One of the possible reasons for this lack of success was that quality men's clothing still had a large handmade element. This meant that buyers had to be highly trained in the cuts and stitches used in the industry. Also, buyers had to decide on color and patterns on the basis of swatches of material, making buying a very specialized field. Possibly another reason was that very few vendors produced desirable merchandise, and thus vendor relations were more important than in most other merchandise lines.

The shoe department, however, was the very epitome of decentralization. There was a general merchandise manager and four regional merchandise managers (because the

---

[3](Long-term debt + capitalized leases) ÷ (Long-term debt + capitalized leases + equity).

California division was still small, the regional manager held the title of buyer). Each store had a department manager with the authority to purchase shoes for the store. The department managers' open-to-buy (OTB) was controlled by the regional merchandise manager, whose OTB was, in turn, controlled by the general merchandise manager.

The delegation of buying authority ranged between these two extremes. For instance, in women's sportswear (under Mr. Jim) in Washington State there were two buyers—one for the downtown store and three additional stores in the state, the other for the Tacoma store and the other three stores. In the other divisions (regions), there was only one buyer each. The department managers in every store had an OTB controlled by the buyers. Whenever sportswear vendors visited a region, all department managers attended a showing of the merchandise and made purchase decisions. If the department managers were unsure of their choices, the buyers would help. Only the buyers and the general merchandise managers would travel to out-of-town buying trips and make all the purchase decisions. The bulk of women's sportswear was purchased by the buyers.

Cosmetics, on the other hand, was more centralized. There were four regional merchandise managers, and the department managers at each store did not have the authority to reorder. Exhibit 5 summarizes the organization and the delegation of responsibilities in the buying organization for key merchandise categories. This organization amplified the diversity in structure. One women's clothing buyer half-jokingly noted that her stiffest competition came from within—other women's departments in the company. Indeed, in recognition of this situation, the company enforced a rule that women's apparel buyers in different departments (as outlined in Exhibit 5), could not buy from the same vendor. One modification not noted in Exhibit 5 was that the regional manager in Oregon felt he needed a merchandise manager for John

McMillan's area, and he made one of the buyers into a regional merchandise manager, coordinating all the buyers of women's clothing in Oregon.

Despite its decentralized organization, Nordstrom's management believed that there was good coordination between buyers where necessary. For instance, there were two women's sportswear buyers for Washington State. If they were going to advertise and/or promote merchandise, they had to concur on which merchandise to advertise and which to mark down. Because it was in each one's best interest, the Nordstroms had found that they always reached an agreement. The difference was that if the buyers were on good terms, agreement was reached sooner; if they weren't it took longer. Thus, even though theoretically the buyers could advertise different merchandise in the same region or not carry advertised merchandise, this rarely happened.

When Nordstrom produced a catalog, all the buyers got together and agreed on which merchandise should go into it; they were then required to carry all the merchandise in the catalog.

KEY SUCCESS FACTORS

There appeared to be three key factors to Nordstrom's success in operating an unorthodox system—getting good people and paying them well, a good and up-to-date financial information flow, and its control system.

People

Nordstrom adhered strictly to a policy of promoting from within. Salespeople were hired at each store by the store manager or department manager. Except for certain stores in Washington (including the downtown store), Nordstrom's stores were not unionized. The company, except where restricted by union rules, met if it did not exceed hourly salaries paid by competition in the area of operation. Salaries within each of the four regions tended to be uniform. The company provided comprehensive health insurance coverage that included dental benefits. All employees who worked over 1,000 hours per year participated in the profit-sharing plan.

The amount paid under the profit-sharing plan depended on three factors—the total amount set aside by the board, length of service, and the employee's income during the year. Monies allocated to the employee were paid into a trust fund administered by a bank, which invested the funds in equities, bonds, and cash equivalents. Thus, an employee would share in any increase (or decrease) in the portfolio in proportion to the amount invested on the employee's behalf. The employee was entitled to the amount in the fund depending on his vesting percentage, which in turn was determined by duration of service. The vesting percentages ranged from 20% after 2 years' service to 100% after 10 years. The amount forfeited by employees who left the company before 10 years was reinvested in the portfolio. Management was proud of this plan, which had been instituted in 1951, and believed it to be an integral part of its philosophy of treating its employees well.

The hourly wages formed the base salary for most sales personnel, who were paid on a commission basis. The commissions varied by department, ranging from 5% to 10%; the median was 6-¾%. A commission was not paid unless the amount due an individual exceeded the base salary on a semimonthly basis. Salespeople in departments such as women's accessories and children's apparel did not receive commissions because merchandise management (which included the concerned Nordstrom)[4] believed that, barring an unacceptably high percentage rate, these salespeople would not earn commissions given their relatively low volume.

Generally, salespeople in the noncommission departments moved to commission departments as soon as there were openings. Nordstrom expected salespeople to reach their commission earning level fairly rapidly. The company maintained a daily record of sales per hour by individual. In fact, department managers, store managers, regional managers, and even the Nordstroms kept track of these data. If salespeople's performance lagged, the department manager would counsel them and point out their weaknesses. If they showed no improvement, then the department manager, after consultation with the store manager and the store personnel manager, would fire the employee. Employees' base wages were between $3.10 and $5.10 per hour. An employee with no previous retail selling experience earned the minimum. An employee with 700 hours of experience earned $3.50; 1,400 hours of experience earned $3.90, and everyone with over 2,100 hours of experience earned $5.10 per hour. Full-time salespeople on commission averaged annual earnings between $12,000 and $15,000.

Turnover at the salesperson level, although fairly high, was not considered a problem. The company estimated salesperson turnover at around 50–60%; most of which was accounted for by seasonal needs.[5] Turnover among permanent salespeople was estimated at around 15–20%, with family situations the primary reason for voluntary resignation. Termination by the company for poor performance or improper behavior accounted for up to 50% of the turnover of permanent employees.

Successful salespeople formed the basis of Nordstrom management. One had to achieve reasonable success as a salesperson to be promoted to department manager—the next step up the ladder. In keeping with the policy of

---

[4] Here Nordstrom means one of "the five" Nordstroms.

[5] Excludes movement due to promotion.

hiring from within, all department managers had been salespeople. The store manager decided whom to promote after taking the advice of the department manager under whom the employee worked. In some instances, the store manager might also ask the advice of the department buyer. However, the decision was made by the store manager. Often an employee would approach the store manager or department manager and express a desire to become a manager.

Department managers received a salary plus a commission on any sales they made. They were also eligible for a bonus, which was generally 1% of the sales increase over the previous year. Department managers' salaries ranged between $14,000 and $40,000; only $6,000 to $8,000 constituted base salary. The average department manager was estimated to earn around $18,000, of which $7,000 was base, $9,500 earned commission, and $1,500 bonus for increased sales. Store managers called on department managers to cover for them when they were not in the store.

The department managers had a dotted line relationship with their merchandise managers or buyers. Although they reported to the store manager, in many instances they had buying authority and had to work closely with the buyers. Store managers were responsible for recommendations on the promotion of department managers, but they always consulted the regional merchandise managers or buyers first.

A department manager could be promoted in two ways: to a larger department or to the position of buyer. The buyer, depending on the degree of autonomy in the department, bought for the region or just bought imports and merchandise not available locally (some merchandise categories had only department managers and regional merchandise managers). Buyers earned between $15,000 and $50,000 per year including bonuses. They earned one bonus on the percentage increase

in sales over the previous year and another on gross margin performance. However, the latter bonus was not awarded for all merchandise categories. For instance, none of the buyers under Mr. Jim received it because he did not believe that this was appropriate for his merchandise categories. The regional manager was responsible for all the buyers in the region and decided on salary increases and, where necessary, the performance criteria for bonuses. However, the regional manager never decided on buyer remuneration without consulting the general merchandise manager. In addition, the regional manager generally informally discussed the buyer's salary increase with the Nordstrom in charge of the merchandise category.

A buyer could be promoted to either merchandise manager or store manager. Most store managers earned between $30,000 and $60,000 per year, with one or two earning more, of which up to 30% could be bonus based. The bonuses were paid on three criteria:

1. Sales increase—averaged 1% of the sales increase over the previous year. In some cases a lump sum was paid for achievement of a dollar increase target.
2. Expenses goals as a percent of sales.
3. Shortage target—a relatively new target.

"The five" felt free to add to or subtract from the bonus criteria as the need arose. For example, if they felt personnel turnover was a problem, they might offer a manager a $5,000 bonus if he or she could achieve a lower specified rate. Regional managers were evaluated for regional performance on basically the same criteria as store managers.

Merchandise managers (general and regional) were evaluated using basically the same criteria as buyers, except they were responsible for inventory turns and in some cases for advertising expenses (net of vendors' promotion allowances) as a percent of sales. Even the general merchandise managers under Mr. Jim were responsible for gross margin and inventory turns. Thus, although the buyers in departments under Mr. Jim were not paid a bonus on gross margin, they were under pressure from their merchandise managers to ensure that gross margins did not get out of line.

Information Flow

"The five" received the following information in the form of printouts:

1. Sales by department by store (daily basis). This printout had daily sales this year; last year; this year as a percent of last year; and month to date this year, last year, and this year as a percent of last year. In summary, the printout gave the combined data for the department for all stores and also provided a comparison with the company as a whole (Exhibit 6 amplifies).

2. Gross margin and inventory by department by store (monthly): The printout provided this year's and last year's figures for the month. The department data included beginning-of-the-month inventory, end-of-the-month inventory, percent change of end-of-the-month inventory, this year/last year, amount on order, sales by month and year to date, percent change in sales over previous year, markdowns, employee discount shown as a percent of sales, stock-to-sales ratio, and inventory turns (see Exhibit 7). The departmental data were also totaled by merchandise division.

3. Gross margin and inventory by department for the company (monthly): The printout listed the same data breakdown as that in Item 2 except for the company as a whole.

4. Sales per hour performance by employee (semimonthly): The printout gave employee name and number, store and department, hours worked, gross sales, returns, net sales, and sales per hour (Exhibit 8).

To ensure that the printouts were up to date, the company had installed a point-of-sale system. Each time a salesperson made a sale, he or she input the following information:

1. Salesperson employee number
2. Department number
3. Classification number
4. Charge account number (if any)
5. Price

Also, Kimball tickets were used at the merchandise manager's request. The following additional information was keypunched on these tickets: vendor, style, month merchandise arrived, color code, and size. However, the printout used by senior management was not dependent on Kimball ticket information. For the future, management was experimenting with a point-of-sale system that would provide information by stockkeeping unit. Here, too, the company expected that these details would not be given to top management and indeed would be provided to the merchandise manager only if he or she requested.

Using the information on the printout, management could quickly pinpoint problem departments and keep track of their progress. However, "the five" rarely intervened directly in a problem. Rather, they waited to be contacted. Because the printouts were also sent to the respective merchandise managers, "the five" knew that the merchandise managers too must be aware of the problem. Store managers received similar printouts, giving them the sales breakdown by department within their stores as well as an overall sales comparison with other stores in their region and the company as a whole. This meant the store managers, too, would be aware of the data reaching corporate. Management reasoned that they would also react to correct a problem. The delegation of responsibilities ensured that top management managed through exception—and generally those exceptions were requests for help or clarification by regional managers, store managers, or merchandise managers.

"The five" met with their respective merchandise managers to work out planned sales and inventory figures for their department categories. They also met with store managers in the state on a monthly basis. Other meetings included regular visits to regions and stores. However, although important, these meetings were only a part of the information flow. The Nordstroms maintained a very informal atmosphere and were readily accessible to their employees. As one of them noted, they had their own offices, but the offices had no doors—this symbolized the openness of the company.

Employees had access to department performance data. For instance, in the downtown store any employee could view the daily sales performance printout for all departments for all stores on microfiche. These data were also made available in other stores, but with a lag for delivery of the fiche. Allowing employees access to sales information helped them feel a part of the team. As one employee put it, "In the company I used to work for, buyers used to get upset but we never knew why they were upset. Here we know if sales aren't doing well and we can do our best to improve sales."

Sales per hour by employee were posted semimonthly by each department manager for the department. Some store managers made available semimonthly sales per employee figures to all employees. In all stores the top sales per hour performances were publicly commended through a letter sent to all employees. In addition to the individuals' names, their sales per hour were shown.

The Control System

The diversity of the Nordstrom organization, the significant variation in responsibilities and duties for the same level of personnel in different merchandise departments, and the extent of decentralization were in the casewriter's opinion quite unusual, if not unique, for an organization of Nordstrom's size. To keep it all functioning smoothly and to ensure that the key management people kept in touch with significant events, the company relied on some equally unique control mechanisms.

Both buyers and store managers were paid bonuses on their percent increase in sales over the previous year. Achievement of a target increase as a prerequisite for the bonus was not a part of the system, but goal setting was achieved through peer pressure. Every year a meeting attended by all regional buyers and store managers was held at each region's headquarters. The regional manager, or in Washington State the Nordstroms, would call on each manager (or buyer), in turn to present his or her sales target for the year. As the figures were called out, the regional manager wrote them beside the individual's name on a large chart. Next to the figures was a space on which the regional manager had written his target for each manager. That figure was kept covered during the initial part of the meeting. Then, amid great suspense, the regional manager tore off the slip of paper that covered his or her target for each manager. If the manager's sales target was under that of the regional manager, the assembly would boo the unfortunate manager. However, if the manager's target was above that of the regional manager, the group would break out in cheers. One manager described the scene as being like a classroom before an exam, or perhaps during an exam, with all the store managers and buyers doing feverish calculations as they heard their peers' targets and were tempted to revise their own. The meeting held in Washington at Nordstrom's headquarters was the largest because, in addition to the managers in Washington State, the regional managers attended. Any employee was welcome at the meetings in each region.

To arrive at their targets, store managers consulted with their department managers. This process was similar to that of the larger meeting. Each department manager read out the target figure for sales in his or her store. Then the store manager revealed his or her figure for each department manager, accompanied by boos or cheers. The store manager, however, did not use the department manager's targets as the only basis for his own goals, but made adjustments wherever he thought necessary. For instance, if the store manager considered a particular department manager's target unrealistic, he/she would scale it down in arriving at a total target for the store.

The buyer, too, would ask each store's department manager for a target. However, this was generally done over the telephone or in individual conversations. This was because a department manager did not report directly to the buyer or the merchandise manager. Once again, the merchandise manager or buyer would use the department manager's target as a guide and adjust it as he/she though it necessary. Thus, if all the buying organization's targets were totaled, they would give a different figure from the sum of all the store managers' targets. This discrepancy was not important, however, because neither the buying organization nor the store managers or regional managers used these targets as their criteria for planning. The buyers or merchandise managers had already agreed or planned on certain open-to-buy figures for the next six months based on more conservative planned sales figures, and the store managers used different and, again, more conservative figures in their expense budgets.

In addition to the annual sales target meeting, there were monthly meetings in each region attended by buyers, all store managers, and all department managers. Various awards were distributed during these meetings. For

instance, there was a customer service award in each region. Every store had to enter the contest for this award. Each store submitted an entry backed up by documentation. There were no set criteria for the entry; selection was left to the store manager. Among the documentation required were all complaint letters received by the store during that month. Two or three stores won prizes, which ranged from $300 to $1,500. These were collected by the store managers who in turn distributed them to outstanding customer service salespeople in their stores.

Also presented was the all-star award. For this each store manager brought a salesperson who had done something to deserve this award. The store managers then described their salespeople's activities to the meeting. A cash award of $100 was presented to the winning individual. A Nordstrom always attended these monthly meetings; they shared attendance responsibilities on a rotating basis.

Buyers, too, were eligible for awards. Each division held a Make Nordstrom Special contest every month, which awarded cash prizes of $200, $100, and $50. The judges looked for good value, unique merchandise, good sales, good promotion, or some combination of the above.

Another award, the Pace Setters Club, recognized outstanding selling performance. Sales targets required to qualify for membership were posted early in the year. To help employees pace themselves, store managers often broke down goals into sales per hour terms. Some department managers asked salespeople to set sales targets and then helped them keep track of their progress. It is important to note that all salespeople who were on commission had the same commission rate, whether or not they achieved targets and/or became a Pace Setter. Pace Setters were recognized through circulation of their names and a separate meeting over a meal with the Nordstroms.

The Nordstroms believed that these cash prizes, although not important in money terms, played an important role in keeping the organization vital and boosting employee morale.

NORDSTROM IN CALIFORNIA

To see how Nordstrom's philosophy worked when transplanted to a distant region where the Nordstrom name was not so well known, the casewriter visited Nordstrom's first (and only) store in California. The company had invested a great deal in the California store because it was their first move outside the Northwest. Management commented on the significance of their move in the 1979 annual report. "Never before had we devoted so much time and money in the planning of a new store because this was a totally new market area for us and it was vital that we get a strong start." The store was located in the South Coast Plaza Mall in Costa Mesa, in southern California. The casewriter interviewed Betsy Sanders, the regional manager for California.

Conversation with the Regional Manager

Sanders recalled with a twinkle in her eye her first interview with Nordstrom. She had returned to Seattle after a long spell in Europe, where she had obtained a degree in German in Munich and a graduate degree in Naples. In Seattle her husband had decided to return to college and Sanders had agreed to support them. However, because she could not get a teaching job she considered retailing. A friend gave her a letter of introduction to Mr. Bruce. She almost didn't go to the interview because she thought she wouldn't enjoy the work. Mr. Bruce almost didn't hire her because he thought she wouldn't be able to work in a department store given her, as he now recalls with a laugh, "dilettante" background. Until her husband completed his studies, Sanders was a salesperson and discovered that she enjoyed her work a great deal. When her husband got his degree, she decided to stay on at Nordstrom and make it a career. She recalled with pride that four years and two days after that decision she was a store manager. When she was offered her present position, her husband agreed to move to Southern California.

Sanders exuded confidence and vitality. It appeared to the casewriter that the employees found working for her a joy and a challenge. She knew most of her employees by name. Because there was only one store, Sanders also filled the role of store manager. She discussed various aspects of her job:

On selection of personnel for the California store Sanders said, "It was my decision on who to have as the buyers for this region. In keeping with our policy of hiring from within, all the buyers have worked for Nordstrom in one of the other three regions. I sent out a bulletin to various people in the divisions and then reviewed the responses. My criteria were basically that the people had to be successful in the positions they were in at that time. They had to prove to me they had knowledge and competence to buy. They also had to be able to manage constructively. By that I mean having the ability to get people to work together and not exercise their authority by fear. I looked for people who had a history of developing people because we will need people here to meet our growing needs. I also looked for a strong record of being customer oriented. Obviously I did not know all the people before and depended on regional managers and store managers to give me their recommendations. I think it worked and worked pretty well because a manager is interested in promoting his or her people, and they [managers] know that if they recommend someone who does not measure up to requirements, the next time I would regard their recommendations with a certain amount of skepticism. Of course, if this were to happen often, I just wouldn't ring them up.

"We have strictly adhered to the policy that all managers must have been salespeople at Nordstrom. We don't hire from outside for two major reasons. On the one hand, we know they (in-house people) can perform because we have their record. On the other hand, they understand the company and the atmosphere within it and have obviously grown comfortable with that atmosphere. Just the other day two buyers from _____ came here to discuss a job at Nordstrom. I told them that I was very interested but that they would have to work on the floor and prove themselves before they could become buyers at Nordstrom. They were rather shocked and horrified. I think that many buyers in other stores regard selling as an operation they don't want to have anything to do with. In this store particularly, we have our buyers on the floor selling."

Expanding on the previous statement, Sanders noted that the buyers in the Costa Mesa store spent a great deal of time on the floor. She felt this was particularly useful because it helped them to get to know the California customers better. Another unusual feature of the California region was that buyers, too, earned a commission on sales they made. Although Sanders had to present the case to corporate to institute that policy, corporate's agreement reflected the extent of decentralization and therefore diversity in Nordstrom's organization.

Another difference in California was that all salespeople could earn commissions; even the accessories and children's apparel salespeople earned commissions if their percent of sales exceeded their base salary. In instituting this change, Sanders reasoned as follows: She believed that noncommissioned status reflected the union's concern that salespeople in certain departments would never really earn their commission and therefore should not be expected to work on a commission basis. However, because the California store was not unionized, Sanders did not believe it necessary to follow Seattle's policy. She also noted that sometimes a salesperson sold 80 handbags and put in a creditable performance yet she would not feel rewarded when her paycheck came around unless she was allowed to earn a commission.

Some of Sanders's other decisions also reflected the degree of freedom given to the regional manager. She determined the level of base pay for sales employees in California, and she decided to keep the union rates used in Seattle (these were much higher than those offered by the competition in California). When this became known to the competition, they expressed their unhappiness at Nordstrom's higher rates because most salespeople Nordstrom hired had substantial experience and therefore earned $5.10 an hour. Another change was Sanders's decision to advertise in magazines, such as *The New West* and *Los Angeles*. Nordstrom had always advertised in newspapers, but Sanders felt that this market required advertisement in magazines. Although corporate questioned her decision, it was her right, she noted, to control advertising within the region.

On the budget process, Sanders commented that Nordstrom worked its budget forward and not backward. By this she meant that she decided on what raises to give various individuals, then worked out the total salaries to arrive at an expense figure for the year. She then looked at the sales target for the year and unless expenses as a percentage of sales were unacceptably high, that was the base she used for expenses. She noted that other stores often estimated their sales increase and then, using a target percentage, worked out the expense level in terms of dollars available for the year. After that they calculated the raises they could give to keep within that expense level. Sanders believed the difference in approach reflected Nordstrom's concept of treating and paying good people well.

On goal setting, she recalled with obvious pleasure the scene at the previous February meeting (1978). She had set a goal of $15 million for the first nine months of operation. When she had given the figure, the Nordstroms had asked if she wished to revise it downward, because they felt it was very ambitious. Their own figure had been $10 million. (Note: for the first year or two of operations the manager of a new store earned a bonus based on a percentage of the amount by which the store exceeded the target.) Sanders noted, "Of course we achieved $15 million in sales last year. Incidentally, in our first full year of operation we achieved sales of $21 million. This year I set a target of $27 million, whereas their target was $25 million. Mine is the highest target for any branch store in the company."

Sanders was asked to comment on the possible dichotomy between customer service and the measurement of employees by sales per hour and the fact that salespeople received a commission on sales. Might that make them less responsive to a customer's needs and more eager to make a sale? Sanders disagreed that a dichotomy existed because the employees' remuneration was dependent on satisfying customers and therefore they had to behave responsibly. She did agree that a few employees became too eager to generate sales and paid less attention to giving customers what they wanted. However, there were at least two means of controlling this. First, the department manager would notice the salespeople's behavior and counsel them to change their pattern; and second, customers would begin to avoid these salespeople and turn to others who were less pushy. Thus, such an aggressive stance was unlikely to pay off in the long run. Sanders added that it was the department manager's role to improve salespeople's customer service posture.

Sanders noted with pride and perhaps a little regret that she had had 7 Pace Setters in the previous year. She had expected only 2 or 3 in the first year and therefore had promised them a breakfast in Seattle with the Nordstroms. Although she was pleasantly surprised that there were 7, she noted that next year she expected 30, and the division overhead would not support a visit to Seattle for breakfast.

Some miscellaneous reflections:

Regional managers could influence the percentage markup for merchandise in their region. Sanders had decided to aim for the same markup as in Seattle, even though she believed that it was lower than that of competition in the area and that the merchandise might support a higher markup.

Sanders noted that a big difference between Nordstrom and other stores in the shopping center was that once you walked into the store and were looking at merchandise, someone would ask if you needed help. That sort of inquiry, she believed, was almost a thing of the past with other stores.

The key to Nordstrom's success, Sanders thought, was the Nordstroms' ability to put people in key positions who knew and understood the company's philosophy and were comfortable in the environment. The role of every manager was to ensure that the atmosphere of vitality and drive was maintained. This was a particularly important goal for store managers because each of them set the tone for a whole unit.

Sanders noted that her store got responses from 1,500 people to its ad for help in the local newspaper (see Exhibit 9). Three people (including herself) did the initial interviewing. Selected applicants were called for a second round of interviews by department managers, who made the final decisions.

Nordstrom did not have a formal training program; it believed in on-the-job training. "We hire what we consider good people and let them get on with their job. Of course the managers are there to help and provide guidance, but we encourage people to take initiative and reward them for doing so."

Other Interviews

The casewriter then talked with some of the buyers. Although at the time they brought only for one store, in a few years their responsibility would grow during Nordstrom's California expansion.

Jeff Cox, buyer of women's shoes, had left the military and joined Nordstrom in 1970 as a salesperson for shoes. He noted that the shoe business was tough. Unlike a buyer of dresses, a shoe buyer had to commit to purchases almost eight months in advance of delivery. This commitment consisted of decisions on style, color, size, and quantities. Cox noted that to order a shoe of one style and color in every size available would result in 72 pairs.

At the moment Cox was the only California buyer for shoes, but once the Brea store opened, each store would have a department manager who would buy the style, color, and size that he or she wanted for the store.[6] Cox would guide them and control their open-to-buy. Cox would buy direct imports, which constituted approximately 5% of total sales.

The shoe department took a weekly inventory by style and size. Stock time was paid for separately, and the hours used were not included in an individual's sales per hour computation. However, setting up displays and keeping them tidy was not paid for separately and had to be done on employees' time.[7] Cox agreed that some employees might

---

[6] Brea would be Nordstrom's second store in California, scheduled for opening in October 1979.

[7] All departments required salespeople to do "maintenance" work on their own time. Exceptions were made for substantial changes and stocktaking.

avoid their share of this "maintenance" work in their desire to maintain their sales per hour. It was his job to see that the load was distributed equitably.

As a buyer, Cox would be evaluated and paid a bonus on (1) gross margin—the bonus on achievement of a gross margin above a certain percentage; and (2) sales increase—1% of the sales increase over the previous year. He also had to watch his expense ratio as a percent of sales, but this was an informal measure on which no bonus was paid. He noted that if the merchandise manager felt a particular department manager's expense ratio was too high, he or she might pay the department manager a lump sum bonus to reduce the percentage below a certain targeted figure.

Michelle Carrig, buyer for cosmetics, had been with Frederick & Nelson and had worked as a fine jewelry buyer. She believed she couldn't achieve growth in that company, and had joined Nordstrom five years before. She had been a buyer in Washington State before moving to California.

In discussing her operating procedures, she noted that she kept an open-to-buy line by vendor, for instance, Estée Lauder, and so on. Inventory by stockkeeping unit count was taken monthly. Every year case space and length were measured and sales per linear foot calculated for every store. If a supplier was not performing satisfactorily in terms of sales per linear foot, its space allocation tended to be reduced. Similarly, if a company did well, it might be granted more space.

Carrig noted that promotional allowances were a key factor in achieving profitability in her business. To encourage aggressive follow-up, the person who processed the invoices allowance was paid a bonus if able to keep promotional allowances above a certain percentage of sales. Such follow-up was necessary because some vendors did not pay promotional allowances unless prodded. Similarly, department managers, although not rewarded through a bonus on promotional allowances, were evaluated informally on this

percentage. Thus, they were encouraged to report accurately all sales by vendor. Department managers also supervised the monthly stocktaking.

Carrig noted that although a department manager did not have an open-to-buy for cosmetics, she as a buyer nevertheless expected good feedback from the department manager through notes and comments. She felt that department managers would be eager to provide good feedback because they would receive a bonus on sales and thus were anxious to ensure that the right products were available at their stores. She also noted that she often tailored needs to suit a department manager's taste. For instance, if a department manager felt more comfortable with pink and other lighter-colored lipsticks it was in Carrig's interest to ensure that she had a better variety of lighter shades.

Carrig herself was evaluated and received a bonus on sales increases, achievement of a gross margin target, and inventory turns. She also had to keep an eye on selling expenses as a percent of sales although she was not formally evaluated on that criterion.

E. N. Goodson, buyer of juniors' coats and dresses, had joined Nordstrom in 1974. There were only six or seven buyers for juniors in the company, and department managers did not have an open-to-buy. Goodson made frequent visits to New York along with the other buyers for U.S. purchases. All imports were bought by the general merchandise manager.

When asked about her buying philosophy, Goodson said she generally bought two to three months in advance. She believed this gave her a great deal of flexibility in timing. She and her merchandise manager mutually agreed every six months to an open-to-buy plan, but she could adjust this in line with sales by telephoning the merchandise manager. She had done this frequently as sales had outstripped all expectations in the first year of operation in California. Goodson characterized her method as buying a few items of each style, but purchasing a wide variety of styles. She compared this with other department stores, which bought a large quantity of items in a certain style. She believed her policy was more effective for juniors, because few juniors wished to wear the same thing as the person next door. If an item was hot Goodson did buy it in somewhat greater depth. Nonetheless, she believed it was worth being unable to reorder a hot item for the sake of providing a wide variety of fresh merchandise. She was not evaluated on gross margin and received a bonus on sales increases.

When asked to comment on working for Nordstrom, Goodson said that the main thing is "you are left to yourself. If you want help, you ask for it. If not, you are on your own. The sales goal is a personal commitment and not really a means of evaluation. It is really up to you what you make of it."

Salesperson Interviews

Person A This employee was a fairly senior woman. She had worked for Bullock's for three and a half years before coming to Nordstrom. She expressed herself freely.

The company (Nordstrom) has a very positive attitude. Everyone is working for the same excellent top management, and I have to say we are paid very well. I think the company takes pride in the people that work for them. For instance, it is a small thing, I know, but everyone was invited to the Christmas party, not just department managers and buyers.

I also like the fact that the buyers are on the floor selling. I think the people like the feel of our store. I know there is a fine line between being helpful and being pushy, and we are very much aware of that.

I keep a book of customers who shop regularly and who have expressed their tastes and desires to me. Whenever there is new merchandise which I feel will suit their needs, I call them up and tell them that it is available. I think there are very few other stores that offer this kind of service.

In terms of rules, I feel there are only two hard and fast rules here: take good care of customers and do not steal. We are allowed a great deal of freedom within these constraints. Just the other day a lady came and bought a dress. Then she wanted a pair of shoes which would match the dress. I could go down and get those shoes for her, so that she had a complete shopping trip without having to move up and down. Besides, I knew that shoes matching her dress were available downstairs, something she may not have known.

Comparing them (Nordstrom to Bullock's), without trying to run down Bullock's, I feel Bullock's almost felt that customer service was not important. They really weren't concerned about employees at the sales level. There was a great deal of emphasis on who was who and following the chain of command. There is no such constraint here, I feel.

Person B

I used to work in I. Magnin and May Company on a part-time basis. I really enjoy working for Nordstrom. They treat employees differently and treat them well. When I used to work for I. Magnin, I didn't know the people on the second floor. Here we get to meet everyone.

Also, in both the (other) companies we didn't know any of the figures (financial data). Therefore, we didn't know why managers got upset at certain times. Here we get a good flow of information. We know how each line is doing and our opinions are often asked for. We are treated like people who can think, and I find this very encouraging.

Our buyer involves us in almost everything. She tells us about new fashions that are coming out, what is in, what we should expect in the future, and what will be moving out. Every month we meet on Sundays for breakfast. In the May Company we never even met on a yearly basis.

Nordstrom managers and employees stressed the fact there was no one organization structure method for doing things. Individuals were given responsibility and left to work things out for themselves in a manner they thought suitable—as long as it was not outrageous. The employees and managers appreciated this freedom and enjoyed working in such an environment.

Conversation with Jim Nordstrom

To conclude his interviews, the casewriter spoke with Mr. Jim, the youngest of the Nordstroms:

We (Nordstroms) have been moving away from the merchandising end of the business, even though we are the nominal merchandise managers. Yes, I guess I do feel a certain sense of loss, but I am really not that unhappy about it. After all, our business has improved since we have moved away, so maybe the people who have taken over are doing a better job than we were.

A great deal of our time now is spent looking for opportunities to locate new stores. However, our number one responsibility is our employees. In fact, normally an organization is depicted as a pyramid with the top management controlling the whole chain of command going down. We look at it the other way. We believe we are at the bottom of the pyramid here to en-

sure that our employees have everything that they need in order to do a good job, and not that the employees are here for us to supervise.

What Mr. Jim said tied in closely with the feelings expressed by the other Nordstroms. Mr. Jim also confirmed the view held by the other Nordstroms that store managers were more important than buyers, though of course both were valued. The Nordstroms viewed buyers as providing a service to the store managers, whose role was to service the customers and conclude the sale.

The casewriter asked if "delegation of responsibility" was the correct expression to use in describing Nordstrom's philosophy. Mr. Jim felt that it was not the best, because "delegation" implied that the Nordstroms retained a certain degree of control, which by and large they didn't have. He said quite candidly:

If I proclaim an edict, I don't know if it will get implemented. For instance, there have been signs in stores which said we don't take merchandise back unless accompanied by receipt. This is just not true. It is our policy to take back merchandise if the customer says they bought it from us, unless we had a valid reason to reject it. I have taken down the signs personally and told several people that this is not our policy. Yet time and again I see the signs. Well, that's life.

Mr. Jim also acknowledged that there was often a certain amount of conflict among buyers and sometimes among buyers and department managers, or others. But he felt very comfortable with the conflict. In fact, he said that "sometimes if there are no conflicts, particularly between buyers, I feel that they are being too kind to each other and not being critical. The conflict, as long as it is within reason, provides a means of competition."

Finally, Mr. Jim said that he didn't think the Nordstrom children would particularly enjoy working for the firm. "By the time they take over we'd be a large company and I think all the fun of growing and expanding will have gone."

CONCERNS FOR THE FUTURE

Summarizing Nordstrom's modus operandi, Mr. Bruce said:

> We offer the customer great variety and depth of merchandise displayed in an attractive environment, with high levels of customer service. All these elements cost money and add to expense, so we compensate that by generating volume. We have to move the merchandise off the floor. We depend on good salespeople to help us do it and we take markdowns whenever we see that merchandise isn't moving as expected.

Nordstrom's sales per square foot figures reflected the emphasis on turnover. Sales per square foot of total space (excluding leased departments operated in other stores) rose from $127 in 1973 to $163 in 1977 and approximately $180 in 1978. This compared with a rise from $58 to $74 per square foot for department stores between 1973 and 1977.[8] Between 1973 and 1978 Nordstrom had more than doubled its space. Total sales had almost tripled in the same period.

Could Nordstrom maintain its pace of growth without detracting from the factors that contributed to its success? Growth would inevitably involve two components: number of stores and geographic dispersion.

Nordstrom had hitherto been identified with the Northwest, and even as late as the mid-sixties the Nordstroms had resisted growth outside the region. The casewriter asked Mr. Bruce, "Why grow?" "We have always had a fairly competitive nature," he said, "and growth is a yardstick of success. We've always had, you might call it, an instinct to do the best we can. Besides, we owe it to our employees to do the best we can for them. By growing we offer them opportunities and succeed in attracting good people."

Profitable growth had been essential to Nordstrom. The company had been able to maintain a conservative balance sheet by tapping the equity markets twice in the last three years in addition to generating funds through retained earnings. The Southern California "experiment" had been a success, and the company planned to build four more Nordstrom stores there over the next two to three years. In addition it planned to open two stores in Oregon, one in Washington, and one in Utah and to expand some existing stores.

The board had set a long-term debt to capital ratio target of 35–40%. (Long-term debt included capitalized leases.) The company estimated that every 100,000 sq. ft. required an investment in land, building, fixtures, and inventory of approximately $10 million in 1978–79 dollars. Of this total, approximately $2–2.5 million consisted of inventory (at cost).[9] Accounts receivable were estimated at 15–18% of sales and working capital needs at 25–30% of sales. Thus, to maintain a conservative balance sheet and still take advantage of all the opportunities available, it was likely that Nordstrom would have to tap the equity markets again. To do this at reasonable cost, it had to continue to be successful.

Was continued emphasis on a decentralized organization, with maximum possible freedom to individual managers, the correct approach? Or would the company run into problems as it expanded?

---

[8] For department stores and specialty stores, published by the National Retail Merchants Association. Figures relate to sales per gross square foot. The 1973 figure is for department stores with sales over $50 million, 1977 for department stores with sales over $100 million.

[9] If payables were taken into account, investment in inventory was estimated at $1.5 million at cost.

EXHIBIT 1

OPERATING STATEMENT AND BALANCE SHEET (AMOUNTS IN THOUSANDS)

Year Ended January 31,	1979	1978	1977	1976	1975
Operations Sales	$297,629	$249,690	$209,882	$179,229	$130,512
Cost of sales and related buying and occupancy costs	195,348	165,561	137,510	119,944	87,475
Selling, general and administrative expenses	72,626	59,099	50,597	43,115	31,510
Interest expense	3,343	2,893	2,641	2,845	2,116
Earnings before income taxes	26,312	22,137	19,134	13,325	9,411
Income taxes	12,645	10,440	9,288	6,375	4,343
Net earnings	13,667	11,697	9,846	6,950	5,068
Net earnings per average share of common stock	1.80	1.60	1.38	1.08	.79
Average shares outstanding	7,579,482	7,318,170	7,123,662	6,418,170	6,418,170
Dividends per share of common stock	.30	.24	.19	.15	.13
Net earnings as a percent of net sales	4.59%	4.68%	4.69%	3.88%	3.88%
Financial Position					
Accounts and notes receivable (net)	$ 56,599	$ 46,855	$ 36,927	$ 31,916	$ 22,269
Merchandise inventories	45,200	33,737	29,047	27,594	20,303
Property, buildings and equipment (net)	66,382	53,718	39,248	38,008	32,069
Total assets	180,950	138,896	116,688	98,864	77,579
Long-term debt	13,367	14,339	14,563	14,636	14,705
Working capital	70,589	51,699	49,256	32,268	28,623
Ratio of current assets to current liabilities	2.61	2.54	2.75	2.13	2.67
Shareholders' Equity					
Book value	$ 97,230	$ 67,618	$ 57,677	$ 39,620	$ 33,654
Per common share	11.83	9.24	7.88	6.17	5.25
Earnings per share of common stock as percentage of book value per share at beginning of year	19.5%	20.3%	20.5%	20.6%	17.2%
Stores and Facilities					
Company-operated stores	26	24	20	17	14
Total square footage	1,585,000	1,406,000	1,167,000	1,114,000	907,000

EXHIBIT 1 (CONTINUED)

OPERATING STATEMENT AND BALANCE SHEET (AMOUNTS IN THOUSANDS)

Assets	January 31, 1979	1978
Current Assets:		
Cash	$ 80	$ 1,216
Short-term investments, at cost (approximates market)	11,025	2,029
Accounts and notes receivable—Customers (net of allowance for doubtful accounts of $1,600 in 1979 and $1,227 in 1978)	53,724	40,798
Licensors and others	2,875	6,057
Merchandise inventories	45,200	33,737
Prepaid expenses and other assets	1,664	1,341
Total current assets	114,568	85,178
Property, Buildings and Equipment	66,382	53,718
	$180,950	$138,896

Liabilities and Shareholders' Equity		
Current Liabilities:		
Accounts Payable	$ 22,146	$ 15,732
Accrued salaries, wages and taxes	9,181	7,490
Accrued expenses	1,452	1,472
Accrued taxes on income—		
Currently payable	2,276	1,341
Deferred	7,413	5,685
Current portion of long-term liabilities	1,511	1,759
Total Current Liabilities	43,979	33,479
Long-term Debt	13,367	14,339
Obligations under Capitalized Leases	26,374	23,460
Shareholders' Equity	97,230	67,618
	$180,950	$138,896

The accompanying financial review and the summary of significant accounting policies are an integral part of these statements. Merchandise inventories are stated at lower of cost (first in/first out basis) or market using the retail method.

(Continued)

EXHIBIT 1 (CONTINUED)

OPERATING STATEMENT AND BALANCE SHEET (AMOUNTS IN THOUSANDS)

	Year Ended January 31,	
	1979	1978
Working Capital Was Provided by:	$13,667	$11,697
Net earnings		
Charge not affecting working capital—provision	6,285	4,721
for depreciation and amortization	19,952	16,418
Working capital provided by operations	—	1,060
Proceeds from long-term borrowings	4,929	10,228
Obligations under capitalized leases	18,216	—
Proceeds from sale of stock	1,643	2,636
Disposition of property and equipment	44,740	30,342
Working Capital Was Used for:	15,663	11,599
Additions to property, buildings and equipment	4,929	10,228
Property leased under capitalized leases	2,268	1,756
Cash dividends paid	972	1,284
Reduction of long-term debt	2,015	3,032
Reduction of obligations under capitalized leases	3	—
Fractional shares redeemed on share distribution	25,850	27,899
	$18,890	$ 2,443
Net Increase in Working Capital		
Changes in Components of Working Capital:	$(1,136)	$ 939
Cash	8,996	(8,628)
Short-term investments	9,744	9,928
Accounts and notes receivable (net)	11,463	4,690
Merchandise inventories	323	809
Prepaid expenses and other assets	(6,414)	(2,983)
Accounts payable	(1,691)	(1,468)
Accrued salaries, wages and taxes	20	(301)
Accrued expenses	(2,663)	225
Accrued taxes on income	248	(768)
Current portion of long-term liabilities	$18,890	$ 2,443
Net Increase in Working Capital		

The accompanying financial review and the summary of significant accounting policies are an integral part of these statements.

EXHIBIT 2

EXTRACT FROM "THE NORDSTROM PHILOSOPHY"

Offering an in-depth selection of quality merchandise and exceptional customer service, Nordstrom has earned a reputation for value and reliability that is perhaps unsurpassed in the Northwest. So, too, has Nordstrom grown to become a fashion leader, gathering together in tasteful contemporary settings a spectacular array of the most sought-after fashions of the day.

Central to the Nordstrom philosophy is a strong belief in an *individualized* approach to fashion. Each Nordstrom store has been carefully tailored to reflect the lifestyles of customers in the surrounding area, showcasing a wide selection of shoes, apparel and accessories in a variety of distinctive "shops" that are rich in color, texture and design. Nordstrom buyers work closely with top-quality manufacturers from both here and abroad to obtain the best values, most unique items and widest selections for their customers; and salespeople, who keep notes on their personal customers' sizes and preferences, are quick to let their customers know when something that may be of interest arrives in the store. It is, in fact, this type of customer service which is perhaps the company's greatest strength—for Nordstrom is a place where friendliness, courtesy and a sincere desire to help are the rule rather than the exception.

An individualized approach is evident *within* the company, too—in a decentralized management structure where ideas and initiative are generated from the bottom up rather than filtered from top management down. Salespeople and department managers are encouraged to implement their own ideas; buyers, who have a great deal of autonomy, are encouraged to seek out and promote new fashion directions at all times. As a result of this distribution of responsibility, Nordstrom employees possess a remarkable amount of enthusiasm—both toward their company and their customers—and motivation is often quickly rewarded, as promotions are made almost exclusively from within.

There is little doubt that the Nordstrom philosophy of selection, value and service—begun in 1901 when John W. Nordstrom opened his first shoe store in Seattle—has contributed tremendously to the company's growth throughout the Northwest and Alaska. It is also the reason Nordstrom believes it can enter new market areas with confidence in the years to come.

EXHIBIT 3

RESULTS OF MARKETING ORGANIZATION SURVEY

WOMEN'S APPAREL

When you think of fashion, what store comes to mind first?

Store	%
Nordstrom	29.3
Bon Marche	24.2
Frederick & Nelson	10.4
Penney's	7.8
Jay Jacobs	3.3
Lamonts	3.3
Sears	3.1
K Mart	2.7
I. Magnin	1.6

Description of Competition

1. Bon Marche = Full line, middle of the road, department store—division of Allied Stores

2. Frederick & Nelson = Full line, better department store with middle to higher price points—division of Marshall Field's

3. Jay Jacobs = Specialty store catering to apparel for young men and women, juniors oriented. Promotional stance. Line includes shoes.

4. Lamonts = Middle of the road department store, similar to Bon Marche but more "bread and butter" oriented

5. I. Magnin = Women's specialty store, with upper-middle price points—division of Federated Department Stores

EXHIBIT 3 (CONTINUED)

RESULTS OF MARKETING ORGANIZATION SURVEY

Location of Last Purchase

Active Sportswear	%
Bon Marche	18.2
Nordstrom	17.2
J. C. Penney	11.7
Frederick & Nelson	6.5
Sears	6.2
Lamonts	4.5
K Mart	4.1
Sportswest	4.1

Denim Jeans	%
Bon Marche	19.9
Nordstrom	10.5
J. C. Penney	9.1
Sears	5.8
K Mart	5.8
Jay Jacobs	5.8
Bernies & Bottoms	4.0
Lamonts	3.3

Tops & Blouses	
Bon Marche	24.0
Nordstrom	14.4
J. C. Penney	11.8
Frederick & Nelson	7.4
Lamonts	7.4
K Mart	6.0
Sears	4.3
Lerner	1.9

Pants	
Bon Marche	20.5
J. C. Penney	14.2
Nordstrom	13.6
Lamonts	6.0
Sears	5.7
K Mart	5.1
Frederick & Nelson	4.3

Dress	
Bon Marche	20.5
Nordstrom	15.5
Frederick & Nelson	11.5
J. C. Penney	8.7
Lamonts	6.2
K Mart	6.0
Sears	4.7

Coat/Jacket	
Nordstrom	18.5
J. C. Penney	12.0
Bon Marche	11.7
Frederick & Nelson	9.7
Sears	6.2
K Mart	4.5
Peoples	2.3
Jay Jacobs	2.3

Lingerie/Foundations	
J. C. Penney	23.1
Bon Marche	21.9
Nordstrom	11.8
Sears	10.3
Frederick & Nelson	9.0
Lamonts	6.3
Fred Meyer	3.3
K Mart	2.8

Hosiery/Pantyhose	
J. C. Penney	16.3
Safeway	16.0
Grocery Store	9.8
Bon Marche	8.3
Frederick & Nelson	6.0
Sears	5.3
K Mart	4.3
Nordstrom	3.8
Pay 'n Save	3.8

Fashion Accessories	
Bon Marche	20.3
Nordstrom	18.2
J. C. Penney	12.7
Frederick & Nelson	6.5
Lamonts	4.8
Fred Meyer	3.8
K Mart	3.8
Sears	2.7

Shoes/Boots	
Nordstrom	34.1
J. C. Penney	7.7
Bon Marche	7.7
Sears	5.0
Frederick & Nelson	4.8
Kinney Shoes	4.1
Leed's	3.6
K Mart	2.6
Lamonts	2.6

EXHIBIT 3 (CONTINUED)

RESULTS OF MARKETING ORGANIZATION SURVEY

MEN'S CLOTHING

When you think of fashion, what store comes to mind first?

Store	%
Bon Marche	21.7
Nordstrom	17.3
Penney's	9.2
Sears	9.2
Frederick & Nelson	6.6
Klopfenstein's	4.0
Squire Shop	3.8
Lamonts	1.7
Finkelstein Goldberg & Feldman	1.4

Location of Last Purchase

Suits	%	Top Coat/Rainwear	%
J. C. Penney	13.6	Bon Marche	13.6
Bon Marche	13.3	Sears	10.0
Nordstrom	10.9	Frederick & Nelson	9.3
Frederick & Nelson	8.5	J. C. Penney	7.9
Sears	8.2	REI	7.1
Klopfenstein's	6.7	Nordstrom	6.4
		Klopfenstein's	5.0

Sport Coat	%	Shoes	%
Bon Marche	16.4	Nordstrom	29.4
J. C. Penney	13.1	J. C. Penney	13.9
Nordstrom	11.3	Sears	10.5
Sears	6.9	Bon Marche	8.7
Klopfenstein's	5.8	Kinney Shoes	8.0
Frederick & Nelson	5.8	Florsheim	4.3
Fred Meyer	2.2	Thom McAn	3.4
		Fred Meyer	2.8
		Raff's	2.8

Dress Slacks	%
Bon Marche	20.7
J. C. Penney	13.8
Nordstrom	10.1
Sears	10.1
Frederick & Nelson	5.2
Squire Shop	3.7
Lamonts	3.2
People's	1.7
Fred Meyer	1.4

EXHIBIT 4

BRIEF BACKGROUND INFORMATION ON "THE FIVE"

	Salariesª	Insurance benefits as reinvestments, profit sharing, and personal benefits
Bruce A. Nordstrom—Cochairman of the board of directors. Graduated from the University of Washington in 1955 with a degree in economics. Started as a shoe salesman; was then responsible for the shoe operation in Portland. Now merchandise manager for the Women's Shoe Division.	$135,500	$16,411
John N. Nordstrom—Cochairman of the board of directors. Graduated from the University of Washington in 1958 with a degree in accounting. Started as a shoe salesman and has since managed several departments and stores. Is now merchandise manager for Men's Clothing and Shoe Division.	$135,500	$15,859
James F. Nordstrom—Director and President. Graduated from the University of Washington in 1962 with a degree in business. Worked as a shoe salesman and manager of shoe stores. Is merchandise manager for Junior Apparel, Women's Sportswear, Children's Apparel, and Women's Shoe divisions.	$135,500	$17,133
John A. McMillan—Director and Executive Vice President. Graduated from the University of Washington in 1957 with a degree in economics. Started in Budget Shoe Department; now merchandise manager for the Women's Ready-to-Wear Division.	$135,500	$17,380
Robert E. Bender—Director and Senior Vice President. Graduated from the University of Washington in 1958 with a degree in marketing. Worked for J. C. Penney for six years. Was hired as manager of the Northgate store in 1964. Now merchandise manager for the Accessories and Cosmetics divisions.	$104,500	$10,430

ªProxy statement, April 20, 1979.

EXHIBIT 5

BUYING ORGANIZATION

Department	Member of "The Five" in Charge	Description of Department Organization
JUNIORS	Jim Nordstrom	A general merchandise manager, under Mr. Jim, two buyers in each region, one each for Sportswear and Ready-to-Wear (RTW). There were two department managers (Sports and RTW) in large stores and one department manager in smaller stores. The department managers had no buying authority.
CHILDREN'S CLOTHING	Jim Nordstrom	A general merchandise manager, one buyer in each state (division), except in Washington, where the department was broken down into Infants, Boys, and Girls with a buyer for each. Only one department manager per store, and they did not have buying authority.
COSMETICS	Robert Bender	A general merchandise manager, a regional merchandise manager for every division except Washington, where there were two buyers, who divided the buying responsibility by vendor. One department manager per store, who did not have the authority to buy. However, they had to take a monthly inventory.
SHOES (MEN'S) SHOES (WOMEN'S)	John Nordstrom Bruce Nordstrom	The organization for each though separate, was similar. Each had a general merchandise manager, and each region had a merchandise manager who controlled the open-to-buys of the department managers in each division. Thus, department managers had full authority to buy for their stores except for imports, which were bought by the merchandise manager in each region.
MEN'S CLOTHING	John Nordstrom	Entirely centralized; one buyer bought for the whole company.
WOMEN'S ACCESSORIES	Robert Bender	No general merchandise manager, but a buyer in each region. Department managers in each store had the responsibility and authority to reorder.

(Continued)

EXHIBIT 5 (CONTINUED)

BUYING ORGANIZATION

Department	Member of "The Five" in Charge	Description of Department Organization
WOMEN's READY-TO-WEAR[a]	Jack McMillan	No general merchandise managers. However, women's clothing was broken down into several departments by name:

1. Point of View:		Three buyers in Washington State (broken down by coats, knits, and dresses). Two buyers in Oregon, and one each in California and Alaska.
2. Town Square: (Modern Missy)		Same structure as in Point of View except in California, where there were two buyers—one for Sportswear and one for RTW.
3. Gallery:		Two buyers in Washington (dresses and coats), two buyers in Oregon, one buyer each in California and Alaska.
4. Collectors: (Better Sportswear)		One buyer in Washington (who also bought for Alaska), one buyer in Oregon, and one in California.
5. Savvy:		One buyer for whole company (a new department).

Department	Member of "The Five" in Charge	Description of Department Organization
WOMEN'S SPORTSWEAR	Jim Nordstrom	A general merchandise manager, then broken down as follows:

1. Blouses:		Five buyers—two in Washington (divided by region), and one each in other divisions.
2. Active:		Four buyers—one in California, one in Oregon, and two in Washington, the latter also buying for Alaska.
3. Sportswear:		Same structure as in Blouses.
4. Equipment: (skis, etc.)		One buyer in California, one in Washington, and one in Alaska.

One department manager per store, who handled all four categories. Department managers in Washington had the authority to buy for their stores from local vendors.

[a]There was a department manager in each store for each department; however, they did not have buying authority.

EXHIBIT 6

DAILY SALES BY DEPARTMENT STORE

REPORT NAME DAILY DEPARTMENT/DIVISION COMPARATIVE NET SALES REPORT NUMBER SA000009
REPORT RUN DATE AND TIME 04/03/79 05:11:24 REPORT PAGE NUMBER 67
DATE AUDITED THROUGH

DAILY COMPARATIVE DATES MONTH TO DATE INCLUSIVE DATES DATES EXCLUDED FROM MONTH TO DATE
THIS YEAR 04/02/79 MONDAY THIS YEAR 04/01/79 THROUGH 04/02/79 THIS YEAR
LAST YEAR 04/03/78 MONDAY LAST YEAR 04/02/78 THROUGH 04/03/78 LAST YEAR

DAILY NET SALES MONTH TO DATE CUMULATIVE NET SALES

DEPT. NO.	DEPARTMENT DESCRIPTION	This Year	Last Year	DIFFERENCE Amount	% of Last Year	This Year	Last Year	DIFFERENCE Amount	% of Last Year
STORE 0001	DOWNTOWN SEATTLE								
0045	MENS POLO SHOP								
0075	MENS BRASS RAIL								
0076	MENS CLOTHING								
0077	MENS SPORTSWEAR								
0078	MENS FURNISHINGS								
0080	LUGGAGE/WORK CLOTHES								
MENS WEAR	TOTAL								
0024	MENS CASUAL SHOES								
0025	MENS DRESS SHOES								
MENS SHOES	TOTAL								
MENS WEAR AND SHOES	TOTAL								
STORE 0001	TOTAL								
STORE 0002	NORTHGATE								
0045	MENS POLO SHOP								
0075	MENS BRASS RAIL								
0076	MENS CLOTHING								
0077	MENS SPORTSWEAR								
0078	MENS FURNISHINGS								

146

EXHIBIT 6 (CONTINUED)

DAILY SALES BY DEPARTMENT STORE

			REPORT NUMBER	SA000009
REPORT NAME	DAILY DEPARTMENT/DIVISION COMPARATIVE NET SALES		REPORT PAGE NUMBER	67
REPORT RUN DATE AND TIME	04/03/79	05:11:24		
DATE AUDITED THROUGH	03/25/79			

DAILY COMPARATIVE DATES			MONTH TO DATE INCLUSIVE DATES			DATES EXCLUDED FROM MONTH TO DATE
THIS YEAR	04/02/79	MONDAY	THIS YEAR	04/01/79 THROUGH 04/02/79		THIS YEAR
LAST YEAR	04/03/78	MONDAY	LAST YEAR	04/02/78 THROUGH 04/03/78		LAST YEAR

			DAILY NET SALES				MONTH TO DATE CUMULATIVE NET SALES			
					DIFFERENCE				DIFFERENCE	
DEPT.	NO.	DEPARTMENT DESCRIPTION	This Year	Last Year	Amount	% of Last Year	This Year	Last Year	Amount	% of Last Year
0080		LUGGAGE/WORK CLOTHES								
		MENS WEAR	TOTAL							
		MENS WEAR AND SHOES	TOTAL							
		PLACE TWO	TOTAL							
		DIVISION ALL GROUPS								
0045		MENS POLO SHOP								
0075		MENS BRASS RAIL								
0076		MENS CLOTHING								
0077		MENS SPORTSWEAR								
0078		MENS FURNISHINGS								
0080		LUGGAGE/WORK CLOTHES								
		MENS WEAR	TOTAL							
0024		MENS CASUAL SHOES								
0025		MENS DRESS SHOES								
		MENS SHOES	TOTAL							
		MENS WEAR AND SHOES	TOTAL							
		DIVISION ALL GROUPS	TOTAL							

EXHIBIT 7

MONTHLY GROSS MARGIN AND INVENTORY BY DEPARTMENT BY STORE

MERCHANDISE INVENTORY REPORT

REPORT AS OF: FEBRUARY 28, 1979
(TY/LY AMOUNTS IN HUNDREDS)

REPORT NUMBER: MIR00020
RUN DATE: 03/14/79   10.56.44
PAGE NO. 1

STORE	INVENTORY				M.T.D. NET SALES		Y.T.D. NET SALES			YTD MD AS % OF SALES	YTD MD %	YTD EMPL DISC SHRINK %	GROSS MARGIN OF SALES	STOCK TO SALES RATIO	INVEN TURN
	BEGINNING OF MONTH	END OF PERIOD	% CHG END INV TY/LY	ON ORDER	AMOUNT	% CHANGE TY/LY	AMOUNT	% OF STORE TOTAL	% CHANGE TY/LY						
01															
DEPT															
01 WOMENS SHOES															
20 WOMENS SHOES															
26															
33															
36															
TOTALS WOMENS SHOES															
DIV TOTALS WOMENS SHOES															
COATS, SUITS, DRESSES															
TOWN SQUARE															
02															
09															
29															
32															
39															
43															
TOTALS TOWN SQUARE															
POINT OF VIEW															
10															
46															
47															
TOTALS POINT OF VIEW															

EXHIBIT 8

SEMIMONTHLY SALES PERFORMANCE BY EMPLOYEE

RUN DATE 04/04/79

PAY PERIOD ENDING 03/31/79
LADIES SHOES

Employee Number	Employee Name	Store/Dept	Selling Hours Worked	Gross Sales	Returns	Net Sales	Sales Per Hour
19554		5 0020	9.00	1,784.20	152.80	1,631.40	181.26
6410		5 0020	83.00	15,831.38	1,307.15	14,524.23	174.99
1622		6 0020	43.40	17,561.62	2,280.80	15,280.82	163.60
6703		1 0001	80.50	11,843.95	624.45	11,219.50	139.37
6518		5 0020	57.60	9,581.83	1,844.32	7,737.51	134.33
1194		21 0020	20.00	2,835.90	182.75	2,653.15	132.65
819		7 0020	35.50	5,035.33	340.45	4,694.88	132.25
22		1 0030	112.60	17,692.31	3,165.64	14,526.67	129.01
4830		21 0020	87.50	12,363.80	1,252.35	11,111.45	126.98
10036		1 0026	96.50	12,861.71	1,128.11	11,733.60	121.59
906		6 0020	35.00	4,352.18	237.60	4,114.58	117.55
4004		25 0020	26.80	3,731.37	654.10	3,077.27	114.82
808		7 0020	96.00	12,260.89	1,313.70	10,947.19	114.03
7408		21 0020	84.00	10,757.49	1,190.57	9,566.92	113.89
6779		1 0001	84.40	10,546.85	1,064.20	9,482.65	112.35
9578		1 0001	97.70	4,688.40	464.50	4,223.90	112.03
2152		1 0036	106.70	14,766.44	2,822.55	11,943.89	111.93
163		21 0020	47.00	5,539.95	282.55	5,257.40	111.85
2449		60 0026	85.70	10,334.93	1,113.56	9,321.37	108.76
8726		25 0020	30.10	3,734.97	473.10	3,261.87	108.36
813		1 0036	91.80	11,775.16	1,850.57	9,924.59	108.11
5666		5 0020	67.10	8,009.15	853.76	7,155.39	106.63
9240		9 0001	73.78	8,361.73	511.40	7,850.33	106.51
229		5 0020	68.00	7,229.72	569.06	6,660.66	105.72
7410		21 0020	48.50	5,738.05	613.20	5,124.85	105.66
2040		1 0026	92.00	11,925.83	2,259.97	9,665.56	105.05
6368		6 0020	39.60	4,179.73	24.95	4,154.78	104.91
2862		4 0020	82.00	9,549.13	976.61	8,592.52	104.78
1608		6 0020	80.80	9,422.11	969.72	8,452.39	104.60
10544		5 0020	68.20	8,103.12	977.15	7,125.97	104.48
4455		20 0020	4.33	513.00	62.00	451.00	104.15
47		4 0020	68.30	7,849.53	855.36	6,994.17	102.43

(Continued)

EXHIBIT 8 (CONTINUED)

SEMIMONTHLY SALES PERFORMANCE BY EMPLOYEE

PAY PERIOD ENDING 03/31/79
LADIES SHOES

Employee Number	Employee Name	Store/Dept	Selling Hours Worked	Gross Sales	Returns	Net Sales	Sales Per Hour
6204		5 0020	82.50	9,529.24	1,098.25	8,430.99	102.19
811		7 0020	112.10	12,489.02	994.25	11,414.77	101.82
9197		5 0020	83.50	9,549.31	1,095.89	8,453.42	101.23
6163		1 0036	54.50	6,624.78	1,131.15	5,493.63	100.80
627		8 0020	34.70	4,517.81	1,023.85	3,493.96	100.69
3250		1 0036	74.80	8,842.03	1,366.41	7,475.62	99.94
4661		21 0020	61.30	6,832.72	713.95	6,118.77	99.81
7493		25 0020	46.90	4,922.83	285.65	4,637.18	98.87
8352		73 0026	47.30	4,943.49	340.40	4,683.09	97.31
72		21 0020	35.30	3,991.51	560.10	3,431.41	97.20
1838		21 0020	80.80	8,131.67	321.45	7,810.22	96.66
97		1 0036	94.70	10,713.81	1,569.59	9,143.42	96.55
8338		8 0020	68.60	7,651.16	1,064.55	6,586.61	96.81
404		4 0020	71.10	8,065.25	1,254.15	6,811.10	95.79
108		21 0020	38.38	4,157.40	493.25	3,664.15	95.66
9868		9 0001	63.00	6,449.16	436.37	6,012.79	94.68

EXHIBIT 9

CALIFORNIA STORE HELP-WANTED ADVERTISEMENT

WANTED: people power

it's something nordstrom feels very strongly about. on may 1, we will be opening our exciting new south coast plaza store at costa mesa... and we are now taking applications in our search for the best possible people to staff it.

we are looking for experienced people who want to learn, grow and expand with us. people who genuinely like people; who find satisfaction in helping others, in going out of their way to be of service.

we need people with an eye for detail, a brain for figures, a will to succeed; experienced people to handle sales, to alter and wrap; to maintain the building and keep it stocked. people to lead and people to follow.

we need people to make things go smoothly. people with ideas, all kinds of people with all kinds of potential. people power, it's the difference at nordstrom. help us make it happen at south coast plaza.

APPLY IN PERSON ONLY:

10:00-5:00 daily beginning march 20. use n.e. entrance to store, follow signs in stairways.

an equal opportunity employer

nordstrom

PART III

LISTENING TO THE CUSTOMER

Chapter 6

METHODS OF LISTENING TO THE CUSTOMER

6.1 THE IMPORTANCE OF LISTENING TO THE CUSTOMER

What does "quality" in a service mean? Engineers who design and manufacture tangible products often use a conformance-to-specifications definition of quality. This is a measure of whether the product performs (or measures or weighs) exactly as it was designed. For example, Motorola, a recognized world leader in manufacturing quality, has instituted a program that calls for fewer than 3.4 operations in a million to fall outside specified tolerances. Some service firms such as American Express Company's Travellers Cheque Group have adopted similar goals. However, controlling overall quality to this level of precision is not realistic for most services, particularly for those in which the customer plays a key role in the completion of the service. Services are performances with many intangible, difficult-to-measure components. A customer of a tax preparation service may agree that her tax form was filled out without mistakes—the firm's quality objective—but be dissatisfied because she found the tax preparer's personality abrasive. The customer would not rate the firm as providing excellent service, even though it met its goals for precision and accuracy.

Defining quality as conformance to specifications leaves out a key decision maker: the customer. It is the customer's specifications, not those of the engineering department, that must be met for the service to be deemed successful and worthy of repeat purchases or recommendations to friends. Therefore, although the term "quality" has many different meanings, service providers are becoming ever more aware that the only quality that really counts is in the eyes of the customer. Precision production processes may be necessary to deliver consistently high quality, but if customers don't notice, or if they are really concerned about other aspects of the service, then high precision doesn't guarantee that customers will consider the quality high.

A firm therefore must be careful that the measurements it takes to monitor quality correspond to the measures of perceived quality that customers use. Customers may have very different views of the service than the provider. Until recently, for example, doctors were notorious for overlooking the customer perspective on the quality of care provided. The medical community believed that the doctor's education and the professional manner he used while interacting with a patient guaranteed quality healthcare. It did not matter that the patient had to deal with a rude telephone receptionist to get an appointment at an inconvenient time, difficulty in parking, long waits in unpleasant waiting rooms, and so on. The doctor may have seemed competent, but cold to the patient, and the entire experience was rated as trying and wasteful. Now that competition is forcing the medical profession to be more customer-oriented, we are beginning to see a change in some of these behaviors.

In the case of credence qualities, described in Chapter 1, customers may have very different evaluation standards because they cannot easily judge service quality. The quality of services such as medical operations, auto repair, or legal representation may be very hard for the average person to judge. In such cases, customers tend to rely on cues they can understand, even though they may have little or nothing to do with the core service being provided. For example, hospital administrators generally find that patients will give high ratings to the overall quality of their care for even the most difficult medical procedures if the staff has smiled at them frequently during their stay. Similarly, automakers find that customers tend to judge overall quality by easy-to-read clues such as whether or not car doors sound solid when being slammed.

Customers and service providers tend to use different language. Successful service firms need to know their customers' vocabulary, because it often carries important information about customers' needs and expectations. For example, retail banking customers frequently rate the service of their bank according to how well the bank "listens to my needs." What does this say about the design of new services or the improvement of old ones? It certainly doesn't relate directly to such concerns of the bank operations officer as turnaround time, average queue length, or statement accuracy. But bankers have come to understand what customers mean by that vague expression and have developed services and training programs to make the staff more attentive listeners, less rigidly bound by rote procedures, and better able to tailor-make services to match the requirements of individual customers. Because service quality (and product quality as well) is largely in the mind of the customer, measuring quality requires talking to customers.

In fact, many organizations tend to measure a different, but related concept—customer satisfaction—rather than perceived quality. The uses of the terms "quality" and "satisfaction" are confusing, because currently there are no generally accepted definitions of them.[1] Some people use them interchangeably, while others see them as distinct concepts. For example, a person may still acknowledge that a hotel deserves five stars, even after a dissatisfying stay there, or can be satisfied with a meal at a low-quality fast-food restaurant. In both cases, the quality affected, but did not determine, the level of satisfaction. We may also suppose that the customer's impressions of the quality of the two establishments was also revised in light of these experiences—somewhat downward for the hotel, somewhat upward for the restaurant. Therefore, in this view, the relationship between the two concepts is conceptualized as in Figure 6.1. Service quality contributes to one's satisfaction with a particular service experience. Then, depending on the level of

FIGURE 6.1

ONE VIEW OF THE RELATIONSHIP BETWEEN QUALITY AND SATISFACTION

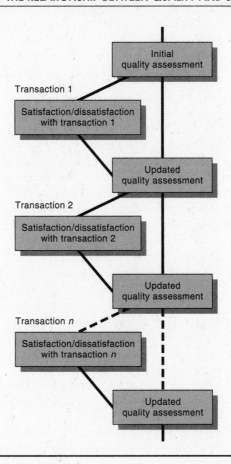

satisfaction, the quality image is revised. Therefore, to understand customers' opinions of an organization's service, one can ostensibly measure customer perceptions of either quality or satisfaction. In fact, most organizations now concentrate on measuring satisfaction or perceived quality with individual transactions—in part, because customer recollections of specific incidents generally prove more useful than statements of their global impressions.

In this chapter we will describe some methods of exploratory research that have been developed to explore the customer's view of a service, specifically to identify the attributes that contribute to one's overall assessment of the firm's service. These methods range from formal research methods such as focus groups and structured in-depth interviews to just doing a better job of listening to what customers say. The objective of these research exercises is to generate an organized list of the many facets of a service that determine customer satisfaction. Once the list is in hand it can be used to construct formal questionnaires to be used in tracking and analyzing customer reactions to the organization's products. The information obtained from these surveys will indicate the relative importance to customers of the various components of the service and will allow management to identify ways to profitably improve service quality.

6.2 THE STRUCTURE OF A SERVICE

Think of a service you recently found dissatisfying. Chances are that not everything about it was terrible, even though your overall opinion of the encounter was low. The company might have been able to change your mind about the service overall by doing better on just one or two key areas, rather than by fixing every problem. Overall satisfaction or dissatisfaction is the result of weighing positive and negative experiences and coming to a net evaluation. Before we can determine how to increase customer satisfaction scores, we must know what these major components are and the relative importance of each to the overall impression. We will also find it useful to learn which subcomponents determine customer satisfaction with each of the components.

Figure 6.2 shows a typical customer organization of information about a service, specifically a hospital. The overall evaluation is determined as a weighted average of the evaluation of the various processes or components of the service. For example, patient evaluations of hospital visits may depend upon their impressions of various components, such as admissions, daily care, the nursing staff, the doctors, the living arrangements, the discharge process, the billing operation, and so on. Each of these components can be broken down further, to help diagnose specific problems or opportunities for improving service. For example, patient satisfaction with billing could depend to varying degrees the willingness of the hospital to provide clear explanations of items, the efficiency of the process, and so on.

How does a firm develop a list of components and subcomponents important to customers? We begin by looking at all the potential needs that a service might fulfill. In the following sections we will describe several exploratory research techniques used to generate lists of the dimensions of a service that determine customer satisfaction. The goal of the first part is to generate a list of 200 to 400 customer needs, which can then be grouped together to form a hierarchical structure of the services components. After this, we will be prepared to look at methods used in grouping these needs.

In terms of the task of getting customers to supply them, customer needs can be grouped into three different categories, each of which has different strategic implications:

Basic attributes are those assumed to be present in any service in the particular industry. For that reason they may not always show up in customer discussions, even though they may be very important. A firm that doesn't offer these attributes could not remain in business. Examples include safe operations by airlines, working rest rooms in a restaurant, and clear connections with a long-distance phone company.

FIGURE 6.2

CUSTOMER ORGANIZATION OF INFORMATION ABOUT A HOSPITAL

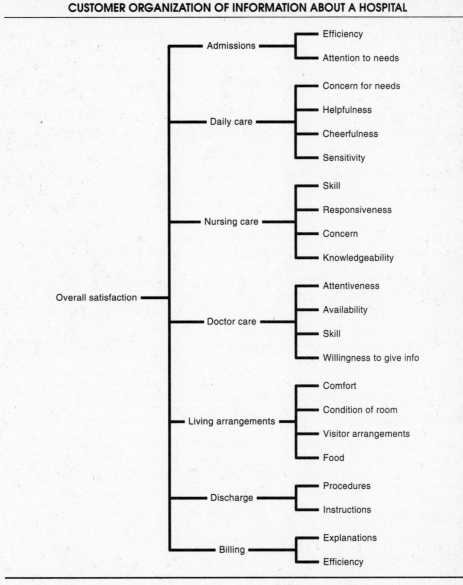

Articulated attributes are those that customers generally mention as desirable or determinant in their choice of a service. These are the attributes on which customers discriminate among competitors. Poor performance on them will lead to customer dissatisfaction, and good performance will lead to satisfaction. They are the bread-and-butter attributes on which firms compete and differentiate themselves: the friendliest bank tellers or the auto repair shop that fixes your muffler on time and at the price promised.

Exciting attributes are those that would delight and surprise customers if they were present. Delivering these attributes can be the key to building strong loyalty among customers, but they are also harder to identify. By definition, customers don't expect them, and so it takes careful questioning to get customers to suggest them. Their power is also fleeting. Attributes that are stunning today become commonplace tomorrow. Auto Zone, a retailer of new replacement parts for automobiles, set new standards in the area of inventory levels and free advice for customers. However, that positioning came under attack from Pep Boys, which carries larger inventories and also offers service bays and installation. Because of this competition, Auto Zone must find new ways to differentiate itself.

Examples of each type of attribute for a veterinary practice are shown in Figure 6.3. By definition, articulated attributes are relatively easy to obtain from customers using standard marketing research interview methods. Basic attributes and exciting attributes are generally revealed by different research methods.

6.3 USING A GROUP OF SUBJECTS: FOCUS GROUPS

We will now describe some specific research techniques used by marketing researchers to identify the customers' view of the processes and subprocess that comprise their interactions with the organization. The most widely used technique for generating lists of consumer-provided service attributes is the focus group. A focus group is a moderated discussion among six to 12 participants. The idea is to

FIGURE 6.3

DIFFERENT LEVELS OF ATTRIBUTES FOR A VETERINARY PRACTICE

Basic Attributes
  Degreed veterinarians
  Waiting room
  Examination rooms
  Supply of basic medications on hand
  Basic procedures offered
  Parking lot

Articulated Attributes
  Appointments taken
  Weekend hours
  Extended weekday hours
  Reasonableness of prices
  Caring attitude of staff
  Friendliness of staff
  Payment plans for expensive procedures
  Assortment of pet supplies and foods for sale
  Reminder notices for vaccinations and treatments

Exciting Attributes
  A pick-up service
  Special tests routinely done for elderly animals
  Availability of rare specialties
  Bandanas for departing "patients"
  Pet shows and contests

generate a free-flowing discussion about the service among members of a target group, using interaction among participants to relax them and to trigger ideas. For example, banks typically run focus groups of their mortgage and installment loan customers to learn firsthand what it is like to deal with the bank processes.

The discussion is typically recorded on both videotape and audiotape for later transcription and analysis. Written transcripts are essential when focus group discussions are used to generate lists of customer needs, because, as we will see, they must be examined in detail by several analysts to identify as many ideas as possible. Many focus groups are also conducted behind soundproof one-way glass so that observers from the company can watch and then discuss the proceedings as they happen.

The success of a focus group depends on the skills and preparation of the moderator, who must put the participants at ease and keep the discussion focused on the topic at hand without injecting personal opinions or inhibiting people's willingness to speak. The moderator must keep overly talkative participants from dominating the discussion and encourage all participants to speak their minds. It is also the moderator's job to see that only one person speaks at a time, so that valuable comments are not misunderstood or lost. As enthusiasm builds among participants side conversations tend to develop. They must be channeled into the main conversation without dampening the group's level of excitement.

The moderator should prepare a loose script in advance, listing the key topics to be covered during the session. As the group runs out of fresh things to say on one topic, the moderator should be prepared to introduce new topics, or to ask follow-up questions to encourage the discussion and to stimulate new ideas among all group members.

Focus groups are the basic procedure for understanding customer views of service.

Practical Considerations   Focus group members are usually recruited by telephone, to ensure that the correct person in the household is contacted and to verify their participation. They are usually offered refreshments and cash for a session of 90 minutes to two hours. For many recruits, the chance to discuss their experiences with a particular product or service will be an inherently interesting experience. Nevertheless, some participants inevitably fail to show up and so recruiters typically contact 10 to 12 people hoping to have eight. Should more people arrive than are needed, the researcher must weigh the disadvantages of running a focus group with too many people, against the danger of alienating potential customers by sending them home without participating. Any persons who are sent home must still be paid.

Professionally designed focus group facilities, with microphones, video cameras, multiple recording facilities, one-way glass, reception area, and so, are obviously best, but can be expensive. Alternatively, a room with a large table will do, provided that participants can be put at ease in the surroundings and that clear recordings of the session can be made.

Limitations   It cannot be stressed too much that focus groups are only exploratory, and that their findings are not statistically projectible to the population at large. Findings from focus group sessions must be formally tested using statistically analyzable surveys before they have any validity. The purpose of a focus group in this context goes far beyond trying to identify how a population feels about a specific, predetermined issue. It seeks to sample the set of all ideas in the minds of the population, a much bigger task, beyond the methodology of group discussions.

This fact tends to get obscured as managers become engrossed in viewing the sessions, reading the transcripts, and studying the reports. There is a tendency to make too much of comments made in focus groups, both good and bad, and to treat them as representative of the general public. But the results are not representative for several reasons. First, focus groups rarely constitute a truly random sample of the population of interest. Even though they are recruited from the target group, sets of participants often tend to be people who were easy to reach, had some time to spare, and were able to get to the sessions. For this reason the sample is inappropriate for statistical projections to the population at large.

Even if the participants are representative of the target population, their comments are probably not. Because of the unstructured nature of focus group discussions and the nature of group dynamics the ideas generated are unlikely to be a random sample of those of the participants, much less of the population at large. For example, in a focus group on checking accounts someone might happen to mention the designs available on checks at their bank. Other customers may pick up on the topic, simply because they have something to say about it, and 15 minutes or more of a 90-minute session will be devoted to a topic that actually has very little bearing on anyone's satisfaction with checking accounts. The moderator must let such a discussion run its course, on the chance that some vitally important, but previously overlooked, attribute of checking accounts is being revealed. Subsequent analysis, perhaps including a question on the importance of check patterns on a formal survey of bank customers, will help to determine whether the matter was due to momentary group sympathies or is a real issue.

One or two participants with dominant personalities can also sway a discussion into unrepresentative areas through social pressure. For this reason focus groups are of limited use in getting candid reactions to socially risky concepts or in eliciting aesthetic judgments. If a dominant member of the group starts the discussion by declaring an introduced concept to be in poor taste, or something only a fool would buy, it tends to severely inhibit those who were about to declare their approval.

Finally, using the focus group format to identify service attributes relies on strength of numbers to produce a full list, rather than on the depth of questioning. In a two-hour session with 10 participants, each participant has an average of only 12 minutes to discuss all he or she feels about the service. This limited "airtime" means that there is very little chance to probe deeply into any one customer's views. As a result, the attributes revealed by any particular individual may be only the most obvious ones.

A variant on the focus group is the minigroup, consisting of just three or four participants. This format provides some of the benefits of interaction from group dynamics and also allows more time to dig in deeply. This size of group is used less than the larger focus group. The smaller group makes the experience less exciting for participants and may not stimulate as much discussion.

6.4 ONE-ON-ONE METHODS: THE IN-DEPTH INTERVIEW

The most effective technique for achieving a deeper understanding of the consumer's view is the one-on-one interview. Interviewing 10 people one at a time obviously takes longer than running a focus group; it also puts greater demands on the interviewer. Without the stimulation of group experiences to trigger ideas or the ability of subjects to sit back and think while others speak, the moderator must use a more structured approach to help the subjects explore their experiences.

Subjects for one-on-one interviews are recruited and rewarded similarly to focus group participants. These sessions must be recorded for future transcription, but are generally not observed in progress, so smaller, more informal facilities can be used. Every effort should be made to make the subject comfortable and at ease, because this format does not offer the strength in numbers or moral support for one's opinions that the larger focus group can provide.

A one-on-one session usually takes about one hour, and in addition to an unstructured discussion of the topic at hand, researchers sometimes use one or more exercises designed to stimulate thinking about service attributes. Some of the most popular are described below. Each of these exercises can be used to stimulate focus group discussions as well.

Triadic Sorting (Kelly's Repertory Grid)

Triadic sorting is a well-established marketing research technique, specifically intended to encourage customers to think about and express the product/service attributes that they use when choosing among competitors in a category.[2] The steps in the exercise are:

1. A list of competitive alternatives in the market is prepared, printed on numbered cards.

2. The subject is asked to go through the cards and remove any completely unfamiliar alternatives.

3. Triples of the cards are then presented to the subject. The subject is asked to think of any basis on which any two members of the triple are similar to each other but different from the third.

   The combinations of cards presented can consist of all possible triples or some subset of them, depending upon how many are involved. The specific subsets presented can simply be a fraction of the set of possibilities, with different subjects getting different sets so that all triples are eventually presented. Alternatively, triples can be based on the researcher's judgment about which combinations are likely to provoke the most thought.

4. The exercise is repeated for each triple in the prespecified sequence. In each case the subject is asked to think of a new way in which any two members of the triple are similar to each other and different from the third.

5. The lists of attributes used to group and separate triples is recorded until the subject is unable to think of new ones for the triples presented.

The list of attributes generated is unlikely to be exhaustive, but the exercise can generate some surprising insights and should stimulate thinking and discussion of attributes. A hypothetical example of a portion of a triadic sorting session is shown in Figure 6.4.

Customer Service Scripts

Marketers often treat physical products as bundles of attributes that are experienced together. For example, a car has a color, a certain number of doors, horsepower rating, trunk capacity, and so on. This approach adequately describes the way most customers view goods; they are things, single entities to be used or consumed as a whole. But services are different from goods in that there is a temporal sequence to the component parts. Services are performances that often occupy time as well as space. They are experienced as well as consumed. A list of a service's attributes, no matter how complete, cannot fully describe the customer's experience with it. The service is a sequence of events whose order and individual qualities define the service.

For services in which customers play an interactive role, such as ordering materials from a supplier or dining in a restaurant, the customer typically has a mental script that facilitates appropriate behavior throughout the performance of the service and evaluation of the service experience. The customer has expectations about the order and duration of each phase of the service and knows what to say and do in response to each action by the service provider. Deviations from the expected script can lead to discomfort and dissatisfaction.

For example, restaurant patrons will evaluate their experience based on how comfortable the entire experience felt. This, in part, is why restaurants tend to follow very rigid scripts. From the opening question at one's first arrival at the restaurant ("How many in your party?" or "Do you have a reservation?"), the inter-

FIGURE 6.4

A HYPOTHETICAL EXAMPLE OF TRIADIC SORTING

A random sample of retail banking customers in a given city was presented with numbered cards, each printed with the name of one of the banks in the area. The banks with which subject #12 was familiar were

> Ace Bank
> 2nd National
> Third American
> Whalers and Miners
> Farmers' Federal

Cards for the other banks were removed from the list for the repertory grid exercise. Ten different triples can be formed from the five remaining banks, a small enough number that all were presented to the subject.

The first triple of banks presented was: Ace Bank, 2nd National, and Third American. The subject split off Ace Bank from the others because it is locally owned, and for its small-town feel and friendliness; she saw the other two as large, impersonal, and based out-of-state. No other divisions or attributes were forthcoming from this triple.
Resulting service performance attributes: Personal, friendly service

The next triple was 2nd National, Third American, and Farmers' Federal. This time the subject set Third American apart for its convenient ATM locations, especially as it is the only bank to have an ATM at the city's airport. On the other hand, the subject could also see setting Farmers' Federal apart from the others because of its image as a good place to get home mortgages.
Resulting service performance attributes: Convenience of ATM locations
　　　　　　　　　　　　　　　　　　　　　　　　Helpfulness in mortgage lending
　　　　　　　　　　　　　　　　　　　　　　　　Mortgage lending rates

When presented with the triple, Ace Bank, Whalers and Miners, and Farmers' Federal, Whalers and Miners was set apart because of its aggressive advertising of a cost-free checking program, the only such program of which the subject was aware. She also split off Ace Bank from the other two, because it was the only one of the three that had a branch office near her home.
Resulting service performance attributes: Free checking
　　　　　　　　　　　　　　　　　　　　　　　　Branch office convenient to residence

From the triple, 2nd National, Third American, and Farmers' Federal, the subject felt that 2nd National and Farmers' Federal had good investment services, but had heard from friends that Third American's performance in that area had not been as good.
Resulting service performance attributes: Variety of investment services available.

And so on for the other six triples . . .

---

change between patron and staff seems unvarying across a wide range of restaurant types and geographic regions. Experienced restaurant-goers "know their lines" when they go out to eat, and can become confused or think poorly of the restaurant if the flow of events and the interchange with the staff is not as expected. For example, a couple having an anniversary dinner at a fine restaurant would expect an attentive waitstaff while trying to decide among specials and menu items, and perhaps when the food first arrives. On the other hand, once the meal is under way and

The service encounter at a restaurant often follows a rigidly followed script, with both parties knowing their own lines and actions and expecting certain cues and behaviors from the other.

the couple is trying to have a private conversation, the hovering presence of a waiter would be considered annoying. The staff must know when to be accessible and when to be unobtrusive.

Service firms must identify the scripts that customers bring to the transaction. The "scenes" of the script usually correspond to the processes of the service described in Section 6.2. The process of eliciting scripts from customers merely involves taking them through a service experience, and probing in detail for what they expect or feel is expected of them at each phase of the experience. To keep the discussion realistic and concrete, the interviewer should concentrate on a specific occasion, perhaps the last time the subject used the service.

Understanding the expected flow of the service script provides important information about where services fail and how the fundamental design of the service operation and the training of the staff can be altered to avoid mishaps and provide pleasant surprises. In Chapter 18 we will describe how the appropriate sequence of events and actual written scripts should be incorporated into actual blueprints of the service process.

The Critical Incident Technique[3]

The critical incident technique (CIT) is a one-on-one exercise to elicit details about services that particularly dissatisfy or delight customers. Data are generally collected from large enough samples of subjects that patterns of responses can be identified. In particular, the questioner asks probing questions to find:

- What makes a service encounter particularly satisfying to customers? Do specific events comprise a satisfying service experience? What do contact employees do that cause these events to be remembered favorably?
- What makes a service encounter dissatisfying to customers? What events occur and what do contact people do that causes them to be remembered unfavorably?
- Are the components that determine satisfactory and unsatisfactory encounters related to each other—for example, opposites or mirror images of each other?

A typical interview script asks a subject to recall an incident when, as a customer of the industry (firm) in question, he had a particularly satisfying (dissatisfying) interaction with an employee. The subject is asked to describe the situation fully: When did it happen? What specific circumstances led up to the incident? What mood or frame of mind were you in? Exactly what did the employee say or do? What result made you feel the interaction was satisfying (dissatisfying)?

Transcripts of the interviews are then compared to identify common problems or sources of delight. Specific points mentioned by the sample of customers provide a list of the key processes and dimensions of the service as customers see them. The specific sources of problems and delight can also be grouped by process and dimension to highlight those components of the service that require attention or where greater customer loyalty can be achieved.

For example, a large study of critical incidents in consumers' experiences with restaurants, hotels, and airlines, found several important patterns throughout the hospitality industry, all dealing with employee behaviors.[4] In particular, employee causes of dissatisfaction and satisfaction were found to fall into three groups. First were incidents in which customers were either delighted or irritated by employees' ability and willingness to compensate for system breakdowns. The second group of incidents involved employee responses (or lack of response) to special customer needs and requests. Finally, the third group dealt with employee actions described as unsolicited or unprompted by the consumer—for example, actions that were surprisingly helpful or disturbingly bizarre. Such patterns of responses across customers and specific industries can provide some useful insights into causes of customer dissatisfaction and delight that should probably be tracked by satisfaction surveys.

Laddering[5]

This exercise goes beyond simply identifying the attributes customers use to classify products. It seeks a deeper understanding of how product attributes are associated with personal beliefs and goals. As such it provides more than just a list of attributes, but gives insights into why the customer thinks they are important. It is based on a psychological theory called Means-End Theory[6] which deals with the connections between product attributes (the "means") and the customer's personal values which the attributes reinforce (the "end").

The interviewer uses a structured series of directed probing questions, typified by the question "Why is that important to you?" The procedure is as follows:

1. An important attribute of a service, perhaps one identified by the Kelly grid procedure described earlier, is selected. The subject is asked which extreme pole of the attribute he or she prefers.

2. The subject is asked why he or she chose that pole. The answer can lead to distinctions among services based on the different reasons customers purchase them and the different consequences they produce.

3. The same procedure of questioning can be continued until customers ultimately distinguish among services not because of their obvious attributes, but based on the personal values they reflect and the consequences that result from using them.

4. When the subject can no longer provide answers, the exercise ends.

5. If the service can be used for different usage occasions, each use can be pursued separately.

Here is a typical ladder obtained from a secretary discussing why she would prefer to use an overnight package delivery service that has drop boxes available:[7]

> Drop box ⇒
>   Convenient ⇒
>   Save time ⇒
>   Can do more ⇒
>   Personal satisfaction ⇒
>   Accomplishment ⇒
>   Self-esteem ⇒

The laddering technique can therefore provide deeper insight into the positioning of a service in the minds of its customers. This depth insight is useful not just for writing compelling advertising copy. Knowing why customers care about certain attributes may suggest the kinds of quality improvements that will be most meaningful to customers.

6.5 LEADING-EDGE USER STUDIES[8]

Questioning customers about their experiences with one's service tends to provide mostly articulated attributes, those features that describe current market offerings, as described in Section 6.1. It is harder to get customers to imagine and to articulate exciting service features, those that would exceed their expectations. And yet, rather than rely entirely on the creativity of one's R&D effort to provide new products for the future, one can look to one's own customers for guidance about what the market wants. For example, many firms in the computer software industry often find that their customers' suggestions for program enhancements provide better insights into the emerging needs of the marketplace than "blue sky" ideas of their own developers.

The key is to identify an important market or technical trend, based on a careful analysis of the business environment: look for economic, demographic, technological, legal, and political changes that can affect your customers and the way they use your services. The firm must next identify those users of the service who lead the trend in terms of their experience with the service and the intensity of their need to adopt it. So-called leading-edge users have two distinguishing characteristics:

1. Their needs for service enhancements are similar to the marketplace as a whole, but they arise months or years before the rest of the marketplace faces them.
2. These users will benefit significantly by finding solutions to those needs.

The leading-edge users must be carefully studied to determine the problems they have with the current market offerings, solutions they suggest, and "wish lists" they have for service suppliers. Very often these intense users are knowledgeable enough to have developed some of their own solutions to their problems, and these home-grown solutions can offer excellent guidance in developing features that should be incorporated into future offerings. For example, a software firm that produces productivity-enhancing graphics programs claims that, even though it has an R&D department, ideas for all of its truly successful new product upgrades have been provided by customers who had pushed the products to their limits and needed specific enhancements.

Finally, the suggestions obtained from the lead-user data must be projected onto the market as a whole to determine the extent to which they really anticipate the coming general demand or are specific to these heavy users. General market reactions to these ideas can be obtained from focus groups during general discussions of product attributes.

6.6 DIRECT OBSERVATION[9]

In addition to these formal marketing research methods, there are many less structured activities that allow a firm to stay tuned in to its customers' needs and experiences. If properly documented, many of these techniques can provide additional insights into the processes and subprocesses of the firm's service that determine customer satisfaction and delight. Mystery shopping is an example of such a technique. Mystery shopping involves hiring individuals to pose as customers of the firm without the employees' knowledge, and to rate the service received. This practice is employed by most fast-food companies (e.g., McDonald's and Burger King), hotel chains (Marriott), restaurants (Shoney's), banks, oil companies (Amoco), and even automobile manufacturers (Ford). Although mystery shopping is intended as a quality control device (and as a motivator to make sure employees deliver good service, because any customer could be a mystery shopper), information gathered in these exercises can be analyzed to identify aspects of the service interaction that are likely to determine customer satisfaction.

Similarly, many companies send mystery shoppers to competitors to experience their services firsthand. For example, Marriott shopped the competitors for its proposed Fairfield Inns to learn directly what the competition was doing. This information can also give insights into potential drivers of satisfaction.

The contents of complaints and comment cards should be tabulated and analyzed as an important source of input from customers. Similarly, many organizations, including Procter & Gamble, American Express, and General Electric have customer hotlines (800 numbers) to answer customer questions and complaints. The issues raised in these contacts need to be captured and organized. As we will discuss later in the book, these forms of unscientifically collected data do not provide statistically valid indicators of general customer sentiment. Nevertheless, they are yet another source of understanding for managers and should be reviewed for insights into key service processes as customers see them.

Exit interviews—interviews of dissatisfied customers who have recently terminated relationships with the firm—are another useful method for appreciating the customer's point of view. Although these discussions can be painful, they are very important for learning what aspects of the service cause customers to defect. Incidentally, the primary purpose of these interviews is to gather information, and they should be treated as such. Their value as opportunities to salvage the relationships is often considerably lower.

The concept of Management by Walking Around (MBWA) has been practiced by good companies for many years, but it gained its capitalized name and a good deal of publicity in Peters and Waterman's book *In Search of Excellence.*[10] MBWA refers to various methods of direct informal observation intended to supplement and breathe life into the statistics that most managers use to monitor the progress of their businesses. The basic idea is that managers must get out of their offices and meet their customers, with the goal of experiencing the business through their customers' eyes. MBWA activities differs from most of the others described in this chapter in that the contact is made by managers and line workers themselves rather than by professional market researchers.

Some firms have required (or at least encouraged) company executives to answer telephone calls from complaining customers.[11] At other companies executives are expected to serve periodically on the front lines of the firm's service outlets. First Union Bank has had its senior management go out into the branches to unobtrusively observe interactions between customers and frontline personnel to provide a better understanding of the customer point of view.[12] Some companies regularly visit their customers to discuss how their relationships are holding up, or they invite customers for detailed visits of the firm's facilities and discussions about what it is like to do business with the firm.[13]

This hands-on understanding of customer needs and desires is important for all of the firm's employees. Quality is ultimately in the hands of the hourly workers who perform the service, and so they too need to experience the service from the customers' viewpoint. For firms that sell to other businesses, Peters and Austin recommend sending hourly workers to meet their counterparts at customer firms to hear how their work is being received.[14] They even cite firms in which managers perform the tasks of hourly workers at a customer firm to gain a better understanding of their service needs.

MBWA activities are often cited as valuable tools to stimulate a firm's employees to take quality more seriously, but they also serve the purpose of this chapter: The insights they provide to managers will give them a much better understanding of how customers perceive the structure of the service.

6.7 HOW MUCH EXPLORATORY RESEARCH IS ENOUGH?

The goal of all these exercises is to compile a complete list of the drivers of customer satisfaction. If critical items are omitted from the list, we may overlook important sources of problems or cost-effective solutions for quality enhancements. But how effective are the above research methods at generating all of the major attributes of a service? A partial answer to this question has been provided by research of Griffin and Hauser,[15] who have performed a number of studies on the effectiveness of these techniques. The reader should be cautioned that these were very limited studies, and that, although the results do give researchers some guidance in designing research, further testing is necessary.

As one would expect, the more focus groups or in-depth interviews are conducted, the greater the number of attributes one is likely to generate. But these sessions take time and can be extremely expensive when one considers the costs of management time spent on viewing interviews, reading transcripts, and discussing the data. There is a trade-off between the mounting costs and the decreasing amount of additional information obtained from doing more interviews. Griffin and Hauser directly addressed this trade-off in a series of studies of exploratory methods applied to two product categories, a proprietary computer product and consumer food-carrying devices.

Comparing the ability of focus groups versus one-on-one interviews to generate lists of customer needs, the authors discovered a surprising relationship. As expected, a given number of two-hour focus groups generated, on average, more needs than the same number of one-hour one-on-one interviews. Surprisingly, the ratio of needs generated per unit of time remained the same for the two methods. The results suggest that it was total interview time, not the number of participants, that determined the number of needs generated. Maybe this shouldn't be too surprising in light of our earlier caution about the limited ability of focus groups to probe as deeply into any one individual's perceptions.

Griffin and Hauser also investigated the average number of interviews necessary to generate a complete list of needs. They found that as the number of interviews increased, the total number of needs revealed seemed to approach a finite upper limit. Then, by fitting a theoretically reasonable curve (the beta-binomial curve) to the increasing number of needs produced by various numbers of interviews, it was possible to estimate that upper limit, that represented the probable total number of needs. Using this value as the total number of needs it was then possible to measure the average percent of total needs generated by various numbers of interviews. For example, they found that it took five interviews, on average, to generate fifty percent of total needs, it took the equivalent of twenty-five interviews to get 98 percent coverage. The multiple sessions did not produce a great deal of duplication of needs among interviews. In fact the bulk of the needs generated were each mentioned in fewer than 20 percent of the interviews. Getting a complete list of attributes requires more than just a few sessions.

A third insight in the Griffin and Hauser studies is that a single reader is unlikely to find all of the needs contained in the transcripts of focus groups and one-on-one interviews. In fact, trained analysts were individually able to identify an average of only 54 percent of the needs contained in a set of transcripts, with a maximum of 68 percent. Preconceptions about needs, and the difficulty in distinguishing among the nuances of certain statements may be partly responsible. The studies found that an average of seven analysts was necessary to identify 99 percent of the needs contained in the transcripts.

An important lesson from this research is that identifying all the customer needs that define a service is not easy or cheap. The data used in these studies represented two narrow categories, and have limited validity to others, but the results show that it is possible to measure the trade-offs between the costs of this research and the completeness of understanding it provides. By replicating the Griffin and Hauser methods, a firm can find out the relationship between costs and understanding for its own products. The studies also found that recent improvements made in interviewing techniques are increasing the efficiency of this activity.

6.8 USING MANAGEMENT EXPERIENCE

Each of the attribute-generating exercises described in this chapter is only exploratory, and we have seen there is no guarantee that they will cover all the important aspects of a service. They are also more likely to generate articulated attributes than basic or exciting attributes. Therefore, before a formal customer questionnaire is finalized, the analyst is advised to look to other sources for possible missing attributes.

The most obvious source is management's common sense about the service, particularly for identifying basic attributes. This develops through experience, including Management by Walking Around. Management should review the list to determine whether any key areas have been overlooked, particularly areas where problems arise and diagnosis and monitoring are desired.

Trade publications occasionally have articles giving advice on quality in their particular industries, including lists of areas to be monitored. Since customer satisfaction questionnaires are often mailed out, it is often quite easy to obtain those used by competitors and by firms in other industries with similar services. These questionnaires can be checked for possibly overlooked service dimensions.

6.9 THE SERVQUAL DIMENSIONS

One final source of service attributes worth mentioning is the SERVQUAL model of Parasuraman, Zeithaml and Berry.[16] These authors conducted focus groups and then formal surveys of customers in several different service industries to develop lists of attributes which define service quality in general. The lists were condensed by correlational analysis into five major categories:

Tangibles The appearance of physical facilities, equipment, personnel, and communications materials.
Reliability The ability to perform the promised service dependably and accurately.
Responsiveness The willingness to help customers and to provide prompt service.
Assurance Knowledge and courtesy of employees and their ability to convey trust and confidence.
Empathy Caring, individualized attention the firm provides its customers.

Customer assessment of each of these dimensions is measured by comparing scales of customers' expectations and actual experiences on a battery of 22 items, approximately four items per dimension. The authors report that Reliability appears to be the most important service dimension for customers across many industries in which they have applied the SERVQUAL methodology.

The classification of these dimensions remains somewhat controversial. Some have criticized the statistical methodology used to identify them as inappropriate.[17] It is also important to remember that the list is intended to describe the dimensions of quality that are common to all services, and is therefore unlikely to encompass all the special properties of any particular service industry. Like product attributes, the SERVQUAL dimensions are also static descriptors of the service rather than components of a dynamic performance. Nevertheless, the five areas have been well accepted by service industry managers as having strong face validity, and no list of customer needs should be considered complete until it has been checked for representation of the SERVQUAL dimensions. For example, one should check the dimensions that describe each process in Figure 6.1 to see whether any of the SERVQUAL dimensions, such as Tangibles, need to be represented in some way on the list.

6.10 ORGANIZING THE LIST OF ATTRIBUTES

Expert Analysis   Once the list of several hundred customer needs has been generated, it must be organized in ways that reflect customers' perception of the structure of the service and that gives management a diagnostic tool for measuring and improving key components of the service. The most useful representation is to represent the service's components as a hierarchical tree diagram, similar to that shown in Figure 6.2, in which the service is seen as a set of discrete processes, each of which is in turn composed of subprocesses. Several methods can be used to organize the long list of customer-generated service components into such a form.

One method, considered to be one of the basic components of Japanese management, is called "K-J analysis."[18] (Japanese quality engineers also refer to such a hierarchical structure as an "affinity diagram.") In this exercise, a multidisciplinary team of experts organizes the list of needs by group consensus. It uses a bottom-up approach, organizing the most detailed levels of needs, and then seeking higher levels of organization in those lower-level groupings. This method is supposed to reduce the influence of the experts' preconceptions about what the structure should look like.

1. The exercise begins with the complete list of expressed needs, often reworded so that each statement is positive: "reasonably priced" vs. "overpriced." The team members are asked to cluster these data into groups of similar topics and to assign a heading that broadly describes each group. The individual statements represent the lowest level of detail, which correspond to design details of the service and form the outermost branches of the tree diagram.
2. At the next stage, these headings are themselves grouped into similar categories, the tactical level of details.
3. These categories are once more clustered into strategic groupings, if possible.
4. Finally, the structure should be assessed for completeness. If management feels that the structure is missing what it knows to be important levels of detail or other branches, it is appropriate to add them to the tree diagram at this stage.

The resulting structure might reflect the service's attribute structure, or perhaps its temporal sequence of processes that make up the service. The key is to find in the data the structure that most closely describes the customers' view.

Using Customers to Do the Groupings In spite of the hope that K-J analysis will be free from the experts' preconceptions, the studies of Griffin and Hauser, cited earlier, also found a "production bias" in the structures developed by experts compared with those of customers. In particular, the researchers conducted an experiment to compare the hierarchical structures obtained by K-J analysis using a panel of engineers to a grouping obtained from customers. A list of over 200 attributes of food-carrying containers (picnic baskets, thermal food containers, etc.) was generated by focus groups, and then organized using K-J analysis by a group of technical experts. The resulting affinity diagram contained five major categories of attributes, all quite technical in flavor: Price, Container Utility, Physical Characteristics, Thermal Attributes, and Convenience. The last category alone included 139 of the attributes.

On the other hand, customer-based groupings of needs tended to reflect the products' functions and uses, and, in particular, divided the engineers' catch-all convenience category into several salient components. This structure had seven major categories, each containing between 20 and 39 of the attributes: Attractiveness, Carries Many Things, Maintains Temperature, Right Size, Easy to Move, Convenience, and Works as Container. The experts themselves conceded that the customer-based structure had stronger face validity as a description of customer behavior.

Griffin and Hauser's method for having customers organize the list of needs combined the individual judgments of a sample of subjects, rather than a group consensus. It also allowed them to have each subject sort far fewer than the full set of several hundred needs, an absolute necessity to getting subject cooperation. The steps used were as follows:

1. Each customer was given a deck of cards, each bearing one item from the list of customer needs. By using multiple subjects, and by carefully choosing overlapping subsets of needs determined according to an experimental design, it is possible to keep the individual decks small.

2. Each subject was asked to sort the cards into piles so that each pile represented similar needs, but so that the piles were somehow different. The number of piles to use was not specified.

3. From each pile, the subject was asked to choose one which best represents the needs in the pile. This need was called an "exemplar" for the pile.

4. The analyst then compiled a co-occurrence matrix, a square matrix with as many rows and columns as there were needs. The number in the i-jth position of the matrix is the number of subjects who placed need i in the same pile as need j. (The analysis must compare these numbers for different combinations of needs, so in designing the decks to give to different subjects it is essential that each pair of needs occurred in an equal number of decks.) A portion of a hypothetical co-occurrence matrix is shown in Figure 6.5.

FIGURE 6.5

AN ILLUSTRATION OF CO-OCCURRENCE MATRIX AND A TREE DIAGRAM

	A	B	C	D	E	F	
A	X	79	36	2	0	0	. . .
B	79	X	22	1	0	2	
C	36	22	X	0	2	4	
D	2	1	0	X	85	11	
E	0	0	2	85	X	6	
F	0	2	4	11	6	X	

. . .

where A = "Manager greets me by name."
   B = "Tellers are friendly."
   C = "I know whom to call when I have a problem."
   D = "They open early in the day."
   E = "Open on Saturdays."
   F = "ATMs are well lit."

with a total of 100 possible matches

Note that A and B should probably be included in the same category, perhaps a "personal relationship" cluster, with C somewhat related; D and E are clearly in a "convenient hours category"; F appears to belong to yet another category, perhaps a "security" or "physical convenience" category.

---

5. The co-occurrence matrix was now interpreted as a similarity matrix. The higher the number in the i-jth position the more often needs i and j were grouped together by subjects, and the stronger the argument for grouping them together near the ends of the tree branches. The mathematical techniques that can perform such similarity-based grouping are called cluster analysis. The application of cluster analysis to the matrix resulted in a hierarchical tree structure of needs that reflected the joint decisions of the subjects. The needs chosen most often as exemplars could be used to name the clusters.

Although the customer-based method produced superior results in the experimental setting, the requirement of computer-based clustering routines makes it far less accessible than K-J analysis, which requires no computer and offers an opportunity for managers to deal in detail with customer statements of their perceptions of the service—a benefit in its own right. If the experts performing the K-J analysis have been practicing Management By Walking Around, as recommended earlier, they might be better attuned to customer thinking than those in the Griffin and Hauser studies were, and may therefore produce hierarchies that more closely reflect customer thinking.

6.11 SUMMARY

In this chapter we have described some techniques used by service firms to begin to understand more effectively the structures of their services as customers perceive them. In particular, the goal of these various exploratory research techniques is to

FIGURE 6.6

THE OVERALL PROCESS OF GENERATING A CUSTOMER-BASED SATISFACTION QUESTIONNAIRE

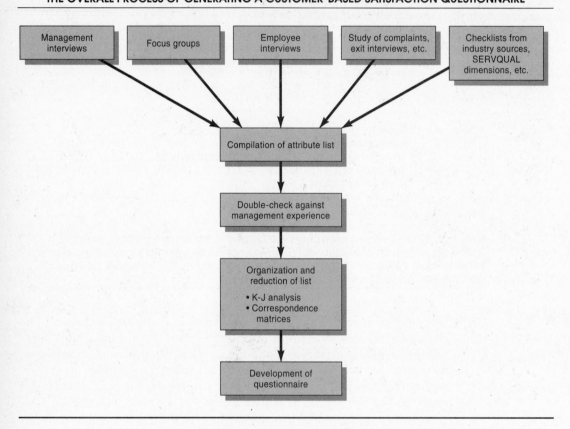

generate lists of customer needs, the building blocks of the mental structures that consumers envision when they evaluate the quality of a service. The overall process is outlined in Figure 6.6.

The most commonly used method may be the focus group, a moderated discussion of the service experience by a group of customers. One weakness of focus groups for the purpose of generating service attributes is that each customer has limited time to speak about his or her perceptions. As a result, discussions may not be able to dig sufficiently deeply to uncover all important determinants of satisfaction. A solution may be to do one-on-one interviews with customers. Without the group synergies of a focus group to spark customer thoughts, there are several exercises that can be used to help subjects think about the service's dimensions. They include triadic sorting, customer service scripts, the critical incident technique, and laddering exercises. Recent research has given some guidance as to the number of interviews necessary to be sure that as many attributes as possible have been obtained, or at least has provided a method that individual firms can adopt for their own individual situations.

There is no guarantee that interviews of customers will generate all the important attributes, so several other sources of ideas were described. Leading-edge user studies can be used to generate exciting service ideas which are beyond the imagination of current customers. Managers should also use their own judgment, based on careful listening to customers. Finally, the SERVQUAL dimensions, a list of generic properties of services, can be used as a final check of the completeness of the list.

We also described two methods for imposing some organization on what is often an enormous list of seemingly trivial comments, a commonly used method based on managerial judgment and the other done by customers themselves. Recent research results suggest that the customer-based approach may be preferable. Later in the book we will show how this organized list is used to compose the formal surveys used to provide statistically valid information about the service and its customers.

REVIEW QUESTIONS

1. Perform the Kelly's grid exercise yourself for the following industries. How representative do you find the resulting list of attributes to be?
   (a) *Fast-food hamburger restaurants:* McDonald's, Wendy's, Burger King, Hardee's, White Castle
   (b) *Rental car firms:* Avis, Hertz, National, Alamo, Budget
2. Consider being asked to perform a laddering exercise to explain your choice of school. How difficult would it be? How difficult would it be to be candid? Would you do this exercise for a stranger?
3. Recall a dissatisfying service experience you had recently. How much specific detail can you remember about it? Could you do a CIT analysis of the service? In particular, structure your recollections in terms of a script. To what extent was the dissatisfaction due to the service provider not following the script you anticipated? Can you recall a service that dissatisfied or confused you because the service provider did not follow your anticipated service script? If you were given the opportunity to manage that service, what steps would you take to avoid this particular problem?
4. Consider your school as a service provider. What do the SERVQUAL dimensions specifically mean for that service. What important attributes of the service (if any) does the SERVQUAL list not cover for this particular service?
5. Your boss wants to know whether the firm should do one-on-one interviews or focus groups to determine the structure of the firm's service. He would like you to handle the operation, whatever you decide. What recommendations would you make?

ENDNOTES

1. For a discussion of the ongoing attempt to clarify these terms see Roland Rust and Richard L. Oliver (1994), "Service Quality: Insights and Managerial Implications from the Frontier," in *Service Quality*, R. Rust and R. L. Oliver (eds.), Thousand Oaks, CA: Sage Publications, 1–20. Another example is A. Parasuraman, Valerie A.

Zeithaml, and Leonard Berry (1994), "Reassessment of Expectations as a Comparison Standard in Measuring Service Quality: Implications for Further Research," *Journal of Marketing*, 58 (January), 111–124.

2. See Paul E. Green, Donald S. Tull, and Gerald Albaum (1988), *Research for Marketing Decisions*, 5th Edition, Englewood Cliffs, NJ: Prentice-Hall.

3. M. Bitner, B. Booms, and M. Tetreault (1990), "The Service Encounter: Diagnosing Favorable and Unfavorable Incidents," *Journal of Marketing*, January, 71–84.

4. Bitner, Booms and Tetreault (1990), *op. cit.*

5. Thomas Reynolds and Jonathon Gutman (1988), "Laddering Theory, Method, Analysis and Interpretation," *Journal of Advertising Research* (January), 11–31.

6. Jonathon Gutman (1982), "A Means-End Chain Model Based on Consumer Categorization Processes," *Journal of Marketing* 46 (2), 60–72.

7. Thomas J. Reynolds and Alyce Byrd Craddock (1988), "The Application of the MEC-CAS Model to the Development and Assessment of Advertising Strategy: A Case Study," *Journal of Advertising Research*, 28 (April/May), 43–54.

8. Eric von Hippel (1986), "Novel Product Concepts from 'Lead Users'," *Management Science* (July), 791–805.

9. For a survey of observational methods used by services marketers in many aspects of marketing research, and the scientific and ethical issues they raise, see Stephen J. Groves and Raymond P. Fisk (1992), "Observational Data Collection Methods for Services Marketing: An Overview," *Journal of the Academy of Marketing Science*, 20 (3), 217–224.

10. Thomas Peters and Robert S. Waterman (1982), *In Search of Excellence*, New York: Harper & Row.

11. Tom Peters and Nancy Austin (1985), *A Passion for Excellence*, New York: Random House.

12. Ron Zemke with Dick Shaaf (1989), *The Service Edge: 101 Companies that Profit from Customer Care*, New York: Penguin Books.

13. For a detailed guide on how to conduct some of these exercises see Edward F. McQuarrie (1993), *The Customer Visit*, Newbury Park, CA: Sage Publications.

14. *Ibid.*, p. 23.

15. Abbie Griffin and John R. Hauser (1993), "The Voice of the Customer," *Marketing Science*, 12 (Winter), 1–25.

16. See A. Parasuraman, Valerie Zeithaml, and Leonard L. Berry (1988), "SERVQUAL: A Multiple-Item Scale for Measuring Consumer Perceptions of Service Quality," *Journal of Retailing*, 64 (1), 12–40. Also, Valerie A. Zeithaml, A. Parasuraman, and Leonard L. Berry (1990), *Delivering Quality Service: Balancing Customer Perceptions and Expectations*, New York: The Free Press.

17. For example, J. Carman (1990), "Consumer Perceptions of Service Quality: An Assessment of the SERVQUAL Dimensions," *Journal of Retailing*, 66 (Spring), 33–55; J. Paul Peter, Gilbert A. Churchill, Jr., and Tom J. Brown (1992), "Caution in the Use of Difference Scores in Consumer Research," *Journal of Consumer Research*, 19 (March), 655–662; Emin Babkus and Gregory W. Boller (1992), "An Empirical Assessment of the SERVQUAL Scale," *Journal of Business Research*, 24, 253–268; A. Parasuraman, Valerie A. Zeithaml, and Leonard Berry (1994), "Reassessment of Expectations as a Comparison Standard in Measuring Service Quality: Implications for Further Research," *Journal of Marketing*, 58 (January), 111–124; J. Joseph Cronin, Jr. and Stephen A. Taylor (1994), "SERVPERF Versus SERVQUAL: Reconciling Performance-Based and Perceptions-Minus-Expectations Measurement of Service Quality," *Journal of Marketing*, 58(January), 125–131; R. Kenneth Teas (1994), "Expectations as a Comparison Standard in Measuring Service Quality: An Assessment of a Reassessment," *Journal of Marketing*, 58 (January), 132–139.

18. For an excellent description of K-J analysis see James L. Bossert (1991), *Quality Function Deployment: A Practitioner's Approach*, Milwaukee: ASQC Quality Press.

Chapter 7

COMPLAINT MANAGEMENT

7.1 OVERVIEW

Despite our best efforts, there are always going to be situations in which a customer becomes unhappy. What a business does when these occasions occur, and how much the organization learns from the experience can have a sizable effect on the organization's future health and vitality. This chapter explores how a business can view complaints as opportunities, how it can manage the complaint process, and how it can use complaint information to target improvement efforts.

The key concept in complaint management is *defensive marketing,* which involves retaining existing customers. (Its counterpart, *offensive marketing,* refers to attracting new customers.) We have seen that the lifetime value of a customer is often much greater than one might anticipate from the size of any individual transaction. This means that an organization can often benefit from making an unhappy customer happy. Although many companies have not learned this lesson very well, many companies have become very good at complaint management. From such examples we can derive several principles to use in guiding the organization's response to a complaint. In addition, statistics about complaints can help us see what areas need attention in the future. This chapter provides some simple approaches for doing this.

7.2 DEFENSIVE MARKETING AND COMPLAINT MANAGEMENT

We are accustomed to thinking of marketing as the attraction of new customers. Tools such as advertising, pricing, sales promotion, and personal selling affect brand choice, and thus market share. This is the traditional way of thinking about marketing, and the "four P's" paradigm, viewing marketing as making decisions about promotion, price, place, and product, assumes the offensive marketing perspective.

Defensive marketing, on the other hand, focuses on retaining existing customers. The business world has become much more aware of defensive marketing in recent years; topics such as customer satisfaction, complaint management, and customer retention have received greater attention.

Because defensive marketing increases customer retention, it has a positive impact on market share. Retaining existing customers also reduces the necessity of attracting new ones (replacements) and can sometimes even reduce offensive marketing cost.[1]

There are other benefits in addition to customer retention. Customers come back only if they are sufficiently happy, which means that a side effect of defensive marketing is positive word-of-mouth, which tends to attract new customers. Also, long-term customers may tend to do more business with the firm (think of older bank customers, for example). Long-term customers are accustomed to how a firm conducts business and so ask fewer questions and cause fewer problems. This reduces the costs of serving them. All of these positive effects of defensive marketing enhance the lifetime value of the customer.

Defensive marketing is not always important. If long-term customer relationships are not possible, it doesn't make any difference if a customer is retained. For example, people only use a national immigration service once, so there is no incentive to improve this service. Monopolists also have less incentive to work hard to retain customers, because the customers have nowhere else to go. For example, the U.S. Postal Service, a government-mandated monopoly, used to be well-known for its inflexible bureaucracy and long service lines. However, when competitors such as Federal Express and UPS sprang up offering services that were close enough to regular mail service to lure away Postal Service customers, the Postal Service then adopted a much more customer-oriented attitude because customers could now be lost.

7.3 THE VALUE OF A CUSTOMER

Consider a young person buying his or her first new car. That customer has not had much time to build financial strength. The car purchased is likely to be small and inexpensive, and the dealer's profit from selling the car is likely to be small. It is tempting to conclude that this customer is not very important.

Some companies realize that this is not the case. Honda, for example, builds its product line and plans its service department to enhance customer loyalty and repurchase. The young customer may buy an inexpensive Civic. But after several years of increased earning power, that same customer may buy a medium-priced Accord. Eventually that same customer may buy Honda's luxury car, the Acura Legend. Figure 7.1 shows this progression. Notice that the profits increase over time, as the customer becomes more established financially.

To determine the current potential value of a customer, based solely on future purchases, we must calculate the net present value of the profit stream represented by the future purchases. Suppose that the dealer profit on a Civic is $500 on average, while the profits on an Accord and Acura Legend are $1500 and $3000, respectively. Let us also suppose that repurchase occurs every five years, and that the discount rate is 10%. The value of the current purchase (Civic) is $500, the value of the second purchase (Accord) is $931, and the value of the third purchase (Acura Legend) is $1157. (Use your finance formulas to check this.) In this case, even the

FIGURE 7.1

THE VALUE OF FUTURE PURCHASES

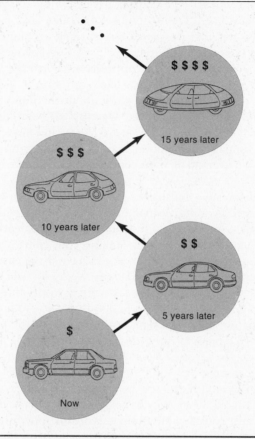

discounted net present value of the purchases increases over time. The total value of the customer, based on future purchases, is $500 + $931 + $1157 = $2588, which is more than five times the $500 that the customer is *apparently* worth, based only on current purchases.

Understanding a customer's value in this light could affect how the customer is treated. If the customer feels mistreated, which is often the case in new car purchases, repurchase from that dealer becomes unlikely. So, wrangling a few extra dollars on a Civic purchase could jeopardize over $2000 in future purchase value. The sales staff clearly must be motivated to enhance satisfaction as well as immediate sales. One way to do this is to compensate the sales force based *both* on sales figures *and* satisfaction with the sales transaction.

A complaint can be a second chance for the company to keep a customer from leaving dissatisfied. If a customer is unhappy but doesn't complain, then the company risks losing that customer, along with the customer's future profit stream.[2] Research indicates that approximately one unhappy customer in twenty actually complains, which means that a complaining customer is just the tip of the iceberg.[3]

Companies should welcome complaints, and view them as a second chance to satisfy a customer.

The urgency with which an organization views a complaint is related to the future value of the customer. Recovery of a dissatisfied customer is possible, and research to date indicates that the benefits of turning around a complaining customer are dramatic. In some circumstances, 95% of complainers will return if the complaint is handled satisfactorily and an unhappy customer who is listened to, regardless of the final outcome, is twice as likely to return.[4]

These numbers tell only part of the story about the importance of complaint management and the value of a customer. We must also consider word of mouth. Happy customers may tell others that they are happy and unhappy customers may tell others that the company is no good. According to one industry report, a dissatisfied customer tells an average of 9–10 people about the bad experience, and 13% will tell 20 or more.[5]

In a previous chapter we considered the example of a customer who did not have a coupon honored by a dry cleaner and then retaliated with negative word of mouth. Let us calculate, very quickly this time, the approximate amount of future business of a customer to this dry cleaner. Suppose that failure to honor the coupon "saved" the company about 50 cents, or would have if the customer had not left. Approximating weekly sales at about $10 per week, of which let us guess that approximately $1 is profit, we see that a customer is worth about $50 of profit per year. Over 40 years this grows to about $2000 in profit. Adding in the *other* customers who may have stopped shopping at this store because of negative word of mouth (let us say two, conservatively) this adds up to $6000 of profit potentially lost. Of course, taking the net present value will reduce this figure somewhat, but it is a safe bet that the amount will still be greater than 50 cents.

Of course, word of mouth can also be positive. Suppose a competitor cleaning establishment "lost" about 50 cents by honoring the customer's coupon. That establishment would receive considerable positive word of mouth, not to mention the possibility of creating a long-term business relationship with the customer.

7.4 THE (UNFORTUNATE) STATE OF COMPLAINT MANAGEMENT

Unfortunately a great many companies and managers do not realize how valuable a customer is, and there are many examples of poor complaint management. Looking at some of these examples can give us an idea of what not to do, and, by contrast, get us started in thinking about what we actually *should* do.

Unfortunate Practice #1—Ignore It

Let us start with the example of an airline phone ticketing service. A professor needed to fly to his grandfather's funeral, and requested a special "bereavement fare." The agent agreed, but required considerable detailed information about the funeral arrangements, which the professor found insensitive and inappropriate. The professor called the airline's main office to complain, and suggested ways in which the situation could be handled with greater consideration. After spending a considerable amount of time elaborating on the complaint and suggested remedies, the following exchange took place:

> **Professor:** What do you do now? How do you intend to respond to my complaint and suggestions?
>
> **Agent:** Well, quite honestly I can't really do very much. I guess I might bring it up in a meeting or something.
>
> **Professor:** But to me, *you* are ABC Airlines. Are you telling me that you screen your complaints and suggestions, only passing along those you agree with?
>
> **Agent:** You have to realize, I'm low person on the totem pole here. To really do anything you'd have to talk to someone higher up, maybe the customer service manager.

At this point the professor asked to talk to the agent's supervisor, who seemed most eager to (1) be agreeable, (2) not actually promise to do anything, and (3) get the professor off the line as soon as possible.

Unfortunate Practice #2—Don't Respond

In 1991 *Advertising Age* magazine did a fascinating study of how quickly the major automakers responded to complaints.[6] They sent the following letter to 26 car companies:

> "Dear [name of appropriate CEO],
>
> I'm a big believer in advertising. I was a big believer in your company's advertising when I bought my car late last year.
>
> When I drove the car off the lot, I noticed some immediate problems. The salesman said, as he was pushing me out the door, 'Don't worry. Just bring it back and they'll fix it.'
>
> I live 35 minutes from the dealer, and it took three visits just to get the factory foul-ups fixed.
>
> Now, a mysterious 'clunking' sound is coming from the right front wheel. The selling dealer hasn't been able to correct it; the dealer in my neighborhood keeps pushing me back to the original dealer, saying it's not his problem.
>
> My salesman has left the dealership; my warranty expires in two weeks, and I have a car I don't even know is safe to drive.
>
> Should I have believed your ads claiming quality, service, and reliability? I'm beginning to think not.
>
> Can you suggest how I can get my car out of this rut?"[7]

The companies have been presented with a crystal-clear case of complaint management. Offensive marketing has *attracted* a customer, and now defensive marketing must *keep* the customer. Given the very high lifetime value of a car customer, one

FIGURE 7.2

AUTO COMPLAINTS: HOW LONG TO RESPOND?

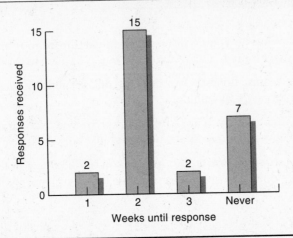

Weeks until response

would expect all of the companies to respond immediately. Figure 7.2, compiled from statistics calculated from the information in the *Advertising Age* article, shows how many companies responded within one week, between one and two weeks, between two and three weeks, and never. Saab and Rolls-Royce were the first to respond. No U.S. company responded until the fourteenth day. Amazingly, seven of the 26 failed to respond altogether! They were: Chrysler, Lincoln-Mercury, Hyundai, Jaguar, Porsche, Subaru, and Toyota.

Apparently things have not gotten much better since then. We recently heard of a woman who had bought a car with an outstanding reputation for quality (we will call it the "Excelsior"), which kept stalling in inopportune and highly dangerous situations. After several months of waiting, corporate headquarters had still not responded to her registered letter requesting a replacement.

Unfortunate Practice #3—Make Them Pay to Complain

If one starts with the unfortunate assumption that complaints are bad, then it is reasonable to want to reduce their number. Improving quality may be an obvious, but difficult, way to reduce complaints. An alternative is to simply make it harder to complain. The ultimate in making it hard to complain is to actually make people pay for complaining!

For example, one software company had a program that was extremely difficult to use and had many problems. As a result, their customer service phone lines became swamped. The company's solution was to set up a subscriber on-line service. Users could ask questions and get complaints resolved, *for a fee*. The company could then feel less guilty about the fact that it was very difficult to reach customer service. In one sense, the needs of the company were served. But in the long run, the company suffers because the needs of the customer are being neglected.

Unfortunate Practice #4—Buy Them Off

Most relatively enlightened companies realize that nothing is gained by ignoring complaints, not responding to complaints, or making complaining more difficult. They realize that retaining the customer is very important because of the lifetime value of the customer, and they try to think of ways to make the customer happy. Usually this is done by making it up to the customer in some way. We refer to this as *"buying the customer off."* Unfortunately, this practice may not have the desired effect on retention.

Several years ago a professor taught a course in marketing research that required the use of a PC statistical package. The package we used was a special student version, which we will refer to as "PC* Pupilware." The problems began when the students, following the manual exactly, got error messages. The software simply would not run. Eventually all of the students in the class, along with the instructor, sent a letter to the software company, requesting a refund. Three months after the semester had ended, the company sent the following form letter to each student:

> Dear [student's first name]:
>
> Professor _____ brought to my attention the fact that you experienced difficulties with PC* Pupilware during the spring term. Unfortunately you encountered several problems that developed with the product, both in terms of its packaging and the documentation. While it may be difficult to prove this point to you given your recent experience, CCCP [not the real company name] prides itself on the level of support it extends to its customers through its products. We have been in the business of producing quality statistical products for over 20 years, and your experience with Pupilware are [*sic*] an exception rather than the rule.
>
> Nevertheless we consider the exception to be an embarrassment, and a situation that should not have occurred. While the problems identified have all been remedied, you are left with a bad experience in your mind. There is nothing that can be done to change that experience, however, I would like to attempt to change your impression of CCCP Inc.
>
> To that end I would like to offer you a CCCP T-shirt in recognition of the trouble you had with the software. I would hope that a T-shirt could help to erase some of the negative experiences you had. . . .

Less foolish examples of buying off the customer are common. If a restaurant doesn't ask you to pay for a meal you found poor, it appears to have responsive service. If a hotel sends a complimentary bottle of wine to make up for problems with the bathtub, that is seemingly considerate. Creatively compensating customers has its place, and is an integral aspect of all successful service guarantees (see Chapter 8). Nevertheless, buying off the customer has an inherent flaw.

Consider what happens when the company engages in this practice. If the company gives something sufficiently meaningful (not a T-shirt), the customer may be appeased. But, what will happen when the customer decides to repurchase? Maybe the customer will remember what nice folks the people at Company X were, and will reward them with business. On the other hand, there is a real danger that this will not take place. The customer was left satisfied not because the company did a good job, but because the company bribed the customer. If the customer thinks about the quality of the job that company did, the perception of the company is still likely to be low. Retention becomes questionable because *the problem was not solved*. When given a choice, the customer may try his luck with another company next time, despite the T-shirt or bottle of wine. Thus it is far better to solve the root problem than it is to compensate for failure.

7.5 PRINCIPLES OF COMPLAINT MANAGEMENT

How does one go about solving the root of the problem? Managerial experience suggests several principles of successful complaint management. These are:

1. Communication links from the front line to the information system
2. Immediate advocacy
3. Authority to settle complaints
4. Responsiveness
5. Not further inconveniencing the customer

We will investigate each of these in turn.

Communications links are invaluable in resolving complaints. For example, through a travel agent one of the authors had arranged for a rental car at a good rate ($25 per day). When he arrived at his destination, he went to the rental counter and asked for his car. The attendant said, "Fine, that will be $35 per day." The author pointed out that he had agreed to *$25* per day. At this point the attendant resorted to her secret weapon, the communication links to the customer database. She was able to show the author that the travel agent had made an error, and exactly how and when the error occurred. This got the rental car company completely off the hook. The problem was between the author and his travel agent. (Interestingly, the author decided not to ask for the difference from the travel agent, because, perceiving himself as the travel agent's customer, he wished to maintain a good relationship rather than creating a problem.)

Another example of the creative use of communication links is the tracking systems that companies like UPS and Federal Express use. At every intermediate location, bar code scanners transmit the package location to central computers. This gives the capability of being able to tell the customer exactly where the package is at any time. Customers need not worry about losing packages and feel reassured about using the service.

Pizza Hut delivery provides another example of using communication links. Whenever a customer places a telephone order, Pizza Hut calls up a computer database, sorted by phone number. The data base includes such information as address, directions, and even previous orders. After hearing about Pizza Hut's system, one executive from another industry said, "If Pizza Hut can do it at a $10 price point, everybody has to do it." Database access, giving all relevant information about a customer, is fast becoming a requirement rather than a competitive advantage.

Immediate advocacy is another important principle. This means that someone from the company is immediately on the customer's side, working to bring about a successful resolution to the complaint. This is not the same as immediate resolution of the problem. Some problems take a long time to solve. However, someone in the company should always represent the complaining customer's interests.

We do not refer to the traditional "Customer Service" department. Usually a small counter staffed by one or two poorly paid and uninformed people, the message is that the rest of the company is not customer service. To see this, try complaining some time about what foods are available at your grocery. If you say this to anyone other than Customer Service, you will be immediately directed to Customer Service. Then Customer Service will smile, thank you for your suggestion, and promise to bring it up with management. Whether they ever do or not is unknown to the customer.

But consider an exception: Whole Foods Market, a chain of natural-foods supermarkets headquartered in Austin, Texas. The Whole Foods approach to complaints and suggestions is that action will be taken on *each one,* and that action will be made known to the store's customers. Their system is low-tech, but effective. They simply post each complaint or suggestion on a bulletin board, along with a description of what they have done in response. Customers have a much more positive attitude about complaining or making suggestions because they know that the store will respond. Of course, suggestions are not always implemented, but each is considered carefully and treated with respect. The store is assuming the role of customer advocate.

Another key principle is the **authority to settle complaints.** The more service-oriented the advanced economies become, the more decentralized complaint resolution becomes. For this reason, and because speed of resolution is important, authority to settle complaints is usually best handled at the front line. For example, American Airlines gives its ticket agents and gate agents broad authority to do just about anything (within reason) to solve a customer's problems. Taking a problem up through channels would simply be too slow. A key to successful delegation of authority is "employee empowerment," which we discuss in greater detail in Chapter 17.

Related to this principle is **responsiveness,** which means that the complaint will be resolved quickly. If the complaint *can't* be resolved quickly, the company must at least communicate this fact to the customer quickly, and indicate exactly what is being done to address the problem. Several of the principles we have discussed so far go hand in hand with responsiveness. For example, the better the communication links and databases the faster the response in many instances. Likewise, an empowered front line tends to have the authority to resolve problems quickly. In general, two things must be done to ensure that the customer considers the company to be responsive, regardless of whether the problem can be solved immediately or not. The company must (1) respond *immediately* to all communications by the customer, preferably by phone, and (2) inform the customer of what is being done to solve the problem and how long it is likely to take.

The final principle of successful complaint management is **don't further inconvenience the customer.** Whenever the organization has made a mistake, it is the organization's sole responsibility to make things right. When this principle is violated, the results can sometimes be comical. One of the authors was attending a meeting in another city, and arrived late at night. Important materials for the next day's presentation were in a checked suitcase. When the suitcase did not arrive, the author waited at the "Customer Service" for about two hours, while the airline tried to track down the suitcase. As it turned out, the suitcase was headed for Boise, instead of Boston, where it should have been. The remainder of the dialog went something like this:

Author: When will I get my suitcase? It's midnight now, and I need my materials for an 8 A.M. presentation.

Attendant: No problem. There's a mail flight arriving from Boise at 4 A.M. You can come out and get it then.

7.6 LEARNING FROM COMPLAINTS

In a large organization there are many complaints over time. These may be sorted, counted, and catalogued to suggest the areas in which the greatest improvement is needed. We can derive some valuable insights using some very simple data analysis and some simple quadrant analysis.

The first step is to obtain a sorted list of all the complaints, grouping similar complaints together. Each type of complaint will now have a count associated with it, reflecting the number of times that complaint occurred. Here is where many managers go wrong. It is tempting to conclude that the most frequent complaint is the most important complaint, and the one that should be addressed first. But some complaints are more serious than others. For example, if an airline passenger complained that there was a gremlin on the wing tearing the engines apart (as was actually depicted on one "Twilight Zone" TV episode) that would presumably be more important than chewing gum wrappers on the floor, even if 1000 people complained about chewing-gum wrappers and only one person complained about the wing-walking gremlin.

Therefore a second step is required. Customers need to be asked which possible complaints have the biggest impact. Each complaint could be rated as to impact on a five-point rating scale, for example, from "very low impact" to "very high impact," or some similar variant. Also, internal records need to be collected as to the effectiveness of resolving complaints. This can be done by recontacting complainers after the fact, and asking whether their complaint was resolved to their satisfaction.

Given the information obtained in the second step, we can now analyze which complaints are most important, and how complaint resolution resources should be allocated. Figure 7.3 shows a quadrant analysis for determining the importance of complaints. First, the complaints are divided into low and high impact and low and high frequency. (A more accurate way to do this would be to plot specific complaints as points determined by average impact and frequency.) The upper-right quadrant reflects frequent problems of high impact. These are the most important problems to solve immediately. The upper-left quadrant, high frequency and low impact, may be important. The many small problems may add up to a big problem. The lower-right quadrant, low frequency and high impact, also may be important. These problems are very important to some people. The lower-left quadrant may be ignored, because the problems are unimportant and infrequent.

FIGURE 7.3

IMPORTANCE OF COMPLAINTS

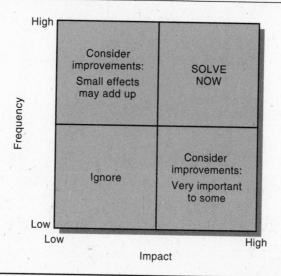

Given the analysis from Figure 7.3, we may then construct Figure 7.4 to address the issue of resource allocation. Dividing the complaints into high and low importance and poor and good resolution (again we could simply plot the points if we chose), the upper-right quadrant of Figure 7.4 represents important complaints that we do a good job of resolving. That is appropriate. Likewise the lower-left quadrant represents problems of low importance that we are not so good at resolving. The problems are relatively unimportant, so effectiveness is not critical. No change is required. On the other hand, the lower-right quadrant represents unimportant problems that we are good at resolving. We may be able to de-emphasize these, if we are spending more than we have to. The upper-left quadrant is where the freed-up money should go. These are problems of high importance that are not being dealt with very well. Our strongest initiatives should be to strengthen this area.

7.7 PROBLEM IMPACT TREE ANALYSIS

So far we have discussed why complaint management is important, how to respond to a complaint, and how to determine which complaints are most important. Now we present an approach for evaluating the complaint resolution process itself and for determining which elements demand the most emphasis. The framework we use is an impact tree,[8] an approach that has been successfully applied at a number of companies.

Figure 7.5 shows the branches of the problem impact tree. Each branch represents the possible outcomes of a customer contact. Either the customer experiences no problem (good), or experiences a problem (bad). If the customer does experience a problem, then the customer either complains (good) or doesn't complain (bad). If the customer doesn't complain, then there is no opportunity to resolve the problem.

FIGURE 7.4

COMPLAINT RESOURCE ALLOCATION

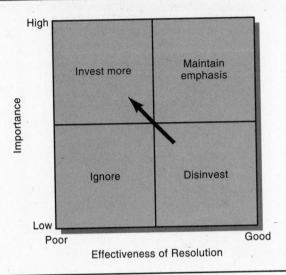

FIGURE 7.5

THE PROBLEM IMPACT TREE

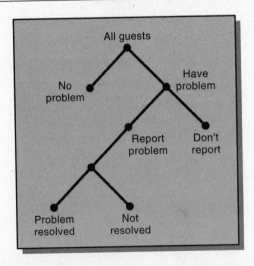

Source: From Roland T. Rust, Bala Subramanian, and Mark Wells (1992), "Making Complaints a Management Tool," *Marketing Management,* 1 (3), pp. 40–45.

If the customer complains, then the problem is either resolved successfully by the company (good) or not (bad).

A problem impact tree analysis is conducted quarterly for all Promus Company (Hampton Inns, Embassy Suites, and Homewood Suites) hotels. The Promus Companies routinely collect data that may be used to determine how many people fall into each category. Their technique involves sending out mail questionnaires to a large sample of customers shortly after these customers have checked out of the hotel. Promus asks, as part of a general customer survey, whether the customer had experienced a problem or not, and, if so, whether or not it was reported, and whether or not it was satisfactorily resolved. Example percentages are given in Figure 7.6. (These numbers are disguised, to protect proprietary interests, but the general pattern of results is preserved.) We see that in this instance 75% of all guests had no problem. Of the 25% who did, only half complained, and 70% of complaints were successfully resolved. From these numbers we can make several useful observations. First, a very high percentage of people with problems do not complain, which removes any possibility of resolving the problem. Also, only 70% of complaints result in successful resolution, which may indicate that problem resolution is not particularly successful.

A further indication of the importance of problem resolution is the large differences in summary measures, such as satisfaction and repurchase intention. Figure 7.7 shows the percentage of people responding in the top two boxes of a five-point customer satisfaction scale, and Figure 7.8 shows the percentage who say they intend to repurchase. We see that if there is no problem, then 95% are satisfied and 95% intend to return. This is very good. On the other hand, among customers who

FIGURE 7.6

COMPLAINT MANAGEMENT RESOLUTION PERFORMANCE

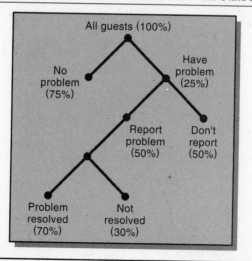

Source: From Roland T. Rust, Bala Subramanian, and Mark Wells (1992), "Making Complaints a Management Tool," *Marketing Management,* 1 (3), pp. 40–45.

FIGURE 7.7

COMPLAINT MANAGEMENT AND CUSTOMER SATISFACTION

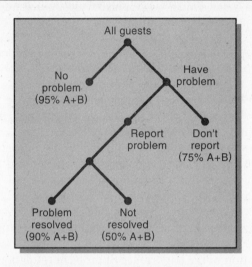

Source: From Roland T. Rust, Bala Subramanian, and Mark Wells (1992), "Making Complaints a Management Tool," *Marketing Management,* 1 (3), pp. 40–45.

FIGURE 7.8

COMPLAINT MANAGEMENT AND REPURCHASE INTENTIONS

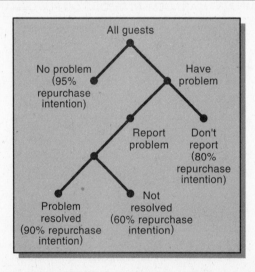

Source: From Roland T. Rust, Bala Subramanian, and Mark Wells (1992), "Making Complaints a Management Tool," *Marketing Management,* 1 (3), pp. 40–45.

experience a problem but don't report it, only 75% are satisfied and only 80% intend to return. This is a big dropoff.

What happens if the customer complains? If the customer complains, and the complaint is resolved, then 90% are satisfied and 90% intend to return. This is almost as good as not having a problem in the first place! On the other hand if a complaint is not resolved, then satisfaction and repurchase plummet. Only 50% are satisfied, and only 60% intend to repurchase. The conclusion is that if a complaint is made, it is very important to resolve it successfully.

We can use the problem impact tree to analyze the value of complaint resolution outcomes, by incorporating the lifetime value of the customer (see Section 7.3). Let us suppose that the lifetime value of a returning customer, in terms of the net present value of future profits, and ignoring word-of-mouth effects (to make things simple), is $200, and suppose that the numbers in Figures 7.6 and 7.8 apply. What is the value of avoiding a problem in the first place? The leftmost branch ("No Problem") has a 95% repurchase rate. Multiplying this by $200 gives an expected value of $190 for a customer in this branch. Now we need to find the repurchase rate for the other side of the tree. This is obtained as a weighted average of the three possible outcomes. The calculation is:

$$\text{Average retention rate} = (.5 \times .7 \times .9) + (.5 \times .3 \times .6) + (.5 \times .8) = 80.5\%$$

Then the expected value of the right side of the tree is $80.5\% \times \$200 = \$161$. This is $29 less than the expected value if there is no problem. Thus it is worth $29 per customer for the company to avoid a problem in the first place. This is quite a lot. Consider for example that the company could justify more than three hours of a $9-per-hour employee to avoid a problem!

We might also consider the value of resolving a problem, given that a complaint has been made. The expected value of the "Problem Resolved" branch is $90\% \times \$200 = \$180$, and the expected value of the "Not Resolved" branch is $60\% \times \$200 = \$120$. Notice that it is worth $\$180 - \$120 = \$60$ to resolve a problem. Notice also that this is more than *six hours* of a $9-per-hour employee, just to resolve one customer's complaint! The company can profit by pampering a complaining customer quite a bit, based solely on the value of future repurchases. Of course, if we factor in the word-of-mouth effect, the numbers get even more impressive.

Another issue is how much we gain from having a customer report a problem. From Figure 7.8 it is easy to calculate the expected value of a customer who has an unreported problem. The value is $80\% \times \$200 = \$160$. Calculating the expected value of a customer who has a problem and reports it involves a weighted average across the "Problem Resolved" and "Not Resolved" branches, using the numbers in Figure 7.6 and Figure 7.8. The value is $70\% \times 90\% \times \$200$ plus $30\% \times 60\% \times \$200$, which equals $162. This is not much more than the value of a nonreporting customer, mostly because 30% of complaints are not successfully resolved. From these numbers it appears that the immediate concern of the company is to resolve a higher percentage of complaints rather than encouraging more complaints. As the percentage of resolved complaints increases, it will then become more important to encourage more complaints.

7.8 SUMMARY

Defensive marketing, the retention of existing customers rather than the attraction of new customers, is increasingly important as the advanced economies become more service-oriented. Defensive marketing activities are justified by the lifetime value of a customer, which is often much larger than one might suspect. Lifetime value arises from future purchases, referrals, and avoiding negative word of mouth.

Complaint management is one of the most direct methods of practicing defensive marketing, because a complaint is a crisis that can result in a large swing in satisfaction and repurchase intention. Unfortunately, there are many companies that still do not understand the value of intelligent complaint management, and many bad business practices exist. Progressive companies manage complaints according to several useful managerial principles, including communication links between the customer database and frontline employees, immediate customer advocacy, authority to settle complaints, responsiveness, and not further inconveniencing the customer.

Smart companies also analyze both complaint data and complaint resolution data. Analyzing complaint data can suggest which are the most important complaints, and to which complaints the most resources should be allocated. Analyzing complaint resolution data is easily managed using the problem impact tree, which yields such insights as the value of problem avoidance, the value of problem resolution, and the value of problem reporting.

REVIEW QUESTIONS

1. A bank wishes to calculate the value of an average customer. The average number of years a customer stays in the market is 10 years, the profit per year starts at $200 per year and increases by $20 per year, and the bank's discount rate is 10%. What is the lifetime value of the average customer?
2. Think of the last time you experienced a problem with a product or service. Did you complain? If not, why not? What would have persuaded you to complain?
3. Think of the last time you complained about a product or service. Was the problem resolved to your satisfaction? Did the company employ any of the "Unfortunate Practices" discussed in Section 7.4?
4. When was the last time you were really impressed with a company's response to your complaint? What did they do right?
5. A car dealer has collected problem impact tree data from customer surveys, and they show that 60% of all customers have no problem. Of those who have a problem only 10% complain, and 90% of all complaints are resolved successfully. The average lifetime value of a returning customer is $5000, including word-of-mouth effects. Customers who don't experience a problem

have a 90% repurchase rate, those with resolved problems have an 85% repurchase rate, complainers with unresolved problems have a 60% repurchase rate, and nonreporters have a 70% repurchase rate. What is the value of avoiding a problem? What is the value of resolving a problem? What is the value of having a customer report a problem?

ENDNOTES

1. Claes Fornell and Birger Wernerfelt (1987), "Defensive Marketing Strategy by Customer Complaint Management: A Theoretical Analysis," *Journal of Marketing Research,* 24 (November), 337–346.
2. Marsha L. Richins (1987), "A Multivariate Analysis of Responses to Dissatisfaction," *Journal of the Academy of Marketing Science,* 15 (Fall), 24–31.
3. TARP (1979), *Consumer Complaint Handling in America: Final Report,* Washington, DC: The Office of Consumer Affairs.
4. Ron Zemke (1989), " Delivering Managed Service," in *Designing a Winning Service Strategy,* Mary Jo Bitner and Lawrence A. Crosby, eds., Chicago: American Marketing Association.
5. TARP (1979), *op. cit.*
6. Therese Kauchak (1991), "A Little Service, Please!" *Advertising Age,* January 21, S8–S10.
7. *Ibid.*
8. Roland T. Rust, Bala Subramanian, and Mark Wells (1992), "Making Complaints a Management Tool," *Marketing Management,* 1 (3), 40–45.

Chapter 8

SERVICE GUARANTEES

8.1 OVERVIEW

With a product warranty the company typically agrees to replace or repair the product. But it is often very difficult or impossible to replace or repair a service, both because of the intangible nature of many services and because the delivery of a service is often transitory. For many years, products have routinely offered warranties to ensure proper performance for a reasonable length of time. The satisfaction guarantee is an extension of the warranty concept to service. Satisfaction guarantees often must be more creative than product warranties in execution. Some offer money back, some offer free future services; a wide variety of compensations are possible. This topic also opens up a new world of opportunity for products. In general, satisfaction guarantees are also useful for products, especially products that involve a large service component.

Much of this chapter's material relies upon the pathbreaking insights of Christopher Hart, the acknowledged leading expert in the field of satisfaction guarantees. We will especially examine one of the most successful proponents of Hart's methods, Hampton Inn. We will see that successful satisfaction guarantees have several characteristics. We will investigate why a guarantee works, and explore some of its drawbacks. We will also see that a successful guarantee can be surprisingly profitable.

8.2 EXAMPLES OF SUCCESSFUL SATISFACTION GUARANTEES

Many companies have used satisfaction guarantees to great advantage. We will look at two of them: Hampton Inn and Delta Dental Plan of Massachusetts. Figure 8.1 reproduces the Hampton Inn 100% Satisfaction Guarantee. Note how short and easy to understand it is. One of the problems with product warranties has always been that when a company's legal staff inserts legal jargon and loopholes, customers are less inclined to trust warranty protection. This makes the product warranties less effective as a marketing tool.

The Hampton Inn guarantee is not an afterthought. It is a key strategic move by the parent, Promus Companies, who have now implemented guarantees in all of their

FIGURE 8.1

THE HAMPTON INN 100% SATISFACTION GUARANTEE

Source: "Hampton Inn 100% Satisfaction Guarantee, Research Justifying the Guarantee" by Promus Companies. Reprinted by permission.

hotel brands. According to Promus CEO Michael Rose, an unconditional money-back guarantee is the "ultimate point of differentiation. The company can set standards of excellence and train personnel to meet them, hence it becomes the tool by which a service culture is molded within the organization and success is measured on a daily basis."[1] It is no coincidence that the name of the company sounds like "promise." The entire company is based on service quality and customer satisfaction.

The idea is that in mature markets all competitors can eventually match each other on product. Thus special aspects of service, such as a satisfaction guarantee, are required to differentiate the firm in the marketplace. Promus's Hampton Inn guarantee, now extended to their Embassy Suites and Homewood Suites, gave the company market momentum. Competitors are now starting to institute similar guarantees to keep up.

Another good example is Delta Dental Care, a dental insurance company from Massachusetts. Their guarantee is shown in Figure 8.2. This guarantee is more detailed than that from the Hampton Inn. It has the disadvantage of being harder for a customer to read and understand, but it has the advantage of being quite specific about exactly what is promised and exactly what the customer will receive if the promise is not met.

Many groups within the company resisted the Delta Dental Plan service guarantee. The marketing group was concerned about the effectiveness of using the guarantee in advertising. The legal group was concerned about losses from the guarantee and wanted to be sure the language of the guarantee adequately protected the

FIGURE 8.2

THE DELTA DENTAL GUARANTEE OF SERVICE EXCELLENCE

Delta Dental Plan of Massachusetts is committed to providing the highest level of service to all its customers. To that end we have instituted a program we are calling the "Guarantee Of Service Excellence." It is our belief that when our people are inspired to seek excellence in servicing our customers, all those who share in Delta Dental Plan of Massachusetts will benefit. To underscore our commitment, we are guaranteeing major areas of service as outlined below and backed by our comprehensive refund policy.

1. The Service: Minimum 10 Percent Savings over the Course of Each Policy Year. These savings reflect the total dollar value of dentists' usual and stated fees, which are not balance billed back to patients.

The Refund: Monetary credit given to the group equal to the difference between 10 percent and the lesser amount actually saved.

2. The Service: No-Hassle Customer Relations. Delta Dental Plan will either resolve your question immediately over the phone or we guarantee you an initial update within one business day and continuous follow-up through resolution.

The Refund: $50 paid to the group per occurrence.

3. The Service: Quick Processing of Claims. Over the course of a policy year, 85 percent of the group's claims will be processed accurately within fifteen calendar days upon receipt of completed claim forms.

The Refund: The administrative fee charged for the group's last month of service.

4. The Service: Smooth Conversion as Defined by the Group. The criteria for each group's successful conversion to Delta Dental Plan is based upon a checklist that is mutually determined between the group and Delta Dental Plan.

The Refund: The administrative fee charged for the group's second month of service.

5. The Service: No Balance Billing of Patients by Participating Dentists. Patients who receive treatment for covered services from a participating Massachusetts dentist will not be inappropriately billed.

The Refund: The group will be reimbursed $50 per occurrence.

6. The Service: Accurate and Quick Turnaround of ID Cards. A complete and accurate identification card for each subscriber will be mailed to the group within fifteen calendar days.

The Refund: $25 paid to the group per ID card.

7. The Service: Management Reports. At the group's request, four standard reports (claims report, cost containment report, and two utilization reports) will be mailed to the group within ten calendar days following the end of each month.

The Refund: $50 per late package paid to the group.

Source: Thomas Raffio (1992), "Quality and Delta Dental Plan of Massachusetts," *Sloan Management Review,* 34 (Fall), pp. 101–110. Copyright © 1992 by Thomas Raffio. Reprinted by permission of Sloan Management Review.

company's interests. (It is a common theme for a legal department not to have a customer-oriented viewpoint.) Almost everyone wondered whether a service guarantee would really work in an insurance company.

Delta's experience has been very positive[2] and the benefits are seen to outweigh the payouts. Benefits from the guarantee have included:

1. More input to the quality improvement program[3]
2. More success in attracting new customers
3. Improved retention of existing accounts

All of these benefits have been documented statistically.

8.3 SATISFACTION GUARANTEES THAT HAVE NOT WORKED

We will give some examples of guarantees we think could be improved, at the risk of offending the cited companies. Let us begin with the guarantee provided by Tune Up Plus, an automotive service company. The guarantee states that "TUNE UP PLUS guarantees all parts and services for a period of 6 months or 6,000 miles . . ." and "Services will be performed or parts will be replaced as needed. . . ", but the customer must first sign an authorization that includes the language that "TUNE UP PLUS assumes no liability whatsoever for theft or any type of damage to the vehicle or its contents." The guarantee itself is not bad; most people can read it, it is fairly clear about what it covers, and explains what will be done. The problem arises in the authorization for service, which is on the same sheet of paper, and which the customer must sign. What good is a guarantee if "TUNE UP PLUS assumes no liability whatsoever for theft or any type of damage to the vehicle or its contents?" In other words, if the repair people damage your car or steal something inside, too bad. The nice-sounding guarantee has a loophole a mile wide.

Another example is Lufthansa Airlines, who guarantee that "if you have a confirmed reservation in first or business class on a transatlantic flight, you're guaranteed seating in that class."[4,5] The benefit of this guarantee is hard to see because the guarantee promises no more than the confirmed reservation does. Lufthansa also guarantees that passengers will be on time for their connecting flights, *unless the delay results from problems with weather or air traffic control.*[6] Unfortunately, most delays occur for precisely these reasons, and thus the customer is unlikely to find this guarantee to be very meaningful.

8.4 CHARACTERISTICS OF A GOOD GUARANTEE

From the preceding examples we begin to see the differences between good and bad guarantees. Hart summarizes these into five main characteristics of a good satisfaction guarantee.[7] A good guarantee is: unconditional, easy to understand, meaningful, easy to invoke, and easy to collect.

When a guarantee is **unconditional,** customers take it more seriously. If a guarantee applies only to left-handed people on Friday in a leap year when there is a full moon, few customers will be very interested. By comparison, consider the Hampton Inn guarantee. It says simply, "If you're not completely satisfied, we don't expect you to pay." This is unconditional and you don't need to be a lawyer to understand it. A guarantee loses power as conditions are placed on it. Consider the Lufthansa on-time guarantee, for example. The conditions exempted 95% of the cases to which it might be applied, reducing its effectiveness by at least that percentage.

A good guarantee is **easy to understand.** If the customer does not understand the guarantee, then that customer will not see any benefit. For maximum effectiveness, the guarantee should be specific. For example, Domino's Pizza guaranteed delivery in 30 minutes. That is much better than guaranteeing "fast delivery," which is hard to pin down.

A good guarantee is **meaningful.** The guarantee must be about things that customers care about. A fast-food restaurant guaranteeing 10-minute service at lunch will probably do better than one guaranteeing to address customers by their first name. This is because fast service at lunch is important to fast-food customers, whereas personal familiarity is not.

A good guarantee is **easy to invoke.** Let us consider the Hampton Inn guarantee, for example. Suppose the customer's air conditioning did not work on a hot summer night, and the problem was not repaired, in spite of bringing it to the management's attention. For the guarantee to be effective, management should make that night free, without waiting for the customer to ask. If it is clear that the customer is dissatisfied, and the problem has not been solved, then management should invoke the guarantee itself.

In most cases, management does not really trust the guarantee, and therefore puts up barriers to invoking it. Management may be concerned about loss of revenues, which may be linked to management compensation. This creates a natural tension between the intended corporate culture, as desired by top management, and the actual corporate culture, as implemented by middle management and the front line. Counteracting an employee's natural reluctance to invoke or carry out the guarantee requires careful training.

A good guarantee should also be **easy to collect;** that is, the remedy should be supplied immediately. For example, a dissatisfied customer at Hampton Inn should receive an immediate credit for the price of the dissatisfying service. The customer should not have to drive across town to obtain payment, nor should the customer have to fill out a laborious form or accumulate a tedious amount of documentation.

A guarantee with the above characteristics is likely to be effective. But exactly why does a guarantee work? What are the benefits, direct and indirect? These questions are explored in the next section.

8.5 WHY A GUARANTEE WORKS

A satisfaction guarantee may appear to be primarily altruistic, but in fact it has a positive effect on the bottom line in several important ways, both indirectly and directly. Indirectly, the guarantee creates more employee sensitivity to the issue of quality. This generates a higher level of quality, which in turn generates greater customer retention as well as increased customer attraction through positive word of mouth (see Figure 8.3). The direct effects include successful advertising through use of the guarantee and improved retention of those successfully invoking the guarantee.

FIGURE 8.3

INDIRECT BENEFITS OF A SATISFACTION GUARANTEE

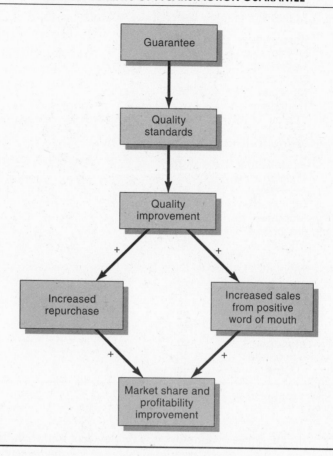

Effect on Employees

Executives at companies employing a strong service guarantee say that the biggest impact of the guarantee derives from its effect on employees. This effect manifests itself in several ways, which have been previously noted by Hart.[8] It causes employees to **focus on customers.** Organizations frequently make the mistake of defining quality only by objective standards or internal measures.[9] A satisfaction guarantee quickly makes it very clear that the only true measure is what the customer thinks.

When the customer determines quality, management must learn as quickly as possible what level of performance will be good enough to avoid causing the guarantee to be invoked. This results in **customer-derived standards** of quality, that the organization may then use as a minimal target of performance. If these standards are not met, the guarantee generates immediate feedback about where the organization's efforts are insufficient. Responding to this feedback and analyzing where the system breaks down forces the company to understand failure.

FIGURE 8.4

THE EFFECT OF A GUARANTEE ON EMPLOYEES: HAMPTON INN

Percent Saying It Makes Company a Better Place to Work

Housekeeper	82
Maintenance	61
Front desk	73
Night auditor	73
Manager	66
Franchisee	62
Total	69

Percent Saying It Motivates Them to Do a Better Job

Housekeeper	93
Maintenance	90
Front desk	87
Night auditor	90
Manager	88
Franchisee	73
Total	90

Percent Saying It Motivates Others to Do a Better Job

Housekeeper	95
Maintenance	88
Front desk	93
Night auditor	95
Manager	90
Franchisee	80
Total	93

Source: The Promus Companies

The effect of the guarantee on employees is very evident to the employees themselves. Hampton Inn surveyed their employees to determine the perceived effects of their 100% satisfaction guarantee. Figure 8.4 shows that 69% of the employees sampled indicated that the guarantee made the company a better place to work, with the housekeepers being the most positive. Not surprisingly, the franchisees were the least positive, presumably because guarantee payouts would appear to be a direct drain on their revenues. Figure 8.4 shows that an even higher percentage of employees, 90% on average, say that the guarantee motivates *them* to do a better job, and an even higher percentage say that it motivates *others* to do a better job. Again, the franchisees are the least convinced.

Effect on Advertising

The guarantee also makes for very **effective advertising.**[10] In an effort to differentiate itself in the marketplace, Hampton Inn made the guarantee central to its advertising. Advertising a strong guarantee projects an image of quality; presumably a company with poor service could not afford to make the number of payouts that would inevitably be required. Advertising the guarantee is also effective because the guarantee reduces customer risk.[11] In other words the customer cannot have a completely unsatisfactory outcome if the guarantee is in effect because the customer will either be satisfied or will get compensation from the guarantee. Decreasing customer risk is particularly important in services, because most services are perceived to be higher in social and psychological risk than the typical product.[12,13]

8.6 WHEN IS A GUARANTEE NOT A GOOD IDEA?

Although the advantages of a satisfaction guarantee are considerable, *a guarantee is not for every company*. Hart[14] points out several reasons a guarantee can backfire. For example, a firm may be **top quality** to the point that a guarantee is essentially implied. The recognized quality leader in an industry whose employees are broadly empowered to solve customer problems might not need a satisfaction guarantee. That is because the company already acts as if it has a guarantee anyway, and the customers know it. For example, Vanderbilt's Owen School runs executive seminars on customer satisfaction measurement and service quality. Occasionally an attendee indicates dissatisfaction with the program. In every case the tuition is promptly refunded or free admission to another seminar of the attendee's choice is provided. Customers simply expect this level of assurance from these seminars. A guarantee might be superfluous and might detract from the previously unquestioned high-quality image of the program by unnecessarily creating doubts about quality.

For other companies, **low quality** makes a guarantee impossible. Suppose half of the customers demanded their money back. How could the company stay in business? The only way poor-service providers can have a guarantee is if it is written in legalese to the extent that nobody can actually invoke it, or is written so vaguely that it does not promise anything. Our favorite is signs which proudly proclaim "100% satisfaction guaranteed!" or, even better, "110% satisfaction guaranteed!!" What does the customer do with such a proclamation? Nothing is promised. If you want to have fun some time, the next time you see such a sign, tell a service provider that you are only 85% satisfied and would like to invoke the guarantee. They will assume that you are joking.

Sometimes low quality is not a problem, but service delivery is still erratic because of **uncontrollable variables.** Suppose, for example, the Denver airport wanted to guarantee air passengers that their planes would leave on time. That would not be feasible, because many of the variables that might cause late departure (snow, airline mechanical problems, etc.) are beyond the airport's control. If the airport wanted to guarantee satisfaction, it could guarantee things that *were* within its control, such as adequate parking and clean rest rooms.

For some companies, a guarantee would not be possible because of **excessive cheating.** Actually this is much less of a problem than most people would suspect, as will be discussed in the next section. Nevertheless, in some circumstances this may be a problem. Consider, for example, what would happen if a satisfaction guarantee was offered by a prison. Imagine something like, "If you are not completely satisfied with your cell and food, we don't expect you to stay." Under those circumstances the incentive to cheat would be too great.

8.7 CHEATING

Probably the biggest reason more companies don't offer service guarantees is that management is concerned too many people will cheat and the payouts will become intolerable. However, the experience of companies that have instituted strong service guarantees indicates that these fears are mostly groundless. In fact, the likelihood of an individual actually invoking a guarantee is fairly small.

In Hampton Inn's case, only about one customer in 400 actually invokes the guarantee. Hampton Inn also has a sophisticated computer system that enables them to track whether there are repeat users (and, by implication, abusers) of the guarantee. Once the company discovered that one individual had invoked the guarantee several times in a row. But when they investigated further, they found that the customer actually had a legitimate reason every time. Hampton Inn's experience has found very few cheaters.

8.8 FINANCIAL IMPACT

One of the amazing facts about satisfaction guarantees is that the direct financial impact is large, and that *a guarantee can be very profitable*. The mechanisms by which a guarantee may directly impact profits are shown in Figure 8.5. We see that

FIGURE 8.5

DIRECT FINANCIAL IMPACT OF A SATISFACTION GUARANTEE

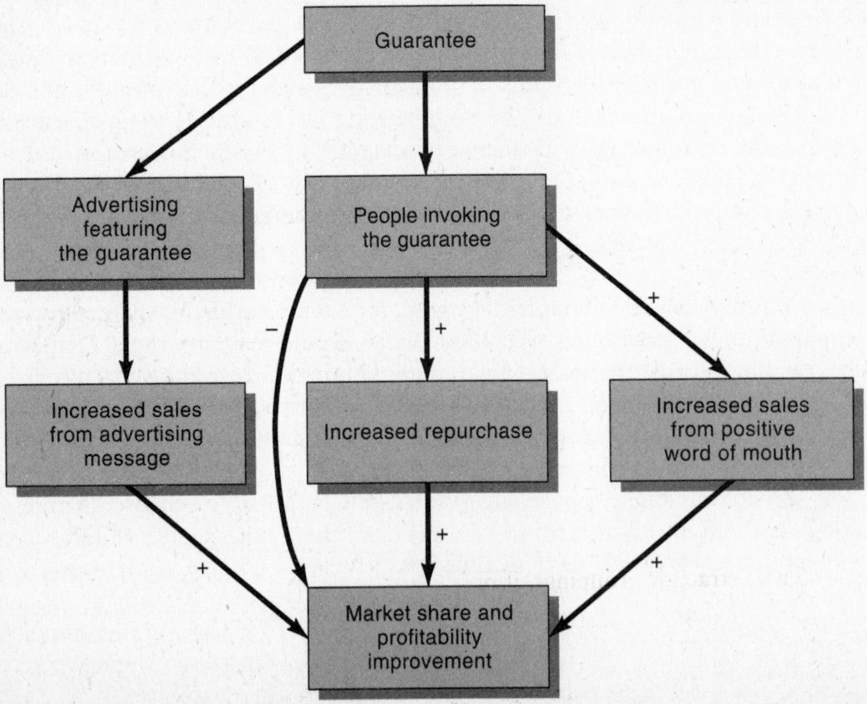

advertising is more effective, which attracts more customers, people invoking the guarantee come back when they might not have, and positive word of mouth from the customers who invoke the guarantee attract still more customers.

Let us walk through some example calculations of the direct profitability of a guarantee. (These calculations are similar to those Hampton Inn has done, but the numbers are disguised to protect proprietary interests.) Let us suppose that 1% of all customers were attracted by the guarantee, and that there were 10 million paid room nights in a year, at an average contribution of $20 per room, on a $50 average room rate. This yields an additional contribution of 1% × 10 million × $20 = $200,000 per year. If one person in 200 (.5%) invokes the guarantee, the lost revenue is .5% × 10 million × $50 = $2.5 million. So far this deal looks like a bad one, because we are down $2.3 million.

Now suppose that without a guarantee 20% of those who are dissatisfied would not return. This 20% is lured back by successfully invoking the guarantee, at an average lifetime contribution of $150. The gain to the hotel is .5% × 10 million × 20% × $150 = $1.5 million. Suppose also that each person who invokes the guarantee has a 20% chance of persuading a new customer to visit the hotel chain, again at an average lifetime value of $150. The benefit is .5% × 10 million × 20% × $150 = $1.5 million. Adding up the positive effects, we have $200,000 from advertising + $1.5 million from returning customers + $1.5 million from customers attracted by word of mouth = $3.2 million. This is much better than the $2.5 million outlay, and does not even include the indirect effects, including the heightened quality culture and its resulting benefits.

8.9 LESSONS FROM THE HAMPTON INN GUARANTEE

Promus Companies' executives have learned a great deal from their experience with the Hampton Inn guarantee. They have distilled their knowledge into 11 practical tips:[15]

1. Focus on customer needs—these drive the invoking of the guarantee.
2. KISS (Keep it simple, stupid)—otherwise the customer won't use it.
3. Deep management conviction is fundamental.
4. Empowerment is key.
5. Train, train, train. Reinforce, reinforce, reinforce.
6. Perpetuate stories of the guarantee in action.
7. Understand the moments of truth. Service failures come from them.
8. Teach customers to complain.
9. Develop tracking systems.
10. Give regular feedback on reasons the guarantee was invoked.
11. Use internal guarantees to support the external guarantees.

These tips are the result of years of experience by perhaps the leading company in service guarantees.

8.10 SUMMARY

Satisfaction guarantees (alternatively, and roughly equivalently called "service guarantees") are a powerful tool for ensuring quality service. They provide assurance to customers and quality standards for service providers. In spite of popular belief, cheaters do not often take advantage of the system, and great benefits are possible. Profits are boosted because of the quality image projected by advertising the guarantee, repeat business from those who invoke the guarantee, and business referred by those who have invoked the guarantee. Most important, the service guarantee establishes a proud quality culture, in which breakdowns are viewed as unacceptable. While not appropriate for every business, service guarantees provide an excellent opportunity for many businesses.

REVIEW QUESTIONS

1. Find an example of a service guarantee in the local Yellow Pages. Evaluate whether it possesses the characteristics of a good guarantee. If it is lacking in one or more areas, rewrite the guarantee appropriately.
2. Think of a company in your community that should not offer a guarantee. Why not? What would they have to do before a guarantee became plausible?
3. Suppose you collect the following data about a restaurant's 100% satisfaction guarantee: there are 5000 diners per year; the average bill is $40, with a contribution of $25; 2% of the customers of the restaurant came because of the guarantee; 1% of all customers invoke the guarantee and of those who invoke the guarantee 30% return who otherwise would not have; the lifetime value of a returning customer averages $150; and each customer who invokes the guarantee on average persuades .5 people to come to the restaurant who would not have come otherwise. Is the guarantee profitable for this restaurant?

ENDNOTES

1. Michael D. Rose (1990), "No Strings Attached," *Chief Executive*, 60 (July-August), 30–33.
2. Delta's experience with the guarantee is chronicled in a 1992 journal article: Robert E. Hunter and Thomas Raffio (1992), "Implementing Service Guarantees—The Delta Dental Plan Study," *Sloan Management Review*, 33 (Spring), 21–22.
3. Thomas Raffio (1992), "Quality and Delta Dental Plan of Massachusetts," *Sloan Management Review*, 34 (Fall), 101–110.
4. James L. Heskett, W. Earl Sasser, Jr., and Christopher W. L. Hart (1990), *Service Breakthroughs*, New York: Free Press, p. 91.
5. Lufthansa Airlines (1987), advertisement in the *Wall Street Journal*, March 9.
6. Christopher W. L. Hart (1988), "The Power of Unconditional Service Guarantees," *Harvard Business Review*, 66 (July-August), 54–62.
7. *Ibid.*
8. *Ibid.*

9. Raymond E. Kordupleski, Roland T. Rust, and Anthony J. Zahorik (1993), "Why Improving Quality Doesn't Improve Quality (Or Whatever Happened to Marketing?)," *California Management Review,* 35 (Spring), 82–95.

10. Dick Berry (1983), "Warranty, Extended Warranty, and Maintenance Agreements: A Marketing Perspective," Chicago: National Association of Service Managers.

11. William R. George, Marc Weinberger, and J. Patrick Kelly (1985), "Consumer Risk Perceptions: Managerial Tool for the Service Encounter," in *The Service Encounter,* John A. Czepiel, Michael R. Solomon, and Carol F. Surprenant, eds., Lexington, MA: Lexington Books, 83–100.

12. W. Lewis (1976), "An Empirical Investigation of the Conceptual Relationship between Services and Products in Terms of Perceived Risk," unpublished Ph.D. dissertation, University of Cincinnati.

13. Dennis S. Guseman (1981), "Risk Perception and Risk Reduction in Consumer Services," in *Marketing of Services,* James H. Donnelly and William R. George, eds., Chicago: American Marketing Association, 200–204.

14. Hart (1988), *op. cit.*

15. From Bala Subramanian, director of corporate research at the Promus Companies.

THE CUSTOMER COMPLAINT LETTER (A)

Following are two actual pieces of correspondence with only names and places changed. They provide an example of how the proprietor of a restaurant dealt with a justifiably angry and disappointed customer.

THE COMPLAINT LETTER

October 13, 1986

123 Main Street
Boston, Massachusetts

Gail and Harvey Pearson
The Retreat House on Foliage Pond
Vacationland, New Hampshire

Dear Mr. and Mrs. Pearson:
This is the first time that I have ever written a letter like this, but my wife and I are so upset by the treatment afforded by your staff, that we felt compelled to let you know what happened to us. We had dinner reservations at the Retreat House for a party of four under my wife's name, Dr. Elaine Loflin, for Saturday evening, October 11. We were hosting my wife's brother and his wife, visiting from Atlanta, Georgia.

We were seated at 7:00 p.m. in the dining room to the left of the front desk. There were at least four empty tables in the room when we were seated. We were immediately given menus, a wine list, ice-water, dinner rolls and butter. Then we sat for 15 minutes until the cocktail waitress asked us for our drink orders. My sister-in-law said after being asked what she would like, "I'll have a vodka martini straight-up with an olive." The cocktail waitress responded immediately, "I'm not a stenographer." My sister-in-law repeated her drink order.

Soon after our waiter arrived, informing us of the specials of the evening. I don't remember his name, but he had dark hair, wore glasses, was a little stocky, and had his sleeves rolled up. He returned about 10 minutes later, our drinks still not having arrived. We had not decided upon our entrees, but requested appetizers, at which time he informed us that we could not order appetizers without ordering our entrees at the same time. We decided not to order our appetizers.

Our drinks arrived and the waiter returned. We ordered our entrees at 7:30. When the waiter asked my wife for her order, he addressed her as "young lady." When he served her the meal, he called her "dear."

At ten minutes of eight we requested that our salads be brought to us as soon as possible. I then asked the waiter's assistant to bring us more rolls (each of us had been served one when we were seated). Her response was, "Who wants a roll", upon which , caught off guard, we went round the table saying yes or no so she would know exactly how many "extra" rolls to bring to our table.

Our salads were served at five minutes of eight. At twenty-five minutes past the hour we requested our entrees. They were served at 8:30, one and one-half hours after we were seated in a restaurant which was one-third empty. Let me also add that we had to make constant requests for water refills, butter replacement and the like.

In fairness to the chef, the food was excellent, and as you already realize, the atmosphere delightful. Despite this, the dinner was a disaster. We were extremely upset and very insulted by the experience. Your staff is not well trained. They were overtly rude, and displayed little etiquette or social grace. This was compounded by the atmosphere you are trying to present and the prices you charge in your dining room.

Perhaps we should have made our feelings known at the time, but our foremost desire was to leave as soon as possible. We had been looking forward to dining at the Retreat House for quite some time as part of our vacation weekend in New Hampshire.

We will be hard-pressed to return to your establishment. Please be sure to know that we will share our experience at the Retreat House with our family, friends, and business associates.

Sincerely,

Dr. William E. Loflin

THE RESPONSE

November 15, 1986

The Retreat House on Foliage Pond
Vacationland, New Hampshire

Dr. William E. Loflin
123 Main Street
Boston, Massachusetts

Dear Dr. Loflin:

My husband and I are naturally distressed by such a negative reaction to our restaurant, but very much appreciate your taking the time and trouble to apprise us recently after dining here. I perfectly understand and sympathize with your feelings, and would like to tell you a little about the circumstances involved.

The Lakes Region for the past 4-5 years has been notorious for its extremely low unemployment rate and resulting deplorable labor pool. This year local businesses found that the situation had deteriorated to a really alarming nadir. It has been virtually impossible to get adequate help, competent or otherwise! We tried to overhire at the beginning of the season, anticipating the problems we knew would arise, but were unsuccessful. Employees in the area know the situation very well and use it to their advantage, knowing that they can get a job anywhere at any time without references, and knowing they won't be fired for incompetency because there is no one to replace them. You can imagine the prevailing attitude among workers and the frustration it causes employers, particularly those of us who try hard to maintain high standards. Unhappily we cannot be selective about employees as we would wish, and the turnover is high. Proper training is not a luxury, but an impossibility at such times.

Unfortunately, the night you dined at The Retreat House, October 11, is traditionally one of the busiest nights of the year, and though there may have been empty tables at the time you sat down, I can assure you that we served 150 people that night, despite the fact that no fewer than four members of the restaurant staff did not show up for work at the last minute, and did not notify us. Had they had the courtesy to call, we could have limited reservations, thereby mitigating the damage at least to a degree, but as it was we, our guests and the employees who were trying to make up the slack all had to suffer delays in service far beyond the norm!

As to the treatment you received from the waitress and waiter who attended you—neither of them is any longer in our employ, and never would have been had the labor situation not been so desperate! It would have indeed been helpful to us had you spoken up at the time—it makes a more lasting impression on the employees involved than does our discussing it with them after the fact. Now that we are in a relatively quiet period, we have the time to properly train a new and hopefully better waitstaff.

Please know that we feel as strongly as you do that the service you received that night was unacceptable, and certainly not up to our normal standards.

We hope to be able to prevent such problems from arising in the future, but realistically must acknowledge that bad nights do happen, even in the finest restaurants. Believe me, it is not because we do not care or are not paying attention!

You mentioned our prices. Let me just say that were you to make a comparative survey, you would find that our prices are about one half of what you would expect to pay in most cities and resort areas for commensurate cuisine and ambience. We set our prices in order to be competitive with other restaurants in this particular local area, in spite of the fact that most of them do not offer the same quality of food and atmosphere and certainly do not have our overhead!

I hope that this explanation (which should not be misconstrued as an excuse) has shed some light, and that you will accept our deep regrets and apologies for any unpleasantness you and your party suffered. We should be very glad if someday you would pay us a return visit so that we may provide you with the happy and enjoyable dining experience that many others have come to appreciate at The Retreat House.

Sincerely,

Gail Pearson

GETTING THE BUGS OUT

Tom Richman

In the extermination business, there is Al Burger and there is everybody else.

What does he know that the others don't?

Howard Roth, born and reared in the Bronx, had to work late one evening at the cheap North Miami Beach, Fla., steak house where he was, temporarily and not by choice, the night manager. A new exterminator was coming to attack the resident cockroaches. Roth let the crew in, went for a drink, and came back later to see how things were going. He opened the door and couldn't believe what he saw. "It was the middle of the night, and here were these five guys, filthy dirty, crawling under and into everything, just doing a super job. Jesus Christ, I said to myself. After a while one guy got up off the floor and we started talking. I didn't know it at first, but he was the boss."

Roth switched jobs.

He hired himself, says the boss, Alvin Burger (rhymes with merger). "We're talking and Roth says, 'I'm gonna go to work for

you. Anybody who can motivate people to do this kind of work, I want to be associated with him.'"

That was 17 years ago. Today, Miami-based "Bugs" Burger Bug Killers Inc. services nearly 12,000 restaurant and hotel accounts spread over 43 states, and the boss doesn't personally supervise every job anymore. No matter. The work gets done just as it would if he were there.

Al Burger has no MBA and little patience for the financial and administrative details of business. But he has overcome the biggest hurdle facing any small, growth-oriented company whose sole competitive advantage is quality of service. The more than 400 service specialists working for "Bugs" Burger (the company) today are just as motivated, and get just as dirty, as the original crew 17 years ago. Al Burger (the man) couldn't do a better job himself.

Says who?

The competition, to begin with. "'Bugs' Burger," says Jim Gillis, owner of All Boston Exterminators, "is number one. There is no number two."

And customers. "Let me put it this way," says Bob Crooks, manager of Gallagher's Restaurant, in Garland, Tex. "You have 'Bugs' Burger, and then you have to go waaay down to get to the second best."

And employees. "I left 'Bugs' Burger and worked for another company," says Alan Rosenberg, a service specialist in Boston who was recently promoted to district manager. "It was a step backward. They had no standards. So I came back. This is the only company I ever saw where the owner and the people on the job all think the same way."

With anticipated 1984 sales of $25 million, "Bugs" Burger is not the largest company in the national pest-control market, estimated at close to $2 billion annually. Orkin Exterminating Co. and Terminix International, both corporate subsidiaries with branch operations or franchises in about 40 states, rack up greater sales: $213 million for Orkin and $160 million for Terminix in 1983. Most of the rest of the industry consists of small, local operators. Indianapolis alone has about 75 pest-control companies. The competition is cut-throat, and the service, according to people with years of experience in the industry, is about the same way everywhere: minimal. Most customers assume they will get the same results no matter who they hire, so they hire on price. "Bugs" Burger doesn't operate in that market. "It's like he's a Mercedes," says Gillis, "and you've got a whole lot of Chevettes driving around out there."

"Bugs" Burger's marketing hook is its audacious guarantee—an unconditional promise to eliminate all roach and rodent breeding and nesting areas on the clients' premises, with no payment due until the pests are eliminated. If the company fails, the guarantee says, "Bugs" Burger will refund the customer's last 12 monthly payments and will pay for one year's service by another exterminator of the customer's choice.

The company doesn't promise that a restaurant diner or a hotel guest will never see another roach, but it does promise that if one shows up, it won't be native-born. Should an immigrant bug ride in with the groceries and stroll across a diner's table, "Bugs" Burger pays for the meal and sends the offended gourmet a letter of apology as well as a gift certificate for yet another free meal. "Customers feel like they've hit the state lottery," says the manager of one client restaurant. "They come in the next time and look for the little things." Hotel guests experiencing a similarly close encounter also get their night's lodging free, an apology, and an invitation to return—on the house. To help the company make good on its promises, "Bugs" Burger customers agree in writing to prepare their premises for monthly servicing and are fined if they don't.

Although the company says it has only once had to honor its full guarantee to a customer, it does spend about $2,000 a month reimbursing diners and room guests for reported pest sightings.

The professors and consultants would say that Al Burger has segmented the market and claimed the upscale commercial customers, those who will pay a premium price for superior service, as his niche. His company's monthly fees run four to six times those of its nominal competitors, sometimes more, and an initial "clean-out" charge alone can run four times the regular monthly fee. But Al Burger has not only created a new price structure, he has also taken a business with about as much prestige as, say, garbage collection, and given it respectability among both customers—". . . 'Bugs' Burger, one of my favorite subjects," responded Boston restaurateur Roger Berkowitz when he was asked about Burger—and employees. "In this company, the serviceman is number one," says Roger Gillen, a "Bugs" Burger employee in the Ft. Lauderdale office.

Al Burger's dad ran a not-very-profitable pest-control business in Albany, N.Y. His older brother bought another marginal operation in Miami. In 1954, after high school, two years in the Army, and a spell of selling vacuum cleaners door-to-door, Al Burger moved south to work for his sibling. He lasted five and a half ("miserable") years, quit, went to work for a competitor, and resigned. Immediately, he and Sandee, his wife of two years, formed their own partnership. Al was the marketing and service department, Sandee was the administration. They had, at first, no customers. "Most buys," says Al, "stole them. They planned their moves [to their own companies] so they could take a percentage of their accounts with them. I started from ground zero. I had to live with myself."

Al Burger has always been hobbled by a conscience. Owning his own company had never been a dream, but six years of working for other people had frustrated him. Employers in the pest-control industry, by and large, paid poor wages, provided no training, and were inured to high annual employee turnover rates. Further, in his experience, the service most companies provided their customers was unforgivably poor. The industry, he says, had convinced its customers that the best they could do was keep the critters—roaches and rodents—under control. Burger knew that with a little more time and effort they could be eliminated.

That conviction became the underpinning not just of "Bugs" Burger's exterminating techniques, but of the company's marketing and personnel management philosophies as well. Unlike the rest of the industry, which talks about "controlling" pests and holding them to an "acceptable" level, Al Burger sets a standard for his people that is unambiguous and requires no interpretation. While an employee might be uncertain about how many roaches is *some* roaches, *no* roaches is pretty easy to understand.

Moreover, it is an unvarying standard. To guarantee "customer satisfaction," as many companies do, is only to say, "We'll do as little as you let us get by with and only as much as you demand." The customer may be happy, but the serviceman on the route is confronted with working to a standard that varies from one customer to another, which is no standard at all. There is nothing to hold him accountable to, except the whim of client complaints.

Companies frequently answer this dilemma by avoiding the issue of quality standards altogether, instructing employees instead to follow a prescribed routine. In the case of pest extermination, that could mean applying the indicated type and quantity of chemicals to a list of likely breeding areas. Follow the routine, the employee is told, and you can't be criticized—whether the rats and roaches are killed or not. After all, the company has promised to do only the best it can, and who is to say what that is?

"Bugs" Burger's quality-control system, an integral part of the company's operations, is extraordinary in itself. But the system exists only to ensure compliance with the unambiguous standard. Take away the standard, or fuzz it up, and the organization, like a basketball team with no hoop to shoot for, loses its purpose.

"I started my business," Al Burger says, "because I thought it was unethical to take money for poor-quality performance. I thought there should be standards and ethics in the industry." When he said so before a meeting of the Florida Pest Control Association in 1960, suggesting to his colleagues and competitors that they could upgrade their service by paying more attention, and more money, to the people they hired, he was hooted off the stage. "I almost cried. I went to the door," Burger says, "and I told 'em I quit."

To this day, Al Burger and the industry he is nominally a part of maintain an unusual relationship. Burger is unforgiving in his criticism. Most owners in the industry, he says, "are former routemen who are thieves and lazy to boot. That's what you've got—a lack of scruples. And why should *their* routemen care? They've probably got their own businesses on the side."

Spokesmen for the industry he reviles don't refute him. "So long as the larger firms demand that their routemen service 18 to 20 accounts a day," says Lee Truman of Indianapolis, a former president of the National Pest Control Association and an industry consultant, "there's no way you can do a professional job. They get by, the customers accept it, and that's pretty much the industry standard. . . . Burger doesn't do anything but use the same techniques all of us could use, and he gets rid of the roaches. . . . We talk professionalism a lot, but we don't practice it."

"In this company," as Roger Gillen, a routeman for 10½ years, says, "the serviceman is number one." Scott Hebenton and Philip Hargrove in Boston, each with less than one year's experience on a route, say much the same. Michelle Kolodny, manager of the company's central office in Miami, says, without prompting, "It's the service specialists that pay my salary." "Nobody is a big shot in this company," says Frank Perez, now the vice president in charge of service but 17 years ago one of the four employees Howard Roth saw working with Al Burger in that greasy steak house. (Roth himself is now executive vice president.) "Our service people," Perez adds, "are the privileged class."

And so it goes. No matter who you talk to in the company, before long he or she pays homage to the men and women (about 7% of the service specialists are female) in the field. It could be just lip service, but it isn't.

On paper, the "Bugs" Burger service organization looks unremarkable. It separates the country into four divisions, each division into regions, and regions into districts headed by managers supervising a dozen or so service specialists each. But superimposed on this ordinary structure is a quality-control system of thoroughly frightening proportions.

Service specialists work unsupervised, at night, on schedules they set for themselves. After each routine monthly service call on every account, however, the routeman files a report in which, if he wants to remain a routeman with "Bugs" Burger, he spills everything. Were there any problems with the customer's sanitation practices? Did the routeman have access to all the premises? Did the customer do the necessary preparation? Did the routeman see a roach or a rodent, or evidence of roaches or rodents? Did he kill any roaches or rodents? Does he need any help with the account? As the routeman is told from the time he first interviews for a job with the company, honesty pays. At "Bugs" Burger, mistakes are forgiven; liars are not.

The information filed by the routeman is checked, not once but several times, by managers at various levels. District managers call each customer a day or two after every monthly service. District managers, regional directors, and divisional vice presidents spend much of their time visiting customers' premises, armed when they arrive with a computer printout of the routeman's reports. The computer printout also includes customer complaints received in Miami. (When customers call "Bugs" Burger from any city in the country except Honolulu, using either the local or toll-free number listed in the phone book, the telephone rings at the Miami corporate headquarters, not at the routeman's home or the local office.) And just to keep all of *those* managers honest, a full-time, two-person quality-control team headed by Al Burger's daughter Susan hopscotches the country calling on customers and filing their own reports. Routemen don't know when or how frequently their clients will be called on by someone from management. The only certainty is that they will be called on, and that if there are complaints, Miami will hear about them first.

Naturally, company managers insist that all this checking up is really done for the routeman's benefit. "Our job," says Tom Schafer, vice president of technical services, which includes quality control, "is to support the service department." Routemen "appreciate" the help these reports and visits give them, assures Perez.

That is exactly the sort of thing you would expect to hear from management. What is surprising, however, is that you get the same story from the field.

"Yeah, it's pressure," says Scott Hebenton in Boston, "but it helps you keep up your standards."

"It gives us that little extra motivation," says Alan Rosenberg. "It would be easy to slack off one night, make it up the next month. But when you think, well, they might call this account *this* month."

Don't they resent it?

"I don't," says Hebenton. "Without it I guess we'd be just like any other company."

An employee-turnover rate of less than 3% last year suggests that most people at "Bugs" Burger feel much the way Hebenton does. Something about this system of management and quality control builds pride instead of resentment among the people whose performance is constantly monitored.

Jack Kaplan, the company's vice president for human resources, thinks it is a "mentality . . . that says, 'You are critical to the success of this company, and I'm going to make you feel that way from day one.' Most people coming here from different backgrounds aren't used to hearing words like that."

Employees first encounter this attitude during the hiring process, which involves two rounds of interviews, elaborate personality and aptitude testing, a polygraph examination, and thorough explanations of the job and the company—all conducted by officials from Miami headquarters, who eventually turn over the names of qualified applicants (2% or 3% of those who answer the ads) to local service managers for the final decision. The people hired already feel part of an elite group just from having survived what they know is an exhaustive selection process. Further, it is a process that doesn't automatically select the young. "I appreciate it," says Hebenton, hired last year at age 37, "because an older guy has just as good a chance." Kaplan recalls interviewing a 45-year-old woman in Roanoke, Va., who asked, he says, "Would you hire an old broad like me?" They did. "Her district manager says she's fantastic," he adds.

New hires undergo a 5-month training program. "It's like boot camp in the Army," says Kaplan, "only it's three times as long and twice as tough." Recently hired service specialists confirm Kaplan's analogy. During the program, they are not assistants, helping someone else. They do real work under the full-time instruction of a field manager. After about three months, new recruits attend a two-week school in Miami, where, one says, "there is no fooling around. You go to class from eight o'clock until six or seven o'clock, then you do your homework and show up again the next morning. It's pretty intense." (Letting no opportunity to exercise a little quality control slip by, company officials test the recruits in Miami, not just to see what they have learned, but also to check the techniques they had been taught by field managers against the company's standards. What public school administrators can't get away with, "Bugs" Burger can.)

Finally, in the sixth month, the new service specialist gets a route. In one sense he is on his own, because the responsibility of keeping customers' premises clear of nesting and breeding pests is ultimately his. Says serviceman Phil Hargrove, "It's like your own little business."

Not quite, but neither are Hargrove and his peers just employees hired to do a high-quality job.

Burger's routemen occupy a unique middle ground. They control the upside of their working lives—their own schedules, their incomes, and, to a large extent, their career paths within the company. What they don't have, in contrast to most workers and all independent business owners, is any downside risk. They can't lose, and that is why they will accept whatever performance standard the company wants them to meet. Once hired and trained at "Bugs" Burger, the only way you can fail is to lie. Cover up a mistake, slack off and don't report it, or ignore a problem, and you are in trouble. But ask for help, and you have it.

Routemen can talk to their district managers on the telephone or ask them to come to the job site, anytime. Regional directors and divisional vice presidents always travel with a working uniform in their bags. "They never look at it as a negative," says Scott Hebenton, "if you ask for help." Recently, the company flew eight out-of-state service specialists to Boston to get their Massachusetts licenses so that they would be available to augment the local forces if a job suddenly demanded a larger army. "They spare no expense," says Hargrove, slightly amazed. "Any serviceman knows," says Jack Kaplan, "that if he wants to talk to Mr. Burger, all he has to do is pick up the phone."

Nor does a "Bugs" Burger service specialist worry about losses from conditions beyond his control:

- If a major customer decides to drop the service at the end of his contract, the company subsidizes the routeman's compensation until a replacement is signed on.
- When a salesman badly underestimates the hours required to service a new account, the company subsidizes the routeman for the time he puts in, because it won't allow him to shortcut the service.
- Customers that won't cooperate with a routeman by maintaining sanitary conditions or by preparing the premises for treatment are dropped. The serviceman, again, is subsidized until a new client is found to fill out his route.

- Promotions from service specialist to district manager—and all other promotions within the company—are made on a three-month, or longer, trial basis, with the salary differential held in escrow during the trial. If a supervisor or, as is more frequently the case, the former routeman decides the promotion isn't working, he gets either his old route back, or a better one. Roger Gillen, an 11-year "Bugs" Burger veteran, tried a management job and left it. "I'm not a management type of person, and you just can't replace a good serviceman." There is no shame at "Bugs" Burger in staying with the job you do well—and for which you are paid well. Servicemen receive $1,200 a month in salary plus 20% of all the monthly gross billings on their routes in excess of $5,100. The average routeman makes $24,000, but $32,000 or more isn't unheard of, according to company sources.

Benefits are impressive, too: full health insurance; disability insurance that pays full salary for three months and 60% thereafter; a pension plan; profit sharing; cost of living adjustments; performance bonuses; and, coming soon, employee equity in an affiliated company selling janitorial supplies.

"An old lady," Al Burger recalls, "told me that if you give without thinking about what you might get back, eventually you'll get back 100 times what you gave. That was Mrs. Lummus. When I was 21, working for my brother, she called. She had a terrible roach problem in Miami Beach, but no money. So I got rid of her roaches, and she made me tea and cookies. I remember what she told me. It's a good thing to carry with you."

High-minded thoughts, of course, do not by themselves ensure business success. While they can inform and influence a management organization, they can't take its place, and Al Burger, he will admit today, is no organizer. In 1978, sales were nearly $6 million, but the business was foundering. Burger realized, with a little help from Howard Roth, that he had reached the limits of his managerial capabilities. "I was panicking, beginning to make mistakes. I was disoriented. I actually had heart palpitations. Too many things were happening that I couldn't cope with. . . . Howard Roth—a guy with a ninth-grade education who really understands people—he sat me down and said, 'Here's a guy that you're going to hire.'"

The guy was Art Graham, who, as president of Pizza Hut Canada Ltd., had just turned the company around. He had worked for "Bugs" Burger briefly in the early '70s, but hadn't appreciated the growth opportunities in the business. In 1978, while Graham was in Miami for the Super Bowl game, Roth persuaded him to come back. Graham built a management structure where none had existed before and pulled the profit margin to 12% of sales within six months, up from 1%. He wrote the company's first business plan and constructed its first annual operating budget.

Al Burger, meanwhile, concentrates on what he does best: marketing and firing up the troops. "Basically," says district director Scott Hebenton, "what Al Burger is, is a service specialist . . . and when he talks to you it's like he's right inside your head. He knows exactly what you're thinking out there on the route. 'Oh, I'm tired. Why not just cut this short and go home.' He's a good motivator."

Both management and motivation remain important. On the marketing front, for example, some of the competition is beginning to catch on to Burger's gimmick—the elimination guarantee—and while they have raised their prices accordingly, "Bugs" Burger is still

the premium-price service. The company loses $2 million or more annually in unrenewed contracts as existing customers switch to lower-cost exterminators.

"Bugs" Burger's response to the competition has been to develop some productivity-enhancing equipment for routemen to use, and to map out some innovative, but still confidential, pricing options. The one thing Burger won't allow is cuts in service. "The minute we start doing that," he says, "our standard falls apart. You can't tell a service specialist not to do a good job on one account and then expect him not to do a bad job on the others. People will strive for that elusive level of perfection. All they need is the right attitude, and that all depends on the goals and standards you set for them."

Al Burger, in short, is still a man with a mission. He won't rejoin the national trade association until it changes its name from pest control to pest elimination. "He was a voice in the wilderness," says Lee Truman of Indianapolis, "but now an awful lot of people think he's been right all along."

And despite the competition, he remains cool and self-confident. The owner of one of Honolulu's most expensive restaurants didn't hide his condescending skepticism when Burger first stopped by on a sales call. But Burger had already toured the dining rooms, kitchens, and work areas. He had seen the thumb-size roaches scampering over the glassware, gone unerringly to where the egg cases were hidden, noted that rats had walked across the floured surface of the piecrust machine leaving paw prints and their distinctive calling cards.

Condescending or not, here was a man, Al Burger knew, who needed and eventually would pay for "Bugs" Burger's kind of service.

CASE

FEDERAL EXPRESS: THE MONEY BACK GUARANTEE (A)

Date: Thursday, March 31, 1988
Time: 10:00 A.M.
Place: Amelia Island Plantation Resort, Florida
Setting: An executive education seminar

Sylvia Cooper, a business school professor, was delivering an executive education seminar for 30 senior managers of a *Fortune 500* company. On the night before her big presentation, she showed participants a Tom Peters video, *A Passion for Customers,* that included a complimentary segment on Federal Express. On the morning of her presentation, she had reason to feel remorse about showing that segment.

Reason The day before, Cooper's secretary had used Federal Express to send her a videotape and some other material she needed for her Thursday presentation. (The videotape had just been completed by the audio-visual department at her school.) A front desk clerk had told Cooper that Federal Express deliveries usually arrived by 10:00 A.M. By that time on Thursday, the daily delivery had indeed been made, but Cooper's package was not there. Her presentation was scheduled for 2:00 P.M.

When Cooper learned that her package had not arrived, she asked whether it could have been overlooked, and suggested that perhaps it was on a delivery truck elsewhere at the resort. The front-desk manager agreed to send someone to check the parcels on all the delivery trucks. When Cooper called the front desk back at 10:30, she was told that a complete search had not turned up her package.

Professor Christopher W. L. Hart prepared this case as the basis for class discussion rather than to illustrate either effective or ineffective handling of an administrative situation.

To order copies, call (617) 495-6117 or write the Publishing Division, Harvard Business School, Boston, MA 02163. No part of this publication may be reproduced, stored in a retrieval system, or transmitted in any form or by any means—electronic, mechanical, photocopying, recording, or otherwise—without the permission of the Harvard Business School.

Cooper then called her secretary, Alice, to make sure she had sent the package. Alice said she had, and offered to check the university mailroom to see if a mistake had been made there. "Call me back in 10 minutes," she told Cooper. When Cooper called back, Alice explained that the mailroom had sent the package, and that everything appeared to be in order on her end. Knowing that Federal Express employed a sophisticated tracking system, Cooper asked Alice to call Federal Express to locate the package. To do so, Alice went back to the mailroom to obtain the air bill number.

When she called Alice back at 11:00, Cooper learned that her package had been a "missort." According to the tracking system, it was sitting at the Federal Express terminal in Savannah, Georgia. The resort was about a three-hour drive from Savannah.

Cooper often cited Federal Express in classes and seminars she taught as an example of service excellence; therefore, she decided to see what she could learn by calling the company herself. She was interested in finding out how Federal Express would "make things right" for her and save her 2:00 presentation.

On the first ring—just as shown in the Tom Peters video—a customer service representative answered.

Cooper:

I have a serious problem. Yesterday, my secretary sent a package that should have reached me at Amelia Island this morning. Apparently it was missorted, and it's sitting in Savannah. I need the material in that package by 2:00 this afternoon. What can you do for me?

Federal Express:

I will need some information, ma'am. What is your air bill number?

C: 619732942.

FE: Thank you. Please hold while I check its status.

C: No, I *know* the status—(Pause).

FE: Ma'am, your package is a missort. It ended up in Savannah, Georgia.

C: That part I know. What I need to know now is what are you going to do about it?

FE: It's our policy that we'll get the parcel to you just as soon as possible. And we won't charge you for it.

C: That doesn't do me any good. I need to know when it will be delivered.

FE: Well, ma'am, we send missorted parcels ASAP. You should have it tomorrow morning.

C: That's too late—I need the material at 2:00 *today*. And I won't even be here tomorrow, I'll be back at home.

FE: That's no problem, ma'am. We'll send it to your home address. What is the address?

C: The address is on the air bill, but that's not the point. I've got to have that material today. Can you get it to me some other way—put it on one of your trucks, or put it in a cab, or in a *helicopter*, for heaven's sake!

FE: (Silence at the end of the line.)

* * *

* What should Federal Express do for this customer?

* In your view, what should Federal Express's general policy be for similar service mishaps?

* What do you think actually happened?

* Federal Express handles roughly 875,000 packages each day. What would you guess its error rate to be?

EXHIBIT 1

FEDERAL EXPRESS MONEY BACK GUARANTEE—SHORT FORM

Two Money-Back Guarantees

Federal Express backs its dependability with *two* money-back guarantees.

First, we guarantee that if we fail to deliver your package by 10:30 A.M. we'll give you your money back.   Even if delivery is only 60 seconds late.

Second, our technologically advanced system allows us to tell you the exact status of your package within 30 minutes of your call. If we can't, you'll get your money back.

EXHIBIT 2

FEDERAL EXPRESS MONEY BACK GUARANTEE—LONG FORM

Money-Back Guarantee Policy

Federal Express offers two money-back guarantees:

1. *Service Failure*-At our option, we will either refund or credit your shipping charges upon request if we deliver your shipment 60 seconds or more after our published delivery commitment.

In order to qualify for refund or credit the following conditions apply:

• For invoiced shipments and for shipments by customers using our automated systems, you must notify us in writing or by telephone of a service failure within 15 calendar days from the invoice date.

• For shipments not invoiced by Federal Express (paid by cash, check or credit card) you must notify us in writing or by telephone of a service failure within 15 calendar days from the date of shipment.

• A service failure will not be deemed to have occurred if within 30 calendar days after you notify us we provide you with:

(a) proof of timely delivery, consisting of the date and time of delivery and name of the person who signed the shipment; or

(b) service exception information reflecting that the failure to timely deliver resulted from an exception described under "Liabilities Not Assumed."

• At the time you notify us, you must provide the account number if any, the airbill or poackage tracking number, the date of shipment, and the recipient's name, address, and Zip Code®.

• Only one refund or credit is permitted per package. In the case of multiple package shipments, this money-back guarantee will apply to every package in the shipment. If a service failure occurs for any package within the shipment a refund or credit will be given for the portion of the shipment charges applicable to that package.

• Package Consolidators are not eligible for this money-back guarantee (see "Package Consolidators" section).

• A refund or credit will not be given for shipments delayed due to incorrect addresses or Zip Codes® or to the unavailability or refusal of a person to accept delivery or sign for the package or due to any of the causes described under "Liabilities Not Assumed." In addition, for shipments to and from Puerto Rico and to international destinations, refund or credit will not be given if failure to deliver is the result of Tax Authority or customs delays arising from inspection requirements or from omissions in documentation.

• This money-back guarantee does not apply to shipments destined outside our primary service areas.

• This money-back guarantee does not apply to requests for invoice adjustment based on overcharges (see "Billing").

• Effective April 1, 1988, for invoiced shipments and for shipments by customers using our automated systems, you must notify us in writing or by telephone of a service failure within 15 calendar days from the invoice date and must within the same 15 calendar days pay for all shipments on the invoice as to which timely delivery occurred based on our records. You must furnish with your payment the invoice numbers to which your payment applies. If an invoice is not paid in full, the reason for each unpaid charge must be noted with its airbill or package tracking number.

2. *Package Status.* At our option, we will either refund or credit your shipping charges upon request if we cannot report the status of your package within 30 minutes of inquiry.

Package status is defined as the most recent electronically scanned location of your package as reflected in our COSMOS computer system.

In order to qualify for refund or credit, the following conditions apply.

• You must telephone us and make your request within 15 calendar days after the date of shipment. Written requests will not be accepted.

• The response period under this money-back guarantee is 30 minutes per package. Where more than one package status inquiry is made in a call, we will respond within 30 minutes of our receiving all package related information.

• You must provide your account umber, if any, the airbill or package tracking number, date of shipment, pieces and weight and the recipient's name, address and Zip Code® on the first call.

• Only one refund or credit is permitted per package. In the case of multiple package shipments, this money-back guarantee will apply to each package in the shipment.

• This money-back guarantee does not apply to shipments destined outside our primary service areas.

• Package Consolidators are not eligible for this money-back guarantee (see "Package Consolidators" section).

• Due to time zone differences, the package status money-back guarantee does not apply to international shipments.

Liabilities Not Assumed

FEDERAL EXPRESS SHALL NOT BE LIABLE, IN ANY EVENT, FOR ANY DAMAGES, WHETHER DIRECT, INCIDENTAL, SPECIAL OR CONSEQUENTIAL IN EXCESS OF THE DECLARED VALUE OF A SHIPMENT ARISING FROM TRANSPORTATION SUBJECT TO THE SERVICE CONDITIONS CONTAINED IN THIS GUIDE, WHETHER OR NOT FEDERAL EXPRESS HAD KNOWLEDGE THAT SUCH DAMAGES MIGHT BE INCURRED, INCLUDING, BUT NOT LIMITED TO, LOSS OF INCOME OR PROFITS.

Federal Express shall not be liable for, nor shall any adjustment, refund or credit of any kind be made as a result of any loss, damage, delay, mis-delivery or non-delivery except such as may result from our sole negligence and the liability for which shall not exceed the declared value of a shipment, incluidng, but not limited to, any such loss, damage, delay, mis-delivery, or non-delivery caused by:

(a) The act, default or omission of the shipper, recipient or any other party who claims an interest in the shipment.

(b) The nature or the shipment or any defect, characteristic or inherent vice of the shipment.

(c) Violation by the shipper or recipient of any of the terms and conditions contained in our Service Guide, as amended from time to time including, but not limited to, improper or insufficient packing, securing, marking or addressing, or failure to observe any of the Service Conditions relating to shipments.

(d) Acts of God, perils of the air, public enemies, public authorities acting with actual or apparent authority on the premises, authority of law, acts or omissions of customs or quarantine officials, riots, strikes or other local disputes, civil commotions, hazards incident to a state of war or weather conditions, national or local disruptions in air or ground transportation networks due to events beyond our control, such as weather phenomena, strikes by government or employees of such organizations or natural disasters.

(e) Acts or omissions of any person or entity other than Federal Express, including our compliance with verbal or written delivery instructions from the shipper or recipient.

(f) Loss of articles loaded and sealed in packages by the shipper, provided the seal is unbroken at the time of delivery and the package retains its basic integrity.

Upon the occurrence of any of the events described in (d) above, we commit to servicing all customers by making all reasonable efforts to transport and deliver packages to their designated recipient as quickly as practicable under the circumstances.

PART IV

MEASURING CUSTOMER SATISFACTION

Chapter 9

THE PSYCHOLOGY OF CUSTOMER SATISFACTION

9.1 OVERVIEW

"The customer has all the votes," says Ray Kordupleski, who heads customer satisfaction measurement at AT&T. What he means is that any business's success ultimately depends on what customers choose to do. Thus it is vitally important to understand the psychology of customers, and why they choose to do what they do. In the context of services, we are primarily interested in what makes a customer satisfied enough to come back (or stay).

Because customer decisions take place in the customer's mind, we must consider perceptions and not just "reality." But more than just customer perceptions are important because customers may have emotional responses as well. Thus we are interested in not just how customers *perceive* service, but also how they *feel* about it. Such feelings, if positive, can range from mild (satisfaction) to extreme (delight). The depth of feeling generally results from the degree to which the customer's perceptions of the service meets or exceeds what the customer expected.

Another factor that impacts customer repurchase is price. The higher the price, the better the expected quality must be to induce repurchase. The concept of "value," sometimes described as "what you get for what you give," represents the trade-off in the customer's mind between quality and price.

9.2 PERCEPTIONS AND REALITY

Traditional quality management arose in manufacturing, through the pioneering quality control efforts of Shewhart, Deming, and others. Their focus was on such things as engineering tolerances and defect rates, measured objectively by scientific instruments. The resulting approach to quality was primarily internally focused.

If we instead view the organization as a service, then what matters is quality as perceived by the customer. If the customer perceives that quality is bad, then it matters little that "objective" quality may be good. For example, if a restaurant customer thinks the restaurant is too cold, it does little good for the matter to argue that the thermometer says 74°F. Because we are dealing with customer perceptions, the relevant domain is psychology rather than engineering. To measure customer satisfaction effectively, we must have some understanding about how satisfaction works.

The disparity between objective quality and perceived quality can be very frustrating to management. For example, in recent years customers in the United States have tended to consider Japanese cars to be of higher quality than American cars. So, when Chrysler marketed a car that was identical (in all but the trim) to a Japanese car, customers consistently rated the American version worse! Everything about the cars was the same, and they were made in the same plant. Objectively, there was no difference between the two cars. Chrysler management knew for a fact that their car was just as good, but customers perceived the quality to be lower.

Another example of the difference between perception and reality involves the psychology of waiting lines. Walt Disney World in Orlando is a well-known example of how to make waiting seem shorter. Tricks to achieve this include having lines make many turns, so no particular segment is too long, and providing entertainment along the way, so the wait feels shorter. Customers don't like to wait. The psychology behind waiting lines can thus be useful to improve the experience. For example:

- Unoccupied time seems longer.
- Preprocess waits seem longer (in other words, it is better to let a patient wait in an examining room instead of the waiting room).
- Anxious waits seem longer (for example, waiting in a hospital emergency room with an injured child can seem to take longer than it actually does).
- Uncertain waits seem longer (for example, waiting for a reply to a job application can seem to take longer than it really does, because it is not clear when a response is expected).
- Unexplained waits seem longer.
- Unfair waits seem longer.
- Solo waits seem longer.

If perceived quality matters more than actual quality, we may wonder why businesses don't simply provide inferior quality but persuade the customer that it was great. Consider the example of a hospital. Suppose that Hospital A has excellent technical treatment, including the latest equipment and the most knowledgeable doctors. But it also has an unpleasant atmosphere and an unfriendly staff. The customer (patient) cannot easily judge technical quality, but is certainly put off by an unpleasant atmosphere and unfriendly staff. Because of this, Hospital A's perceived quality is likely to be poor.

Hospital B isn't as good as A on the technical aspects. Its equipment is older, and its doctors are a little bit behind the times. Yet it will invariably receive very good perceived-quality scores because of its pleasant atmosphere and friendly staff. If quality, as perceived by the customer, is the true indicator of quality, should we conclude that Hospital B is a better hospital because its perceived quality is higher?

We can resolve this paradox by adding the element of time. Presumably the patients of Hospital A will have better clinical outcomes, meaning that they will be healthier and happier as time goes by. Their perceived quality rating for Hospital A will tend to reflect their improved health. Hospital B's patients, initially happy, will become less enamored with Hospital B as their health deteriorates over time. *When viewed in the long term,* perceived quality does tend to converge on objective quality, when objective aspects are important and if they become known.

The element of time also becomes important when there are repeated transactions over time. In the hospital example there are two kinds of perceived quality: the perceived quality of the individual transaction and the perceived quality of the service provider overall. We can see the difference very easily. Suppose, for example, that you go to dinner at your favorite restaurant, which has been a pleasant experience many times before. But on this night the food is inferior. The perceived quality of that particular service encounter is negative, but the overall perceived quality of the restaurant is still likely to be good, although perhaps not quite as good as before.

What are the elements of perceived quality? Some authors have claimed to reduce the psychological facets of perceived service quality to a handful of service satisfaction dimensions, which are presumed to be universal across all people. Some authors propose ten dimensions, whereas another author proposes six.[1] These categorization schemes turned out to not be as universal as the authors had hoped, because of the profound differences between different service scenarios. Current thought is that it would not be possible to list a set of universal service quality dimensions. Different services involve different wants and needs that do not fit into broad categories.

9.3 SATISFACTION: AN EMOTIONAL RESPONSE

Many applied researchers treat service quality and customer satisfaction as though they were interchangeable concepts.[2] However, theorists in customer satisfaction are in agreement that the concepts are quite distinct.[3,4] In particular, perceived quality is a rational perception, whereas satisfaction is an emotional or feeling reaction.[5] Satisfaction states may include contentment (the phone works), surprise (I won the lottery!), pleasure (the wine is good), or relief (the dentist has finished drilling).[6]

Perceived quality does *influence* satisfaction. For example, if a new Rolls-Royce is delivered with a slight nick in the paint, then perceived quality is still likely to be high (higher than just about any other car), but satisfaction will be low. That is because the Rolls-Royce buyer has very high expectations. Absolutely nothing should be wrong. Consider on the other hand the buyer of a used Yugo. The car can be a complete wreck (very low perceived quality). But because expectations are very low, if it still runs at all, the buyer is likely to be very happy (high satisfaction).

The word "satisfaction" comes from the Latin words *satis* (enough) and *facere* (to do or make).[7] These words suggest the true meaning of satisfaction, which is fulfillment. Managerially, fulfillment usually translates to solving problems. But many businesses have found that merely solving problems and satisfying the customer is not enough. To produce high levels of customer loyalty, businesses need to move beyond mere satisfaction, to customer delight.

9.4 DELIGHT

Going beyond mere satisfaction involves doing more than eliminating problems. It involves the concept of delight. Delight is positive surprise. It is the highest level of satisfaction and it translates into better outcomes (higher customer retention levels, etc.) than can be achieved through other levels of satisfaction.

Delight has not received much attention in the academic literature, but the trade press is full of references to "delighting the customer." Yet, there is considerable confusion among managers about what delighting the customer really means. It is often referred to as some sort of complete problem solving, as in "The customer is satisfied with a defect rate of .01%, but if we could eliminate defects altogether, then the customer would be delighted!" Actually, at such a small defect rate, it would likely be some time before the customer even noticed. Eliminating problems may satisfy the customer, but delight requires surprise.

Consider, for example, an airline flight leaving from Nashville. If the plane left on time, customers would probably be satisfied. On the other hand, suppose all families traveling with small children were given Nashville coloring books to take home. That would be a positive (presumably) surprise, and could produce delight.

Delight is possible only if the customer is satisfied to begin with. For example, suppose an airliner had all its engines go out, and was crashing to earth, out of control. This would make most passengers very dissatisfied. Suppose now that the flight attendants went up and down the aisle giving out gourmet chocolates. This positive surprise, which might ordinarily produce delight, would not work in this instance, because the base level of satisfaction had not been established. This hierarchy of satisfaction has been well-established in research.[8]

Delight leads to behavioral outcomes that are substantially better than mere satisfaction can provide. These include repurchase, positive word of mouth, and so on. This relationship is "nonlinear."[9] That is, there are thresholds of satisfaction beyond which little benefit is obtained. Looking at Figure 9.1, we see that improvement in satisfaction first has considerable impact (steep slope of the impact curve) because problems are being solved. Beyond this stage, the satisfaction level remains the same until the point at which positive surprise (delight) is reflected. Delight is very effective at building loyalty and devotion, much more so than mere satisfaction.[10]

FIGURE 9.1

THE EFFECT OF SATISFACTION AND DELIGHT

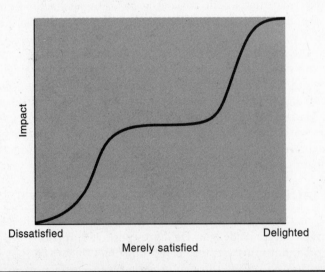

Dissatisfied   Delighted

Merely satisfied

9.5 EXPECTATIONS

Satisfaction and delight are both strongly influenced by customer expectations. By "expectations," behavioral researchers mean an array of possible outcomes that reflect what might, could, will, should, or had better not happen. There are several different kinds of expectations. Figure 9.2 shows a hierarchy of expectations that might exist for a typical customer.

The **will expectation**[11] comes closest to the mathematics definition. It is the average level of quality that is predicted based on all known information. This is the expectation level most often meant by customers (and used by researchers). When someone says that "service exceeded my expectations," they generally mean that the service was better than they had predicted it would be.

The **should expectation**[12] is what customers feel they deserve from the transaction. Very often what *should* happen is better than what the customer actually thinks *will* happen. For example, a student may think that each lecture *should* be exciting, but doubts that a particular day's lecture actually *will* be exciting. Or, professors may think that students *should* be lively and intelligent, but think that actually they *will* sit in class like lumps!

The **ideal expectation**[13] is what would happen under the best of circumstances.

FIGURE 9.2

THE EXPECTATIONS HIERARCHY

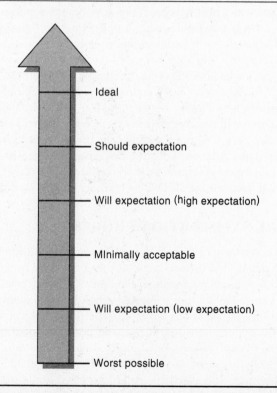

- Ideal
- Should expectation
- Will expectation (high expectation)
- MInimally acceptable
- Will expectation (low expectation)
- Worst possible

It is useful as a barometer of excellence. On the other end of the scale are the minimally acceptable level[14] (the threshold at which mere satisfaction is achieved), and the worst possible level (the worst outcome that can be imagined).

Expectations are affected strongly by experience. For example, if the customer has a bad experience, then the will expectation will decline. A good experience will tend to raise the will expectation. Generally speaking, the should expectation will ratchet up, but never decline. Very good experiences tend to bring the should expectation up to that level. Thus expectations change over time, often for the better.

An example of this is the U.S. auto industry. General Motors, Ford, and Chrysler had instilled a level of quality expectations in the U.S. population that was low by today's standards. Then the Japanese started exporting cars of significantly higher quality. Expectations jumped, as customers saw that a higher level of quality was possible. The complacent U.S. automakers, making cars of the same quality as always, suddenly found themselves faced with millions of customers who had significantly higher expectations. The result was disastrous for the auto manufacturers.

Experience is not the only thing that shapes expectations. Expectations may also be affected by advertising,[15] word of mouth,[16] and personal limitations.[17] However expectations are formed, they are a very important influence on satisfaction, through the mechanism of disconfirmation.

9.6 DISCONFIRMATION (GAPS)

"Expectancy disconfirmation," the gap between perceived quality and expected quality, is a very powerful predictor of satisfaction.[18] In fact, this link is so strong that satisfaction itself has often been (incorrectly) *defined* as the gap between perception and expectation.[19] The importance of disconfirmation in explaining satisfaction and other behavior has been demonstrated in many contexts, including sales force interactions,[20] restaurant service,[21] security transactions,[22] and telephone service.[23]

Consider, for example, Figure 9.3. Here perceived quality is higher than expected. This situation will usually result in satisfaction, and will almost always result in expectation being raised. Figure 9.4 shows the opposite; perceived quality is not as good as expected. This situation will probably result in dissatisfaction, and will very likely result in lowered expectations for the service. These disconfirmations (gaps) form the conceptual basis for the SERVQUAL[24] model for service quality and satisfaction.

9.7 THE SATISFACTION PROCESS

Now that we have discussed quality, expectations, disconfirmation, and satisfaction in some detail, it is time to step back and consider how these elements fit together. Figure 9.5 presents a simplified diagram that nevertheless includes the most important linkages. We see that perceived quality results from both objective quality and expectations. Expectations have a direct effect on perceived quality. In particular, the higher the expectations, the higher the perceived quality. Perceived quality is then compared to expectations, resulting in a disconfirmation, either positive or negative. Perceived quality also updates the expectations to produce new expectations, which are either raised (because higher than expected quality was experienced) or lowered

FIGURE 9.3

POSITIVE DISCONFIRMATION

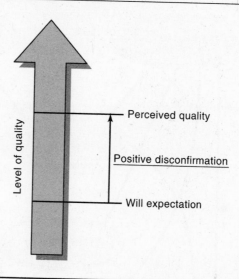

FIGURE 9.4

NEGATIVE DISCONFIRMATION

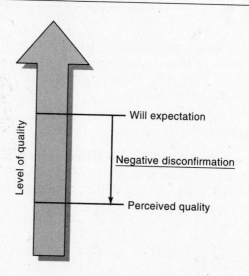

FIGURE 9.5

THE SATISFACTION PROCESS

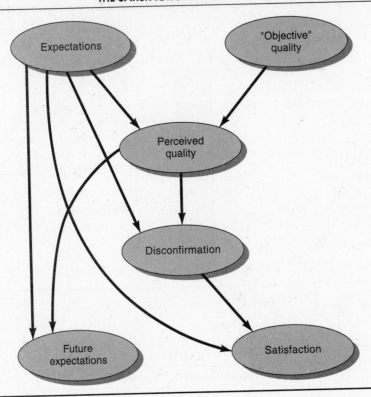

(because lower than expected quality was experienced). At the same time, satisfaction results primarily from disconfirmation, but also (secondarily) expectations. That is, there is also a direct effect of expectations on satisfaction—the higher the expectations, the higher the satisfaction.

9.8 VALUE

Ultimately, perceived value drives purchase and repurchase. Value is formed by the relationship between quality and price. Figure 9.6 shows how quality, price, and value are related. The higher the quality, the higher the value. The higher the price, the lower the value. In colloquial usage, "value" is often used as a code word for price. Thus, "value" really refers to low price in many advertisements. However, this use of the word "value" is correct only if quality is constant, which rarely is the case.

Thus we see that there are many ways to obtain value. A product/service may be of relatively low quality, but because it is also very cheap, it is a good value. Likewise a product/service may be very expensive and yet still be a good value because its quality is so high. Ultimately, individual preferences dictate whether there is a good value or not. We explore this in the next section.

FIGURE 9.6

PRICE, QUALITY, AND VALUE

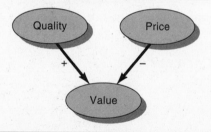

9.9 UTILITY AND CHOICE

Economic utility is a useful way to visualize the relationship between quality, value, and choice.[25] We may think of utility as being some sort of quantifiable "goodness." As quality increases, utility increases (Figure 9.7). As price increases, utility (usually) decreases (equivalently, disutility increases, see Figure 9.8). Utility functions vary with individuals and this helps explain why people make such different decisions. For example, Figure 9.9 graphs the disutility of price to two people, one rich and one poor. It is easy to see that price A is simply beyond the resources of the poor person, while it incurs very little disutility for the rich person.

The concept of value has often been used to represent this tradeoff between quality and price. Viewed from an economic utility point of view:

$$\text{Value} = \text{Utility of quality} - \text{disutility of price}$$

Choice is then based primarily on getting the best value. Figure 9.9 shows clearly that there will be market segments in terms of quality. Some people will be happy to pay for more quality because they will perceive the corresponding increase in

FIGURE 9.7

THE UTILITY OF QUALITY

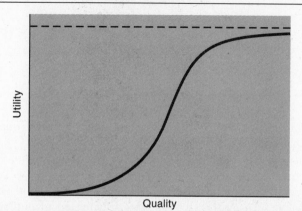

FIGURE 9.8

THE DISUTILITY OF PRICE

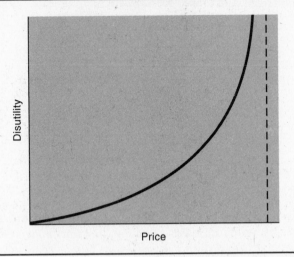

FIGURE 9.9

THE DISUTILITY OF PRICE—INDIVIDUAL DIFFERENCES

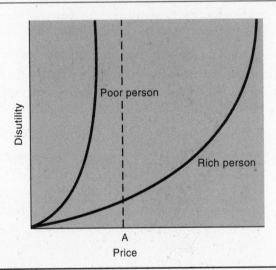

price as having little disutility. Others will refuse to pay for more quality because the price increase has great disutility to them.

Another aspect that becomes important in determining choice is **uncertainty.** Figure 9.10 shows two persons' expectations of quality outcome. Person 1 is experienced with the product/service, and thus has little doubt about what quality level will ensue. That is seen by the fact that the distribution of outcomes expected is

FIGURE 9.10

UNCERTAINTY IN EXPECTATIONS

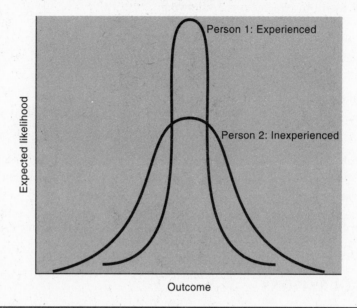

tightly bunched. Person 2, on the other hand, is not really sure exactly what will happen, because of inexperience. This is seen by the broad, unfocused, distribution of expected outcomes.

This contrast is important because there may be *downside risk*. That is, people generally find the potential losses from worse-than-expected outcomes to outweigh the potential gains from better-than-expected outcomes. That is, a worse-than-expected outcome hurts more than a better-than-expected one helps. If we look at Figure 9.10, even though Person 1 and Person 2 have the same will expectation, Person 1 is most likely more positive than Person 2, because of less downside risk.

This observation explains an interesting paradox. Under some circumstances it is perfectly rational for an individual to choose an option that is actually expected to be worse (on average), if the downside risk for that option is less. For example, in the early days of personal computers it was widely believed that PCs made by Apple were superior technically to those made by IBM, yet IBM PCs sold better because IBM was a "safe" choice. This situation changed as customers gained more experience with PCs. As customers learned more, they feared the "downside risk" of the upstart computers less, and IBM's market share declined. Thus, as experience increases, knowledge about the product/service increases, and the distribution of expected outcomes tightens up to look more like Person 1 in Figure 9.10. Downside risk is reduced, and probability of repurchase therefore increases, even if the perceived quality is only what was expected. In other words, customers often appear loyal when they are being rational and avoiding risk.

9.10 SUMMARY

When managing customer satisfaction and putting together customer satisfaction surveys, it is useful to remember the following:

1. The customer's perception is what counts. Measure that.
2. Satisfaction is not the same as perceived quality.
3. Quality perceptions are rational. Satisfaction is emotional.
4. Delight is more than just complete satisfaction.
5. Expectations vary across individuals and change over time.
6. Disconfirmation is the most important driver of satisfaction.
7. Value is utility of quality minus disutility of price.
8. Expectations have distributions, which change shape with experience.
9. Customers avoid downside risk by displaying loyalty.

Use of these psychological principles and findings can help produce an effective customer satisfaction survey, as we will see in the following chapter.

REVIEW QUESTIONS

1. Think of a service you have experienced, which you were happy (unhappy) with at first, but after the fact became unhappy (happy)? Why did that happen?
2. What was the last time you were truly delighted with a product or service? What was it that caused your expectations to be greatly exceeded?
3. Think about a trip to your regular dentist to get an impacted wisdom tooth pulled. Describe your ideal visit, your should expectation, will expectation, minimally acceptable experience, and worst possible outcome. Be as specific as possible.
4. Draw the quality-utility curve of an uncultured customer; of a refined customer. What impact will these utility curves have on product choice, using a utility maximization argument, if they have an equal amount of money?

ENDNOTES

1. See, for example, A. Parasuraman, Valarie A. Zeithaml, and Leonard L. Berry (1985), "A Conceptual Model of Service Quality and Its Implications for Future Research," *Journal of Marketing*, 49 (Fall), 41–50, and Christian Gronroos (1988), "Service Quality: The Six Criteria of Good Perceived Service Quality," *Review of Business*, 9 (Winter), 10–13.
2. William Boulding, Ajay Kalra, Richard Staelin, and Valarie A. Zeithaml (1993), "A Dynamic Process Model of Service Quality," *Journal of Marketing Research*, 30 (February), 7–27.
3. J. Joseph Cronin and Steven A. Taylor (1992), "Measuring Service Quality: A Reexamination and Extension," *Journal of Marketing*, 56 (July), 55–68.
4. Richard L. Oliver (1993), "A Conceptual Model of Service Quality and Service Satisfaction: Compatible Goals, Different Concepts," in *Advances in Services*

Marketing and Management: Research and Practice, Vol. 2, Teresa A. Swartz, David E. Bowen, and Stephen W. Brown, eds., Greenwich, CT: JAI Press.

5. Robert A. Westbrook, Joseph W. Newman, and James R. Taylor (1978), "Satisfaction/Dissatisfaction in the Purchase Decision Process," *Journal of Marketing,* 42 (October), 54–60. It should also be noted that although satisfaction is an affective summary, it can be influenced by cognition.

6. Richard L. Oliver (1989), "Processing of the Satisfaction Response in Consumption: A Suggested Framework and Research Propositions," *Journal of Consumer Satisfaction, Dissatisfaction, and Complaining Behavior,* 2, 1–16.

7. Oliver (1993), *op. cit.*

8. John E. Swan and Linda Jones Combs (1976), "Product Performance and Consumer Satisfaction: A New Concept," *Journal of Marketing,* 40 (2), 25–33.

9. Kevin Coyne (1989), "Beyond Service Fads—Meaningful Strategies for the Real World," *Sloan Management Review,* 30 (Summer), 69–76, and Terence A. Oliva, Richard L. Oliver, and Jan C. MacMillan (1992), "A Catastrophe Model for Developing Service Satisfaction Strategies," *Journal of Marketing,* 58 (July), 83–95.

10. Dave Ulrich (1989), "Tie the Corporate Knot: Gaining Complete Customer Commitment," *Sloan Management Review,* 30 (Summer), 19–27.

11. Boulding *et. al.* (1993), *op. cit.,* and John A. Miller (1977), "Studying Satisfaction, Modifying Models, Eliciting Expectations, Posing Problems and Making Meaningful Measurement," in *Conceptualization and Measurement of Consumer Satisfaction and Dissatisfaction,* H. Keith Hunt, ed., Cambridge, MA: Marketing Science Institute, 72–91.

12. *Ibid.*

13. Miller (1977), *op. cit.*

14. Miller (1977), *op. cit.,* and Valarie A. Zeithaml, Leonard L. Berry, and A. Parasuraman (1993), "The Nature and Determinants of Customer Expectations of Service," *Journal of the Academy of Marketing Science,* 21 (Winter), 1–12.

15. Raymond P. Fisk and Kenneth A. Coney (1981), "Postchoice Evaluation: An Equity Theory Analysis of Consumer Satisfaction/Dissatisfaction with Service Choices," in *Conceptual and Empirical Contribution to Consumer Satisfaction and Complaining Behavior,* H. Keith Hunt and Ralph L. Day, eds., Bloomington: Indiana University.

16. Robert E. Burnkrant and Alain Cousineau (1975), "Informational and Normative Social Influence in Buyer Behavior," *Journal of Consumer Research,* 2 (December), 206–215.

17. Westbrook *et. al.* (1978), *op. cit.*

18. Richard L. Oliver (1980), "A Cognitive Model of the Antecedents and Consequences of Satisfaction Decisions," *Journal of Marketing Research,* 17 (November), 460–469.

19. John A. Howard and Jagdish N. Sheth (1969), *The Theory of Buyer Behavior,* New York: Wiley.

20. Richard L. Oliver and John E. Swan (1989), "Equity and Disconfirmation Perceptions as Influences on Merchant and Product Satisfaction," *Journal of Consumer Research,* 16 (December), 372–383.

21. John E. Swan and I. F. Trawick (1981), "Disconfirmation of Expectations and Satisfaction with a Retail Service," *Journal of Retailing,* 57, 49–67.

22. Richard L. Oliver and Wayne S. DeSarbo (1988), "Response Determinants in Satisfaction Judgments," *Journal of Consumer Research,* 14 (March), 495–507.

23. Ruth Bolton and James Drew (1991), "A Multistage Model of Customers' Assessments of Service Quality and Value," *Journal of Consumer Research,* 17 (March), 375–384.

24. A. Parasuraman, Valarie A. Zeithaml, and Leonard L. Berry (1988), "SERVQUAL: A Multiple-Item Scale for Measuring Consumer Perceptions of Service Quality," *Journal of Retailing,* 64 (1), 12–40.

25. William D. Perreault, Jr. and Frederick A. Russ (1976), "Physical Distribution Service in Industrial Purchase Decisions," *Journal of Marketing,* 40 (April).

Chapter 10

DESIGNING CUSTOMER SATISFACTION SURVEYS

10.1 OVERVIEW

Focusing the efforts of the organization on the things that matter most to its customers is the surest path to retaining customers and to increasing revenues and market share. Yet how do we know, scientifically and reliably, which aspects are most important? To find out it is essential to conduct customer surveys, carefully designed and scientifically administered. These surveys can be used to determine the extent to which customers are satisfied and delighted, and the extent to which this influences customer retention. They can also be used to pinpoint processes and subprocesses within the company where resources should be targeted.

If we follow some basic principles, it is fairly easy to design a very useful survey. Designing a good customer satisfaction survey is a skill, but one that can readily be acquired through diligent study and practice. This chapter presents one method for designing and writing a customer satisfaction survey. There are many possible approaches to take, but this particular method has been used frequently with great success. Regardless of the particular approach taken in designing the survey, use of the principles discussed in this chapter will ensure the survey's validity, relevance, and actionability.

Figure 10.1 summarizes the steps in designing and implementing a customer satisfaction survey. We begin with obtaining top management support and conducting exploratory research. From there, the sampling and data collection details should be worked out and the key business processes identified. Making the survey relevant to business processes is the foundation of our approach, and it is at that point where most surveys fail most completely. The survey is written according to a structure dictated by the business processes, the results are analyzed, and the main findings are synthesized. The main findings are then used to improve the business processes, and subsequent surveys are planned, to monitor progress and identify areas of further opportunity.

FIGURE 10.1

THE CUSTOMER SATISFACTION SURVEY PROCESS

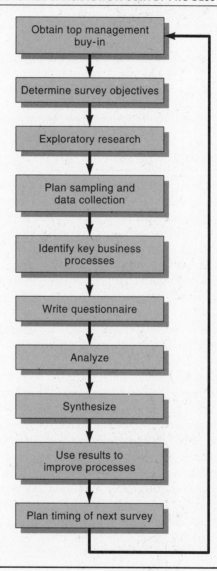

10.2 PREPARING TO SURVEY

Purpose

First, we must be clear about why the customer satisfaction survey is being conducted. Answers such as "to listen to the customer," or "because everybody has one," indicate a lack of clear motivation. Good reasons for doing a customer satisfaction survey include:

1. To help focus process improvement efforts (for example, a bank might determine that it is important to improve teller friendliness).
2. To determine whether previous improvement efforts have worked (if a teller friendliness program worked, then satisfaction with teller friendliness should have improved).
3. To discover strategic advantages or disadvantages (for example, the bank may discover that it has the friendliest tellers in the industry, making a people-oriented ad campaign believable and effective).

With a clear goal in mind, it will be possible to move on to the next step.

Ensuring Buy-In

Customer satisfaction survey results will not help a business unless top management is interested in obtaining the information. Thus it is essential that the survey project have top management buy-in. Top management should agree with the purpose of the research, and share the understanding of what actions will result from the survey. One way to achieve this is to involve management in the design and construction of the survey. It should be helpful for management to see drafts of the questionnaire and have the opportunity to suggest changes. This prevents the research results from getting rejected after the fact by a manager who feels the questions should have been asked differently.

In designing a survey, remember that in any service it is the frontline employees who have the bulk of the customer contact, and thus have the greatest opportunity to implement process improvements that directly affect the customer. Because the frontline employees will implement most of the important changes, their voice must be represented in the construction of the survey. They should be involved from the very beginning all the way through the final stages.

Involving both management and frontline employees is essential because it lays the groundwork for effective implementation of the survey's findings. Advance effort is also needed to ensure that the survey is relevant to customers. One of the most common errors in designing a customer satisfaction survey is to simply write the survey "cold," without adequately exploring the wants and needs of the customer. For example, a common approach is for a group of managers to sit down in a room and try to imagine what would be important to the customer. The problem with this approach is that real customers are often very different from what management imagines them to be like. This "shortcut" approach may appear to save time and money, but actually in the long run it is a foolish waste of energy, because the survey is sure to be worthless.

Exploratory Research

The exploratory research phase, conducted prior to writing the questionnaire, ensures that the issues covered by the questionnaire are relevant to the customer. (Many techniques that are useful for this purpose are discussed in Chapter 6.) In general, the idea is to structure the questionnaire around business processes, but *within process* the issues covered should be those that are "top of mind" to customers, and those issues should be worded in the customers' own words, as derived from focus group transcripts, complaints, and suggestions.

10.3 SAMPLING

Once the preliminaries are out of the way, it is time to consider the important sampling decisions. These are to determine what the sample population should be and how the sample should be drawn. The sample population, depending on the purpose of the survey, could include an organization's current customers, former customers, competitors' customers, or prospective customers.

Choosing The Sample Population

Current customers are a good place to start. They are familiar with the service provided, and also represent potential future profits, through repurchase and word-of-mouth considerations. But it may be difficult to sample a firm's current customers. If we are a retail bank, we know our customers well and have all sorts of information about them, including name, address, phone number, and account information. It is very easy to contact them. On the other hand, suppose we are in the summer boat rental business. Who are our current customers, especially if it is winter? We might suspect that a customer who has returned for several consecutive summers is a current customer, but we do not know for sure. That same customer may not be back the next year. In such a case it is best to sample customers as they conduct their transaction, perhaps contacting them two or three days after they have returned home. Alternatively, if the questionnaire is short enough, we may be able to administer the questionnaire as they prepare to leave, perhaps as part of the payment process.

If we sample only current customers, we may get too rosy a picture of how we are doing. Therefore, former customers are also a good source. Presumably we did something wrong that caused them not to return. In some cases it is possible to question former customers as they leave. For example, when a customer closes a bank account, the bank can ask some satisfaction questions, and also ask directly why the customer is leaving. If a business has customer addresses or phone numbers, it can also contact customers after they have left. A business such as a restaurant that conducts business on a transaction basis will have the most difficulty contacting former customers. Because the business does not keep detailed customer information, the only recourse is to sample the general population, or perhaps sample a more targeted version of the general population to uncover former customers. But this is generally too expensive to be practical.

Comparison with Competitors

Talking to competitors' customers is also a good idea, if the budget permits. It is very useful strategically to know where the competition is strong and where it is weak. One method often used is to administer the same questionnaire to both the competitor's customers and one's own customers. For example, suppose that on a five-point satisfaction scale, with 5 the best, reliability of phone service averages 3.5 for our customers and 2.5 for the competition. We might then conclude that we are perceived as more reliable and say that we had a one-point advantage on reliability.

Unfortunately, this method of analysis to evaluate performance relative to the competition can be misleading. Suppose, for example, that our customers are predominantly American, and the competition's customers are predominantly Japanese. Suppose also that, on average, Japanese are more demanding. In such a case our competitor's 2.5 may be just as good or better than our 3.5; we may be misled if we think we are better.

Few people would compare customer satisfaction levels across different countries, without making some sort of adjustment for national differences. But what about within-country satisfaction? Suppose, for example, that our customers are predominantly from the South, and the competitor's customers are predominantly from the North. If the northern customers are more demanding, our apparent advantage may be illusory. One must adjust the ratings by considering regional variation. Geographic differences are not the only factors that must be taken into account, however. We still may have bias in our comparison. For example, if our customers are older, and older people are less demanding, a bias will exist. Comparisons are not accurate unless age differences are considered.

These examples take us to a general point: any customer characteristics that might influence ratings must be considered when making a comparison with competition. Their customers are not the same as ours, and we should not pretend that they are if we wish to make valid comparisons.

Prospective customers are another group to question. They will not be able to respond to satisfaction questions because satisfaction requires experience. But they will be able to respond to questions about perceived quality. This is useful in evaluating marketing opportunities and weaknesses. Why are they not our customers already? What must we do to strengthen our image?

Drawing the Sample

Regardless of which group we survey, the sample must be drawn in a scientific manner so that a probability sample results. A *probability sample* is one in which any member of the population has a known (at least in principle) probability of being selected. For example, if two people were being chosen randomly from a list of ten people, then each person would have a selection probability of 2/10. It is not correct to do statistical analysis on samples drawn in any other way because the results will not be projectable to the full population.

The simplest way to ensure a probability sample is to generate a complete list of the population (the set of people we wish to find out about), and then use random numbers to select the sample. Such a sample is known as a *simple random sample*. An even simpler alternative is to take a random starting place on the list, and then sample every *n*th person (every 10th, every 500th, or whatever is necessary to draw a sample of the size required). This is known as a *systematic random sample*. Unless there is some sort of recurring pattern in the list, this method will result in samples that are almost as good as simple random samples. There are many other types of probability sampling techniques, such as stratified sampling and cluster sampling. Although we do not detail them here, you may read about them in marketing research texts.

One sampling method seems scientific, but it does not result in a probability sample. That is *quota sampling*. To collect a quota sample, the researcher tries to categorize people into groups defined by classifier variables, such as age and sex. Then the number to be surveyed in each age-sex cell is obtained based on the percentage of the population that should be in each age-sex category. The researcher then tries to find people who would fit in the cells. Because this search process is rarely random (have you ever seen interviewers in shopping malls trying to chase down a man 60–69 years old, to complete their quota?) some individuals inevitably have a higher probability of being selected. For example, someone who looks dangerous, insane, different, or just in a hurry, will almost certainly be skipped. Quota sampling should be avoided if at all possible.

10.4 DATA COLLECTION

How the survey data are collected can have a strong influence on their quality and usability. The first major decision that must be made is that of the *mode of data collection,* or what technical means will be used to collect the data.

Telephone surveys are popular for customer satisfaction measurement. A response rate of 80% or better is not unusual if the survey is interesting and well-designed. Telephone interviewing is also very fast. A typical setup is for the telephone interviewer to be seated at a computer or terminal, with the questionnaire projected on the screen. The interviewer can log responses immediately, sending data into the database automatically. Because data entry is incorporated directly into the interviewing process, data can be analyzed almost immediately. To maintain the integrity of the sample, it is important to call back those respondents who have not answered, several times, at different times of day, until their response is finally obtained. Otherwise the sample becomes biased in favor of people who are home a lot, such as retirees and housewives, and biased against those who are rarely home, such as business people and two-career households. One disadvantage of telephone interviewing can be cost, because interviewer time is not cheap, and long-distance phone bills can add up. Also, some people don't have phones.

Mail surveys are also popular, especially because they are relatively inexpensive. The main argument against mail surveys is the typically very low response rate, often in the 15 to 20% range. A naive researcher might conclude that this is not a problem. For example, if 200 completed surveys are needed, and a 20% response rate is expected, then 1000 surveys can be sent out. However, the real problem with a low response rate is not the actual number of respondents, but nonresponse bias. The fact that only 20% of the sample responds may create a bias. It may be the least busy 20%, the most interested 20%, etc. These respondents may differ from the population in important ways that will seriously damage the validity of the survey results. On the other hand, if 90% of the sample responds, the respondents will match the sample (and thus, by inference, the population) almost completely. This potential for nonresponse bias is such a problem that some major marketing research firms refuse to conduct mail surveys.

Nevertheless there are occasions in which budget constraints dictate that a mail survey be employed. In those cases it is imperative that everything possible be done to increase the response rate. Some of the ways this can be done include keeping the questionnaire short, enclosing a postage-paid return envelope, enclosing a cover letter that encourages responding, sending prior notification the week before, and reminders the week after, enclosing some sort of incentive, such as a quarter ("to brighten the day of a child you know"), making the survey easy to fill out, and making sure the mailing list is up to date. Mail surveys are the least expensive way to conduct customer satisfaction surveys, but they are a last resort.

Personal interviews are another method. Sometimes interviews are the only adequate way to collect data. For example, how else could one sample the customers of a fast-food restaurant? The only feasible alternative would be to hand out surveys to be filled out later, but handout surveys generate *extremely* low response rates (about 5%). Personal interviews generally have a good response rate, but it can be difficult to maintain a probability sample. The way to do that is to have very careful rules about exactly who will be sampled. Using the fast-food example, one might sample every tenth customer through the door, for example. This would be one way to make sure that interviewers did not pick only the friendliest, best dressed, or most attractive customers.

Response by interactive media (e.g., the Internet) is a mode of data collection that is going to be more popular in the future. As two-way cable systems become widespread, the potential for interactive questionnaires by cable is sure to increase. The biggest challenge will be how to get the attention of the sample, over all of the other information that is likely to bombard them over the cable. The strategy for using this medium will depend greatly on the details of the system, which are still evolving.

Comment cards are a poor, but frequently used, method of collecting data. These are often seen in hotel rooms, on restaurant tables, and in shops. There are several fatal problems with using comment cards to collect customer satisfaction survey data. First, although every customer is a potential respondent, there is no serious attempt to induce customers to respond. In effect, the entire population is being halfheartedly sampled. The result is an extremely low response rate. That alone would cause a serious nonresponse bias problem. Moreover, there is a bias in that the people who use comment cards tend to have extremes of opinion. Either they are ecstatic (occasionally) or they are furious (almost always). Thus the respondent pool is also drastically biased in favor of hotheads and grumps. Comment cards are appropriate only as an exploratory device to generate hypotheses about areas of concern. These hypotheses can then be implemented in customer satisfaction surveys that are appropriately designed to sample properly and minimize nonresponse bias.

Given that we have decided how to administer the questionnaire, the question remains as to who should administer it. It is tempting to reduce cost by administering the survey in-house. This approach rarely works. To understand why, let us consider some examples. Suppose we are conducting a sample of internal customer satisfaction and we decide to save money by having management conduct the survey with personal interviews. It is likely that the respondents will be intimidated and will be unable to give honest responses. Or, suppose customers are to be given questionnaires by the sales force. If these questionnaires ask for an evaluation of the sales force, sales people may be tempted to give the questionnaire only to customers who are happy or to fill out some of the questionnaires themselves. In both cases the administration of the questionnaire causes bias, because the people administering the questionnaire are not disinterested parties. The best way to overcome these problems is to commission an outside researcher or company to administer the questionnaire. Generally this practice will cost more, but the increase in unbiasedness and professionalism will usually make the investment worthwhile.

10.5 WORDING

The wording of the items in a customer satisfaction questionnaire is crucial to the questionnaire's success. There are many ways mistakes can be made. Most important, the questionnaire must be written in language relevant to the customer—that is, by using the words of the customers themselves. It is easy to forget that company employees develop their own jargon, which diverges badly from common language usage. For example, bankers may talk about "ATM machines" but customers may talk about "cash machines" or "bank machines." Computer people may talk about "bits, bytes, RAM, and ROM," where customers may talk about whether the computer "is big enough to hold my programs." The gap in language can be huge, and the questionnaire must reflect the language of the customer, not the jargon of the company. One way to accommodate customers' terminology is to use transcripts of focus group interviews. If several focus group participants talk about something in the same way, then that way is probably the customers' vernacular.

One innovative way of discovering the customers' language is to put all of the statements obtained from customer verbatim responses into a computer database. The database can then be used to count which words are used the most, and how words are used together. Obviously a computer must be used to perform this onerous counting task.

Once we are confident that we know how customers talk about things, the next step is to decide what mix of closed-end (multiple-choice) and open-end (essay) questions to use. You know from school that multiple-choice tests are faster and easier. The same thing holds for customers. If the questionnaire is full of open-end questions, it will look lengthy and difficult. This generally means that the number of open-end questions should be severely constrained. Sometimes there is no way of avoiding an open-end question, but often an open-end question can be converted into a closed-end one. For example, the open-end question, "At what kind of store did you buy the computer?" could be changed to "Where did you buy the computer?: (a) computer store, (b) discount electronics store, (c) mail order, (d) phone order, or (e) other."

Usually a great deal can be learned from one or two strategically worded open-end questions, at the end of the questionnaire. The purpose of these questions is exploratory in nature, which means the questions might be marked "optional." One very useful question is, "What is the single biggest problem you have had as a customer?" Another is "What is the single most important thing we could do to improve our service?" Either question will provide a wealth of information. The verbatim responses from just one of these questions will keep a manager busy for hours, and deeply enrich that manager's intuitive understanding of the most important customer issues. We recommend making the responses available to management, unedited and uncensored.

Closed-end questions generally retain a standard form in a customer satisfaction survey. Every question should be worded roughly the same, with only the subject of the question changing. If, as is typical, we are wishing to measure the level of performance, we will want to know if performance meets expectations with quality, satisfaction, or as expected. Figure 10.2 shows some of the main ways in which the satisfaction question can be worded. The first two examples in the figure are quality questions. In the first case, the researchers seek to measure the reputation of the company overall. This measure should not change much over time, although it may slowly drift up or down. The second case measures quality of a particular transaction. It is important that the researcher realizes whether the overall reputation of the company or the quality of specific transactions is sought. Generally it is preferable

FIGURE 10.2

WORDING THE SATISFACTION QUESTION

Quality (cumulative)

Please rate the quality of this restaurant:

☐ Excellent   ☐ Good   ☐ Fair   ☐ Poor

Quality (transaction-specific)

Please rate this visit to the restaurant:

☐ Excellent   ☐ Good   ☐ Fair   ☐ Poor

Satisfaction

How satisfied were you with this visit to the restaurant?

☐ Very satisfied   ☐ Satisfied   ☐ Dissatisfied   ☐ Very dissatisfied

Disconfirmation

Please rate this visit to the restaurant:

☐ Much better than expected   ☐ About as expected   ☐ Worse than expected to measure the quality of transactions. This is because quality improvement (or deterioration) will be detected more quickly by a transaction-specific question, because a reputation question involves not only recent transactions, but also to some extent *all* past transactions.

The next example is a satisfaction question. Note that satisfaction, by its very nature, is transaction-specific. It also implies experience, where quality questions can measure perceptions of quality even without experience. We show a scale from "Very Satisfied" to "Very dissatisfied," but other scales are possible, such as, for example a "Delighted" to "Terrible" scale.[1] The last example is a disconfirmation question, measuring comparison with expectations. This last question is the one we advocate.[2] This is because, under some fairly reasonable assumptions, it can be shown mathematically that comparison with expectations will correlate higher with customer retention than either a quality question or a satisfaction question.[3]

Note also the way the categories of this question are set up. It is well-known among customer satisfaction researchers that the typical customer satisfaction or quality question produces very skewed responses, with an inordinate number of responses at the very top end of the scale.[4] Essentially too many people say "Excellent" or "Very Satisfied" when they really just mean that they didn't experience any problems. By making the top category "Much Better than Expected," it is much more difficult for the respondent to check the top box. We have found that the skewness of the scale decreases dramatically, thereby increasing the information imparted by the scale and ensures that the people checking the top box really are delighted. Although this question is a comparison with expectations question and not a satisfaction question, for convenience we will generally refer to the "Worse than Expected" respondents as "Dissatisfied," the "About as Expected" respondents as "Satisfied," and the "Much Better than Expected" respondents as "Delighted." Because of the very strong link between disconfirmation and satisfaction, this relabeling is not too much of a stretch.

One key issue is how many scale points (response categories) to use. Good results may be obtained from three, four, five, seven, ten, or just about any number of scale points. We recommend using three scale points, in association with a disconfirmation scale, because this enables us to model the effects of satisfaction and delight separately.[5]

10.6 UNNECESSARY QUESTIONS

Some questions that frequently appear in customer satisfaction surveys are not really necessary. These include expectations questions and importance questions. Figure 10.3 shows examples of each. The idea behind the expectations question is to measure methods of performance separately, and then subtract expectations from performance to get a "gap," which indicates performance versus expectations.[6] Unfortunately there are statistical and methodological problems with this practice.[7] The suggested remedy would be to measure disconfirmation directly.[8] This has the double advantage of being more statistically reliable and cutting the length of the questionnaire.

In the case of importance questions, the motive is to concentrate on issues important to customers. Unfortunately, including importance questions not only

FIGURE 10.3

EXAMPLES OF UNNECESSARY QUESTIONS

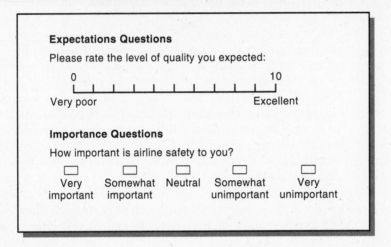

adds length to the questionnaire; it does not work. Take, for example, the question in Figure 10.3. It is hard to imagine a customer who will not report that airline safety is "Very Important." At the same time, airline safety is not *determinant* of either initial choice or satisfaction. Because just about all airlines have indistinguishable safety records (except for commuter airlines), airline safety will hardly ever lead to any important behaviors. For our purposes, airline safety can be ignored. This is not to say that the maintenance crews should be laid off, but rather that the status quo is appropriate, because an incremental shift in safety measures would have little effect on anything measurably important. Determining which dimensions of quality have an impact is still important, of course, but it turns out that this can be done very efficiently using statistical methods on only the satisfaction questions (see Chapter 11).

10.7 QUESTIONNAIRE STRUCTURE

The most important element of effective questionnaire design (and the element most often done badly) is structuring the questionnaire around business processes. Figure 10.4 shows a typical questionnaire structure. At the top are summary questions. These are then linked to overall satisfaction questions on each of the processes. The overall process satisfactions are then linked to satisfaction on dimensions within the process. The reason for building a structure of this sort is that the context of customer satisfaction measurement is quality improvement, and improving quality demands ownership, which is only possible if the results of the survey are linked to business processes. Thus we *structure* the questionnaire around the structure of the business, but within the process we consider the issues the *customer* considers relevant, and we *word* the questions in the customer's language.

FIGURE 10.4

QUESTIONNAIRE STRUCTURE

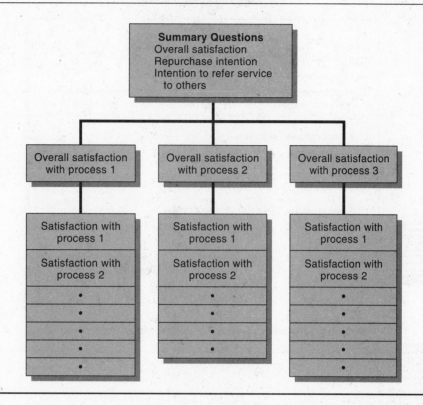

Ultimately we wish to create overall attitudes and behavioral intentions toward our business. Thus we include summary questions on the questionnaire (see Figure 10.5) that will have the closest relationship with actual behavior. The first example question in Figure 10.5 is an overall comparison-with-expectations question. This will be an overall question, regardless of whether quality, satisfaction, or comparison with expectations is being measured.

The second summary question is a repurchase-intention question. In many cases this question can be calibrated against actual repurchase behavior by tracking the respondents over time to check whether they actually repurchase or not. For example, suppose 90% of the people who check "100% repurchase intention" actually repurchase. This finding calibrates the meaning of the "100%" box at 90%. Note that this question involves several categories. Another common way of wording the repurchase intention is a yes-no question. Statistically it is possible to show that the information contained in a yes-no question is much less, which means that a much larger sample size is required to obtain a similar amount of information. For this reason it is always better to use several categories.

The third summary question is a word-of-mouth question. The idea is to see

FIGURE 10.5

EXAMPLES OF SUMMARY QUESTIONS

Overall Satisfaction/Quality/Disconfirmation

Please rate this visit to the dentist:

☐ Much better than expected   ☐ About as expected   ☐ Worse than expected

Repurchase Intention

How likely are you to visit this dentist the next time you need dental care?

☐ 100%   ☐ 80%   ☐ 60%   ☐ 40%   ☐ 20%   ☐ 0%

Intention to Refer Service to Others

How likely are you to refer this dentist to others?

☐ Very likely   ☐ Somewhat likely   ☐ Neither likely nor unlikely   ☐ Somewhat unlikely   ☐ Very unlikely

FIGURE 10.6

EXAMPLES OF PROCESS QUESTIONS

Process Overall Questions

Please rate the in-flight meal you were served:

☐ Much better than expected   ☐ About as expected   ☐ Worse than expected

Process Dimension Questions

Please rate the vegetables in your in-flight meal:

☐ Much better than expected   ☐ About as expected   ☐ Worse than expected

Please rate the dessert in your in-flight meal:

☐ Much better than expected   ☐ About as expected   ☐ Worse than expected whether the service was good enough to generate positive word of mouth, which can produce secondary financial benefits through the attraction of new customers. Since it is difficult to calibrate this question, its usefulness is limited.

Under the summary questions are those about individual business processes (see Figure 10.6). They include overall questions for the process and detailed questions about the various dimensions of the process. These various questions form a chain that can be used to explain overall satisfaction, repurchase intention, and behavior. The idea is that satisfaction on the process dimensions drives overall satisfaction with the process. The overall process satisfactions then drive overall satisfaction, which drives repurchase intention, which drives repurchase behavior.[9]

Finally, the questionnaire generally includes classification questions, which are used to segment the respondents. They may include any of a wide variety of possible questions, including demographics, geography, usage occasion, type of customer, or other questions relevant to the managerial scenario being inspected.

10.8 OTHER ISSUES

There are a number of other issues that influence the effectiveness of the customer satisfaction measurement process. One issue is questionnaire length. A long questionnaire hurts the response rate. But how long is too long? As a rough rule of thumb, a questionnaire should not be longer than about two pages. We have used questionnaires as short as 8–10 questions with very good results. It is better to start with what is absolutely necessary, and then to stop! The enemy of the effective questionnaire is the "nice to know" question, as in "As long as we're doing a survey, it would be *nice to know* whether they've seen our advertising or not." "Nice to know" questions are generally mildly interesting to managers but have no impact on management.

A second issue is how often to survey. This may be dictated by budget. If there is enough money to sample every two years, then sample every two years, even if six months would produce better information. One rule of thumb is that the interval of measurement should be roughly equal to the time it takes to implement a quality improvement effort. More frequently than that may not be useful, because things will not have had time to change. However, it is often important to sample frequently, if only to monitor competitive advances. Large companies typically survey continuously, but report results on a monthly or quarterly basis. Small companies may find sampling once per year an appropriate trade-off between cost and benefit.

Companies that begin a customer satisfaction measurement program should be very careful about changing the survey. One of the key benefits of customer satisfaction monitoring is to see whether there is improvement (or deterioration) over time. It is difficult to compare results if the questions or the scale are changed. It is advisable to maintain continuity in the wording of the questions, to the extent possible. Likewise, it is advisable to maintain the same scale. If the wording or scale needs to be changed, then it is important to do a split test, using each version at the same time, for the same population, to see how the old and new versions map into one another.

Many companies are using customer satisfaction scores as one input to the compensation of employees. This is a proven way to make employees care about customer satisfaction, but great care must be taken to ensure that the measures are used fairly. For example, suppose Salesperson A has a bad bonus this quarter because factors outside his/her control caused the customer satisfaction ratings to drop. The shipments to Salesperson A's region might have been late. In this case, the salesperson will have a great deal of resentment toward the satisfaction measurement program and probably will do anything possible to rig it or sabotage it in the future.

Or suppose, similar to the problem of comparing satisfaction with competitors, Salesperson A's customers are simply more difficult to please because of some personal characteristic that is prevalent in A's region. A's scores will be bad, all other things being equal, and it is really outside A's control. Again, Salesperson A will feel as though the system is not fair and will fight the system every chance he/she gets. Plans linking satisfaction scores with compensation must be very careful about adjusting for factors that make the comparison unfair.

Often to get honest responses, especially when sampling internal customers, suppliers, or channel customers, it is necessary to promise anonymity or confidentiality. These two things are not the same. *Anonymity* means that the researcher will not know who the respondent is. Thus tricks such as coding each "anonymous" mail questionnaire with an identifying ID number are unethical and could lead to legal action against the company. *Confidentiality* means that the researcher knows who the respondent is, but won't tell. This is a feasible possibility when the questionnaire is being administered by a third party. It should be made clear to the respondent whether the responses are anonymous or confidential, and then the researcher should scrupulously stick to the bargain. Generally speaking, a promise of confidentiality (or, even better, anonymity) will increase the response rate and make the responses more candid.

Another ethical issue arises with the use of the questionnaire for purposes other than its stated purposes. For example, suppose the real reason the questionnaire is being given is to qualify sales leads. The conversation might go like this:

Interviewer (INT): How satisfied are you with the performance of your vacuum cleaner?

Respondent (RESP): It's OK, I guess.

INT: How long have you owned it?

RESP: About 10 years.

INT: Were you aware that the average life of a vacuum cleaner is 5.7 years?

RESP: Why, no.

INT: Let me tell you about our new vacuum cleaner. . . .

Such a use of a "customer satisfaction survey" is a gross ethical violation and due cause for investigation by consumer protection agencies.

Another ethical violation is the use of a "customer satisfaction survey" to impart information about available services. A dialog might be:

INT: How would you rate your life insurance policy, on a 1 to 5 scale?

RESP: 5, I think.

INT: How would you rate your awareness of our homeowners' policies?

RESP: Gee, I didn't know you had homeowners. 1, I guess.

INT: How would you rate your awareness of our car insurance policies?

RESP: You have car insurance, too? I didn't know that. 1?

INT: How would you rate your awareness of our personal liability policies?. . .

With more and more "questionnaires" like these, it is no wonder that compliance rates are dropping like a rock.

10.9 SUMMARY

In summary, we will emphasize those aspects of designing a customer satisfaction survey that are most often done incorrectly. Key points to remember in survey design are:

1. Always do exploratory research before writing a questionnaire.

2. Make sure you have a probability sample.

3. Minimize nonresponse bias. Use phone surveys if possible.

4. Have an objective third party administer the survey.

5. Use transaction questions rather than cumulative questions.

6. Minimize the number of open-end questions.

7. Use a three-point disconfirmation scale, if possible.

8. Word the scale in such a way that top box usage is minimized.

9. Don't use separate expectations questions or importance questions.

10. Structure the questionnaire around business processes.

REVIEW QUESTIONS

1. Suppose you manage a grocery store.
   (a) Design a sampling plan for conducting a customer satisfaction survey.
   (b) Plan and defend an appropriate mode of data collection.
   (c) Determine the relevant business processes.
   (d) Write a repurchase intention question and an overall satisfaction question.
   (e) Write an overall process question and two process dimension questions.

2. Think of a company for which a mail survey would be appropriate.
3. Find a customer satisfaction survey from your daily life and criticize it according to what you have learned from this chapter.

ENDNOTES

1. Robert A. Westbrook (1980), "A Rating Scale for Measuring Product/Service Satisfaction," *Journal of Marketing*, 44 (Fall), 68–72.
2. A similar form is recommended in James M. Carman (1990), "Consumer Perceptions of Service Quality: An Assessment of the SERVQUAL Dimensions," *Journal of Retailing*, 66 (Spring), 33–56.
3. Roland T. Rust and Anthony J. Zahorik (1992), "A Bayesian Model of Quality and Customer Retention," presented at the ORSA/TIMS Joint National Conference, San Francisco.
4. Robert A. Peterson and William R. Wilson (1992), "Measuring Customer Satisfaction: Fact and Artifact," *Journal of the Academy of Marketing Science*, 20 (Winter), 61–71.
5. Wayne S. DeSarbo, Lenard Huff, Marcelo M. Rolandelli, and Jungwhan Choi (1994), "On the Measurement of Perceived Service Quality: A Conjoint Analysis Approach," in *Service Quality: New Directions in Theory and Practice*, Roland T. Rust and Richard L. Oliver, eds. Thousand Oaks, CA: Sage Publications, 201–222.
6. A. Parasuraman, Valarie A. Zeithaml, and Leonard L. Berry (1988), "SERVQUAL: A Multiple-Item Scale for Measuring Consumer Perceptions of Service Quality," *Journal of Retailing*, 64(1), 12–40. The authors refer to this difference as "quality," but it would be more accurate to call it disconfirmation.
7. See Carman (1990), *op. cit.*, and S. Paul Peter, Gilbert A. Churchill, Jr., and Tom J. Brown (1993), "Caution in the Use of Difference Scores in Consumer Research," *Journal of Consumer Research*, 19 (March), 655–662.
8. Carman (1990), *op. cit.*
9. Raymond Kordupleski, Roland T. Rust, and Anthony J. Zahorik (1993), "Why Improving Quality Doesn't Improve Quality (Or Whatever Happened to Marketing?)," *California Management Review*, 35 (Spring), 82–95.

Chapter 11

ANALYZING CUSTOMER SATISFACTION SURVEYS

11.1 OVERVIEW

The primary purposes of analyzing customer satisfaction surveys are not only to give management a clearer idea of how satisfied customers are, but also to pinpoint areas in which customer satisfaction improvement is likely to generate desirable customer behaviors, such as higher customer retention. For example, suppose an airline finds out that satisfaction with in-flight meals is low. That information alone is not enough to justify action, because satisfaction with meals may have very little affect on customer retention.

We have seen in the previous chapter how grouping questions by business process (e.g., in-flight meals) can result in managerially relevant information. Using statistical methods, it is possible to determine which processes have the greatest impact. It is also possible to assess statistically the most important process dimensions (e.g., perhaps main course, beverages, or service, within the process of in-flight meals).

Further, statistical methods can be employed to find out whether solving problems (moving customers from dissatisfaction to satisfaction) or adding extras (moving customers from satisfaction to delight) has the larger affect. This chapter also shows some specific techniques for turning questionnaire results into actionable information that can improve customer retention.

11.2 PREDICTING REPURCHASE INTENTION

Repurchase intention usually has a very direct link to customer retention. If the information is collected as a percentage and if we accept those percentages at face value, we may see an immediate link to market share and profitability. But usually these numbers are not exactly right. For example, fewer than 100% of those saying they have a 100% likelihood of returning will actually return. But historical data can be used to validate these categories. So, for example, we might be able to say that 93.4% of the "100%" category do repurchase. This information allows us to make a clear link to market share and profitability.

FIGURE 11.1

EFFECT OF OVERALL SATISFACTION AND DELIGHT

	Repurchase Intention
Delighted	95.2%
Merely satisfied	84.7%
Dissatisfied	31.3%

Effect of delight = .952 − .847 = .105

Effect of satisfaction = .847 − .313 = .534

How do overall satisfaction and overall delight relate to repurchase intention? This relationship is easily determined by examining the average repurchase intention of the "Dissatisfied," "Satisfied," and "Delighted" categories. Figure 11.1 shows sample data. We see that Delighteds are likely to return 95.2% of the time, Satisfieds are likely to return 84.7% of the time, and Dissatisfieds are likely to return only 31.3% of the time. Simple subtraction allows us to see the incremental effects of moving a customer from satisfied to delighted, or from dissatisfied to delighted: an added 10.5% from delighting a customer, and an added 53.4% from satisfying a customer.

11.3 PREDICTING OVERALL SATISFACTION

It is nice to know that overall satisfaction has a big effect, but that information is meaningless unless we can figure out what *produces* overall satisfaction. The technique involves analyzing satisfaction data from the business processes.

Separating the effects of satisfaction and delight means that we have to create two new variables, a satisfaction variable and a delight variable, from every three-point scale response. Figure 11.2 shows how to build the new variables. The new variables are constructed as "dummy variables," indicating that their value is either "0" for "no" or "1" for "yes."

If the response was "1 = Dissatisfied," then the customer was neither satisfied nor delighted. In this case, both the satisfaction and delight variables are coded "0." If the response was "2 = Satisfied," then the customer was satisfied but not delight-ed. Thus we set the satisfaction variable to "1" and the delight variable to "0." If the response was "3 = Delighted," then the customer was both satisfied and delight-ed. Both variables are thus coded as "1." These operations are easily accomplished using the "recode" options of any standard statistical package.

A data set prepared for analysis will have the general form of Figure 11.3. The respondents (customers) are rows, and the satisfaction and delight variables are columns. We can see that the columns should include the overall satisfaction score, the process satisfaction scores, and the process dimension satisfaction scores. They should also include overall delight, the process delights, and the process dimension delights. The columns do not have to be in the order shown in Figure 11.3, but they must be present somewhere.

Because every respondent will have answered every question, there will be *missing data* that must be represented in some way. Typically it is appropriate to choose

FIGURE 11.2

CONVERTING THE RAW SATISFACTION SCORES TO DUMMY VARIABLES

Raw Score	Satisfaction Dummy	Delight Dummy
1 (dissatisfied)	0	0
2 (satisfied)	1	0
3 (delighted)	1	1

FIGURE 11.3

PREPARING THE DATA SET FOR ANALYSIS

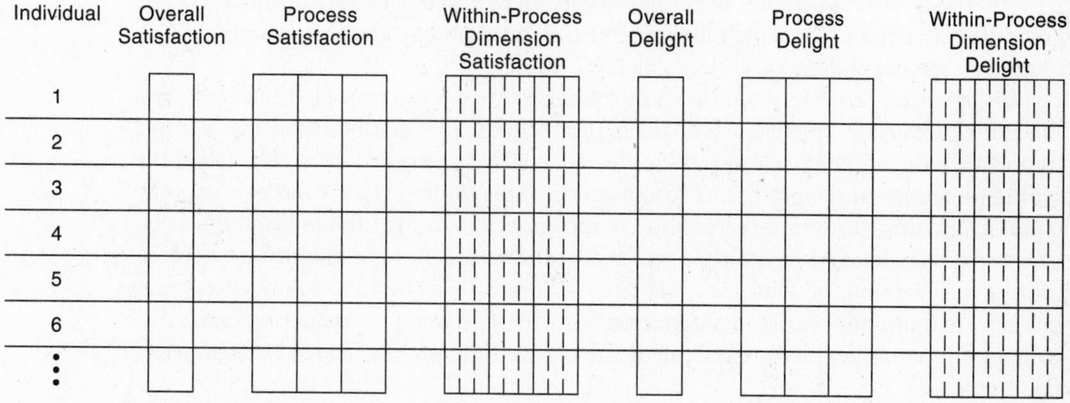

one particular way in which a missing observation will be denoted. The researcher may designate a symbol, or the statistical package may indicate which symbol to use.

Given that missing data exist in the data set, which they generally do, some sort of strategy must be devised for dealing with them in the analysis. There are several missing data options typically available in statistical packages. Often the default option, the option which happens automatically unless you override it, is the "listwise deletion" option. That is, any row (respondent) that contains a missing variable is thrown out of the analysis. This is the appropriate missing data option for bivariate analyses. However, for multivariate analyses, this option is often a very bad one, because most of the data set will end up getting thrown out. Another option, often used by customer satisfaction researchers for multivariate analyses, is *mean substitution,* in which a missing value is replaced by the mean for that variable. This option preserves the size of the data set, but at the expense of including some "data" that do not actually exist. Other, more elaborate methods include *data imputation,* which uses the other variables to predict what the missing value would be. This sophisticated approach is not available on all statistical packages. (We recommend mean substitution unless a data imputation option is available.)

If a complete data set has been constructed, there are both simple (bivariate) and more complex (multivariate) ways to relate the process satisfactions to the overall satisfaction. The simplest technique is to run regression analyses, one predictor at a time, relating each process satisfaction to the overall satisfaction. An example is shown in Figure 11.4. We would pay particular attention to three statistics in the printout. The R^2 tells us the proportion of the variance of the dependent variable that is explained statistically by the independent variable. In this case we see that BILLING explains 25% of the variance of OVSAT. We would also take a close look at the sign of the t statistic. In this case it is positive, which indicates that an increase in billing satisfaction (BILLING) should have a *positive* impact on overall satisfaction (OVSAT). Finally we would look at the p-value, which reports the result of a hypothesis test on the regression coefficient. Given a typical alpha value used to test hypotheses, .05 for example, the p-value can be compared to this number. In this case .00 is less than .05, which means that the independent variable is significantly related to the dependent variable, at the .05 level.

If the correlations between the independent variables are roughly the same, then the above bivariate approach will do a pretty good job of obtaining the relative importance of the predictor variables. An alternative approach explicitly takes the multicollinearity of the predictors into account. This multivariate approach uses the equity estimator[1] to obtain regression coefficients that control for multicollinearity. The appealing alternative, multiple regression analysis, is not a good idea under conditions of severe multicollinearity, because the regression coefficients are too unstable. Severe multicollinearity is a common feature of customer satisfaction data, due to halo effects. A detailed treatment of the equity estimator is beyond the scope of this book.

Figure 11.5 shows an example of output from the equity estimator. Notice that all predictors are included at once, rather than running one regression per predictor. The interpretation of the standardized equity estimator coefficients is essentially equivalent to that of beta coefficients in multiple regression analysis, but not all of the statistical hypothesis tests are available. We can see at a glance, though, that SALES and BILLING have the biggest effects, based on the size of the coefficients. Also, the signs are all positive, indicating that all predictors have a positive relationship with overall satisfaction.

11.4 PREDICTING OVERALL DELIGHT

The approach here is similar to predicting overall satisfaction, with one key exception. Remember that our psychological framework dictates that it is possible to delight only a customer who is already satisfied. This means that dissatisfied customers are not really prospects for delight, and thus they should be deleted from the analysis. (They should not be permanently removed from the data set—only excluded from this analysis!) Figure 11.6 shows an abbreviated view of the data set, highlighting the cases that should be tossed out. We can see that any respondent who has a "0" for the overall satisfaction dummy variable is by definition dissatisfied and not a candidate for delight. Deleting these respondents is easy to do in any standard

FIGURE 11.4

PREDICTING OVERALL SATISFACTION: EXAMPLE WITH BIVARIATE RESULTS

DEPENDENT VARIABLE = OVSAT

Independent Variable	Beta Coefficient	Standard Error	t	p
Billing	.50	.15	3.33	.0

$R^2 = .25$

FIGURE 11.5

PREDICTING OVERALL SATISFACTION: EXAMPLE WITH MULTIVARIATE RESULTS

DEPENDENT VARIABLE = OVSAT

Independent Variable	Standardized Equity Estimator Coefficient
Billing	.45
Sales	.50
Product	.25
Repairs	.19

statistical package. Figure 11.7 shows an example bivariate regression analysis relating billing delight (BILLDEL) and overall delight (OVDEL). In this case the R^2 is very low (.02) and the p-value indicates that the predictor variable is not significantly related to the dependent variable. Figure 11.8 shows the multivariate version of the analysis, using the equity estimator. We can see that repair delight (REPDEL) and sales delight (SALEDEL) are the most significant predictors.

11.5 PREDICTING PROCESS SATISFACTION

The analyses in Section 11.3 showed how the process satisfaction scores could be related to the overall satisfaction score. Ultimately, though, we will need to know what drives the overall process satisfaction. Thus we relate the process dimensions to the overall process satisfaction. Again, we may do this simply using bivariate regression or in a more sophisticated way using equity estimator regression.

Figure 11.9 shows the results of a bivariate regression analysis relating billing accuracy (ACCURATE) to billing satisfaction (BILLING). The significant p-value indicates that there is a significant relationship, and the sign on the beta coefficient indicates that the variables are positively related. The corresponding multivariate analysis is shown in Figure 11.10. Here we only have collected data on two process dimensions, billing accuracy (ACCURATE) and whether the bill is easy to understand (EZ). Billing accuracy appears to be somewhat more important, based on the relative sizes of the coefficients, but both have a positive effect on billing satisfaction, as we would expect.

FIGURE 11.6

PREDICTING OVERALL DELIGHT: PREPARING THE DATA

Individual	Overall Delight	Overall Satisfaction	Process 1 Delight	Process 2 Delight	•••
1	1	1	1	0	•••
2	0	1	0	0	•••
3	0	0	0	0	•••
4	1	1	0	1	•••
5	0	0	0	0	•••
⋮	⋮	⋮	⋮	⋮	⋱

(Delete all cases for which overall satisfaction = 0)

FIGURE 11.7

PREDICTING OVERALL DELIGHT: EXAMPLE WITH BIVARIATE RESULTS

DEPENDENT VARIABLE = OVDEL

Independent Variable	Beta Coefficient	Standard Error	t	p
BILLDEL	.15	.12	1.20	2.0

$R^2 = .02$

FIGURE 11.8

PREDICTING OVERALL DELIGHT: EXAMPLE WITH MULTIVARIATE RESULTS

DEPENDENT VARIABLE = OVDEL

Independent Variable	Standardized Equity Estimator Coefficient
BILLDEL	.18
SALEDEL	.30
PRODDEL	.10
REPDEL	.42

11.6 PREDICTING PROCESS DELIGHT

Again, as in Section 11.4, we must weed out the respondents who are not prospects for delight. Figure 11.11 shows a schematic of the data set, illustrating that all individuals who are dissatisfied with the process overall should be eliminated from this stage of the analysis. As before, we may use bivariate regressions to get a rough idea of the relative impact of the predictors. Figure 11.12 shows an example. In this case

FIGURE 11.9

PREDICTING PROCESS SATISFACTION: EXAMPLE WITH BIVARIATE RESULTS				
DEPENDENT VARIABLE = BILLING				
Independent Variable	Beta Coefficient	Standard Error	*t*	*p*
ACCURATE	.32	.09	3.56	.00

$R^2 = .10$

FIGURE 11.10

PREDICTING PROCESS SATISFACTION: EXAMPLE WITH MULTIVARIATE RESULTS	
DEPENDENT VARIABLE = BILLING	
Independent Variable	Standardized Equity Estimator Coefficient
ACCURATE	.36
EZ	.24

FIGURE 11.11

PREDICTING PROCESS DELIGHT: PREPARING THE DATA

Individual	Process Delight	Process Satisfaction	Dimension 1 Delight	Dimension 2 Delight	...
1	1	1	1	0	...
2	0	0	0	1	...
3	0	1	0	0	...
4	1	1	0	1	...
5	0	0	0	0	...
⋮	⋮	⋮	⋮	⋮	⋱

(Delete all cases for which process satisfaction = 0)

it is clear that accuracy delight (ACCDEL) does not have much impact on billing delight (BILLDEL). The *p*-value is insignificant and the R^2 is very low. The multivariate analysis, shown in Figure 11.13, also shows little impact based on either predictor. In fact, one of the predictors actually has a slight negative relationship, which is probably equal to zero, within sampling error.

11.7 ESTIMATING RELATIVE IMPORTANCE

So far we have seen how to quantify relative impact, but this is not the same as determining managerial importance. A simple example will explain why. Suppose,

FIGURE 11.12

PREDICTING PROCESS DELIGHT: EXAMPLE WITH BIVARIATE RESULTS

DEPENDENT VARIABLE = BILLDEL

Independent Variable	Beta Coefficient	Standard Error	t	p
ACCDEL	.01	.13	.08	.4

$R^2 = .00$

FIGURE 11.13

PREDICTING PROCESS DELIGHT: EXAMPLE WITH MULTIVARIATE RESULTS

DEPENDENT VARIABLE = BILLDEL

Independent Variable	Standardized Equity Estimator Coefficient
ACCDEL	.01
EZDEL	− .02

for example, that complaint recovery is one of the processes we are analyzing, and that we wish to determine its importance. Further, suppose that regression analysis shows that moving customers from dissatisfied to satisfied in complaint recovery has a large impact on customer retention. By itself, this information would seem to suggest investing in complaint recovery systems. However, suppose we also knew that only one tenth of one percent of our customers ever had a complaint. Then we would realize that any improvements in complaint recovery would affect very few customers. Our measure of importance must reflect not only the size of the statistical link, but also how many customers will be affected.

With the results of the bivariate or multivariate regression analyses, calculating relative importance is fairly easy. Figure 11.14 shows a simple calculation that may be used in the bivariate case, assuming the listwise deletion option was used for missing data. An importance score (0 to 100) is calculated by multiplying the bivariate R^2 by the percentage of cases present. In the figure we see that the R^2 was .40, and 10% of the cases were missing. This finding yields an importance score of 36. This approach works because R^2 is the percentage of variance of the nonmissing cases that is explained. Cases are presumably missing because that aspect was not relevant to the respondent. Thus the variance explained for *all* of the cases would be the R^2 times the percentage of cases present.

As we have seen, if the pattern of multicollinearity is complex, then the multivariate analysis using the equity estimator is more appropriate. In this case, assuming that the mean substitution option has been used for missing data, the square of

FIGURE 11.14

CALCULATING RELATIVE IMPORTANCE: SIMPLE (BIVARIATE) METHOD

Bivariate R^2	.40
$\times$	$\times$
% cases present	90%
Importance (0–100)	36

FIGURE 11.15

CALCULATING RELATIVE IMPORTANCE: MULTIVARIATE METHOD

Standardized equity estimator coefficient squared	.25
$\times$	$\times$
100	100
Importance (0–100)	25

the standardized coefficient, multiplied by 100, gives an importance weight on a 0 to 100 scale. An example is shown in Figure 11.15. The resulting importance weights give a good sense of *"which buttons to push" to get the most impact.*

11.8 IMPORTANCE-PERFORMANCE MAPPING

The importance-performance map is another data presentation device that many managers find appealing. The idea is derived from standard quadrant analysis, which has been used for many years in business strategy. In general, this approach argues, we should be most concerned about those issues for which the importance is high, and our performance (typically measured by average satisfaction) is poor. These issues yield the greatest potential for gain.

We make one key change to this widely used approach, however. Because converting satisfied to delighted typically requires different programs from converting dissatisfied to satisfied, we analyze them separately. So, we measure performance as either percent satisfied, or percent of satisfied who are delighted. To implement this approach, we start with importance and performance data such as those shown in Figure 11.16. This addresses the issue of converting dissatisfieds to satisfieds. We then map the processes in Figure 11.17. The quadrants are roughly defined by the averages on the two axes.

The upper-left quadrant is where we are doing well, but the importance is low, and thus maintaining the status quo is suggested. In some cases, there may be opportunities for transferring resources from the processes in this quadrant. The upper-right quadrant is where we are doing well, and importance is high. This area represents our competitive strengths. We should trumpet this competency in advertising and personal selling. The lower-left quadrant is an area in which we are not doing

FIGURE 11.16

IMPORTANCE-PERFORMANCE IN DRIVING SATISFACTION: OVERALL PROCESS DATA

Process	Importance	% Delighted
Billing	45	40
Sales	50	70
Product	25	80
Repairs	6	50

FIGURE 11.17

IMPORTANCE-PERFORMANCE IN DRIVING SATISFACTION: QUADRANT MAP

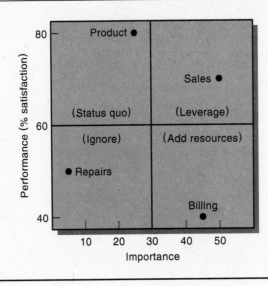

FIGURE 11.18

IMPORTANCE-PERFORMANCE IN DRIVING DELIGHT: OVERALL PROCESS DATA

Process	Importance	% of Satisfied Who Are Delighted
Billing	18	5
Sales	30	30
Product	10	40
Repairs	14	50

FIGURE 11.19

IMPORTANCE-PERFORMANCE IN DRIVING DELIGHT: QUADRANT MAP

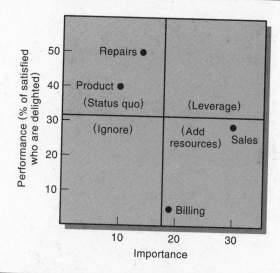

particularly well, but it doesn't matter. It is better to ignore these areas. The lower-right quadrant represents our area of greatest opportunity. It is important, and we are not doing well. Resources should be added to this area.

One caveat should be mentioned with regard to quadrant maps. Remember that the quadrants are defined in a somewhat arbitrary manner. Therefore, processes that are near a borderline should be examined carefully. For example, Product is close to the upper-right quadrant. There may be some leverage opportunities. Also, if there is not much variance on a dimension (e.g., *all* of our processes have very high and roughly equal performance), then dividing that dimension may be questionable.

Figures 11.18 and 11.19 show the data for deriving a quadrant map for driving delight, and the map. Comparison with Figure 11.17 shows that the satisfaction quadrant map may be very different from the delight quadrant map. For example, Repairs changes position on the map. Apparently we are doing something right to delight repair customers, even though we have some trouble getting our customers satisfied in the first place.

The quadrant analysis can also be employed at the process level. Figures 11.20 and 11.21 show the importance-performance maps of satisfaction and delight about whether the bills are accurate and easy to understand. The maps show pretty clearly that making the bills more accurate should be a high priority in improving satisfaction with billing; however, neither of these dimensions seems to have much ability to delight the customer.

FIGURE 11.20

IMPORTANCE-PERFORMANCE IN DRIVING PROCESS SATISFACTION

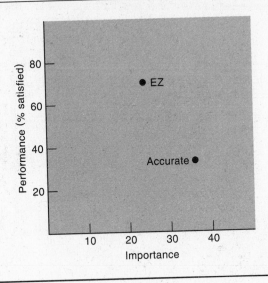

FIGURE 11.21

IMPORTANCE-PERFORMANCE IN DRIVING PROCESS DELIGHT

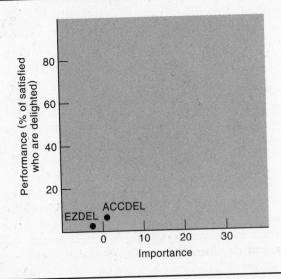

11.9 SUMMARY

We have seen that it is possible to derive some very valuable insights from customer satisfaction survey data, but these results are possible only when the questionnaire is organized around business processes. We can also benefit by differentiating between the conversion of customers from dissatisfied to satisfied and the conversion of satisfied customers to delighted.

Analyses may be conducted in either a simple or sophisticated manner, although greater accuracy is associated with the more sophisticated approach. In either case, importance scores show the impact of each variable in driving satisfaction (or delight). The importance scores may be mapped in an importance-performance quadrant chart, which yields managerial recommendations about which variables to emphasize.

REVIEW QUESTIONS

1. Out of 100 respondents to your customer satisfaction survey, 1 is dissatisfied, 98 are satisfied, and 1 is delighted. The importance scores show clearly that overall satisfaction is more important than overall delight in predicting repurchase intention. Which would you emphasize? Why?
2. If you found out that accuracy in billing was an area in which you had a high importance score and many dissatisfied customers, what would you do next?
3. You are VP of marketing at a major hotel chain. Your customer satisfaction researcher brings you the results of his/her customer satisfaction survey analysis. It includes a multiple regression of the process satisfaction scores (on a 1-to-5 scale) versus overall satisfaction (also on a 1-to-5 scale). What questions or comments do you have?

ENDNOTE

1. Lakshman Krishnamurthi and Arvind Rangaswamy (1987), "The Equity Estimator for Marketing Research," *Marketing Science*, 6 (Fall), 336–357.

STATISTICAL QUALITY CONTROL OF CUSTOMER SATISFACTION

11A.1 THE PHILOSOPHY OF QUALITY CONTROL

All outputs, whether they represent the thickness of a machined part or the satisfaction of customers, have random variation which occurs naturally. That is, even a precision drill press does not produce exactly the same result every time, and a service provider will not satisfy every customer equally, even if the service is essentially the same. In statistics we refer to this random fluctuation as *random error,* and all statistical models include this random error explicitly. This chapter applies the statistics of random variation to determine when outcomes are different from what would be expected by random chance. This approach is essentially equivalent to statistical hypothesis testing in concept, but the use of multiple samples makes the statistical formulas differ from those of typical hypothesis testing.

If we acknowledge that random variation exists, then it also is implied that apparent differences may in fact be based solely on random chance. For example, if Alan and Barbara are service providers and Alan's average customer satisfaction rating is higher than Barbara's, this result may reflect nothing more than random chance. Even if the difference actually does reflect ability, such interpersonal differences are completely normal because the distribution of abilities itself has random variation in it. In fact, if the population is symmetrically distributed, half of the population is certain to be below average. With this in mind, statistical quality control does not look at the individual but rather examines the success or failure of the *process* as a whole.

Analysis of the variation within a process is facilitated by the use of multiple samples. That is, information can be gained by repeating the sampling process several times in different locations or time periods, giving some insight into how and why results vary across different samples. Examining samples that produce results that are far out of the ordinary leads to asking how those samples are different. That in turn leads to identifying the factors that make those samples different. These factors are referred to as "assignable causes" or "special causes."

We begin the chapter by showing how to build and use control charts to identify samples that are out of the ordinary. We show how the use of these charts in services is very different from how they are used in manufacturing. We show how assignable causes can be identified and how that information can be used to improve business processes.

The purpose of statistical quality control is to facilitate continual quality improvement. The process shown in Figure 11A.1 is used. We start by selecting

FIGURE 11A.1

THE STATISTICAL QUALITY CONTROL PROCESS

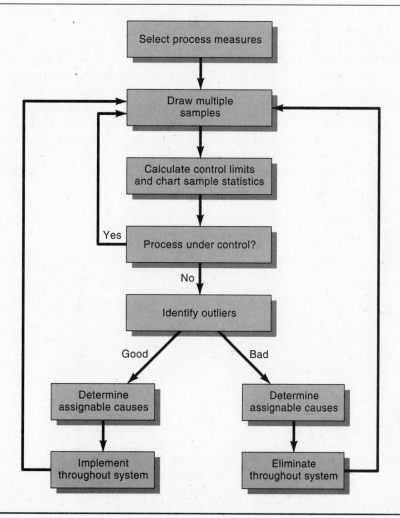

measures of success or failure (e.g., customer satisfaction scores), and then draw multiple samples (e.g., samples from different time periods, different stores, etc.). We then use statistical methods to determine whether or not the process is "under control." (If there are samples that produce widely discrepant results, then the process is assumed to be "out of control.") If the process is out of control, then we examine the most extreme ("outlier") samples to try to figure out why they are different from the other samples. These outliers may give us information that we can use to implement improvements throughout the organization. The remainder of the chapter details how a statistical quality control approach can be applied to customer satisfaction measures.

11A.2 CONTROL CHARTS

Control charts are used to depict graphically the normal range of the data and to highlight the exceptional observations. They always have the general form shown in Figure 11A.2. The vertical axis represents the outcome, and the horizontal axis refers to the particular sample (or replication). Each point plotted on the chart represents a summary statistic from a sample such as the mean customer satisfaction rating, for example.

The U line represents the upper control limit. This line represents three standard deviations above the average (denoted as CL for centerline). The L line represents the lower control limit, which is three standard deviations below the average. Only about one observation in 400 should fall outside the control limits. Figure 11A.3a shows a typical process which is exhibiting a normal amount of random deviation. We say that such a process is "under control."

FIGURE 11A.2

CONTROL CHART AND OUTLIERS

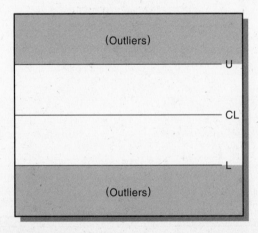

FIGURE 11A.3

DETERMINING WHETHER A PROCESS IS UNDER CONTROL

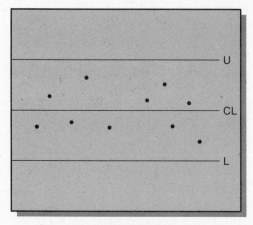

a. Under Control

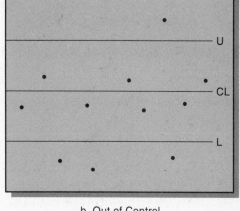

b. Out of Control

Given that we expect to find almost no observations outside the control limits, when we do find an observation out there, we should immediately ask ourselves what is going on. Such an outlier may be different from the other observations; random variation is not adequate to explain that much deviation. When several observations are outside the control limits, they are probably not being produced in the same way (it is statistically unlikely) and we say that the process is "out of control." Figure 11A.3b shows an example. When a process is out of control, a greater-than-expected number of bad outcomes tends to result. Bringing a process under control often facilitates a decrease in variation among outcomes and *improves the average outcomes.*[1]

There are several kinds of control charts, and we will see examples throughout. We will also see that the way control charts are used in services is in some ways different from the way they have traditionally been used in manufacturing.

11A.3 QUALITY CONTROL IN MANUFACTURING

Statistical quality control was originally developed to improve manufacturing operations. A typical scenario might involve a machine that produces parts of a particular size, let us say .52 mm wide. The actual manufactured parts must be quite close to this intended width to work properly. The goal of quality in the manufacturing arena is thus **adherence to specifications.** Quality is usually gauged by whether or not the measurements stay within the control limits. Taguchi refers to this as the "goalpost syndrome" (because it implies that anything within the control limits is good enough), and recommends instead a "loss function" in which further from specifications is always worse, even if measurements are within the control limits.[2]

If too many outliers are found, the process is judged to be out of control and the search for an assignable cause begins. In manufacturing this process involves examining the defective parts to see what might have gone wrong and looking at the production records for any pattern that might explain the problems. The search for assignable causes is highly centralized and is focused on the factory floor.

Once an assignable cause is found, implementing change is a matter of changing whatever was producing the defects. If, for example, defects become more numerous as time since an equipment inspection passes, inspections might be scheduled more often. This solution assumes that too long a period between inspections causes the machines to go out of adjustment and is implemented in a centralized way, on the factory floor.

11A.4 QUALITY CONTROL IN SERVICE

Statistical quality control should be conducted very differently in services. Consider a typical services scenario: a regional bank has dozens of branches, each of which has several tellers. Quality will depend on performance that is very decentralized. So, even if top management devises a perfect method for serving the customer, quality will not be achieved if the tellers don't implement it properly.

Managers of services may be tempted to apply the statistical quality control ideas directly from manufacturing. This procedure involves setting service specifications. For example, a teller might be permitted an average of no more than five minutes per transaction or be expected to answer the telephone in two rings or less. But specifications such as these do not really look like manufacturing specifications. They are somewhat arbitrary. For example, why not four minutes per transaction, or six? Why not one ring, or three? Also, deviation from specifications is not necessarily a bad thing. For example, if the specification is five minutes per transaction, and a particularly fast or efficient teller averages three minutes, the performance should be considered good, even though it does not match the specification.

To use statistical quality control in services, we must first realize that the key measure of importance is not the internal process but the satisfaction of the customer. The more satisfied the customer is, the higher the quality is. So, quality control should emphasize satisfaction rather than specifications. This can be done by charting the mean satisfaction scores of samples of customers. For example, in the bank scenario above, the average customer satisfaction at each branch can be charted. If the process is out of control, we can take advantage of the fact that the outliers are samples of people rather than machine parts. In many cases we can actually ask those people what made their satisfaction so low (or high). For this reason, identifying assignable causes is often easier than in manufacturing.

Implementation of change is somewhat more difficult, however. Unlike manufacturing, where changes are made in a central location, services usually require that changes be made in many locations at once. For example, if process improvements are to be adopted by bank tellers at bank branches, then those changes typically must be made at every branch, and this result may not be easy to accomplish.

11A.5 MULTISAMPLE STATISTICS FOR QUALITY CONTROL

We will proceed from the assumption that elementary statistical inference, including hypothesis testing, tests of means, and tests of proportions are familiar to the reader (or can be relearned quickly!). We also assume that the reader can calculate a sample mean, sample variance, and sample proportion.

Where statistical quality control departs from elementary statistics is the use of multiple samples. Every point on a control chart represents a sample. We thus need some new sample statistics to accommodate the multiple-sample case. For example, let us define the mean of the sample means $\overline{X}$ as $\overline{\overline{X}}$, and the mean of the sample proportions p as $\overline{p}$. The double line means that we have the average of averages. Also, let us define the mean of the standard deviations S as $\overline{S}$. These new sample statistics, along with control chart constants which we can look up from a table, are all we need to calculate the control limits on any of the control charts we will discuss in this book.

11A.6 INVESTIGATING MEANS

When we calculate the averages of quantitative variables (such as customer satisfaction), we are computing means. By random chance alone, we will get somewhat different means from different samples, even if the underlying process is identical. However, the control limits can be used to tell us which means are very different from what would be expected. The control limits, CL, L, and U, are calculated by the simple formulas shown in Figure 11A.4. Note that the only inputs are the average sample mean $\overline{\overline{X}}$, the average sample standard deviation $\overline{S}$, and a control chart constant A_3, which can be looked up in the table in Figure 11A.4.

To see how this works, consider the data in Figure 11A.5. This figure shows the average customer satisfaction rating for an airline (on a 1-to-5 scale) and the sample standard deviation of those ratings, for each of 20 cities. Note that the n (15 in this case) refers to the *number of customers* in each sample (city), and *not* the *number of samples* (cities). (You should verify the computed values of the sample statistics and control chart constants shown at the bottom of the figure.) Figure 11A.6 shows the resulting control chart. Note that there are many "good surprises" (satisfaction averages greater than U) and "bad surprises" (satisfaction averages lower than L). With this large number of outliers we are forced to conclude that the process is out of control.

The control chart in Figure 11A.6 assumes that there is the same sample size in each sample (as do almost all control charts in manufacturing). This assumption does not often hold true with customer satisfaction surveys. Even if the same number of questionnaires are sent out, chances are that different numbers will return. For this reason we need an approach for building a control chart when there are unequal sample sizes. Such a chart is shown in Figure 11A.7. The horizontal axis is now sample size, and the control limits, being dependent on sample size, become tighter as the sample size increases. We can also observe this from the formulas in Figure 11A.4. This format enables us to show the results from samples of different size in one figure. In Figure 11A.7 the variable being plotted is the percent (or, equivalently, proportion) of people checking the "top box" (most positive response) on a customer satisfaction survey.

FIGURE 11A.4

CONTROL CHART CONSTANTS

n	A_3	B_3	B_4	n	A_3	B_3	B_4
2	2.659	0	3.267	14	.817	.406	1.594
3	1.954	0	2.568	15	.789	.428	1.572
4	1.628	0	2.266	16	.763	.448	1.552
5	1.427	0	2.089	17	.739	.466	1.534
6	1.287	.030	1.970	18	.718	.482	1.518
7	1.182	.118	1.882	19	.698	.497	1.503
8	1.099	.185	1.815	20	.680	.510	1.490
9	1.032	.239	1.761	21	.663	.523	1.477
10	.975	.284	1.716	22	.647	.534	1.466
11	.927	.321	1.679	23	.633	.545	1.455
12	.886	.354	1.646	24	.619	.555	1.445
13	.850	.382	1.618	25	.606	.565	1.435

	CL	L	U
Mean ($\overline{X}$)	$\overline{\overline{X}}$	$\overline{\overline{X}} - A_3 \overline{S}$	$\overline{\overline{X}} + A_3 \overline{S}$
Standard deviation (S)	$\overline{S}$	$B_3\overline{S}$	$B_4\overline{S}$
Sample proportions ($\overline{p}$)	$\overline{\overline{p}}$	$\overline{\overline{p}} - 3\sqrt{\dfrac{p(1 - \overline{\overline{p}})}{n}}$	$\overline{\overline{p}} + 3\sqrt{\dfrac{p(1 - \overline{\overline{p}})}{n}}$

Source: Adapted from Irving W. Burr (1976), "Statistical Quality Control Methods," New York: Marcel Dekker, Inc. Copyright © 1976 by Irving W. Burr. Reprinted by permission of Marcel Dekker, Inc.

FIGURE 11A.5

AIRLINE SATISFACTION DATA

City	$\overline{X}$	S	City	$\overline{X}$	S
1	4.7	.1	11	3.3	.7
2	3.8	.3	12	3.5	.3
3	3.6	.5	13	3.6	.4
4	4.9	.0	14	3.4	.5
5	4.2	.2	15	4.1	.2
6	3.8	.3	16	4.2	.1
7	1.0	.9	17	3.1	.5
8	3.7	.3	18	3.5	.5
9	3.9	.4	19	3.7	.6
10	3.1	.6	20	4.6	.1

$\overline{\overline{X}} = 3.685$ U = 3.685 + .789(.375) = 3.981

$\overline{S} = .375$ CL = 3.685

$n = 15$ L = 3.685 − .789(.375) = 3.384

Source: "Statistical Quality Control Methods," by Irving W. Burr. Copyright © 1976 by Irving W. Burr. Reprinted by permission of Marcel Dekker, Inc.

FIGURE 11A.6

CONTROL CHART FOR MEANS

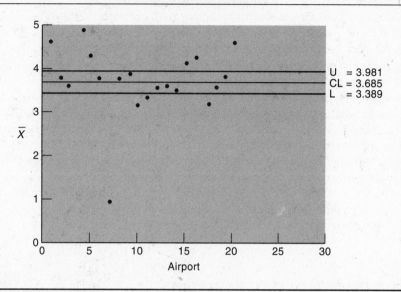

U = 3.981
CL = 3.685
L = 3.389

FIGURE 11A.7

CONTROL CHART WITH UNEQUAL SAMPLE SIZES

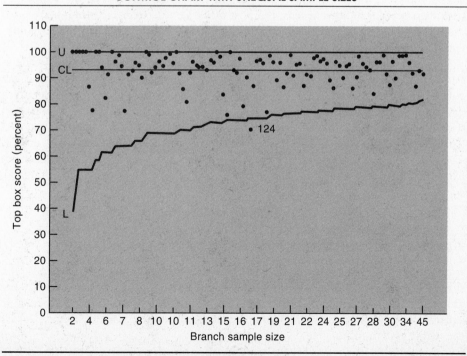

11A.7 INVESTIGATING PROPORTIONS

Proportions arise from yes-no questions. The general approach to plotting proportions on a control chart is essentially similar to the process for means, except that the control limits are calculated differently. The average proportion, averaged across the multiple samples, is denoted $\bar{p}$. It is the mean of the p's from the individual samples. The control limits are then calculated according to the formulas in Figure 11A.4.

As an example, consider the data in Figure 11A.8. A hotel chain with 30 hotels has sampled its guests and asked whether they have patronized the hotel restaurant. The result is a proportion for each hotel, listed in the second column. The average of the proportions, $\bar{p}$, is then calculated. From $\bar{p}$, along with the (same) sample size from each hotel, we can construct the control limits. The resulting control chart is shown in Figure 11A.9. In this case we presumably want the hotel guests to use the restaurant. Any points that are above the upper control limit are good surprises, and points below the lower control limit are bad surprises. Again, the fact that there are more outliers than one would expect indicates that the process may be out of control. Note especially Hotel 24, which is an extreme outlier.

11A.8 INVESTIGATING VARIATION

Control charts can also be used to analyze whether variation within samples is greater than one would expect. The statistic plotted is often the sample standard deviation S.[3] As an example, consider the data in Figure 11A.10. Thirty post offices have sampled 15 hours of service to find out the variation between the number of customers served. In other words, if a post office serves a very large number of customers in some hours and a very small number in other hours, then the variation, measured by the sample standard deviation S, will be high.

From the data in Figure 11A.10, we calculate the average sample standard deviation $\bar{S}$. From this and the control chart constants we look up, we can construct the control chart in Figure 11A.11. Because more-than-usual variation is generally a bad sign, points that are above the upper control limit should be regarded as bad surprises, and those below the lower control limit should be regarded as good surprises. It is not so clear in this case whether the process is out of control or not. There is only one outlier, and it may be unique. Still, the existence of such an extreme outlier should arouse suspicions.

11A.9 ASSIGNABLE CAUSES (SPECIAL CAUSES)

If the process is out of control, we would like to know why. Factors that cause the system to be out of control, "assignable causes," are important because we may be able to affect them. For "bad surprises," we would like to remove any assignable cause. For "good surprises," we would like to duplicate the assignable cause across the whole system, if possible.

FIGURE 11A.8

HOTEL RESTAURANT PATRONAGE DATA

Hotel	p		Hotel	p
1	.62		16	.80
2	.75		17	.67
3	.71		18	.73
4	.96		19	.81
5	.72		20	.64
6	.68		21	.66
7	.71		22	.69
8	.73		23	.67
9	.65		24	.02
10	.54		25	.70
11	.69		26	.70
12	.72		27	.68
13	.71		28	.54
14	.73		29	.69
15	.68		30	.73

$\overline{\overline{p}} = .68$ $n = 90$

$$\sqrt{\frac{\overline{p}(1 - \overline{p})}{n}} = .05$$

$U = .68 + 3(.05) = .83$
$CL = .68$
$L = .68 - 3(.05) = .53$

FIGURE 11A.9

CONTROL CHART FOR PROPORTIONS

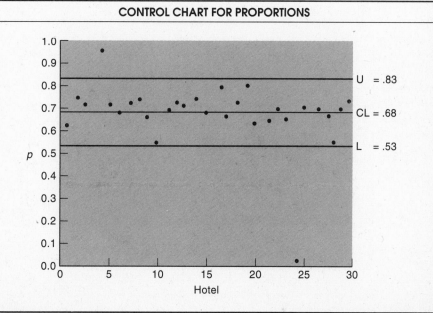

FIGURE 11A.10

HOURLY VARIATION IN POSTAL CUSTOMERS' SERVICE

Post Office	S		Post Office	S
1	6.5		16	6.9
2	6.8		17	6.5
3	7.1		18	6.5
4	5.9		19	6.3
5	5.7		20	6.7
6	6.0		21	12.4
7	6.3		22	6.1
8	6.7		23	6.3
9	6.5		24	6.7
10	6.6		25	6.6
11	6.6		26	3.1
12	5.8		27	6.4
13	7.1		28	7.0
14	4.9		29	6.8
15	6.1		30	6.5

$\overline{S} = 6.51$ $U = 6.51(1.572) = 10.23$

$CL = 6.51$

$n = 15$ $L = 6.51(.428) = 2.79$

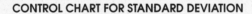

FIGURE 11A.11

CONTROL CHART FOR STANDARD DEVIATION

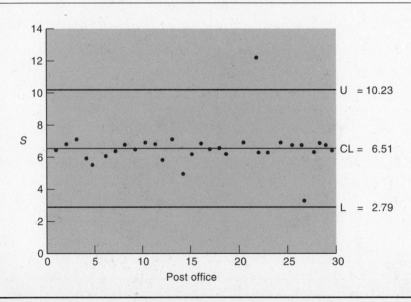

To see how this approach might work, let us look again at the example in Section 11A.6. Figure 11A.6 shows that without a doubt the process is out of control, and there are both good surprises and bad surprises. The next step is to study the outliers to see what makes them special. In this case it turns out that cities 7, 10, 11, and 17 had the lowest customer satisfaction, below the lower control limit. Cities 7, 10, and 17 also had very low on-time percentages. The implication is that the low on-time percentages at these airports must be improved. Also, greater attention to on-time percentage *across the entire system* may be beneficial. One possible way to improve the on-time percentage (actually used by American Airlines) is to stretch the scheduled flight time. For example, if a flight is scheduled for an hour and a half, but is often 15 minutes late, then it could be scheduled for an hour and 50 minutes. This approach might have the effect of improving customer satisfaction, *even without making any operational improvements*. Of course, the efficiency of arrival and departure procedures should also be carefully scrutinized.

On the good-surprise side, it turns out that cities 1, 4, 5, 15, 16, and 20, the outliers beyond the upper control limit, are all southern cities with mild weather, meaning that there are few winter weather delays. This finding points out an important lesson. The assignable causes are not always under management's control. Chicago's O'Hare Airport cannot be made warm in the winter, just because we know it would help!

Now consider the example in Section 11A.7, shown in Figure 11A.9. Hotel 4 is an outlier, with extremely high restaurant usage. It turns out that Hotel 4 is eight miles from the nearest competing restaurant. That is great for restaurant patronage, but not easily duplicated, because it is not usually a good idea to locate a hotel in an out-of-the-way location. The bad surprise is Hotel 24. Further investigation shows that Hotel 24 has its restaurant entrance behind the restrooms, down a back hallway. Maybe something can be done about this. For example, it might be possible to create a more convenient entrance. If that is not possible, then maybe the entire restaurant can be moved. If that is not possible, maybe the hotel can emphasize room service. This entrance convenience problem also sensitizes us to whether the restaurant entrances at *other* hotels in the chain might be made more convenient.

The post office example in Section 11A.8 (and Figure 11A.11) shows a process that looks like it is probably under control, with one outlier post office that is probably doing something wrong. Further investigation reveals that that particular post office sends all but one of its counter employees to lunch at noon, thus drastically reducing capacity and leading to excessive variation in service capability. Although not reflected in the control charts, we might also expect that this practice is enormously inconvenient for the postal customers, many of whom can come by only during the lunch hour.

How did investigation reveal these assignable causes? In general, we first generate a list of possible assignable causes, from talking to both customers and frontline personnel from the outliers. Focus group interviews are a good way to do this. From this process, the 8 to 10 most likely causes can be identified. The customers and frontline employees are then asked directly about the possible effect of these 8 to 10 causes. The positive assignable causes can be promoted throughout the system, and the negative causes can be eliminated. Many quality control people devote their attention solely to negative assignable causes, but when we are dealing with customer satisfaction data, positive surprises are just as meaningful, and potentially just as useful. Promoting positive surprises generally involves publicizing them, and making heroes out of the people responsible.

11A.10 SUMMARY

Statistical quality control results from a process orientation. That is, when things go wrong, blame the process, not the people. Then find out why the process is out of control.

There are some major differences between how statistical quality control is generally employed in manufacturing and how it should be employed with services. In particular, quality control in manufacturing involves conformance to specifications, whereas quality control in service involves maximizing customer satisfaction. If service quality is perceived as conformance to service specifications, the result is an artificially mechanical conceptualization of service that will tend to overemphasize internal processes and underemphasize customer satisfaction.

If, on the other hand, we do our statistical quality control on customer satisfaction itself, then positive surprises become very important. It is as important to understand the causes of good surprises as it is to understand the causes of bad surprises. We gain both by encouraging the causes of good surprises and eliminating the causes of bad surprises. The supplement, Computer Exercises for Service Marketing, includes a case that will provide practice on these methods.

REVIEW QUESTIONS

1. Check the control limit calculations in the examples in Sections 11A.6, 11A.7, and 11A.8.
2. For the data in Figure 11A.5, calculate the mean and standard deviation of the X's. Construct a confidence interval three standard deviations above and below the mean. Is this the same as the control limits calculated in Figure 11A.5? Why or why not?
3. Are there good surprises in manufacturing control charts? Why or why not?
4. Devise examples where means, proportions, and standard deviations could usefully be charted on control charts. What specific managerially useful information might arise from each chart? Think of a possible assignable cause for each and what management might do to improve the situation.

ENDNOTES

1. W. Edwards Deming (1986), *Out of the Crisis,* Cambridge, MA: MIT Center for Advanced Engineering Study, 380–387.
2. Phillip J. Ross (1988), *Taguchi Techniques for Quality Engineering,* New York: McGraw-Hill, 3–6.
3. The range, the difference between the maximum and the minimum, is another measure of variation that is often charted, but we will not discuss it here.

CASE

A MEASURE OF DELIGHT: THE PURSUIT OF QUALITY AT AT&T UNIVERSAL CARD SERVICES (A)

In the lobby of the headquarters building of AT&T Universal Card Services Corp., a crystal Malcolm Baldrige National Quality Award rotates silently on a pedestal within a glass case. On one marble wall, above a sheet of flowing water, are the words, "Customers are the center of our universe." The inscription on the opposite wall reads, "One world, one card." Despite a steady stream of visitors and employees, the lobby has the hushed and serene atmosphere of a shrine.

But on the upper floors of the building—in the heart of the operation that brought home the nation's top quality award—it is never silent. In a honeycomb of open and brightly lit cubicles, about 300 men and women are speaking intently but pleasantly into telephone headsets while deftly keying information and instructions into the computer terminals before them. In all directions, one phrase is repeated so often that it seems to hang in the air: "AT&T Universal Card, how may I help you?"

The workers appear private and autonomous, connected only to their customers on the other end of the line. Yet at any moment, day or night, there may be someone else listening. It may be a co-worker, monitoring the call in order to suggest how a request might be handled differently. It may be a team leader, gathering the information that will figure in next year's raises. It may be a senior

This case was written by Research Associate Susan Rosegrant as part of a joint effort between the Kennedy School of Government and the Harvard Business School. The case was prepared as the basis for class discussion rather than to illustrate either effective or ineffective handling of an administrative situation.

To order copies, call (617) 495-6117 or write the Publishing Division, Harvard Business School, Boston, MA 02163. No part of this publication may be reproduced, stored in a retrieval system, used in a spreadsheet, or transmitted in any form or by any means—electronic, mechanical, photocopying, recording, or otherwise—without the permission of Harvard Business School.

manager, putting on a headset to listen to calls while working out in the company gym. Or it may be a quality monitor in another building, scribbling ratings and comments on a one-page sheet that will help determine whether everyone in the company gets a bonus for that day. And all the while, as the pleasant voices talk on, a computer tracks every call that comes in, continually measuring how long it takes to answer each call, how many seconds are spent on each conversation, and whether any customers hang up before their calls are answered. In the eyes of the executives who designed the company's operating philosophy and strategic plan, the monitored calls were an indispensable component in boosting AT&T Universal Card over its competitors, and making it a true quality company.

The Challenge

In the summer of 1993, Universal Card Services (UCS) was, by most standards, in an enviable position. The wholly owned AT&T subsidiary had broken into the highly competitive credit card business in 1990, determined to build on the AT&T name with a philosophy of "delighting" customers with unparalleled service. To help do that, the company had created an innovative measurement and compensation system to drive the pursuit of quality and customer satisfaction. Now just three years later, UCS, with nearly 12 million accounts, was the number two credit card issuer in the industry. Not only that; in 1992 UCS was the youngest company ever—and one of just three service firms—to win the coveted Malcolm Baldrige National Quality Award.

But despite these successes, there was a sense within the Jacksonville, Florida–based company that some fundamental changes were in order. In particular, Rob Davis, vice president of Quality, was searching for ways to push UCS's quest for quality one step further. A number of factors triggered this critical self-examination. Competitors had begun to

close the gap opened by UCS when it pioneered its innovative policies and practices three years earlier. The departure of two key architects of company policy underscored the fact that now, with more than 2,700 employees and three new sites across the country, UCS was no longer in a startup, entrepreneurial phase. Finally, Davis and other senior managers were questioning many of the basic concepts underlying the measurement system that had helped the company achieve so much. Nearly everyone agreed that changes were needed in what the company measured, how it measured, and what it did with the information. There was no consensus, however, on exactly what to do.

The Founding

When AT&T recruited Paul Kahn in 1989 to lead its foray into the credit card business as UCS's president and CEO, the information technology giant had two main goals. It wanted to offer a combined credit card and calling card that would bolster its long-distance calling revenues. Perhaps more important, it wanted to regain the direct link to the customer that it had lost in 1984 when a court decision forced the spin-off of its regional Bell operating companies. With the backing of AT&T, Kahn, a 10-year veteran of First National Bank of Chicago and Wells Fargo Bank, developed a bold plan for breaking into the market, where unchallenged pricing practices and highly profitable operations were the norm. First, the new company did away with the annual membership fee, saving cardholders who signed up during the first year the $25 or more typically charged by issuing banks. Second, UCS set its interest rate on unpaid balances below what most bank issuers were charging, pegging it to the banking industry's prime lending rate.

In addition to such pricing strategies, AT&T and Kahn shared a vision of the kind of company they wanted to create: an organization where motivated and empowered employees would set new standards for quality in customer service. To achieve this ambitious goal, the new company set out to measure almost every process in sight. "We decided that we had to create an environment where the net takeaway to both the parent company and to the consumer was an experience superior to anything they'd had before," explained Kahn.

On March 26, 1990, during the Academy Awards, UCS aired its first ad. The combination of the AT&T name and the waived annual fee proved more potent than anyone had imagined. In the first 24 hours, UCS's 185 employees received 270,000 requests for applications or information. The company opened its one millionth account 78 days after launch.

Pillars of Quality

In contrast to many established companies that have struggled to superimpose "quality" on an existing corporate culture, UCS had the luxury of establishing quality as an overarching goal from the start. In fact, quality was less a goal than an obsession. The seven core company values—customer delight, continuous improvement, sense of urgency, commitment, trust and integrity, mutual respect, and teamwork—were emblazoned on everything from wall plaques to T-shirts and coasters. Senior management was convinced that quality processes—with the end result of superior customer service and efficiency—would give UCS a key competitive advantage in the crowded credit card marketplace. As a company brochure noted:

> Each time a customer contacts UCS, it's a moment of truth that can either strengthen our relationship with them or destroy it. Each call or letter is an opportunity to create a person-to-person contact that makes the Universal Card, and AT&T, something more than another anonymous piece of plastic lost in a billfold.

In order to provide such unprecedented customer service, the Business Team, an executive committee of a dozen top vice presidents headed by Kahn, took a number of steps (see organization chart, Exhibit 1). They made sure that the telephone associates—Universal's designation for its customer service representatives—were carefully selected, and then trained to "delight" customers. They set up benchmarking studies, comparing UCS both to direct competitors and to other high-performing service companies. They conducted a Baldrige-based quality assessment in the very first year, as well as each successive year, and used the results as the basis for a companywide strategic improvement process.

But the most unusual mechanism built into the organizational pursuit of quality was a unique and multifaceted measurement system, designed to measure performance on a number of levels both within the company and without. While it was not unusual for credit card issuers to monitor certain aspects of customer service, UCS's efforts went far beyond industry standards. Nor were most measurement systems designed to achieve so many purposes: to locate problem processes; to promptly address any problems discovered; to constantly assess how well customers were being served; and to reward exceptional performance. "We had an expression here, 'If you don't measure it, you can't move it,'" recalled Mary Kay Gilbert, a senior vice president who helped develop the original business plan for AT&T. "If you're not measuring a key process, you don't even know if you have a problem." UCS was determined not to let that happen.

The Quality Organization

As one of its first initiatives, Rob Davis and his Quality team developed two extensive surveys. The Customer Satisfier Survey was a questionnaire to gather market research data on what the company termed "customer satisfiers," the products, services, and treatment—including price and customer service—that cardholders cared about most. An outside market research firm conducted the survey, talking to 400 competitors' customers and 200 UCS customers each month. More unusual were the Contactor Surveys, for which an internal team each month polled more than 3,000 randomly selected customers who had contacted the company, querying them within two or three days of their contact. UCS's survey team administered 10 to 15 different Contactor Surveys, depending on whether a customer had called or written, and on the customer's particular reason for contact, such as to get account information or to challenge a bill. Survey questions such as, "Did the associate answer the phone promptly?" and "Was the associate courteous?" were designed to gauge overall satisfaction as well as the quality of specific services.

But the effort most visible to telephone associates and other employees, and the one that had the most profound effect on the company's day-to-day operations, was the gathering of the daily process performance measures. Senior managers had debated every aspect of this so-called "bucket of measures" at the company's formation, and it was at the heart of how UCS operated.

The Business Team had agreed that the best way to drive quality service and continuous improvement was to measure the key processes that went into satisfying the consumer—*every single day*. Building on the experience of credit card industry veterans recruited at startup, such as Fred Winkler, executive vice president for Customer Services, and adding information gleaned from the Customer Satisfier and Contactor Surveys as well as additional benchmarking studies, the Business Team assembled a list of more than 100 internal and supplier measures it felt had a critical impact on performance (see Exhibit 2 for an example of how UCS linked internal process measures with key satisfiers).

The original list was top-heavy with actions directly affecting cardholders—such as how soon customers received their credit cards after applying, and whether billing statements were accurate. But the list gradually expanded to include key production, service, and support processes from every functional area of the company, many of which were invisible to customers but which ultimately impacted them (see Exhibit 3 for a list of such processes). By the middle of 1991, Vice President Jean Collins and her Relationship Excellence team, the independent monitoring group within UCS charged with collecting the measures, were tracking about 120 process measures, many considered confidential. Indicators ranged from the quality of the plastic used in the credit cards to how quickly Human Resources responded to job resumes and issued employee paychecks, and to how often the computer system went down.

UCS did more than measure, though; it set specific standards for each measure and rewarded every employee in the entire company when those standards were met on a daily basis. To make clear the importance of quality, the bucket of measures was linked directly to the company's compensation system: If the company as a whole achieved the quality standards on 95 percent of the indicators on a particular day, all the associates—or nonmanagerial employees—"earned quality" for the day, and each "quality day" meant a cash bonus, paid out on a quarterly basis.[1] Although some top managers questioned the compensation/quality link, arguing that, in essence, the achievement of quality should be its own reward, Kahn felt the tie to compensation was essential. "I think we ought to put our money where our mouth is," he declared. "We wanted quality, and we ought to pay for it." The financial incentives were not insignificant: The bonus system gave associates the ability to add more than $500 to their paycheck every quarter, and managers could earn 20 percent above base salary.

The daily push to earn quality—and to earn a bonus—was an omnipresent goal.

Video monitors scattered around the building declared the previous day's quality results. Every morning at 8:00, Fred Winkler, in charge of operations, presided over a one-hour meeting of about a dozen senior managers to discuss the latest measures, identifying possible problems and proposing solutions. A summary of the "Fred meeting," as one manager dubbed it, could be dialed up on the phone later that morning. In each functional area, managers convened a similar quality meeting during the day, examining the measures for which they were responsible and, if they had failed to meet a particular indicator, trying to figure out what went wrong (see Exhibit 4 for a sample report showing telephone associate performance). Furthermore, the bucket of measures figured prominently in monthly business meetings, the Baldrige assessments, focus groups, and other regular process improvement meetings. According to Deb Holton, manager of Quality, the daily measures were on everyone's minds: "It is virtually impossible to be in this building for 10 minutes without knowing how you did the day before."

The Empowered Employee

At UCS, customers were referred to as "the center of our universe." At the center of the business, however, were the telephone associates who, although entry-level workers, had the highest pay and status among nonmanagerial employees. They, after all, were the frontline representatives who determined what impression customers took away from their dealings with UCS. Indeed, telephone associates were responsible for almost all customer contact—answering phones, taking applications, handling correspondence, and even collecting from overspenders and trying to intercept fraudulent card users.

To make sure that it had the right people for the job, UCS put applicants through a grueling hiring process: Only one in 10 applicants won an offer of employment after the two-part aptitude test, customer service role-playing, handling of simulated incoming and outgoing calls, credit check, and drug testing. Once hired, telephone associates received training for six weeks and two more weeks on the job. Instruction began with a two-day cultural indoctrination dubbed "Passport to Excellence," introducing concepts such as mission, vision, quality objectives, and empowerment. But the main purpose of the lengthy training was to give associates detailed coaching in telephone skills and the management of all phases of a customer inquiry, from initiation to conclusion.

UCS did not expect to get commitment and excellent customer service from the telephone associates, however, without giving them something in return. In fact, the company's vision of "delighting" customers rested on having "delighted" associates. Much of what the rest of the organization did—from Human Resources management to information support systems design and the measurement system itself—revolved around ensuring that telephone associates were able and motivated to provide the quality service that was the company's stated goal.

The Information Services group, for example, developed and continually upgraded U-WIN, an information management system tailored to the specific needs of the telephone associates. Drawing in part on the company's U-KNOW system—which gave managers online access to the customer, operational, and financial information in UCS's database, known as UNIVERSE—the U-WIN system allowed associates to pull up on their workstation screens information ranging from cardmember files, to form letters, to special product offers (see Exhibit 5 for an overview of the information management system). U-WIN even gave associates a head start on serving customers by automatically calling up cardmembers' accounts as their calls were being connected. "We're high touch, high tech," explained Marian Browne, vice president of Customer Relationships, the service area in which telephone associates handled general correspondence and responded to customer calls. "That means we work with our people and focus on our customers, but we can't do either unless we have leading-edge technology."

UCS top management was also determined to involve associates, listen to their ideas and concerns, and draw them into most facets of the business. Associates served side by side with senior managers on teams deciding issues ranging from what awards the company should bestow to how computer screens should be designed for maximum efficiency. They were encouraged to ask questions at monthly business reviews and at "Lakeside Chats"—quarterly question-and-answer sessions with Winkler held in the company cafeteria. And the UCS employee suggestion program, "Your Ideas ... Your Universe," was broadly publicized, with impressive results: in 1991, more than half the workforce participated, and management accepted and acted on almost half of the more than 5,000 suggestions.

In addition to these "empowerment"-oriented activities, the company looked for concrete ways to please associates. UCS provided generous fringe benefits, for example, including a free on-site fitness center for employees and their spouses, and reimbursement for undergraduate and graduate courses. The company supported a substantial reward and recognition program, sponsoring 6 companywide awards, 3 companywide recognition programs, and more than 30 departmental awards. And the Business Team encouraged managers to look for reasons to celebrate. Indeed, boisterous ceremonies in the cafeteria marking such events as all-company achievements or the bestowal of specific awards were a regular occurrence. "The culture we've developed is very focused around rewards and celebration and success," said Melinda Stickley, compensation/recognition manager. "We've got more recognition programs here than any company I've ever heard of."

The far-ranging programs and activities appeared to be paying off. According to annual employee opinion surveys, associates rated the company significantly higher in such categories as job satisfaction, management leadership, and communication than the norm for employees at high-performing companies. Not only that, absenteeism was low, and employee attrition was far below the average for financial services companies (see Exhibit 6 for selected employee opinion survey results and attrition and absenteeism rates).

Despite the efforts of senior managers to create a positive environment, however, the telephone associate's job was not easy. Many stresses arose simply from working for a 24-hour customer service operation—stresses that may have been particularly trying for UCS's well-educated employees.[2] Telephone associates, organized in teams of about 20, spent long days and nights—as well as periodic weekends and holidays—on the phone, performing a largely repetitive task. There was often mandatory overtime, particularly during unexpectedly successful card promotions, and associates knew their schedules only two weeks in advance.

Along with these largely unavoidable downsides, the particular culture of UCS imposed its own stresses. The pressure to achieve quality every day was an ever-present goad. Furthermore, the company's determination to continuously improve—captured in an oft-used phrase of Fred Winkler, "pleased, but never satisfied"—frequently translated into increased performance expectations for the associates. As the telephone technology systems got better, for example, managers expected associates to take advantage of the increased efficiencies by lowering their "talk time," the average amount of time they spent on the phone with each customer.

Finally, there was the monitoring. About 17 process measures were gathered in Customer Relationships, the general customer service area. To begin with, the information technology system tracked the average speed of answer, the number of calls each associate handled, and how long each associate spent on the phone. As a result of their exposure to the daily printouts detailing these statistics, most associates could rattle off with deadly accuracy how many calls they handled in a day—typically about 120—as well as how many seconds they spent on an average call—in the range of 140 to 160.

Perhaps more daunting, telephone associates were directly monitored by a number of people both inside and outside of Customer Relationships. As part of the gathering of the daily measures, specially trained monitors in both the Relationship Excellence group and an internal quality group listened in on a total of 100 customer calls a day.[3] The monitors—or quality associates—rated telephone associates on accuracy, efficiency, and professionalism, recording their comments on a one-page observation sheet (see Exhibit 7 for a description of these measures and how they were gathered).

Any "impacts"—UCS's term for a negative effect on a customer or the business—were reported at Customer Relationship's daily quality meeting, attended by representatives from both Relationship Excellence and the internal quality group.[4] Negative reports were then passed on to the team leaders of the associates involved to discuss and keep on file for performance reviews.

Other parts of the organization monitored calls as well, each with a slightly different purpose. Team leaders listened to 10 calls a month for each of the approximately 20 associates in their groups, using the observations to review and "develop" the associates. And *all* managers at UCS, regardless of their function, were encouraged to monitor at least two hours of calls a month to stay in touch with services and practices. Rob Davis, vice president of Quality, for example, held a regular monthly listening session with all his staff, followed by a discussion period to analyze the quality implications of what they had heard. Finally, the results of the Customer

Contactor Surveys, including verbatim remarks from cardholders about how associates treated them, were turned over to managers in Customer Relationships who could easily identify which associate handled a particular call if there was an "impact" or other problem to resolve.

The combination of high corporate expectations and these multiple forms of monitoring and feedback created considerable pressure at UCS not only to perform well, but to do so under intense scrutiny, at least for telephone associates. Some managers felt this took a toll. "The quality process, daily sampling, and feedback were not without pain," claimed Mary Kay Gilbert, who as senior vice president of Cardmember Services oversaw the Customer Relationships operation. "I had to stop people and say, 'Wait, we're here to make sure we're delivering the right service to customers. This isn't personal.'"

But others argued that the way the associates were monitored, and the way team leaders and managers delivered feedback, kept it from being a negative or stressful experience. Company policy dictated that all supervisors and managers were to treat associates with respect and to view mistakes as a learning opportunity. If an associate were overheard giving inaccurate information to a customer, for example, the team leader was not to rebuke the associate, but to explain the error and provide additional training, if necessary, so that the mistake would not occur again. "The positive stress for workers here is high risk, high demand, high reward," asserted Deb Holton, manager of Quality. "It is not the stress of coming in in the morning and checking their brains at the door."

Raising the Bar

Thanks in large part to the customer-pleasing work of the telephone associates, by the close of 1991 financial analysts had declared UCS a major success for AT&T. During that year, holders of the UCS card had dramatically increased AT&T calling-card usage. And after less than two years in business, UCS ranked a stunning third in the dollar volume of charges on its card, with $3.8 billion in receivables, $17.2 billion in total sales volume, and 7.6 million accounts. Industry kudos included a "Top Banking Innovation" award from American Banker and "Best Product of 1990" from *Business Week*.

Despite this stellar performance, the Business Team was convinced that it was time to shake things up—that everyone could do better. Although some executives initially balked at the prospect of a change, after a series of debates the Business Team agreed to "raise the bar" on the number of indicators the company had to achieve to earn quality. A compelling argument for the increase was the fact that associates were meeting or exceeding standards so consistently. During 1991, associates had made quality at least 25 days out of every month, and in August they had earned quality every day, often achieving 97 percent or more of the indicators. Managers, too, were doing well. "We wanted to take it up," explained Davis, "because of our strong commitment to continuous improvement."[5] Added Marian Browne, vice president of Customer Relationships, "Everything was going fine, but if you look at perfect service every day, we weren't giving perfect service every day."

With the Business Team's blessing, Kahn sent the following letter to all employees on December 26, just five days before the change was to take effect:

Dear UCS Colleague,

In the spirit of continuous improvement, UCS will take another step in our never-ending commitment to customer delight. Beginning Jan. 1, 1992, the quality objective for associates will move from 95 percent to 96 percent. The quality objective for managers will move to 96 percent for the target goal and 97 percent to 100

percent for the maximum goal. UCS's Excellence Award program will continue to reward quality as it has in the past—the only difference will be that the objective will be moved up for both managers and associates.

UCS people have demonstrated our value of customer delight since "day one." As we continue to improve our ability to delight customers, we'll also continue to evaluate and revise our quality standards and measurements. I'm extremely proud of the work each of you performs. Your dedication to our seven values continues to make UCS a leader in the industry.

What the letter didn't mention was that the raising of the bar was actually a double challenge: Not only did employees have to achieve a higher percentage of measures, but individual standards had been raised on 47 of the indicators, making each of them harder to earn. In addition, Collins and her Relationship Excellence team took advantage of the start of the calendar year and the relative lull after the holiday season to retire and replace a substantial chunk of the measures. While only 15 indicators had been dropped in all of 1991 and 26 added, the monitoring group abruptly cut out 48 indicators, many of them among the most consistently achieved, and replaced them with 46 new ones. In effect, this meant that close to half of the measures by which associates judged their daily performance—and were judged—were now different.

The reaction to the change was immediate. Associates earned only 13 quality days in January and 16 in February, and managers fared even worse. Not only was the company failing to make the new goal of 96 percent, it was missing quality by as much as six percentage points on a given day, well below the worst daily performance of the previous month. "We fell flat on our faces as far as the number of days we were paying out as a business," Davis recalled. Added Collins, "For most of the days we were well below even the old standard."

The abrupt dropoff took management by surprise. According to Robert Inks, who started as a telephone associate in May 1990, associates weren't so much mad as they were concerned—concerned that higher standards of efficiency might make it harder to deliver quality service, and concerned that regular bonuses might be a thing of the past. "The associates looked at it as, well, this is my money," explained Inks, "I'm not going to be getting my money." Added Pam Vosmik, vice president of Human Resources: "There was probably some grousing in the hallways."

It was no consolation that UCS was on the verge of logging its first profit. In fact, at a business meeting open to all employees, associates accused management of having raised the bar as a cost-cutting measure to avoid paying compensation. Nor was the timing of the slump propitious. UCS was ready to make an all-out push to win the Baldrige award, and although the site examiners would not arrive until September, it was critical that employees be motivated and on board. "I went to the Business Team," recalled Gilbert, "and I said, 'Look, we raised all these indicators and measures and I don't think the people around this table understand the impact. But if we start beating people up as a result of this, you can kiss the Baldrige good-bye.'"

Senior managers took the performance plunge to heart. In fact, according to Davis, some managers were so concerned by the apparent associate disaffection that they were ready to lower the bar to its previous level. Instead of backing down, however, the Business Team concocted an alternate scheme to reignite associate enthusiasm. In March, the same month that UCS submitted its Baldrige application, the company announced the "Triple Quality Team Challenge." The special incentive program allowed associates and managers to earn triple bonuses that

month for each quality day they achieved beyond a base of 20 quality days. If employees earned 22 quality days, for example, they would get credit for 26. A four-foot by 16-foot calendar board mounted in the cafeteria and small boards in each functional area displayed daily progress toward the goal. In explaining the incentive program, *HOTnews*, an internal publication reserved for important communiqués, noted:

> . . . quality results in January and through February 26 show UCS not doing as well as it did even before we raised our quality standards in 1992. Many of the current problems have nothing to do with our new standards or indicators, but are failures of basic courtesy and accuracy. "I know we can do better," says Kahn. "The results concern me and I know they concern you. It's important that we work together to meet our quality goals and delight our customers. The 'Triple Quality Team Challenge' must be a team effort—we need to help each other achieve our indicators, not look around for who's not making theirs and punish them."

Softening the System

The Triple Quality Challenge was a rousing success. Associates' quality days spiked back up to 25 in March, and managers earned 19 days (see Exhibit 8 for an overview of quality days achieved over time). But the organizational upset engendered by the raising of the bar, along with fears that telephone associates—on whose dedication the company's success depended—could become disillusioned, prompted a harder look at making both measures and feedback more participatory and more palatable. In the months that followed, UCS even abandoned the "pleased but never satisfied" expression because it gave associates a sense of inadequacy and futility.

Efforts to reach out to associates took a number of forms. Managers in Customer Relationships continued to coach team leaders, one-third of whom had been promoted from the associate level, to make sure they were comfortable and skilled at giving feedback. "We've got a lot of young, inexperienced team leaders, and what you have to teach your team leaders is that you can't use feedback as a club," noted Marian Browne. "You use it as a development tool. You don't do it to beat people up, or to catch people." Customer Relationships also began to experiment with peer monitoring, having telephone associates critique each other rather than relying solely on team leaders for developmental review.

Relationship Excellence, which had already been sharing the gathering of the daily measures with Customer Relationships since the end of 1990, helped other functional areas set up internal quality departments to co-sample, with the plan that they might eventually take over the measures entirely. Although some executives were concerned that this shift might hurt the integrity of the sample, Ron Shinall, a Relationship Excellence team leader, insisted it was a necessary evolution. "There's going to be a natural aversion to someone telling you how to make your process better if that person hasn't worked with you or been in that process," he declared.

Relationship Excellence also changed what it did with call observations. The daily Customer Relationships quality meeting, which had served largely as a chance for quality associates to report the mistakes they had caught, became, instead, a forum for discussion and learning. Telephone associates from the floor were invited to join the internal and external quality representatives, and the entire group debated whether negative impacts had occurred without ever identifying those who had handled the questionable calls. "It's helped get a lot of buy-in from the associates," remarked Darrin Graham, who had led Customer Relationships's internal quality department. "Back at the beginning, when you would hear that there is this group out there listening to my calls, you just naturally started to get an us/them mentality, and they're out to get us. Now that mentality is going away."

As part of this overhaul, Relationship Excellence experimented with no longer giving associates—or their team leaders—feedback on calls monitored for the daily measures. But although the experiment had been urged by an associate focus group, the so-called Nameless/Blameless program lasted only a few weeks. "The majority of the people wanted to know if they'd made a mistake," Browne explained. Feedback resumed, but with two important differences: negative impacts no longer went into associates' files, and team leaders received, and handed on, both good news and bad. The internal quality group also worked harder to stress the positive. "We used to walk up to people's desks and we'd have a piece of paper in our hand, and they'd be like, 'Oh no, here they come,'" recalled Paul Ferrando, team leader of Customer Relationships's first internal quality group. "And I'd say, 'Someone on your team had an excellent call.' When you bring good news, they don't grimace when you walk up to them anymore. People aren't afraid of quality, and they aren't afraid of this monitoring anymore."

The steady evolution of the system appeared to have increased associate acceptance of the measures. There would always, of course, be some employees who balked at being measured, as the following response to the June 1992 employee survey indicated:

A big handicap is being monitored constantly. The people are not relaxed. They are under so much stress that they will get a variance, that they don't do their job as well as they could. Monitoring should be used as a learning tool—we're all human and sometimes forget things.

But most telephone associates professed their support. "The reason that we're measuring is to find out what we're capable of, and what we're doing right, and what we can improve on, and what we don't need to improve," declared Cheryl Bowie, who took a large paycut from her former managerial position to become a telephone associate in 1992. "There is no problem here with the feedback. You're not branded or anything. It's just a learning experience."

On October 14, 1992, near the end of a challenging year of growth and change, Universal Card was awarded a Malcolm Baldrige National Quality Award. At a black-tie celebration party recognizing employees' part in the companywide effort, associates received a $250 after-tax bonus and a Tiffany pin, and a small group of associates, selected by lottery, traveled to Washington, D.C., for the actual Baldrige presentation. But the award did not lessen the sense of urgency at UCS. "When we learned we had won the Baldrige," recalled Quality manager Deb Holton, "our second breath was, 'But we will not be complacent.'"

In truth, UCS would have had to change, whether it sought to or not. Paul Kahn announced his resignation in February 1993 over differences within the company as to whether UCS should expand into new financial products, and Fred Winkler defected for archrival First Union Corp. in April. Although David Hunt, the banking industry executive who replaced Kahn, and Winkler's successor, AT&T veteran Gerald Hines, quickly won widespread acceptance, the departure of these two critical and charismatic leaders created anxiety about the company's future direction.

The competitive landscape within which UCS operated was also changing. Although by early 1993, the company had captured the number two ranking among the 6,000 issuers of credit cards, with almost 12 million accounts and 18 million cardholders, it was becoming increasingly difficult for UCS to make its product stand out. Competitors such

as General Motors Corp. had introduced their own no-fee cards, and the variable interest rates pioneered by UCS had become common. "The sad part is, our competition is catching up with us," lamented Mark Queen, manager of Customer Listening, and overseer of the Customer Contactor Surveys. "Where we need to continue to distinguish ourselves is in service."

But continuous improvement—finding ways to motivate associates beyond what they had already accomplished—was not an easy task. For one thing, with the company's growth slowing, it would no longer be possible for as many associates to quickly ascend the corporate ladder to team leader and other managerial positions. Moreover, the current measurements no longer seemed to be driving the quest for improvement, and Davis and others had become convinced that it was time to retool a system that no longer fit the needs of the company. Ironically, considering how much Universal Card had already done to create meaningful and effective measures, among the Business Team's top 10 goals for 1993 was the development of a world-class measurement system.

WEIGHING THE OPTIONS

By the summer of 1993, Davis's Quality organization was assessing a range of new approaches to measuring. In particular, a specially convened Measures Review Committee under Thedas Dukes, a senior manager now responsible for the daily measures, was taking a hard look at what to change.

Customer-Centered Measures

A project of particular interest to Davis was the company's early experimentation with customer-centered measures (CCM). While CCM might not change what UCS was measuring, advocates argued it would more concretely and powerfully express how the company was serving cardholders by stating this performance in terms of customer impacts.

Instead of reporting that 98 percent of cardholder bills were accurate on a given day, for example, a CCM report might state that 613 customers did *not* get a correct bill. "We are trying to change the language away from percentages and indexes to a language of customers," explained Davis. Added Ron Shinall, quality team leader, "It's hard to tell the difference between 99.8 percent and 99.9 percent, but in some of the high-volume areas, that can mean a tremendous number of people are actually impacted. Fractions of a percent mean a lot when you're talking about 40,000 daily calls."

UCS had been considering customer-centered measures since visiting early Baldrige winner Federal Express Corp. in the summer of 1991. Unlike UCS, with its 100-plus measures, Federal Express had selected just 12 processes it deemed critical to serving customers, and had based its reward system on that 12-component CCM index. In January 1993, Universal began a six-month test of CCM, reporting customer impacts on 13 existing process indicators that measured different aspects of accuracy and professionalism. The now 30-member Relationship Excellence group, which had changed its name to Quality Applications in December, sent out its first CCM report in March.

But the jury was still out on what impact CCM would have. Linda Plummer, a senior manager in Customer Relationships, applauded the idea of expressing error in human terms. Yet she found the initial reports, which simply listed the number of customers impacted in each category along with the effects per thousand contacts, to be meaningless. "Someone needs to tell me at what point I have a concern," she complained. "Is it when 100 customers are impacted, or 2,000 customers are impacted? I don't even look at them anymore because I don't know how to interpret them." Jean Wentzel, another senior manager in Customer Relationships, agreed: "Until we've really communicated it effectively and tied it back to the compensation system, it's not going to have the same buy-in or impact."

But increasing the relevance of CCM by tying it to the compensation system would not be easy. In fact, the cross-functional CCM group responsible for the pilot project had recently agreed to shelve temporarily the issue of whether to create a compensation link, concluding that the points raised were too complicated to tackle all at once. Unresolved questions included how to set standards for customer impacts; whether the compensation system should include both business-centered measures reported the old way and customer-centered measures reported the new way; and whether UCS should retire its bucket of measures and move instead to a system more similar to that at Federal Express, with compensation based on just a dozen or so service measures, rather than on a broad range of company functions. This last possibility, which would result in many people and processes no longer being measured, fundamentally challenged the company's founding philosophy of having all employees work together, be measured together, and earn quality together.

Statistical Process Control

Statistical process control was another tool Quality Applications was examining. There was a growing conviction within UCS that the company needed to adopt a more long-term outlook in quality measurement. This belief was further fueled by feedback, late in 1992, from a committee that had evaluated UCS for AT&T's prestigious Chairman's Quality Award, noting that "there is no evidence of a statistical approach to data analysis, including determining out-of-control processes, identifying special and/or common causes, and the approach to prioritizing improvement opportunities."

In fact, the gathering of measures on a daily basis, as well as UCS's commitment to a "sense of urgency"—one of its seven values—had contributed to the focus on the short term. Only recently had Universal switched from monthly to quarterly business reviews, and the group that met every morning to discuss the daily measures, now headed by Fred Winkler's replacement, Jerry Hines, was for the first time adding a quarterly quality review. Remarked Davis, "With our daily focus on measurements and our fix-it-today mentality, the thing that sometimes suffers is looking at the long-term trends in the data."

Statistical process control (SPC) seemed to provide at least a partial answer to this shortcoming. The quality improvement methodology, developed at Bell Laboratories in the 1920s to chart manufacturing processes and identify events that affect product output, had been broadly defined in recent years to include such tools as cause-and-effect diagrams and Pareto charts, as well as control charts to statistically examine process capability and variation. But SPC had only rarely been applied in a service environment. The challenge at UCS, therefore, was to adapt the manufacturing tool to its customer service business.

Pete Ward, a process engineer within Quality Applications, was confident this could be done. He had already begun to prepare individualized reports for associates, allowing them to use SPC to chart and trend such daily productivity measures as talk time and number of calls handled. In contrast to mere daily statistics, Ward explained, the SPC charts would help telephone associates see the impact that one action—such as spending too much time on the phone with customers—had on another, as well as aid them in spotting cyclical patterns in their own performances.

But SPC, like CCM, raised questions about the existing measurement system. It was unclear, for example, whether it was valuable to apply statistical tools to something as ambiguous and subjective as deciding whether an associate had been courteous enough or had spent too much time with a customer. In addition, SPC charts, which allowed a more meaningful and long-term look at performance than the daily measures, presented ammunition for the argument that it was time for Universal Card to switch from its obsession with daily goals and rewards to a reliance on more statistically significant trends.

A Link to External Results

These and other questions had revived old complaints that the measures did not accurately reflect how customers actually viewed Universal, nor how the company was performing. Mark Queen, manager of Customer Listening and overseer of the Customer Contactor Surveys, acknowledged that although the internal measures were designed to measure processes important to customers, missing quality days internally didn't necessarily show up in dissatisfied customers. When internal quality results took a nosedive after the bar was raised in early 1992, for example, the Customer Contactor Surveys indicated only a slight blip in customer satisfaction—a fact, Queen says, that "was driving everybody crazy."

Similarly, Queen noted that although recent customer feedback indicated that cardholders viewed associates as somewhat less courteous than before, the internal quality monitors listening in on phone calls had not logged an increase in negative impacts. "There is not a clear enough linkage," Davis admitted. "What people would really like would be for me to say, 'OK, if you can take this internal customer measure and raise it from 96 percent to 99 percent, I guarantee it will take customer satisfaction up by X amount.' But we can't say that, yet."

Linkage aside, on occasion, the internal measures seemed to be at cross purposes with the company's financial goals. Greg Swindell, who in late 1992 became vice president of Customer Focused Quality Improvement, for example, described an unexpectedly successful marketing promotion for a new credit card product that left understaffed telephone associates unable to keep up with the rush of calls. Although the surge of new business was good for the company, the telephone associates were, in effect, doubly punished: first by having to frantically field additional calls, and second by missing their quality indicators and losing compensation. "The question is, is that high response rate a bad thing?" Swindell asked. "And my answer is no. We're here to bring on more customers, to become more profitable. So how do we balance this focus on these metrics and our business and strategic objectives? For me, this offers a very perplexing problem."

A NEW LOOK AT THE MEASURES

Spurred by these and other questions, there was talk at UCS of a radical rearrangement of the bucket of measures. Although it was not clear what would take the bucket's place, more and more managers were beginning to feel that UCS's drive for continuous improvement was being held hostage by the relentless and short-term push to bring home the daily bonus. What had originally been designed as a means for identifying and improving processes and as a motivational tool, critics charged, was now holding the company back rather than driving it forward.

Greg Swindell was one who questioned the status quo: "Perhaps it is a very good tool to help us *maintain* our performance, but I'm not sure it's the kind of tool that will help take us into the next century and really get a lot better at what we're doing." Swindell was particularly concerned about how inflexible the system

had become in the wake of associates' intense reaction to the raising of the bar. Managers rarely suggested adding new measures, even when they spotted an area in need of improvement, he remarked, because they did not want to make the goals too challenging and jeopardize the all-important bonus. Mary Kay Gilbert agreed: "The more focus and pressure you put on your quality standards, the less people are willing to raise their hand and say, 'I think this process should be measured,'" she declared. "Tying compensation to it just kind of throws that out the window."

Similarly, associates had grown to resist having measures retired, not only because that usually meant the loss of an "easy win," but also because it required workers to realign their priorities and goals (see Exhibit 9 for charts illustrating the decline in measurement system changes after 1992). In part to address the issue of stagnation in the system, Quality Applications, in a just-released draft on measurement methodology, urged managers to regularly review old measures and create new ones, noting particularly that "danger lies when the primary reason for a measurement is to adapt to the [compensation program] rather than to improve the performance of the team or process. . . . Our measures should be used to aid in our continuous improvement programs."

To keep the measures flexible, Davis was considering a "sunset law" on measures that required all indicators to be retired and replaced after one year. But although he had heard the compensation plan referred to as "an entitlement," he remained a supporter of the basic concept. "Some people in our business believe that if we didn't have measurements tied to compensation, then people would be more willing to measure the right things," he mused. "My feeling, though, is that I'll take all the negatives that go with it any day in order to get the attention." Telephone associate Robert Inks agreed: "I don't think we would have gotten as far as we have today without it, because people can look at our monitors and say, 'We didn't do too good yesterday, we're not getting that money.' And then they look at the future and say, 'Well, we have eight more days in the quarter. We're going to really focus on quality and make it, because if we don't get those eight days, that's $100 I lose.'"

Although Davis was well aware of the measurement debates, he doubted that Universal would abandon its daily measures any time soon. In fact, he had more down-to-earth concerns: In January 1994, UCS was planning to raise the bar again, and Davis was already planning how to make the transition smoother this time around. Although he anticipated some resistance, Davis was convinced that the ongoing quest for continuous improvement was necessary. "We'll have to hit hard on the fact that we're going to keep raising the standards, it's not going to stop," he declared. "And if we think it is, we're just fooling ourselves."

But Pam Vosmik, vice president of Human Resources, voiced a separate concern. Recalling Winkler's "pleased but never satisfied" expression, she made a plea for balance. "You need to keep people focused," Vosmik asserted, "but by the same token, in the worst-case scenario, you can make an organization dysfunctional if there is never a hope that you're going to be satisfied."

ENDNOTES

1. For managers to earn quality, they also had to meet standards on a separate set of indicators tied to vendors' products and services. Managers' bonuses were then based on three components: quality days, individual performance, and the company's financial performance.
2. Because of underemployment in the Jacksonville area, and the desirability of working for AT&T, UCS had been able to recruit a highly qualified workforce: Sixty-five percent of telephone associates had college degrees.
3. Relationship Excellence originally did the entire 100-call sample, but Customer Relationships began cosampling when it created its internal quality department in November 1990.
4. The ten areas in which impacts could occur had been identified as (1) telephone contact, (2) correspondence contact, (3) application contact, (4) change of address, (5) claims, (6) credit line increase, (7) payment receipt, (8) statements, (9) plastic card production accuracy/timeliness, and (10) authorization availability/accuracy.
5. In fact, the threshold for managers had already changed: Since January 1991, managers had to achieve 96 percent of their quality indicators for full compensation, receiving only three-quarters of the bonus for 95 percent.

EXHIBIT 1

UCS ORGANIZATION CHART, AUGUST 1992

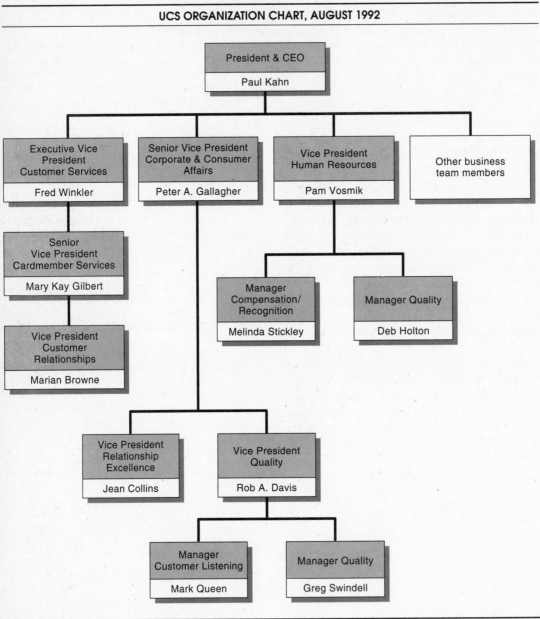

EXHIBIT 2

INTERNAL PROCESS MEASUREMENT LINKAGES TO CUSTOMER SATISFIERS

Primary satisfiers	Secondary satisfiers	Tertiary satisfiers	Internal measurement samples
	Professionalism	Service 24 hours/day 7 days/week	System availability
		Not getting a busy signal	
Customer service	Accessibility		Average speed of answer
		Answering your call quickly	
	Efficient handling	Not being put on hold	Abandon rate (% of customers who hang up)
		•	•
		•	•
	Attitude	•	•

Source: Universal Card Services.

EXHIBIT 3

KEY UCS AND SUPPLIER PROCESSES

Key Processes	UCS or Supplier
Business processes	
Strategic and business planning	UCS
Total quality management	UCS
Support services processes	
Collections	UCS
Management of key constituencies	UCS
Customer acquisition management	UCS
Financial management	UCS
Human resource management	UCS
Information and technology management	UCS
Product and service production and delivery processes	
Application processing	Supplier
Authorizations management	Supplier
Billing and statement processing	UCS
Credit card production	UCS
Credit screening	Supplier
Customer acquisition process management (Prospective customer list development and management)	Supplier
Customer inquiry management	UCS
Payment processing	UCS
Relationship management (Service management, communications management, programs and promotions, brand management)	UCS
Transaction processing	Supplier

Source: Universal Card Services.

EXHIBIT 4

SAMPLE DAILY RELIABILITY REPORT—TELEPHONE ASSOCIATE PERFORMANCE

Measure	Standard	Wednesday 06/30/93		Month-to-Date	
		Sampled	Performance	Sampled	Performance
Average speed of answer (ASA)	20 seconds	39,278	12.42 seconds	1,114,722	11.70 seconds
Abandoned rate	3%	39,278	1.24%	1,114,722	1.25%
Accuracy	96%	100	100%	2,400	98.58%
Professionalism	100%	100	100%	2,350	99.91%

Source: Universal Card Services.

EXHIBIT 5

UCS'S INTEGRATED DATA AND INFORMATION SYSTEMS

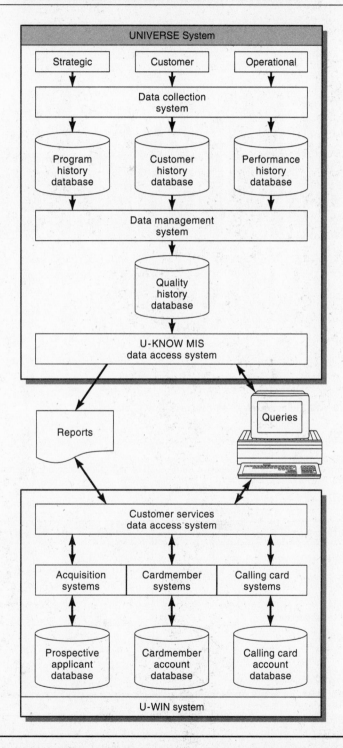

EXHIBIT 6

EMPLOYEE SATISFACTION DATA

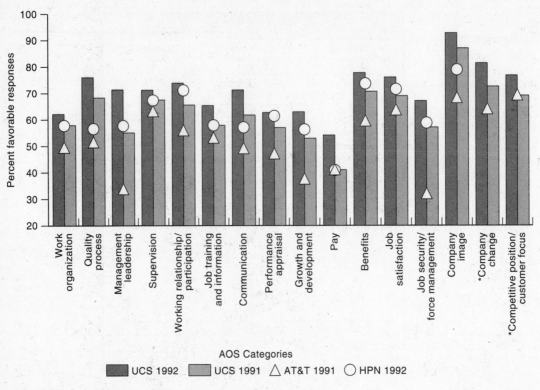

AOS Categories

■ UCS 1992　　■ UCS 1991　　△ AT&T 1991　　○ HPN 1992

Note: 1992 data for AT&T unavailable; AT&T conducts its AOS biannually.　　*HPN not available.

Note:
AOS = Annual opinion survey
HPN = High-performing norm (average response for a group of high performing organizations that use the same survey)

Adverse indicators	1990	1991	1992	Benchmark
Employee turnover				
UCS total	9.7%	10.1%	12.3%	N/A
Managers	8.7%	9.0%	7.2%	14%
Associates	10.1%	10.5%	14.1%	23%
Customer contact associates	10.2%	10.7%	13.5%	23%
*Absenteeism rate**				
Managers	N/A	1.3%	1.1%	1.3%
Associates	N/A	2.2%	3.3%	1.9%
* includes pregnancy and disability				

Source: Universal Card Services.

EXHIBIT 7

TELEPHONE ASSOCIATES MEASUREMENT REGIME

Measure	Description	Sampling and scoring regime	Performance standard (1Q93)
Average speed of answer (ASA)	Average time between completion of customer connection and answer by telephone associate	100% sample by automated call management system (CMS)	20 seconds
Abandon rate	Percentage of calls initiated by customers, but abandoned prior to being answered by telephone associates	100% sample by automated call management system (CMS)	3% of incoming calls
Accuracy	A qualitative measure of the level of accuracy of information given by associates to customers	Random sample of 100 calls per day evaluated by quality monitor Scoring system includes predefined criteria for evaluating customer impacting errors, business impacting errors, and non-impacting errors	96%
Professionalism	Professionalism (courtesy, responsiveness) shown by telephone associate	Random sample of 100 calls per day evaluated by quality monitor Scoring system includes predefined criteria for evaluating customer impacting errors, business impacting errors, and non-impacting errors	100%

Source: Universal Card Services.

EXHIBIT 8

QUALITY DAYS PERFORMANCE AND BONUSES

Associate quality days and bonus performance

Quarter	# Quality days as % of total	Bonus as % of salary
4Q90	76.1%	6.4%
1Q91	87.8%	11.4%
2Q91	92.3%	9.9%
3Q91	96.7%	12.0%
4Q91	95.7%	11.6%
1Q92	70.3%	10.6%
2Q92	75.8%	7.5%
3Q92	76.1%	7.9%
4Q92	95.7%	10.8%
1Q93	84.4%	9.4%

Management quality days and bonus performance

Period	# Quality days as % of total	Bonus as % of salary
1991	87.9%	5.6%
1992	66.1%	4.7%
1Q93	76.7%	5.6%

Source: Universal Card Services.

EXHIBIT 9

CHANGES IN STANDARDS AND MEASURES

Number of increases in standards for existing measures

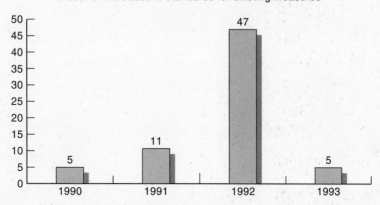

Note: Data for 1993 is year-to-date through June 30, 1993.

Number of additions and deletions of measures

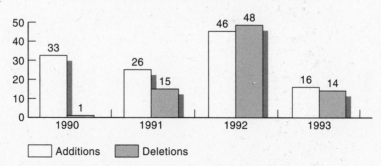

Note: Data for 1993 is year-to-date through June 30, 1993.

Source: Universal Card Services.

PART V

DETERMINING FINANCIAL IMPACT

Chapter 12

MEASURING THE BENEFITS OF SERVICE IMPROVEMENT: TRADITIONAL METHODS

12.1 HOW QUALITY GENERATES PROFITS

Quality is an important concern for service firms, for several reasons. First, as we have seen, monitoring quality requires that customer perceptions be monitored. In addition, quality control is generally just more difficult in service settings, since production is often decentralized and subject to many influences including the customer's ability to perform his or her role well. Therefore, customer satisfaction and, with few exceptions, customer retention are always at risk. Managers must be vigilant to maintain sufficiently high quality to maintain customer loyalty, but how much can they afford to spend to do so? Is it always worthwhile to spend more on improving the quality of one's goods and services?

High quality and profitability do appear to go together—*on average*. Since the publication of *In Search of Excellence* in 1982,[1] there has been a steady stream of books from the business press describing firms for whom quality programs have led to new levels of financial success. Trade magazines regularly have special issues on quality, describing the successes of industry quality leaders.

However, quality-oriented companies aren't invincible. Florida Power & Light, the only U.S. company to win Japan's prestigious Deming prize for quality, found itself with morale problems and financial difficulty the next year. Wallace Co., the first small business to win the Malcolm Baldrige National Quality Award, was out of business in two years, in part because of the overhead it incurred in improving its customer service levels. Quality experts agree that high quality may be necessary to be profitable in many industries, but it is not a guarantee of profits. It is certainly possible to overspend on quality, particularly if it gets the company too far beyond what consumers believe they need. Companies that spend money on quality must be careful to think about where the benefits of quality programs will be coming from.

In spite of the exceptions, there is some scientific evidence of a positive relationship between quality and profits. The Strategic Planning Institute in Boston maintains a large data base, called the PIMS data (for "Profit Impact of Marketing Strategy") containing information on profitability and a large number of strategic variables for companies in many industries. In a series of cross-sectional studies of the PIMS data researchers have found strong positive relationships between ROI (see Figure 12.1) and self-reported quality levels and between quality and market share growth.[2]

Where do the higher profits come from? Figure 12.2 shows the general effect of quality on the costs and sales of a firm. The main effects of quality on profits are through lower costs due to efficiencies achieved, increased sales from current customers, greater attraction of new customers, and the possible ability to charge higher prices. These effects aren't necessarily the same for all firms and industries. Studies of the PIMS data found that the relative importance of each of these factors varied widely across different industries.[3] For example, in some industries the high-quality firms fill high-priced niche markets; in others, the demand for high-quality products can be the basis for a high-volume, low-price market domination strategy as a result of the lower costs caused by efficiencies and experience curve effects.

However, it appears that not many companies carefully track the source of profits from their quality programs, and fewer try to predict the effects before spending. The U.S. General Accounting Office found that only five of 22 finalists for the Baldrige Award—firms that must be considered among the country's elite quality-oriented firms—had measured the cost savings from their quality programs. There are several reasons for this lack of measurement. First, there is a general feeling among many managers that the value of quality is not quantifiable. Many of the

FIGURE 12.1

THE PIMS DATA SHOW A POSITIVE RELATIONSHIP BETWEEN ROI AND QUALITY

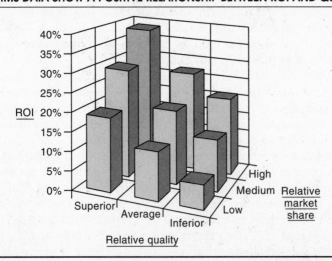

Source: Robert D. Buzzell and Bradley T. Gale, "Quality and Share Both Drive Profitability," from *The PIMS Principles: Linking Strategy to Performance,* New York: Free Press. Copyright © 1987 by Robert D. Buzzell and Bradley T. Gale. Reprinted by permission of The Free Press. All rights reserved.

FIGURE 12.2

QUALITY AFFECTS COSTS AND REVENUES IN SEVERAL WAYS

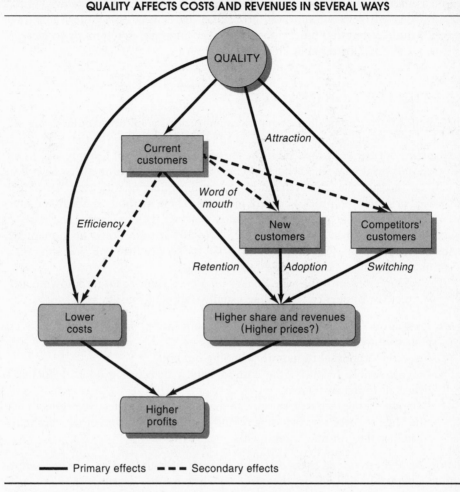

——— Primary effects   – – – Secondary effects

effects are hard to measure and require very subjective cost estimates. Second, many quality-oriented managers simply don't feel that quality should be subject to financial criteria. For example, a director of quality assurance for Motorola's computer group was quoted as saying, "I have a problem with anyone who asks for a cost/benefit analysis. . . . We don't allow defects to be characterized as minor or major. They all must be eliminated [because] we simply can't afford to have poor quality." In a survey of electronics industry executives, profits were rated a distant third as an anticipated benefit of quality programs—behind product quality and customer satisfaction.[4] Even W. Edwards Deming, who many see as the initiator of the quality revolution, believed that many of the financial benefits from quality are "invisible and unknowable." The higher-order effects of improved morale and multiplied efficiency can't be measured, and measurable effects will include only a trivial part of the process.[5] This question remains an area of open debate in quality management circles.

Despite the problems in measuring the effect of quality, companies must manage their limited resources and direct their spending where it most counts. In this chapter we briefly review the overall problem of measuring the financial impact of quality, and describe what practitioners and academics are doing to try to measure the various effects illustrated in Figure 12.2.

12.2 THE COST OF QUALITY

The initial enthusiasm for quality improvement processes in the manufacturing sector was the result of cost reductions achieved by revising systems so that procedures were carried out correctly the first time. The influential work of Deming and Juran, two U.S. industrial engineers whose teachings on statistics and quality control are heavily credited for the improvement in Japanese product quality after World War II, focused primarily on process control methods. These methods enabled manufacturers to detect quality problems early in a process, thereby saving the costs of rework and scrap, which can amount to 25% to 30% of sales revenue in manufacturing companies and as much as 30% to 50% for service firms.[6] Eliminating these wasteful costs can have a dramatic effect on profits.

The resources spent to provide quality on a consistent basis are known collectively as "the cost of quality." Spending usually occurs in four areas:

1. Prevention of problems: training, communication, installation of delivery systems to reduce the chance of problems.
2. Inspection/appraisal to monitor ongoing quality.
3. Internal failure recovery: the cost to redo a defective product before it is delivered to the customer.
4. External failure recovery, the cost to make good on a defective product identified by the customer, including refunds, replacements, and other steps taken to restore the customer's good will.

Identifying and estimating these costs can be very difficult, particularly in a service setting. Chapter 13 will discuss the cost of quality in more detail.

12.3 THE VALUE OF CUSTOMER RETENTION

The second influence on profits is the retention of current customers. Think of a firm's customer base as water in a bucket, as in Figure 12.3. Customer defections correspond to leaks in the bucket, causing the level of sales to drop. To replace them the firm must attract new customers. These may be newcomers to the market or customers of the competitors. To make the level rise, the inflow at the top must be greater than the outflow at the bottom. There are two ways to achieve this goal: the firm can turn up the tap by seeking new customers more aggressively, or it can take steps to plug leaks by keeping its current customers from leaving.

The standard approach to marketing has been the former. For the last several decades, basic marketing courses have focused on taking the offensive. Marketing students have been taught to manipulate the marketing mix of product, price,

FIGURE 12.3

MARKET SHARE, AS REPRESENTED BY THE WATER LEVEL IN A BUCKET

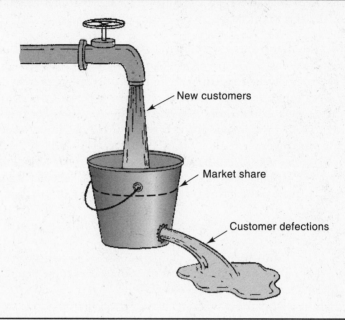

distribution, and marketing communications to attract and to win new customers. There has been an assumption that the marketing mix must also satisfy current customers, but after-sale service, complaint management, and other key elements of customer retention programs—defensive marketing—have not received as much emphasis.

That is unfortunate. A commonly quoted rule of thumb based on a series of frequently quoted studies is that that the cost of winning a new customer is on average about five times greater than the cost of retaining a current customer. For example, some magazine publishers claim that subscription price doesn't pay back the average costs of signing the subscriber until into the second year. And in mature, increasingly competitive markets, firms are finding that they simply can't assume they will be able to find customers easily to replace those they lose. Customer retention is beginning to receive much more attention. For example, Xerox now includes the opportunity costs of lost sales due to poor quality in its cost-of-quality calculations.[7]

Bain and Co., a strategic consulting firm, has studied the value of customer retention among many of its clients. Bain claims that an increase in customer retention rates of 5 percentage points can increase profits by 25% to 80%.[8] This is the result of several effects:

1. It is more expensive to win new customers than old ones, as mentioned above.

2. Tracking studies over time have shown that longer-term customers tend to purchase more.
3. In some industries, servicing a familiar customer becomes generally more efficient and therefore cheaper.

Bain also finds that there are second-level, though harder-to-measure, benefits. Long-term, satisfied customers are more pleasant for employees to work with and contribute to the employees' sense of pride and job satisfaction, thereby reducing the costs of employee turnover. High customer retention makes a firm a more formidable competitor as well. Competitors cannot easily measure another firm's retention, or even know that it is the source of the firm's growth. Highly satisfied customers are not easy to woo away.

The empirical findings of the Bain study suggest that investing in quality programs to improve customer retention can be worthwhile, whether it includes programs to improve quality and customer satisfaction initially or programs to address customer complaints.

We are certainly not surprised to learn that, over a wide range of product categories, satisfied customers have a higher probability of repurchase than dissatisfied customers. But it has also been found that customers who had problems that the firm redressed were almost as willing to return. Sometimes these people were more loyal than customers who never had problems.[9]

Many kinds of quality programs can have an effect on retention rates. What are firms doing to try to estimate the impact on profit that such programs are likely to have? In spite of the evident value of customer retention, few companies have developed ways to explicitly measure its value. Several of concepts in use include:

Problem impact tree analysis. In Chapter 7 we described how some firms use the concept of the lifetime value of a customer and the probabilities of return at different points of the problem impact tree to determine the expected value of solving or preventing problems. For example, suppose the lifetime value of a loyal customer is $1000, and that customers having no problems have a 95% retention rate, while customers with problems have, on average, only a 60% retention rate. Then the expected lifetime value of the two customers are, respectively, $950 and $600. This suggests that it would be profitable to spend up to $350 per complaining customer to resolve problems.

   This analysis can give firms a good idea of the scale of solutions that should be undertaken, but it does not pinpoint the specific service attributes that are likely to pay the biggest dividends. It also does not address the value of delighting the customer, which is the basis for true loyalty.

Segmentation schemes. Many industries segment their customers on the basis of demographic or other variables that correlate with lifetime value, retention probability, and so on. They use the averages to analyze the amount worth spending on satisfying customers in each group. For example, banks use a number of criteria, such as account age, to segment their customers into groups whose value and retention probabilities are meaningfully different. One banking expert found a relationship between account value and customer propensity to switch around: The more loyal the customer, the greater the account balance kept in the bank. The average balances of stayers to leavers was 2:1 for accounts less than three years old, 1.5:1 for accounts of four to seven years old, and 1:1 for accounts of seven to twelve years.[10] So, loyal customers appear to be worth more by generally measurable amounts. Caution should be exercised in imputing cause and effect, however, since the results don't include information on customer satisfaction with the banks in question. The results could just as well be telling us that customers with large balances find it harder to switch. A complete explanation for the observed relationship probably involves effects in both directions. Nevertheless, the different ratios provide a starting point for experiments to determine reasonable amounts to spend on improving account retention. Other industries also use segmentation schemes to identify differences in retention repurchase intention or willingness to recommend across customers who differ in identifiable and manageable ways

Other methods of analysis. If a firm keeps adequate records of its costs, client value, and sales transactions, it is possible to estimate the value to profits of quality spending on a case-by-case basis. For example, Xerox has expanded its cost-of-quality accounting to keep track of the opportunity costs of lost sales and canceled contracts. This method uses straightforward cost-of-quality analyses. When problem causes are identified, relevant staff members attempt to compare the financial value (revenues, costs) of an account when there are no problems to the value given the current level of the problem. They subtract the cost of the problem from the cost of the solution to determine the value of addressing the problem.[11] Companies like IBM also now monitor the effect of quality spending on such retention-related measures as installed base and customer satisfaction as part of an overall "quality payback formula."

The debate over the ability to measure the value of quality goes on. Certainly many quality analysts are aware of the value of retention, and have developed ways to measure it. However, aside from the types of general, straight-ahead analyses described above, it appears that few comprehensive systems for measuring the value of retention have been developed. In Chapter 14 we will describe a different approach, the ROQ perspective, which seeks to determine the impact of individual quality programs through their effect on retention rates.

12.4 THE VALUE OF NEW CUSTOMERS

Improved quality also increases profits by attracting new customers. New customers can become aware of higher levels of quality through formal marketing communications or from word of mouth from current customers. Word of mouth is particularly critical for some services, such as banks and other financial services: research has found that personal referrals are responsible for 20% to 40% of bank customers[12] and are a key factor in selecting financial service providers.[13] Because of this, many businesses measure "willingness to recommend" as part of their quality tracking program.

For services in which repeat purchases are impossible or very unlikely, such as college degrees and some medical procedures, getting the customer to give an enthusiastic testimonial to other potential customers is the logical equivalent of a retention objective. Organizations that track this measure tend to analyze the extent to which it is correlated with satisfaction with particular attributes, to help them direct their quality improvement efforts toward the most effective programs.[14] However, the financial value of improving the willingness to recommend is very difficult to assess. It is so far removed from the actual generation of sales from new customers that it is probably impossible for the typical firm to determine the expected benefits associated with the costs necessary to increase this measure.

Some data are available to measure the impact and velocity of word of mouth indirectly. AT&T's General Business Systems Division, the division that sells telephone switching equipment to small commercial customers, takes monthly surveys of how customers perceive the value of its equipment and services relative to those of its competitors. It also tracks its share of new installations by month. Time-series analysis of share and relative quality showed a lagged relationship between quality changes and share, with the greatest increase occurring approximately six months later. Figure 12.4 shows the size of the lagged effects at various intervals.[15] Again, quality appears to generate sales, but the presence of a lagged effect is important. Customers buy systems at all times of the year, and one assumes that AT&T salespeople describe the new changes to potential customers as soon as they happen. So why should there be such a lag? It may reflect the average amount of time for word-of-mouth communication, a potentially powerful influence in selling these high-involvement systems, to spread personal testimonials about significant product and service improvements.

FIGURE 12.4

THE LAGGED EFFECTS OF QUALITY ON NEW SALES AT AT&T

Source: Adaped from Ray Kordapleski, Roland T. Rust, and Anthony J. Zahorik (1993), "Why Improving Quality Doesn't Improve Quality," *California Management Review,* 35 (Spring), 82–95.

FIGURE 12.5

QUALITY AND MARKET SHARE ARE BOTH IMPROVING AT FORD MOTOR COMPANY

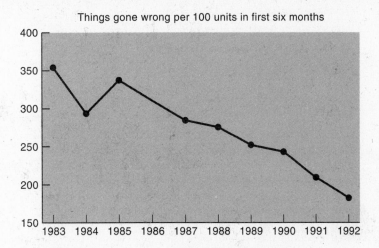

Things gone wrong per 100 units in first six months

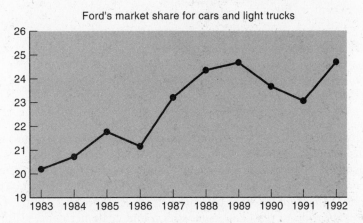

Ford's market share for cars and light trucks

Source: James Welch, senior analyst, Arthur D. Little, Cambridge, MA, July 1993.

However customers learn about quality, there is no shortage of empirical evidence that it has an impact on sales to new customers. For example, customers and analysts have attributed the tremendous inroads into the U.S. market Japanese automakers achieved during the 1970s and 1980s to the high quality of their cars relative to U.S. models. Figure 12.5 shows that the same effect has worked in the other direction. Ford Motor Company has worked hard to increase the quality of its products and services, instituting problem-solving work teams in its own plants and forcing its suppliers to meet rigorous quality standards under its Q1 certification plan. The effort appears to have had some success. The graphs show a steady increase in share with a customer-based quality measure, reduction in problems

Ford Motor Company has instituted extensive programs to improve the quality of all of its products and services.

reported by customers (TGW, or things gone wrong per 100 cars) during the first six months of ownership.

Predicting the ability of higher quality to attract customers is no different from predicting sales based on other changes in product positioning, for which a large literature exists.[16] Perceptual maps of a market, as described in Chapter 4, will provide some indication of the likely competition and customer demand for products with changed quality attributes. Services will differ somewhat from products, in that many of the attributes are intangible and much harder to control and communicate, but the principles are the same.

12.5 CONCLUSIONS

In the tough competitive arena in which most service firms compete today, maintaining high quality is not a guarantee of success but rather a minimum requirement for survival. And yet service quality is extremely hard to measure. Quality is in the mind of the customer, whose standards are continually rising, and can depend on many things, most of them intangible and difficult to control precisely. Determining where to spend the firm's limited resources to maintain a level of service quality that is attractive to customers is a major, ongoing problem facing management.

In this chapter we have described some of the methods currently in use. Many firms now realize that tracking financial data alone is insufficient. Such tracking tells us how we have done in the past, but says very little about our likely success in the future. Therefore efforts are being made to identify the impact on profits of different kinds of quality initiatives. In particular, the effects of quality programs on profits take time to develop, and so some means must be found to predict and track their effectiveness. To anticipate future corporate performance, managers are turning to measures that are seen as leading indicators of financial performance, such as customer satisfaction, competitive quality, customer perceptions of the firm's stature, and market share.[17]

As we have seen, the payback from quality programs can come from many sources, and is not always easy to measure. It doesn't help that many firms fail to track easily obtainable data that could greatly assist them in making these estimates. Many fail to do exit interviews with departing customers to find out what problems have caused them to leave.[18] We have found that even large, sophisticated companies do not keep sales records that distinguish among new customers, switchers, and repeat customers. Such data could be extremely useful in tracking the relative effectiveness of offensive and defensive marketing programs.

However, given the stakes involved, data collection and measurement techniques for certain aspects of the problem are improving. In the next chapter we will describe some of the basic concepts of measuring the cost of quality. In Chapter 14 we will describe a new approach for measuring the value of customer retention on profits.

REVIEW QUESTIONS

1. Describe all the ways in which quality improvements lead to higher profits.
2. Do all quality improvements necessarily lower costs? If not, how can one measure whether they are worth making?
3. A firm currently has 80,000 regular customers, each relationship worth an average of about $150 per year in contribution margin (revenues less variable costs). Currently approximately 20% of its customers defect to competitors per year. These losses are made up for by the attraction of customers who enter the market or switch from competitors, but management would like to stem this loss. It has identified a quality problem that accounts for customer dissatisfaction leading to 15% of these defections. How much could management profitably spend on this problem to stop these defections? What additional effects of this quality improvement might justify an even higher level of spending?
4. The ripple effects of quality on profits described in Figure 12.2 will not all take the same amount of time. Rank the effects in terms of how soon each of them is likely to become evident. How fast are they likely to manifest themselves for a bank, a restaurant, a hospital, a consulting firm?

ENDNOTES

1. Thomas Peters and Robert Waterman, Jr. (1982), *In Search of Excellence,* New York: Harper & Row.

2. Robert Buzzell and Brad Gale (1987), *The PIMS Principles: Linking Strategy to Performance,* New York: Free Press.

3. L. Phillips, D. Chang and R. Buzzell (1983), "Product Quality, Cost Position and Business Performance: A Test of Some Key Hypotheses," *Journal of Marketing,* 47 (Spring), 26–43.

4. E. B. Baatz (1992), "What is return on quality and why should you care," *Electronic Business,* 18 (October), 60–66.

5. W. Edwards Deming (1986), *Out of the Crisis,* Boston: MIT Press.

6. Lawrence P. Carr (1992), "Applying Cost of Quality to a Service Business," *Sloan Management Review,* Summer, 72–77.

7. *Ibid.*

8. Frederick F. Reichheld (1992), "The Truth of Customer Retention," *Journal of Retail Banking,* 13 (4), 21–24; Frederick F. Reichheld and David W. Kenny (1992), "The Hidden Advantages of Customer Retention," *Journal of Retail Banking,* 13 (4), 19–33.

9. Claes Fornell, Roland T. Rust, Bala Subramanian, and Mark Wells (1992), "Making Complaints a Management Tool," *Marketing Management,* 1 (3), 41–45.

10. Peter Carroll (1991), "The Fallacy of Customer Retention," *Journal of Retail Banking,* XIII (Winter), 15–20.

11. Lawrence P. Carr (1992), *op. cit.*

12. Frederick F. Reichheld and David W. Kenny (1990), "The Hidden Advantages of Customer Retention," *Journal of Retail Banking,* XII (Winter), 19–23.

13. *Quality as Consumers See It,* prepared for Travelers Insurance Companies by Yankelovich, Skelly and White, Inc., September 1984.

14. For healthcare examples, see R. Carey and E. Posavac (1982), "Using Patient Information to Identify Areas for Service Improvement," *Health Care Management Review,* 18 (Spring), 43–48 and Arch Woodside, L. Frey and R. Daly (1989), "Linking Service Quality, Customer Satisfaction and Behavioral Intention," *Journal of Health Care Marketing,* 9 (December), 5–17. For an analysis applied to graduate MBA programs, see William Boulding, Ajay Kalra, Richard Staelin, and Valerie A. Zeithaml, "A Dynamic Process Model of Service Quality," *Journal of Marketing Research,* 30 (February), 7–27.

15. Ray Kordupleski, Roland T. Rust and Anthony J. Zahorik (1993), "Why Improving Quality Doesn't Improve Quality," *California Management Review,* 35 (Spring), 82–95.

16. For example, see Glenn L. Urban and John R. Hauser (1993), *Design and Marketing of New Products,* 2nd Ed., Englewood Cliffs: Prentice-Hall.

17. Robert G. Eccles (1991), "The Performance Measurement Manifesto," *Harvard Business Review,* (January-February), 131–137.

18. Reichheld and Kenny (1990), *op. cit.*

Chapter 13

THE COST OF QUALITY

13.1 QUALITY-COST TRADE-OFF

Quality improvement leads to profits at least in part because of cost savings achieved through increased efficiency. Before a firm can calculate its return on investment in quality, it must determine the costs associated with poor quality and what, if any, cost reductions it can expect from its quality improvement efforts. The understanding that high levels of quality can lead to cost savings has required a shift in management thought about the cost of quality and its return. Managers used to believe that for any process there was a trade-off between cost and product or service quality. Common belief held that it could not be economical for any process to reduce defects to zero. Every process there was a theoretical optimum where the marginal benefit of improved quality was less than its marginal cost (see Figure 13.1).[1]

The traditional view underestimated (or failed to identify) all the costs associated with poor quality. By some estimates, these costs average 20% to 30% of sales for manufacturing companies and 30% to 50% of sales for service companies.[2] Businesses that have established total quality programs have found that when the full costs of poor quality are recognized, the most economical process is one where all products produced meet specifications (see Figure 13.2).[3] Although management has come to accept the fact that higher quality results in lower costs, the value of setting up programs to measure these costs is not universally accepted. While quality "gurus" such as Juran and Crosby advocate measuring such costs, Deming considers the idea a waste of time.[4] Such programs do provide one important benefit, however: they translate quality problems into dollars. Because these numbers are usually quite large, they can help convince of the need for quality improvement. Further, such programs can cost justify particular quality improvement efforts.

13.2 COST OF QUALITY

All firms recognize the need to identify and track the costs of their operations. Most firms, however, do not aggressively monitor their quality-related costs. Although some quality-related costs are usually tracked, there is seldom a full accounting (nor are they viewed holistically as the cost of poor quality).

FIGURE 13.1

CLASSIC MODEL OF OPTIMUM QUALITY COSTS

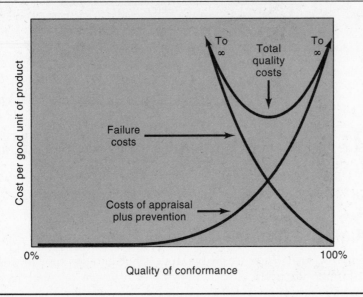

Source: Frank M. Gyrna (1988), "Quality Costs," in *Quality Control Handbook,* 4th ed., J. M. Juran, ed., New York: McGraw-Hill.

FIGURE 13.2

NEW MODEL OF OPTIMUM QUALITY COSTS

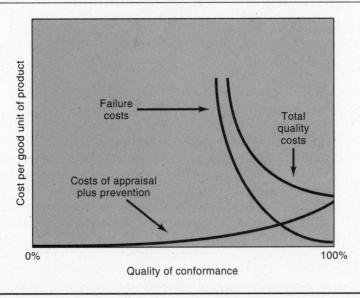

Source: Frank M. Gyrna (1988), "Quality Costs," in *Quality Control Handbook,* 4th ed., J. M. Juran, ed., New York: McGraw-Hill.

"Cost-of-quality" programs attempt to determine the financial impact associated with preventing, testing, or repairing defective products or services.[5] Generally, they determine a single dollar figure associated with poor quality. In addition to quantifying the financial consequences of quality problems, such programs strive to identify areas for quality improvement and cost reduction.

The cost of quality can be divided into four main categories (see Figure 13.3):[6]

1. **Internal failure costs.** The costs associated with errors that are discovered and corrected before the product is delivered to the customer. Examples include scrap, rework, downtime, and discounts on the selling price of goods resulting from substandard quality.
2. **External failure costs.** The costs associated with errors that are discovered after the product or service has been delivered to the customer. Examples include warranty and replacement costs, refunds or rebates, and customer complaint handling costs.

FIGURE 13.3

ASSIGNMENT OF COST ELEMENTS TO QUALITY COST CATEGORIES

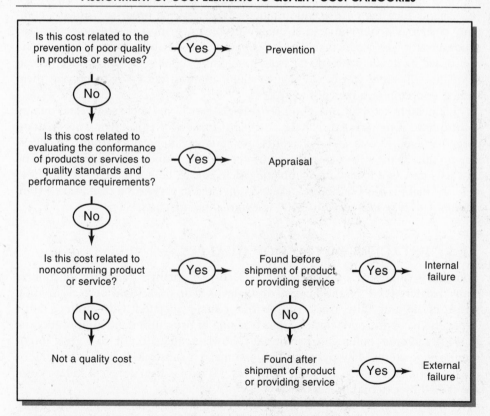

Source: Excerpt from *Principles of Quality Costs* by Jack Campanella. Copyright © 1990 by Jack Campanella. Reprinted by permission of ASQC Quality Press.

3. **Appraisal costs.** The costs associated with ensuring that the product or service meets specifications. Examples include inspections, lab tests, and field tests.
4. **Prevention costs.** The costs associated with avoiding errors. Examples include training, preventive maintenance, and process planning.

All businesses incur costs associated with each of these four categories of the cost of quality. Although quality expert Philip Crosby has popularized the notion that "quality is free," there is no way to reduce the cost of quality to zero.[7] Firms that have not embraced total quality control tend to find that most of their quality costs occur in the failure and appraisal categories. Quality-conscious firms have found that it is much more cost-effective to focus on preventing errors. Although focusing on prevention may sound intuitive, it is not the standard procedure in most firms. Usually when a firm begins experiencing quality problems, its first response is to increase inspection activities. This method fails, however, because the cause of the problem has not been addressed. One of the reasons companies address quality problems through inspection rather than prevention is that inspection can easily be added to the end of the process and so requires no real change to a process. On the other hand, focusing on prevention requires restructuring processes. But if a company is serious about eliminating quality problems, it must design processes that produce error-free products or services. Quality experts claim that 80% of defects are caused by design problems or from purchasing supplies based on price instead of quality.[8] In other words, the way to eliminate most defects is to prevent them from ever becoming a part of the process.

Eliminating errors makes good economic sense. Firms engaged in total quality control have demonstrated that the cost-benefit trade-off is in favor of prevention costs over failure costs. In other words, it is more economical to produce a defect-free product than to have to rework and repair the product (see Figure 13.4). The cost savings associated with eliminating defects can be substantial. It has been reported that for most businesses, every $1 invested in prevention could save $10 in internal failure costs and up to $100 in external failure costs.[9]

13.3 OBSTACLES TO COST OF QUALITY

Companies interested in measuring their cost of quality frequently encounter many barriers. One of the biggest obstacles is that traditional cost accounting measures do not fully track or identify costs associated with poor quality. Typically, accounting systems do some tracking of prevention and appraisal costs, as well as internal failure costs. Normally, however, they do not do a good job of monitoring external failure costs. This can mean a substantial underreporting of the cost of quality since, by some estimates, 70% of a firm's typical failure costs are caused by external failures.[10]

Further, most accounting systems ignore the strategic implications of quality improvement. For example, high defect rates may cause disruption to the production process, longer lead times, and the need to expedite items. These strategic costs are an important part of the cost of quality and should not be ignored. Not recog-

FIGURE 13.4

FAILURE COST AS A FUNCTION OF DETECTION POINT IN A PROCESS

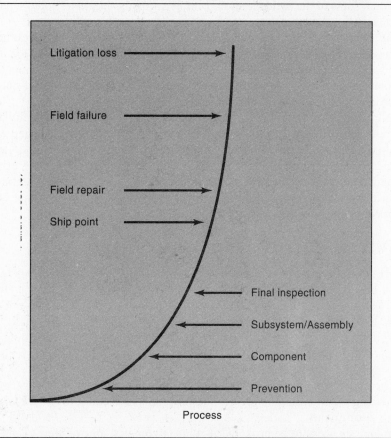

Process

Source: Excerpt from *Principles of Quality Costs,* 2nd ed., by Jack Campanella. Copyright © 1990 by Jack Campanella. Reprinted by permission of ASQC Quality Press.

nizing the strategic implications can make it difficult or impossible to identify areas that will provide the maximum benefit to the company from quality improvement.[11]

The way to handle these accounting problems is to use what information is available from the current accounting system. Estimates can then be made for elements not currently monitored. This practice leads to an important point regarding cost-of-quality analysis. Cost-of-quality studies are not designed to replace a company's accounting system. Instead, they are a tool designed to demonstrate the financial importance of quality and to help identify areas where quality improvement can benefit a company financially. Being reasonably close will serve the company just as well as being exact. In fact, if being precise means using an inordinate amount of time and/or disrupting operations, then approximating these costs will be better for the company.

Companies also face the problem of deciding how to allocate uncommon but large costs. For example, a product liability claim may be an unlikely occurrence, but should it happen, the costs would be significant. Including such costs in the cost-of-quality analysis would distort the figure and may cause management to discount the reasonableness of the entire analysis. Still, it probably should be noted separately as an unlikely but potential cost.

Some categories in a cost-of-quality study can be controversial. Examples of such categories might include overhead, depreciation on equipment used for inspection, and loss of customer goodwill. Including controversial costs without agreement from those affected in the company is not a good idea. The cost of quality is usually a large enough figure without including controversial categories.

Finally, firms that are not involved in manufacturing may have difficulty explicitly defining conformance quality. Also, frequently these firms have not had experience using quantifiable performance measures. In such cases it is essential to determine process specifications that affect customer satisfaction. For example, when the U.S. marketing division of Xerox measured its cost of quality, it defined its product as "100 percent customer satisfaction," meaning that anything causing less than complete satisfaction was a defect.[12]

13.4 IMPLEMENTING COST-OF-QUALITY PROGRAMS

There are several ways to begin implementation of a cost-of-quality program. All, methods, however, require the commitment of senior management for the effort to succeed. Because senior management acceptance and support is imperative, it is best to begin by demonstrating to them the magnitude of the cost of quality. This approach requires an analysis of the primary costs associated with providing quality products or services.

This analysis can be conducted through a review of the company's financial data. Where costs are unavailable, estimates can be used. The focus of this review is on uncovering major costs; the review does not have to account for all costs associated with poor quality.

The analysis needs to be broken down into two parts: an overview of the entire company and an overview of a particular area of the company. The overview of the company will demonstrate the magnitude of the cost of quality. The overview of a specific operation will show management how to calculate and eliminate these costs. Therefore, when selecting an example area, it is best to select the section that represents the most obvious opportunity for improvement.

After the review has been conducted, the information must be presented to management. The presentation should do the following:

- Demonstrate the need for action given the size of costs associated with poor quality.
- Recommend the creation of a task force, chaired by someone in management and including individuals from all major departments, to calculate the cost of quality.
- Suggest that an area of the organization be used as a pilot study. (The logical area would be the one used as an example in the presentation.)

Quality experts have found that it is not uncommon for initial cost estimates to account for greater than 20% of sales.[13] Management may be surprised and perhaps skeptical because of the size of the figure. Given that the majority of this information will come from their own financial data, however, management will probably accept the findings. Hopefully, this will cause management to create a task force and implement a pilot program.

The first objective of the task force should be to determine the categories comprising the cost of quality. After a list has been created, management needs to agree to the categories. Getting management to agree to the categories used in the analysis increases the likelihood that they will accept the figures presented to them from the study.

Once agreement has been reached regarding the categories, the next step is to assign responsibilities and a schedule for collecting data for the pilot area under study. The data will come from several disparate sources. Examples of such sources are:[14]

Cost accounting data. Included are data on things that reflect quality costs such as scrap and rework. The main problem with this data is that it could be dated, and therefore not reflect the current situation.

Payroll data. Included is a full or partial assignment of employees' salaries for work on quality-related activities.

Estimates from knowledgeable personnel. Estimates from appropriate individuals can be sought on things such as calculating the time to repair a product or allocating the percentage of time an employee is engaged in quality related activities.

After the data have been collected, the information needs to be charted over time. It is wise to collect data for a reasonable period of time before drawing conclusions or planning actions. Because costs can vary with the level of activity, it is important to track these costs as both the total dollars used and a some percentage of one or more measurement bases that represent indicators of business activity. Otherwise, it is impossible to determine whether cost changes are the result of particular actions taken or are simply the result of changes in business activity. Examples of cost-of-quality measures that reflect business activity include: (1) quality costs per unit produced, (2) quality costs as a percent of sales, (3) quality costs as a percent of cost of goods sold, and (4) quality costs as a percent of total manufacturing costs. It is also important to track quality costs by the category to which they correspond: prevention, appraisal, internal failure, or external failure. After the quality cost information has been tracked for a sufficient time period, the next step is to identify opportunities for improvement. Because prevention costs are less expensive than appraisal or failure costs, the logical areas to focus the company's quality improvement efforts are on areas requiring inordinate appraisal costs or causing internal or external failures.

At this point, the results of the program need to be summarized and presented to management. Assuming the results are positive, the presentation should also recommend the following:

1. The company's employees should be informed of the results of the program.
2. Key members of each department should be educated in the concepts of a cost of quality system.
3. The program should be implemented throughout the company.

Getting management to inform the employees of the results of the program should not be difficult, because good news is easy to tell. Further, since the task force contains individuals from all key departments and a knowledgeable individual is located in each section, educating members of the various departments should be relatively easy. Although management should commit to implementing a cost-of-quality program throughout the entire company, it should not move too quickly by installing the program in all areas at once. The program should progress at a reasonable pace, moving from department to department so that the organization can learn from each area and devote attention to the program's success. One advantage of this approach is that both management and employees can see successful implementation of the program over time and under a variety of circumstances. This practice serves to reinforce their commitment to the program. Also, including all departments in the design and implementation of the program prevents the analysis from becoming viewed as the "product" of the quality department.

13.5 LIMITATIONS

Cost-of-quality analysis is an effective tool for getting management's attention regarding the amount of money a company currently spends to correct or prevent errors. It also shows how shifting spending from appraisal and failure categories to prevention can result in substantial financial benefits. Cost-of-quality analysis cannot, however, be the primary means of monitoring a company's quality efforts. More timely, nonfinancial measures are needed to establish targets for quality improvement.

There are several problems with relying on cost of quality as a performance measure. First, measuring the cost of quality in and of itself will not solve quality problems. Solving problems requires the action of management. Second, cost of quality programs are vulnerable to short-term management practices. It is often possible to reduce quality costs in the short term without improving quality. In fact, eliminating prevention and appraisal costs will result in immediate, but short-lived cost savings.[15]

Also, the cost figure will almost always underestimate the actual cost of quality. It is difficult, if not impossible, to determine the costs associated with things like customer ill will and plant disruptions. Further, it is impossible to determine an optimum cost-of-quality level. There will always be some cost associated with providing a quality product or service, but there is no way to determine accurately whether too much is being spent. Finally, although prevention costs are generally presumed to be more cost-effective than appraisal and failure costs, there is no optimum distribution of costs over the four categories of cost of quality.

As a result, even though cost-of-quality analysis provides important information regarding a company's quality efforts, it is not a good measure of actual performance. Therefore, if an area has been identified as needing improvement from a cost-of-quality analysis, it is extremely important for nonfinancial methods that will accurately monitor the process to be determined and tracked.

13.6 SUMMARY

Because cost savings are one of the ways that quality leads to profits, companies should determine their cost of quality before calculating their return on investment in quality. Quality costs fall into four categories: prevention, appraisal, internal failure, and external failure. External failure costs are the most expensive quality costs to the company, followed by internal failure costs. Prevention costs, quality costs that focus on preventing errors, are the most cost-effective quality costs. A company's quality costs are usually quite large, often exceeding 20% of a firm's sales. As a result, the size of these costs can focus management's attention on the need to improve quality. Therefore, management should be made aware of the costs the company incurs as a result of poor quality.

When implementing a cost-of-quality program it is best to use a task force made up of individuals from all major departments, as well as management. The task force should determine the categories that will comprise the company's quality costs. Once the categories have been resolved, the task force should begin the program by focusing on a particular department to serve as a pilot study.

The pilot program should begin by uncovering the current cost of quality for the area. These costs should be tracked over a reasonable time period before any conclusions are drawn. The results should point to potential opportunities for improvement. The company should then take action on the most promising areas. Once the pilot program has been completed, the results need to be presented to management, as well as to the employees. The program should then be instituted company-wide; however, this procedure should be done slowly.

Cost of quality may be an effective tool for getting management's attention regarding the need for quality improvement and for isolating opportunities for cost savings, but it cannot be the primary means of overseeing a company's quality efforts. Therefore, it is extremely important to use nonfinancial methods to monitor a company's quality efforts.

REVIEW QUESTIONS

1. Why is it impossible to reduce the cost of quality to zero?
2. Why is it important to use measures other than simply the total dollar figure associated with quality costs when tracking the cost of quality?
3. Think of a problem not mentioned in the chapter that could occur with the use of cost-of-quality analysis as a performance measurement tool.

ENDNOTES

1. Robert S. Kaplan and Anthony A. Atkinson (1989), *Advanced Management Accounting,* 2nd ed., Englewood Cliffs, NJ: Prentice-Hall.
2. E. B. Baatz (1992), "What is return on quality, and why should you care," *Electronic Business* (October), 60–66.
3. Kaplan and Atkinson (1989), *op. cit.*

4. D. A. Garvin (1987), Competing on the Eight Dimensions of Quality," *Harvard Business Review* (November-December), 101–109; P. Crosby (1979), *Quality is Free,* New York: McGraw-Hill; and W. Edwards Deming (1986), *Out of the Crisis,* Boston: MIT Press.

5. Lawrence P. Carr (1992), "Applying Cost of Quality to a Service Business," *Sloan Management Review* (Summer), 72–77.

6. Frank M. Gyrna (1988), "Quality Costs," in *Quality Control Handbook,* 4th ed. (J. M. Juran, ed.), New York: McGraw-Hill, pp. 4.1–4.30.

7. P. Crosby (1979), *op. cit.*

8. "The Push for Quality," *Business Week,* June 8, 1987, p. 135.

9. George P. Bohan and Nicholas F. Horney (1991), "Pinpointing the Real Cost of Quality in a Service Company," *National Productivity Review* (Summer), 309–317.

10. Lawrence P. Carr (1992), *op. cit.*

11. P. Nandakumar, S. M. Datar, and R. Akella (1993), "Models for Measuring and Accounting for Cost of Conformance Quality," *Management Science,* vol. 39, no. 1 (January), 1–16.

12. Lawrence P. Carr (1992), *op. cit.*

13. *Principles of Quality Costs* (1990), 2nd ed., Jack Campanella, ed., Milwaukee: ASQC Quality Press.

14. Frank M. Gyrna (1988), *op. cit.*

15. Wayne J. Morse, Harold P. Roth, and Kay M. Poston (1987), *Measuring, Planning, and Controlling Quality Costs,* Montvale, NJ: National Association of Accountants.

Chapter 14

RETURN ON QUALITY

14.1 INTRODUCTION

Managers in virtually all industries have come to recognize the importance of service to their firms' continued success. However, whereas service quality is an important element to a firm's operations, it is not a magic wand for which cost is no object. Furthermore, not every customer-pleasing service enhancement is equally important in building loyalty or in generating cost savings. Consequently, given limited resources to invest, spending on service improvement becomes a classic resource allocation decision.

As a result, many managers are now estimating the return on proposed service improvement efforts before committing their resources. This investment-oriented approach is frequently referred to as the "return on quality" method.[1] The approach is based on the premise that it is possible to measure the impact on profits through the improved retention of the firm's current customers due to improved service. There are, in fact, many improvement initiatives, such as increased variety at a restaurant, for which improved customer satisfaction, and not lower cost, is the primary effect and primary source of increased profits. Because its goal is to retain current customers, it is called "defensive" marketing. The chain of effects by which service improvements increase loyalty, repeat purchases, and ultimately profits is shown in Figure 14.1.

Although improved service can also make the firm more attractive to new customers in the market and to competitors' customers, these "offensive" effects take longer to build, and their timing is far more difficult to predict. They are dependent upon the efficiency of word of mouth among customers and the extent to which the firm spends money on promotion. Therefore, the return-on-quality approach focuses on the "defensive" impact of service improvement. This restriction means that estimates may underestimate the eventual total financial impact. Nevertheless, they provide a conservative lower limit for the value of such programs.

So how is a manager to decide which areas warrant spending, and how much should be spent on them? Many of the data needed to answer these questions are near at hand, in customer satisfaction data collected through questionnaires, in corporate records on the internal costs of poor service quality, and in the judgment and intuition that the firm's managers have developed through years of experience.

FIGURE 14.1

THE CHAIN OF EFFECTS OF SERVICE QUALITY ON PROFITS THROUGH RETENTION

(1) Spending on service quality $\Rightarrow$
   (2) Improved service performance $\Rightarrow$
      (3) Increased customer satisfaction $\Rightarrow$
         (4) Increased customer retention $\Rightarrow$
            (5) Increased market share $\Rightarrow$
               (6) Increased revenues $\Rightarrow$
                  (7) Increased profits

14.2 PUTTING THE INFORMATION TOGETHER

Determining how improving service will impact customer retention, market share, and profits requires the development of a model that ties relevant data together in a managerially meaningful way. The model should be designed so that a manager can quickly and easily test different programs and different assumptions about their likely effectiveness. However, pulling all of these facts and judgments together to estimate the consequences of different actions is a daunting task. It would be helpful to have an interactive computer model, known as a decision support system, which pulls all the data together and produces logically consistent estimates and forecasts of the likely financial effects of service improvement programs. In this chapter we describe the necessary components of such a decision support system.[2] The structure of the model's inputs and outputs are shown in Figure 14.2. The model is based on the chain of effects in Figure 14.1. The technical details of how the components are linked together is in the appendix following this chapter.

Linking Customer Satisfaction to Retention

Several of the model's relationships are considered to be outside management's control in the short run, and form the backdrop against which the impact of various quality programs can be tested. In particular, a survey of the firm's customers is required, asking them about how various aspects of the firm's services meet their expectations and their likelihood of remaining a loyal customer during the next period of time.

    Figure 14.3 shows the structure of a hypothetical firm's customer satisfaction questionnaire following the format described in Chapter 9. Figure 14.4 shows the customer satisfaction data collected from the survey, and Figure 14.5 shows the relationship between customers' average retention rate and their satisfaction with the firm's overall level of service.[3] From this information, we can estimate the relationships from (3) to (4) in Figure 14.1 using statistical methods; that is, we can estimate how satisfaction and delight drives retention. Determining the relationship between customers' satisfaction levels and retention is especially important in choosing areas for attention. The most important areas are those that cause customers to leave or to be loyal, not necessarily those that receive the largest number of complaints, or those for which satisfaction is rated the worst. We must also estimate the relationships that describe how satisfaction and delight at lower levels of the service drive satisfaction and delight at higher levels. We can then follow the

FIGURE 14.2

THE LOGICAL FLOW OF A RETURN-ON-QUALITY DECISION SUPPORT SYSTEM

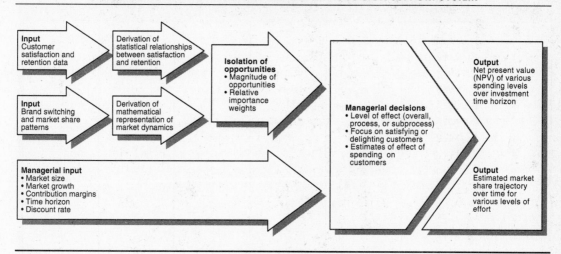

FIGURE 14.3

LAYOUT OF CUSTOMER SATISFACTION QUESTIONNAIRE

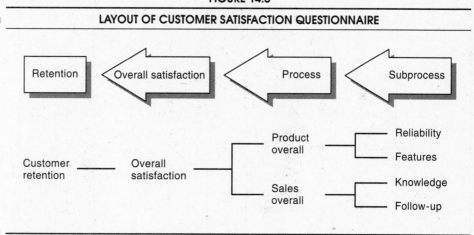

chain of relationships from satisfaction or delight at the subprocess level up through retention. In order to separate the effects of satisfaction and delight, it is necessary to recode the data set by creating two new variables, a satisfaction variable and a delight variable, from every response on the three-point scale used. The new variables are constructed as "dummy variables," indicating that their value is either 0 for "No" or 1 for "Yes." Figure 14.6 shows the recoded data set.[4]

After the recoded data set has been constructed, statistical methods can be used to relate the process satisfaction levels to the overall satisfaction level. The methodology necessary to determine these relationships was described in Chapter 10.

FIGURE 14.4

RESPONSES TO CUSTOMER SATISFACTION SURVEY

Overall satisfaction	Product overall	Reliability	Functions	Sales overall	Knowledge	Follow-up
1	1	2	2	2	2	2
1	2	0	0	3	3	2
1	2	1	1	2	2	2
1	1	1	0	1	1	2
1	1	2	2	1	1	2
1	2	3	0	2	2	2
1	1	0	1	2	2	2
1	0	2	0	2	3	2
2	0	0	0	3	3	3
2	2	2	2	2	2	2
2	0	2	0	2	1	1
2	2	0	0	1	1	1
2	2	2	2	2	2	2
2	2	2	0	0	0	0
2	1	0	1	1	1	3
2	2	2	2	2	3	2
2	0	0	0	3	3	3
2	2	2	2	2	2	2
2	2	2	0	0	0	0
2	2	3	2	2	2	2
2	2	2	2	2	2	2
2	2	2	1	2	2	2
2	2	2	2	3	3	2
2	2	2	2	2	2	2
2	2	2	2	2	2	2
2	3	2	2	2	2	2
2	2	2	2	3	3	1
3	2	2	2	2	3	3
3	3	3	3	2	3	3
3	2	3	2	3	0	2
3	2	2	2	3	3	3
3	3	3	3	3	3	3
3	3	3	3	3	3	3
3	3	2	2	3	3	3
3	3	3	3	3	3	3
3	2	0	2	2	3	2
3	3	3	3	3	3	2
3	2	3	3	3	3	3
3	2	2	2	3	3	2
3	3	2	0	3	3	3
3	2	2	2	3	2	3
3	3	3	3	3	3	3
3	3	2	3	2	3	1
3	3	2	3	2	3	3
3	3	3	3	2	2	3
3	2	2	3	3	3	3
3	3	3	3	3	2	3
3	2	2	1	3	3	3
3	3	0	0	3	3	3
3	2	3	1	3	3	2

Note: 0 indicates missing data
1 indicates service was "worse than expected" (referred to as "dissatisfied")
2 indicates service was "about as expected" (referred to as "satisfied")
3 indicates service was "much better than expected" (referred to as "delighted")

FIGURE 14.5

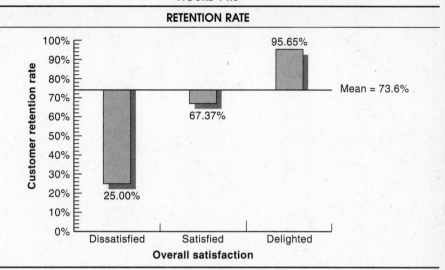

RETENTION RATE

Choosing Between Service Improvement Initiatives

The data should then be analyzed to create a series of importance-performance tables. The tables present the importance of the various processes and subprocesses, as well as the percentages of customers who are currently dissatisfied, satisfied, or delighted (see Figure 14.7). The importance score indicates how strongly the customer response at any lower level is related to the response at the next higher level (e.g., subprocess to process, or process to firm overall). A firm's service performance is shown by the percentage of dissatisfied, satisfied, or delighted customers it has with various processes and subprocesses.

Each importance score in Figure 14.7 is a number between 0 and 100 that indicates relative impact. The higher the score, the greater the impact. By examining information at the firm level, the process level, or subprocess level, the manager can consider programs that are targeted at narrow aspects of the service or broader programs that affect customer attitudes about processes or even the service overall. In this case, the importance score was determined using bivariate ordinary least-squares regression to get a rough idea of the relative impact of the processes and subprocesses.[5] The R square from each bivariate regression was multipled by the percentage of respondents who answered the question on the customer satisfaction survey. This number was then multiplied by 100 to get a number between 0 and 100.[6] This works because R^2 applies only to the nonmissing portion of the data. Cases are presumed to be missing because they were not relevant to the respondent. Therefore, the importance score for all respondents would be the R^2 times the percentage of cases present.

Managers should be careful not to focus only on importance scores. If the firm has a small percentage of dissatisfied customers or a high percentage of delighted customers, the subprocess or process with the highest importance score may not represent the best opportunity (because there are few people left to be shifted). Therefore, managers need to consider whether there is the potential to

FIGURE 14.6

RESPONSES TO CUSTOMER SATISFACTION SURVEY (USING DUMMY VARIABLES TO SEPARATE BETWEEN SATISFACTION AND DELIGHT)

Overall		Product		Reliability		Functions		Sales		Knowledge		Follow-up	
Sat	Del	Sat	Del	Sat	Del	Sat	Del	Sat	Del	Sat	Del	Sat	Del
0	0	0	0	1	0	1	0	1	0	1	0	1	0
0	0	1	0	NA	NA	NA	NA	1	1	1	1	1	0
0	0	1	0	0	0	0	0	1	0	1	0	1	0
0	0	0	0	0	0	NA	NA	0	0	0	0	1	0
0	0	0	0	1	0	1	0	0	0	0	0	1	0
0	0	1	0	1	1	NA	NA	1	0	1	0	1	0
0	0	0	0	NA	NA	0	0	1	0	1	0	1	0
0	0	NA	NA	1	0	NA	NA	1	0	1	1	1	0
1	0	NA	NA	NA	NA	NA	NA	1	1	1	1	1	1
1	0	1	0	1	0	1	0	1	0	1	0	1	0
1	0	NA	NA	1	0	NA	NA	1	0	0	0	0	0
1	0	1	0	NA	NA	NA	NA	0	0	0	0	0	0
1	0	1	0	1	0	1	0	1	0	1	0	1	0
1	0	1	0	1	0	NA	NA	NA	NA	NA	NA	NA	NA
1	0	0	0	NA	NA	0	0	0	0	0	0	1	1
1	0	1	0	1	0	1	0	1	0	1	1	1	0
1	0	NA	NA	NA	NA	NA	NA	1	1	1	1	1	1
1	0	1	0	1	0	1	0	1	0	1	0	1	0
1	0	1	0	1	0	NA	NA	NA	NA	NA	NA	NA	NA
1	0	1	0	1	1	1	0	1	0	1	0	1	0
1	0	1	0	1	0	1	0	1	1	1	1	1	0
1	0	1	0	1	0	0	0	1	0	1	0	1	0
1	0	1	0	1	0	1	0	1	0	1	0	1	0
1	0	1	0	1	0	1	0	1	0	1	0	1	0
1	0	1	1	1	0	1	0	1	0	1	0	1	0
1	0	1	0	1	0	1	0	1	1	1	1	0	0
1	1	1	0	1	0	1	0	1	1	1	1	1	1
1	1	1	1	1	1	1	1	1	0	1	1	1	1
1	1	1	0	1	1	1	0	1	1	NA	NA	1	0
1	1	1	0	1	0	1	0	1	1	1	1	1	1
1	1	1	1	1	1	1	1	1	1	1	1	1	1
1	1	1	1	1	0	1	0	1	1	1	1	1	1
1	1	1	1	1	1	1	1	1	1	1	1	1	1
1	1	1	0	NA	NA	1	0	1	0	1	1	1	0
1	1	1	1	1	1	1	1	1	1	1	1	1	0
1	1	1	0	1	1	1	1	1	1	1	1	1	1
1	1	1	0	1	1	1	0	1	1	1	1	1	0
1	1	1	1	1	1	NA	NA	1	1	1	1	1	1
1	1	1	0	1	1	1	0	1	1	1	0	1	1
1	1	1	1	1	1	1	1	1	1	1	1	1	1
1	1	1	1	1	1	1	1	1	0	1	1	0	0
1	1	1	1	1	1	1	1	1	0	1	1	1	1
1	1	1	1	1	1	1	1	1	0	1	0	1	1
1	1	1	0	1	1	1	1	1	1	1	1	1	1
1	1	1	1	1	1	1	1	1	1	1	0	1	1
1	1	1	0	1	1	0	0	1	1	1	1	1	1
1	1	1	1	NA	NA	NA	NA	1	1	1	1	1	1
1	1	1	0	1	1	0	0	1	1	1	1	1	0

Note: NA indicates missing data
1 in *Sat* category indicates respondent was "satisfied or delighted"
1 in *Del* category indicates respondent was "delighted"

FIGURE 14.7

RESULTS OF STATISTICAL ANALYSIS (USING BIVARIATE ORDINARY LEAST-SQUARES REGRESSION)

Relationship to Overall Satisfaction

	Coefficient	t-statistic	R Square	Response %	Importance	% Dissat.
Product	0.7268	5.379	0.3967	90.00%	35.70	10.90%
Sales	0.3636	1.899	0.0727	94.00%	6.84	8.30%

Relationship to Product Satisfaction

	Coefficient	t-statistic	R Square	Response %	Importance	% Dissat.
Reliability	0.4474	2.456	0.1370	78.00%	10.69	5.00%
Functions	0.2708	2.039	0.1036	74.00%	7.66	15.80%

Relationship to Sales Satisfaction

	Coefficient	t-statistic	R Square	Response %	Importance	% Dissat.
Knowledge	0.8000	12.683	0.7814	92.00%	71.89	10.60%
Follow-up	0.1818	1.254	0.0331	94.00%	3.11	8.30%

Relationship to Overall Delight

	Coefficient	t-statistic	R Square	Response %	Importance	% Only Sat.
Product	0.6161	4.565	0.3214	90.00%	28.93	58.70%
Sales	0.5826	4.862	0.3394	94.00%	31.91	43.80%

Relationship to Product Delight

	Coefficient	t-statistic	R Square	Response %	Importance	% Only Sat.
Reliability	0.4890	3.540	0.2480	78.00%	19.34	60.00%
Functions	0.7564	6.939	0.5722	74.00%	42.34	52.60%

Relationship to Sales Delight

	Coefficient	t-statistic	R Square	Response %	Importance	% Only Sat.
Knowledge	0.6740	6.080	0.4510	92.00%	41.49	34.00%
Follow-up	0.5500	4.383	0.2946	94.00%	27.69	50.00%

shift a significant percentage of customers from dissatisfied to satisfied, or satisfied to delighted for a particular process or subprocess, as well as the corresponding importance score.

The two sets of information together give the manager some initial indications of where to most effectively allocate resources and the trade-offs involved. The obvious place to begin would be a critically important service aspect with which many customers are dissatisfied. However, companies with ongoing service improvement programs will probably have identified such "low-hanging fruit" and be trying to decide among less obvious choices. It is with those choices that the model will be most helpful. For example, just because a large number of customers express dissatisfaction with some subprocess doesn't necessarily make it a priority problem if it has very little to do with customers' satisfaction with the process. On the other hand, a highly important process may not be worth further investment if most customers are already delighted with it. Trade-offs must be made, but the model will help in the decision by giving profit information for each alternative.

Linking Retention to Market Share

For a firm to determine the relationship between its customer retention rate and its market share, it must have an understanding of the dynamics of the market under current competitive conditions. Simply tracking revenues, profits, or market share will not provide enough information to link retention to market share. Therefore, to accurately model the dynamics of the market, companies must track the following information:

- The extent of brand/firm switching by customers in the market.
- The rate of entry of new customers into the market.
- The percentage of customers that are new to the market that are attracted to your firm.
- The percent of customers who leave the market.

These figures are assumed to represent (or must be judgmentally adjusted to represent) the levels of offensive and defensive activity in the market under current competitive conditions. The ebb and flow of customers to and from our brand/firm provide the projections of market share and contributions if no new actions are taken. These values will serve as a baseline for comparing the net present value of programs intended to change our retention rate. It provides information for estimating the link from steps (4) to (5) in Figure 14.1.[7]

Figure 14.8 shows how these components fit together to affect market share. Basically a firm improves its market share by attracting new customers at a rate greater than its market share percentage and/or increasing its retention rate as a result of improving customers' satisfaction levels through improved service. However, the firm's attractiveness to new customers is assumed to be unrelated to the customer satisfaction of existing customers (for this reason the faucets have no valves in Figure 14.8). Therefore, the only way we increase market share through customer satisfaction is by raising the firm's retention rate. Improving customer satisfaction increases the retention rate (i.e., the hole in the bucket in Figure 14.8 gets smaller), which allows the firm to keep a larger percentage of its customers and thereby improve its market share.

Linking Market Share to Revenues

Once the dynamics of the market are understood, it is relatively easy to link market share and revenues. Two additional pieces of information are necessary: the size of the market and the average profitability per customer of the segment under investigation. By multiplying the market share by the number of people in the market times the average profit per customer, it is possible to convert market share forecasts into dollars—that is, steps (5) to (6) in Figure 14.1.

FIGURE 14.8

LINKING RETENTION TO MARKET SHARE

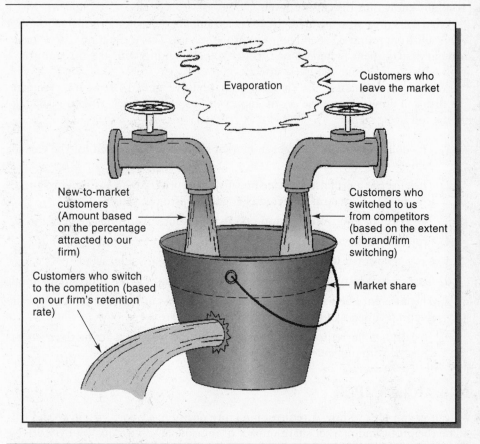

Evaporation

Customers who leave the market

New-to-market customers (Amount based on the percentage attracted to our firm)

Customers who switched to us from competitors (based on the extent of brand/firm switching)

Customers who switch to the competition (based on our firm's retention rate)

Market share

Linking Service Improvement Programs to Customer Satisfaction

Once the links between customer satisfaction and revenues are understood, it then becomes possible to estimate how changes in customers' satisfaction levels will impact market share and revenues. What is needed is a way for the manager to explore the profit impact of various proposed service improvement programs. However, these programs usually have some cost associated with their implementation (even if ultimately they produce a net cost savings). Therefore, the expected changes in the percentage of dissatisfied, satisfied, or delighted customers must be linked to various levels of spending to improve service. This information corresponds to the link between steps (1), (2) and (3) in Figure 14.1.

Managers should have some idea what the firm currently spends on various processes and subprocesses to "keep customers satisfied" (i.e., reduce dissatisfied customers) and to exceed their expectations (i.e., increase delighted customers). Further, the customer satisfaction surveys show how many customers are dissatisfied,

satisfied, or delighted with various aspects of the firm's service. Therefore, the level of customer satisfaction that corresponds to spending on service for a process or sub-process is known for the current level.

Managers must also estimate the expected impact on customer satisfaction that will result from proposed spending to improve service. This estimation can be made through management judgment or through experimenting with the program on a small scale to determine the likely effect.

With this information, the chain of causation in Figure 14.1 is now complete. The firm can now estimate the profit impact of proposed service programs, by taking the following steps:

1. The dollar impact of changes in market share are determined for the current competitive situation.
2. The effect of a proposed service improvement program on customer retention is estimated (based on expected changes in customer satisfaction).
3. The effect of improved retention on market share over time is determined.
4. Projected changes in market share are translated into dollars.
5. Costs associated with implementing the program are subtracted.
6. Cost savings resulting from improved "cost of quality" are added to the total.
7. The difference between the baseline profit figure and the new dollar figure is the profit impact of the proposed program.
8. To calculate the return on investment divide the profit impact by the costs associated with implementing the program.

14.3 AN EXAMPLE

We can get an idea of how a return-on-quality decision support system would calculate the profit and market share impact of improving service quality by working through a simple example. Examination of the data set in Figure 14.4 reveals that 16% of respondents were "dissatisfied," 38% were "satisfied," and 46% were "delighted" with the firm's overall level of service. Figure 14.5 shows that the retention rate for dissatisfieds was 25%, satisfieds was 67.37%, and delighteds was 95.65%. Therefore the average retention rate for all customers is

$$(16\% \times 25\%) + (38\% \times 67.37\%) + (46\% \times 95.65\%) = 73.6\%$$

Suppose the firm initiated a service improvement effort that would reduce the number of dissatisfied customers to 5%, then the expected retention rate resulting from this effort would be

$$(5\% \times 25\%) + (49\% \times 67.37\%) + (46\% \times 95.65\%) = 78.26\%$$

If we know the number of customers in the market and the firm's market share, we can then estimate the resulting market share impact. If the market has 800,000 customers and the firm has a 10% share then the expected gain in customers for the next time period resulting from the change in retention rates would be

$$(800,000 \times .10) \times (.7826 - .7360) = 3728$$

To determine the profit impact for the next time period, the firm needs to know

- The average profit per customer.
- The expected costs associated with improvement effort.
- The expected costs savings (if any) asssociated with the improvement effort.
- The firm's discount rate.

If the average annual profit for each customer is $200 and the firm uses a 10% discount rate to determine the net present value of the investment, then the profit impact for the next time period, if there were no costs to implement the program and no cost savings resulting from the program, would be $3,728 \times 200 = \$745,600$. Therefore the present value (PV) would equal:

$$PV = \frac{\$745,600}{(1 + 0.1)} = \$677,818$$

If we assume that there was an upfront cost of $475,000 to implement the program, then the net present value (NPV) of the expected profit impact is $677,818 – $475,000 = $202,818 and the expected return on investment (ROI) is:

$$ROI = \frac{\$202,818}{\$475,000} = 42.7\%$$

14.4 SUMMARY

The return-on-quality approach attempts to measure what has until now generally been considered unmeasurable, the impact of service improvement on profits through increased customer retention and market share. The start-up costs to measure this impact are not great, given that a firm is already monitoring its standing among its customers. The program requires data from the sort of customer survey that many firms are now already doing, as well as other essential measures of competitive performance. In return, the program enables a manager to organize his or her thinking about how service quality programs will justify their expense through improved revenues. The program requires some possibly difficult managerial judgments, but these judgments are made anyway, and are implicit in decisions being made without the model. The model shows managers the logical implications of those assumptions.

Several vivid lessons have been drawn from using the model on actual corporate data. The first is that quality programs aimed at customer retention take time to pay off. Net present value (NPV) calculations of many programs computed over just one year often show the most profitable course is to spend nothing. However, when the NPV is calculated over horizons of two or three years, spending on retention programs frequently pay off handsomely if given time to develop.

The second lesson is that many programs don't ever pay off through increased retention alone. However, that is not to say that they shouldn't be instituted. If they generate suitable cost savings, they may well be worth the expense. Therefore, cost savings must be incorporated into the calculation.

By using a return-on-quality approach, managers can now rely on more than the belief that service quality leads to profits. They can project the expected profit impact resulting from their programs. As a result, managers can make sure that the effect of their programs show up on the bottom line.

REVIEW QUESTIONS

1. Why have many firms adopted an investment-oriented approach to service improvement?
2. Why is it possible that the return-on-quality approach may underestimate the financial impact of improving service?
3. Why is it important not to focus only on importance scores of a process or subprocess when determining where to improve service?

ENDNOTES

1. Examples include: E. B. Baatz (1992), "What is Return on Quality, and Why Should You Care?" *Electronic Business* (October), 60–66; David Greising (1994), "Making Quality Pay," Business Week (August 8), pp. 54–58; Roland T. Rust, Anthony J. Zahorik, and Timothy L. Keiningham (1994), *Return on Quality: Measuring the Financial Impact of Your Company's Quest for Quality,* Chicago: Probus Publishing Co.
2. This decision support system was introduced in: Roland T. Rust, Anthony J. Zahorik, and Timothy L. Keiningham (1994), *Return On Quality (ROQ): Making Service Quality Financially Accountable,* Marketing Science Institute (April), Report Number 94–106.
3. The labels dissatisfied, satisfied, and delighted are used to describe respondents who rated service as worse than expected, about as expected, and much better than expected. Although these responses are comparisons relative to expectations and not direct measures of satisfaction, they are used for convenience. Further, because of the very strong link between disconfirmation and satisfaction, this relabeling is not too much of a stretch.
4. Note: Using "dummy variables" will require larger data sets than the example here in order to keep the model's error within acceptable levels.
5. Note: Using bivariate ordinary least-squares regression does not control for the problem of multicollinearity. As a result, the sum of the R squares from the various bivariate regressions can total more than 100%. Therefore the regression coefficients for the various processes and subprocesses can be larger than is warranted. To control for multicollinearity, using the statistical techniques such as the equity estimator or ridge regression is more appropriate. For information on the equity estimator, see Arvind Rangaswamy and Lakshman Krishnamurthy (1991), "Response Function Estimation Using the Equity Estimator," *Journal of Marketing Research* 28 (February), 72–83, and Lakshman Krishnamurthy and Arvind Rangaswamy (1987), "The Equity Estimator for Marketing Research," *Marketing Science,* 6 (Fall), 336–357. For information on ridge regression, see Arthur Hoerl and Robert Kennard (1970), "Ridge Regression: Biased Estimation for Non-Orthogonal Problems," *Technometrics,* 12 (February), 55–63.
6. Another method of estimating importance using multivariate regression techniques is shown in the appendix to this chapter.
7. The technical details regarding how to use this information to model a firm's market dynamics is shown in the appendix.

TECHNICAL DETAILS OF THE RETURN-ON-QUALITY MODEL

It is important to remember that decision support systems are tools that provide useful inputs to a manager's decision, but their findings must be considered along with many other objective and subjective factors. They seldom provide definitive answers by themselves because the outputs of any model are dependent upon the model's assumptions; moreover, all decision models are based on a simplified view of reality. Therefore, before we use any decision model, it is important to have at least an intuitive understanding of how the model works. This understanding should give users more confidence in using the model's forecasts, because they know when these forecasts are likely to be accurate and when they are unlikely to reflect some key aspects of reality. Often, in the latter cases, the user may be able to put the appropriate "spin" on the model's output to account for the missing factors. In this section we describe several of the key assumptions (simplified, in some cases, to accommodate a minimal technical level) underlying the return-on-quality model developed by Rust, Zahorik, and Keiningham so that the user will better understand what data must be collected and how the results should be interpreted. We present them in the order in which the user encounters them.

14A.1 ESTIMATING THE IMPORTANCE WEIGHTS

The satisfaction importance scores are derived from regression analysis between measures of satisfaction at different levels. These measures are derived from the customer satisfaction survey, by converting customer choices on the three-point scale ("worse than expected," "about as expected" and "much better than expected") into two dummy variables S and D. S is an indicator that the customer is at least satisfied:

- If a customer rates an item as worse than expected, then $S = 0$.
- If the item is about as expected or much better than expected, $S = 1$.
- D is an indicator of delight.

- If a customer rates an item as about as expected, then $D = 0$.
- If the item is rated much better than expected, $D = 1$.

The overall process importance weights are obtained by using regression methods to estimate the relationship between the dummy variable for overall satisfaction and the satisfaction dummy variables for the processes. Assuming we were examining a hotel with six customer contact processes (room, bath, staff, service, grounds, and restaurant) then the predictor equation would be as follows:

$$S_{overall} = a_0 + a_1 S_{room} + a_2 S_{bath} + a_3 S_{staff} \\ + a_4 S_{service} + a_5 S_{grounds} + a_6 S_{rest} \tag{14A.1}$$

The coefficients of this equation are used as importance weights, provided they are positive. Negative coefficients are presented as zero, since we are interested only in those variables that can have a positive influence on overall satisfaction.

Customer satisfaction surveys are often plagued by the statistical problem of multicollinearity; that is, customers tend to rate several of the processes or their sub-processes similarly, almost always high or low together. There are several possible reasons for this. First of all, different people have different levels of acceptance: some may be very critical or very enthusiastic about everything, and tend to use only one end of the scale. This behavior is much less common with the three-point comparison-with-expectations scale than with the traditional five-point poor-to-excellent rating. A second cause of multicollinearity is due to "halo effects," in which delight or disappointment with some central aspect of the service tends to color customer attitudes about other aspects. For example, if there is a problem with the bath, the customer may be very critical of the room as well.

Both of these reasons assume that multicollinearity is a spurious phenomenon, but there is always the possibility that two variables really are correlated. This situation is not as likely if the processes are truly independent processes of the service. However, if because of administrative structure, two processes generally perform well or poorly together, then it will be much harder to separate the effects of each process on overall satisfaction. In that case, the data should perhaps be grouped together and the two processes treated as a single unit.

Multicollinearity poses problems for the estimation of importance weights, because when scores on several processes vary together it is impossible to know which ones are relatively more important in driving the overall score. As a result, the estimates of the coefficients of the processes' scores in Equation (14A.1) are subject to a great deal of uncertainty. To minimize the effect of multicollinearity and to obtain the most stable estimates possible from the information supplied, the Rust, Zahorik, and Keiningham return-on-quality model estimates Equation (14A.1) using techniques designed to control for multicollinearity instead of ordinary least-squares methods.

14A.2 THE CHAIN OF EFFECTS FROM PROCESS TO RETENTION

The coefficients in Equation (14A.1) and those relating processes with their sub-processes are linked together to predict the effect on retention that is likely to occur given a change in satisfaction levels at the process or subprocess level. For example, from Equation (14A.1) we have the relationship

$$S_{\text{overall}} = c_{\text{room}} + a_1 S_{\text{room}} \qquad (14A.2)$$

where c_{room} is a constant. In particular, in a regression relationship it must be true that

$$\overline{S}_{\text{overall}} = c_{\text{room}} + a_1 \overline{S}_{\text{room}} \qquad (14A.3)$$

where $\overline{S}_{\text{overall}}$ and $\overline{S}_{\text{room}}$ are the mean values of S_{overall} and S_{room}, respectively. From Equation (14A.3) it is easy to solve for c_{room}.

Because these are both 0/1 variables, their means equal, respectively, the percent of customers satisfied with the hotel overall and the percent satisfied with the room. That is, Equation (14A.2) is not just a relationship between individual satisfaction ratings. It relates percentages of customers satisfied with different levels. The return-on-quality model uses this relationship to predict changes in the percent of customers satisfied with the hotel overall from changes in the percent of customers satisfied with the room. The return-on-quality model derives similar relationships at each of the subprocess levels, such as

$$S_{\text{room}} = c_{\text{TV}} + a_{13} S_{\text{TV}} \qquad (14A.4)$$

or

$$D_{\text{room}} = d_{\text{TV}} + b_{13} D_{\text{TV}} \qquad (14A.5)$$

the corresponding equation for delighted customers. [A more sophisticated way to do this is to consider the effect of several processes or subprocesses at once (see Chapter 11)].

To complete the linkage to retention, the return-on-quality model determines the average retention rates, for each group, those dissatisfied, those satisfied, and those delighted, respectively, with the overall service. If we call them R_1, R_2, and R_3, respectively, then the mean retention rate among the hotel chain's customers is

$$\overline{R} = (1 - \overline{S})R_1 + \overline{S}R_2 + \overline{D}(R_3 - R_2) \qquad (14A.6)$$

where $\overline{S}$ is the mean value of S, or the percent of customers who are at least satisfied overall, and $\overline{D}$ is the mean value of D, or the percent of customers who are delighted with the hotel overall.

This discussion completes the chain of equations. For example, Equations (14A.2) and (14A.4) show how a change in percent satisfied with a subprocess affects the percent satisfied overall, and Equation (14A.6) shows how these changes in the percent satisfied overall are translated into new average retention figures.

14A.3 THE NPV CALCULATION

The net present value calculation for a particular spending pattern measures not the absolute NPV of all sales, but the NPV of the change in sales from the current level, regardless of the source of the change. As was explained above, some of the "drift" in sales may result from better or worse retention rates by our competitors or may be the result of differences in the relative attractiveness of the various firms in the market. Therefore, sales may rise or fall, regardless of what we do to improve restaurant variety, for example. Therefore, what is important in comparing quality programs is their relative effectiveness. A program may be unable to reverse a drop in market share, but if it can slow that drop more cost-effectively than other programs, it is worth considering. In particular, the formula computes the net sales for the nth period out as sales in the nth period due to market growth and change in market share minus the current number of sales per period:

$$DS_n = MS_n(N_0T)(1 + g)^n - MS_0(N_0T) \qquad (14A.7)$$

where MS_n = market share in period n
MS_0 = current market share
N_0 = current market size = number of individuals
T = number of sales per individual per period
g = market growth rate

The NPV of cash flows in the nth period is then computed as

$$NPV_n = (1 + r)^{-n}(pDS_n - K_n + R_n)$$

where r = firm's discount rate
p = individual contribution per purchase
K_n = cash outlays for the quality program in period n
R_n = savings due to quality program in period n

14A.4 COMPUTING MARKET SHARE OVER TIME

The focus of the return-on-quality model is on the improvement in sales due to improved customer retention rates. Higher retention rates cause higher sales as defections slow market share increases, all else being equal. Therefore the key to the return-on-quality calculations is the projection of market shares in future periods as a function of retention rate. The return-on-quality model projects market share formulas forward one step at a time, from period t to period $t + 1$, using the information gathered beforehand and that supplied in the input screens.

First some notation. Let

N_t = market size in period t
G = $(1 + g)$ = market growth factor
MS_t = market share in period t
MS_{t+1} = market share in period $t + 1$
c = churn or percent of customers that leave the market each period
r_t = percent of customers retained by our firm after period t
r_t' = competitors' collective retention rate
A_{t+1} = our relative attractiveness to new customers in period t, i.e., the percent of new customers in the market who choose us.

Then the number of new customers in period t is

$$r_t \, MS_t \, N_t \qquad\qquad\qquad \text{(retained customers)}$$

$$+ \, (1 - r_t' - c) \, (1 - MS_t) \, N_t \qquad \text{(switchers)}$$

$$+ \, A_t + 1 \, (GN_t - (1 - c) \, N_t) \quad \text{(new customers)} \qquad (14\text{A}.8)$$

The total number of new customers in the market in period $t + 1$ will be GN_t, so our share will be the value in Equation (14A.8) divided by GN_t, or

$$MS_{t+1} = [r_t \, MS_t + (1 - r_t' - c) \, (1 - m_t) + A_{t+1} \, (G - 1 + c)]/G \quad (14\text{A}.9)$$

In the model, all parameters in Equation (14A.9) are assumed fixed for the near term except retention, r_t, which is assumed to be a function of spending on quality, as described in Equation (14A.6). Although historical measures may provide some guidance about the values of these other parameters, an important role of managerial judgment is to adjust the key variables such as market growth, competitive retention rates and relative attractiveness to reflect the most likely values over the planning horizon.

PART VI

IMPROVING SERVICE

MOMENTS OF TRUTH

15.1 MANAGING THE MOMENT OF TRUTH

Several years ago, the *Wall Street Journal* did a survey of consumers to determine what their biggest complaints were about service.[1] The most frequently mentioned complaints were instances with which many of us can relate:

Staying home for delivery people who fail to show	40%
Salesclerks who are on the phone while waiting on you	37
Salesclerks who say, "It's not my department"	25
Salespeople who talk down to you	21
Salesclerks who can't describe how a product works	16

How can a service firm that wants to delight its customers and improve its retention rate avoid these common service failures?

Customer satisfaction surveys may reveal areas of a service with which customers are dissatisfied, but determining what steps can be taken to fix the problems requires that one look at the design of all aspects of the service, including those the customer experiences and the operations behind the scenes. We have seen that the intangible portion of a service is often a fleeting, temporal performance. It can't be inventoried or inspected in advance. It's produced as it is consumed by the customer. Intangibility greatly increase the difficulty of controlling service quality as delivered by different people and at different times. And yet it is often the brief encounters with customers during a service that are the most important determinants of overall customer satisfaction. In this chapter we will describe methods for increasing customer satisfaction by designing and controlling the quality of customer/server interactions.

In a period of three years, Jan Carlzon, the president of the Swedish airline SAS, transformed the company from a major loser to *Transport World*'s "Airline of the Year." In his book, *Moments of Truth,* he explains:

"Last year, each of our 10 million customers came in contact with approximately five SAS employees, and this contact lasted an average of 15 seconds each time. Thus SAS is 'created' in the minds of our customers 50 million times a year, 15 seconds at a time. These 50 million 'moments of truth' are the moments that ultimately determine whether SAS will succeed or fail as a company. They are the moments when we must prove to our customers that SAS is their best alternative."[2]

The term "moment of truth" had been applied to service encounters before,[3] but Carlzon's eloquent description of the importance of these key moments has popularized the term. Many services face the same situation as SAS. A customer's experience with the service will be defined by brief interactions with service personnel and the firm's systems. It is these interactions that we seek to understand by the methods of listening, described earlier, and around which most customer satisfaction surveys are structured. These moments are fleeting. The design and management of the service must be carefully planned to ensure that the interactions go well. Continuously producing successful moments of truth is not a lucky accident, but the result of hard work aimed at understanding the needs of customers and employees alike.

Christian Gronroos, a pioneer thinker in the marketing of services, postulates that perceived service quality consists of two parts: technical quality and functional quality.[4] Technical quality refers to what customers receive during the service, or what remains when the service is over: a completed tax form, the use of a rental car, a night's lodging. Discussions of this dimension of quality are similar to those of Crosby[5] and others in the goods-manufacturing industries who define quality as conformance to specification. Often customers can objectively measure whether the results of the service, the technical service quality, was within the promised tolerances. For example, they can see whether or not the rental car was ready as promised, that the haircut was competently done, or that the tax form passed the scrutiny of the IRS.

However, because customers are often either direct observers of the production process or active participants, how the process is performed also has a strong influence on the overall impression of the quality of the service. This is functional quality. The rudeness of a receptionist, the disconcerting mannerisms of the tax preparer, the sloppy appearance of the waiter, or the abruptness of a clerk can alter one's overall attitude toward a service, perhaps reversing the impression formed by high technical quality. A well-performed service encounter may even overcome the negative impression caused by poor technical quality, particularly if customers can see that the employees have worked very hard to satisfy them in the face of problems outside their control.[6] For example, by offering a free meal to a patron who has had a dissatisfactory dining experience a restaurant may well be able not only to salvage the relationship but also to generate a lot of positive word of mouth. Functional quality can also be affected by other customers. For example, if one must stand in line at a supermarket behind many customers who write checks without appropriate identification, the service will leave a poor impression. The importance of functional quality therefore makes it essential to understand the full scope of the customers' point of view when designing services.

Controlling the perceived quality is further complicated when multiple people

A customer's impression of a service is often determined by short interactions with the service firm's hourly employees.

are involved on both the provider and receiver sides. For example, to care for a sick child, a parent may call a particular doctor's receptionist for an appointment, the parent and child may both interact with the nurse and doctor, and the parent may have to deal with the billing office through an insurance firm. The family's impression of the visit will be determined by the impressions of both parent and child with each of the individuals contacted. In fact, marketers identify as many as five different roles in the buying process even for consumer purchases: the initiator of the purchase, key influencers, the person who makes the final decision, the person who actually uses it, and the party who pays. For simple purchases these roles are all played by the same person, but, as illustrated above, they can be played by separate people. For purchases by organizations, the roles are usually much more complicated, involving many different persons on both sides. The people in the buying unit can be expected to pool their impressions, and bad experiences in one part of the service can ultimately destroy the overall relationship. Therefore, it is very important to identify all the moments of truth perceived by customers and to manage them carefully to keep them of high quality.

Components of the Service Process

A service process can be thought as having several parts, each of which has different management requirements to maintain quality, as in Figure 15.1.[7] The consumer sees the interactive part of the service, the additional three P's of the service marketing mix described in Chapter 1: the people, procedures and systems, and physical components encountered in using the service. The people—such as waiters, ticketing agents, telephone receptionists, and other customer contact personnel—may be the most important, because they are better able to discern customers' special needs and to overcome weaknesses in the other parts of the service. Procedures and systems are the operating routines and the ways of doing business that the firm uses and expects its customers to follow in delivering its services. For example, the system used by an automobile repair facility to schedule appointments for service, determine customers' problems and authorize repairs, keep them informed as the service progresses, and provide accurate billing must be designed to minimize customer frustration while maximizing efficiency. Finally, the physical component consists of the tangible resources that the firm uses to deliver its services: computer systems, the physical decor of its facilities, the appearance of its written correspondence, and the like, all of which can influence the perceived quality of the service. The components that make up the interactive part of the service all fall above the customer's "line of visibility." They are all directly observable by the customer, and generally correspond to the questions on the customer satisfaction survey.

Below the line of visibility are the support functions that enable the firm to provide quality in the interactive components. Gronroos identifies three support functions. Management support makes sure that the interactive components are working properly by guaranteeing that the frontline personnel get the resources they need and by setting examples that keep the quality culture alive in the organization. This support role is provided by executives and supervisors with the authority to allocate resources, direct the efforts of the frontline personnel, and motivate them using "internal marketing" methods. Support systems are the behind-the-scenes operations, such as computer and data management services, accounting, and logistics, that serve the frontline personnel to guarantee that their

FIGURE 15.1

THE STRUCTURE OF SERVICE PRODUCTION

Interactive part:

Customers interact with
  Contact personnel
  Systems
  Physical component

Line of visibility ————————————————————————

Support:

Management support
Support functions
Technological/knowledge support

Unrelated functions

services are timely, accurate, correct, and so on. The third component, technological/knowledge support, includes the investments in technical and physical resources that make the service possible, as well as investment in a knowledge base (hiring specialists or getting training for personnel) so that the systems are used as effectively as possible. Overall quality service in the organization requires that the support functions must think of the frontline personnel as internal customers, know their needs, and deliver the highest quality of internal service possible. Most of the support functions contribute in some way to the quality of the service perceived by the external customers. In fact, they may well represent the bulk of the service-producing activity. Their careful management is no less important to the quality of the firm's overall service than that of the frontline operations.

Finally, some internal functions of the firm may be invisible to the customers, such as the operation of the employee dining room. The quality of these functions might have no influence on the firm's production of services. However, one must be very careful before classifying a particular function as invisible, particularly if it results in a lessened emphasis on quality. There are fewer functions with no customer service impact than one might think. For example, if the employee dining room is a source of low morale, or causes delays because of poor organization, it can affect the quality of customer experiences.

How can we design services to guarantee that they will be as satisfying as possible to the consumer? There are three components to the service design problem. The first component addresses the structure of the core service process itself. We will describe two commonly used techniques to ensure that service elements meet customer needs, *blueprinting* and *quality function deployment*. Blueprinting borrows techniques from logistics, decision theory and computer systems design to "engineer" the flow of a service to make sure that all activities are done properly, in the appropriate sequence, and by the persons responsible. In the next section we will discuss the concept of blueprinting and describe how it is done. Quality function deployment is another method used to ensure that customer needs are being met, and will be described in Section 15.3. The second component, based on research in human resources and organizational behavior, uses findings about the dynamics of personal interaction to train frontline personnel to deal with customers during moments of truth. We will address some of these issues in Section 15.4, and discuss them in further detail in Chapter 17. Finally, the third component deals with the design of the physical evidence to support and enhance the delivery of the service. We will describe some issues in designing the physical setting of the service, or servicescape, in Section 15.5.

15.2 DESIGNING THE PROCESS: BLUEPRINTING SERVICES

Most services are dynamic systems. Operations must take place in a defined sequence, often with responsibilities handed off from one person or subsystem to another. Poorly designed flows of operations in these systems can cause missed handoffs, miscommunication, or other structural failures, and may fail to devote adequate attention to key moments of truth. Blueprinting (also called "flowcharting.") is a technique that helps to understand the totality of a service as a process, so that "fail points," those stages of the service that have a high statistical probability of generating problems, can be identified, understood, and possibly redesigned. The blueprint is an objective, graphical depiction of the service, as in Figure 15.2. In addition to a diagnostic role, it can also serve as a valuable communication device to allow people in the firm with very different perspectives to converge on a single understanding of what the firm does, and what it should do. The National Health Service in the United Kingdom has used blueprinting of hotel services within its healthcare delivery systems to understand consumer perceptions of quality and to involve employees in suggesting improvements in service quality.[8]

G. Lynn Shostack, an executive who has done much to popularize the use of service blueprinting, breaks service systems into three components: the process, the means, and the evidence.[9] The *process* refers to the sequential flow of steps in both visible and support systems. The logical flow of the service process is fundamental to its ability to deliver consistent quality. *Means* refer to the resources used to accomplish each of the tasks in the process—whether physical assets or people. They are often illustrated by symbols in the blueprint to highlight the particular investment choices that have been made to accomplish each task. As the blueprint is examined for ways to improve the service, choosing different means may have a greater impact than restructuring the flow of the system. For example, in a department store an interactive, menu-driven computer terminal may be a better choice for giving directions than a person. Finally, *evidence* refers to the set of clues that customers use to assess the quality of the firm, such as the appearance, professionalism, and demeanor of the frontline personnel; the look of the firm's letterhead and the readability of the statements; its delivery trucks, and so on. For complex, hard-to-judge services these clues can play a major part in setting customer attitudes about the quality of the service delivered. They should also be symbolically represented in the service blueprint.

A full understanding of a service may require blueprinting at several levels of increasing detail, starting with a general blueprint of the overall service process and then filling in details on subsidiary blueprints. The blueprint should show the logical sequence of steps and all points at which the service can diverge into different directions depending upon decisions by customers and managers or as dictated by the outcomes of service processes. It should show responsibility for each activity and all contacts between parties in the process. Fail points should be clearly indicated. The blueprint should be detailed enough to enable the firm's services to be distinguished from those of competitors.

Developing a Blueprint

There is no single best approach for generating a blueprint of a service, but there are some useful guidelines.[10] It is best to make blueprinting a group exercise, including only those who are fully involved in the process. The ideal group probably contains between three and eight participants. This is large enough to generate sufficient cross-fertilization of insights, but small enough to let everyone participate. In the case of the automobile repair facility, an ideal team would include people from management, billing, and the parts department, as well as a service representative, a mechanic, and a garage assistant.

The analysis should start with a specific instance of a service encounter and track precisely what happened. (When Ms. Jones brought her car in for a transmission repair yesterday, exactly what happened throughout the process?) The goal is to depict how the system really works, rather than to create an idealized version of

FIGURE 15.2

A BLUEPRINT OF AN AUTO DEALER'S SERVICE DEPARTMENT

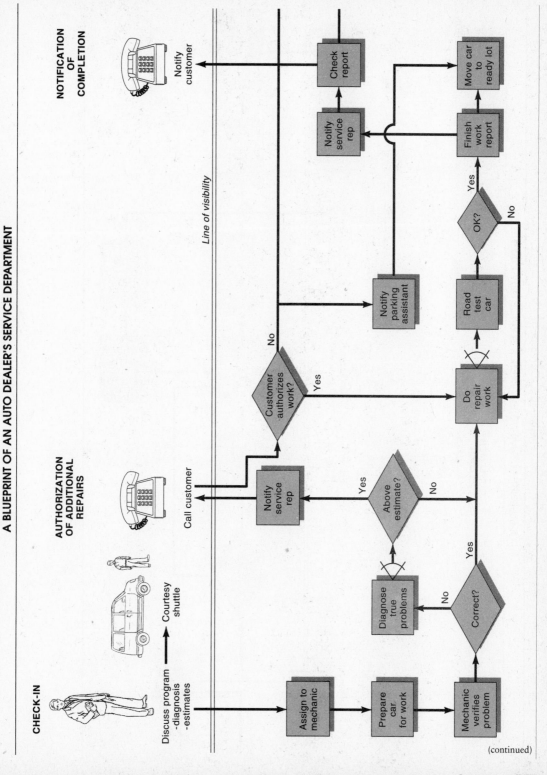

(continued)

FIGURE 15.2 (Continued)

A BLUEPRINT OF AN AUTO DEALER'S SERVICE DEPARTMENT

how it is supposed to work. Development of an ideal system will come later. Note that the candor necessary to get participants to describe what actually goes on can be threatening unless a truly participative atmosphere has been established for the session. If participants fear being blamed for service failures, they will be reluctant to provide accurate accounts of events. To provide a full understanding of the process, other specific examples may also need to be tracked to cover other common contingencies not addressed in the first one.

Once a particular service incident has been chosen for blueprinting, the team must decide where to begin the process. For example, should the blueprint for the auto garage begin with the approach of the service representative to the customer and her car, or should it begin with the customer's approach to the dealership, or even earlier? This can be a point of disagreement, but once the basics of the blueprint are on paper, it is easy to add earlier steps, if necessary. It is more important to get the exercise productively under way than to debate where the service encounter started.

A useful technique for organizing events and tracking responsibility is to create a diagram which some people call a process *flowchart,* as distinct from a service blueprint. (Terminology is not yet settled in this area.) Figure 15.3 traces a typical process for a customer at the auto dealership. To begin, write the names of each department or persons involved in the service delivery across the top of a large sheet of paper. The list should also include the customer (as a single entity, or each of the separate buying roles if they are played by different people—for example, if the college student who brings in the car wants his or her parents to be billed). Then the steps of the process should be mapped in sequence on the paper from top to bottom, listing each activity under the name of the person or department responsible for it. This format is more natural for participants than attempting to directly design a service blueprint. Certain conventions of symbolism from computer flowcharting are often used. In particular, diamonds indicate branching points, in which the future actions are chosen depending on the answers to questions. If no one at the meeting knows about an important area of the flowchart, a person from that area should be recruited to complete that part of the figure. It is also possible to discover that no clearly defined procedures exist for certain operations—an indication of potential trouble spots.

Figure 15.3 shows that customers take their cars to the service garage in the morning, and service is generally done the same day, if possible. The service representative gives the customer an estimate of the time of completion and an estimate for the service bill at the time of drop-off. If the customer decides to have the service done at that time, the process follows the steps shown in the flowchart.

When the process flowchart is complete, it can then be rearranged into the form of a service blueprint, as in Figure 15.2. The sequence of events should be arranged around the line of visibility, and organized in the order in which the customer experiences them. Customer contacts and activities that are visible to the customer should be represented above the line by symbols that depict all of the forms of evidence observed by the customer. The flow of supporting systems below the line is usually depicted more formally as a sequence of boxes, arrows, and divergence diamonds. However, a large number of sophisticated notations have been developed to make blueprints as informative as possible. For example, Shostack[11] recommends

FIGURE 15.3

A FLOWCHART OF ACTIVITIES FOR AN AUTO DEALER'S SERVICE DEPARTMENT

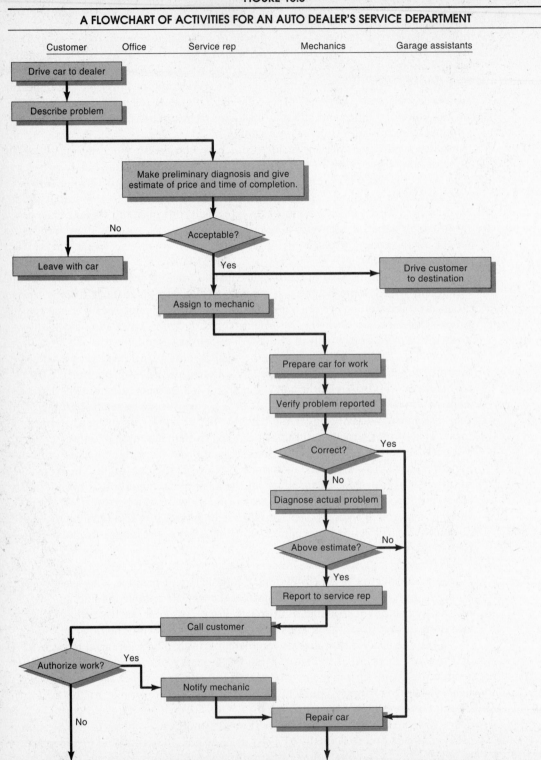

FIGURE 15.3 (Continued)

A FLOWCHART OF ACTIVITIES FOR AN AUTO DEALER'S SERVICE DEPARTMENT

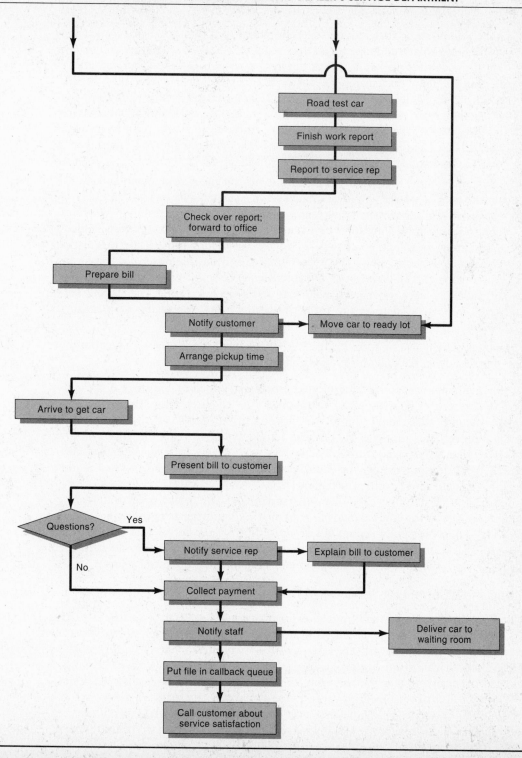

the use of special symbols to highlight sensitive points in service blueprints such as:

Dialogue points, those that require carefully prepared scripts to elicit information from the customer, and may themselves require detailed blueprinting and scripting if the contact person must ask different questions or take different actions depending upon the customer's answers. In Figure 15.2 a carefully written script might be devised when informing customers that work will exceed the original estimate, since this is a source of potential mistrust and ill will. Service representatives would need to be trained in how to approach customers with the bad news and in how to respond to possible customer anger or mistrust in a way that maintains the firm's reputation for honesty.

Problem points, those that require problem solving, diagnosis, judgment, and choice on the part of service employees. Such service steps might be highlighted on a blueprint if management is currently concerned about its training programs aimed at preparing employees to make such decisions. On the auto repair blueprint, there are several points where employee discretion is used, specifically the original estimate by the service representative and the diagnosis and testing by the mechanic. Well-trained personnel will be necessary to maintain the quality of these key steps, or management may wish to design some checks and balances into the system, in the form of oversight and approval by supervisors before employees are allowed to proceed further.

Fail points should also be specifically denoted in some fashion, for easy location by those studying the diagram for possible improvements.

Another enhancement to the blueprinting process suggested by Shostack is the concept of divergence. This is the extent to which a process step allows for many possible outcomes depending upon the customization needs of the customer.[12] Attempting to blueprint the many possible actions available under this circumstance could require an artificial intelligence system to describe. Instead, a symbol borrowed from decision theory, the "fan," can be used. This symbol is used at the repair stage and several others in Figure 15.2.

Blueprinting notation has not been standardized. The point is accurate depiction of the service for internal analysis, and most exercises are for proprietary, internal use rather than for communication with the outside world. Therefore, practitioners should feel free to develop any symbolism that works to describe the firm's service process in terms that are understandable to all relevant parties.

Using the Blueprint for Service Improvement

The blueprint can serve many purposes in managing a service. It can be used to make improvements to the design of an existing service or to design a new service. Its focus is on the service delivery system, and is therefore consistent with Deming's philosophy that most quality problems are with the system, rather than the workers' level of effort.[13] Using the blueprint for service redesign is straightforward. Once the group feels that the blueprint captures the actual service process currently in use, it should be compared to the desired level of service. The preferred level of service may require eliminating steps to improve response time, or giving frontline employees more leeway to satisfy customers. The blueprint should reveal steps that contain unnecessary loops, bottlenecks, and potentially problematic customer/server interactions. It may clarify points where simpler sequences of activities would be less likely to break down. As mentioned earlier, if the auto repair facility finds that it consistently underestimates the costs of repairs, perhaps due to a lack of experienced service representatives, then an additional level of oversight by a manager may need to be built into the system until current personnel can be better trained.

A blueprint can also serve as a guide to the implementation of a service plan by clearly explaining the appropriate sequence of steps needed to deliver a quality service. In particular, the service blueprint can be a great educational tool for illustrating that each employee plays a key role in an overall system, rather than performing isolated jobs. This larger perspective on the service process often helps customers to achieve higher levels of performance by convincing them why each contact person in a service firm must be a "part-time marketer."[14] In the auto repair facility, for example, the clerk whose job it is to post customer names in the callback queue at the completion of a service may be more careful to do so accurately after seeing that operation laid out as a critical step in monitoring customer satisfaction on the far right of the blueprint.

The blueprint also suggests the stages in the process where measurements are needed to monitor service quality and to keep it in control. For example, just downstream from fail points and bottlenecks are obvious places to monitor the service, both internally and from the perspective of customers.

By providing an understanding of the entire service, blueprinting also serves as a bridge between technical and functional quality. The quality of personal interactions that make up functional quality can't be fully specified in a blueprint. Writing carefully devised scripts for the points of interaction above the line of visibility is not enough to guarantee that service employees will be personable or responsive to unusual contingencies. But the blueprint does facilitate the development of functional quality because the interactions mapped in there pinpoint those moments on which training must be focused, such as how to notify customers that the actual repair work will exceed original estimates. And many of the aspects of functional quality can be determined by how some systems are designed in the blueprint. For example, a blueprint can support functional quality by guaranteeing that support systems provide contact people with all the information necessary to be helpful and responsive, for example, by making sure that the service representative has all the relevant information from the mechanic's diagnosis of the problem, so that a detailed description of the new findings are possible. (An alternative would be to have the mechanic call the customer, a process which would put entirely different stresses on the system.)

15.3 DESIGNING THE PROCESS: QUALITY FUNCTION DEPLOYMENT

While blueprints help to ensure that service processes run smoothly and that all contact points with the customer are well thought out, further research is usually necessary to ensure that the service meets customer needs. A complicating factor in the design of quality services is the imperfect relationship between the technical design elements of a service and customer impressions of the service. Managers don't always know what level of effort will be necessary to decrease the percent of customers who are dissatisfied with some level of a service. For example, how much faster does restaurant service have to be before it is noticed as better? What does a bank have to do to improve customer perceptions that it "listens to their needs"? What elements of office decor will contribute most to an atmosphere that supports perceptions of "professionalism" and "competence"? How can we find the proper balance between providing quick response to waiting customers and taking sufficient time with the customer currently being served? In Chapter 6 we described various methods of collecting and organizing the needs that customers hope to have satisfied when purchasing a service. But, even with such a list in hand it is not always clear how the service blueprint should be designed or altered so that the service is perceived to satisfy those needs. In this section we will briefly describe a design exercise called Quality Function Deployment (QFD) that was developed to help designers find the links between customer needs and design elements.

QFD was developed in Japan in the 1960s and was first used at Mitsubishi's Kobe shipyard in 1972.[15] It was subsequently adopted by Toyota and its suppliers, where it began to receive worldwide notice. It has been in use in the United States for more than a decade, primarily by manufacturers of automobiles, electronic equipment, and other products. Its use in the service sector has been less extensive, but it offers benefits there as well. The purpose of QFD is to translate customers' vague statements into actionable design specifications. It also provides an objective, structured forum in which people from various functions of the design and production process can communicate their needs and opinions on the structure of the service. QFD is an approach, not a rigidly designed set of procedures. But although firms must adapt the methods of QFD to suit their own particular needs, certain common tools are employed by all users of QFD.

The central tool of QFD analysis is a diagram called the House of Quality.[16] The general layout of such a diagram is shown in Figure 15.4. (The figure actually shows a small portion of a diagram for the design of a new chain restaurant.) The central part of the diagram is a matrix whose rows correspond to the list of customer needs developed and organized into a hierarchical structure as described in Chapter 4. In this case, we see portions of two major categories of customer needs, Service and Variety. The column labels are the technical components of the service design, also organized in a hierarchical fashion. Components of several categories, staff training, kitchen operations, and menu design are shown. Entries in the matrix are symbols or numbers that indicate the strength of the effect that a design component (column) is likely to have on customer perceptions of a particular need (row). For example, restaurant customers have stated that a knowledgeable waitstaff is an important factor in determining satisfaction with the restaurant. What should the restaurant do to improve its score on that dimension? It could train its waitstaff to understand the preparation of the dishes, including recommendations about combinations, tastings, and so on. Researching customers and intensive discussions with restaurant personnel will help management to understand important relationships among all the

FIGURE 15.4

THE HOUSE OF QUALITY: AN ABBREVIATED EXAMPLE

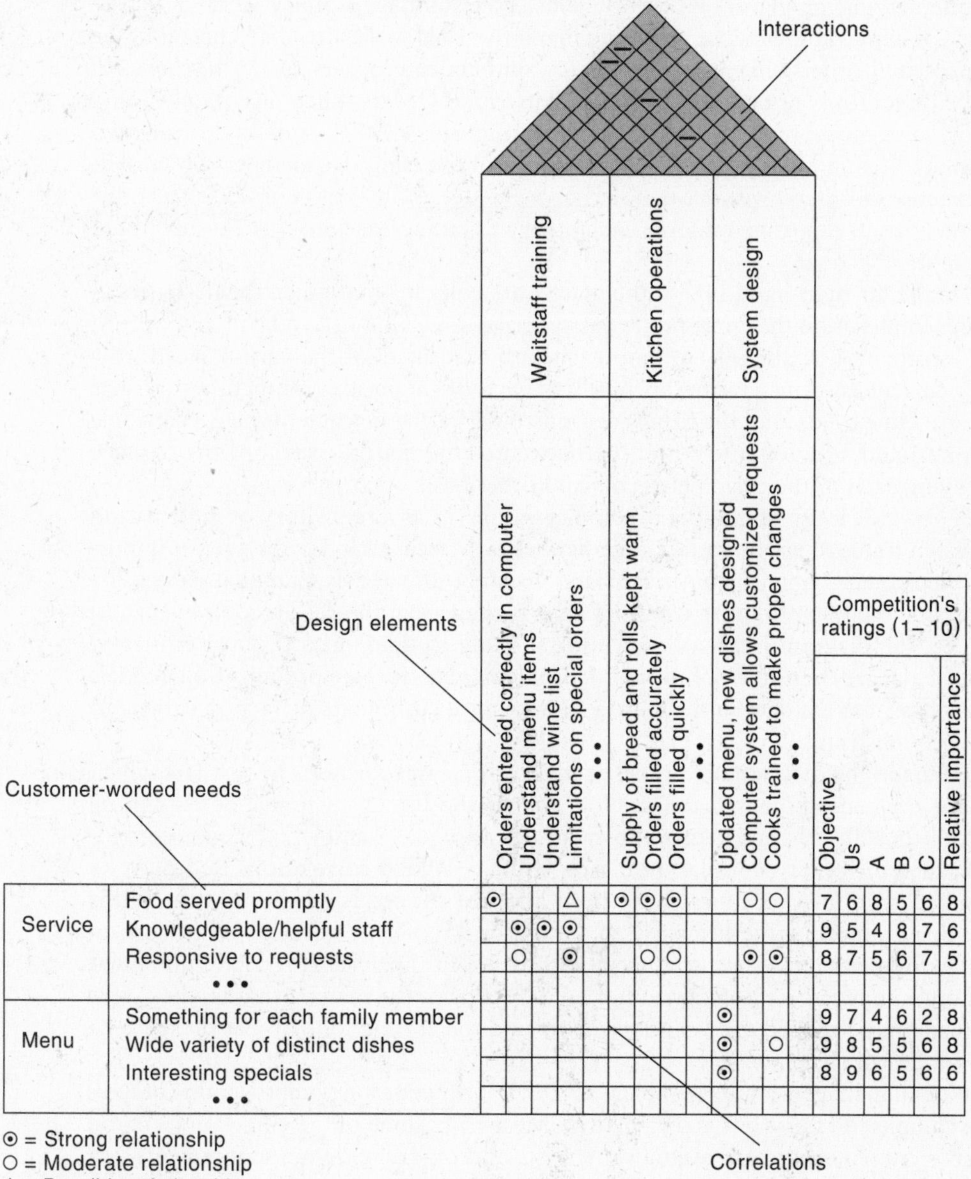

		Waitstaff training: Orders entered correctly in computer	Waitstaff training: Understand menu items	Waitstaff training: Understand wine list	Waitstaff training: Limitations on special orders	Waitstaff training: •••	Kitchen operations: Supply of bread and rolls kept warm	Kitchen operations: Orders filled accurately	Kitchen operations: Orders filled quickly	Kitchen operations: •••	System design: Updated menu, new dishes designed	System design: Computer system allows customized requests	System design: Cooks trained to make proper changes	System design: •••	Objective	Us	A	B	C	Relative importance
Service	Food served promptly	⊙			△		⊙	⊙	⊙			○	○		7	6	8	5	6	8
	Knowledgeable/helpful staff		⊙	⊙	⊙										9	5	4	8	7	6
	Responsive to requests		○		⊙			○	○			⊙	⊙		8	7	5	6	7	5
	•••																			
Menu	Something for each family member										⊙				9	7	4	6	2	8
	Wide variety of distinct dishes										⊙		○		9	8	5	5	6	8
	Interesting specials										⊙				8	9	6	5	6	6
	•••																			

⊙ = Strong relationship
○ = Moderate relationship
△ = Possible relationship
= No relationship

various customer needs and design elements. The values discovered are entered in the appropriate cells of the matrix.

The "roof" of the matrix is a separate table used to indicate positive and negative interactions among design components. For example, a policy to offer a wide variety of items on the menu, including made-to-order variations may confound the computerized order entry system used to communicate orders to the kitchen. An indication of this negative interaction between "Orders filled accurately" and "Allow customized requests" can be entered into the cell at the juncture of the two columns to remind designers of the limitations of stressing one element too hard at the expense of others, without major changes in design. It is of course also possible that two design elements reinforce each other in that increasing one makes the other even more effective.

On the far right-hand side of the matrix are columns that guide the designers in placing emphasis on the appropriate customer needs. Columns can be used to record such information as the relative importance to customers of the various needs, the firm's current customer rating on fulfilling each of the needs, competitors' ratings on those same needs, and the firm's ideal customer rating on each of the needs. Some users also add additional rows on the bottom of the matrix to record the costs of improving each of the design elements and other costs.

When the House of Quality is complete, it serves as a repository of information for design teams to use in putting together better services. It indicates what is important to customers, how customer satisfaction can be affected by changing service elements, and the limitations or synergies among changes in the design components. In practice, the diagram is used in an informal way to guide and support efforts to design balanced, sensible solutions to problems. No formal optimization models exist to, say, use the data in the matrix to maximize customer satisfaction subject to a budget constraint.

Filling in the diagram on a realistic scale can be an enormous task, a fact which has put off many potential users. Note that if the list of customer needs can be reduced to 100 different items, and there are an equal number of design components, then the central correlation matrix still has 10,000 correlations that must be estimated. Various procedures have been adopted for reducing the burden of this task. For example, some firms assign sectors of the matrix to teams who work in parallel to research the specific correlations. In a QFD exercise at Digital Equipment Corporation, teams were assigned horizontal strips of the matrix; that is, they were assigned sets of related needs and asked to find the correlations of just those needs with all design elements.[17]

Not all managers embrace the use of QFD, in spite of the potential value of having a completed House of Quality matrix. Measuring some of the correlations in the matrix between customers' vague statements and objective design components can be very difficult. As already noted, the task can be enormous and can take a great deal of time to complete. And of course, it doesn't supply specific answers, just organized information for those who must seek the answers. Nevertheless, interest in QFD remains high. The organization and discipline that the exercise brings to the planning function, perhaps after being modified to reduce the burden of time and effort, has been deemed to be well worth the trouble by many satisfied adherents.

15.4 MANAGING PEOPLE: USING "INTERNAL MARKETING" TO IMPROVE SERVICE

For many services, employees remain the primary ingredient of success in the moment of truth. A 1988 Gallup survey of consumers found that the most common definition of quality for services was employee contact skills such as courtesy, attitude, or helpfulness.[18] This result should come as no surprise to service marketers. In many service industries any competitive advantages obtained through innovative service design are usually momentary or impossible. The real source of competitive advantage is in the unmatched service attitude of the firm, specifically its frontline personnel. For example, retail bank customers often find the financial specifications of the offerings of competing banks to be relatively similar. The real basis for loyalty to one's primary bank usually lies in the personal relationships developed over time.[19] Therefore, formal designs of the service process are not enough to guarantee the quality of moments of truth. Management must be sensitive to the intangible aspects of the service, particularly the service orientation of its frontline personnel. In this section we will briefly describe what is necessary to foster this attitude.

Management is a key factor. One of the critical behind-the-scenes elements of Gronroos' service structure described in Section 15.1 was management support. It is management's job to engender and continuously rejuvenate a customer-oriented culture at every level of the firm. Managers and supervisors are responsible for establishing the organization's common values about service through strong leadership. By setting a good example and offering meaningful support and constant encouragement, the firm's management can do much to determine the attitude of employees when they face customers. We will discuss the motivation of employees further in Chapter 17, when we discuss empowerment.

A quality revolution cannot be maintained only by management's demonstrations of enthusiasm. Formal programs are also needed. "Internal marketing" is a term commonly used to describe the programs necessary to instill and maintain a strong service mentality throughout an organization. Internal marketing programs have several purposes.[20] First, they guarantee that all employees have a firm understanding of the structure of the business, its mission, and its customer-orientation. Secondly, these programs should be designed to keep employees motivated and suitably trained to act in service-oriented ways. Finally, they can be very helpful in attracting and keeping good employees.

Gronroos described the needs for these programs in his "internal marketing concept" which states that

> The internal market of employees is best motivated for service-mindedness and customer-oriented performance by an active, marketing-like approach, where a variety of activities are used internally in an active, marketing-like and coordinated way.[21]

Given the importance of the contact person's interaction in moments of truth, it is essential that the firm market the concepts of its services internally to its own employees before it can successfully market them to external customers. The strategy of internal marketing programs should be as well coordinated as the firm's external marketing strategy. For example, an unconditional service guarantee, an increasingly popular service offering, will not be successful unless employees have a clear understanding of how it works and are committed to fulfilling its promises.[22] Typical components of an internal marketing campaign include the following:[23]

Training. Training must focus on two different types of programs to keep employees in top shape as part-time marketers. They need to be given the technical know-how to do their jobs, but they also need to be steeped in the customer-based culture of the firm. To produce the kinds of employees necessary to deliver top-quality service, neither can be overlooked. Training frontline personnel in high-contact services should include interpersonal skills as well as technical performance skills. In particular, a good server must be able to identify what a customer wants by asking questions and listening carefully, and should be able to communicate to customers a sincere concern for their satisfaction. The manager of a chain of restaurants posed the issue this way in describing how they train their frontline personnel to deal with customer concerns: ". . . we advise new employees to take action before the guest has to ask for a remedy."[24]

Continuous interaction with management. Training can only go so far. Each employee has different personal needs for information and motivation that uniform training programs can't be expected to identify. It is management's job to extend the formal training through continual support, assistance, motivation, involvement in decision making, setting of examples, and rewarding of good performance.

Internal mass communication. Internal communication is one way to reach large numbers of employees with information that supports the service environment, shares information on new ways of satisfying customers, and so on. Distributing or posting a regular newsletter recognizing excellent performance by employees and containing letters of complaint and praise from customers is a good way to keep employees informed. Many large firms, such as Kmart and Home Depot, have their own internal television networks to broadcast important news and programs that support the overall corporate culture to employees throughout their facilities.

Marketing research. Just as t would be foolish to attempt to market to end customers without researching their needs, desires, and perceptions, it is just as foolhardy to fail to research one's employees. Employee attitudes and their willingness and ability to perform certain roles in the planned marketing strategy must be understood if the internal marketing program is to be effective. Moreover, research into employee experiences and opinions about the service delivery is also a vital, and too-often overlooked, source of information about how to improve the service to external customers.

Other human resource activities. Many activities ensure that the proper personnel are being hired and retained. Therefore, it is difficult to separate personnel policies from marketing strategy in a service firm. We will have more to say about these other human resource activities in Chapter 17.

15.5 MANAGING THE PHYSICAL EVIDENCE

In addition to the logical flow of the system and the motivation of the staff, the physical environment in which the service takes place, "servicescape," can also have an important influence on both customer and employee satisfaction.[25] The atmospherics of the physical setting in which a service is delivered can greatly enhance or detract from its quality. Scientifically determined results on this topic come from diverse fields and address only small parts of the puzzle. But they suggest that physical surroundings can play an important role in managing the moment of truth in several ways. First, physical surroundings can play a key role in providing cues about the expected level of quality. A plushly furnished lawyer's office with expensive original artwork on the walls communicates a different level of performance (and price) than a sparsely furnished messy office. The postal service in the United Kingdom has made radical changes in its operations to improve efficiency and customer service, but also felt it must support that effort by making major changes in the appearance of its postal stations, an effort that will cost 50 million pounds through 1998.[26]

Second, the servicescape can affect the actual delivery of the service. For example, we know that the environment of retail stores can influence people's willingness to stay and browse, to spend money and to socialize with others.[27] The tempo of background music can influence traffic flow and people's degree of spending.[28]

Pleasant surroundings can improve a customer's overall impression of the service, and can even influence their willingness to shop longer and spend more money.

Researchers have found that some seating arrangements, such as that in airports, can discourage social interactions.[29] Certainly a physically uncomfortable setting can inhibit an employee's performance and can affect his or her emotional state.[30] Finally, unique physical surroundings can be a source of differentiation for a firm, such as a restaurant whose walls serve as an art gallery for local painters, or an insurance firm like Transamerica whose unique headquarters has become a widely recognized landmark of the San Francisco skyline.

Comprehensive research still needs to be done to identify the interactions between environment and customer and employee behavior and how they affect customer satisfaction. Nevertheless, Bitner has provided a framework to guide managers in structuring the elusive problem of designing an appropriate servicescape.[31] She suggests first classifying services by who performs them within the servicescape: customers only (self-service operations, such as ATM machines or golf courses), customers and employees (interpersonal services such as hospitals, airlines, barbershops, and newsstands), or employees only (remote services such as electric utility offices and telephone answering services). Where a service is classified on this dimension determines whether the focus of the servicescape design should be on attracting, stimulating and guiding customers, on fostering interactions between customers and employees, or on maximizing productivity and accurate task completion by workers, respectively.

Bitner's summary of diverse results on this subject provide some other insights for understanding the role that the servicescape plays in influencing the behavior of customers and/or employees. There are three basic dimensions of a servicescape that can be manipulated: the ambient conditions such as temperature, lighting, and noise level, which become increasingly important the more time people spend in the facility; the spatial layout and functionality of the environment, which affect the ease and efficiency with which employees or customers can accomplish their tasks; and, signs, which instruct and guide service participants; and symbols and artifacts, which communicate nonverbal cues to them.

These dimensions affect customers and employees in three ways. First, there is a cognitive response as people interpret the cues. Customers may deduce the quality of the service offered by the firm, and employees may draw conclusions about the firm's internal culture or their personal importance to the firm from the physical surroundings they observe (a top-floor corner office, vs. a basement cubicle.) Second, there can be an emotional response to the surroundings, that can greatly influence a person's satisfaction level and intention to return. For example, facilities can be stimulating and exciting rather than boring, can give customers a feeling of independence and control rather than confusion and dependence on others. Finally, there is a physiological response, such as a discomfort from hard seating at a concert or to a too-cold temperature in a classroom. These responses can affect both customer enjoyment and the ability of service providers to do quality work.

Ultimately, these responses affect customer and employee behaviors. A well-designed servicescape, by generating appropriate beliefs, emotions and physiological reactions on the part of the relevant people, will provide an effective environment for the service encounter. For example, in the case of a self-serve facility such as a movie theater, will the cognitive and emotional responses to the appearance and image of the place attract people in the first place? Once inside, will their emotional and physiological reactions to the dimensions of the interior of the theater (the temperature, the seat comfort, the decor) cause them to stay and consider returning? For interpersonal services, will the dimensions of the servicescape encourage the appropriate interactions necessary for effective services? At the Shouldice Hospital in Toronto, a facility that specializes in hernia operations, the facility has low-rise stairways, common rooms at the ends of hallways, and gardens to encourage patients to get up and walk as soon as possible. Ronald McDonald Houses, low-priced residences for families who must travel out of town to visit their hospitalized children, consist of apartments with no kitchens. Each family must make use of kitchen facilities in a common area, to encourage social interaction with other families.

Because of the importance of servicescapes, Bitner makes the point that their design should not be left to "facility planners." A service's physical facilities should be tied into the strategies of marketing, human resources, and operations. All groups should be represented in the design process, and all decisions should reflect research on both the customers and the employees who will use the facilities.

15.6 SUMMARY

Managing the moment of truth is a complex task, and none of the approaches described above completely captures its essence by itself. Blueprinting helps to describe the dynamic aspects of the service and puts the key moments of truth into context. However, it cannot address some of the complex, intangible interpersonal and environmental aspects of those moments. An analysis of the psychological complexity of the interactions between customers and employees is also necessary to develop training programs that can teach service personnel how to better interact with customers. QFD is conceptually a very useful tool, but it can be difficult to implement and does not easily capture the dynamic aspects of the flow of a service. A better understanding of the effect of physical surroundings is also needed, although some frameworks for analyzing the problem have been suggested. Finally, each specific tool for quality improvement suggested by these tasks must be costed out, and its cost must be weighed against the likely effect on customer satisfaction, retention, and, ultimately, the firm's profits.

The dimensions of the problem of managing the moment of truth and their importance for improving overall customer satisfaction are clear. What to do about them to make the most of each specific instance is not. We have presented some tools to help the manager in this formidable, all-important task. But it is the manager's job to use them in creative ways to solve his or her particular problems. It's what management is all about, and what makes it fun.

REVIEW QUESTIONS

1. What is the difference between technical and functional quality? What are some measures of each for the following services, and which type of quality is more important?
   (a) an airline
   (b) a grocery store
   (c) a dentist's office
   (d) a mail-order marketer of music tapes and CDs

2. Describe the six components of service above and below the line of visibility for
   (a) a fast-food restaurant
   (b) a hospital
   (c) an overnight parcel service

3. Design a blueprint for the drive-through window operation of a typical fast-food restaurant. In your experience, are there any fail points? How would you redesign your blueprint to reduce the probability of these service failures?

4. Add a service system that would allow customers of the auto dealer described in Figure 15.2 to make service appointments.

5. How does internal marketing differ from external marketing? Can you find analogies to each of the four P's of marketing management?

ENDNOTES

1. David Wessel (1989), "Sure Ways to Annoy Customers," *The Wall Street Journal,* (Nov. 6), B1ff.
2. Jan Carlzon (1987), *Moments of Truth,* Cambridge, MA: Ballinger Publishing Co.
3. R. Norman (1984), *Service Management,* New York: Wiley.
4. Christian Gronroos (1990) *Service Management and Marketing,* Lexington, MA: Lexington Books, p. 37.
5. Philip Crosby, *Quality Is Free,* New York: McGraw-Hill
6. Richard L. Oliver (1989), "Processing of the Satisfaction Response in Consumption: A Suggested Framework and Research Propositions," *Journal of Consumer Satisfaction/Dissatisfaction and Complaining Behavior,* 2, 1–16.
7. Gronroos (1990), *op. cit.* and G. Lynn Shostack (1984), "Designing Services that Deliver," *Harvard Business Review,* (January-February), 133–139, and G. Lynn Shostack (1987), "Service Positioning Through Structural Change," *Journal of Marketing,* 51 (January), 34–43.
8. See Lyn Randall (1993), "Perceptual Blueprinting," *Managing Service Quality,* (May), 7–12.
9. Shostack (1984), *op. cit.*
10. See e.g., Murray W. Janzen (1991), "Total Quality Through Process Flowcharting," *1991 AACE Transactions,* F.8.1–F.8.4.
11. G. Lynn Shostack (1992), "Understanding Service Through Blueprinting," in *Advances in Services Marketing and Management,* T. Swartz et al., eds., 75–90.
12. G. Lynn Shostack (1987), "Service Positioning Through Structural Change," *Journal of Marketing,* 51 (January), 34–43.
13. W. Edwards Deming (1986), *Out of the Crisis,* Cambridge, MA: MIT Press.
14. Evert Gummesson (1987), "The New Marketing—Developing Long-Term Interactive Relationships," *Long-Range Planning,* 20 (August), 10–20.

15. Robert King (1987), "Listening to the Voice of the Customer: Using the Quality Function Deployement System," *National Productivity Review* (Summer), 277–281.
16. John R. Hauser and Don Clausing (1988), "The House of Quality," *Harvard Business Review,* 66 (May-June), 63–73.
17. Louis Cohen (1988), "Quality Function Deployment: An Application Perspective from Digital Equipment Corporation," *National Productivity Review,* (Summer), 197–208.
18. The Gallup Organization, Inc. (1988), "Consumers' Perceptions Concerning the Quality of American Products and Services," survey conducted for the American Society for Quality Control, ASQC Publication No. T711, October.
19. See Roland Rust and Anthony Zahorik (1993), *Journal of Retailing,* 69 (Summer), 193–215.
20. William R. George (1990), "Internal Marketing and Organizational Behavior: A Partnership in Developing Customer-Conscious Employees at Every Level," *Journal of Business Research,* 20, 63–70; also Gronroos (1990) *op. cit.,* p. 225.
21. Christian Gronroos (1983), *Strategic Management and Marketing in the Service Sector,* Cambridge, MA: Marketing Science Institute.
22. Gronroos (1990), *op. cit.,* p. 222
23. George (1990), *op. cit.;* Gronroos (1990), *op. cit.*
24. Timothy W. Finstahl (1989), "My Employees Are My Service Guarantee," *Harvard Business Review* (July-August), 28–32.
25. Mary Jo Bitner (1992), "Servicescapes: The Impact of Physical Surroundings on Customers and Employees," *Journal of Marketing,* 56 (April), 57–71.
26. Suzanne Bidlake (1993), "Counter Revolution at the Post Office," *Marketing,* (Sept. 2), 18–19.
27. Robert Donovan and John Rossiter (1982), "Store Atmosphere: An Environmental Psychology Approach," *Journal of Retailing,* 58 (Spring), 34–57.
28. Ronald Milliman (1982), "Using Background Music to Affect the Behavior of Supermarket Shoppers," *Journal of Marketing,* 46 (Summer), 86–91; Ronald Milliman (1986), "The Influence of Background Music on the Behavior of Restaurant Patrons," *Journal of Consumer Research,* 13 (September), 286–289.
29. R. Sommer (1984), *Tight Spaces: Hard Architecture and How to Humanize It,* Englewood Cliffs: Prentice-Hall.
30. Albert Mehrabian and James A. Russell (1974), *An Approach to Environmental Psychology,* Cambridge, MA: Massachusetts Institute of Technology, chap. 4.
31. Mary Jo Bitner (1992), *op. cit.*

Chapter 16

RELATIONSHIP MARKETING

16.1 INTRODUCTION: THE GROWTH OF RELATIONSHIP MARKETING

For several decades marketing theorists have drawn a clear difference between marketing and selling.[1] Selling conjures up for us the image of a door-to-door peddler who tries to sell us something we don't want, and then gets out of town as quickly as possible. The marketing concept, on the other hand, teaches firms to profit by selling what customers really want for a value that competitors can't match. The rationale for this second approach is twofold: First, it assumes that the marketer represents a going concern with every intention of remaining in business in the same market. Second, it supposes a goal of satisfied customers who will be a source of repeat purchases and positive recommendations. In spite of this underlying concept, the focus of marketing education and marketing practice has been on the attraction of new customers through the use of the four P's (product, price, promotion/communication, and place/distribution), rather than on the retention of current customers. Until recently, then, marketing efforts have been focused on "creating exchanges" rather than managing long-term relationships with customers.

Maturing markets, lower population growth, and global competition have forced managers to examine the costs of winning new customers versus retaining their old ones. We now see the focus of marketing shifting to managing relationships with customers. The following definition of marketing captures the new spirit:

> Marketing is to establish, maintain, enhance (usually but not necessarily always long-term) relationships with customers and other partners, at a profit, so that the objectives of the parties involved are met. This is achieved by a mutual exchange and fulfillment of promises.[2]

The concept of promises made and kept by both sides is a key to this definition. The promises made by the seller include the obvious ones that are part of any selling contract, such as product quality, delivery and inventory management, attendant services, and others, but for a long-term relationship they must also cover deeper commitments to the buyer's success. The promises made by the buyer also must be beyond those of the contractual terms of payment. One British executive described his understanding of the role of the customer in a strong relationship:

> I describe 'loyal' customers as those who will call me as a supplier immediately [when] they receive a visit from a competitor with a new product and feel that they have a unique relationship with me and my staff.[3]

The role of services marketing is critical in relationship building. Consider the following quote from Raymond Langton, the head of SKF North America, a firm in an industry that many would consider to be as far from the "service sector" as any could be (it manufactures bearings for industrial customers): "In today's world, to retain business you cannot look at is as if you were selling a product. You are providing a value-added service." In addition to selling bearings the firm now provides its customers with assistance in the mounting and maintenance of its bearings to reduce downtime in their factories.[4] It is particularly in this critical area of relationship marketing that any organization begins to realize that it is in the business of marketing services. Relationships, whether with consumers or industrial customers, are built on service.

In fact, in spite of the obvious benefits of relationships to sellers of establishing long-term markets for their products, much of the impetus for closer ties has come from industrial buyers who have found that partnerships with their suppliers are essential to producing high-quality products while cutting costs. After all, continuous quality improvement is difficult when a firm frequently changes suppliers. On the other hand, long-term, stable relationships are important to building and maintaining quality by allowing both parties to learn each other's businesses and develop cooperative solutions to problems.

Levitt called this form of relationship "reciprocal dependency" and insisted that the seller is responsible for initiating and nurturing it.[5] Research has shown that buyer firms tend to consider the granting of further sales in the future to be a privilege earned through careful attention to the buyer/seller relationship.[6] In fact, buyers in large transactions often see themselves as having granted the sellers special favors, rather than having participated in mutually profitable exchanges. Moreover, having "awarded" these contracts, they expect to be appreciated and further rewarded to even the debt, perhaps by extraordinary service, continued investment in quality improvements, and discounts on further purchases.

Because of the level of commitment required for these relationships, the decision cycle for firms choosing suppliers has become much longer. For example, banks that used to evaluate and choose providers of stationery supplies in three to six months now take up to 18 months.[7] This is because the decision to buy is not just for a single transaction, but has become a commitment to enter a long-term relationship, with the attendant risks. In fact, Levitt compared this decision to a romantic encounter. Doing business is no longer a decision to have a "one-night stand," but a commitment to a marriage, which will require cooperation, nurturing, mutual problem solving, and conflict resolution to keep the arrangement productive and mutually beneficial.

Baxter International, the healthcare products and services giant, demonstrates how far relationship building has gone. Its hospital customers have felt tremendous pressure on their earnings due to the growth of alternative healthcare delivery systems, government restrictions, and insurance company pressures. Baxter has negotiated arrangements with some hospitals in which cost targets for supplies are determined and Baxter shares the savings or the costs depending on how well it does in meeting that target. It provides consultants who advise the hospitals on standardizing products and streamlining inventory procedures. In fact, Baxter now manages the inventory systems for some of its clients and may deliver supplies to individual floors many times a day. The companies sales through the inventory management program rose by more than a third in 1993, while the supply costs to its hospitals decreased—by about $300,000 for one hospital. Baxter and its customers now have a common goal in bringing down costs, because they share the same profit and loss.[8]

Not all relationships are such strong partnerships. In many industries, the burden is on the seller to develop the relationship. For example, firms that originally supplied checks and stationery items to banks have found other ways to make themselves valuable partners with their clients. Most now offer such additional services as marketing research, sales training, assistance with direct marketing programs, and development of other printed sales materials. Providing such important strategic services helps to develop a close partnership between the two firms, thereby making competitive inroads very difficult.[9]

Baxter International shares profits and losses from its supply and inventory management programs with its hospital customers.

Consumer Relationships

The concept of relationships has become particularly popular in describing these new arrangements between corporations, but, as we will see, it can also be applied to consumer marketing. Relationship building in consumer markets tends to put most of the burden on the seller, since it is generally not as contractually based as business-to-business marketing. But the idea for the seller is the same—to develop reasons for the buyer to consider the seller more than the source of single transactions, but rather as a dependable source for solving many needs. For example, banks offer products and services to meet evolving customers' needs over the life cycle, and many assign "personal bankers," individuals who take responsibility for keeping in personal touch with sets of customers, cross-selling new products and handling customer problems. Bank One, headquartered in Columbus, Ohio, uses its extraordinary database of information on its customers to track their financial and life-cycle progress, so that it can offer appropriate services. For example, its systems are programmed to identify customers with large checking account balances as prime candidates for the sale of investment products.[10] This relationship makes it more difficult and undesirable for customers to switch banks. In another category, Anne Klein, the designer of women's business clothing offers an "At Your Service" hotline, that promises to "create a look just for you," with the help of fashion consultants who can assist in shopping at more than 900 stores.[11]

Benefits

Developing a strong relationship marketing orientation is not without costs in money, time, and effort. So, before a firm rushes out to establish stronger relationships with customers, it is good to identify the benefits that it is likely to realize. Advocates list many. One of the most obvious is familiar from earlier chapters: customer retention. Higher retention means higher market share, which in turn means higher revenues. In addition, sales calls or other contacts are more efficient and productive with familiar customers, than with new ones. New arrangements can require complex, costly negotiations. Long-time customers often purchase greater quantities than new customers, and it is easier (and less costly) to sell new products to them.[12] In high-contact industries, customer service representatives who are switched from lost accounts may require significant retraining to make them of value to new customers.[13] Reichheld proposes that a cycle of success can begin here as the improved economies lead to better profits, allowing higher pay to workers and improved morale. Satisfied employees will deliver better service, which leads to further productivity, and so on.

In addition to the benefits of improved retention, offering customers the advantages of close relationships can have other benefits to the seller. In particular, for products that are sold through distribution channels, providing customers with an incentive to establish a direct relationship with the manufacturer will circumvent the difficulty that many producers have with channel members who refuse to share their customers' names. For sales to industrial buyers, where most negotiations go through a purchasing agent, the establishment of relationships with individual users allows the seller to identify and learn the needs of key influencers in the organization's buying center that may otherwise be hard to reach.[14]

Degrees of Relationship Building

However, before getting too swept up in the possibilities, we need to consider the costs of building relationships as well. Kotler identified five different levels of relationship marketing at which a firm may choose to operate.[15]

basic No lasting relationship is really established. The transaction is made and both parties go their own ways.

reactive The seller offers to respond if the buyer has any problems.

accountable The seller contacts that buyer after the sale to find out how the product has been received and whether it could have been better.

proactive The seller calls the customer from time to time with updates on improvements to the product and other services to make the product's consumption more satisfying.

partnerships Both parties work together to find solutions to mutual problems and opportunities for mutual success. This arrangement is generally limited to business-to-business marketing.

The ideal level for a particular firm depends upon several things, particularly on the number of customers and the margins on products. Due to the sheer numbers of customers buying small quantities at low margins, most package goods marketers operate at the basic level. However, Procter & Gamble and some others have operated at the reactive level for many years, by providing 800-number customer complaint and advice lines for each of their products. It has not been feasible for P&G to operate at a higher level, although, as we will discuss later in this chapter, database management and telecommunications technology may allow consumer products firms to improve communication with and learn about their customers. In Chapter 19 we will discuss in more detail the effects of technology on the future of marketing.

Knowing that relationship marketing is important is not the same as knowing how to do it well. We will now turn to particular steps firms can take to improve their relationship marketing.

16.2 DEVELOPING RELATIONSHIPS

Reichheld maintains that strong relationship marketing depends on the development of four components: products that will build loyalty, employees who are adept at relationships, the appropriate set of customers, and measurement to monitor and improve.[16] We will explore each of these components in turn.

Products

The basis of the new marketing concept is still delivering products that customers want. But sellers no longer think about needs as static; they consider the evolution that needs are likely to follow over time. Because winning new customers is harder than keeping familiar ones, the marketer's best strategy is to develop products and services for the evolving needs of current customers, rather than passing them

Procter & Gamble and many other manufacturers seek relationships with their customers through the use of 800-number help lines that solve problems and offer advice on product usage.

off to other sellers and trying to find new customers for the same old products. For example, insurance companies provide a range of products that become relevant at different times in a customer's life. They may be able to initially sell a young individual automobile and renter's insurance. As the person matures and his or her needs change, the company should be alert to the opportunities for selling homeowner's insurance and investments. As the person reaches maturity, services such as health insurance and retirement planning assistance become more important. AT&T's Universal Card is developing its services to meet the changing needs and technological capabilities of its credit card customers. It is currently developing what it calls a "21st Century Personal Servant," an individualized computer account that will extend its current credit service by pulling together all of a consumer's monthly bills into a single statement, allowing the cardholder to pay them electronically, balancing the checkbook, making reservations, and even making recommendations about sales.[17]

This evolution of customer needs over time is typical of most products. Most students today find it hard to imagine that 50 years ago there were retail stores that sold only radios, later adding television sets, because the average customer was intimidated by the technology and wanted a great deal of advice and after-sale service. As the products became commonplace and easier to use, the need for attendant services disappeared and these items could be sold through discount stores with no clerical assistance.

Companies pass through similar life cycles with the products they buy from vendors. A subcomponent may be of keen interest to top management when initially purchased. Its quality, the availability of technical support, and timely delivery schedules will provide the basis for frequent discussions and relationship building between corporate executives at the beginning. However, these concerns will eventually become the routine responsibility of the purchasing agent and the customer firm's own technical staff. If the supplier wishes to remain an important partner in the buyer-seller relationship it must continually enhance the product with value-added enhancements and services. We have seen how check and stationery suppliers have managed to add services to their product lines that keep their relationships of interest to the top managers of their clients. Similar activity is necessary for any firm that seeks to keep partnerships vibrant and closed to competitive inroads.

In addition to the inevitable evolution of any customer's needs, larger trends are at work as supplier firms throughout the economy have realized the importance of providing products that "entangle" customers in longer-term relationships. Levitt anticipated most of these changes a decade ago. As he predicted, sales over time have progressed from selling core products, to augmented products (products with service, installation, guarantees, etc.), integrated systems of products and services that will address many buyer needs. This type of evolution requires expanded commitments by both parties. These relationships are intended to maintain frequent, meaningful contact between partners. The implications for the product offerings necessary to compete in this environment are daunting. No more small ideas or hit-and-run selling. Relationship marketing requires continued attention to the needs of customers, and constant development of new products and services to address their evolving needs.

Employees

Relationship marketing obviously involves the efforts and skills of more individuals than just those in the sales or marketing departments. The need for service and support implies that employees in design, engineering, and manufacturing and/or service delivery must also be intimately acquainted with the needs of the customer and be prepared to deal with individuals from the customer firm. This observation is true for almost any support function in the company. For example, information systems may need to be coordinated to enhance ordering, billing, and other data exchange with customers. Each of the people involved will contribute to the image of the vendor among the buyer's employees. Gronroos has spoken of the need to train all employees of service firms to be "part-time marketers," because their interactions with customers are important in maintaining corporate relationships.[18] But it is also true for many employees of manufacturing firms, given that relationships are built upon personal interactions and serving the customers' needs.

What are the implications for human resource policies of this new approach? Reichheld[19] insisted that the key to loyal customers is maintaining loyal employees. Long-term employees know the organization's systems better, know how to deal with customers better, and build up personal relationships with customer employees that form the basis of trust so important to the interfirm partnership.

Therefore it is important to design jobs that encourage employees to stay.

Higher compensation can help, of course, but it isn't the only requirement. Career advancement opportunities and empowerment (to be discussed in Chapter 17) are also important to attracting and keeping top-performing employees. Firms should be aware of the value of personal relationships that employees have with their customers and seek to keep them in contact with the same people. Companies that routinely rotate managers destroy this opportunity for long-term relationships to develop, making it easier for customers to consider defecting. Our research in the banking industry found that many customers become very dissatisfied when personnel are switched from one branch to another.

Reichheld also recommended that firms hire employees on the basis not only of skills and experience, but also of their expected long-term service to the company. For example, he pointed out that the Olive Garden restaurant chain prefers to hire as prospective managers people with strong ties to the communities in which they are expected to develop businesses, and they are kept in those positions to leverage the relationships they develop with the local community. The chain also rewards its staff for loyalty by paying higher wages to those with longer experience with the firm.

Hiring should also consider certain personal characteristics of salespeople and others who will have high interactions with customer personnel. Research has shown that salespeople who are perceived as similar to clients with respect to appearance, lifestyle, and socioeconomic status tend to be more successful,[20] although a rigid policy in this regard could be the basis for discrimination suits. The same research also suggested that potential hires be screened for social abilities that promote long-term interpersonal relationships.

In general, employees with expected longer tenure with the firm also justify a greater investment in training, which is likely to further increase customer satisfaction. This training must include information and skills necessary to building long-term relationships, lessons that are evidently not part of many current training programs. A recent study of life insurance agents in the United Kingdom found that a large majority of the sample did not feel that suggestions for change and service improvement should come from the needs of the client base. Moreover, most said that they gave a higher priority to attracting new customers than to servicing existing ones.[21] These attitudes against relationship building had not been addressed in their training, which tended to concentrate primarily on the technicalities of insurance. But, such attitudes can be changed. In the United States, State Farm Insurance has a training program and an incentive system that put equal weight on servicing new and current policies, and the firm is an industry leader in customer loyalty.[22]

A study of the role that sales representatives play as relationship managers between firms found that their training should specifically address several skills.[23] In particular, training in trust-building activities, and skills in questioning and listening to customers are necessary. This includes preparing salespeople to deal with some common ethical dilemmas. In particular, customers occasionally disclose selective information to contact people to test their trustworthiness and honorable intentions, as well as the willingness of the seller firm to reciprocate with equivalent disclosures. To help employees deal with such situations and to maintain cordial relationships with customer firms, training should emphasize rigid corporate standards of integrity regarding the use of such information.

To manage, expand, and grow the relationship, the study's authors also recommended that sales reps be trained in a broader set of disciplines than those narrowly defined by the current product line. Training in related disciplines such as financing methods or other service management areas that may be of value to customers (again, as in the case of the bank check suppliers) can help the sales staff to become truly valuable problem solvers for customers.

Finally, if employees are to be allowed to nurture long-term relationships with customers, the structure of their jobs and organizational responsibilities may need to change. For the past decade major consumer product firms, such as Procter & Gamble and Kraft/General Foods, have experimented with new operating structures that cut across brand lines. The traditional brand management structure doesn't suit itself well to the management of relationships with ever more powerful retail chains and special-needs market segments. In response, manufacturers have experimented with positions such as "segment manager," an individual or team whose job is to coordinate the firm's marketing efforts to address the needs of important customers or segments. Due to the confusion of responsibilities, no single standard has achieved universal acceptance, as the P&G brand management model did for over fifty years. Companies are each seeking their own solutions to the organizational problems of managing products and customers simultaneously. Assigning responsibilities for profit and loss and setting corresponding incentives in these multiply structured environments is likely to remain unsettled for a long time.

Employees must also be trained to calculate the value of customer relationships, so that they can allocate their efforts appropriately. Not every customer is worth the cost of establishing a long-term relationship.

Customers

Not all customers are suitable for long-term relationships. Customers worth pursuing are those that have the greatest lifetime value, and, in particular, those for whom the lifetime value exceeds the cost of acquiring them as customers. We have spoken with bankers who insisted that they lose money on most checking accounts, but then offer large price and merchandise inducements to all customers who open accounts with them. These programs may well attract some customers who will establish long-term relationships with the bank, but in the short-run they will also attract a large number of expensive, nonloyal customers who may put the financial viability of the total program in jeopardy.

Loyalty-based marketing should not be confused with short-term price promotions that seek to generate momentary bursts in sales. They should be carefully focused to identify customers who are likely prospects for long-term relationships. Demographic factors and past purchase histories can be useful in this search. In particular, by identifying segments of similar customers, the firm improves its prospects of tailor-making services that generate high loyalty. For example, older people tend to be more loyal banking customers and also have many similar service needs, whereas younger customers with low balances can be notorious brand switchers. Sometimes a firm may identify a customer segment whose loyalty is counterintuitive and turn its attitudes to its own advantage. For example, USAA, an insurance firm, specializes in policies to military personnel, a community that makes frequent moves and has been notoriously unprofitable to insure. However, USAA created a system that specializes in this group's unique needs, including an immense centralized database that keeps track of clients around the world. This tracking system has provided great convenience to clients who have rewarded the firm with an astonishing 98% retention rate on its automobile insurance policies.[24] Incidentally, the firm's products have also evolved to meet its customers' needs, now including credit cards and investment products.

Based on information obtained from doctors, hospitals, and prenatal training programs, Kimberly Clark, the manufacturer of paper products including Huggies diapers, spent more than $10 million on a database system containing over three-fourths of the names of expectant mothers in the United States.[25] During pregnancy the women receive a series of mailings containing information on maternity and child care, and upon the birth of the baby a coupon for Huggies—which can be tracked to determine whether it is used. How can Kimberly Clark justify this expense? It is the company's feeling that it is building a relationship with the mothers which will result in loyalty to the firm's products. The prize: an average $1400 per year spent on disposable diapers, enough to justify significant expenditures on relationship building.[26]

Keeping Information on Customers Identifying and keeping in touch with potentially loyal customers is essential, and computer technology now makes it possible on a scale unimaginable just a few years ago. In fact, an excellent database and the capability to organize, analyze and segment it are absolutely essential to make relationship marketing work. The file must not only contain basic names and addresses but purchase histories and other relevant information that will allow the firm to anticipate a customer's future needs.[27] Vendors are rushing to fill this information need. For example, Equifax Check Services, known to many as a clearinghouse for authorizing consumer purchases by check at retail stores, actually captures information about each purchase and enters it into the database using the purchaser's driver's license number. The database now contains purchase records on 92 million individuals, including the amount of each purchase, the specific store and the time of day. Equifax can manipulate the database on behalf of its clients to produce lists or even direct mailings. We will discuss the future of database marketing further in Chapter 19.

Determining the Value of a Customer How can one decide which customers are profitable enough to keep or to pursue? Myer recommended a measure of customer value called Customer Return on Assets (CRA).[28] The basic idea is to measure the profitability of relationships with individual customers, something often overlooked by accounting systems that tend to focus more on product performance. Systems that measure revenue only, combined with a dedication to high service levels at any cost, are likely to lead to terrible misallocations of effort by the sales force and other customer relations personnel. Relationship managers should also be tracking the costs of maintaining relationships. These costs can be traced to individual accounts and include sales costs, service costs, and other costs related to serving the particular account. The formula for computing CRA was developed primarily for manufacturers selling to wholesale and retail chain customers, but the formulas can be computed for other sellers of products and services as well.

The formula is calculated in Figure 16.1 for a hypothetical customer of a firm providing cleaning and maintenance services, including the sale of supplies and certain equipment. The CRA for this client is 24.6%, slightly lower than the 30% average for many of the actual customers in Myer's study. The first category of costs contains the usual measures of costs of sales, indicating a 48% gross margin on sales. The second category includes the costs of marketing to the particular customer. Specifically, it consists of the costs of selling, promotion, the development of specific products, storage and transportation, and extra service required to keep the account satisfied. Note, for example, that this customer is receiving extra services amounting to 10% of revenues. When these marketing costs are subtracted from the gross margin, the result is the contribution of the customer's sales to corporate overhead. This amount is the return on the manufacturer's investment in the customer.

FIGURE 16.1

THE COMPUTATION OF CUSTOMER RETURN ON ASSETS

	Amount	Percent of Sales
Revenue	$5423,893	100
less:		
Cost of labor (sales, equipment, materials) +	291,018	54
Reserves for damaged and returned merchandise +	7,573	1
Discounts and allowances	36,287	7
	334,878	62
= Gross margin	208,015	48
less:		
Selling cost +	27,145	5
Promotion cost +	86,863	16
Product development cost +	5,423	1
Direct warehousing cost +	4,859	1
Customer freight cost +	3,435	1
Postsale service cost +	55,144	10
	182,869	34
= Customer contribution to overhead	25,156	5
divided by:		
Accounts receivable +	90,577	17
Inventory (finished goods)	11,531	2
	102,108	19
= Customer return on assets:	25,156 / 102,108 = <u>24.6%</u>	

The manufacturer's investment in the customer is the amount of capital tied up in maintaining the account. In particular, the manufacturer is carrying accounts receivable from the customer, and holds certain finished goods in inventory for later shipment to the customer. For this particular client, average accounts receivable amount to 17% of annual revenues, equal to more than two months of sales, indicating that this customer is slow in paying bills. The average value of equipment and materials held in inventory for this customer represent 2% of sales.

What levels are appropriate for a given seller will depend on the nature of the product and its stage in the life cycle, competition, the state of the economy, and other factors. So each firm must determine what standards are acceptable for its own situation. Even without identifying ideal objective standards for the CRA items, the calculations are useful in comparing the costs to serve different customers. Firms that applied this formula found wide variation in costs of serving customers, particular in promotion expenses because of the fact that some customers bought only on promotions. Other wide variations were discovered in selling costs and in accounts receivable. Interestingly, the analysis also found that the fastest-growing customers were generally the least profitable.

Myer recommended several actions to take to deal with the variability in demands and profitability of different customers, based on the calculation of CRA for each account. Some customers may not be worth the expense of keeping, but others may be attractive long-term partners if the pricing schedules they now pay can be adjusted to reflect more accurately the higher costs of serving them. The challenge is to make those with low CRA more profitable without scaring them away. In particular,

1. The firm should decide what range of CRAs is acceptable. The key is long-term viability more than the current immediate return.
2. A menu of highly flexible options should be drawn up to reflect the range of service options required by different customers, including a greater number of discount schedules, delivery options, promotional packages, and electronic ordering options than the one or two now generally offered.
3. Prices should then be assigned to each service option to reflect the cost of providing it. This will allow customers to specify the services they need and are willing to pay for on an *à la carte* basis. The different prices should be defensible to customers as reflecting the costs of offering the options.
4. Finally, selling the new pricing schedule to customers may be difficult, particularly to those who in the past demanded and received lots of services for no extra cost. Myer recommended a two-pronged strategy to help customers accept the new pricing option: First, rather than positioning additional services as extra charges, present the deletion of services as discounts from the full-service price. Second, these programs must be phased in gradually over time, with a small initial spread that is gradually widened over time.

Although many marketing firms don't do analyses of this type, such calculations are clearly prerequisites to choosing and developing profitable relationships. A CRA analysis may also reveal segmentations based on account service needs that will enable the seller to serve them more profitably than would the usual segmentation based on size or region. Specialty teams can be assigned to deal with customers with similar service needs, a practice that may help reduce the costs of selling to them and managing their accounts. The result can also be improved quality of the relationship.

Measurement

As with any investment, measures of outcome are necessary to control the process, to assess its success, and to provide feedback for assessing the relative effectiveness of various programs. Reichheld asserts that most relationship-building programs will not produce measurable bottom-line results for several years.[29] Instead, his recommendation is to track a leading indicator of profits, customer retention, as described in Chapter 14 in the discussion of the ROQ model. As we have warned, monitoring satisfaction alone is insufficient, since satisfaction levels are often very high, even though retention is not.

Myer recommended that market share with key accounts be tracked.[30] Because of his recommendation that financial data be kept for each account, he also suggests that CRA be tracked by account. However, he also recommends keeping some softer measures that directly address relationship marketing. For example, to what extent have we improved the cooperation and participation of key accounts? Have all members of the supply chain benefited, and are customers sufficiently aware of those benefits? These last measures are not easy to define objectively, but they seem well worth following.

Unfortunately, evaluating expenditures in terms of their long-term value to the firm runs counter to standard accounting practice. Currently there are no standardized approaches to measuring the value of a firm's customer relationships. The subjectivity of the judgments necessary to quantify this concept makes it an unlikely prospect for standardized accounting standards in the near future. Therefore marketing must press forward in its effort to find useful measures to track and control this key activity.

Other Implementation Issues

In summary, successful relationship marketing is a three-stage process.[31] First of all, the company must have an excellent knowledge of its customers. For consumer marketers and industrial marketers with large numbers of customers, an extensive database containing information on current and potential customers is required. Secondly, the company must have the capability of tailoring its marketing programs to individual customers based on customer characteristics and preferences. Finally, it must be able to track individual purchase histories to be able to assess the costs of acquiring and servicing each customer compared to the customer's lifetime value.

For many years Sears Roebuck & Company has been at the forefront in tracking sales to individual customers and in running loyalty programs for many of its retail customers. Programs such as its Mature Outlook, New Movers, College Advantage, and its recently launched Sears Best Customer program are all intended to increase customer loyalty to the chain and to add a more personal touch to its customer dealings, in spite of the firm's image as a retail giant. A Sears executive recently outlined three important factors in establishing relationships with individual customers.[32] These are:

1. Keep it local. Because a relationship implies person-to-person contact, all of the Sears programs are the responsibility of individual store managers, rather than of the chain itself.

2. The program must include both "hard" and "soft" benefits. Hard benefits include discounts, promotions, etc. that are available only to program members that give the program meaning. Soft benefits include giving special priority attention to program members with problems and special requests.

3. Communication is essential. Sears continually reinforces its message to its better customers that they are special, using between six and eight communications per year, including announcements, promotions, and surveys.

Managers insist that the value of these programs are cumulative, and that the impact on loyalty becomes more powerful each year.

16.3 THE FUTURE OF RELATIONSHIP MARKETING

Technology holds the key to the future of relationship marketing, particularly with individual consumers. Marketers in many consumer categories now have the technical capability to track purchases of individuals and build databases from these records. The cost of doing so has fallen to a thousandth of what it was in 1970.[33] Firms like Lands' End, L. L. Bean, and American Express consider their databases to be among their most valuable assets. Artificial intelligence programs as well as simpler models can be used to infer individual customer needs and preferences from these databases. In this way, customer purchases are the equivalent of a continuous conversation with the seller.

The seller's ability to speak directly back to the buyer is also improving. The databases can be combined with new printing technologies to communicate with consumers on an individual basis. It is now technically possible for a firm like Lands' End to print individual catalogs for each customer on its mailing list, although the cost is probably yet too great to make it practical. Nevertheless, the day is coming. Magazine publishers already print thousands of slightly different editions of their publications targeted to customers with different needs and backgrounds. Coming developments in telecommunications technology, to be discussed further in Chapter 19, will also give marketers the ability to communicate directly and interactively with customers. The potential for relationship building is enormous. The deciding factor will be how fast costs fall to make these activities feasible.

The future of relationship marketing is hard to predict with certainty because the tools on which it will rely are evolving so rapidly. At the same time, relationship marketing does not have a particularly long history on which to base assessments of its strategic potency or to justify massive expenditures. Nevertheless, the natural next step for marketing to take would seem to be getting back to the one-on-one interactions that marketers thought they had lost when their markets expanded beyond their local communities.

16.4 SUMMARY

The importance of relationship marketing has arisen for several reasons. Throughout this book we have stressed the importance of customer retention to corporate profits. Particularly in the area of business-to-business marketing, many firms have found that retaining customers requires more than simply providing prompt, friendly service: it requires the establishment of long-term, mutually beneficial relationships. Sellers benefit from these arrangements because they are guaranteed stable, long-term sales. Buyers benefit because their suppliers can justify long-term investments in technologies that produce higher quality at lower costs.

In practice, the development and nurturing of long-term relationships is up to the seller. Becoming an attractive partner requires attention to four areas. First, the firm must continually develop its products to meet the evolving needs of its customers, and to seek new ways of remaining strategically important to its customers. Second, the firm must hire and train its personnel to deal effectively with customers, and perhaps reorganize job roles so that employees are given the necessary authority to develop and maintain relationships. Third, the firm must be somewhat selective about the customers it chooses to develop relationships with. Not all customers are equally profitable, and the firm must determine that its investment in customer service will be appropriately rewarded by its customers. The final component in a successful relationship-building program is measurement, a careful tracking of key indicators to monitor the long-term health of the partnership.

Relationship marketing is not a passing fad. If anything, the development of communications technology and addressable media are making it possible for firms to establish relationships not only with large institutional customers, but with individuals. The profit advantages of improving customer retention through long-term alliances mean that relationship marketing is here to stay.

REVIEW QUESTIONS

1.
   (a) Does the CRA provide a suitable measure of the value of a customer? In particular, do you agree with the denominator used to compute CRA in the last line of the formula?
   (b) How would you adjust the formula to make it more appropriate for a service firm, such as a CPA firm or an institutional cleaning service?
   (c) Does the CRA formula address the long-term value of the customer?
2. How might technology be expected to enable firms to move up Kotler's ladder of levels of relationship marketing?

3. At one time IBM dominated the computer industry because customers wanted the exceptional support that the firm had to offer. Now many customers feel confident enough about computer systems that they are willing to save money by buying clones or by buying through discount brokers who offer no support. What steps do you think IBM will have to take to reestablish itself as a high-involvement purchase for computer customers?

4. Can you think of any services where high employee turnover is not a problem to maintaining customer relationships? Where do these services fall on Kotler's five-point scale? Do you agree that employee longevity is necessary for firms to achieve the highest level of relationship marketing?

5. Relationship among firms can last for 30 or more years, often well beyond the careers of those who initially started the relationship. What can firms do to institutionalize relationships so that they endure even when the people involved change?

ENDNOTES

1. Philip Kotler (1991), *Marketing Management: Analysis, Planning, Implementation and Control,* Englewood Cliffs, NJ: Prentice-Hall.
2. Christian Gronroos (1990), *Service Management and Marketing: Managing the Moments of Truth in Service Competition,* Lexington MA: Lexington Books, p. 138.
3. Alan Barrell (1992), "Relationship Marketing: Way Ahead for the 90s?," *Business Marketing Digest,* 17(3), 49–54.
4. Rahul Jacob (1994), "Why Some Customers are More Equal Than Others," *Fortune* (September 19), 215–224.
5. Theodore Levitt (1983), "After the sale is over...," *Harvard Business Review* (September–October), 87–93.
6. Lawrence A. Crosby, Kenneth R. Evans, and Deborah Coles (1990), Relationship Quality in Services Selling: An Interpersonal Influence Perspective," *Journal of Marketing,* 54 (July), 68–91.
7. Barry I. Deutsch (1992), "Supplier Relationships That Make the Difference," *Bank Marketing* (July), 20–23.
8. Jacob (1994), *op. cit.*
9. Deutsch (1992), *op. cit.*
10. Jacob (1994), *op. cit.*
11. Barbara van Gorder (1991), "The New Age of Relationship Marketing," *Credit Magazine,* (March/April), 22–24.
12. Frederick F. Reichheld and David W. Kenny (1990), "The Hidden Advantages of Customer Retention," *Journal of Retail Banking,* 12 (Winter), 19–22.
13. Deutsch (1992), *op. cit.*
14. Bob Donath (1994), "Sell 'subscriptions' instead of 'products'," *Marketing News* (September 12), p. 12.
15. Philip Kotler (1992), "Marketing's New Paradigm: What's Really Happening Out There," *Conference Executive Summary* (September–October), 50–52.
16. Frederick F. Reichheld (1993), "Loyalty-based Management," *Harvard Business Review* (March–April), 64–73.
17. Faye Rice (1993), "The New Rules of Superlative Service," *Fortune* (Autumn/Winter) 50–53.

18. Christian Gronroos (1983), *Strategic Management and Marketing in the Service Sector,* Cambridge, MA: Marketing Science Institute.
19. Reichheld (1993), *op. cit.*
20. J. L. Wiener and J. C. Mowen (1985), "Source Credibility: On the Independent Effects of Trust and Expertise When Attractiveness is Held Constant," Working Paper 85–3, Oklahoma State University.
21. Robert E. Morgan and Sanjay Chadha (1993), "Relationship Marketing at the Service Encounter: the Case of Life Insurance," *The Service Industries Journal* 13 (January), 112–125.
22. Reichheld (1993), *op. cit.*
23. Crosby, Evans, and Cowles (1990), *op. cit.*
24. Reichheld (1993), *op. cit.*
25. Jonathon R. Copulsky and Michael J. Wolf (1990), "Relationship Marketing: Positioning for the Future," *Journal of Business Strategy,* 11 (July–August), 16–20.
26. Incidentally, the Kimberly Clark program has also been attacked by some critics as an example of an egregious invasion of privacy by Big Business, particularly after incidents in which congratulatory messages were sent out to women who had suffered miscarriages.
27. For an example of the use of databases in insurance marketing, see John J. Harrison (1993), "Relationship Marketing—A Strategy for Survival," *National Underwriter [Property/Casualty/Employee Benefits]* (June 21), 9ff.
28. Randy Myer (1989), "Suppliers—Manage Your Customers," *Harvard Business Review,* (November–December), 160–168.
29. Reichheld (1993), *op. cit.*
30. Myer (1989), *op. cit.*
31. Copulsky and Wolf (1990), *op. cit.*
32. Greg Gattuso (1994), "Relationship Marketing: A Two-Way Street," *Direct Marketing* (February), 38–39.
33. Robert C. Blattberg and John Deighton (1991), "Interactive Marketing: Exploiting the Age of Addressability," *Sloan Management Review* (Fall), 5–14.

Chapter 17

EMPLOYEE EMPOWERMENT

17.1 INTRODUCTION[1]

John Weaver, the vice president of human resources at Guest Quarters Suites Hotel, recently reported the following incident about employees at the chain's hotel in Philadelphia. A couple had made repeated trips to the city in the process of arranging to adopt an infant, always staying at the hotel. For the visit on which they were to pick up the baby and return her to the hotel, they were astonished to find that the hotel staff had converted their suite into a nursery, complete with crib, balloons, a teddy bear, and a giant card signed by every employee of the hotel staff.[2] The action was motivated not by managers, but by employees who take pride in delighting the hotel's customers. How does a service firm foster an atmosphere where employees are motivated to make an extra effort on the customer's behalf?

We have emphasized throughout this book the importance of people to the delivery of outstanding service. The personal interaction component of services is often a primary determinant of the customer's overall satisfaction. Even highly automated services occasionally develop problems, and in those cases customers typically want to speak to a real person who can help them. Their satisfaction with the service will be strongly affected by the skill, promptness, and accuracy with which the contact person does his or her job. Finding ways to encourage employees to identify with the organization and to take extra steps to ensure customer satisfaction is a major challenge facing service marketers.

During the 1970s, U.S. companies scrambled to understand and emulate market-winning strategies of their newly emerging rivals from Japan. The concept of participative management was identified as a potential key to Japanese firms' high quality and productivity. The dominant paradigm for manufacturing success in Western firms had been tight, hierarchical control structures. Managers told workers what to do and monitored workers to make sure they carried out instructions correctly. But when they discovered the nature of organizational cooperation in Japanese corporations, U.S. managers began to question the old paradigm. Spurred on by images of Japanese workers putting in long days for their companies, volunteering valuable suggestions for product and service improvements, and meeting regularly to share ideas, U.S. managers began instituting quality circles, and delegating responsibility and authority to workers. The initial efforts were not entirely successful. It took these firms a while to understand that procedures developed in the context of Japanese culture could not simply be adapted without modification. They also began to learn that getting workers to commit themselves to producing high-quality work requires a fundamental shift in the entire culture of the organization, from the top to the bottom—a much bigger job than it was initially perceived to be.

Nevertheless, the goal remains attractive: Imagine employees who are highly committed to doing their best, eager to root out quality problems, willing to offer solutions from their highly informed vantage points on the front line: service workers who take initiative and go the extra distance to meet customers' special needs, thereby building loyalty and high retention among the clientele. It sounds great, but how to get there? *Empowerment* is a term that has evolved for programs intended to promote these behaviors in employees and to push decision making and involvement to the front line. In the next section we will discuss some of the basics of empowerment, its benefits and costs, its pros and cons. In Sections 17.3 and 17.4 we will describe some of the attempts to define what empowerment is and the research that justifies the effort. In Section 17.5 we will describe the steps management must take to introduce empowerment into an organization. The chapter will conclude with some final thoughts about empowerment.

17.2 THE BASICS OF EMPOWERMENT

Although empowerment programs were initially applied in the manufacturing sector, the idea also works well for the service sector, particularly for those requiring a high degree of personal contact with customers. High-contact services give the server the opportunity to "read" customer needs and tailor-make more satisfying experiences. A knowledgeable, sensitive, and caring service provider can anticipate a customer's needs and provide a special level of customization that leads to customer delight. In addition, service quality tends to be variable, and employees may be able to help the firm recover from service problems if given adequate leeway to find satisfying remedies. Employee initiative has not always been regarded as the way to improve service, however. In the 1970s Theodore Levitt wrote two articles castigating the service industry for being far behind manufacturing in efficiency and customer satisfaction precisely because it was too "humanistic" rather than "technocratic."[3] He recommended redesigning services on more of an assembly-line basis: simple, clearly defined tasks with minimal decision making required of workers. This approach has worked well for some service firms, notably in the fast-food industry. But many do not feel their services should be run this way. Jan Carlzon, the president of SAS, expressed a very different opinion about the role of his airline employees during the 15-second-long moments of truth, those brief encounters between customers and service providers that are so important to forming customer opinions about the entire service:

> If we are truly dedicated to orienting our company toward each customer's individual needs, then we cannot rely on rule books and instructions from distant corporate offices. We have to plan responsibility for ideas, decisions, and actions with the people who *are* SAS during those 15 seconds:

ticket agents, flight attendants, baggage handlers, and all the other frontline employees. If they have to go up the organizational chain of command for a decision on an individual problem, then those 15 golden seconds will elapse without a response, and we will have lost an opportunity to earn a loyal customer.[4]

Carlzon's comment captures the spirit of the empowerment movement: organizations that enable their frontline employees to be committed to serving customers, to make decisions rather than refer to their supervisors, to show individual accountability and a willingness to take risks rather than adhering rigidly to procedure manuals, and to have access to the information and technology necessary to do their jobs.

But because the term has no universally accepted formal definition, there is occasionally some confusion as to what empowerment is and is not. Some users of the term miss the point.[5] Programs intended to reduce the workforce and to redistribute the duties of those let go among those who remain are not empowerment. Empowerment may make reduction in the workforce possible, but that is a side effect, not its goal. Nor does empowerment mean giving employees free reign to do whatever they feel is appropriate, even though Zemke and Shaaf have described it as "turning the front line loose" and "in many ways the opposite of doing things by the book."[6] Obviously, some constraints are necessary to keep employees from giving away the store, but these constraints should be communicated through an understanding of the organization's culture through careful training. Also, empowerment should not be seen as a substitute for fixing quality design problems. The best products and services are those that are done right the first time, and relying on the initiative of workers to make good on poorly designed products is costly and unlikely to satisfy customers in the long run.

Empowerment in service firms tends to focus on developing a corporate culture and organizational structure in which frontline employees eagerly perform their tasks of satisfying the customers by using their best judgment to tailor-make solutions that satisfy the customer and are in the firm's best interests. Consider Wal-Mart, a company that has been particularly successful in convincing employees that their interests are the same as those of the firm's. Typical of employee attitudes is the following quote from an employee (or "associate" in Wal-Mart's system) at the company's 1992 Store of the Year in Mansfield, Ohio: "I don't have to ask somebody what to do. I know what needs to be done. If there is a piece of tile missing from the floor, I fix it. If the light bulbs are out, I replace them. Got to keep it looking nice for the customers."[7]

This cooperation has been achieved because Wal-Mart really does treat its employees as partners in a common drive for success. Witness the comments of another employee who had worked her way up from part-time employee to a supervisory position: "I made it known from the beginning that I wanted to advance, to prove myself, to get training, to become an assistant manager. They have worked with me, showing me what I am doing well, what I can do better. They have given me room where I can improve. They have given me the opportunity."[8] The concern shown by the company for the success of its employees through the success of the firm has won the loyalty of this and many other employees.

Wal-Mart employees are well known for their eagerness to please customers.

"Inverting the pyramid" is a expression commonly used to describe the difference between the empowerment approach and traditional management styles. In a classical hierarchical organization, as depicted in Figure 17.1a, orders flow from the top of the organization and are carried out by the people at "the bottom." They have little discretion in changing services because the expertise, and therefore decision-making authority, is considered to reside at the top of the organization. In an empowered organization, as in Figure 17.1b, the hierarchy (often drawn as a pyramid) has been inverted. Serving customers is considered to be the most important function in the organization, and the people on the front line who provide it are considered to be the most important people. They need training to do their jobs, but once educated in their jobs and the organization's goals they are given the authority to do what is necessary to serve the customer. The role of management in this structure is that of facilitator—to support the service providers with necessary resources, including information, training and other tools necessary to do the best possible job of satisfying the customer.

Firms using the traditional hierarchical structure in which orders are dictated down the chain of command often find the transition to employee empowerment a formidable task. Dennis Longstreet, the president of Ortho Biotech, a division of Johnson and Johnson, successfully managed such a transition in his firm after he found that listening to people was the key to success. However, at first it was difficult for him and his staff to accept the apparent loss of management power that goes with empowerment. His advice to others, in retrospect, was that the risks may be less than they appear: "When you start something like this, you give up a lot of ability to make firm, hard decisions, and you take a chance that employees may lead

FIGURE 17.1

(A) A STANDARD HIERARCHICAL ORGANIZATION AND (B) AN "INVERTED PYRAMID"

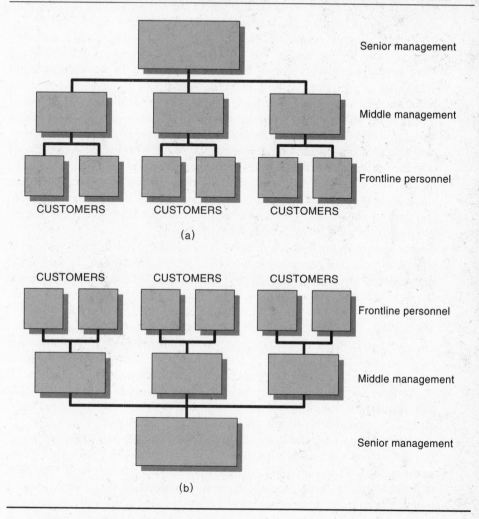

you someplace you don't want to go. But then you learn that most of them want the same things you want. Everyone wants to succeed."[9]

Benefits of Empowerment

Several types of benefits accrue from successfully empowering the workforce:

- **Greater employee satisfaction.** Proponents of empowerment insist that employees want to make a difference and to feel respected. People want to have a sense of control so that they can take personal pride of accomplishment in the results of their hard work. Noble ambition, but what's in it for the company? Actually, plenty. In addition to the fact that such employees are likely to be more productive and provide much more satisfying service for customers, enormous cost savings can be realized from lower absenteeism and less employee turnover. In industries where the costs of hiring and training service workers are high, this can have a substantial effect on profits.

General Electric's Financial Services Operation, its centralized accounting unit, faced declining morale and decreasing productivity in 1988, and set about revolutionizing its service orientation as part of a firm-wide program of cultural change dictated by CEO Jack Welch. The program included the formation of customer-focused work teams with the authority to identify and fix problems on their own. Periodic surveys of employee morale and job satisfaction showed strong improvement, including increases in feelings of motivation, responsibility and empowerment. Over 85% said they were eager to take the initiative to make changes when they identified better ways of doing things. The effects on the unit went far deeper than just having happier employees. Productivity improvements included a 34% increase in invoices paid per employee, a 19% decrease in the costs per employee paid, and an increase in the employee/manager ratio of 71%.[10]

- **Greater customer satisfaction.** Employees who identify with their company's goals are more likely to provide attentive, personable service. Research has shown that when bank tellers felt well treated, their customers tended to rate the service better.[11] Southwest Airlines believes that its employees must be happy if they are to provide service levels that exceed customer expectations. The airline's Executive Vice President, Customers, wrote, "At Southwest, there are two kinds of customers: passengers and employees. If passengers are satisfied, they'll fly Southwest. If employees are satisfied, they'll provide the type of service guaranteed to positively, outrageously satisfy customers."[12] Many firms report similar correlations. Guest Quarters hotels found that those hotels with the highest levels of employee satisfaction also had the highest rates of intention to return among surveyed customers.[13]

    If employees have the authority to respond quickly to a customer's special needs, they can heighten customer satisfaction or avert problems, by customizing the moment of truth to delight the customer the first time. However, when problems do occur, the ability to fix problems on the spot can turn a potentially angry customer into a loyal one. Reduced employee turnover can also be a source of improved customer satisfaction. For example, many retail banking customers prefer to develop personal relationships with bank employees whom they can seek out for advice or call to resolve problems. Banks with high employee turnover tend to alienate such customers.

- **Good ideas for improvement.** Frontline service workers know from experience which policies and procedures work and which don't work. They also may have good ideas on how to do things better. However, if they don't believe they will be listened to and taken seriously, they are unlikely to go to the trouble of communicating their ideas. One of the cornerstones of empowerment is open lines of communication between the front line and management. Firms that take advantage of this valuable resource will be much better off than those that force solutions from the top. For example, when Beth

Israel Hospital began putting employees on problem-solving teams, they were able to make extremely valuable suggestions to improve the efficiency of operations and the quality of care provided. Ideas included more efficient procedures for delivering drugs from the hospital pharmacy as well as restructuring jobs to allow staff to become better acquainted with smaller groups of patients. Costs are down, and the hospital is regarded as one of the best companies in the United States.[14] At AT&T's Universal Card division, a highly empowered workplace, employee suggestions saved the division more than $600,000 in 1992 alone.[15]

- **Cost Savings and Productivity Improvements.** The attraction of empowerment for many companies is the potential financial benefits. Dedicated employees work harder than those who don't care about their work. Research has shown that when superiors share power and control with their subordinates, organizational effectiveness increases.[16] Employees thus empowered don't need constant supervision, making some levels of management unnecessary. These long-term benefits take a significant investment in time and money to achieve. Firms that make half-hearted efforts at empowerment in hopes of quickly realizing a profit are doomed to fail.

Costs of Empowerment

In some cases, offsetting costs may outweigh the benefits:

- **Recruitment and training costs.** Empowerment puts new demands on employees. They are responsible for determining customer needs and in showing initiative to solve service problems. Not everyone wants these responsibilities or is capable of performing the tasks required.[17] An associate of Gore & Associates, an extremely unstructured firm that is famous for producing Gore-Tex waterproof fabric and for its high levels of employee empowerment, recently said, "You have to take a lot of responsibility to work here, and not everybody is willing to do that. This place is for people with bound wings who want to fly."[18] Therefore, recruitment must be organized to identify and attract people who will thrive in an empowered organization. This process is more costly than standard recruitment. After hiring, employees in an empowered organization will need training to make sure that they understand the company and its products, their roles and the limitations of their discretion, and have the teamwork and communication skills needed to work effectively in such a culture. These training costs are also must higher than those of a nonempowered employee.

- **Labor costs.** Hiring and retaining employees with the initiative and abilities to work successfully in an empowering organization may require higher wages. Also, the higher training costs for employees means that the use of temporary workers is often not practical, and thus it may be necessary to keep on a larger, periodically underutilized trained workforce.[19]

- **The costs of errors.** Empowering workers also means allowing them to make mistakes, which can also be costly. For example, employees may be overly generous to aggrieved customers when helping the organization to recover

Extensive training of empowered employees is necessary to help them understand how to use their authority wisely.

from mistakes. The Ritz-Carlton Company has authorized each hotel employee to spend up to $2000 to satisfy a dissatisfied guest, a policy that could obviously bankrupt the company if invoked too often.[20] Nevertheless, the policy is important to guarantee satisfied customers, and it is essential that employees feel empowered to use it, rather than feel fear of being chastised by supervisors for occasionally being too free with the firm's funds. In some closely regulated industries, such as international airlines, employees may offer solutions that violate laws or legal agreements.

Empowering employees requires that the firm absorb such mistakes as learning experiences, rather than use them as grounds to "punish the guilty." It is the role of training to reduce the occurrence of such errors of judgment in the future. For this reason Ritz-Carlton employees receive extensive training in doing their jobs, in teamwork, and in the corporate culture, as well as in quality and quality control techniques.

- **Service inefficiencies and inequities.** The reduction of standardization and increase in employee discretion that empowerment brings can also lead to ill will and claims of unfairness if customers feel that some servers are more generous or helpful or accommodating than others. The person at the airline ticket counter receiving extra time to accommodate a special request to reroute his flight may be delighted by the attentive and resourceful agent. The long line of people waiting behind him for service may be less enthusiastic. There are times when customers prefer a machine-like system that moves high volumes of customers efficiently. In these circumstances, customers will accept limited options as the tradeoff for smoothly run operations. Once the planning process has decided upon the proper service level for the firm's strategic positioning the limits of employee discretion must be clearly taught in training sessions.

- **Role stress on employees.** When workers are empowered, middle managers must make the transformation from being a supervisor of frontline workers to a facilitator, motivater, and coach of frontline workers. This can become a very difficult, even threatening change for many managers. Frontline workers also feel stress, as they must now learn to make judgments between alternatives that satisfy customers vs. those that protect the company's profits.

Degrees of Employee Involvement

For employees to be empowered they must feel they have a role in the success of the organization. However, employee involvement in the organization is not an all-or-nothing proposition. Different levels of employee involvement may be appropriate for different industries and corporate cultures. Lawler[21] identified three different levels of employee involvement that a firm can adopt as it leaves behind the controlling, production line view of employees. The lowest level he called *suggestion involvement,* where the employees' ability to affect the business is limited to that of quality circles or formal suggestion programs. Their day-to-day jobs are not affected directly by these programs, but the employers do have the ability to provide some input about their circumstances. The second level is *job involvement,* in which job enrichment and teamwork are used to give employees a wider range of meaningful tasks and to achieve a greater sense of achievement and satisfaction. While frontline workers' jobs are richer at this level, senior management need not change its behavior to engender this transformation in the organization. Finally, in *high-involvement* organizations, employees at all levels are fully involved in the quality effort, share information, work on teams to solve problems and share in the success of the company. The number of organizations successfully achieving this ideal level is small. The costs and efforts involved are enormous, and there aren't many managers with experience in this very innovative approach.

Should every company empower its workers, and if so, how much? There is no clear-cut answer to this question, but some characteristics of a business make it more or less a candidate for empowerment. Bowen and Lawler[22] suggested five contingencies or dimensions, depicted in Figure 17.2, on which firms vary that can be used to determine the appropriateness of employee empowerment in a specific organization. They are described in the following paragraphs.

- **Basic business strategy.** For low-cost, high-volume businesses empowerment may be impractical and may actually get in the way of what customers want and will pay for. For example, the core concept of a concession stand at a busy stadium is the delivery of a limited menu of products quickly. Customers do not expect to be able to receive specialized orders, and would not tolerate the time spent delivering such services to others. Employees are expected to exchange products for cash as fast as possible, and have no need for

FIGURE 17.2

BOWEN AND LAWLER'S DIMENSIONS AFFECTING THE NEED TO EMPOWER WORKERS

Dimension	Empowerment Important?	
	Yes	No
Basic business strategy	Customized for individual customers	High-volume, low-cost; standardization
Ties to customers	Long-term relationships	Infrequent transactions
Technology	High personal component	Highly automated
Business environment	Unpredictable	Highly predictable
Employee attitudes	Risk takers, challenge seekers, ambitious	Risk-averse employees, no initiative or ambition for challenge

For services designed for maximum throughput and low margins there may be little room for employees to exercise discretion in their dealings with customers.

much discretion in satisfying customers beyond providing items on the menu. However, the more a firm provides differentiation, customization and personalized service, the greater the need to empower frontline workers.

- **Ties to customers.** The more the firm must establish a long-term relationship with its customers, as opposed to engaging in short, infrequent transactions, the greater the value from empowering employees. Concession stands at tourist resorts can perhaps afford to be brusque with customers. The tellers at a neighborhood bank branch cannot.

- **Technology.** To the extent that technology removes or replaces human interaction in the service delivery, empowerment in the usual sense becomes less necessary. However, other means to keep these employees enthusiastic about their jobs are still required. For example, at many organizations automated, menu-driven telephone answering systems are taking over most of the duties of the human operators. And yet, there always remains the need to have operators available to deal with exceptions and problems. As the opportunities to interact with and serve customers become reduced to overseeing the operations of a machine, employee morale can fall, and jobs must be redesigned to offer stimulation and a sense of pride.

- **Business environment.** Unpredictable environments often require frontline employees with the discretion and ingenuity to respond to unanticipated situations. A stockbroker who is bound to offering a fixed set of investment opportunities under any economic conditions would not keep many customers. Empowerment is essential for businesses that require innovation to survive. Stable situations make empowerment much less necessary because they allow management to design ideal responses to anticipated situations in advance.

- **The people in the organization.** Not all managers are able to function in a participative atmosphere, and not all employees are looking for responsibility and personal growth. Providing exceptional service often requires that an employee make an extra effort to listen and understand the customer's problem, to seek solutions, and to step outside the basic job description to complete the task. Not everyone has the ambition to make this effort or is willing to risk possible reprimands from superiors for going too far. Barring a complete replacement of its workforce, a firm must adopt an empowerment level that is comfortable for its employees.

Other conditions that advise against empowerment are those where turnover is high and pay is low, because the cost of training simply isn't worth it. There are also industries where government regulations or technical requirements severely limit the breadth of employee discretion, such as accounting practices or the management of nuclear power plants.[23]

To decide on the level of empowerment that is appropriate for a particular firm, one should weigh each of these five contingencies, and any other compelling data, to determine the net effect.

17.3 DESIGNING EMPOWERED ORGANIZATIONS

We noted earlier that there is no agreed-upon definition of the term *empowerment*. In this section and the next we will examine some of the definitions that academics and practitioners have proposed. Most definitions tend to fall into two different categories, both of which provide insights regarding management's role in introducing empowerment and managing empowered workers. The first category focuses on how to redefine tasks and reallocate resources in an organization so that workers have the knowledge and discretion to make decisions for themselves. The second category, to be discussed in Section 17.4, focuses on the psychological and motivational needs of employees in empowered positions.

Perhaps because managers need practical information on how to get empowerment programs started, most studies have treated empowerment as a set of participatory management techniques—ways to share power with subordinates by decentralizing decision-making authority. Conger and Kanungo called this approach "empowerment as a relational construct."[24] The theoretical research on which this approach is based deals with the roles of power and control in organizations. Specifically, it explores the relationships among individuals or groups when the performance outcomes of one are dependent on the actions of another. For example, how can an organization successfully restructure its divisions of responsibility to transform the manager/frontline employee relationship from that of order giver/follower to that of facilitator/problem solver? The specific structures and incentive systems that are likely to be most effective depend on many complex factors. The objective of research in this field is to understand the sources of formal authority and control in organizations, and to develop strategies and tactics for reallocating those sources to make the distribution of power among the organization's members more equal. This category of empowerment research starts with the premise that sharing power with subordinates improves an organization's effectiveness.[25]

Bowen and Lawler[26] define empowerment as the sharing of four commodities with frontline employees:

1. Information about the organization's performance
2. Rewards linked to the organization's performance
3. Knowledge that allows the workers to understand the organization's performance and make contributions to it
4. Power to make decisions that influence the organization's performance

The model predicts that the employees, armed with an understanding of the effects they can have on the organization's performance and the power to take actions, can act for the good of the firm and reap rewards for doing so.

Pailin's alternative view of empowerment allows him to measure it through a battery of questions posed to both managers and employees.[27] This ability to measure empowerment with a reliable scale allows management to determine if managerial efforts to increase empowerment are having an effect. He defines empowerment as having three major dimensions:

- **Influence over standards/ participative decision making.** Frontline employees know best what must be done to improve customer service. They have first-hand experience with the wide range of customer requests, and they know what is required to satisfy them. Employee input is essential to job design and setting of appropriate performance standards, and it should be taken seriously. Therefore, decision making should be participative so that employees can give continuous feedback to management on how to improve service delivery.

- **Resource availability.** To be truly empowered, employees must be given adequate tools to do the job. They need information about customers, about their organization, its products, and its performance. They must have access to the basic equipment and supplies necessary to serve customers well. They may also require the assistance of support personnel to expedite their tasks, and they definitely need the full support of senior management. In other words, the organizational structure should be an "inverted pyramid."

- **Decision-making authority.** Empowered employees must have the authority to make timely decisions so as to be able to take the appropriate actions during the initial moment of truth. Such decisions might have clearly identified limits that are instilled through training. This component of empowerment affects customer satisfaction most directly.

Every employee at Ritz-Carlton Hotels is empowered to spend up to $2000 to satisfy a guest.

This description of empowerment focuses on implementation through job structure and resource allocation. The motivation of workers to use this power is implied, but not explicitly addressed, in this definition, nor are rewards specifically mentioned.

These two working definitions provide a number of suggestions for what an organization must do to empower its employees. They also provide a framework for measuring the success of efforts to do so, through the perceptions of both managers and the employees themselves. The majority of management recommendations to be drawn from these models deal with organizational structure and task redesign. They also have implications for human resource management, particularly for recruiting and training. We will discuss these recommendations in Section 17.5.

17.4 MOTIVATING EMPOWERED EMPLOYEES

The models of empowerment that focus on delegation of authority generally assume that employees will be self-motivated to use this newly obtained power. What are the psychological components of empowerment?

Building Self-Confidence

In their model of employee motivation Conger and Kanungo[28] point out that delegating authority to employees may be necessary to empower them, but it doesn't guarantee that they will have the will or incentive to use it. They propose that empowerment should be thought of as a "motivational" construct, the act of giving a person a sense of power. They defined empowerment as a process of psychologically enabling employees by creating conditions that give them a greater feeling of self-confidence and a greater belief in the power of their actions to make a difference. Employees must be convinced that they are not victims. To achieve this state of affairs, management must act to strengthen employees' beliefs in their ability to accomplish meaningful tasks (self-efficacy).

The founder of a restaurant chain that evolved into an empowered organization found that its employees progressed through several stages. At first they were wary of using the broad authority they were told they had to delight customers. Only after considerable coaxing and demonstrations of sincerity on the part of senior management did employees come to believe in its stated commitment and embrace it wholeheartedly.[29]

Why is this important? Research in the areas of expectancy theory[30] and self-efficacy theory[31] has shown that a person's motivation to work harder at a task depends on separate expectations about two stages of task completion, as in Figure 17.3: (1) *the self-efficacy expectation,* a belief that the effort will provide an acceptable level of performance ("I am able to do the job required."), and (2) *the outcome expectation,* a belief that the performance level will be sufficient to yield the desired outcome (Doing this will make a difference). Conger and Kanungo's definition of empowerment is concerned with building up the first stage, self-efficacy expectation.

Separating the influences on motivation into these two expectations implies that a person's self-confidence is not necessarily linked to outcomes. So employees can

FIGURE 17.3

THE TWO-STAGE EXPECTANCY MODEL OF MOTIVATION

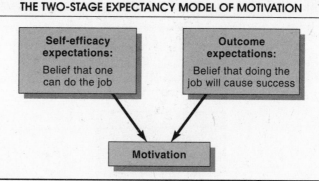

feel good about themselves and the efforts they are making, even if the business results of their actions are not favorable. This has important implications for motivating employees. If managers continue to build up their employees' expectations for their own abilities, the employees will continue to take on challenges and show initiative even under trying circumstances.[32] Once employees believe they are doing a good job, they will be likely to continue to deliver quality work, even if sales fall or other potentially discouraging events occur.

General Electric's Financial Services Organization, described earlier, provides an example of how an empowered workforce can maintain a commitment to quality under even the most extreme conditions. FSO underwent considerable reorganization a few years after its highly successful empowerment program had been put in place. In particular, the unit shifted most of its operations from the northern United States to Florida to save costs. When the employees in the Bridgeport, Connecticut, center were told that their operation was to be closed, their immediate response was to organize a team to write a new mission statement with three primary objectives: to successfully end operations by the end of 1992, to continue to achieve high levels of customer satisfaction, and to assist employees in finding new jobs.[33] These workers believed in themselves and refused to do less than their best.

Using this self-efficacy definition, Conger and Kanungo propose that the process of empowerment must go through five stages, as shown in Figure 17.4. In the first stage, managers must identify the factors that lead to feelings of powerlessness among employees, specifically those conditions that make employees feel that they have no control over their own situations and that their efforts cannot change how the firm operates. These factors can include formal organizational structures and policies; management styles of superiors; reward systems that do not recognize effort, innovation, or initiative; and the specific nature of the jobs. Such inhibitors must be addressed before employees will be self-motivated enough to extend themselves to performing high-quality work.

The second stage of the empowerment program involves the firm's taking actions that will promote feelings of self-efficacy among employees. These include many of the activities of job design that were described in Section 17.3, except that they now have a more narrowly defined purpose. Providing participative decision-making opportunities, training programs to build up skills, improving

FIGURE 17.4

CONGER AND KANUNGO'S STAGES OF EMPLOYEE EMPOWERMENT

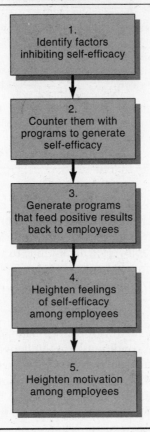

Source: "Five Stages in the Process of Empowerment," *Academy of Management Review,* Volume 13, Number 3. Reprinted by permission.

communication programs, decentralizing the control of resources, and instituting reward systems that encourage innovation are all recommended here, as before. But so are programs that explicitly encourage and express confidence in employees, that design more interesting, meaningful jobs, and set challenging but attainable goals.

The third stage of this empowerment process is the development of feedback programs to inform employees of their self-efficacy. The most effective feedback programs let employees discover their own abilities. They start by assigning employees to easy tasks and then slowly increase task difficulty, thereby guaranteeing that employees will experience early success and realize their increasing potential. Other forms of feedback are also useful, but less effective, such as formal recognition programs and the informal encouragement and support of supervisors. In addition, management must also be prepared to contend with the emotional stress that these changes can generate in the workforce. Providing a supportive, trusting environment has also been shown to improve self-efficacy.[34]

Ideally, the final two steps in the process are the achievement of strengthened feelings of self-efficacy among employees, followed by heightened levels of effort and persistence in accomplishing tasks. A scale such as Pailin's can then be used to measure and track the level of empowerment over time to determine if the program is effective.

Enthusiasm for the Work

Thomas and Velthouse pursued the approach of Conger and Kanungo by digging more deeply into the determinants of employee motivation.[35] After all, self-confidence alone isn't enough to ensure that a person will make the effort to do a good job. Their research asked the question, what energizes people to pursue particular tasks? Their definition of empowerment is "intrinsic task motivation," a person's intrinsic commitment to do a good job—motivated by the "pull" of the task, not the "push" of management.[36] Their model of motivation also has important implications for management's role in implementing empowerment programs.

The core of the Thomas and Velthouse model, seen in Figure 17.5, is a cycle of three events that can either build or reduce motivation among employees: task

FIGURE 17.5

THE THOMAS AND VELTHOUSE MODEL

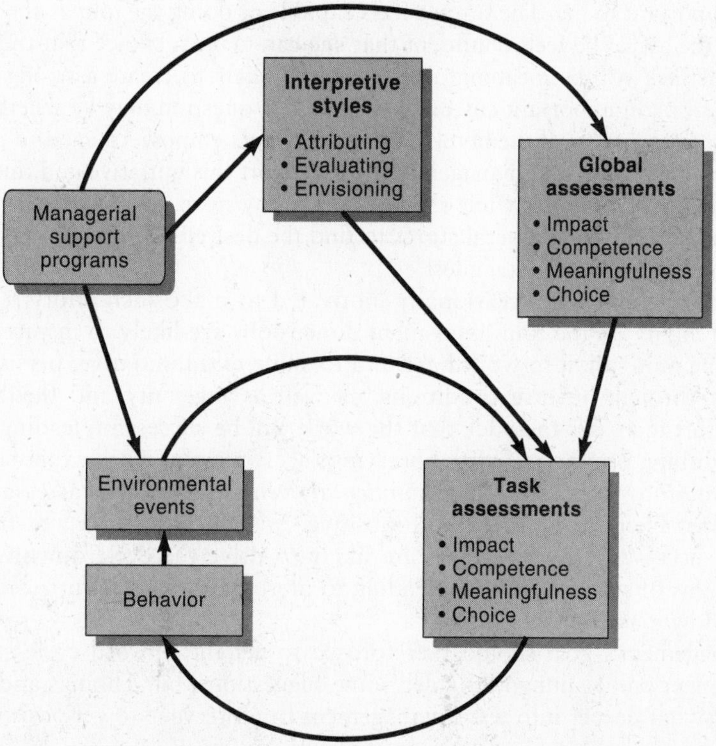

Source: "Cognitive Mode of Empowerment," by Kenneth Thomas and Betty Velthouse, *Academy of Management Review*, Volume 15, Number 4. Reprinted by permission.

assessment, environmental events, and behavior. The core determinant of whether a person will be motivated to make an effort is *task assessment,* or judgments about a particular task being considered. These judgments cover four dimensions of the task: Will it produce the desired effect? Does the person believe that he or she has the skills necessary to do the task? Is the task meaningful enough to care about? Does the person have a choice? Many scholars consider this last component, choice, to be an essential component of intrinsic motivation.[37] Of course, choice is primarily what is offered to employees by the definitions of empowerment that emphasize participatory management (see Section 17.3). Perspectives to assess the task come in part from *environmental events,* or observations of the results of previous actions, training, communication with other employees, and so forth. Task assessments directly affect the person's *behavior.*

Consider, for example, the case of a trainee working at the front desk of a hotel who overhears a businesswoman guest lamenting that she will be meeting her young niece for dinner, but, because she will be in business meetings all day, will not be able to purchase a stuffed animal that the child would love to receive. The trainee sees an opportunity to delight a frequent guest of the hotel and spends an hour shopping for the toy, so that it can be presented to the guest before the end of the day. In deciding whether or not to undertake this initiative, she will explicitly or implicitly assess the task on the four dimensions. This action will have a major impact on the guest's satisfaction with the hotel, inasmuch as the meeting with her niece was clearly important to her. The trainee feels capable of doing the job; as she knows the stores in the area, she feels confident that she can make a choice that the guest will enjoy. The task will be meaningful, in that it is likely to create a strong emotional response from an important customer. The largest question may be whether she has the choice of doing so. If the hotel is one that fosters empowerment and a customer orientation, it's likely that management will support this initiative and find someone to cover her normal duties while she goes to the toy store. In spite of terrible weather and the need to go to several stores to find the desired toy, she returns to present the gift to the delighted hotel guest.

Why are employees occasionally motivated to make such efforts? Tasks that are rated highly on the four assessment dimensions are likely to inspire the worker with the motivation to work hard and to show extra initiative, persistence, and resiliency through adverse conditions, as well as ingenuity and flexibility. This added effort increases the odds that the work will be successful, leading to a cycle of self-fulfilling prophecies; after observing this successful work experience (a positive addition to the cache of *environmental events*), a worker's assessment of the next task is likely to be even more positive, raising motivation and the odds of another successful effort. Failures are likely to drive the cycle downward: lower expectations of success next time leading to more-halfhearted efforts, poor results, and still lower assessments.

Management's goal should therefore be to get the upward cycle started, but how? Conger and Kanungo provided some suggestions, but Thomas and Velthouse dug somewhat deeper into ways management can intervene to get positive results.

Global Assessment For example, employee assessment of a particular task is influenced by general attitudes formed over a wide range of experiences. Past experience with his or her performance on other tasks gives a person an additional basis for assessing new ones, and on the same four dimensions at a more general level: Is the person pessimistic or optimistic about the usual effect of tasks like this? How does the person feel about his or her general competence to accomplish tasks? How much does the person care about work as a rule? How much autonomy does a person feel that he or she has in general? These global impressions are built up over time by assessing and observing the history of other efforts. After each experience a person is likely to adjust his or her overall outlook. A failure may cause a generally optimistic person to be a little more wary next time. A failure may cause a pessimist to have a bit more hope. In the long run, one's overall attitude is the cumulative effect of many past experiences. Including these global assessments in the model suggests certain types of management activities and training programs that might influence employees' overall views of success, such as inspirational programs designed to make employees feel better about themselves and about their general competence in achieving success. These programs in turn will improve employee assessment of each specific task and get the empowerment cycle started.

Individual Style The fact that individuals interpret their experiences very differently can also influence the directions of a particular person's empowerment cycle. For example, people who tend to attribute failures to environmental conditions beyond their control, instead of seeking out ways to fix specific problems, tend to get easily discouraged by setbacks and to lose motivation. Some people set unrealistically high performance standards for themselves and regard everything less than perfection as failure, another drain on sustained motivation. Successful people are often able to imagine success and block out images of failure, whereas unsuccessful people often cannot do so.[38] Understanding the individual employee's ways of dealing with experiences provides management with opportunities to overcome some of these negative effects and to improve the odds of positive task evaluations. In particular, it has been demonstrated that people can be made aware of their styles of interpreting events and can be taught how to change negative habits.[39]

By the admission of researchers in this field, the psychological side of empowerment has received much less scientific investigation.[40] The models that have been proposed to describe the factors affecting employee response to empowerment are built mostly upon research in other settings than management environments. Therefore, although the models have general support in the psychological literature, many of their key provisions must still be validated for business organizations. Nevertheless, this ongoing research addresses an important issue. Given the costs involved in instituting empowerment programs, no area should be left to chance. It is necessary to develop a firm understanding of the factors that underlie motivation as well as measures to monitor it and interventions to improve it.

17.5 MANAGERIAL IMPERATIVES

The models of empowerment processes presented in Sections 17.3 and 17.4 are based on research results pulled together from a variety of fields, and their overall validity for management settings remains untested. Nevertheless, they are summaries of the best available information we currently have about the factors that affect employee attitudes toward their work. From these models we can draw a number of inferences about what management can do to bring about the cultural changes necessary to empower organizations. To complement and reinforce those deductions we have the practical experiences of many organizations that have tried empowerment. In this section we draw on both theory and experience to suggest the steps management must take to introduce and manage empowerment in organizations.

Creating the Change Assuming that an organization has determined that empowerment is desirable, what do these scholars and practitioners have to tell us about the process of introducing it?

Management's first job is to plan the change with care. The task of strategic quality planning and the structure of the resulting plan will be described more fully in Chapter 18. Briefly, the process consists of learning the dynamics of the marketplace (including the needs of "internal" customers, the employees), determining the new mission of the firm, setting clear objectives, and devising strategies to reach them, including the design of the service and the tasks of employees. When AT&T designed its Universal Card Services (UCS) division, its objectives were to create "a great work environment and a highly skilled organization." Planning focused on four key steps: every employee was involved in continuous improvement, a formal structure was set up for continuous education and training, employee recognition and performance monitoring were designed to be related to the firm's financial goals, and a concern for employee well-being and morale was made central to the design.[41] New monitoring and control methods may be needed in order to establish a continuous check that the business is on the right track. At UCS, monitoring methods included annual surveys on job satisfaction, teamwork, management leadership, and blind monthly telephone surveys to employees' homes on the same topics. The process by which the plan is written is as important as the plan itself; it should be the result of both top-down and bottom-up initiatives, so that all relevant parties have a chance to contribute and to understand the direction that the company wants to take. Planning issues relating specifically to implementation are described next.

Job Design Redesigning jobs to empower employees requires a great deal of thought. Conger and Kanungo[42] tell us that if employees are to be motivated to do quality work, jobs must be designed to provide a feeling of power and self-efficacy. The following factors inhibit an employee's self-esteem and so reduce motivation:

- **Lack of role clarity.** Jobs with unclear duties and boundaries tend to confuse and discourage workers and lead to conflicts. Clear boundaries of responsibilities need to be developed and communicated. Limits of discretion that employees have to take independent actions should also be communicated. For example, one restaurant owner developed the following suggested responses to service failures: If guests have to wait between 10 and 20 minutes beyond their reservation time, they should be offered free drinks. If the wait is longer than 20 minutes, the entire meal might be free. However, employees were also told not to quibble about boundaries. These guidelines communicated the approximate value the restaurant put on these problems, but the staff was allowed to use their own judgment to deviate from these suggestions.[43]

- **Unrealistic goals.** Jobs must be designed to be manageable. Thomas and Velthouse also imply that jobs with unrealistic goals are likely to lead to high failure rates and therefore diminished motivation. To avoid this problem at AT&T's UCS division, for example, employees meet with their managers annually for the purpose of mutually determining personal objectives and performance standards.[44]

- **Lack of appropriate authority, high rule structure.** One of the objectives of empowerment is to delegate decision-making authority to frontline workers. They won't feel empowered to do their jobs if they are unnecessarily constrained and must clear all decisions with superiors. (This practice also inhibits service quality by making it far less responsive.) Rather than rigid rules, training should be used to instill appropriate boundaries around the areas in which employees can exercise discretion, as in the restaurant guidelines described earlier. The importance of giving employees the discretion to make decisions is also supported by the model of Thomas and Velthouse. Remember that choice is one of the dimensions of task assessment, and that intrinsic task motivation is reduced when an employee's feeling of self-determination is diminished. On the other hand, being given authority instills pride, which leads to motivation to do a good job.

- **Lack of resources.** Employees will not feel able to do the job if they don't have the appropriate tools. These tools could be information (providing the airline ticket agent with a computer terminal giving accurate information on alternative flights), adequate training (instructing waiters on the restaurant's wine list), or other means necessary to serve their customers.

- **Limited participation in decision making and limited contact with senior management.** Employees need to feel they are a part of the team, and receive feedback and recognition for jobs well done. At L. L. Bean, employees from all levels of the organization serve on problem-solving teams. Each person's input is encouraged and respected, and every attempt is made to develop the participatory skills of each member. Indeed, the role of managers on these teams is that of coach and developer, rather than of team chairman.[45]

- **Lack of meaningful goals.** Motivation is partly driven by a feeling that one is doing something substantial. This also follows from Thomas and Velthouse's dimensions of task assessment. The best goals are simple and clearly understood. Federal Express's goal is clear in its guarantee, "Absolutely, positively overnight." To the extent that employees can see how their individual goals relate to the overall corporate mission they will be motivated to pursue them.

- **Low task variety, highly established work routines.** Highly repetitive, undemanding jobs are unlikely to instill a sense of self-efficacy. Empowerment usually means doing whatever it takes to please the customer, which implies that employees are expected to step outside of narrow job categories if the situation requires it. This also implies that they must be prepared through training to have a broader set of skills.

- **Low advancement opportunities.** It's hard to feel highly capable in a dead-end job. For that reason, empowerment programs are often accompanied by extensive training programs, and a promote-from-within policy. Guest Quarters, for example, fills 75% of its management positions from within the company. Its stunningly motivated staff also has a much lower turnover rate: 45% compared to an industry average of 89%.[46]

The model of Thomas and Velthouse also suggests that jobs without clearly discernible impacts on the firm's success are unlikely to inspire employees to give their best. The task for managers may be one of communicating to employees just how critical their roles are.

Recruiting and Training   We have already noted that not all employees want these jobs. Empowered jobs require personnel who have a desire to be challenged, to assume responsibility, and to succeed. This motivation can be measured, using a battery of psychological tests designed to measure growth-needs strength.[47] Testing of potential employees for highly empowered positions should include the measurement of these traits, as well as the social skills necessary to succeed in an interactive environment.

Frontline employees who are accustomed to following rigid procedures and obtaining authorization for all exceptions may require preparation for participative management. The models of Bowen and Lawler and Pailin point out the need for training. To be able to exercise discretion with customers, for example, we have seen that they must have a firm idea of what is permissible, and what levels of redress are simply too much for customers to ask. They may need training in interpersonal skills, and in using the information systems or technology that is needed to support their decisions. An empowered organization works through cooperation and influence rather than by control, so employees must learn how to deal with other employees, and how to work in teams. Employees at AT&T's UCS division receive training in four major areas:

1. Basic job skills, such as dealing with customers, office computers, etc.
2. Career-based skills, such as leadership, mentoring, and career development.
3. The use of quality techniques.
4. Personal development, including time management and wellness.

The concern for the whole person and his or her feelings of self-efficacy are clearly evident in this program.

Psychological Support   The models also provide some guidance for giving psychological support to employees to make them comfortable with their new roles and responsibilities. Many managers who have successfully implemented empowerment programs suggest easing employees into the new culture by gradually making them responsible for solving bigger and bigger problems that management had previously handled.

Thomas and Velthouse suggested other management activities that research has indicated will address the four dimensions of task assessment that they see as so important to motivation. It is up to the leadership of the firm to convince employees that their jobs are significant and meaningful and, through encouragement and positive feedback, that they have the skills to do well. Programs that are designed to improve employees' general self-image of their abilities to overcome adversity, such as Outward Bound, can also affect their assessment of their ability to achieve in the new work roles being asked of them. Clearly the AT&T training program described above addresses these issues. Rewards for good efforts can also be used to reinforce the feelings of self-efficacy of employees.

Their model also indicates the need for monitoring employees' task assessment activities for dysfunctional styles of attributing causes, in evaluating the outcomes of their work, and in their ability to envision success. To the extent that overly negative attitudes inhibit employee confidence in the ability to achieve success, training programs can be developed to help them be more rational and upbeat.

Reward Systems Many firms adopting empowerment programs seek to reward excellent performance through monetary incentives. For example, after Zurich-American Insurance determined that its policyholders considered it important that their phone calls were quickly answered, it set up a policy of rewards and penalties for its customer service representatives based on the number of rings of a phone before it is answered. In the words of the president, now when a phone rings in the service center "people dive for it."[48] Most empowered organizations find it necessary to boost the enthusiasm of their employees for their expanded roles by offering monetary incentives for work well done.

Nevertheless, management should not underestimate the value of kind words that build self-confidence, and public recognition that reinforces feelings of self-efficacy and can serve to inspire other employees.[49] For example, at the AT&T UCS

Public recognition and individual encouragement by supervisors can be powerful motivators.

division, the Power of One award, one of many forms of public recognition, is given to an employee for exceptional effort in helping a customer. The award is presented as a surprise by senior executives at the person's work area, complete with blowing horns.[50]

Support for Middle Managers The drastically changed role of lower- and middle-level managers cannot be overlooked. In the newly designed organization, their jobs, their apparent importance to the organization, and their relationships to other levels of the organization are all changed. The fact that the new corporate structure requires them to give away a lot of their power may make them feel very insecure. Under empowerment, decision making is supposed to flow downward, and much of the rest tends to flow upward, so job security is a major concern for middle managers. These people require a great deal of training to do their new jobs, and probably also need a great deal of support to deal with the stress. New communication skills will be needed to help them relate to employees in a more supportive and less commanding manner. Managers need to be taught how to *help* employees solve their own problems, rather than doing all the problem-solving themselves. They must understand how to manage the new systems, including monitoring employee performance, and how to use new compensation schemes.

L. L. Bean has instituted an extensive system to help managers make this adjustment. Training and counseling sessions are coupled with regular surveys of each manager's performance as a coach and facilitator (as opposed to a bureaucratic order giver) filled out by the people he or she supervises. The surveys consist of a battery of questions dealing with nine dimensions of a total quality climate:

- aspiring and focused
- ethical and compassionate
- customer focused and aligned
- effective and efficient
- challenging and empowering
- open and innovating
- objective
- rewarding and developing
- team-oriented

The surveys are anonymous and only average scores are revealed, but supervisors are required to discuss the results with the people who filled them out and explore solutions to problems.[51] Other companies offer similar support to help middle managers adjust to their new roles.

Overcoming Other Problems The transition to empowerment is not easy for a traditional U.S. company. The emphasis on the individual in the United States may be too much at odds with the team-based decision making necessary for participatory management.[52] What works well in Japan will not necessarily work well in other parts of the world.

Internal problems can also inhibit a firm's ability to change the culture. Financial strains can cause managers to revert to the old, safe ways.[53] We have seen that when managers give up power to employees they often hear suggestions that they may feel are ill-advised. Therefore, when managers are under pressure to deliver profits, there is a strong temptation to take back decision-making authority and to insist on imposing their views of what must be done. An atmosphere of strong internal politics may make some people unwilling to give up power over private fiefdoms within the firm and may lead them to resist the shift of power. For example, cross-training employees in multiple skills enables them to take ownership of and solve a wider variety of customer problems, but it may also mean that certain specialty departments can be downsized. The Medical University of South Carolina Medical Center found that it had a large and expensive inventory of "idle-but-ready" skills on its staff that it could reduce by cross-training employees in other departments. However, MUSC faced opposition to empowerment programs from some of these departments precisely because they would lead to staff and budget reductions.[54] Instituting empowerment programs in large, bureaucratic companies can be especially difficult due to problems in developing good interdepartmental communication.[55]

Managing the Empowered Corporation

Once empowerment has been introduced, the job of managing is very different from that of the supervisory role in a traditional, hierarchical company. The role of the lower and middle managers is now to support the frontline staff in their efforts to satisfy customers. Their new duties include:[56]

Mentoring employees in problem solving, decision making, and teamwork skills. Managers must foster a spirit of trust, treat workers with respect, and listen carefully to their ideas. They must be able to help teams and individuals make decisions for themselves.

Coaching employees to do their work better. This approach requires that managers recognize achievement and provide encouragement and psychological support. They must also get away from the mindset of punishing "wrong-doers," and rather help employees to build from successes and learn from mistakes.

Setting goals and providing incentives through compensation and special awards, both monetary and otherwise. Managers must ensure that the goals of lower-level units are consistent with the goals of the organization as a whole. This requires an open flow of information, for which these managers are also responsible.

Facilitating the work of the front line by making sure necessary resources and training are available to them. The need for adequate resources to do the job required is clear. Continuous learning is also essential in a company that hopes to produce quality. But teams and individuals should be responsible for their own learning. It is the manager's job to help them identify their training needs and to teach them how to learn and how to train others.

Coordinating the work of teams, helping to resolve problems within and between teams, allocating resources among them, and helping them to share their best practices with other parts of the company.

Monitoring and evaluating internal and external performance. Producing consistent quality requires that diagnostic measures be regularly monitored. Several measures seem to be obvious candidates for tracking the progress of an empowerment system. Measures of the effectiveness of the process itself should include surveys of employee satisfaction and employee turnover, and measures of employees' perceptions of the extent of their empowerment. These findings can be related to output measures such as customer satisfaction and measures of productivity.[57]

These duties require a host of new skills that have not been part of the traditional manager's tool kit.[58] Managers must be able to know when to give direction to subordinates and when to let them make their own decisions. They must be able to build self-confidence in others, to listen well, and to empathize with them. They must be able to achieve goals through negotiation and influence, rather than by giving orders. Successful managers must be able to generate ideas, to deal with uncertainty, and to face conflict and channel it productively. They must be able to spark change and to create an environment that inspires subordinates to take risks. They also need to know how to pass these same skills on to others. Finally, good managers must have integrity. They must be honest in their discussions and forthright in keeping their commitments. Is it little wonder that many middle managers feel enormous job stress?

17.6 CONCLUSIONS

The empowerment of employees forces the organization to foster coordination between departments that have historically had little to do with each other. In particular, marketing and production must work closely with human resources in hiring, training and managing personnel, because people now become central to the organization's products and, indeed, its overall strategic position.

It also requires a new perspective on the old view of service jobs as "low-skilled" positions. Empowered frontline employees must indeed have skills, but mostly communication and other interpersonal skills, rather than the traditional technical skills of the manufacturing sector. Some of these skills are hard to teach, and many of them require extensive training, of both front-line personnel and their managers.

For this reason, empowerment of service workers is not a decision to be taken lightly. In spite of the unbridled zealotry expressed by some proponents of empowerment, who insist that it is the only way for firms to survive in the new, highly competitive global economy, the costs can be high and the rewards uncertain. For example, Conger and Kanungo warned that

> Although we have focused on the positive effects of empowerment, it is conceivable that such management practices may have negative effects. Specifically, empowerment might lead to overconfidence and, in turn, misjudgments on the part of subordinates. Because of this sense of false confidence in positive outcomes, organizations might persist in efforts that are, in actuality, tactical or strategic errors.[59]

Bowen and Lawler, in their discussion of the benefits and costs of empowerment in different types of organizations, also warned that "precious little research on the consequences of empowerment"[60] has been done. In fact, their parting words serve as a suitable cautionary final note to this chapter:

> Before service organizations rush into empowerment programs, they need to determine whether and how empowerment fits their situation.[61]

Empowering employees may be a critical component of service quality, but the complex organizational and interpersonal dynamics involved in adopting the new mindset must be managed very carefully. Otherwise, the firm may never survive to enjoy the fruits of the effort.

REVIEW QUESTIONS

1. If one purpose of empowerment is to make work more enjoyable and rewarding for employees, why are many labor unions suspicious of empowerment programs? Do you think they have a point?
2. What are some of the benefits a company receives from empowering its workers? What costs and risks must it incur?
3. Why do middle managers often resist empowerment programs in their firms?
4. Give an example of a service business where a high level of empowerment is essential; where a low level of empowerment is optimal.
5. What insight about employee motivation do Conger and Kanungo provide by separating the concepts of self-efficacy expectation and outcome expectation?
6. What are the components of the principal recurring cycle in the Thomas-Velthouse model? What can managers do to begin a cycle of positive reinforcement of this cycle?
7. List the new duties a middle manager must assume in a newly empowered organization.

ENDNOTES

1. The authors wish to thank Jim Pailin of Vanderbilt University for his invaluable advice in writing this chapter.
2. John J. Weaver (1994), "Want Customer Satisfaction? Satisfy Your Employees First," *HRMagazine* (February), 112ff.
3. Theodore Levitt (1972), "Production-Line Approach to Services," *Harvard Business Review* (September-October), 41–52; Theodore Levitt (1976), "Industrialization of Services," *Harvard Business Review* (September-October), 63–74.
4. Jan Carlzon (1987), *Moments of Truth,* Cambridge, MA: Ballinger Books, p. 3.
5. James E. Pailin, Jr. (1992), "Empowerment: Increasing Customer Satisfaction with Service Encounters Through Service Job Redesign," paper presented at "Frontiers in Services," Service Marketing Conference, Vanderbilt University, Nashville, September 25.
6. Ron Zemke and Dick Shaaf (1989), *The Service Edge: 101 Companies That Profit from Customer Care,* New York: New American Library.
7. Jay L. Johnson (1993), "How Wal-Mart's People Make a Difference," *DM* (August), 60–63.

8. *Ibid.*

9. John Huey, "The New Post-Heroic Leadership," *Fortune,* February 21, 42–50.

10. Robert Frigo and Robert Janson (1994), "GE's Financial Services Operation Achieves Quality Results Through "Work-Out" Process," *National Productivity Review* (Winter), 53–61.

11. David E. Bowen and Edward E. Lawler III (1992), "The Empowerment of Service Workers: What, Why, How and When," *Sloan Management Review* (Spring), 31–39.

12. Colleen Barrett (1993), "Giving Customers P.O.S.," *Sales & Marketing Management* (November), 52.

13. Weaver (1994), *op. cit.*

14. David Holzman (1993), "When Workers Run the Show," *Working Woman* (August), 38ff.

15. Pamela Vosmik (1993), "In Pursuit of Quality Human Resources at AT&T Universal Card Services," *Employment Relations Today* (Spring), 29–35.

16. See, e.g., R. J. House (1988), "Power and Personality in Complex Organizations," in L. L. Cummings and B. M. Shaw (eds.), *Research in Organizational Behavior,* vol. 10, Greenwich CT: JAI Press, 305–357; R. M. Kanter (1979), "Power Failure in Management Circuits," *Harvard Business Review,* 55(4), 65–75.

17. J. R. Hackman and G. R. Oldham (1980), *Work Redesign,* Reading MA: Addison-Wesley.

18. Huey (1994), *op. cit.*

19. Bowen and Lawler (1992), *op. cit.*

20. Charles G. Partlow (1993), "How Ritz-Carlton Applies 'TQM'," *The Cornell Hotel and Restaurant Administration Quarterly* (August), 16–24.

21. Edward E. Lawler III (1988), "Choosing an Involvement Strategy," *Academy of Management Executives,* 2, 197–204.

22. Bowen and Lawler (1992), *op. cit.*

23. Kathleen M. Cahill (1993), "The Many Faces of Empowerment," *Enterprise,* 6 (January), 26–29.

24. Jay A. Conger and Rabindra N. Kanungo (1988), "The Empowerment Process: Integrating Theory and Practice," *Academy of Management Review,* 13 (3), 471–482. This article provides an extensive review of the academic literature supporting models of empowerment as a relational construct.

25. Kanter (1979), *op. cit.*; A. S. Tannenbaum (1968), *Control in Organizations,* New York: McGraw-Hill; Pailin (1992), *op. cit.*; Thomas J. Peters and Robert H. Waterman (1982), *In Search of Excellence,* New York; Harper & Row; Tom Peters and Nancy Austin (1985), *A Passion for Excellence,* New York: Random House; Zemke and Schaaf (1989), *op. cit.*

26. Bowen and Lawler (1992), *op. cit.*

27. Pailin (1992), *op. cit.*

28. Conger and Kanungo (1988), *op. cit.*

29. Timothy W. Firnstahl (1989), "My Employees Are My Service Guarantee," *Harvard Business Review* (July-August), 28–32.

30. Edward E. Lawler III (1973), *Motivation in Work Organizations,* Monterey CA: Brooks/Cole.

31. A. Bandura (1977), "Self-Efficacy: Toward a Unifying Theory of Behavioral Change," *Psychological Review,* 84, 191–215; A. Bandura (1986), *Social Foundations of Thought and Action: A Socio-cognitive View,* Englewood Cliffs, NJ: Prentice-Hall.

32. Bandura (1977), *op. cit.*

33. Frigo and Janson (1994), *op. cit.*

34. E. Neilsen (1986), "Empowerment Strategies: Balancing Authority and Responsibility," in *Executive Power,* S. Srivastava, ed., San Francisco: Jossey-Bass, 78–110.

35. Kenneth W. Thomas and Betty A. Velthouse (1990), "Cognitive Elements of Empowerment: An 'Interpretive' Model of Intrinsic Task Motivation," *Academy of Management Review,* 15 (4), 666–681.
36. D.E. Berlew (1986), Managing Human Energy: Pushing vs. Pulling," in S. Srivastava (ed.), *Executive Power,* San Francisco: Jossey-Bass, 33–50.
37. For example, R. de Charms (1968), *Personal Causation: The Internal Affective Determinants of Behavior,* New York: Academic Press; E. L. Deci and R. M. Ryan (1985), *Intrinsic Motivation and Self-Determination in Human Behavior,* New York: Plenum.
38. R. Harrison (1983), "Strategies for a New Age," *Human Resource Management,* 22, 209–235; W. Bennis and B. Nanus (1985), *Leaders,* New York: Harper & Row.
39. L. Y. Abramson, M. E. P. Seligman, and J. D. Teasdale (1978), "Learned Helplessness in Humans: Critique and Reformulation," *Journal of Abnormal Psychology,* 87, 19–74; A. Ellis (1980), "Rational-Emotive Therapy: Research Supports the Clinical and Personality Hypotheses of RET and Other Modes of Cognitive Behavior Therapy," *Counseling Psychologist,* 7, 2–42.
40. Conger and Kanungo (1988), *op. cit.*
41. Vosmik (1993), *op. cit.*
42. Conger and Kanungo (1988), *op. cit.*
43. Firnstahl (1989), *op. cit.*
44. Vosmik (1993), *op. cit.*
45. Dawn Anfuso (1994), "L. L. Bean's TQM Efforts Put People Before Processes," *Personnel Journal* (July), 72–83.
46. Weaver (1994), *op. cit.*
47. Pailin (1992), *op. cit.;* Bowen and Lawler (1992), *op. cit.*
48. Sally Roberts (1994), "Translating Quality Goals into Results," *Business Insurance* (May 16), 46–47.
49. Pailin (1992), *op. cit.*
50. Vosmik (1993), *op. cit.*
51. Anfuso (1994), *op. cit.*
52. Donna Brown (1992), "Why Participative Management Won't Work Here," *Management Review* (June), 42–46.
53. Conger and Kanungo (1988), *op. cit.*
54. "Patient-focused Care Aims to Counter Institutional Culture," *Modern Healthcare* (December 6, 1993), 48–52.
55. Donna Brown (1992), *op. cit.*
56. Pailin (1992), *op. cit.;* Clay Carr (1991), "Managing Self-Managed Workers," *Training & Development* (September), 37–42.
57. Carole Congram and Joby John (1993), "How to Empower Front-Line Service Employees: A Continuous Improvement Model." presented at the 47th Annual Quality Congress, Boston MA, May.
58. Carr (1991), *op. cit.*
59. Conger and Kanungo (1988), *op. cit.,* p. 480.
60. Bowen and Lawler (1992), *op. cit.,* p. 35.
61. Bowen and Lawler (1992), *op. cit.,* p. 39.

Chapter 18

THE SERVICE-BASED BUSINESS PLAN

18.1 INTRODUCTION

For more than a decade U.S. firms have tried to emulate the quality programs they saw being developed by their Japanese competitors. Early on, many seized upon the use of quality circles as being the key to salvation, only to be disillusioned when these exercises failed to bring about the hoped-for results, and employees became cynical about being used. Others have sought to adopt statistical process control without adequately training employees to interpret data and find solutions to quality problems. In some cases, quality improvement efforts have not been adequately translated into customer-defined quality. In all such firms, quality programs inevitably fall into disrepute as yet another useless passing fad.

But even in those firms in which customer satisfaction has become the company watchword, near-religious zeal, rather than fiscal responsibility, has often driven corporate activities, resulting in a flurry of expensive and poorly coordinated programs that have brought down the wrath of corporate budget keepers. Lavish service may produce happy customers, but the firm's shareholders are often less pleased. When quality managers are unable to justify their activities in tough economic times, these quality programs also become at risk.

To create a successful quality program, companies need a financially accountable quality mindset that focuses on the *return on quality,* the financial benefit that they will realize from investments in quality improvements. Responsible management of quality—real customer-defined quality—cannot be achieved by halfhearted, piecemeal, or cosmetic means. Converting a firm to a customer-driven mindset, while managing the return on quality improvement expenditures, requires tightly coordinated planning throughout the entire organization, from top to bottom, with the profitable improvement of customer-defined quality as the overall driving force. This objective should define the direction of the organization as a whole and guide the development of specific objectives and strategies at each lower level. In particular, strategies at all levels should be selected on the basis of their contribution to higher-level goals, as well as on their ability to contribute profitably to customer satisfaction.

It is possible for the plan to link quality improvement efforts throughout the organization to financial outcomes by focusing on the extent to which they improve customer retention. In Chapter 15 we demonstrated how this can be done by presenting a decision support system that can be used to link service quality improvements efforts to the bottom line. The full linkage of effects was described as: Service delivery—customer satisfaction with subprocess—customer satisfaction with processes—overall customer satisfaction—customer retention—market share—profits. The basic idea is that customer dissatisfaction or delight with subprocesses can be statistically related to their dissatisfaction or delight, respectively, with higher-level processes and overall satisfaction and with customer intentions to return. Therefore, if these linkages are understood, one can estimate the extent to which various service improvements will result in higher rates of retention, leading to improvements in market share and contribution margin. However they are calculated, the ratio of gains in contribution to the costs of achieving them is a measure of the return on quality, or ROQ.

In the sections that follow we will illustrate a planning process that is rooted in the concepts of improved customer retention and the return on quality. The chapter will review all aspects of planning, highlighting those that are novel to ROQ.[1] In Section 18.2 we will describe the general planning cycle and the evolutionary procees a firm must go through to become proficient at ROQ planning. In Section 18.3 we describe the planning process itself, the tasks that must be performed to produce a sound quality-focused plan. Section 18.4 presents an outline of the contents of a quality-based business plan, emphasizing those components that are essential to keeping the organization focused on profitable customer service improvement. The chapter is not intended to be a self-contained planning template, but a complement to books devoted to planning, which tend to ignore or underemphasize return on service quality.

18.2 THE PLANNING CYCLE

Whatever the objective, planning should be a continuous process, following the cycle shown in Figure 18.1: Plans are drawn up and implemented. Results are then monitored to provide input for the next plan, which will be designed to fix problems or to build upon successes. The cycle is actually much more complex than the simple diagram would suggest. Between the planning and implementation stages, there is often a great deal of negotiation; managers may find certain aspects of the plan unworkable, and suggest alternative strategies that must then be coordinated with the efforts of other parts of the organization. In fact, while many plans are done on a large scale perhaps once a year, reviews of results are often made quarterly, or even monthly. This permits mid-course corrections to objectives and strategies. Such monitoring of programs should be carried out continuously on a smaller scale for programs at all levels of the organization. Shewhart called this the *PDCA cycle* for Plan–Do–Check–Act.[2]

Planning for return on quality takes time, given the deep understanding of operations necessary to do it well. Figure 18.2 shows the stages that a firm must pass through on its way to becoming skilled at ROQ planning. Initially, managers will have little understanding of the likely effect of quality improvements on customer satisfaction, and so estimates of the changes in customer retention resulting from

FIGURE 18.1

THE PLANNING CYCLE

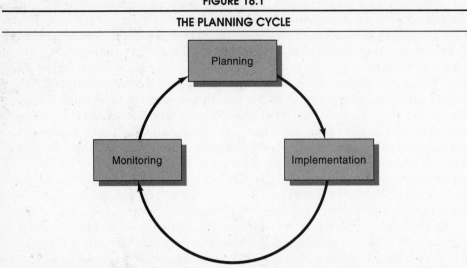

quality programs will depend entirely upon management estimation. However, as calculations based on those estimates reveal the most promising areas for improvement, experiments can be run to improve management understanding of customer response. These experiments will lead to more solid estimates that can be used to guide full-scale rollouts of programs. The figure simplifies the actual situation, since competitive and market conditions always change, and forecasts are never completely correct. Thus, past data are never a certain guide to the future, and some managerial estimation is always necessary. Nevertheless, the figure suggests how management must build up a fund of experience over time to improve its understanding of market response to quality improvements.

18.3 BENEFITS OF PLANNING

Planning provides several important benefits. First, planning directed primarily toward achieving a high return on quality continually communicates the organization's need to consider financially justifiable customer satisfaction as the ultimate objective of every employee. This focus on financial return need not be an inhibitor to customer service. In fact, service based on maximizing the lifetime value of customers is usually better than the usual transaction-focused service with which most of us are familiar. Employees that understand the value of customer retention should be willing to provide quality service.

Planning also serves as a basis for coordinating activities at lower levels. Through planning, employees can see where their efforts fit into the top management's vision for the company and with the activities of other departments, and can therefore take initiatives that are consistent with the overall efforts of the firm. ROQ planning ensures that all members of the organization see the service in terms

FIGURE 18.2

STAGES OF CORPORATE LEARNING

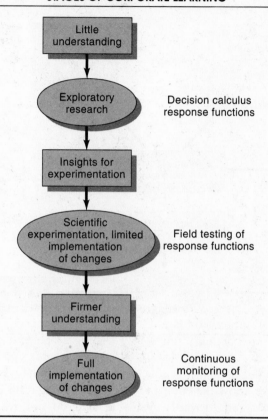

of the processes and dimensions that are important to the customer. It gives them a basis to argue for support and to gain commitment for the programs they see as necessary to achieve organizational goals and objectives.

Planning processes, such as the one we will describe, force management to design programs that have an organized, logical basis and are directed toward the firm's overall objectives. In particular, the plan should start with a thorough analysis of the firm's business environment, followed by goals and strategies derived from that analysis to provide the strongest results possible. This logical sequence, depicted in Figure 18.3, is more likely to result in the identification of true sustainable sources of differential advantage and return on quality.

Finally, the plan can serve as the basis for monitoring and control. The plan identifies those in the organization responsible for achieving particular goals and the data that must be monitored. The plan forces the firm to think through actions in specific terms, and provides deadlines and benchmarks against which to measure progress.

The ideal planning organization, as envisioned by Baldrige consultants Hart and Bogen, does indeed seem like a formidable competitor:

FIGURE 18.3

THE PLANNING PROCESS

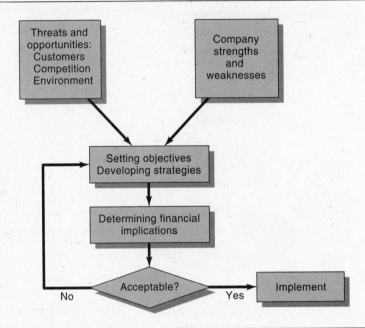

The strategic value of quality is now recognized at all levels of the organization. Employees know the company's short- and long-term quality initiatives backwards and forwards. Valuable data do not rot in the attic anymore. Instead, information from operations personnel on the shop floor and the sales force in the field is fed back up the organization to become part of the corporate plan. The same thing happens to input from customers and suppliers. No longer internally focused, the company is a true citizen of the marketplace, using world-class benchmarks to drive the goal-setting process. Quality plans confront and root out failure in all functional areas, including support functions. Senior executives are actively involved in mapping out strategy and linking objectives and logistical support. Interlocking quality councils at all levels of the organization speed up the communication process. The company consciously plans for continuous improvement. Episodic and narrowly focused plans are replaced by bold initiatives such as cycle-time reduction, uniform reduction of defects across the organization, and the improvement of fundamental processes. Long-term quality initiatives, such as meeting educational needs in the workforce, are now undertaken.[3]

Careful planning alone is not a guarantee of success. The "Do" stage of the PDCA cycle is at least as important as having a plan. Firms that institute planning programs without thoroughly understanding their appropriate implementation and use are likely to generate more problems than they solve.[4] We have seen that even Baldrige award winners can fall on hard times, particularly if the financial consequences of quality programs are not understood in advance. But intuition would suggest that firms with strong planning processes should do better. In fact, although research results are few in number, studies have shown a positive relationship between the level of planning and financial success in organizations.[5]

18.4 STAGES IN THE PLANNING PROCESS

The key to making a plan work is less in the contents of the plan, than in the manner in which it is developed. The forecasts on which a plan is based can be wrong, or the environment can change. Therefore, no plan should be cast in stone. But the exercise of preparing the plan should make the organization attuned to the requirements for success in its chosen markets and improve its ability to respond appropriately to changes. Moreover, involving as many people as possible in the planning process has the beneficial effect of developing feelings of individual "ownership" of programs by those concerned and helps to maintain a much higher level of involvement in the delivery of quality service.

Although each organization must design a planning process that fits its own culture and personality, experienced planners and planning consultants agree on several key steps.

Review of Current Plans   Planners must be keenly aware of how well the last plan has fared. This is the "Check" phase of the Shewhart PDCA cycle. Are its objectives being met? If not, why? Have customer satisfaction levels with processes and dimensions responded to programs as predicted? Both failures and successes should be carefully noted and learned from so that action programs and research studies for next period can be designed.

Data Collection   The objective of planning is to determine the best course of action possible given the business conditions facing the firm. Hence, collecting information about the threats and opportunities facing the company is an essential part of any planning exercise. The data needed follow directly from the questions that the plan is intended to answer:

1. What are the prospects for profits and growth in this industry?
2. What do our customers want?
3. Where do we stand vs. our competition?
4. What do we have to do to achieve corporate objectives, particularly, profitable customer satisfaction?

Specific areas on which data should be collected are the following:

- **Market dynamics.** To track the profit impact of quality improvements the firm must keep track of, and be able to predict changes in, several key measures. These include the market's growth rate and its components, such as the number of new customers and the number of customers leaving the market (the "churn"). These numbers are particularly helpful in assessing the profitability of retaining customers rather than attracting new ones. External trends that can affect the business should also be tracked and future turning points predicted. These include economic, demographic and social trends, new advances in technology, and relevant regulatory and political developments. The firm should have ongoing monitoring systems in place to keep track of these important influences in the market and the environment.

- **Sales analysis.** Gauging the success of quality improvement programs also requires that the firm be able to determine what part of its growth (or decline) is attributable to various quality efforts. Is growth the result of retaining customers or of replacing high defections through expensive programs to attract new customers? So, in addition to the usual analysis of sales, costs and profits, managers should also monitor retention rates and brand switching patterns. All of these data should be available by market segment, by product, by distribution channel, by region—whatever division is likely to provide useful insights to management in identifying problems and opportunities.

  Availability of sales data should therefore be a major ongoing part of the firm's MIS function. (Note that this area is the second criterion of the Baldrige Award.) Unfortunately, in many cases, this support is not available. Information on products and accounts is often collected and organized for cost accounting purposes and is not readily usable by marketing managers for decision making. We have found major companies with strong customer orientations that were nevertheless unable to identify which components of their sales were due to renewals, new customers, and switchers from competitors.

- **External customers.** Since satisfying customers is a major thrust of the plan, managers need to monitor customer satisfaction with current products, as well as their future needs and desires, using separate analyses for each key segment. The firm should also be careful that its understanding of each segment's perceptions of the service's constituent processes and dimensions remains current. If market growth and brand-switching patterns differ by segments, this finding should also be noted. Regularly administered customer satisfaction surveys, as described in Chapter 11, will provide much of the information, but additional research projects to answer specific questions may also need to be commissioned.

- **Internal customers.** Any service-oriented firm should also be monitoring employee satisfaction and other measures that provide feedback on the development of empowerment programs and other human resources initiatives. Analysis of employee satisfaction with services provided by other departments should be an ongoing part of quality monitoring, along with more operationally defined quality measures of support quality, such as number of defects or processing time. After all, delays or errors in billing can be just as detrimental to the salesforce's efforts to serve clients as product quality problems. Specific unanswered questions may warrant marketing research studies.

- **Product and service quality.** Regular tracking of customer reactions to product quality as well as statistical process control of internal quality measures will provide this information, which will indicate areas for particular attention in the next plan. It may be possible to identify internal quality measures that are closely linked to customer satisfaction ratings, so that problems can be spotted at the earliest possible stage.[6]

- **Suppliers.** Measures of supplier quality and assessment of relationships with suppliers will be used to identify quality problems and to determine future quality initiatives.

- **Competition.** All plans must contain thorough analyses of the firm's chief rivals—as defined by customers—to predict what their likely future moves will be. ROQ analysis is particularly concerned with the ability of competitors to attract and retain customers and with the quality initiatives they are taking to raise the general level of expectations among customers in the market in general. Have they matched our quality programs? Have they gone beyond them in ways that will raise the expectations of our own customers or the ways in which the market perceives services to be structured? For example, a fast-food chain developing an efficient means to accept credit cards for payment at all establishments would shake up the status quo and give customers a new process on which to base overall satisfaction of fast-food establishments: the payment process.

  Competitive analysis requires a regular program of market structure analysis to identify those firms that customers feel offer the closest substitutes to our products and services. These companies must be monitored to understand their strategies, strengths, weaknesses, and future intentions. Assembling this information requires an ongoing program of competitive intelligence, including a range of activities from the use of clipping services to monitor news about rival firms to primary research designed to understand their operations, costs, and future plans.[7]

- **Benchmarks for processes.** To improve its processes continuously the firm must compare itself to the best in the world. Given that the firm is looking for ways to do things better, it must seek world leaders in specific processes, study them thoroughly, and "borrow" ideas that will improve operations. As we have stated before, a firm should not limit itself to its own industry but should study any firm in the world from which it can learn how to improve. The areas to be benchmarked should be closely linked to quality strategy goals, so that time and money are not wasted, but there is no limit to the number of areas that may be benchmarked in a quality-driven company. Xerox benchmarks well over 250 different processes, including billing processes at American Express, marketing against Procter & Gamble, and distribution against L. L. Bean.[8]

- **Environmental monitoring.** Trends in environmental forces must be anticipated, and the likely threats and opportunities they may spawn should be analyzed. These forces include changes in the economy, in demographic patterns, cultural and social trends, the regulatory and political climate, and developments in technology. In some industries, such as nursing homes, regulatory changes occur regularly, and can have profound effects on how firms operate and compete. Of particular concern for ROQ analysis is the likely effect of any environmental changes on the size and growth rates of the markets in which the firm competes, on customer needs and the level of their expectations, on profit margins, and on the horizon over which the return on investments should be calculated.

- **Cost of quality.** The cost of poor quality and of preventative measures are essential components of managing the return on quality. Continuous efforts should be made to identify sources of poor quality and to find cost-effective ways of reducing them.

How can a manager make sense of the enormous amount of data this monitoring process produces? Some firms do clog their planning processes with too much data. Systems for tracking the environment also can be expensive and complex and are not necessarily available to companies with limited resources. Nevertheless, by knowing what sources of information are on the ideal list, a firm that cannot afford them all will at least know what it is giving up and where its decision making may be vulnerable.

Forecasts and Assumptions After gathering detailed records of past and current activities, the planning staff must next look to the future. Like all planning, ROQ analysis, is based on forecasts; it attempts to foresee the effects of proposed marketing actions. Although the analysis of historical data provides some understanding of likely market dynamics and brand-switching patterns, the future is always subject to change. Extensive analysis of environmental trends and competitive behavior allows managers to adjust historical figures to estimate anticipated future changes. Some of these estimates can be obtained from experts at governmental agencies or trade associations, but some may need to be derived specifically for the firm, either internally or by research vendors.[9] Given the high level of uncertainty in environmental forecasts, companies without sophisticated expertise should be extremely careful when using them. The planning process should, to some extent, supplant the need to have precise forecasts by providing a range of contingencies for various possible environmental outcomes.

In predicting the effect of service improvement efforts on changes in sales, estimating the likely reaction of customers to specific marketing programs is the most subjective and is often the most sensitive. For example, if 14% of restaurant customers are currently dissatisfied with the menu selection, to what extent will a new proposed restaurant format reduce that number? If it has an effect, will the percent dissatisfied drop to 10% or to 2%? Managers must be able to provide reasonable values to these questions, since they directly affect the estimates of relative financial attractiveness of alternative objectives and strategies on which program choices will be based. Therefore, during the planning cycle, managers should be encouraged to think in terms of customer reactions to marketing activities. Measures that track customer satisfaction with processes and dimensions over time in response to quality-related actions should be provided to help managers develop a feel for the magnitude and time delay of these reactions in their markets. Where possible, experiments should be run to isolate and measure customer reactions to various levels of quality improvement. This deliberate activity is necessary if management is to develop understanding of the effects of different levels and forms of spending on quality and on customer satisfaction and retention rates that will allow it to allocate funds responsibly. This experimentation is part of the organizational learning described in Figure 18.2.

Situation Analysis Finally, the data must be analyzed to answer some key questions. In particular, have our processes slipped over time? How do our measures compare to those of competitors? How are customer needs changing? Are we prepared to meet their emerging needs better than competitors? What opportunities do we have to make significant, and profitable, increases in customer retention?

The result is often called a *SWOT analysis,* for strengths, weaknesses, opportunities, and threats. In other words, the firm's abilities must be matched to opportunities available to optimize its prospects for competitive success. The analysis should focus on the key elements that will give the firm a profitable differential advantage with customers, rather than providing a laundry list of many unrelated points. The results will serve as the platform from which objectives and strategies are to be developed.

Development of Objectives and Strategies   The heart of the planning process is the setting of objectives and formulation of strategies based on the data analysis, guided by the firm's vision and mission statements. To ensure that return on customer-oriented quality is central to every department's goals, the corporate-level mission and objectives must stress quality, customer satisfaction and customer retention among the overriding concerns. For example, consider the customer and quality emphasis in the mission statement of General Motor's Saturn Division:

> Market vehicles developed and manufactured in the United States that are world leaders in quality, cost and customer satisfaction through the integration of people, technology and business systems and to transfer knowledge, technology and experience throughout General Motors.

This statement is made available to all employees on wallet-sized cards. A carefully drawn mission statement, well understood by all employees, provides guidance for making decisions about all further planning details.

Next, developing clearly stated, quantified corporate objectives is essential in guaranteeing coordination in the many activities planned throughout the organization. Then, goals for individual departments and products must be made consistent with this overall direction. Short-term strategies and actions proposed for the plan should be evaluated by how much they are positive steps toward longer-term goals. Once these higher-level, long-term objectives are established, then lower-level and shorter-term objectives that are logically linked to them can be developed.

Planning Roles and Procedures   The planning process must start with the top managers. They decide the overall direction of the firm and establish the values and culture of the organization. They must provide inspiration for a customer-based quality orientation through their actions and leadership. However, specific operational details must be the responsibility of those who will have to implement them and who are most familiar with customer demands. Therefore, after the wishes of top management are carefully communicated to the line managers lower in the organization, the line managers must set their own objectives and design strategies to accomplish them. Note that if the firm's actions are to be guided by an ROQ perspective, then the dissemination of responsibility for planning requires that decision makers throughout the organization understand the key concepts of customer retention and customer response to quality.

Frequent cooperative vertical communication is necessary throughout the process. Departments and product managers need to let top management know what they're planning, and top management should use its expertise to help lower-level managers set priorities and to guide and suggest improvements before unacceptable initiatives are developed too far. Many firms also encourage the use of cross-functional teams to ensure coordination and cooperation among departments. For example, in developing a new line of fashion eyewear, all major roles should be involved throughout the planning process, although their relative influences will vary over time: design's role is to provide styling ideas; engineering must verify that the designs have adequate strength and optical properties; manufacturing must make sure that proposed products can be efficiently produced; and marketing must make sure that the customer's needs and wants will be met.

To guarantee that quality is given suitable attention and to provide expert support and coordination among all line and support departments, some companies establish high-level quality councils to which all top executives are expected to belong.[10] Through their highly visible efforts of approving lower-level quality and ROQ goals, reviewing ongoing progress toward those goals, giving public recognition for jobs well done, and in serving on various project teams, executives can contribute greatly to establishing the quality culture throughout the organization.

Objectives   Managing return on quality requires that some objectives specifically address the defensive marketing issues of customer retention and satisfaction—at the level of the firm overall and with specific processes and dimensions. In particular, to improve the retention rate of current customers management must decide whether to emphasize solving problems or enhancing services. The first will decrease the number of dissatisfied customers, whereas the second will delight customers with various aspects of the product or service. These objectives can in turn be translated into internal operational objectives, once the relationships between operations and customer reactions are understood. All objectives should be quantifiable—that is, related to specific measures that are spelled out in the plan, and they should have definite time frames.

Determining objectives and strategies is not a linear process; objectives, the mission statement, and the creative development of strategies must be formulated simultaneously. There may simply be no way to accomplish some objectives with the firm's resources, so the set of feasible strategies and their estimated financial return must be kept in mind when goals are being set. For example, a firm with limited cash flow may be unable to achieve aggressive market share growth goals because of its inability to finance new service outlets.

From a practical standpoint, care must be taken to choose objectives appropriate to the organization's level of sophistication, particularly if quality principles are new to management. Quality experts often recommend that companies start with objectives that call for small increases in quality and then work up to larger jumps.[11] But don't be afraid to try a few big jumps to really stretch the troops. To inspire truly innovative thinking an organization needs objectives that call for a performance much better than current levels. Sometimes bold objectives with no obvious way to reach them can inspire employees to innovate and to discover breakthrough levels of quality delivery that the previously considered set of strategies would never have achieved. For example, a goal of reducing defects by 10% is likely to produce suggestions to work harder in traditional ways. A goal of reducing defects by 95%

requires a thorough evaluation of how processes are performed. But this device must be used selectively. A plan consisting entirely of stretch objectives and unfamiliar strategies is not likely to be taken seriously as a guide to action. Nor are managers likely to be able to supply sound estimates of costs or likely customer responses for estimating the return on quality of these activities.

The role of objectives is under debate. Deming insisted that they are counter-productive. He assumed that empowered employees will do their best to improve quality anyway, and that pressure to meet specific quantified objectives, often based on very soft forecasts, might only shift their focus away from more productive activities.[12] For example, a dictate to improve customer satisfaction by answering 99% of all phone calls by the second ring may actually hurt the company image as operators rush current callers so that they can answer the next call. On the other hand, many managers find objectives a useful way to communicate the firm's priorities and to encourage innovative thinking.

Strategies and Operating Plans   Generating strategies is a mixture of art and a science. Strategies should be appropriate to the objectives they are meant to reach as well as financially responsible. At the same time creativity and innovation are essential to break new ground in service design. Ross and Silverblatt described strategic planning as "a combination of trend spotter, number cruncher, and financial planner overlaid with intuitive decisions aided by an emerging kit bag of [Strategic Marketing Planning] techniques."[13]

The initial stages of the strategy genteration process should attempt to produce a wide array of possible solutions for consideration. This requires a firm understanding of the SWOT analysis and access to a broad range of ideas. As many sources of insights as possible should be used from inside and outside the firm. Senior management and the quality council should ensure that communication, among personnel from different functions and different divisions within the company takes place to share experiences and ideas. They company should also use its contacts outside the company for fresh perspectives. Sources might include ad agencies, marketing research firms and consultants who have a good understanding of the company and its markets, but are less likely to be bound by the company line. And of course, the firm should borrow ideas liberally from the companies it is benchmarking. After managers have studied these sources of ideas, formal brainstorming techniques can be used to generate additional strategies. Although it might be tempting to stop as soon as one or two acceptable ideas have been proposed, participants should keep going, pushing harder to generate a wide list of alternatives.

Quality managers have found that the biggest gains can be obtained from projects generated and carried out by interdepartmental teams.[14] Major improvements in quality can rarely be accomplished by single departments. For example, training frontline personnel to be more friendly won't help much if the underlying service is too slow. Spending more on advertising may attract some customers willing to give the product a try, but it won't retain them if the underlying product isn't what they expected. All departments involved must understand the idea so that their efforts can be coordinated.

From the list of strategies generated, managers must choose those they wish to pursue. Several criteria are helpful in making this decision:[15]

- Is the strategy consistent with the objectives and the SWOT analysis, and does it provide the firm with some sustainable competitive advantage?
- Are the potential rewards of the strategy sufficient to warrant the effort? An analysis of the strategy's impact on customer retention and profits can assist here in determining the likely financial consequences of alternative programs.
- Are each of the individual programs consistent with overall goals and with those of other departments and corporate functions? For example, plans to increase customer service while reducing personnel may be at cross-purposes unless the system is being fundamentally restructured. Assumptions about costs and returns that underlie the impact on retention for one program may be invalidated by the implementation of others. The use of high-level cross-functional teams is intended to reduce this type of problem.
- Is the program feasible given the company's strengths and weaknesses and those of the competition? Do the personnel who must carry it out understand it and believe in it?
- How solid are the key assumptions on which the strategy is based? Does the strategy's success depend upon uncertain outcomes, such as major changes in economic trends, or exceptional performance by departments of the company or the passage of particular legislation? If so, how acceptable are the negative consequences if the assumptions are wrong? Can the strategy be reversed?

Other Parts of the Plan   The remaining parts of the plan include the financial projections and the contingency plans. The financial section should include pro forma income statements and cash-flow projections for the firm, given the proposed strategies. Output from the ROQ model, described in Chapter 15, or other analyses of retention data can be used to develop the revenue and profit projections for proposed defensive strategies.

Contingency plans should be drawn from the discussions that selected the proposed strategies. The purpose of contingency planning is to have alternative strategies ready to go should key planning assumptions fail to materialize. A great deal of time will be saved later if planners use the strategy meetings to discuss alternative actions while everyone is deeply engaged in the planning process and while institutional understanding of the SWOT analysis is at its most intense.

Review and Approval   The process of review and approval should be ongoing throughout the planning process. Most firms still require a formal presentation to, and approval by, corporate leadership, but in the ideal process this session is a review and fleshing out the details of already agreed-upon strategies, rather than an initial sales presentation to senior management. The final presentation should be largely ceremonial, with no surprises. Developing plans in the lower echelons without the guidance and participation of the senior management is unlikely to to be successful for the same reasons that designing products without input from engineering, manufacturing, and marketing is likely to be a problem. Both instances of insulated planning can be commonly found in the "real world," but they are extremely wasteful, because the process can go too long before critical errors are identified, causing time-wasting rework. Continuous communication between upper and lower echelons is equivalent to small batch processing in manufacturing.

Problems are detected and fixed early, resulting in a timely, fully acceptable, better quality final product. Upper management and the quality council should be kept informed and provide guidance throughout the development of the plans, and drafts should be reviewed by other parts of the organization.

Implementation   Planning is one thing. Actually making the plan work is another. A survey of executives at Fortune 100 companies found that a majority of them felt disappointment and frustration with their planning systems, mostly due to problems in implementation of their plans.[16]

Monitoring   A well-crafted plan should have clearly defined areas of responsibility and deadlines so that sources of shortfalls or unexpectedly effective performance can be identified. However, spotting trouble or locating exceptional success requires continuous monitoring. Measurements to be tracked should be clearly specified in the plan itself, since in many cases they provide the operational definitions of what is expected of employees. Some data are available from standard secondary sources, such as sales reports and other basic accounting documents. Some are available from outside vendors such as Nielsen store audits and other market monitoring firms. In general, these measurements are related to the objectives stated in the plan.

In addition to tracking the usual barometers of the progress of the business plan, such as sales, profits, market share, response to advertising, and the like, quality programs obviously require that internal quality measures be charted and analyzed to spot difficulties and opportunities for improvement. For tracking the return on quality the following regular monitoring programs of external customers are also recommended.

- Satisfaction measures: overall, with each process and with each of their dimensions, particularly in those areas where estimated response functions indicated changes in levels of dissatisfaction or delighted customers.
- Switching patterns, including rates of customer retention and percent of new customers, and other "background" values of the ROQ model.

In addition, the firm should be monitoring the following:

- Employee satisfaction with levels of empowerment, compensation and rewards, working conditions, and other aspects, tracked through anonymous surveys.
- Internal customer satisfaction, using surveys that measure the level of support services provided by departments for each.

18.5 AN OUTLINE OF A PLAN

Every organization has its own ideas about the specific format its planning documents should follow, depending upon what issues need particular emphasis in its industry, the sophistication of planning in the organization, and how the planning responsibility is delegated. In this section we will describe the general contents of a planning document that embodies the principles of customer orientation and return on quality. The specific order and format of the plan's structure is not important and should be shaped to needs of the individual user, but the basic issues addressed by the plan are essential to be sure that profitable, customer-oriented service is maintained.

Plans should be read and used. The specific length of a plan depends upon a firm's situation, but a document of less than 20 pages is probably too sketchy, whereas a document of more than 50 pages may be too intimidating to be "user-friendly." The writing should be accessible and make use of outlines and bullet points to organize ideas. Subheadings make it easy for the reader to locate specific pieces of information. Numerical data in tables and graphs are more useful than long expository paragraphs.

The typical strategic business plan is typically organized according to the following sections.[17]

Executive Summary

This section is a concise summary (no more than 3–4 pages) of the plan's major recommendations and their anticipated results. It should be considered the primary document submitted to senior management. The rest of the plan provides support and operational details for the executive summary should anyone need to consult them, but reading this section alone should provide a clear picture of exactly what actions the plan proposes.

Historical Update

This section should bring the reader up to date on important trends that have determined the current state of the industry and offer some insights about where it might be heading. Possible trends to cover include:

- The market's size, growth, profitability, costs, etc.
- Competitive activity, including changes in quality-related activities, pricing approaches, distribution channels, promotion methods, etc.
- Changes in the nature of demand and supply.
- Influences of technology.
- Changing political and regulatory climate.

Situation Analysis

This section should present an analysis of pertinent data to understand the current and future dynamics of the market. This analysis serves as a platform to support the choice of objectives and strategies. The list of topics to consider includes the following:

A. Industry Attractiveness Analysis

- How big is the market, its growth rate, stage of the product life cycle, the average profit level and its variance over time?
- What competitive forces put pressures on profit levels in the industry, including the costs of quality programs and the prices customers will pay

for quality? In particular, extending the concepts of Michael Porter to include return-on-quality concerns:[18] the intensity of interfirm rivalry, the threat of entry by other firms, the amount of negotiation leverage possessed by suppliers and buyers, threats of substitute products, and the amount of slack capacity in the industry.

- What is the future of relevant trends in the environmental such as demographic shifts, technological development, and political and regulatory restrictions, and how will they affect the firm's ability to profitably improve customer satisfaction?

B. Customer Analysis. This section presents an analysis of the factors that attract and retain customers, to provide the support for customer-oriented actions. First should come a clear description of the major segments into which the company separates its customers:

- Who are they?
- How do they use the product?
- What motivates them to buy?
- What is their buying process?
- How often do they buy?
- What is the average contribution margin per period of customers in this segment?

An analysis of the effect of marketing on each segment should follow.

- What are the switching patterns in this segment? Over the planning horizon, what are the expected growth and mortality rates of the segment?
- What offensive initiatives are necessary to attract new customers from the segment?
- What are each segment's view of the service processes and dimensions and which have the greatest effect on customer retention?

C. Sales Analysis. What percent of profit increases have been due to market size growth, market share growth, price increases, cost reductions, and productivity improvements?[19] How do profits and costs differ by product, segment, distribution channel, territory, etc.?

D. Competitor Analysis. This section presents an analysis of key competitors. It should summarize their objectives and current strategies, their strengths and weaknesses on the dimensions that will affect their ability to compete effectively, and their likely future actions. This section is often presented in tabular form, with short, concise summary entries describing each dimension of the included companies.

E. Self-assessment. To make the competitive analysis meaningful, a similar analysis of the company should be done. Brutally honest candor is necessary here, although this approach can be politically sensitive. We must have an objective side-by-side comparison of our firm and our competitors if we are to choose realistic goals and effective strategies. This comparison should also include customer satisfaction with each level of the service or product.

F. **Forecasts and Assumptions.** Any other forecasts of important environmental and market factors that are necessary to proceed with ROQ strategy development should be included in this section as well.

Objectives

Objectives must be consistent if they are to lead to success. Therefore, the plan should present the entire "cascade" of objectives, from those at the corporate level to those of the various functional areas. The plan should list:

- The firm's mission statement/vision
- Corporate objectives
- Objectives for lower-level units, if the plan is being done for a division or other subunit of the corporation
- Functional area objectives for each of the following:
  1. Marketing
     (a) Could include sales, profit, share, retention rates, etc., perhaps by segment.
     (b) Penetration of new target markets, withdrawal from current targets.
     (c) Satisfaction objectives can be provided for each of the service processes and dimensions used in the ROQ analysis, specifying whether the objective is to solve problems (increase the percent satisfied) or to raise service quality to new levels (improve the percent delighted).
  2. Management
     (a) Organization structural changes.
     (b) Objectives relating to leadership.
     (c) Hiring, training, turnover, empowerment objectives.
     (d) Satisfaction and delight objectives for internal customers.
  3. Operational
     (a) Internal quality measure goals.
     (b) Process capabilities.
     (c) Supplier capabilities.
  4. Financial
     (a) Financial goals, such as profits, ROI, ROA, etc.
     (b) Return-on-quality objectives.

Strategies and Program Details

In this section are described the action programs that have been chosen to reach the various objectives.

Marketing Strategies Marketing strategies should be formulated by market segment if possible, to keep customer service foremost. However, concern for production and marketing efficiency may also require that production and service delivery be coordinated across segments.

Typical *offensive strategies* include programs in

- Positioning
- Product/service line changes
- Pricing
- Distribution outlets
- Sales force
- Advertising
- Sales promotion

Defensive strategies are those related to improved retention of customers:

- Programs to improve satisfaction or delight with individual processes and dimensions. The profitability of selected programs should be analyzed using ROQ analyses.
- Other after-sale service programs.
- Satisfaction-monitoring programs.
- Complaint-handling programs.

Other marketing strategies include programs for

- Research and development
- Marketing research

Management Strategies   Among the marketing strategies are the following:

- Leadership and management improvement plans
- Programs to revise the organizational structure
- Employee recruitment programs
- Training programs
- Compensation plans
- Empowerment and motivational programs

Operational Strategies   The operational strategies should consider:

- Programs to describe how operations will be managed, what materials and equipment will be used
- Quality measurement programs
- Programs to measure the cost of quality

Financial Strategies   The main financial concern has to do with how money needs will be met with programs for raising funds through debt or equity.

Financial Statements

This section projects the financial consequences of the proposed strategies under the assumptions about the future presented earlier. It should include proposed budgets for all proposed marketing, human resources, and operations programs, as well as pro forma statements. These budgets and statements should reflect projected costs, revenues, and profits. Supporting tables should include cost-of-quality analyses and ROQ analyses of the likely profit impact of marketing programs.

Monitors and Controls

Some of the variables that need monitoring to guarantee service quality and to manage its financial return are:[20]

1. Measures of marketplace performance
   - Market growth rate, and our sales growth compared to it
   - Market shares and share changes of all firms in the market
   - Profit margins and earnings as a percent of sales
   - Number of customers who are new to the market
   - Number of new customers who are brand switchers from competitors
   - Our retention rate
   - Number of customer defections, and their reasons for doing so

2. Data necessary to improve the use of ROQ analysis
   - Customer satisfaction changes in response to marketing programs to calibrate ROQ response functions more effectively in the future

3. Management climate
   - Measures of managers' satisfaction with various aspects of their jobs
   - Turnover rates of management, supervisors and employees

4. Employee opinions about
   - Job satisfaction
   - Corporate support (i.e., anticipation and planning to meet individual job performance needs)
   - Feelings of empowerment
   - Employee concern with improving his or her own service effectiveness

5. Internal service climate
   - Quality and timeliness of service between departments
   - Clearly defined goals for internal service
   - Appropriateness of rewards for excellence in internal service

6. Customer satisfaction
   - Satisfaction scores for processes and dimensions
   - Number of complaints
   - Resolved complaints
   - Number of customer compliments

7. Internal quality measures
   - Resolution of complaints
   - Returns and allowances
   - Time required to settle a complaint
   - Delivery cycle times
   - Other measurements relevant to specific processes and dimensions

Contingency Plans

There should be a quick sketch of the basic strategies to be employed in the event that key assumptions of the primary plan should prove to be in error.

18.6 SUMMARY

This chapter is intended to emphasize those aspects of planning most important for developing a strong customer-oriented culture in an organization that is also financially accountable. In so doing we have only sketched out the contents of certain sections, such as the financial projections. However, we also have provided suggestions for objectives, measures, and controls that might be more extensive than a given organization may choose to use.

The success of ROQ-focused strategic quality planning depends upon how well the process is deployed throughout the organization, a very difficult task in most companies. Successful deployment requires new thinking about the role of employees and how they are rewarded. It requires teaching new skills to managers. And it requires a new cooperative spirit among employees so that they are willing to put the greater good of the firm ahead of individual goals.

Achieving this culture is not a simple process for many U.S. workers; many firms have been unable to sustain TQM programs. This communal spirit is at odds with two common characterizations of U.S. society. On the one hand, Americans are often described as independent and self-absorbed, ready to jump to a new company for personal advancement. On the other hand, companies have long operated on the Taylor principles that prescribe rigid hierarchical management structures and unbending work rules, a culture that fosters distrust and confrontation on both sides.

Leading the revolution to overcome these barriers requires the sincere, tireless commitment of the CEO in all statements and actions. He or she should continuously endorse strategic quality planning, and if not actually play a role in designing the system, then certainly take part in regular reviews of the process and provide funding, time, and other support necessary to ensure high-quality planning activities. However, even a committed top manager cannot impose an ideal planning structure on an organization. McDonald cautioned that all planning interventions have political ramifications.[21] Some employees will lose power and others will gain. Long-standing power relationships will be affected. Therefore, when designing the planning process the personalities and management styles of the firm's personnel and the firm's current stage of development must be kept in mind.

It takes time to instill a sound planning process into the culture of an organization. Doing it well requires total commitment from the entire organization, and lots of communication, both vertically and horizontally. It requires commitments of time and resources. And it takes patience to learn how to do it properly because it is unlikely to be satisfactory the first few times. A specialist in writing business plans for small firms claimed that even for such limited exercises it takes at least three years to get proficient at writing plans.[22] For a large organization requiring cooperation from many participants, the learning process will surely be much longer.

REVIEW QUESTIONS

1. Why is planning beneficial, even if circumstances change, making the resulting plan unworkable?
2. Since you have studied marketing and planning a friend managing a small (87 employees) software business has invited you to help him out. In particular, he would like you to sit down with him and write a quality-focused marketing plan for his firm. What would you tell him?
3. Consider the Saturn mission statement quoted in the chapter. What manner of changes, if any, would you suggest to improve it? How does the mission statement distinguish Saturn? In other words, what processes and products found at other auto manufacturers would not be consistent with Saturn's mission statement?
4. What is the difference between strategies and objectives? Your staff has generated a long list of possible strategies to consider for the next plan. What criteria would you use to select the ones you choose to pursue?
5. What are the major components of a quality-based business plan?

ENDNOTES

1. For an excellent treatment of marketing planning in general, see Donald R. Lehmann and Russell S. Winer (1988), *Analysis for Marketing Planning,* Homewood, IL: BPI-Irwin.
2. Walter A. Shewhart (1931), *The Economic Control of Manufactured Product,* New York: D. Van Nostrand Company, Inc.
3. Christopher W. L. Hart and Christopher E. Bogan (1992), *The Baldrige,* New York: McGraw-Hill, p. 122.
4. Malcolm H. B. McDonald (1990), "Ten Barriers to Marketing Planning," *The Journal of Services Marketing,* 4 (Spring), 5–18.
5. Stanley F. Stasch and Patricia Lanktree (1980), "Can Your Marketing Planning Procedures Be Improved?" *Journal of Marketing,* 44 (Summer), 79–90; McDonald (1990), *op. cit.,* p. 7.
6. Raymond E. Kordupleski, Roland T. Rust, and Anthony J. Zahorik (1994), "Why Improving Quality Doesn't Improve Quality," *California Management Review,* 35 (Spring), 82–95.
7. See Leonard Fuld (1985), *Competitor Intelligence,* New York: Wiley.
8. Hart and Bogan (1992), *op. cit.*
9. The complexities of forecasting are beyond the scope of this book, but many excellent articles and books on forecasting are available. We recommend John C. Chambers, Stinder K. Mullick, and Donald H. Smith (1974), *An Executive's Guide to Forecasting,* New York: Wiley; David M. Georgoff and Robert G. Murdick (1986), "Manager's Guide to Forecasting," *Harvard Business Review,* 64 (January-February), 110–120.
10. G. Howland Blackiston (1988), "A Renaissance in Quality," *Executive Excellence* (September), 9–10.
11. Blackiston (1988), *op. cit.;* Hart and Bogan (1992), *op. cit.*
12. W. Edwards Deming (1986), *Out of the Crisis,* Cambridge, MA: MIT Press.
13. Joel E. Ross and Ronnie Silverblatt (1987), "Developing the Strategic Plan," *Industrial Marketing,* 16, 103–108.

14. Blackiston (1988), *op. cit.*
15. For example, see George S. Day (1984), *Strategic Market Planning: The Pursuit of Competitive Advantage,* St. Paul, MN: West Publishing.
16. Ross and Silverblatt (1987), *op. cit.*
17. For other detailed descriptions of planning documents, see Lehmann and Winer (1988) *op. cit.,* and Karsten G. Hellebust and Joseph C. Krallinger (1989), *Strategic Planning Workbook,* New York: Wiley.
18. Michael E. Porter (1980), *Competitive Strategy: Techniques for Analyzing Industries and Competitors,* New York: Free Press.
19. McDonald (1990), *op. cit.*
20. Some of these measures were suggested in Robert L. Desatnick (1987), "Service: A CEO's Perspective," *Management Review* (October), 41–45.
21. McDonald (1990), *op. cit.*
22. Charles J. Bodenstad (1989), "Directional Signals," *Inc.* (March), 139–141.

au bon pain.
THE FRENCH BAKERY CAFÉ

The Partner/Manager Program

Au Bon Pain has tried every progressive human resource strategy or policy available—we've had them all. Quite honestly, I don't believe that any incremental strategies work long term in the multisite service business, particularly in a labor market—like Boston—that is characterized by low unemployment levels. I'm convinced that developing new solutions for human resource management at the unit level is the basis of competitive advantage. Instituting our Partner/Manager Program throughout the company now could give us an important edge. This is our chance to blow the company out, or to blow ourselves up.

This is how Len Schlesinger, executive vice president and treasurer of the Au Bon Pain (ABP) Company, described the situation he and company president Ron Shaich faced in January 1987. Six months earlier, in July 1986, 2 of the 24 company-owned stores had embarked on an experiment that could lead to a revolutionary change in the company's store-manager compensation system. The Partner/Manager Program Experiment ran for six periods of four weeks each (the first period of the experiment, period 8, ran from July 13 through August 9). The experiment concluded on December 20, 1986. Now, Schlesinger and Shaich had to decide whether to roll out the program in all of the company's stores, run it on a trial basis involving only some of the stores, withdraw it to make needed improvements, or abandon it.

Research Assistant Lucy N. Lytle prepared this case under the supervision of Professor W. Earl Sasser as the basis for class discussion rather than to illustrate either effective or ineffective handling of an administrative situation. To order copies, call (617) 495-6117 or write the Publishing Division, Harvard Business School, Boston, MA 02163. No part of this publication may be reproduced, stored in a retrieval system, used in a spreadsheet, or transmitted in any form or by any means—electronic, mechanical, photocopying, recording, or otherwise—without the permission of Harvard Business School.

HISTORY

Au Bon Pain, a chain of upscale French bakeries/sandwich cafes, opened its first store in Boston's Faneuil Hall in 1977. This store was originally developed as a marketing vehicle for Pavallier, a French manufacturer of ovens and other bakery equipment. In 1978, Louis Kane, an experienced venture capitalist, bought the store and the rights to the concept. Two years later, Kane teamed up with Ron Shaich, a Harvard MBA who had worked as the director of operations for the Original Cookie Company, a national chain of over 80 retail cookie stores, and who had just opened The Cookie Jar, a cookie store in a high-traffic location in downtown Boston. The two agreed to merge their businesses, enabling Kane to utilize his extensive real estate skills while Shaich handled the operational end of the business.

ABP quickly became known both for the high quality of its croissants and baguettes and for its prime locations. Although the company was based in Boston, Massachusetts, the chain expanded rapidly during the next six years to include stores in New York, New Jersey, Maine, Pennsylvania, Connecticut, and New Hampshire. By 1986, there were 24 company-owned units in the ABP chain. (For a complete list of ABP store locations and sizes, see Exhibit 1.)

Originally, each of the ABP units operated as a self-contained production bakery in the back, with a retail store and seating area in the front. A bakery chef was assigned to each store to handle the demanding process of rolling out croissants and baking breads in the classic French style. In addition to croissants and breads, sandwiches, coffee, and beverages were also sold. Some test stores offered soups, salads, omelettes, cookies, and sorbets as well. Generally, 65% of a unit's business was takeout.

In 1980, Shaich and Kane decided to centralize production, and they fired 15 of the company's 18 bakers. They transferred the remaining three to the Prudential Center store, where the dough was prepared, frozen, and then shipped to the other units. This change eliminated the need for a highly trained chef in each unit, improved inventory control, increased product consistency, and reduced the size of each unit's production area. Three years later, production was moved to ABP headquarters in South Boston. Frozen dough, which had a shelf life of eight weeks, continued to be shipped to all the units on a weekly, or semiweekly basis.

Len Schlesinger, formerly an associate professor in organizational behavior at the Harvard Business School, joined the company as its executive vice president and treasurer in early 1985. He was charged with the task of systematizing efforts to increase sales and improve quality throughout ABP by increasing employee ownership—both financial and psychological—in the organization.

ABP's major competitors included Vie de France, PepsiCo's La Petite Boulangerie, and Sara Lee's Michelle's Baguette and French Bakery. By 1986, however, all three were suffering from a combination of low profitability and decreased sales.

"THE CYCLE OF FAILURE"

According to Schlesinger and Shaich, in 1985 ABP's retail operations confronted for the first time a set of human resource problems endemic to the fast-food industry. These problems included a continuing crew labor shortage, a chronic shortage of associate managers, an inability to attract and select high-quality management candidates, an inadequately trained management staff, and what Schlesinger referred to as the tendency of many district managers to play "super GM" (general manager)—meaning that they focused obsessively on following up day-to-day activities (a GM's responsibility) at the expense of defining clearly the district manager's role. Labeled by Shaich as "the cycle of failure," the problems interrelated systematically to induce a pattern of poor performance at the store level.

Shaich noted:

Our lack of attention to these issues had created problems at the crew level that remained unsolved. These, in turn, magnified managerial problems, and vice versa. It created a vicious cycle—the cycle of failure—and led to a significant degradation of the customer experience. Len and I concluded that if Au Bon Pain was to achieve its objectives of delivering a high-quality customer experience which resulted in sales and profitability, we had to break out of this cycle once and for all.

Schlesinger added:

It was clear, especially in the Boston market, that the labor crisis had engendered a serious decline in the quality of the crew candidates we attracted and ultimately hired. In the past, we had focused on simply staffing our stores rather than on attracting desirable candidates. All of our energies were devoted to the short-term operational needs of the business in this area.

At the same time, training for the crew was practically nonexistent and, where it did exist, poorly executed. Development, too, tended to follow a Darwinian "survival of the fittest" approach. The problem was compounded by the fact that we were committed to a promote-from-within policy which precluded the opportunity to acquire skilled talent from outside.

Beyond that, considerable work remained to be done to develop our reward system into a long-term compensation system which more directly tied the managers into the success of their stores.

EXISTING COMPENSATION SYSTEM IN 1986

Our existing compensation system, which we devised in 1985, goes a long way toward addressing the problems contributing to the cycle of failure. It's a simple system under which managers are paid according to their level of responsibility and the sales activity of their stores.

Shaich made this observation as he outlined the two basic components of ABP's existing compensation system (i.e., the system in place prior to the development of the Partner/Manager Program): base pay and a volume adjustment. Under the plan, general managers earned a base salary of $375 a week. Salaries rose as weekly sales volumes increased, up to $633.75 a week at the highest-volume store.

Base Pay A manager's base pay was determined by his or her level in the organization: general manager, senior associate manager, first associate manager, or second associate manager (which included manager trainees). In July 1985, the base pay levels were as follows:

Level	Weekly Pay	Annual Pay
General manager	$375.00	$19,500
Senior associate manager	350.00	18,200
First associate manager	341.54	17,760
Second associate manager	336.54	17,500

Volume Adjustment In addition to base pay, a volume adjustment was calculated each week for first associate, senior associate, and general managers. (Second associate managers were not eligible for a volume adjustment). Because ABP had a wide range of store volumes with varying managerial responsibilities and workloads, it established three categories of stores:

Store Volume	Weekly Sales
Low	$4,000–$10,000
Medium	$10,000–$20,000
High	over $20,000

The formulas for determining salaries for general, senior associate, and first associate managers (i.e., base pay plus volume adjustment) are presented in Exhibit 2.

THE DEVELOPMENT OF THE PARTNER/MANAGER PROGRAM

In the spring of 1986, Schlesinger and Shaich developed a draft of a new compensation/incentive system—the Partner/Manager Program—for the managers of ABP's stores. Shaich explained:

> Len and I had identified the problems inherent in the cycle of failure. The next step was to figure out how to pay people more. Since 1985, under our existing compensation system, we had tried to develop a pay system which allowed the managers to make more money than they had before while still tying them to the success of their stores and the company.

In brief, the Partner/Manager Program would reclassify general managers as "partner/managers" and provide them with a base salary of $500 per week. Each partner/manager could choose an associate manager, who would be paid $400 per week. The partner/manager would be entitled to a 35% share of the unit's incremental profits under the new system; the associate manager would receive 15%; and ABP would receive the remaining 50%.

A store-lease payment would be deducted monthly from the store controllable profits to cover unit-level fixed expenses, corporate overhead, and reasonable profit expectations. The amount of the store-lease payment would be guaranteed for 13 periods (i.e., one year), with the following exceptions, which would require an adjustment. First, the addition of fixed assets would trigger an increase in the store-lease payment of 25% of the total fixed asset cost divided across 13 periods. Second, additional sales, which triggered a percentage rent clause in the real estate lease, would increase the store-lease payment by the percentage specified in the real estate lease.

Incremental profits would be equal to a unit's net controllable profits minus its store-lease payment. These profits would be distributed to the managers at the close of each period (i.e., every four weeks). ABP would hold in reserve $7,500 for the partner/manager and $2,500 for the associate manager until the end of their contracts, which could last one, two, or three years.[1]

The managers would be required to work a minimum of 50 hours per week, and the partner/manager and/or the associate manager would have to be on duty in the store during 90% of its operating hours. The quality of each store would be monitored through "mystery-shopping" reports, "white-glove" inspections, and 100% customer satisfaction "moment-of-truth" indicators. A violation of any of the listed rules could result in the dismissal of either or both of the managers if the problem was not corrected within a specified amount of time. (See Appendix A for a working draft of the Partner/Manager Program.)

GOALS OF THE PARTNER/MANAGER PROGRAM

Product of Research   The Partner/Manager Program was the result of research and careful thought, according to Schlesinger:

---

[1]During The Partner/Manager Program Experiment, which is described in detail later in this case, Schlesinger and Shaich opted to distribute the managers' share of the incremental profits in a lump sum at the end of the six-month trial period.

It's not something that we developed overnight. We looked into the compensation systems of a number of fast-food chains, including Sambo's, Chick-Fil-A, Golden Corral, and Kentucky Fried Chicken. The Partner/Manager Program is a customized imitation of the processes we studied. In some ways, it is revolutionary—but it is not without precedent in this industry.

Under this system, we would manage our partner/managers with loose controls and less overhead, hold them tightly accountable to outputs (i.e., customer satisfaction as determined by mystery shopping) rather than inputs, and require them to invest themselves in their stores. Hopefully, through their efforts, the good managers would earn considerably more than they do now.

Shaich added:

We want to hire people who really care ... the kind of person you'd want on your side when you go into a street fight. A person who does a good job for the people beneath him, not to impress somebody higher up. This is an organization that has rewarded trying for years. Now it's time to reward results.

One of the aims of this program would be to employ fewer managers, who would work harder, and make more money than their predecessors. We want people willing to pay the price to earn big bucks.

Personally, I believe that people earning less than $30,000 per year should be managed through individually based incentive/compensation plans.[2] People higher up in an organi-

zation, with a longer time horizon and broader responsibilities, should have a low salary and stock options, like at People Express. The problem at People was that while stock ownership is meaningful, it's money that gets results.[3]

The Role of the District Manager Not only would the Partner/Manager Program change ABP's compensation system, but it also would alter the ways in which the individual units were supervised. Schlesinger explained:

Under this program, the district managers would function as coaches, rather than as policemen—and they would supervise 8 to 10 stores rather than the traditional 3 or 4. The district managers would serve as consultants by generating ideas for sales building and cost reduction, and as support people by helping out during busy seasons and assisting with the training of new associate managers. They would earn perhaps 5% of the incremental profits generated by each of the units they supervise. Of course, we haven't worked out all the details yet.

One of the factors necessitating the change in the district managers' role was what Shaich termed the "Stockholm effect" (psychological phenomenon that occurs when, over time, hostage victims develop sympathetic feelings toward their captors). He noted:

In the past, the district managers, like the general managers, became excuse-givers. Instead of holding the general managers accountable to Au Bon Pain's standards—as customers do—the district managers began to

---

[2]For an example of such a company, see HBS case no. 376–028, "The Lincoln Electric Company."

[3]For further information, see HBS case no. 483–103, "People Express (A)."

sympathize with the managers' excuses. They became agents of the status quo rather than agents of change.

Now it's clear that the partner/managers would be primarily responsible for handling any problems that arise. I expect that 90% of the problems we used to deal with at headquarters, the managers would now figure out on their own.

Increased Stability One of the goals of the Partner/Manager Program would be to increase stability at the unit level by reducing turnover and by encouraging managers to commit themselves to working at a specific unit for at least one year. Shaich discussed this idea:

The program would require each manager to have a real financial commitment to his or her store in the form of his or her share of the incremental profits—some of which would be held back by Au Bon Pain until the end of the contract. We expect that after working in the same unit for at least a year, a manager would have the chance to become very familiar with the store's cycle—what its sales volume is like, when its peak periods are, and so on. In the long run, this knowledge would increase the quality of each store's operations.

At the same time, the managers would get to know their customers and crew on a personal basis. Significantly, consulting psychologists have found that the most important single variable that keeps a customer coming back to a store is whether or not someone in the store knows that customer's name. There are employees at Golden Corral, for example, who know the names of 2,700 customers.

This "retention quotient" has major implications for a company like Au Bon Pain as our research indicates that some of our customers—the ones we refer to as the "Au Bon Pain Club"—visit our stores up to 108 times per year.

QUALITY CONTROL

Although the Partner/Manager Program would reduce the degree of corporate supervision of the individual stores, quality control measures remained in place. For example, units were mystery shopped at least once a week. Mystery shopping involved having a professional shopper hired from outside ABP evaluate the store from a customer's perspective. The mystery shopper judged a store on the basis of "moment-of-truth" indicators, generated in customer focus groups, which were aimed at achieving 100% customer satisfaction. Although they were subject to change, one set of indicators is shown in Exhibit 3. Mystery shoppers encountering "perfect service" carefully noted the names of those responsible and reported their experiences back to headquarters. According to Len Schlesinger, this was happening about once per month, and when it did "it set off all kinds of bells, awards and recognition." Stickers were frequently attached to cash registers reminding employees that their next customer could be the mystery shopper.

In addition, white-glove inspections, using a 140-item checklist covering all phases of store operations, were conducted by an Au Bon Pain auditor every accounting period. The inspections lasted eight hours, and the days when they occurred were not announced in advance.

Decreased Recruiting Budget Schlesinger expected a dramatic decrease in ABP's recruiting budget as a result of the publicity surrounding the news that it would be changing its compensation system. He predicted:

> If we go public with this program, the resulting newspaper and trade journal articles would help us to attract and stockpile a new group of managerial candidates. We could cut our annual recruiting budget from $230,000 to $60,000 by substituting press for want ads.

POTENTIAL PROBLEMS

Burning Out   Shaich and Schlesinger both raised the issue of managers burning out during the program. They agreed that being a partner/manager or an associate manager under the new program would be a potentially stressful experience—sufficiently stressful that it could cause some managers to drop out before their contract ended. Schlesinger, however, was philosophic about it:

> Burning out managers would be one concern. But the way I see it, we're all adults entering into a business contract. We understand the benefits and the risks.

Physical Limitations   At least three physical factors limited productivity and sales: (1) each unit's proofing capacity (i.e., the capacity of the machines in which the dough rose for approximately two hours), (2) each unit's freezer capacity, and (3) the limitations of Au Bon Pain's product line.

Schlesinger predicted:

> If Au Bon Pain adopts the Partner/ Manager Program, people will claim that we have come up with a new way to con people—but that wouldn't be true. The program would establish a clear, tangible link between the results the managers achieved and the money they would make.

We wouldn't hold up goals that aren't attainable, because we would need to create a base of heroes. Under the Partner/Manager Program most people would make about $40,000 a year. The heroes would make between $60,000 and $100,000, and they would set an example for which everyone would strive.

THE PARTNER/MANAGER PROGRAM EXPERIMENT

Eager to discover if the program would be successful in a real-life situation, Schlesinger and Shaich invited the general and associate managers of two stores to participate in a six-month trial run of the Partner/Manager Program. Gary Aronson, the general manager of ABP's Burlington Mall store (30 miles west of Boston), and Frank Ciampa, his associate manager, agreed to give it a try. So did Brian McEvoy, the general manager of the CityPlace store in Hartford, Connecticut (100 miles south of Boston), and his associate manager, Stephen Dunn.

The managers did not feel that they were coerced into participating in the experiment. "We were able to choose whether or not we wanted to participate," McEvoy said. Before the experiment began, both Aronson and McEvoy met with Schlesinger and Shaich to discuss a rough draft of the program. "We gave them our input, and they incorporated our suggestions into a revised version," Aronson explained. Later, all four managers met with Schlesinger and Shaich to review the changes and discuss any questions about the program.

Aronson explained why he agreed to participate in the experiment:

> Frank and I decided that our number one priority was to show that a program like this could work. We wanted to convince people that this was something revolutionary, and

that it would not only turn around this company, but that it has the potential to change the whole industry. The way I see it, this program is going to turn us all into a bunch of professionals.

McEvoy was motivated both by the "financial incentives of the program" and by his perception that it was an alternative to following the traditional career path—which would have involved moving to Boston and trying to get promoted to the position of district manager. He noted, "First of all, my wife and I didn't really want to relocate because it would have upset her career. At the same time, even if we did move, there wouldn't have been any guarantees that I would have been able to move up in the company."

MANAGERS' BACKGROUNDS

What initially attracted me to Au Bon Pain was that they allowed their managers more mobility and more access to upper-level management than most fast-food chains. They also let their managers have an input into the decision process.

I believe that the only way you can grow as a manager is to work in a less structured environment. At Au Bon Pain, you can't run on buzzers and bells like you can at McDonald's or Burger King; you have to be able to think.

This is how Stephen Dunn, associate manager of the CityPlace store in Hartford, recalled his first impression of ABP. Dunn graduated from the University of Massachusetts in 1981 with a business degree in hotel/restaurant/travel administration, and he had experience working in full-service, fast-food, catering, and banquet situations. In 1985, he was recruited by a headhunter retained by ABP and accepted a position as the associate manager of the CityPlace store.

Ironically, Brian McEvoy, Dunn's partner and the general manager of the CityPlace store, never intended to work for ABP. After graduating from the University of Massachusetts in 1980 with a degree in history, followed by two years of teaching experience and a brief stint in the Navy, he viewed his original meeting with Shaich as a "practice interview." Later, impressed with the company, he took an entry-level job as an associate manager. At the start of the Partner/Manager Program Experiment, he had been with the company for three years.

Gary Aronson, the general manager of the Burlington Mall store, dropped out of college after one semester, and worked for Kentucky Fried Chicken for eight years before joining ABP in 1983 as an associate manager. He explained, "I switched jobs because I saw a lot of opportunity for me at a place like this. I didn't feel that the management team I was training with was that experienced, and I knew I'd find a way to shine real quickly."

Aronson's associate manager, Frank Ciampa, graduated from Bentley College in 1984 with a bachelor's degree in marketing management and an associate's degree in accounting. He joined ABP in 1985 as a manager trainee—in the hope that he could use this position as a stepping stone to a job in the corporate side of the business. He admitted:

If you'd asked me a year ago what I wanted to be after working here for several months, it sure wasn't to be a partner/manager. But since I've been working with Gary under the Partner/Manager Program, my whole mentality has changed. Now, I'm in no hurry to work in the office—I enjoy being a manager.

Managers' Activities During the Experiment "Len tells people that I run the place like a family deli, and I suppose that could be true," Aronson admitted. Both his wife and Ciampa's mother worked in the store, and Ciampa's father, a manufacturing equipment mechanic, helped with maintenance.

Originally, Aronson employed two associate managers. When the experiment began, however, he took the opportunity to have one of the two transferred to another unit. He explained that, according to the program, he didn't need three managers to run the store. "It means that Frank and I have to work longer hours," he conceded, "but it's worth it." The Burlington Mall store was open from 9:00 A.M. until 10:00 P.M. Monday through Saturday, and 11:00 A.M. through 6:00 P.M. on Sunday.

During the experiment, Aronson took on a number of wholesale accounts, noting:

The store doesn't open until 9:00 A.M., but Frank and I get here by 4:30 or 5:00 most mornings to prepare our wholesale products. We've even begun to do a little catering. If we can keep the four or five accounts we've got right now, I bet we could make about $40,000 worth of sales next year just on the wholesale line.

Aronson and Ciampa also took advantage of the increased managerial responsibility called for in the program and initiated some money-saving repairs. Ciampa recalled:

During the first week of the experiment, we decided to knock out a platform built against one wall in order to make room for eight more seats in the cafe area. Of course, making this change wasn't high on the list of priorities for the company's construction department, so Au Bon Pain estimated it would cost $10,000. We found a guy who'd do it for only $3,000, and we did it right away.

Similarly, when it was time to repaint the store, headquarters esti-

mated it would cost $1,200 to paint one wall. We had the whole store painted ourselves for about $800.

At the same time, Aronson began calculating food cost on a monthly, rather than daily, basis. "It drives the people at headquarters crazy," he grinned, "but I'm running the best food cost of any of the stores. As long as I'm alert, and trust the people I'm working with, I've never had a problem with stealing or cheating." He added that the turnover rate in his store was close to 0%.

The CityPlace store was open from 6:30 A.M. until 6:00 P.M. Monday through Friday. It was closed on the weekends. McEvoy admitted, "I don't want to work 80 hours a week the way Gary does now. I'm starting to like having my weekends off." He alternated shifts among himself, Dunn, and Barbara Jones, his shift supervisor. Dunn observed:

Au Bon Pain provides us with a labor grid to guide us in making decisions about how many people to schedule to work at different times during the day. We generally employ more people than the grid specifies. For example, they say that in the morning we should be able to run the store with four people. We always try to schedule six in an attempt to decrease the amount of time it takes to fill a customer's order.

McEvoy added:

In order to schedule extra crew members to work during peak hours, we had to pay them more because they were only working a two-hour-long shift. However, having the extra workers allowed us to improve our service and decrease the time customers had to wait for their order, so it paid off in increased sales.

Approximately three months into the experiment, McEvoy and Dunn began a telephone express service. Under the new system, office workers called in orders of $25 or more, which they picked up a little while later. "It's a lot quicker than having to stand in line and wait while the order is filled, and it helps us to serve all our customers more efficiently," McEvoy explained. The telephone express service was currently available to only the office workers in the CityPlace building, but McEvoy was considering expanding it to other areas.

Managers' Evaluation of the Partner/Manager Program All four managers agreed that one of the program's benefits was less corporate supervision of the units. This change was most apparent in the new role assumed by the district managers. Schlesinger acted as the district manager for both stores, and Ciampa noted that he had visited the Burlington Mall store no more than three or four times in as many months, although he kept in contact over the telephone.

McEvoy predicted, "The district managers will become less like policemen, and more like advisors and coaches. Instead of being told 'You must do this,' managers will hear comments like 'How can we build sales?' and 'How can we improve the store?'"

Aronson added:

Some managers love to have the district manager come around so that he or she can admire how clean the floor is. Frank and I don't need that. We know exactly what to do. Having someone else around actually brought down the quality of our work because we were busy explaining everything.

Aronson and Ciampa believed that the program had the potential to reduce the tendency of many managers in the fast-food industry to move from one job to another, starting at the ground level each time and slowly working their way up. Aronson explained:

In most professions, if you're good at what you do, when you change jobs you start out making more money than you did before. The fast-food industry's mentality is different. For example, when I left International Food Services, I was the highest-paid manager there and I was working in the highest-volume store. But when I decided to join Au Bon Pain, I had to start at the ground floor again and work my way up. It's the same story everywhere. I had to take a $135/week cut in pay in addition to going through the emotional upheaval of moving from one job to another. The prevailing attitude seemed to be "Well, maybe you're a whiz with fried chicken, but you don't know anything about croissants."

Now, Ron and Len have realized that they can't operate the way the Wendys and the Burger Kings deal with people. To be successful in the future, this company will have to bring in established people who've shown that they can do the job. A manager with five or six years' experience in the fast-food industry has to be worth a lot more than someone just out of school. If we start paying people what they're worth, I believe we can pick up some prime-time players and make this a really interesting company.

Aronson felt that, in the past, some of the instability generated by managers moving from store to store was the result of decisions made at the company headquarters. He asserted:

Once a manager had a store running smoothly, BINGO! They suddenly wanted to transfer you to a problem store. The better a manager you were, the more problems you had to take care of. After a while you began to ask, "What am I? A clean-up crew?"

Dunn believed that holding back part of the managers' share of the incremental profits until the end of their contract would reduce the desire to store-hop. He said, "Now, I'm a lot less company oriented, and a lot more store oriented. I'm less willing to leave the unit where I'm working and move to another store." McEvoy pointed out, however, that "the way for an ambitious person to make even more money would be to move to a higher-volume store. Personally, I'm not interested in relocating right now, but the temptation is always there."

Despite the decreased corporate supervision of the units under the program, the managers still perceived a continuing corporate overemphasis on details and paperwork. Aronson complained:

There's too much emphasis on the detail end, not enough on the meat-and-potatoes end. The majority of my customers want good food, quality service, and they want it fast. But every time we've been mystery shopped during the experiment, we've received the same basic criticism. Although our overall score is quite high, the mystery shopper generally objects that the floor hasn't been swept. Frankly, during lunchtime this place is a zoo. If we tried to sweep then, we'd get complaints from the customers about the dust flying in their food.

McEvoy generally agreed with Aronson's point, but admitted that he was more concerned that he was close to reaching maximum output on much of his equipment.

Dunn brought up another issue:

Under this new program, an associate manager's greatest fear will be that everything that he or she can make or lose hinges on the partner/manager they're working with. The partner/manager calls the shots, that's the bottom line, even though you've got your money tied into this thing too.

The managers also discussed the length of their workweek. Aronson reported that he and Ciampa were each working an average of 80 hours per week—25 hours more per week than they had been working before.

Aronson recalled:

I knew that during the experiment I wouldn't have much time left over for anything else, and that was a real consideration. I finally told my family to put up with it for six months, and in the end I would make it worth their while. In the first 16 weeks, we had two days off. I've worked some days from 4:30 in the morning until 11:00 at night.

McEvoy and Dunn each worked 50 to 55 hours a week. McEvoy explained, "The amount of hours we're working hasn't really changed that much." Dunn added: "We work as long as it takes to get the job done. Whenever we've worked extra hours, it has been because we were understaffed, not because we decided to work long hours because of the experiment."

Dunn summarized his evaluation of the experiment:

To be blunt, parts of the program are good, and parts are bad. Burnout, particularly in this industry, is high.

If someone is going to be locked into this thing, and they're going to have the added pressure of knowing that their money—a large part of their share of the bonus—is tied up in whether or not they can last out their contract, well, in my opinion, that kind of stress could actually cause a person not to perform as well as they could. I'm not trying to be negative, but they've got to be careful who they choose to be managers and how they monitor them.

There are also the shift supervisors to deal with. A lot of them act like managers in every degree but in the paperwork, including sales building. In fact, when we began this experiment, Brian decided to pay our shift supervisor 2% of our half of the incremental profits. When other shift supervisors hear about the phenomenal amounts of money being made by the managers, how will that affect their motivation?

Finally, even if this program dramatically improves the quality of our applicants for managerial positions, what are we going to do about the turnover rate for lower-level employees? It's close to 400% a year in this store. High turnover is an industry norm. How does that affect the quality of the customer experience?

Results During the experiment, sales in the Burlington Mall and CityPlace stores increased dramatically. The operating statements for both units during periods 1 to 7 and during the experiment (periods 8 to 13) are shown in Exhibit 4. Exhibit 5 summarizes the

stores' performance against the company's plan and compares it to their 1985 performance. While both McEvoy's and Aronson's base salaries remained at $500 per week, their actual, annual earnings were closer to $50,000 and $70,000, respectively.[4] A memo outlining the final distribution of profits is presented in Exhibit 6.

The Decision Shaich considered the experiment a resounding success, and suggested that:

The problems don't lie in the concept, which I'm convinced is basically sound. The challenges will be in its execution. There are a lot of implementation issues we still have to deal with—that's one of the costs of being in the vanguard on an issue like this—but I think the potential gain is worth the risks.

The key to success will be for us to get out of the way once this thing starts. We've developed the concept, and now we have to stand back and let the managers operate it. In time, I believe we'll witness startling results. In my opinion, at least 25% more sales can be made. Len puts the figure closer to 50%, and Louis Kane thinks it's even higher. I'd love to flip the switch tomorrow and set the program in motion.

Schlesinger added, "In time, this plan will be broadly applicable to any multiunit service concept on the face of the earth."

Aronson was more guarded, asserting:

With the right people, this program can work. But to suddenly turn it over to all the stores—personally, I

---

[4]Art Veves, Burger King's regional director of Human Resources in Boston, reported in a telephone conversation that the average Burger King manager earned between $24,000 and $30,000 annually, plus a bonus of approximately $2,500. The salary expectations for a McDonald's manager were roughly equivalent to these figures.

think that would be a big mistake. There are some people who would try and squeeze it dry. In the short term they could show fantastic results, food and labor costs down, etc., but in the long term you wind up with underportioning and dirty stores.

McEvoy agreed:

I don't think they should roll out this program to every store right away, especially if they're hiring a lot of new managers. It takes a while for a person to settle in. The strict deadlines for solving problems set out in the Partner/Manager document would put too much pressure on new managers who aren't used to handling everything by themselves. Holding them accountable could blow them right out of the water.

Ciampa added:

Even under the best of circumstances, the company will be lucky if 50% of the people working for them now make it under the new program. People are used to getting a lot of supervision. It used to be that the louder you cried, the more attention you got.

Dunn added a final caution:

During the experiment, we've had phenomenal sales growth. But, and I've said this to Len and Ron, 85% of that growth would have occurred in any case because of the type of individuals Brian and I are. It just happened that the experiment began when we were starting to get things together. Specifically, at that point, Brian and I had been working together for nine months. We were comfortable with each other and we knew our customers. It was the middle of the summer and we were fully staffed because a lot of high school kids wanted summer jobs. Our equipment was functioning correctly for the first time in a long time, and we had just converted from an inefficient cafeteria-style system to one in which the person working the cash register automatically keyed in the sandwich order to the kitchen.

When asked if they planned to sign up for the long-term deal, Aronson, Ciampa, and McEvoy indicated they would if certain conditions were met (e.g., Aronson would sign up for only a one-year deal). Dunn replied, "No comment."

After a meeting in early January, during which he reviewed both his own and Shaich's comments and the reactions of the managers involved in the experiment, Schlesinger concluded:

From an MBA viewpoint, it's an interesting situation. We've got two hand-picked managers and six months of data on which to base a decision whether or not to shake up this whole company. Are we foolish if we grab at this opportunity?

EXHIBIT 1

COMPANY-OWNED STORES

Location	City	State	Year Opened	Square Footage	Number of Managers
Faneuil Hall Marketplace	Boston	MA	1977	1,400	4
Burlington Mall	Burlington	MA	1978	1,400	2
Logan Airport	Boston	MA	1981	800	4
Cherry Hill Mall	Cherry Hill	NJ	1984	1,000	2
Harvard Square	Cambridge	MA	1983	2,500	4
Park Plaza	Boston	MA	1984	1,000	4
Arsenal Mall	Watertown	MA	1984	2,300	3
CityPlace	Hartford	CT	1984	2,400	2
2 Penn Center	Philadelphia	PA	1985	2,700	2
Riverside Square	Hackensack	NJ	1984	1,800	3
Crossgates Mall	Albany	NY	1984	1,400	1
Cape Cod Mall	Hyannis	MA	1985	1,000	3
Crystal Mall	Waterford	CT	1984	600	2
Rockefeller Center	New York	NY	1985	2,500	5
Prudential Center	Boston	MA	1985	3,000	4
Filene's	Boston	MA	1984	800	3
Filene's (Franklin St.)	Boston	MA	1985	50	4
Filene's (Basement)	Boston	MA	1984	600	
Copley Place	Boston	MA	1984	2,500	4
Copley Place (Stuart St.)	Boston	MA	1985	1,000	2
Maine Mall	South Portland	ME	1983	500	1
Cookie Jar	Boston	MA	1980	700	2
Newington	Newington	NH	1984	800	2
Kendall Square	Cambridge	MA	1986	2,600	3
Dewey Square	Boston	MA	1986	2,400	2

EXHIBIT 2

WEEKLY MANAGER SALARIES FOR GIVEN WEEKLY SALES VOLUMES (COMPENSATION SYSTEM PRIOR TO THE PARTNER/MANAGER PROGRAM)

Volume/ Week	General Manager (Base = $375)		Senior Associate Manager (Base = $350)		First Associate Manager (Base = $341.54)	
	Volume Adjustment	Weekly Total	Volume Adjustment	Weekly Total	Volume Adjustment	Weekly Total
$1–4,000	$ 0.00	$375.00	$ 0.00	$350.00	$ 0.00	$341.54
5,000	13.12	388.12	5.25	355.25	2.53	344.07
10,000	78.75	453.75	31.50	381.50	15.21	356.75
15,000	118.00	493.00	47.25	397.25	22.81	364.35
20,000	157.50	532.50	63.00	413.00	30.42	371.96
25,000	174.38	549.38	69.75	419.75	33.67	375.21
30,000	191.25	566.25	76.50	426.50	36.93	378.47
35,000	208.13	583.13	83.25	433.25	40.19	381.73
40,000	225.00	600.00	90.00	440.00	43.46	385.00
45,000	241.88	616.88	96.75	446.75	46.71	388.25
50,000	258.75	633.75	103.50	453.50	49.97	391.51

To compute the weekly salary for general managers, the following formulae were used:
- Low-volume store: base pay + .013125 (volume − $4,000)
- Medium-volume store: base pay + $78.75 + .00785 (volume − $10,000)
- High-volume store: base pay + $157.50 + .003375 (volume − $20,000)

For senior associate managers, the formulae were:
- Low-volume store: base pay + .00525 (volume − $4,000)
- Medium-volume store: base pay + $31.50 + .00315 (volume − $10,000)
- High-volume store: base pay + $63.00 + .00135 (volume − $20,000)

For first associate managers, the formulae were:
- Low-volume store: base pay + .002535 (volume − $4,000)
- Medium-volume store: base pay + $15.21 + .001521 (volume − $10,000)
- High-volume store: base pay + $30.42 + .000652 (volume − $20,000)

EXHIBIT 3

PEGS (PRODUCT, ENVIRONMENT, GREAT SERVICE)

STORE NAME: _____ # _____   COMPLETED BY: _____

DAY: s m t w th f s DATE: _____ / ___ / ___   SHIFT MANAGER: _____

TIME: ____:____ am/pm   MGR. SIGNATURE: _____

PRODUCT	Yes	No

I. ALL PRODUCTS AVAILABLE ALL DAY. SIGN SPECIFIES SOUPS/SANDWICHES AS OF 10:00 A.M. (Especially watch for fresh O.J., all croissants including almonds, big breads, and petit pain/hearth rolls.)

II. ALL ITEMS MUST BE FRESH AND PREPARED TO ABP SPECIFICATIONS. NO BAKED GOODS OUT OF THE OVEN MORE THAN SIX HOURS (COOKIES AND MUFFINS EIGHT HOURS.) NO WARM CROISSANT IN OR ON THE WARMER FOR MORE THAN 4 HOURS. (Check times on trays and talk with customers about the quality of food when completing #VI. Sample different items.)

III. TEMPERATURES: SOUPS 155-165°, WARM CROISSANT MINIMUM OF 145°, COLD BEVERAGES 36-42°, HOT BEVERAGES 185°. (Must be checked with a thermometer.)

ENVIRONMENT

I. NOTHING ON FLOORS OR CARPET MORE THAN FIVE MINUTES, BOTH FLOORS AND CARPET MUST BE CLEAN. (Identify a specific piece of trash and note the time...recheck after five minutes.)

II. DISPLAY PRODUCTS: ALL ITEMS PROPER SIZE, COLOR, CLEAN AND ORGANIZED. (All items properly identified with product description cards, observe.)

III. NO CONDIMENTS STATIONS PUT OF STOCK. (Salt, pepper, sugar, sweet & low, stirrers, napkins, creamers with ice or icepack, comment cards, menus, water, cups, straws.)

IV. ALL UNOCCUPIED SEATS/TABLES CLEANED WITHIN TWO MINUTES. ALL TABLES BALANCED PROPERLY SO THEY DON'T TILT WHEN FOOD IS PLACED ON THEM. (Identify a specific table and note the time...recheck after two minutes. Actually check five tables to make sure they don't tilt.)

V. BATHROOMS CLEANED AND STOCKED ALL DAY. (Toilet paper, soap, towel.)

GREAT SERVICE

I. NO MORE THAN THREE MINUTES IN LINE. (Identify, by description, a minimum of five customers. List their entry time, counter departure time, and when appropriate, the time they leave the sandwich pick-up area. Calculate the difference for total wait time.)

II. PLEASANT GREETING AND EYE CONTACT THREE SECONDS OR LESS WHEN A CUSTOMER HAS REACHED THE COUNTER. REGISTER CLOSED SIGNS CLEAN AND IN USE. (Observe a transaction at each register.)

III. WHAT THE CUSTOMER ORDERED IS WHAT THEY RECEIVE. CORRECT CHANGE GIVEN FOR THEIR PURCHASE. (Talk with at least five customers. Sandwich expediter calls out ticket number and reads off entire sandwich order. Observe.)

IV. BOTH CSR / MGR EXHIBIT A "WANT TO SERVE" ATTITUDE. (All register people must be able to speak and understand English. Talk with at least five customers.)

SCORE THE NUMBER OF ACTUAL "YES" OUT OF TWELVE   /12

customer description	error time	leave time	leave sand. bar	sand. bar wait	total time serve

GENERAL COMMENTS: _____
_____
_____

EXHIBIT 4A

STORE OPERATING STATEMENT, BURLINGTON MALL (PRE-EXPERIMENT): PERCENTAGE OF NET SALES (NUMBERS HAVE BEEN DISGUISED)

	Periods						
	1	2	3	4	5	6	7
Regular sales	100.0	98.5	98.9	100.0	100.0	100.0	100.0
Wholesale	0.0	0.0	0.0	0.0	0.0	0.0	0.0
Promotions	0.0	1.5	1.1	0.0	0.0	0.0	0.0
Net sales	100.0	100.0	100.0	100.0	100.0	100.0	100.0
Discounts	0.4	0.4	0.6	0.7	1.0	0.9	0.5
Net net sales	99.6	99.6	99.4	99.3	99.0	99.1	99.5
Management	9.1	9.8	11.7	11.4	7.8	9.0	8.9
Shift supervisor	0.0	0.0	0.0	0.0	0.0	1.2	1.1
Crew	15.1	14.3	14.9	13.8	14.1	13.2	13.9
Benefits	2.6	3.0	2.9	4.1	3.1	1.6	3.1
Total labor	26.8	27.1	29.5	29.3	25.0	25.0	27.0
Food cost	29.4	30.1	31.1	30.0	30.5	30.2	32.0
Paper cost	1.8	1.2	1.4	1.2	2.0	1.4	1.8
Controllables	1.5	1.4	1.1	2.0	2.1	1.8	2.3
Utilities	1.9	2.8	2.3	2.3	1.8	2.1	2.2
Controllable profit	38.2	37.0	34.0	34.5	37.6	38.6	34.2
Fixed expenses	3.4	3.6	3.5	3.4	3.0	3.1	3.3
Occupancy	9.3	9.5	9.6	9.5	12.3	10.3	10.4
Store profit	25.5	23.9	20.9	21.6	22.3	25.2	20.5

EXHIBIT 4B

**STORE OPERATING STATEMENT, BURLINGTON MALL (EXPERIMENT): PERCENTAGE OF NET SALES
(NUMBERS HAVE BEEN DISGUISED)**

	Periods					
	8	9	10	11	12	13
Regular sales	97.0	97.1	96.0	95.2	93.9	95.8
Wholesale	3.0	2.9	4.0	4.8	6.1	4.2
Promotions	0.0	0.0	0.0	0.0	0.0	0.0
Net sales	100.0	100.0	100.0	100.0	100.0	100.0
Discounts	0.4	0.3	0.2	0.2	0.2	0.2
Net net sales	99.6	99.7	99.8	99.8	99.8	99.8
Management	6.4	5.6	5.7	5.4	4.9	3.7
Shift supervisor	1.8	0.8	0.1	1.3	2.4	2.3
Crew	13.0	12.9	12.9	12.5	11.9	11.3
Benefits	2.0	1.7	1.7	1.6	1.6	1.0
Total labor	23.2	21.0	20.4	20.8	20.8	18.3
Food cost	28.7	29.1	29.7	29.4	29.4	28.6
Paper cost	1.7	1.5	2.0	1.6	1.9	1.7
Controllables	1.3	0.8	1.1	0.9	1.1	1.5
Utilities	3.4	2.7	2.8	2.2	1.3	0.4
Controllable profit	41.3	44.6	43.8	44.9	45.3	49.3
Fixed expenses	3.0	2.9	2.8	2.8	2.4	2.0
Occupancy	11.8	9.2	9.5	9.5	11.2	9.2
Store profit	26.5	32.5	31.5	32.6	31.7	38.1

EXHIBIT 4C

**STORE OPERATING STATEMENT, CITYPLACE (PRE-EXPERIMENT): PERCENTAGE OF NET SALES
(NUMBERS HAVE BEEN DISGUISED)**

	Periods						
	1	2	3	4	5	6	7
Regular sales	100.0	96.5	97.8	100.0	100.0	100.0	100.0
Wholesale	0.0	0.0	0.0	0.0	0.0	0.0	0.0
Promotions	0.0	3.5	2.2	0.0	0.0	0.0	0.0
Net sales	100.0	100.0	100.0	100.0	100.0	100.0	100.0
Discounts	0.3	0.3	0.4	0.4	0.3	0.3	0.4
Net net sales	99.7	99.7	99.6	99.6	99.7	99.7	99.6
Management	7.0	6.8	7.3	6.5	7.1	7.1	6.8
Shift supervisor	1.8	2.0	1.9	2.1	2.3	2.0	1.5
Crew	12.2	13.1	13.6	13.2	12.4	13.2	14.6
Benefits	2.3	2.9	2.1	2.9	2.3	2.3	2.8
Total labor	23.3	24.8	24.9	24.7	24.1	24.6	25.7
Food cost	28.0	29.1	29.9	31.2	27.5	29.1	30.9
Paper cost	2.4	2.7	2.8	2.8	3.1	3.2	3.2
Controllables	1.3	1.5	1.9	3.8	2.0	4.7	1.8
Utilities	1.6	1.5	2.1	1.6	1.8	1.7	1.7
Controllable profit	43.1	40.1	38.0	35.5	41.2	36.4	36.3
Fixed expenses	8.5	8.9	9.9	8.3	8.8	9.1	7.8
Occupancy	12.4	12.9	12.4	12.2	12.1	12.1	11.7
Store profit	22.2	18.3	15.7	15.0	20.3	15.2	16.8

EXHIBIT 4D

STORE OPERATING STATEMENT, CITYPLACE (EXPERIMENT): PERCENTAGE OF NET SALES (NUMBERS HAVE BEEN DISGUISED)

	Periods					
	8	9	10	11	12	13
Regular sales	100.0	100.0	100.0	100.0	98.6	98.1
Wholesale	0.0	0.0	0.0	0.0	1.4	1.9
Promotions	0.0	0.0	0.0	0.0	0.0	0.0
Net sales	100.0	100.0	100.0	100.0	100.0	100.0
Discounts	0.3	0.3	0.3	0.4	0.5	0.3
Net net sales	99.7	99.7	99.7	99.6	99.5	99.7
Management	6.0	5.8	6.2	5.0	5.7	5.7
Shift supervisor	1.9	2.0	2.0	1.7	1.9	1.8
Crew	14.6	14.6	13.4	15.0	13.9	14.3
Benefits	2.2	3.0	2.1	3.0	2.1	2.0
Total labor	24.7	25.4	23.7	24.7	23.6	23.8
Food cost	27.6	29.6	29.6	29.9	31.0	30.6
Paper cost	2.8	3.1	2.9	2.9	3.0	3.1
Controllables	2.6	2.3	1.6	2.1	1.7	1.6
Utilities	1.2	1.7	9.6	0.6	9.7	3.8
Controllable profit	40.8	37.6	32.3	39.4	30.5	36.8
Fixed expenses	6.9	7.6	11.3	7.2	5.9	7.4
Occupancy	9.6	10.3	9.7	9.2	13.0	8.9
Store profit	24.3	19.7	11.3	23.0	11.6	20.5

EXHIBIT 5

PERFORMANCE AGAINST PLAN AND PRIOR YEAR (CURRENT DOLLARS)

		Periods 1–7	Periods 8–13
Sales vs. plan	Burlington	(11,695)	56,719
	CityPlace	12,903	69,311
	Total	1,208	126,030
Sales vs. last year	Burlington	(1,600)	70,478
	CityPlace	33,512	93,558
	Total	31,912	164,036
Controllable profits vs. plan	Burlington	(3,844)	53,562
	CityPlace	4,613	18,580
	Total	769	72,142
Controllable profits vs. last year	Burlington	(2)	57,449
	CityPlace	2,706	29,741
	Total	2,704	87,190

EXHIBIT 6

PARTNER/MANAGER PROFIT DISTRIBUTION

MEMORANDUM

TO: Gary Aronson, Frank Ciampa, Steve Dunn, Brian McEvoy

FROM: Len Schlesinger

DATE: January 15, 1987

RE: Partner/Manager Profit Distributions

cc   Ron Shaich

        Louis Kane

	Burlington	CityPlace
Store Lease Payment	$127,526.25	$103,619.50
Fixed Asset Additions	110.62	45.49
Percentage Rent	3,556.28	0.00
TOTAL DUE ABP	131,193.35	103,664.99
CREDITS		
Period 8	23,225.00	23,680.65
Period 9	28,740.00	20,218.65
Period 10	27,705.00	23,444.46
Period 11	29,445.00	23,809.65
Period 12	33,172.00	24,071.65
Period 13	45,122.00	23,024.65
TOTAL CREDITS	187,409.00	138,249.71
LESS TOTAL DUE ABP	131,193.35	103,664.99
PROFIT POOL	56,215.65	34,584.72
ABP Share	28,107.82	17,292.36
P/M Share	19,675.48	12,104.65
Assoc. P/M/ Share	8,432.35	5,187.71
P/M Weekly Wage		
Salary	500.00	500.00
Share	819.81	504.36
TOTAL	1,319.81	1,004.36
ANNUALIZED	68,630.12	52,226.72
Assoc. P/M Weekly Wage		
Salary	400.00	400.00
Share	351.35	216.15
TOTAL	751.35	616.15
ANNUALIZED	39,070.20	32,039.80

AN INTRODUCTION TO THE PARTNER/MANAGER PROGRAM

I. Company Objectives

As Au Bon Pain moves into the future, we must develop for our bakery/cafe managers a compensation/incentive system that is second to none in our industry segment. The foundation of ABP's success is talented people who achieve results and, in turn, share in the financial rewards of their efforts. The Partner/Manager Program provides the opportunity for a select group of managers to be in business for themselves, but not by themselves. The company provides support by monitoring the quality standards, which will be vigorously enforced, and by refining and expanding our retail concept and system. Our ability to attract talented and enthusiastic people who thrive in our environment is nothing less than the prime ingredient necessary to achieve all the goals that we have set.

Au Bon Pain believes fundamentally that the individual bakery/cafe units' sales and profitability are strongly influenced by their retail operations' quality. Furthermore, we believe that the retail operations' quality is directly affected by the presence of:

- A management team that truly cares about the quality of the customer experience
- A management team that has experience and is committed to working at a specific unit for an extended period of time
- A management team that is committed to the Au Bon Pain operating system but that is flexible enough to make some of its own decisions and adaptations to build sales in its market
- A crew with strong interrelationships and a commitment to the management team, and thus to the customer
- An explicit focus on managing outputs (service, sales, food costs, controllable costs, labor costs) vs. inputs
- A store-manager/company "you win-we win" approach

Developing these traits has been very difficult, however, due to Au Bon Pain's internal structure and to the following dynamics of the fast-food labor market, specifically:

Drafted in the Spring of 1986 by Len Schlesinger and Ron Shaich. Abridged by Research Assistant Lucy N. Lytle under the supervision of Professor W. Earl Sasser, January 1987.

- A managerial labor pool that forces us to take more "chances" in hiring entry-level talent, in addition to significant turnover at the associate manager level
- A centralized, system-wide orientation toward the operations and marketing functions in our bakery/cafes which currently stifles our ability to exercise initiative at the store level
- Excessive crew turnover and sloppy hiring, which severely degrade the quality of the customer experience and exacerbate the day-to-day problems of the management team

To address these problems and to move toward reaching an idealized version of our retail operations, we are proposing a radically reconceptualized framework for managing human resources in Au Bon Pain bakery/cafe units. It is titled the Partner/Manager Program.

II. Objectives of the Partner/Manager Program

- To develop a management compensation system that enhances dramatically our ability to attract and retain the finest managers in the industry
- To shift our organizational focus from being promoted to district manager as the desired career path to achieving partner/manager status (a terminal general manager's position)
- To increase dramatically a store management team's tenure and thus its feelings of "local ownership"
- To lessen our top-down management approach to retail operations by:
  1. increasing local unit responsibilities for decision making and execution, with an accompanying reward system that increases management commitment to unit results
  2. encouraging partner/managers to "push" the corporate office to respond to local needs
- To reduce dramatically district manager supervision of retail stores and to shift the district manager's role from a policeman/checker to a business/sales consultant
- To provide a human resource mechanism that frees ABP to grow at an accelerated rate without great pain ("hyperphased growth")
- To maximize simultaneously store-level profits, ABP return on investment, and management salaries
- To provide the opportunity for our partner/managers to build financial "nest eggs"
- To provide job security to those people who perform for ABP and for themselves

III. Management of the Partner/Manager Experiment

The experiment will run for six periods, from July 13 until December 20, 1986. Len Schlesinger will assume direct responsibility as the district manager for the two stores selected to participate.

Experimentation at the Burlington Mall store will test our abilities to revive a mature shopping mall location and to tap into area offices as a growth vehicle in the face of increased competition. The CityPlace experiment will provide us with considerable data on how best to leverage an office building location to its fullest potential.

IV. The Economics of the Partner/Manager Program

A. Each store's general manager will be reclassified as a partner/manager at a base salary of $500 per week. Each will be authorized to hire/retain one associate manager at a base salary of $400 per week. Any additional management support can be added at the partner/manager's discretion. All managers must, however, take their bonus (i.e., their 50% share of the store's incremental profits) from a fixed pool.

B. Au Bon Pain will determine a "store-lease" payment required to support a unit's fixed expenses, corporate overhead, and reasonable profit expectations. During the experiment, this payment will be $127,526 for the Burlington Mall unit, and $103,619 for the CityPlace unit.

C. The store-lease payment will be guaranteed for the period of the experiment, with the following exceptions, which will require adjustments:

1. The addition of fixed assets will trigger an increase in the store-lease payment of: $.25 \times$ total fixed asset cost.
    Example: A new counter is added to Hartford at a cost of $10,000. On an annual basis, this addition would increase the store-lease payment by $2,500.

2. Additional sales, which trigger a percentage rent clause in the real estate lease, will increase the store-lease payment by the percentage specified in the real estate lease.
    Example: The rent for the Burlington unit assumes that the store will achieve the 1986 plan. All sales over this plan will increase the store-lease payment to Au Bon Pain by 8% of the incremental sales dollars.

D. Profits will be distributed to the partner/manager and associate manager as follows: actual store controllable prof-

its – store-lease payment = incremental profits or losses.

> incremental profits $\times .50$ = ABP share
> incremental profits $\times .35$ = partner/manager share
> incremental profits $\times .15$ = associate manager share

E. The partner/manager's and associate manager's share of the incremental profits will be distributed at the close of each period. Au Bon Pain will hold in reserve $7,500 for the partner/manager and $2,500 for the associate manager until the end of their contracts.

F. For the Partner/Manager Program Experiment, profit distributions will occur after the final review of the experiment is completed (approximately February 1, 1987).

V. Supervising and Managing the Partner/Manager Experiment

A. The two stores will be "mystery shopped" at least once a week, and the mystery-shopping reports will serve as critical indicators of store-level quality standards.

B. The two stores will be subjected to three "white-glove" inspections. These will be conducted by an independent ABP auditor who is not connected with the experiment. The inspections will cover all phases of store operations and will be a major input to the overall evaluation of the experiment.

C. The two stores will be expected to comply with the 100% customer satisfaction "moment-of-truth" indicators and will be evaluated against them.

D. The partner/manager, associate manager, or a certified ABP shift supervisor must be on duty in the store during all store hours. The partner/manager and associate manager must each work in the store a minimum of 50 hours a week, and the partner/manager and/or the associate manager must be on duty in the store during 90% of its operating hours.

E. Au Bon Pain reserves the right to discharge, remove, or replace the partner/manager or associate manager at any time. All store managers, crew, and shift supervisors will remain employees of Au Bon Pain.

VI. "The Rules"

Violation of the following conditions will engender a default and/or the termination of the partner/manager's and/or associate manager's experiment.

A. The partner/manager shall use the Au Bon Pain bakery/cafe premises solely for the operation of the business, keep the business open and in normal operation for such minimum hours and days as ABP may from time to time prescribe, and refrain from using or suffering the use of the premises for any other purpose or activity at any time.

B. The partner/manager shall maintain the bakery/cafe in the highest degree of sanitation, repair, and condition. In connection therewith, he or she shall make such additions, alterations, repairs, and replacements thereto as ABP may require, including without limitation, periodically repainting the premises; repairing impaired equipment, furniture, and fixtures; and replacing obsolete signs.

C. The partner/manager further understands, acknowledges, and agrees that—to ensure that all products produced and sold by the bakery/cafe meet ABP's high standards of taste, texture, appearance, and freshness, and to protect ABP's goodwill and proprietary marks—all products shall be prepared by only properly trained personnel in strict accordance with the Retail Baker's Training Program.

D. The partner/manager shall meet and maintain the highest health standards and ratings applicable to the bakery/cafe operation.

E. The partner/manager shall operate the bakery/cafe in conformity with such uniform methods, standards, and specifications as ABP may from time to time prescribe to ensure that the highest degree of quality and service is uniformly maintained.

F. Unless transferred at Au Bon Pain's request, the partner/manager and/or associate manager will not be eligible for the profit-sharing disbursements unless he or she completes the full time-period of the experiment. If transferred, the affected manager will receive a pro-rated share based on the percentage of total controllable profit contributed while he or she was employed in the store.

The partner/manager agrees:

1. To maintain in sufficient supply, and use at all times, only such products, materials, ingredients, supplies, and paper goods as conform with ABP's standards and specifications. The partner/manager shall not deviate from these standards by using nonconforming items.

2. To employ a sufficient number of employees to meet the standards of service and quality that ABP may prescribe.

3. To comply with all applicable federal, state, and local laws, rules, and regulations with respect to ABP employees.

4. To permit ABP or its agents or representatives to enter the premises at any time for the purposes of conducting inspections; to cooperate fully with ABP's agents or representatives in such inspections by rendering such assistance as they may reasonably request; and, upon notice from ABP or its agents or representatives, to take such steps as may be necessary to correct immediately any deficiencies detected during such inspections.

The partner/manager agrees further that failure to comply with the requirements of this paragraph will cause ABP irreparable injury and will result in the subject termination of his or her employment and the loss of any incremental profit funds held in reserve.

In addition, the partner/manager shall be deemed to be in default and ABP may, at its option, terminate this agreement without affording him or her any opportunity to cure the default, upon the occurrence of any of the following events:

A. The operation of the bakery/cafe results in a threat or danger to public health or safety that is not corrected by the partner/manager within one week of notice.

B. The partner/manager is convicted of a felony or any other crime or offense that is reasonably likely, in the sole opinion of ABP, to affect adversely the ABP system or goodwill associated therewith.

C. The partner/manager fails to comply with the covenants in A–E above provided, however, that for any correctable failure he or she has 30 days after notice from ABP to correct the failure.

D. The partner/manager, after correcting any default, engages in the same activity, giving rise to the same default, whether or not the deficiency is corrected after notice.

E. The partner/manager repeatedly is in default of or fails to comply substantially with any of the requirements imposed by this agreement, whether or not the deficiencies are corrected after notice.

CASE

CUMBERLAND HOTELS(C)

Planning for Quality

Roland T. Rust, Anthony J. Zahorik,
and Timothy L. Keiningham

INTRODUCTION

Ron Nichols, Vice President of Quality Planning for Cumberland Hotels, Incorporated (CHI) was excited. His staff was ready to prepare the last draft of CHI's business plan for the next year, and Ron was feeling elated that this plan promised one of the best years that the firm had experienced in some time. Since arriving at CHI three years ago from a large West Coast hotel chain, he had worked hard to develop a new planning process in the organization. His goal for the process was to help the organization develop strategies which would help it break out from its customary place in the pack by changing the static thinking of everyone in the company and instilling a true, customer-oriented culture. He had met initial resistance, but had gradually convinced even the rank and file that their interests would be best served by making the effort to carefully develop fact-based strategies that would move the organization forward. Moreover, because his charge from management also included a warning to

keep profits up, he wanted to make sure that his spending on quality had impact on the firm's financial health. This required that management also begin considering the return on quality from its spending.

The first two plans he attempted fell far short of his goals, largely because relevant managers throughout the organization had to learn his systematic process and become convinced that management was serious about quality and customer service. This plan was significantly better. Ron felt that his people had finally "gotten it," and they were excited about the entire exercise, although they still needed training to know what to do about infusing the empowerment of employees, internal marketing and ROQ analysis throughout the organization. Top managers were now firmly committed to the profitable improvement of quality, and were eager to teach the necessary skills to the rest of the organization. They felt confident that it could be done. Employee morale was generally good, and, thanks to careful preparation by Nichols' staff,

This case was prepared by Roland T. Rust, Anthony J. Zahorik, and Timothy L. Keiningham. Some information in the case is real, but has been disguised to protect proprietary interests. Cumberland Hotels is a fictitious brand, and any similarity to any existing company is unintentional.

employees were generally eager to play a larger role in the running of the organization.

Now Ron Nichols was eager to assemble all of their hard work into a finished product to be presented to the board of directors in two weeks.

CUMBERLAND HOTEL'S SITUATION

Cumberland Hotels had been founded in 1959 by Cook Welch as a single hotel and restaurant catering to business and leisure travellers in Nashville, Tennessee. Over the years the chain had grown to consist of 24 units across the Southeastern U.S. with annual sales of over $57 million. (See Table 2 for this year's projected income statement.) The firm had not built any new units in four years, since an earlier economic boom in the Southeast, followed by an economic downturn, had caused the market to stagnate with significant overcapacity, and with limited growth projected for the next few years as well. Cumberland's occupancy rates were currently averaging only about 60%, although it was more profitable than several other rivals, and had held its market share at about 2.5% for the last four years—up from 1.9% before its last building phase. However, a few of its primary competitors had begun serious quality improvement programs, and Ron Nichols saw that he would have to similarly upgrade CHI's standards or it would rapidly be at a serious competitive disadvantage.

To assure that quality planning decisions were based on facts, CHI had begun surveying samples of recent guests to determine their satisfaction with all important aspects of the firm's services. A random sample of customers was routinely surveyed by mail within a week of their stays on a continuous basis. Results were tabulated by unit, and bimonthly results were sent to managers. The MIS department was working to ensure that managers received these results within one month of collection. The collected data were also used for ROQ analyses of current and proposed quality improvement efforts.

In a highly competitive market CHI had been able to keep within range of its toughest competition by upgrading its restaurants and installing several innovative services for its business customers. CHI was in pretty good shape financially to make additional improvements. The firm had strong cash reserves and a good credit rating which meant that the firm would be able to finance several projects under consideration for next year.

Corporate Goals

In fact, Nichols had been brought in by CHI's board, because of some serious quality improvements made by two of its major competitors, Arlington Inns and Devon Hotels, and the feeling of some new shareholders that CHI had the potential for significant growth. Nichols' charge had been to bring the quality movement to Cumberland's organization, and to find ways to grow the business in spite of the slow growth of the Southeastern market overall.

CHI's corporate mission statement was written by Cook Welch many years earlier, and stated that "Cumberland Hotel's mission is to provide travelers with comfortable, reasonably priced lodging and dining. We strive to provide an atmosphere of old-fashioned Southern hospitality while maintaining modern standards of efficiency. Cumberland Hotels also believes that it must treat its employees with the same courtesy and respect that it wishes to show to its guests." This mission still provided overall direction for the firm, but CHI had become a bit more specialized over time. In particular, the chain's comfortable, low-priced hotels and restaurants had become favorite stopovers for business travelers, and CHI began to cater to this market segment by establishing corporate discounts and by being one of the first area chains to have fax machines available for use by clients.

As stated earlier, specific corporate objectives for the next year were for aggressive growth. In particular, the firm wanted to increase its market share to 3% within two years without building any more units, and to increase its sales by at least 10% next year—all while maintaining profits of at least 5% of sales. Management specifically wanted to take a longer, customer-oriented view in achieving these increases, significantly improving customer satisfaction with the chain while maintaining at least a 15% return on quality. Top management felt that these rather stiff objectives were reachable, and early in the planning process challenged the firm's managers to come up with some innovative ways to deliver on these goals.

THE PLANNING PROCESS AT CHI

The planning cycle at CHI began with the February directors' meeting at which the final numbers on the previous year's performance were presented and the current year's plans were reviewed. The general direction of the firm for the next two to three years was discussed as the basis for setting corporate goals for the following year. The president of the company worked with his planning staff to translate the board's wishes into firm objectives for the next year (contingent, of course, upon the current year's performance). The general spirit of these objectives was then communicated to department and unit managers to assist them in their planning processes. The planning process was coordinated by the vice presidents of marketing and of planning and strategy, but was designed to involve all those in the organization who would have to take initiatives and make decisions.

Each unit manager was expected to understand the market conditions of his or her unit—the economic environment, competitive behavior, and consumer trends—and to report them back to the home office. For efficiency CHI's units were highly standardized, and individual units were not allowed to deviate from the corporate operating pattern. Nevertheless, individual unit managers were considered to be excellent sources of information and creative ideas, given their constant exposure to customers. They were therefore expected to meet with corporate staff early in the process to propose and request permission for marketing initiatives which would generate growth and profits in their own markets. Good generalizable ideas were considered possibilities for inclusion into the general marketing plan for the entire chain.

DATA COLLECTION

Nichols' staff had compiled a lot of data during the year to assist the corporate planners, something that had been sorely lacking in the past. Corporate staffers had regularly monitored government forecasts, industry trade association figures, news clippings, and other secondary sources to obtain solid information about the market and CHI's competitors. They had also analyzed CHI's own customer survey data, and had commissioned several marketing research studies to provide information about key planning issues. As results of all these efforts became available they had been passed on to relevant parties involved in the planning process.

The Industry

The lodging industry in the area of the Southeast covered by CHI had experienced slow, steady growth for the last few years, and was expected to continue at the same pace for the next few years. This growth rate was due to a mixture of continued population and business movement to the region, tempered by a difficult economy which tended to suppress both business and leisure travel. Specifically, the annual growth rate of room nights across the market was about 1.5%, with the total market currently at approximately 42 million room nights per year. Within the region there was considerable variation among cities in economic health and market growth, necessitating a certain amount of local as well as corporate-level planning. Specific plans for individual units' responses to their local conditions were done under the guidance of the corporate planning staff to ensure consistency with corporate strategies, but only major unit-level initiatives, such as large capital expansion programs, were spelled out in the corporate plan.

Technology was forcing changes on the hospitality market, particularly the market for business travellers. Centralized computerized reservation systems had been a must for years, and had greatly improved the efficiency and customer tracking abilities of those competitors who adopted them. Customers were now also demanding their own access to technology, particularly the availability of FAX machines on a 24-hour basis and the ability to use high speed computer modems in their rooms.

Security was a growing concern, particularly for the growing number of women travelling on business. Catering to these customers required that hotels provide improved lighting in public areas, randomized door locks, and expanded room service hours, among other things.

Government regulations, particularly those regarding fire safety, to say nothing of the insurance industry, had forced hoteliers to upgrade their buildings, a particular hardship for several chains with venerable old downtown hotels. Changes in the tax deductibility of certain business entertainment expenses several years earlier had reduced revenues of some hotels, particularly the upscale hotels. CHI had been only mildly affected.

Competitors

The flat growth in the industry, and the chronic overcapacity in many markets had made competition particularly acute in CHI's southeastern market. Competitors had responded by cutting prices and by scrambling to upgrade their facilities and services. This flurry of costly marketing activity in the last few years had caused the demise of several smaller chains, which had either gone out of business, or had been swallowed up by several national chains which had increased their presence in the area in the last few years by acquiring and upgrading the facilities of the distressed firms.

Cumberland's market niche was that of a reasonably priced hotel emphasizing special services for business travellers. Research on customers in CHI's targeted business and leisure segments indicated that its primary competition consisted of three different hotel chains, Arlington Inns, Budget-Rest Inns and Devon Hotels. CHI's planning staff had followed these companies closely for the last few years.

Arlington Inns Arlington Inns was a recent but formidable competitor. Begun just five years ago as a division of a large firm which runs several other successful national hotel, resort, and restaurant chains, Arlington had none of the baggage of older chains. It had been built from the ground up, rapidly covering the region with new, well-designed buildings and a management dedicated to instilling a strong customer-oriented quality culture. By starting with a clean slate, the corporation was able to design a modern, innovative organization. The sophistication and extensive experience of the parent corporation was evident in the chain's operations. Arlington's hotels were known throughout the industry for their generally smooth operations and well-trained staffs. Units provided adequate, but minimal, amenities. To minimize expenses they did not have restaurants, but did offer complimentary breakfast buffets in the lobby. The chain tried instead to locate its units near a variety of restaurants.

Within five years it had acquired a 5.8% share of the entire market, and undoubtedly had aspirations for more. It had achieved this rapid growth by emphasizing high value backed up with an unconditional satisfaction guarantee, one of the first such guarantees in the industry. To support its guarantee, Arlington had begun a regular program for monitoring customer satisfaction, sampling customers by mail questionnares throughout the year. This effort was tied to the database on the chain's computer system, which ran the centralized reservation system and kept extensive records on purchase records of individual customers. Results of the satisfaction surveys were quickly analyzed and distributed to relevant unit managers within several weeks. The firm insisted that these results be used for continuous quality improvement.

Arlington's advertising budget was small, but it had an excellent word-of-mouth reputation, and had courted the favor of travel agents as a safe (and guaranteed) recommendation for leisure clients.

Budget-Rest Inns One competitor which had been severely wounded by the industry shakeout was Budget-Rest Inns, a small no-frills chain, built up by the Curry family over the last thirty years. Budget-Rest Inns currently had a 3.1% share of the market, but that share was falling rapidly.

Often employing his own family members as construction crews to keep costs down, Harold Curry had built a chain of twenty-seven aging motels along interstate highways throughout the South. His first unit had been built in 1961 as the interstate highway system was just developing in the region, and his units multiplied along with the highway system, rising at key exits on the outskirts of major cities and tourist destinations. Low construction costs and spartan, no-nonsense designs had allowed Budget-Rest to offer extremely low prices, and had succeeded in attracting a loyal following of price conscious business and leisure customers. A small but memorable radio advertising campaign had been used to build and maintain awareness. Units served no food, except from vending machines, although their highway exit locations usually had restaurants nearby. The centralized reservation system was rudimentary.

This strategy had served the Currys well until several forces combined to put their business in peril. The growth of population and business activity in the South during the eighties had attracted the attention of much more sophisticated national chains which had moved into the market and increased the competitive pressure, including bidding up the price of land at new choice locations. At the same time, customer demands for services and value grew. Budget-Rest's low tech, low service positioning had become a liability, as more sophisticated competitors found ways to close the price gap while offering a far better product. Budget-Rest's initial response was to cut budgets and work its employees harder to keep costs low, but morale and service had suffered. The chain was now strapped for cash, and its survival was somewhat in doubt.

Devon Hotels Devon Hotels had a 4.7% market share in the region. Devon was a national full-service hotel chain in the moderate price range. Customer research confirmed that Devon occasionally attracted CHI's customers in spite of its higher prices because of its convenience and broader range of product offerings. The chain's hotels were generally located in city centers. For the business segment Devon's hotels offered more than just accommodations, modems, and FAX machines. Most had several public rooms which could accommodate meetings or business banquets of up to 150 people. Devon had also chosen locations to be attractive to tourists who would stay at the hotel while visiting nearby sites. The hotels had swimming pools, and most had recently upgraded their restaurants and lounges.

Devon Hotels was highly regarded as a well-managed organization, and its managers were often hired away by other firms for their state-of-the art knowledge of the hospitality industry. The organization had a strong quality culture which had been been fostered by the use of its decentralized decision-making structure. Managers of individual hotels and even managers of departments within them were expected to develop strategies to make the most of the threats and opportunities in their individual markets, and all had roles in the corporate planning process. Devon had adopted a TQM philosophy several years earlier, and had been quite successful in getting general adoption throughout the organization. The firm regularly monitored its customers' satisfaction with many dimensions of its services, and provided timely feedback on its findings to unit managers.

Devon was a good marketer. Its customer analysis had allowed it to keep ahead of customer needs with sound investments in physical facilities and personnel training. Its advertising program was primarily an impressive campaign of print advertising in highly targeted magazines.

The publicly held company appeared to be on a firm financial footing. It had grown carefully, invested wisely and been able to regularly pay out dividends to its stockholders. Recent land purchases by Devon and comments by the firm's CEO suggested that it now planned to leverage its reputation by getting into the resort business. CHI executives felt that that diversion would keep Devon from greatly expanding its number of regular hotels for the time being.

Other Competitors Other competitors in the area, ranging from a few single-unit hotels to national chains, were considered less immediate threats to CHI's core business than the above three because of their positioning and their price ranges. Because of the current overcapacity of rooms, the lack of market growth, and the high cost of startup, CHI planners saw little concern for new entrants such as Arlington in the foreseeable future. It was more likely that established firms might up the facilities of some of the financially weakened chains when the economy improved, although their physical plants would require extensive upgrading to compete successfully.

Customers

CHI had two major target markets, budget conscious business travelers and leisure travelers, although business travelers accounted for fully 78% of room nights. The two markets had different buying processes and staying patterns, but in general were quite similar in terms of services desired and competitors used. As a result, CHI tended to group them together for purposes of ROQ analysis, although they continually monitored the segments for differences.

Business Customers The typical business customer was a sales representative who used the hotel as a base of operations to meet with clients in the local community. After a difficult day of travelling and selling, these clients wanted a conveniently located hotel with comfortable rooms, adequate work space and good lighting. They often preferred Cumberland Hotels to Arlington Inns because of the convenience of the in-house restaurants. The average stay was 1.23 days and the typical customer stayed in a Cumberland Hotel 2.85 times per year.

Many of these customers had their travel plans made by corporate travel offices, which preferred to negotiate corporate rates for their personnel and also preferred to make all reservations through centralized scheduling services. The volatile nature of selling also required flexibility in scheduling, so many rooms were sold on extremely short notice. This forced a short planning horizon on hotel chains, and made good demand forecasting essential for proper planning. Business customers also required detailed, readable printouts of their bills for their expense accounts. The demand for access to telecommunications services, especially facsimile services and in-room computer modem capability was growing rapidly, as was the need to be able to make photocopies at almost any time of day or night.

Women made up an increasing percentage of business travelers, and they tended to demand several enhancements to service that male guests had generally considered less important. In particular, safety was the biggest concern, especially lighting and security in parking lots, elevators and hallways.

CHI sold many of its rooms to this group via personal selling to corporate travel departments. The primary concerns of these buyers were price and convenience, since their charge was to support sales staff productivity at the lowest reasonable cost. Business travelers who purchased by themselves were strongly influenced by word-of-mouth recommendations and, to some extent, by advertising which stressed comfort, convenience and value.

Profit analysis of individual customers estimated that the average contribution margin from business customers was about $30.75 per visit.

Leisure Travelers Most leisure travelers who stayed at Cumberland hotels considered them to be good stopover sites on their way to other places rather than as vacation destinations. This segment of travelers was looking for comfortable, low-priced accommodations while passing through, or as a convenient base while pursuing activities away from the hotel. The average stay by a member of this segment was just 1.1 days. As a result, the lack of swimming pools and other recreational amenities were not considered to be critical drawbacks to continued popularity with this segment, although some budget hotels were adding them, and could change customers' expectations about the acceptable level of amenities in the future.

These customers were not heavy users of CHI services. The average leisure customer visited a Cumberland Hotel only 0.80 times per year. Most did not make reservations in advance, but tended to stop when they became tired of driving and saw a hotel along the highway. Name recognition and clear positioning due to advertising were considered important in stopping these travelers. Most purchases were paid for by credit card. The average contribution margin of these customers was $27.50 per visit

Contract Customers CHI had recently been pursuing some other ways to use excess capacity, to lock in some long-term revenues, and to reduce the volatility of demand to improve planning. In particular, hotel managers in several cities, with the encouragement and support of headquarters, had contracted with several major corporations to house personnel who were attending programs at local corporate training centers. These programs guaranteed revenues months in advance, and provided significant contribution, although less than would have been realized from the same number of individual customers. While not wanting to book so many of these programs that it would have to turn away many "full fare" guests, they were seen as a good way to fill otherwise idle rooms while contributing to "keeping the lights on."

Personal selling would be necessary to sell these programs. The primary concern of corporate purchasing agents who negotiatied these contracts with hotels was price. They were also concerned that the facility be within a reasonable distance from their training facilities and that the trainees had comfortable rooms, but price was clearly the driver.

If CHI were to expand this program very much the local nature of these markets meant that the natural person to make these sales would be the local unit managers. However, this would require training the managers in selling skills and adding a set of duties rather different from those for which these people had been hired and promoted. Another plan might be for unit managers to identify possible customers, but to rely on sales reps from corporate headquarters to help them close the sales. Part of the cautious nature of this roll-out program was to determine the best way to proceed on this point.

Another reason for caution was to take time to learn what special needs such groups might have, and what effect it would have on the image of the hotel. The company planned to accommodate about 960 people the next year, each staying for an average of 12 days and at an average contribution of $492 per person. For now, CHI planners wanted to incorporate limited testing of the contracts into the marketing plan, but it was unlikely to make a serious impact on the bottom line for several years.

ROQ-Based Analysis of Customer Satisfaction Cumberland had undertaken extensive surveys of customer satisfaction with its services for several years, and, as stated earlier, business customers and leisure travelers tended to have few differences in the way they viewed or rated the firm's services. Customers tended to regard their experience with CHI as consisting of six different processes, each consisting of up to five subprocesses, as shown below.

Levels of customer dissatisfaction with the processes and subprocess and their relative importance as drivers of satisfaction can be found in Table 1. They revealed that Cumberland was still suffering from some unacceptably high levels of dissatisfaction with several key components of its services. Management was determined to fix causes of dissatisfaction before embarking on any new initiatives to delight customers. Cumberland already had extremely high levels of delighted customers. However, under the current competitive climate, management felt that the identified problems must be addressed quickly, or Cumberland could fall irreversibly behind some its most aggressive rivals.

Market Dynamics

Calculating ROQ for proposed spending required that CHI keep a careful accounting of the dynamics of the market in its coverage area. The staff had used its own surveys as well as figures from trade associations and government documents to assemble the necessary estimates. In particular, in the last year the market had grown from 41,385,248 room nights to a projected 42,004,785 for the current year. The average individual stayed for 1.2 room nights per visit, both for Cumberland and the industry as a whole. The net growth in the market was about 1.5% per year. However approximately 1% of the industry's customers left the market each year, so the number of new customers each year was about 2.5% of the previous year's total, or 863,000 transactions this year. CHI's analysts felt that these aggregate growth rates were likely to persist for at least the next three years.

Cumberland anticipated selling 1,058,552 room nights this year, or 884,311 individual transactions. This represented a share of 2.52%, up from 2.49% the previous year. Survey data suggested that Cumberland had retained about 65% of its customers, or 559,306, from the previous year; 34% had switched to competitors; and 1%, the market average, had left the market. Current projections and recent experience suggested that 303,422 transactions this year would be from customers who had switched from other firms. The remaining 21,583 transactions represented customers who were new to the market. They represented 2.5% of the market's new customers, so Cumberland was attracting new customers at a rate very close to its current market share.

PROGRAM DEVELOPMENT

Having compiled the above information on its marketplace, Nichols and his staff had worked with the managers in the various

I. Room	II. Bath	III. Staff	IV. Service	V. Grounds	VI. Restaurant
1. Carpet	1. Tub	1. Knowledge	1. Wakeup calls	1. Landscaping	1. Service
2. Bed	2. Cleanliness	2. Friendly	2. Messages	2. Lighting	2. Cleanliness
3. TV	3. Supplies	3. Professional	3. Checkout/in		3. Variety
4. Workspace	4. Vanity				4. Quality
5. Lighting					

TABLE 1

THE DRIVERS OF SATISFACTION FOR CUMBERLAND HOTELS

	Relative Importance	Percent Dissatisfied
Room	.05	5.9%
Carpet	.13	2.1
Bed	.16	3.4
TV	.15	8.7
Workspace	.13	9.6
Lighting	.08	5.0
Bath	.23	10.3%
Tub	.07	6.0
Cleanliness	.25	6.5
Supplies	.32	10.7
Vanity	.00	4.9
Staff	.08	4.4%
Knowledgeable	.00	10.5
Friendly	.04	4.5
Professional	.00	4.8
Service	.10	3.2%
Wakeup calls	.00	4.4
Messages	.19	6.3
Checkout/in	.01	12.4
Grounds	.00	5.4%
Landscaping	.19	5.3
Lighting	.17	5.3
Restaurant	.22	16.8%
Service	.01	5.7
Cleanliness	.01	25.3
Variety	.03	9.6
Quality	.05	4.3

parts of the company to develop objectives and strategies to help the firm reach its overall objectives. Initially, managers felt that meeting the firm's growth goals would be a challenge in the current economic climate. However, as they became comfortable with their enhanced role in the planning process, enthusiasm grew for generating new approaches, and there was now a good deal of excitement about the possibilities and eagerness to get on with new programs. Nichols' primary task at this point was to make certain that the number of proposed programs from each unit and functional area of the company

were consistent with each other and with the overall direction of the firm.

Everyone realized that Cumberland had to tighten up its operations significantly before great strides could be made. The current 13% overall dissatisfaction level was unacceptable. However, the ROQ analysis had identified specific problem areas, and the relevant departments and unit managers had worked to develop quality improvement strategies that they believed would resolve the most important ones quickly and profitably. With a common sense of confidence in the firm's ability to deliver an improved product in the next year, specific objectives and strategies had been developed.

Marketing's Contribution The marketing department saw that it could assist the drive for growth in several ways. First was an increase in offensive marketing. CHI had some important advantages over its competitors which had not been adequately exploited in the past, particularly with new quality programs in place to eliminate the problems which had reduced customer satisfaction in the past. Marketing managers felt that an advertising program proclaiming CHI's range of services, new high-quality standards, and low prices would generate increased trial among its competitors' customers and new entrants to the market. Specifically, marketing's objective was to increase the trial rate among new customers to 4%, a 60% increase over the current level. A recently completed marketing research study, commissioned to determine what customers were looking for, strongly supported the feasibility of this objective. The theme would be "the new spirit of service and value" at Cumberland Hotels. The marketing department had worked out the details of the advertising program, including specific copy claims, budgets, and media schedules. To support the value claim, marketing also recommended that the price of a single room be increased by at most 2.5% to $52 per night. This would maintain a contribution margin per room night of about $25, or approximately $30 per transaction.

A second offensive thrust was the development of the market for corporate training programs, in which companies rented blocks of rooms for out-of-town employees who were involved in extended educational programs. Because the trial programs with contract sales seemed to be working out, the marketing department proposed building these revenues up to 5% of corporate sales in three years. Contract sales were expected to be additional revenues, not replacements for "retail" sales. The rationale for the program was that CHI's business emphasis meant that its hotels already offered many of the specialized services needed by trainees, and that no other hotels were specifically targeting this market, although many of them sought it out for marginal income when they had slack capacity. At the same time, the economic growth of the Southeast meant that the demand for training in the region was growing. CHI could compete for this price-driven business without greatly reducing its margins, and, by specializing on the needs of corporate trainers, it could keep costs down to the point where these training programs could provide a steady source of reliable and predictable income. Marketing also thought that this service could ultimately improve retail sales if trainees were significantly impressed to choose Cumberland Hotels for their personal or business use. Strategy details involved developing a workable personal selling program and training for unit managers.

Analysis of the return on quality (ROQ) of various quality improvement proposals had also provided insight into areas for profitable defensive marketing efforts, and a major corporate goal was set to reduce the percent of customers dissatisfied with the hotel overall by at least half, i.e., to less than 6.5%. Strategies to reduce customer dissatisfaction with rooms and restaurants were to receive

particular attention. Relevant managers met to evaluate the ROQ viability of various strategies. CHI used a three-year planning horizon with a 15% discount factor in computing ROQ. In particular, several programs were evaluated and proposed:

A program to increase customer satisfaction with various bathroom supplies, including built-in hair dryers as well as the quality of complementary items such as shampoos and soaps, had been tested at two units the previous year. Customer reactions to various combinations had been measured at these sites to give management a better understanding of customer desires. Computer analysis of the estimated ROQ from several alternatives found that the most profitable package was one averaging about twenty cents more per night than the amount currently spent. The systemwide costs for these upgrades would add about $210,000 to the budget each year. However, the improvements were expected to reduce the percent of customers dissatisfied with this subprocess from 6.5% to a hardcore 2%, add a net present value of $87,218 over three years, and an ROQ of 18.2%.

Several unit managers, who shared customers' dissatisfaction with the message system, demonstrated that purchasing several upgraded components for unit computer systems would take care of most of the problems. For an initial investment of $48,000 plus expected maintenance of $2000 per year the source of most problems with the current message system would be eliminated, reducing the number of dissatisfied customers from the current 5.8% to about 2%. This program would have a three-year NPV of $18,728 and an ROQ of 35.6%.

A management trainee at one hotel also proposed a small but effective solution to dissatisfaction with TV sets which was adopted by the chain. She had determined that almost all compaints were due not to malfunctioning TV sets, but to guest inability to operate the remote control device. Her suggestion that the hotel place laminated cards in each room containing clear instructions on the operation of the TV sets had received limited testing in her hotel unit. Complaints about television sets had indeed almost disappeared. Systemwide costs were minimal. Just $4800 worth of cards was expected to reduce the percent dissatisfied with televisions from 7.1% to just 2%. The plan had an expected ROQ of 276%.

Dissatisfaction with rooms and the restaurants also needed immediate attention, but management had few data or even good estimates about the likely effect of specific programs. They did have some estimates of the effect on overall satisfaction with the hotels of various combinations of programs, including those already mentioned, based on some variation among units that had crept into the system over the years. In particular, a $1 million increase in the budget, if properly spent, was estimated to drop the overall dissatisfaction rate of 13% to just 7%, and an additional million could drop it to about 4%. The ROQ analysis indicated that $1 million was about the right amount, given CHI's financial requirements. In particular, the $2 million investment was computed to have a lower net present value and a lower ROQ than the $4 million dollar program. Based on experience at the most successful hotels, the management advised allocating the rest of the budget as follows:

$460,000 in additional spending to replace worn out furniture, TVs, lights, etc. and to teach housekeeping staff to recognize defunct items. Although CHI had a regular schedule to identify and replace furnishings, the current budget was evidently insufficient to catch all the defective items, and this additional amount was thought to be sufficient to reduce most of the sources of complaints. However, this effort illustrated the interdependence among quality initiatives: the

success of this program to reduce complaints depended upon housekeeping staff to spot potential problems or, if necessary, on the complaint management system to notify the proper individuals.

$65,000 was to be used to improve the acceptability of restaurant menus. In spite of generally poor ratings for the restaurants, headquarters did not think that great amounts of money need be spent to improve the variety and quality of the food, the two major areas of customer complaints. Rather, the problem was the fact that menus had not changed with the times, and emphasized the fried foods and highly cooked vegetables that reflected the chain's traditional Southern roots, but were less appealing to a younger and more demographically diverse population. The money would be spent to test a broader, healthier, more varied menu and train kitchen staffs in its preparation. This was generally considered to be a relatively easy and long overdue change.

Improved customer satisfaction would not just come from better physical facilities. Good personal interaction was considered essential before customers would rate other aspects of the service favorably. Therefore, to make sure the rest of the money did not go to waste $210,000 would be spent for additional training and motivation programs for hotel contact personnel to continue to improve their skills and enthusiasm in dealing with guests.

Other ongoing defensive strategies included a project to improve the ease with which customers could file complaints to make sure that key feedback was not being lost. This project was being undertaken by a taskforce reporting directly to the VP of Marketing. Management had also commissioned a study to track customer response levels following quality changes, so that CHI planners could better predict the speed with which customer satisfaction might reach new levels.

Management's and HR's Contribution

As is evident from the ROQ analysis conducted by marketing, management and human resources would have to play a vital role in achieving corporate objectives. Management saw that it would have to continue to increase top and middle management involvement in quality programs. In particular, it was clear to Nichols that further training in leadership skills would be necessary to establish the quality culture he envisioned.

Management established objectives regarding specific skills and levels of enthusiasm among contact personnel. To reach these objectives HR planned to offer several new training programs in interpersonal skills, problem resolution, and corporate policy. New hiring policies would also be explored, particularly to better determine the compatibility of new recruits with the requirements of the new empowerment programs. HR was also expected to arrange training of desk personnel with the new message/wakeup call system and to instruct housekeeping on identifying worn out room furnishings. Enthusiasm for the new quality culture would also be fostered by a new program of recognitions and rewards for employees who took special initiatives to provide exceptional customer service.

One of the specific objectives that CHI hoped to reach with these programs was to reduce turnover among front desk and housekeeping staff by 10%.

In addition, to support the quality effort it was considered essential that CHI begin to monitor the quality of its internal processes as well as those of its services for guests. HR was therefore charged with developing an internal survey instrument to monitor staff satisfaction with the various support functions, and to begin developing benchmarks for these service levels based on the best practices that could be found.

Operations' Contribution

At CHI, as at most successful service operations, marketing and operations worked very closely together. Nevertheless, the planned improvements put a number of specific demands on the operations department, which developed a number of objectives in support of corporate objectives. For example, operations was charged with determining optimal inventory levels of supplies for both hotels and restaurants. It also had the responsibility of designing the new message systems and the general flow of operations at the front desk.

Although the ultimate measure of quality is in the mind of the customer, CHI management realized that it needed to develop internal measures which would warn it of problems before customers became dissatisfied. Therefore operations was given the task of devising and monitoring a set of measures of service quality which were closely related to customer satisfaction. Some were obvious, such as the number of garbled messages or the number of dinner customers who had to wait more than 15 minutes before being served, but an objective for the next year was to develop a more complete set which covered the full range of service dimensions.

The details of the operations department's strategies were critical to the success of the overall strategy.

Financial Estimates

Financial projections for the current year looked good, and next year looked even better. The projected income statements for the current and next years are shown in Table 2. The anticipated improvements in defensive and offensive marketing efforts were anticipated to have a dramatic effect on CHI's income statement for the following year. In particular, ROQ analysis suggested that the improvements on overall satisfaction would result in an

TABLE 2

PROJECTED INCOME STATEMENTS FOR CURRENT AND NEXT YEARS		
REVENUES		
Rentals	$57,675,181	$69,095,017
Beverage	9,286,682	11,144,018
Food	24,047,618	28,857,142
Telephone	2,443,864	2,932,636
Minor departments	1,368,564	1,427,218
Rental and other income	2,932,636	3,020,615
Total	$97,754,544	$116,476,646
EXPENSES		
Payroll	$35,387,145	$40,695,217
Departmental expenses	11,926,054	13,803,963
Energy	4,985,482	5,733,304
Food	7,527,100	9,032,520
Beverage	1,955,091	2,346,109
Property opn and maint	3,225,900	4,651,080
Administration and general	4,503,445	5,073,790
Marketing	3,421,409	6,158,536
Interest	6,451,800	6,774,390
Rent and insurance	3,812,427	4,117,421
Depreciation	5,963,027	6,261,179
Taxes	3,421,409	4,076,683
Total	$92,580,290	$108,724,191
Net income	$5,174,254	$7,752,455

increase in retention from 65 to 68.15%. Because the rate at which these new programs could be adopted was uncertain, Nichols' planners used a value of 67% for their forecast for the next year, for an estimate of 709,230 room nights sold to retained customers next year.

The improvements in offensive marketing programs had been anticipated to increase the number of brand switchers and new customers by 60%. If equally successful with both groups, this would account for another 534,592 room nights. The contract programs were expected to provide another 11,520 room nights. The total forecasted sales was 1,255,342 room nights, an 18.6% increase over the current year, and a 2.94% market share.

This ratio was used as the basis for forecasting several lines in the next year's *pro*

forma income statement. Given a slight increase in prices planned for next year, planners used a round figure of 20% as the growth in actual dollar sales of Room rentals, less $10 per room night for contract sales. They also forecast 20% increases for Beverage, Food, and Telephone revenues. Revenues from minor departments were expected to increase only 4.3% and other rental income would go up by no more than 3%.

On the expense side Food, Beverage, and Property Operations and Maintenance were also expected to increase by 20% to support the increased customer traffic. In addition, POM was also to be charged for the bathroom supplies upgrades programs and the facilities renovation effort. The same rate of growth was not seen in all cost categories, since CHI was currently below capacity and somewhat overstaffed. Payroll, Departmental, and

Energy expenses were predicted to increase by 15%, perhaps a conservative overstatement of the actual amounts necessary to service the anticipated increase in sales. In addition to the 15% increase, Departmental Expense was to be charged for the upgraded message systems and restaurant improvements.

Among overhead items, administration was estimated to increase by at most 10% plus the cost of the training and motivation programs. The greatest increase was to be in the marketing budget, including $752,710 for selling and central support functions and a near doubling of the advertising budget to $5,405,826 for a total of $6,158,536. Interest, Rent and Insurance, and Depreciation were calculated to each be approximately 5% higher. Finally, the preliminary estimate of taxes was $4,076,683.

The forecasted net income was therefore a record high $7,752,455 as well as a record high 6.7% of sales.

The Final Step

The pieces were now all in place. People throughout the organization had contributed some very exciting ideas and everywhere in the firm people were eager to get started on these new quality initiatives. Ron Nichols was also looking forward to presenting the plan to the board in two weeks. But first he had to pull all the material together into the final draft. He called his staff together to begin assembling the document.

PART VII

THE FUTURE OF SERVICE MARKETING

chapter 19

IMPLICATIONS OF TECHNOLOGY

19.1 OVERVIEW

Technology is the skeleton of the economy, around which marketing institutions form like muscle. If technology changes, then marketing inevitably changes as well. For example, when television was invented, marketing changed itself to take advantage of the new medium, through commercials and program sponsorship. When the interstate highway system was built, marketing adjusted to that by building suburban shopping centers. When supermarket scanner technology emerged, marketers devised ways of exploiting the new technology, by inventing point-of-sale couponing and store-level databases. Many of the technological changes of the recent past have involved the blossoming of the information age, which has made the entire economy more information-oriented, and therefore more services-oriented. This broad trend continues today.

    The important changes in marketing in the coming years are almost certain to be driven primarily by changes in information technology. In fact, several very important technologies now beginning to be implemented will soon have a profound impact on marketing. These technologies, taken collectively, form what we will term *the digital age,* an age in which digital communications technologies merge with digital computer technology.[1]

    In the digital age marketing will become faster and smarter. By this we mean marketing will meet customers' needs quicker and more accurately. Consumers will gain power, as they obtain more access to large amounts of information. For example, any customer who has complete knowledge about prices will never overpay. Knowledge translates to economic power. Advertising and retailing, meanwhile, will suffer greatly, while customer service will become more important than ever. The new prevailing paradigm of marketing will be *adaptive marketing,* in which products (very often information services) will be customized to suit individual customers and will be continually updated. Marketing will be radically transformed as a result of this technological revolution. The remainder of this chapter explores the surprising marketing implications of the digital age.

19.2 THE DIGITAL AGE

Digital storage of information was a powerful invention because it made possible the storage and manipulation of vast amounts of information by computer. In fact, digital storage of information became widespread with the invention, in the 1940s, of the practical digital computer, which stored information electronically in binary bits (one or zero, on or off). Telephone lines, and cable television, transmitted information in analog; the sound waves themselves were transmitted in electronic form. Digital transmission of sound and pictures required too much "bandwidth" (amount of information transmitted at one time) to be feasible.

Since the 1980s, however, two developments have changed this situation. First, the use of fiber-optic cable has greatly increased the bandwidth available for data transmission. Second, data compression technologies have made it possible to transmit sound and pictures using far less bandwidth than before. The net result of these two technological developments is that the transmission of vast amounts of information to the home is now technologically feasible. The biggest remaining hurdle is the economics of laying fiber-optic cable to the home. Once this feat is accomplished, there will essentially be no practical limit to the amount of information traveling to and from a home, and hence there will be profound consequences on how marketing is done.

Let us consider how the technological skeleton of marketing will be different in the coming years. Figure 19.1 shows the history of two modes of communication to the home: telephone and television. We see that roughly every 20 years there has been a major revolution in this technology. For the year 2000, the feasibility of transmitting vast amounts of data to (and from) the home should result in the videophone (a telephone with a television-like picture) finally catching on (as real-time video, instantaneous video transmission, becomes possible). Then interactive cable television will become widespread, with a vast number of available channels and options. Currently it appears as though this network may evolve directly from the Internet.

The digital age blurs the line between media such as telephone and cable TV. If the telephone transmits pictures and cable TV is interactive, what is the difference between the two? Figure 19.2 shows a schematic of the digital environment, as it is likely to unfold. In the home, the consumer controls a combination TV/telephone/computer (and probably newspaper, on-line database, and anything else

FIGURE 19.1

THE HISTORY OF COMMUNICATION TO THE HOME		
Year	Telephone	TV/Radio
1880	(none)	(none)
1900	Party line	(none)
1920	Private	Radio
1940	Private	Black-and-white TV
1960	Private	Color TV
1980	Private	Cable TV
2000 (projected)	Videophone	Interactive cable

FIGURE 19.2

THE DIGITAL ENVIRONMENT

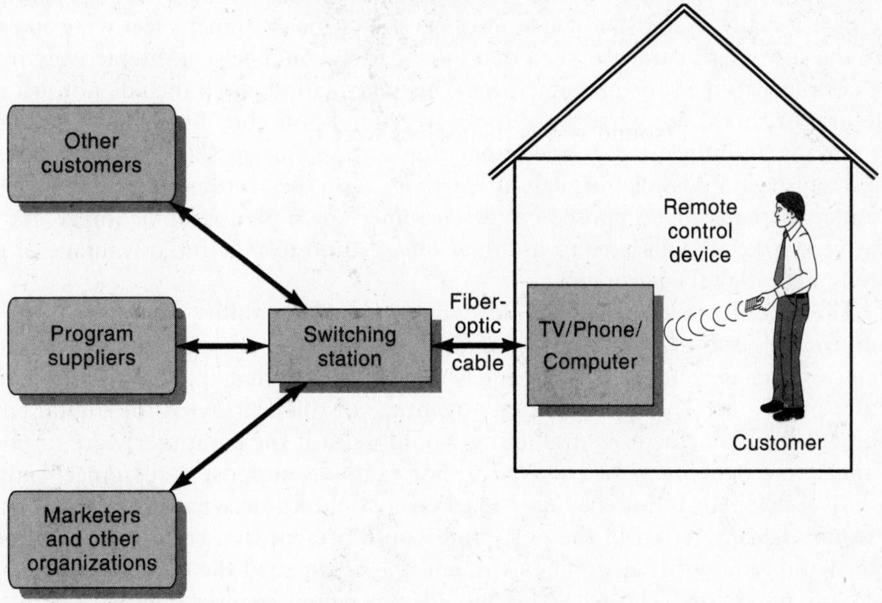

involving information) using a personal remote device, much like an existing TV remote control. The TV (to conveniently label the TV/telephone/computer) is connected to an information network via fiber-optic cable. Connections may be made, using the network, to other customers (friends, business contacts, relatives, etc.), program suppliers (TV networks, radio stations, newspapers, databases, etc.), or marketers and other business organizations (for product information, home shopping, bill paying, etc.).

19.3 MARKETING: FASTER AND SMARTER

These technological changes have the general impact of making it possible for marketing to become faster and smarter. Of course, if being faster and smarter is possible, it *must* be done so as to remain competitive in the marketplace.

Marketing must become **faster** because communications technologies make it possible. An example of this is banking by TV. Initially, customers had to visit the bank, during normal banking hours. Then banks created drive-through windows, to make visiting the bank faster. When computer technology became sufficiently advanced, automatic teller machines made it even faster to bank, by permitting transactions at any hour. The new interactive TV environment makes banking even faster, by permitting banking transactions in the home, without even having to drive to the automatic teller. The waiting time for conducting banking transactions has shortened steadily and dramatically over time.

Marketers will be on the right track by imagining what would happen if their service could be provided *immediately* and by considering how to use the new technology to do that. For example, consider purchasing new shoes. Immediate shoe purchase would require some way of immediately determining fit, and inspecting the shoe visually. If statistics concerning the size of the customer's feet were entered into the customer's database, then that information could be sent interactively from the customer to the shoe manufacturer. This information could include not just the size of past shoes, but what those shoes were, and how they fit, providing a basis for making an immediate size determination for the current shoe. Visualization of the shoe is again possible through interactivity, with the customer requesting to see the shoe, perhaps superimposed on the customer's own photographic image. As we can see, marketers will have to use their imagination to take full advantage of the speed of the digital environment.

The preceding example also takes advantage of the ability of the digital environment to permit marketing to become *smarter*. The computer knew the customer's purchase and fit history and was able to use that information to guide future purchases. The key to taking advantage of this feature of the digital environment is to imagine how marketing would work if the computer were *infinitely smart* and had *complete knowledge*. For example, suppose a customer wanted to buy a shirt. An infinitely smart marketer would know what style of shirt the customer had preferred in the past, and would present that style first. The marketer would know the customer's size and the credit card the customer generally used for purchases. The marketer would also know exactly where to ship the merchandise.

The digital environment makes all of this feasible. A purchase history would contain a data file that included past shirts purchased, with sizes and prices. These figures could then be matched with existing product offerings, by checking the data network. The customer's credit card and address are easily collected and stored on a data file. Notice that this transaction no longer includes a retailer, a fact we will explore in more detail in Section 19.6. Of course some customers may not like the idea that all of this personal information exists on a computer database, but we will see in the next section that the database itself might be kept by the customer rather than by the company.

19.4 CONSUMER POWER

The technological shifts of the digital age will have important implications with respect to shifting power in the distribution channel. Figure 19.3 shows a remarkable historical shift in power from the manufacturer to the retailer, and eventually to the consumer. As recently as the 1970s, the manufacturer enjoyed primary control power—based on the manufacturer's access to national or regional market surveys and extensive sales data. Retailers could not match this. If a manufacturer told a retailer that a certain item would sell because it sold in similar markets around the country, the retailer was in no position to disagree. Thus the manufacturer could largely dictate the retailer's merchandising strategy, resulting in inefficiencies such as the wrong goods being pushed in a market, thus hurting the consumer.

The advent of retail scanner data around 1980 changed all of this. It gave the

FIGURE 19.3

THE LOCUS OF CHANNEL POWER

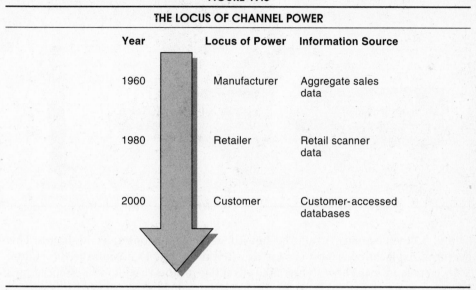

Year	Locus of Power	Information Source
1960	Manufacturer	Aggregate sales data
1980	Retailer	Retail scanner data
2000	Customer	Customer-accessed databases

retailer access to actual purchase records, by customer, by product. If the manufacturer tried to push a particular product, the retailer might refer to scanner data that indicated that product (or similar products) had failed previously. The effectiveness of sales promotions was also more clearly evident from this new information. Thus retailers gained an advantage in negotiations with manufacturers.

In coming years, power will shift even further down the channel. In the digital environment, the customer has extensive amounts of data available. For example, the customer will be able to check prices easily. No retailer (or manufacturer) will be able to charge uncompetitive prices, because that fact will become known to the customer through a simple database search. Prices will tend to drop, reflecting this new power of information enjoyed by the customer.

Quality will also rise. Databases and information searches will also provide the customer information about quality. Imagine a consumer magazine like *Consumer Reports,* on-line and covering every imaginable product and service. Widespread use of these resources will result in better customer decision making.

The sheer quantity of information to be navigated will require that the customer get some help. One way to visualize this is a "knowledge robot" or "knowbot" that can help narrow down information into an amount which is digestible. Figure 19.4 shows schematically how this might work. Such a knowbot is identical in function to the "reducing valve," which author and mystic Aldous Huxley hypothesized as being a primary function of the human brain.[2]

We foresee much of the knowbot's function as being proactive in nature. For example, the knowbot might suggest which television programs or movies might most interest the viewer. Or, if a sale came along that would be likely to interest the customer, the knowbot could let the customer know.

We also foresee that the knowbot, along with other databases and computers

FIGURE 19.4

THE FUNCTION OF THE KNOWBOT

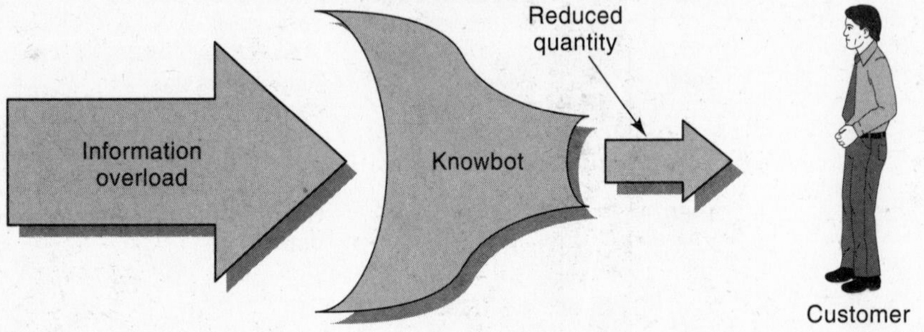

helpful to the customer, would be housed with the customer, in the home. This decentralized location is most consistent with the knowbot's decentralized function. Marketers must learn how to best take advantage of this situation. In essence, marketers are going to have to learn how to market to knowbots. One marketing course of the twenty-first century might very well be "Computer Behavior"!

19.5 THE DEATH OF ADVERTISING

One of the implications of the digital environment is the death (or extreme decline) of advertising as we know it. This trend may be seen historically. The conduits for advertising are media, and media are changing drastically. From the 1950s through the 1970s it was easy to obtain a large audience by advertising on network television. There were only three networks, and thus each could gather a large audience. There were also a few main magazines (*Life, Look,* etc.) which could also be counted on to reach a wide cross section of people.

In the 1980s this situation began to change very rapidly. Cable television proliferated, resulting in an increasingly fragmented media environment, and a relative decline of the broadcast networks. A similar change was occurring in magazines, with new titles appealing to very specific segments (gun collectors, competitive distance runners, etc.) putting general magazines like *Life* and *Look* out of business. Not coincidentally, the advertising industry went into a tailspin during this period, with the major advertising agencies laying off large numbers of employees, as marketers looked for new ways, such as sales promotion and direct mail, to drum up business.

The digital age that is forming now will greatly accelerate this trend. The media environment will fragment into tiny pieces, with television increasing its channels by approximately 500%, based on current technology, and magazines deliverable electronically becoming individualized. Media will eventually not be able to reach enough people to justify advertiser sponsorship. Ultimately the result will be both a shift of promotional funds to other methods, such as outdoor advertising and event sponsorship, and the creation of shopping programs that can be selected *voluntarily* by customers.

19.6 THE DECLINE OF RETAILING

Just as advertising will fall on hard times, retailing will suffer as well because one of the main reasons for the success of retailing, convenience, will be removed. Shopping on the TV will simply be easier than going out to a retail store. Also, TV shopping will be cheaper, because manufacturers selling direct do not have to pay the overhead of a retail store. This means that customers placing a high value on price and convenience (which is probably most customers) will opt for TV shopping.

That leaves retailers with the segment of customers who are not price- or convenience-sensitive. To be successful, retailers will have to provide a shopping environment that is itself a memorable experience, and emphasize personal service with a uniquely human touch. One might imagine that upscale boutiques would probably survive, but discount stores are probably in for a tough time. With retailers in decline, there will be a major increase in the need for delivery companies (e.g., Federal Express and UPS) that can facilitate direct delivery from the manufacturer to the customer. In essence, delivery companies will assume much of the role currently played by distributors and retailers.

19.7 CUSTOMER SERVICE: MORE IMPORTANT THAN EVER

Interestingly, even as retailing fades, customer service is likely to become increasingly important—mainly because greater technology provides better capability. For example, suppose a product isn't working properly. A customer service representative could show the customer, over the interactive television, how to use the product and evaluate problems with the product. Customer service is inherently interactive, and the biggest problem is adequate communication. This problem is addressed by the inherent interactivity of the media environment. A much closer relationship between the manufacturer and customer is facilitated, leading to a new level of expectations in service, and a further shift in emphasis away from the physical product, toward service delivery. Needless to say, complaint management is also facilitated, by being made both faster and smarter.

19.8 ADAPTIVE MARKETING: THE NEW PARADIGM[3]

Modern marketing has had several major eras, defined by the degree to which products were customized. The first era (see Figure 19.5) was the mass marketing era. This era extends roughly from 1850 (when standardized parts became increasingly

FIGURE 19.5

THE ERAS OF MODERN MARKETING		
Time Period	Era	Strategy
1850–1930	Mass marketing	Standardized products
1930–1990	Market segmentation	Differentiated products
1990s	Relationship marketing	Differentiated products/ Individualized service
2000+	Adaptive marketing	Individualized products/ Continual improvement

common in manufacturing) until about 1930. The best example of this era was Henry Ford's Model T. The Model T was very successful, because uniformity of manufacture, combined with the assembly line, reduced manufacturing costs. Standardized parts made the Model T easy to repair and maintain. Ford boasted about the Model T's lack of customization, exclaiming that customers could have any color they wanted, *as long as it was black.*

The advent of radio helped to stimulate a greater interest in consumer choice, by highlighting the many possibilities available. The result of this was the development of groups of people with very different wants, even within the same product category. General Motors was quick to recognize this, and moved to offer consumers a wide variety of colors and features. Ford, until that point the unquestioned leader of the auto industry, sacrificed several future generations of possible market leaders by gamely sticking to the old strategy. The era of market segmentation had begun. This era required differentiated products that would appeal to different customer segments.

Some time around 1990 (or possibly a few years before), another era became dominant. Widespread access to computer databases and easy-to-use computer software programs made it possible to keep track of individual customers on an ongoing basis. Relationships were then maintained by such techniques as direct mail, telephone calls, or personal visits. Customers were contacted about offerings that (according to the database) they would be likely to desire. Businesses learned as much as possible about customers, and stored the information in customer databases. Essentially the relationship marketing era provided individualized service, although the products themselves were not typically individualized.

The next step is *adaptive marketing,* in which both the product and service are individualized. What makes this individualization possible is the ability to customize products, plus the ability to obtain and process ongoing information about usage

FIGURE 19.6

ADAPTIVE MARKETING

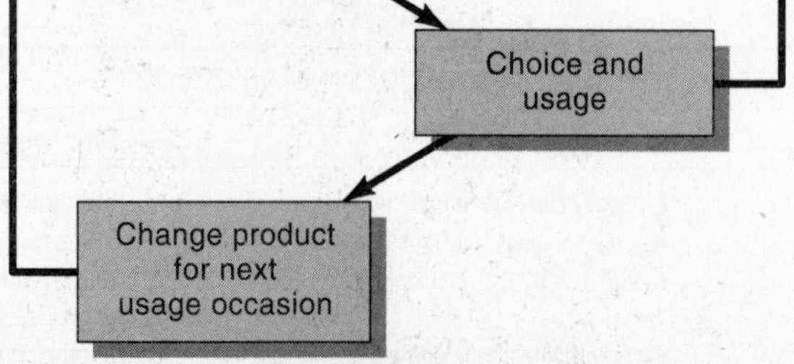

and choice. Figure 19.6 shows how adaptive marketing works. The expansion of the economy in the digital age will primarily be the result of the growth of information services. Information services have the characteristic of potentially being altered for every individual usage occasion, for every individual customer.

Consider, for example, an electronic newspaper, such as is likely to be available in the digital environment. There is potentially a new usage occasion every day. The knowbot provides the stories in the order in which they are likely to be desired, based on that individual's preferences and reading history. The individual then chooses which stories to read, and how much time to spend on each story. Based on this "choice and usage" pattern, the knowbot then updates its database about what this individual customer is likely to prefer in the future. This results in a revised, and continually improved, product offering for the next usage occasion.

Essentially, adaptive marketing is the ultimate form of marketing to segments of size one. The product itself is customized to best please an individual customer, and the product is updated for every usage occasion.[4] Increasingly, marketing will be done this way in the twenty-first century.

REVIEW QUESTIONS

1. Consider university education. How could digital technology make university education faster and smarter? How could healthcare become faster and smarter? How could restaurant service be made faster and smarter?

2. What if you wanted to buy a car, but there were no television, radio, or magazine advertisements to inform you. Suppose, though, that you had a huge, very intelligent, database at your disposal, through your TV. What kind of information would you like to have? How much would you pay to get it? Who would find it to their advantage to supply the information?

3. Some people have argued that the digital age will result in a population of "information haves" and "information have-nots." Will such be the case? If so, what will be the implications on society? How could that be prevented from happening?

4. Which will be among the first specific industries to embrace adaptive marketing? Which will be among the last?

ENDNOTES

1. For a thorough discussion of these issues, and their marketing implications, see Roland T. Rust and Richard W. Oliver (1994), "Video Dial Tone: The New World of Services Marketing," *Journal of Services Marketing,* in the Readings at the end of the chapter.
2. Aldous Huxley (1954), *The Doors of Perception,* New York: Harper.
3. Thanks to Sajeev Varki for many of the insights in this section.
4. Adaptive marketing differs from mass customization in that the customization of product/service is an *ongoing* process, rather than a one-shot affair. Adaptive marketing differs from relationship marketing in that the product/service is customized for the individual, not just for a segment or market niche to which the customer has been assigned.

CREDITS

Unless otherwise acknowledged, all photographs are the property of Scott, Foresman and Company. Page abbreviations are as follow: (T) top, (C) center, (B) bottom, (R) right.

Page 6: Courtesy Citibank.

Page 7: Courtesy State Farm Insurance.

Page 14: Courtesy Lexus

Page 27: Doris DeWitt/Tony Stone Images

Page 33: Jim Daniels/The Picture Cube

Page 35: SuperStock, Inc.

Page 77(L): Courtesy of Holiday Inn Worldwide.

Page 77(R): Courtesy of Holiday Inn Worldwide.

Page 85: Library of Congress.

Page 161: Michael Kraswoitz/FPG.

Page 166: Uniphoto.

Page 318: Courtesy Ford Motor Company.

Page 353: Frank Siteman/The Picture Cube.

Page 369: Peter Menzel

Page 376: Comnet/West Light.

Page 379: Bruce Ayres/Tony Stone Images.

Page 394: Copyright ©1993 Dennis Brack/Black Star.

Page 398: Bob Daemmrich/The Image Works.

Page 400: Eric R Berndt/Unicorn Stock Photos.

Page 403: Reprinted here with the express Permission of The Ritz-Carlton Hotel Company. Ritz Carlton is a registered trademark of the Ritz-Carlton Hotel Company.

Page 413: Courtesy of Wendys International.

INDEX